Engineering Graphics with AutoCAD® 2006

James D. Bethune
Boston University

Upper Saddle River, New Jersey
Columbus, Ohio

Library of Congress Cataloging-in-Publication Data

Bethune James D., 1941
    Engineering graphics with AutoCAD 2006/ James D. Bethune.
        p. cm.
    Includes index.
    ISBN 0-13-171391-4
    1. Engineering graphics. 2. AutoCAD. I. title

T357.B464   2006
620'.0042'0285536—dc22   2005050949

Executive Editor: Dehbie Yarnell
Managing Editor: Judith Casillo
Production Editor: Louise N. Sette
Production Supervisor: Lisa Garboski, bookworks
Design Coordinator: Diane Ernsberger
Cover Designer: Rod Harris
Art Coordinator: Janet Portisch
Production Manager: Deidra Schwartz
Marketing Manager: Jimmy Stephens

This book was set in Times and Arial by *The GTS Companies*/York, PA Campus and was printed and bound by Banta Book Group. The cover was printed by Coral Graphic Services, Inc.

Pearson Education Ltd.   Pearson Education Australia Pty. Limited
Pearson Education Singapore Pte. Ltd.   Pearson Education North Asia Ltd.
Pearson Education Canada, Ltd.   Pearson Educación de Mexico, S. A. de C.V.
Pearson Education—Japan   Pearson Education Malaysia Pte. Ltd.

10 9 8 7 6 5
ISBN: 0-13-171391-4

Preface

This book teaches technical drawing and uses AutoCAD® as its drawing instrument. This book updates *Engineering Graphics with AutoCAD® 2005* for AutoCAD® 2006. It follows the general format of many technical drawing texts and presents much of the same material about drawing conventions and practices, with emphasis on creating accurate, clear drawings. For example, the book shows how to locate dimensions on a drawing so that they completely define the object in accordance with current national standards, but the presentation centers on the Dimension toolbar and its associated tools and options. The standards and conventions are presented and their applications are shown using AutoCAD® 2006. This integrated teaching concept is followed throughout the book.

Most chapters include design problems. The problems are varied in scope and are open-ended, which means that there are several correct solutions. This is intended to encourage student creativity and increase their problem-solving abilities.

Chapters 1 through 3 cover AutoCAD Draw and Modify toolbars and other commands needed to set up and start drawings. The text starts with simple Line commands and proceeds through geometric constructions. The final sections of Chapter 3 describe how to bisect a line and how to draw a hyperbola, a parabola, a helix, and an ogee curve. Redrawing many of the classic geometric shapes will help students learn how to use the Draw and Modify toolbars, along with other associated commands, with accuracy and creativity.

Chapters 2 and 3 also show how to use the new dynamic input options. This is a significant change in the program.

Chapter 4 presents freehand sketching. Simply stated, there is still an important place for sketching in technical drawing. Many design ideas start as freehand sketches and are then developed on the computer. This chapter now includes extensive exercise problems associated with object orientation.

Chapter 5 presents orthographic views. Students are shown how to draw three views of an object using AutoCAD. The discussion includes projection theory, hidden lines, compound lines, oblique surfaces, rounded surfaces, holes, irregular surfaces, castings, and thin-walled objects. The chapter ends with several intersection problems. These problems serve as a good way to pull together orthographic views and projection theory.

Chapter 6 presents sectional views and introduces the Hatch and Gradient commands. The chapter includes multiple, broken-out, and partial sectional views and shows how to draw an S-break for a hollow cylinder.

Chapter 7 covers auxiliary views and shows how to use the Snap, Rotate command to create axes aligned with slanted surfaces. Secondary auxiliary views are also discussed. Solid modeling greatly simplifies the determination of the true shape of a line or plane, but a few examples of secondary auxiliary views help students refine their understanding of orthographic views and eventually the application of UCSs.

Chapter 8 shows how to dimension both two-dimensional shapes and orthographic views. The Dimension command and its associated commands are demonstrated, including how to use the Dimension Styles tool. The commands are presented as needed to create required dimensions. The conventions demonstrated are in compliance with ANSI Y32. The exercise problems for Chapter 8 have been extensively revised and are all presented on grids so that the dimensions can be easily derived.

Chapter 9 introduces tolerances. First, the chapter shows how to draw dimensions and tolerances using the Dimension and Tolerance commands, among others. The chapter ends with an explanation of fits and shows how to use the tables included in the appendix to determine the maximum and minimum tolerances for matching holes and shafts.

Chapter 10 continues the discussion of tolerancing using geometric tolerances and explains how AutoCAD® 2006 can be used to create geometric tolerance symbols directly from dialog boxes. Both profile and positional tolerances are explained. The overall intent of the chapter is to teach students how to make parts fit together. Fixed and floating fastener applications are discussed, and design examples are given for both conditions.

Chapter 11 covers how to draw and design using standard fasteners, including bolts, nuts, machine screws, washers, hexagon heads, square heads, set screws, rivets, and springs. Students are shown how to create wblocks of the individual thread representations and how to use them for different size requirements.

Chapter 12 discusses assembly drawings, detail drawings, and parts lists. Instructions for drawing title blocks, tolerance blocks, release blocks, and revision blocks, and for inserting drawing notes are also included to give students better preparation for industrial practices. Several new exercise problems have been added to the chapter.

Chapter 13 presents gears, cams, and bearings. The intent of the chapter is to teach how to design using gears selected from a manufacturer's catalog. The chapter shows how to select bearings to support gear shafts and how to tolerance holes in support plates to maintain the desired center distances of meshing gears. The chapter also shows how to create a displacement diagram and then draw the appropriate cam profile.

Chapter 14 introduces AutoCAD® 3-D capabilities. It teaches students about AutoCAD® 3-D commands and coordinate system definition before introducing them to surface and solid models. Both WCS and UCS are explained and demonstrated along with Preset and View commands. 3-D primitives are introduced and used to create simple shapes. The chapter concludes by showing how to create orthographic views from the drawn 3-D shapes.

Chapter 15 extends the discussion of Chapter 14 to cover surface modeling. The basic geometric shapes of the Surfaces toolbar are presented as well as the Revsurf, Tabsurf, Rulesurf, 3D Face, and 3D Mesh commands. All the surface commands are demonstrated and used to create 3-D shapes.

Chapter 16 introduces solid modeling and includes the Solids Editing commands. The Solid and Solids Editing toolbars are demonstrated and used with the Union and Subtract commands to create 3-D shapes. Orthographic views are then created from the solid shapes. More complex shapes are created using the Extrude, Section, and Slice commands. The chapter concludes with several exercise problems that demonstrate a solid modeling approach to intersection problems as originally introduced at the end of Chapter 5. The chapter also includes several design exercise problems.

Chapter 17 presents a solid modeling approach to descriptive geometry. For example, a plane is drawn as a solid that is 0.00001 inch thick. AutoCAD®'s solid modeling and other commands are then used to manipulate the plane. The true lengths of lines and shapes of planes, point and plane locations, and properties between lines and planes are discussed. Piercing points and line visibility are also covered.

Online Instructor Materials

To access supplementary materials online, instructors need to request an instructor access code. Go to **www.prenhall.com,** click the **Instructor Resource Center** link, and then click **Register Today** for an instructor access code. Within 48 hours after registering you will receive a confirming e-mail including an instructor access code. Once you have received your code, go the site and log on for full instructions on downloading the materials you wish to use.

Autodesk Learning License

Through a recent agreement with AutoCAD publisher, Autodesk®, Prentice Hall now offers the option of purchasing *Engineering Graphics with AutoCAD 2006* with either a 180-day or a 1-year student software license agreement. This provides adequate time for a student to complete all the activities in this book. The software is functionally identical to the professional license, but is intended **for student or faculty personal use only.** It is not for professional use. For more information about this book and the Autodesk Learning License, contact your local Pearson Prentice Hall sales representative, or contact our National Marketing Manager, Jimmy Stephens at 1 (800) 228-7854 x3725 or at Jimmy_Stephens@prenhall.com. For the name and number of your sales rep, please contact Prentice Hall Faculty Services at 1 (800) 526-0485.

ACKNOWLEDGMENTS

I would like to thank the following reviewers. Their comments and suggestions were most helpful in creating this and previous editions: Anthony Duva, Wentworth Institute of Technology; Dale M. Gerstenecker, St. Louis Community College at Florissant; John Loebach, Spoon River College; N. S. Malladi, Ph.D., University of South Alabama; and Jack Zhou, Drexel University.

Thanks to Debbie Yarnell and Judy Casillo, the managing editor who pulled it all together; to Lisa Garboski; and to David, Maria, Randy, Lisa, Hannah, Wil, Madison, Jack, Luke, and Cheryl for their continued support.

James D. Bethune
Boston University

Contents

Chapter 3—More Advanced Commands

Chapter 4—Sketching

Chapter 5—Orthographic Views

Chapter 14—Fundamentals of 3-D Drawing

Chapter 15—Surface Modeling

Chapter 16—Solid Modeling

Chapter 17—Descriptive Geometry

Appendix

CHAPTER 1

Getting Started

Figure 1-1

1-1 INTRODUCTION

This chapter explains the various aspects of the AutoCAD 2006 for Windows drawing screen and shows how they can be manipulated. Figure 1-1 shows a typical initial AutoCAD Windows screen. Your screen may look slightly different because of your selected screen resolution values.

The top line displays the Windows pull-down menus for exiting a program and changing a program. It is assumed that the reader is familiar with basic Windows operations.

The second line is the Standard toolbar and contains a group of the most commonly used commands.

The third line contains some command icons and an area that shows the current, or docked, object properties that are active.

The line below the drawing portion of the screen displays the name of the current drawing. Since no drawing has been named, the line reads "Drawing1.dwg". Once a drawing name has been defined, it will appear at the bottom of the screen.

The bottom left corner of the drawing screen shows the coordinate display position of the horizontal, vertical crosshairs in terms of an X,Y coordinate value, whose origin is the lower left corner of the drawing screen.

The commands listed on the bottom line (status line) are displayed in light gray when they are off, and in black when they are on.

The horizontal and vertical scroll bars can be used to move the drawing screen up, down, right, or left; they function as they do with other Windows applications.

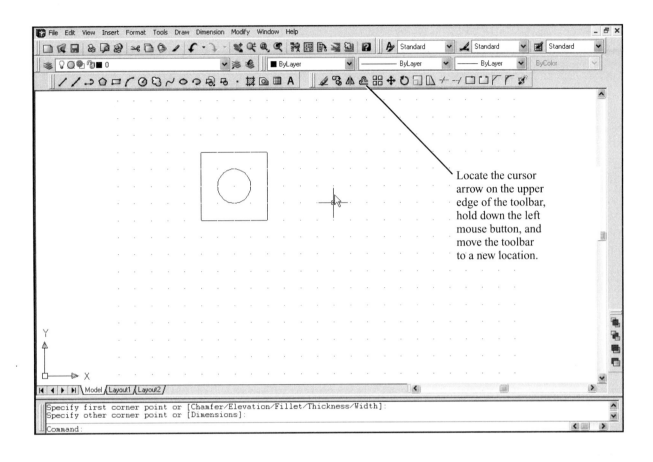

Locate the cursor arrow on the upper edge of the toolbar, hold down the left mouse button, and move the toolbar to a new location.

Figure 1-2

The large open area in the center of the screen is called the *drawing screen,* or *drawing editor.* The two rectangular boxes of command icons located along the left edge of the drawing screen are the Draw and Modify toolbars. They can be moved around the screen as shown in Figure 1-2.

1-2 TOOLBARS

An AutoCAD toolbar contains a group of command icons located under a common heading. The initial AutoCAD as screen, shown in Figure 1-1, contains six toolbars: Layers, Standard, Object Properties, Styles, Draw, and Modify. There are 24 additional predefined toolbars, and you can create your own user-specific toolbars as needed.

To move a toolbar

See Figure 1-2.

1. Locate the cursor arrow on the heading Modify.
2. Press and hold down the left mouse button.

A light gray broken-line box appears around the edge of the toolbar.

3. Still holding the left mouse button down, move the gray outline box to a new location on the screen.
4. Release the left button.

The toolbar will appear in the new location.

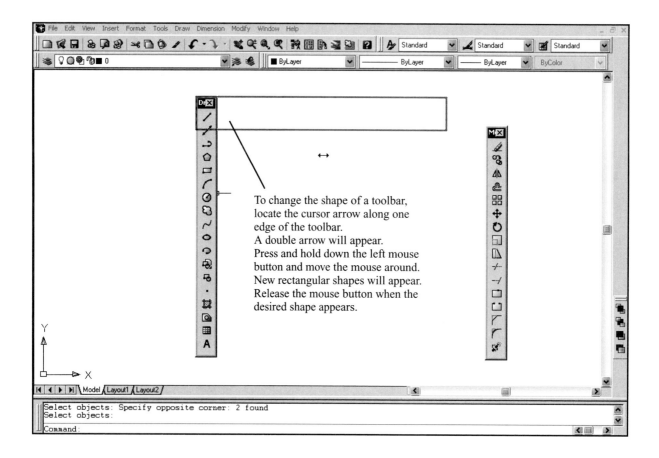

To change the shape of a toolbar,
locate the cursor arrow along one
edge of the toolbar.
A double arrow will appear.
Press and hold down the left mouse
button and move the mouse around.
New rectangular shapes will appear.
Release the mouse button when the
desired shape appears.

Figure 1-3

To change the shape of a toolbar

See Figure 1-3.

1. Locate the cursor arrow along the right edge of the Modify toolbox.

   A double arrow will appear.

2. Press and hold the left mouse button.

   A light gray broken-line box will appear around the outside of the toolbar.

3. Still holding the left mouse button down, move the mouse around and watch how the gray box changes shape.

4. When the gray toolbar shape is a long, vertical rectangle, release the left mouse button.

   A reshaped toolbar will appear.

To return the toolbar to its original location and shape

1. Locate the cursor arrow along the bottom or edge lines of the toolbar and return the toolbar to its original shape using the procedure outlined in Figure 1-3.
2. Move the reshaped toolbar to its original location along the left side of the drawing screen using the procedure outlined in Figure 1-2.

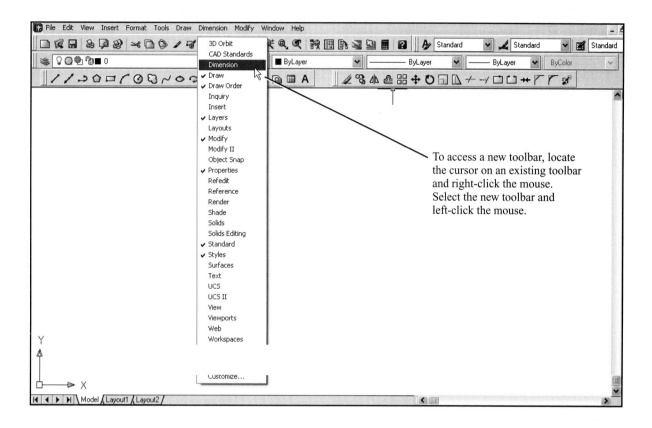

To access a new toolbar, locate the cursor on an existing toolbar and right-click the mouse. Select the new toolbar and left-click the mouse.

Figure 1-4

To add a new toolbar to the screen

See Figures 1-4 and 1-5.

1. Locate the cursor on any one of the existing toolbars and press the right mouse button. In this example the Standard toolbar was selected.

A list of the available toolbars will cascade down the screen.

2. Select a new toolbar and click the left mouse button. In this example, the Dimension toolbar was selected.

The selected toolbar will appear on the drawing screen. See Figure 1-5. You can move any toolbar or change its shape as described in Figures 1-2 and 1-3.

To remove a toolbar from the screen

1. Locate the cursor arrow on the check mark located in the upper right corner of the toolbar and press the left mouse button.

Figure 1-5 shows the Draw and Modify toolbars docked horizontally at the top of the drawing screen. The Dimension toolbar will initally appear within the drawing area of the screen, as will any other toolbar activated. Toolbars can then be moved to different locations, as explained. If the toolbar is located close to either the top or sides of the drawing screen, it will blend into the area surrounding the drawing area and will no longer be within the drawing area.

The Dimension toolbar

Figure 1-5

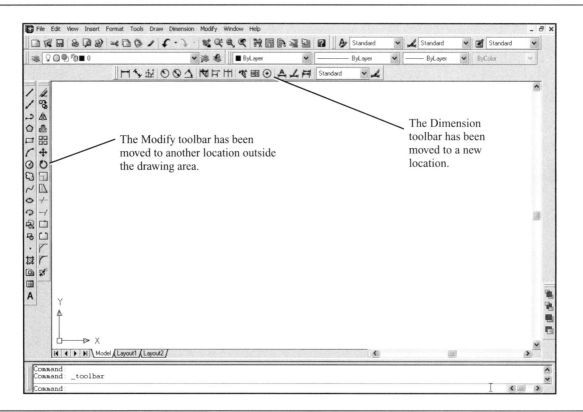

The Modify toolbar has been moved to another location outside the drawing area.

The Dimension toolbar has been moved to a new location.

Figure 1-6

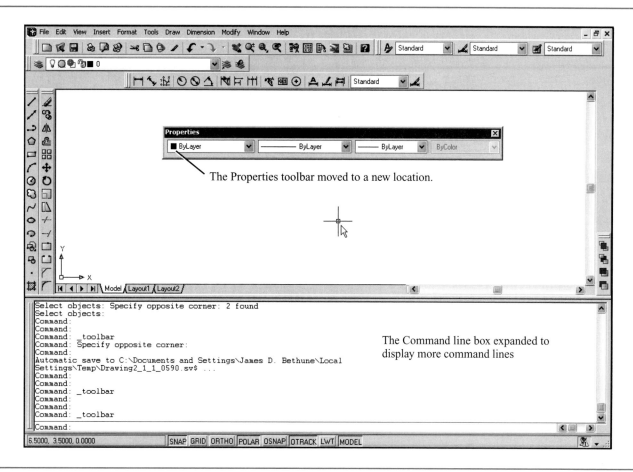

Figure 1-7

To relocate the toolbars from positions outside the drawing area

1. Locate the cursor arrow above the icons, but still below the horizontal line that defines the toolbar area, and press and hold down the left mouse button. A rectangular box will appear around the toolbars that will move with the cursor arrow. Release the left button when the new location is reached.

Figure 1-6 shows the Dimension toolbar located at the top of the screen, and the Modify and Draw toolbars located outside the drawing area. Note how they have blended into the area outside the drawing screen.

1-3 THE COMMAND LINE BOX

The size of the Command window, located at the bottom of the screen, may be changed to display more or fewer command lines. It is recommended that at least two command lines be visible at all times.

To resize the Command Line box

See Figure 1-7.

1. Locate the cursor arrow along the top edge of the Command Line box. A double arrow will appear.
2. Still holding the left mouse button down, move the cursor arrow to a new location on the drawing screen.

The Command Line box will expand as the double arrow is moved upward.

3. Release the left mouse button to relocate the Command Line box.

The Command Line box may now be moved and reshaped just like a toolbar. Figure 1-7 also shows the Object Properties toolbar moved from its original position above

A toolbar contains tools (icons that allow access to commands).

To determine the command a tool represents, locate the cursor arrow on the tool, but do not press a mouse button. The name of the command represented will appear.

Figure 1-8

the drawing area to a location within the drawing area. AutoCAD allows you to customize the screen to whatever configuration suits your work best.

1-4 COMMAND TOOLS

A *tool* is a picture (icon) that represents an AutoCAD command. Most commands have equivalent tools.

To determine the command a tool represents

See Figure 1-8.

1. Locate the cursor arrow on the selected icon (tool).

In the example shown, the Line command tool within the Draw toolbar was selected.

2. Hold the arrow still without pressing any mouse buttons.

The command name will appear below the tool. This name is referred to as a *tooltip*.

1-5 STARTING A NEW DRAWING

When a new drawing is started a drawing name is assigned, the drawing units are specified, the drawing limits are modified, if needed, and Grid and Snap values are defined. The following four sections will show how to start a new drawing.

1-6 NAMING A DRAWING

Any combination of letters and numbers may be used as a file name. Either upper- or lowercase letters may be used, since AutoCAD file names are not case-sensitive. The symbols $, -, and _ (underscore) may also be used. Other symbols, such as % and *, may not be used. See Figure 1-9.

All AutoCAD drawing files will automatically have the extension *.dwg* added to the given file name. If you name a drawing FIRST, it will appear in the files as FIRST.dwg. Other extensions can be used, but the .dwg is the default setting. (A default setting is one that AutoCAD will use unless specifically told to use some other value.)

Drawings may be saved to any drive and directory. The defaults for Windows XP Professional are the C: drive and the My Documents directory.

Correct drawing names:

    FIRST   **EK-130-1**   **PA1-1a**

Incorrect drawing names:

    100%   ***.***

To locate a file on a disk in the A: drive:

    A:FIRST

Figure 1-9

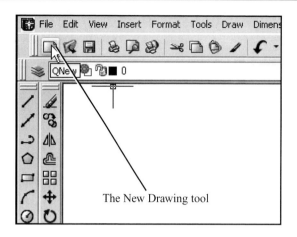

The New Drawing tool

Figure 1-10

If you want to locate a file on another drive, specify the drive letter followed by a colon in front of the drawing name. For example, in Figure 1-9 the file specified A:FIRST will locate the drawing file FIRST on the A: drive.

For large drawings, that is, drawings that have very large databases likely to exceed the capacity of the specified drive, it is better to work on a drive that you are sure has sufficient space to accept the drawing file and then transfer the drawing to another drive as part of the saving process.

To start a new drawing

There are four ways to access the Create New Drawing dialog box that is used to name a new drawing:

Select the File pull-down menu, then New.

Figure 1-11

1. Select the New Drawing tool in the Standard toolbar (see Figure 1-10).
2. Select the File pull-down menu, then select New (see Figure 1-11).
3. Type the word *new* in response to a Command prompt.
4. Hold down the Control key and press N.

Any of these methods will cause the Select template dialog box to appear on the screen. See Figure 1-12. The acad template will set up a drawing using inch values and ANSI style dimensions. The acadiso template

This template will set up a drawing with millimeter values and iso style dimensions.

This template will set up a drawing with inch values and ANSI style dimensions.

Figure 1-12

Figure 1-13

will set up a drawing using millimeter values and ISO style dimensions.

To save a new drawing file

A drawing name is entered as a file name by using the Save As option under the File pull-down menu. See Figure 1-13. It is recommended that a drawing name be assigned before a new drawing is started.

1. Select the File pull-down menu.
2. Select Save As.

The Save As dialog box will appear. See Figure 1-14. Note that the operating system for the computer used to create Figure 1-14 was Microsoft Windows NP. This dialog box may look different if a different operating system is used.

Figure 1-14

The Save Drawing As dialog box will list all existing drawings. Click on the thumbnail option under the Views heading to change the list to thumbnail drawings.

3. Enter the drawing name.

In this example, the drawing name "First" was used.

4. Select OK.

The name of the drawing will appear at the top of the screen. See Figure 1-15.

1-7 DRAWING UNITS

AutoCAD 2006's Select template dialog box allows for either English or metric units to be used as default values; however, AutoCAD can work in any of five different unit

Figure 1-15

Figure 1-16

Select the Architectural units.

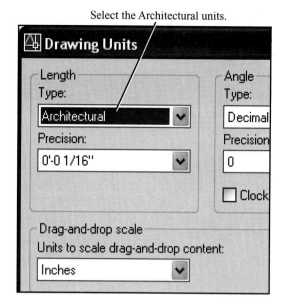

Figure 1-17

systems: Scientific, Decimal, Engineering, Architectural, or Fractional. The default system is the Decimal system and can be applied to either English (inches) or metric values (millimeters).

To specify or to change the drawing units

1. Select the Format pull-down menu.
2. Select Units (see Figure 1-16).

The Drawing Units dialog box will appear. See Figure 1-17.

3. Select architectural units by clicking the arrow to the right of the Type box.

A listing of the five unit options will cascade down.

4. Select Architectural.
5. Select OK.

The original drawing screen will reappear. Note that the coordinate display box now displays the cursor location in terms of feet and fractional inches.

6. Repeat the procedure and set the units back to decimal.

To specify or change the precision of the units system

Unit values can be expressed from zero to eight decimal places or from 0 to 1/256 of an inch.

1. Access the Drawing Units dialog box as explained previously.

2. Select the arrow to the right of the current precision value display box below the word Precision.

A listing of the possible decimal precision values will cascade from the box. See Figure 1-18.

3. Select 0.0000.

The value 0.0000 will appear in the Precision box.

4. Select OK.

The original drawing screen will appear. If the unit precision had been changed, the change could be checked

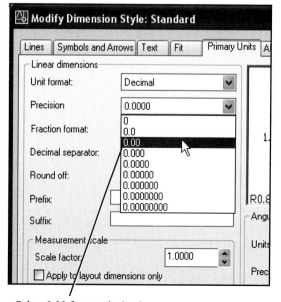

Select 0.00 for two decimal place precision.

Figure 1-18

```
┌─────────────────────────────────────┐
│                                       │
│   Standard Drawing Sheet Sizes—Inches │
│                                       │
│        A = 8.5 × 11                   │
│        B = 11 × 17                    │
│        C = 17 × 22                    │
│        D = 22 × 34                    │
│        E = 34 × 44                    │
│                                       │
└─────────────────────────────────────┘
```

Figure 1-19

by looking at the coordinate display box in the lower left corner of the screen. The values displayed should reflect the new precision specification. Figure 1-18 shows how to select a coordinate display with a precision of two decimal places.

To specify or change the Angle units value

Angles may be specified in one of five different units: Decimal Degrees, Degrees/Minutes/Seconds, Gradians, Radians, or Surveyor units. Decimal Degrees is the default value.

Change the angle units by selecting the desired units in the cascade menu under Angle Type. The precision of the angle units is changed as specified for linear units.

1-8 DRAWING LIMITS

Drawing limits are used to set the boundaries of the drawing. The drawing boundaries are usually set to match the size of a sheet of drawing paper. This means that when the drawing is plotted and a hard copy is made, it will fit on the drawing paper.

Figure 1-19 shows a listing of standard flat-size drawing papers for engineering applications, Figure 1-20 shows

```
┌─────────────────────────────────────┐
│                                       │
│                                       │
│   Standard Drawing Sheet Sizes—Millimeters │
│                                       │
│        A4 = 210 × 297                 │
│        A3 = 297 × 420                 │
│        A2 = 420 × 594                 │
│        A1 = 594 × 841                 │
│        A0 = 841 × 1189                │
│                                       │
└─────────────────────────────────────┘
```

Figure 1-20

```
┌─────────────────────────────────────┐
│                                       │
│   Standard Drawing Sheet Sizes—Architectural │
│                                   USA │
│        A = 9 × 12                     │
│        B = 12 × 18                    │
│        C = 18 × 24                    │
│        D = 24 × 36                    │
│        E = 36 × 48                    │
│                                       │
└─────────────────────────────────────┘
```

Figure 1-21

standard metric sizes, and Figure 1-21 shows standard architectural sizes.

A standard 8.5″ × 11″ letter-size sheet of paper as used by most impact and laser printers is referred to as an *A-size* sheet of drawing paper.

To align the drawing limits with a standard A4 (metric) paper size

1. Create an acadiso template, then select the Format pull-down menu.
2. Select Drawing Limits.

See Figure 1-22. The following prompts will appear in the Command Line box.

Reset Model space limits:
Specify lower left corner or [ON/OFF]
<0.0000,0.0000>:

Figure 1-22

Click here to set values for Grid and Snap.

Figure 1-23

3. Press the Enter key or the right button on the mouse.

This means that you have accepted the default value of 0.0000,0.0000, or that the lower left of the drawing screen is the origin of an X,Y axis.

Specify upper right corner <420.0000,297.0000>:

4. Type 297,210; press Enter.

This changes the upper right corner of the drawing screen to an X,Y value of 297,210. There will be no visible change to the screen. The new limit extends beyond the cur-

rent screen calibration. The screen must be recalibrated to align with the new drawing limits.

5. Type Zoom.

Specify corner of window, enter a scale factor (nX or nXP) or [All/Center/Dynamic/Extents/ Previous/Scale/Window] <real time>:

6. Type A; press Enter.

The Zoom All command will align whatever drawing limits have been defined to the drawing screen. You can verify that the new drawing limits are in place by moving the cursor around the screen and noting the coordinate display box in the lower left corner of the screen. The values should be much larger than they were with the original inch default screen settings.

1-9 GRID AND SNAP

The Grid command is used to place a dotted grid background on the drawing screen. This background grid is helpful for establishing visual reference points for sizing and locating points and lines.

The Snap command limits the movement of the cursor to predefined points on the screen. For example, if the Snap command values are set to match the Grid values, the cursor will snap from grid point to grid point. It cannot be located at a point between the grid points.

The default Grid and Snap setting for the acad template is 0.50 inch, and the default setting for Grid and Snap for the acadiso template is 10 millimeters.

To set the Grid and Snap values

1. Create an acadiso template, then select the Tools pull-down menu.
2. Select Drafting Settings.

See Figure 1-23. The Drafting Settings dialog box will appear. See Figure 1-24. If necessary, click the Snap and Grid tab.

3. Click on the Grid and Snap boxes.
4. Place the cursor on the Snap X spacing box to the right of the given value under the Snap heading.

A vertical flashing cursor will appear.

5. Backspace out the existing value and type in 5.
6. Click the Snap Y spacing box.

The Y spacing will automatically be made equal to the X spacing value. Nonrectangular snap spacing can be created by specifying different X and Y spacing values.

Define the X and Y values for Snap and Grid here.

Figure 1-24

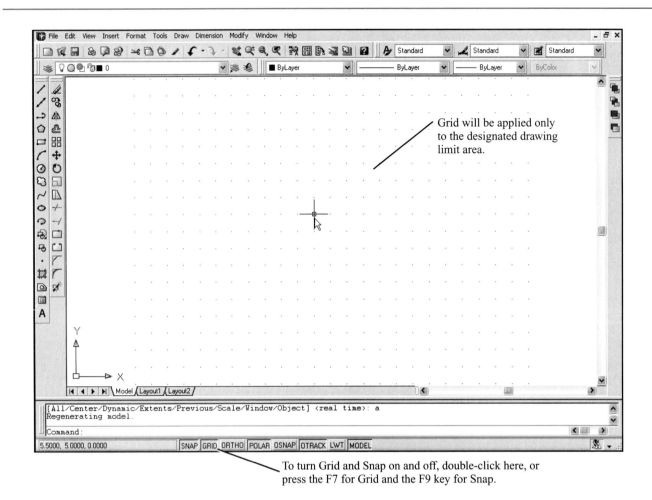

Grid will be applied only
to the designated drawing
limit area.

To turn Grid and Snap on and off, double-click here, or
press the F7 for Grid and the F9 key for Snap.

Figure 1-25

7. Select the Grid X spacing box under the Grid heading.
8. Backspace out the existing value and type in 10 (just 10).
9. Click the Grid Y spacing box to make the X and Y values equal.
10. Select OK.

The original drawing screen will appear with a dotted grid. See Figure 1-25. Since the Snap values have been set to exactly half the Grid values, the cursor can be located either directly on grid points or halfway between them.

The grid will first appear in the lower left corner of the drawing screen. Use the All option of the Zoom command or the Zoom Window command to increase the size of the grid to match the drawing screen. See Figure 1-25.

The grid can be turned on and off by either double-clicking the word GRID at the bottom of the screen or by pressing the F7 key on the keyboard. Snap can be turned on and off by double-clicking the word SNAP at the bottom of the screen or by pressing the F9 key on the keyboard.

Figure 1-26

1-10 SAMPLE PROBLEM SP1-1

Set up a drawing that will use millimeter dimensions and the following parameters:

Sheet size = 297,210
Grid = 10 spacing
Snap = 5 spacing
Whole-number precision

To specify the drawing units

1. Select the New tool from the Standard toolbar.

The Select template dialog box will appear. See Figure 1-26.

2. Select the acadiso template, then OK.

To define the drawing precision

1. Select the Format pull-down menu, then Units.

The Drawing Units dialog box will appear. See Figure 1-27. In this example only whole numbers will be used, so the "0" option is selected.

2. Select the desired precision, then OK.

To calibrate the sheet size

1. Select the Format pull-down menu, then Drawing Limits.
2. Set the lower limit for 0.0000,0.0000 (accept the default values), and the upper right limit for 297,210.

The limits are given in terms of their X,Y coordinate values.

Figure 1-27

To set the Grid and Snap values

1. Select the Tools pull-down menu, then Drafting Settings.

The Drafting Settings dialog box will appear. See Figure 1-28.

2. Enter the designated Grid and Snap values.

The screen is now ready for starting a drawing using millimeter values. Note that the grid fills only the 297 × 210 area specified as the drawing limits.

Define the X and Y values for the Grid and Snap.

Figure 1-28

1-11 SAVE AND SAVE AS

The Save and Save As commands are used to save a drawing. The Save command is also called the *quick save* command. It is used primarily while you are working on a drawing to save your work as you go. Save can also be used to save a finished drawing, but only under the original file name of the drawing. The Save As command allows you to save a drawing under a different file name.

To use the Save command

The Save command can be accessed in one of three ways:

1. Click the Save icon on the Standard toolbar.
2. Select the File pull-down menu and select Save.
3. Press Control + S.

The Save Drawing As dialog box will appear with the drawing name listed as the File name. See Figure 1-29.

4. Click the Save box.

To use the Save As command

The Save As command is used to save a drawing just as the Save command does, but under a name that is different from the original drawing name. For example, you named a drawing FIRST and then decided to save it on a floppy disk on the A: drive under the name BOX.

1. Select the File pull-down menu, then Save As.

The Save Drawing As dialog box will appear. See Figure 1-30.

2. Scroll down the Save in box and select the 3 1/2 Floppy (A:) option.
3. Type the new file name in the File name box.
4. Click the Save box.

1-12 OPEN

The Open command is used to call up an existing drawing so that you may continue working on it, or revise it.

To use the Open command

The Open command may be accessed in one of three ways:

1. Use the Open tool on the Standard toolbar.
2. Select the File pull-down menu, then select Open.
3. Press Control + O.

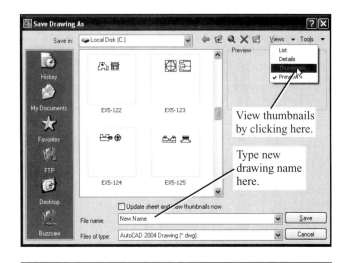

Figure 1-29

The Select File dialog box will appear. Select the Preview option under the Views heading. See Figure 1-31. Drawings will be listed and a preview of each presented. Click the desired drawing's preview, and the file name will appear in the File name box, then click Open.

1-13 EXIT

The Exit command allows you to exit AutoCAD.

1. Select the File pull-down menu, then Exit.

See Figure 1-32. The system will exit the AutoCAD program and return to Windows.

Figure 1-30

Figure 1-31

Figure 1-32

1-14 EXERCISE PROBLEMS

EX1-1

Create a drawing screen as shown. Include the Object Snap, Zoom, Draw, Modify, and Dimension toolbars in the orientation and format shown.

EX1-2

Create the following drawing screen setup.

Decimal units
Drawing Limits = 594,420
Grid = 25
Snap = 12.5

EX1-3

Create the following drawing screen setup.

Decimal units
Drawing Limits = 17,11
Grid = 1.00
Snap = 0.50

EX1-4

Create the following drawing screen setup.

Architectural units
Drawing Limits = 48,36
Grid = 6
Snap = 3

EX1-5

Create the following drawing screen setup.

Fractional units
Drawing Limits = 36,24
Grid = 1
Snap = 1/2

EX1-6

Create a drawing screen as shown. Include the Text, Zoom, Modify II Draw, and Modify toolbars in the orientation and format shown.

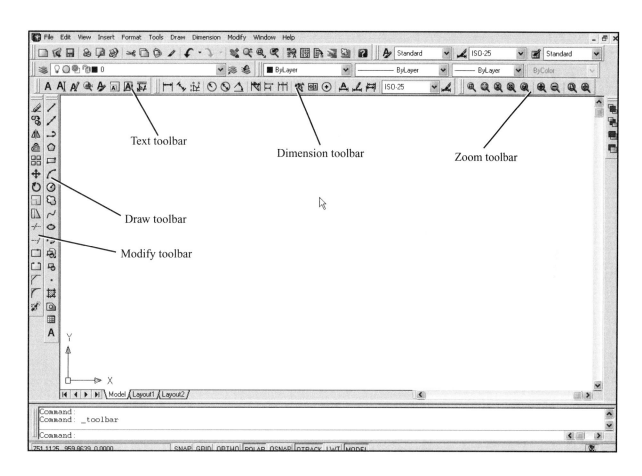

EX1-7

Create the following drawing screen setup.

Decimal units
Drawing Limits = aligned with an A3 sheet size
Grid = 10
Snap = 5
Precision = one decimal place

EX1-8

Create the following drawing screen setup.

Decimal units
Drawing Limits = aligned with a C sheet size
Grid = 0.50
Snap = 0.25
Precision = two decimal places

EX1-9

Create a drawing screen as shown. Include the Text, Zoom, Draw, Modify, Modify II, Dimension, and Viewports toolbars in the orientation and format shown.

C H A P T E R 2

Fundamentals of 2-D Construction

2-1 INTRODUCTION

This chapter demonstrates how to work with AutoCAD commands. AutoCAD commands are executed by using command tools, toolbars, and a series of prompts. The prompts appear in the Command Line box and ask for a selection or numeric input so that a command sequence can be completed. The Line command was chosen to demonstrate the various input and prompt sequences that are typical with AutoCAD commands.

Most of the commands contained in the Draw and Modify toolbars will be demonstrated in this chapter. The purpose is to present enough commands for the reader to be able to create simple 2-D shapes. The next chapter will present more advanced applications for these commands and will present some new commands as well.

2-2 LINE—RANDOM POINTS

The Line command is used to draw straight lines between two defined points. Figure 2-1 shows the Line tool on the Draw toolbar.

There are four ways to define the length and location of a line: randomly select points; set a specific value for the Snap function and select points using the Snap spacing

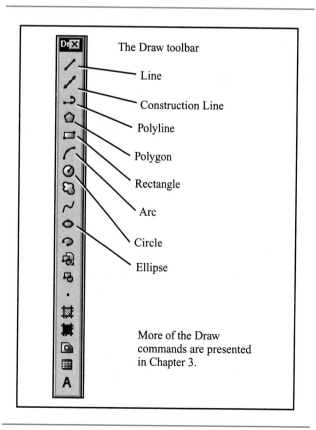

The Draw toolbar

— Line

— Construction Line

— Polyline

— Polygon

— Rectangle

— Arc

— Circle

— Ellipse

More of the Draw commands are presented in Chapter 3.

Figure 2-1

21

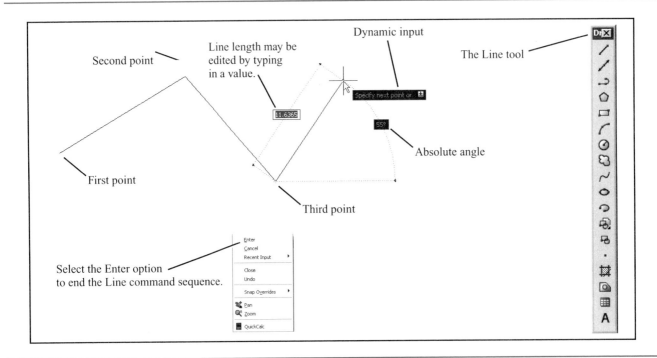

Figure 2-2

values; enter the coordinate values for the start and end points; or use relative inputs and specify the starting point, the length, and the direction of the line.

To randomly select points (See Figure 2-2.)

1. Select the Line tool in the Draw toolbar.

   You can also access the Line command by typing the word *line* in response to a command prompt.
   The following command sequence will appear in the Command Line box.

   Command: _line Specify first point:

2. Place the cursor randomly on the drawing screen and press the left mouse button.

   Specify next point or [Undo]:

   As you move the cursor from point to point dynamic inputs will appear on the screen. See Figure 2-2. Dynamic inputs include an absolute angle and length change box. Dynamic inputs will be discussed in Section 2-6.

3. Randomly pick another point on the screen.

   Specify next point or [Undo]:

   AutoCAD will keep asking for another point until you press either the Enter key or the right mouse button.

4. When the right mouse button is pressed a small dialog box will appear. See Figure 2-2.

5. Click the Enter option to end the Line command sequence.

   The Line command may be reactivated by pressing the right mouse button immediately after selecting the Enter option. A dialog box will appear. See Figure 2-3. Select the Repeat Line option to restart the Line command.

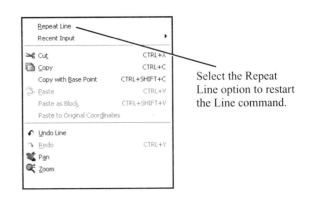

Select the Repeat Line option to restart the Line command.

Figure 2-3

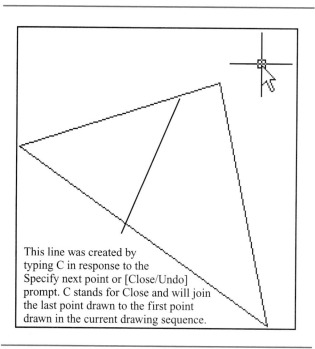

This line was created by typing C in response to the Specify next point or [Close/Undo] prompt. C stands for Close and will join the last point drawn to the first point drawn in the current drawing sequence.

Figure 2-4

To exit a command sequence

If, as you work, you need to exit a command sequence, press the Escape key, which will return you to a command prompt. The Escape key allows you to exit almost all AutoCAD commands.

To create a closed area (See Figure 2-4.)

1. Select the Line tool from the Draw toolbar.

   Command: _line Specify first point:

2. Select a random point.

   Specify next point or [Undo]:

3. Select a second random point.

   Specify next point or [Undo]:

4. Select a third random point.

   Specify next point or [Close/Undo]:

5. Type C, then press Enter to activate the Close option.

   A line will be drawn from the third point to the starting point, creating a closed area.

2-3 ERASE

You can erase any line by using the Erase command. There are two ways to erase lines: select individual lines or window a group of lines. The Erase tool is located on the Modify toolbar. See Figure 2-5.

To erase individual lines

1. Select the Erase tool on the Modify toolbar.

   The following prompt will appear in the Command Line box.

   Command: _erase
   Select objects:

   The cursor will be replaced by a rectangular cursor. This is the select cursor (*pickbox*). Any time you see this

Figure 2-5

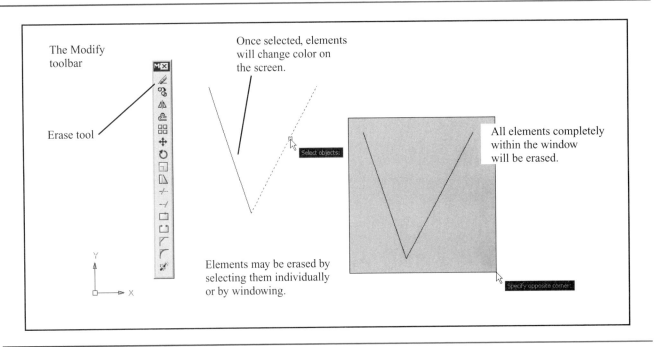

The Modify toolbar

Erase tool

Once selected, elements will change color on the screen.

All elements completely within the window will be erased.

Select objects:

Specify opposite corner:

Elements may be erased by selecting them individually or by windowing.

Figure 2-6

cursor, AutoCAD expects you to select an entity—in this example, a line. See Figure 2-6.

If you change your mind and do not want to erase anything, select the next command you want to use, and the Erase command will be terminated.

2. Select the two open lines by placing the rectangular cursor on each line, one at a time, and pressing the left mouse button.

The lines will change color from black to a broken gray pattern. This color change indicates that the line has been selected. The selection is confirmed by a change in the prompt.

Select objects: 1 found
Select objects:

3. Press the right mouse button or the Enter key to complete the Erase sequence.

The two lines should disappear from the screen.

To erase a group of lines simultaneously (See Figure 2-6.)

1. Select the Erase tool.

Command: _erase
Select objects:

2. Place the rectangular select cursor above and to the left of the lines to be erased and press the left mouse button.

3. Move the mouse, and a shaded window will drag from the selected first point.

4. When all the lines to be erased are completely within the window, press the left mouse button.

All the lines completely within the window will be selected and will change to broken gray lines. The number of lines selected will be referenced in the Command Line box.

5. Press the right mouse button or the Enter key to complete the command sequence.

The lines will disappear from the screen. The Undo tool will return all the lines, if needed. If the Erase window was created from right to left, any line even partially within the Erase window would be erased.

2-4 LINE—SNAP POINTS

Lines can be drawn using calibrated Snap spacing. This technique is similar to drawing points randomly, but because the cursor is limited to specific points, the length of lines can be determined accurately. See Figure 2-7.

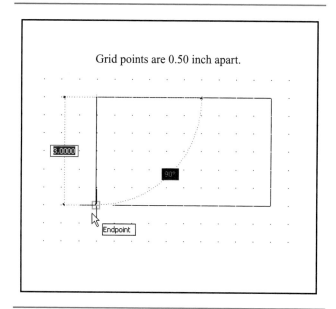

Grid points are 0.50 inch apart.

Figure 2-7

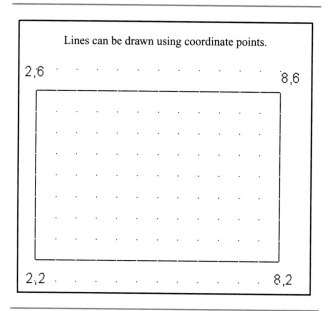

Lines can be drawn using coordinate points.

2,6   8,6

2,2   8,2

Figure 2-8

Problem: Draw a 3″ × 5″ rectangle.

1. Set the Grid spacing for .5 and the Snap spacing for .50, and turn both commands on. Zoom the grid to fit the screen.
2. Select the Line tool from the Draw toolbar.

   Command: _line Specify first point:

3. Select a grid point.

   Specify next point or [Undo]:

4. Move the cursor horizontally to the right 10 grid spaces and press the left mouse button.

   The Grid spacing has been set at .5, so 10 spaces equals 5 units. Watch the dynamic input readings as you move the cursor. The X value should increase by 5, and the Y value should stay the same.

   Specify next point or [Undo]:

5. Move the cursor vertically 6 spaces and press the left mouse button.

   Specify next point or [Close/Undo]:

6. Move the cursor horizontally to the left 10 spaces and press the left mouse button.

   Specify next point or [Close/Undo]:

7. Type c; press Enter.

   Save or erase the drawing as desired.

2-5 LINE—COORDINATE VALUES

AutoCAD will also accept locational inputs, the start and end points of a line, in terms of X,Y coordinate values. The 0,0 origin is located in the lower left corner of the drawing screen.

Problem: Draw a 4″ × 6″ rectangle starting at the 2,2 coordinate point. See Figure 2-8.

1. Select the Line tool from the Draw toolbar.

   Command: _line Specify first point:

2. Move the cursor to the right of the word point: in the command line and left-click the mouse. Type 2,2; press Enter.

   Specify next point or [Undo]:

3. Move the cursor to the command line and type 8,2; press Enter.

   The X value has been increased 6 inches.

   Specify next point or [Close/Undo]:

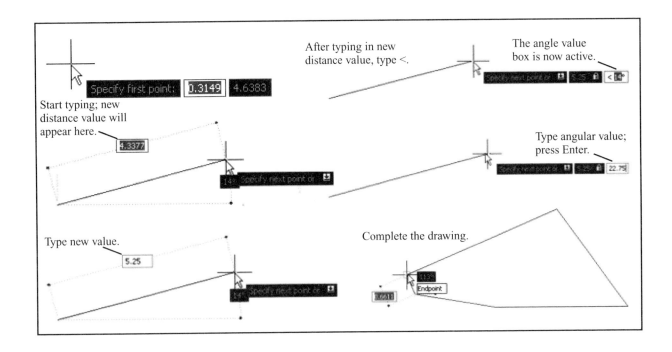

After typing in new distance value, type <.

The angle value box is now active.

Start typing; new distance value will appear here.

Specify first point: 0.3149 4.6383

Type angular value; press Enter.

Type new value.

5.25

Complete the drawing.

Endpoint

Figure 2-9

4. Move the cursor to the command line and type 8,6; press Enter.

   The Y value has been increased 4 inches.

   Specify next point or [Close/Undo]:

5. Move the cursor to the command line and type 2,6; press Enter.

   Specify next point or [Close/Undo]:

6. Type c; press Enter.

   Save or erase the drawing as desired.

2-6 LINE—DYNAMIC INPUTS

Dynamic Input is a new command. It allows both angular and distance values to be added to a drawing using screen prompts.

To create lines using Dynamic Input

This example was created using inch values.

1. Click the Line command tool and select a starting point.

   Figure 2-9 shows the dynamic input for the selected first point.

2. Move the cursor to the approximate location of the second line point.

   The distance and angular values for this new point will be displayed in boxes.

   Angular values assume that 0° is a horizontal line to the right of the first line point.

3. Type in the desired distance value.

   The new value will appear in the distance value box.

4. Continue typing (do not press Enter) and type the < symbol.

   The line distance will change to the typed value, and the angle box will become active.

5. Type the desired angular value; press Enter.

Figure 2-10

The angular value will be applied to the line, and the dynamic input command will prepare for the next line point input.

6. Complete the desired shape; press Enter.

To access the Dynamic Input Settings

See Figure 2-10.

1. Right-click the DYN box located at the bottom of the screen.

    A small dialog box will appear. See Figure 2-10.

2. Click the Settings option.

    The Dynamic Input settings box will appear.

2-7 CONSTRUCTION LINE

The Construction Line command is used to draw lines of infinite length. Construction lines are very helpful during the initial layout of a drawing. They can be trimmed during the creation of the drawing as needed.

1. Select the Construction Line tool from the Draw toolbar.

    Command:_ xline Specify a point or [Hor/Ver/ Ang/Bisect/Offset]:

    The Specify a point command is the default setting.

2. Select or define a starting point.

    You can position the direction of the line by moving the cursor or by using dynamic input, as defined in Section 2-7, to define the line's direction.

3. Select or use dynamic input to define a through point.

    Specify through point:

    A line will pivot about the designated starting point and extend an infinite length in a direction through the cursor. You can position the direction of the line by moving the cursor. See Figure 2-11.

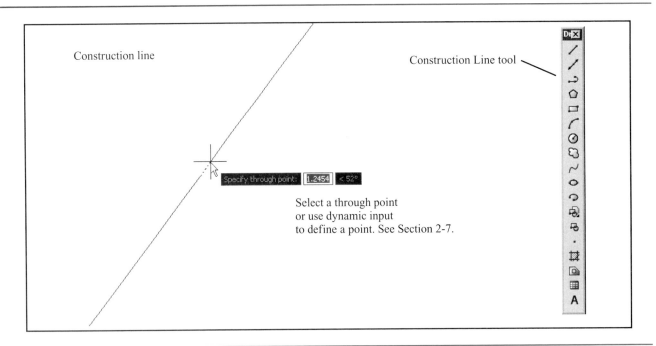

Construction line

Construction Line tool

Specify through point: 1.2454 < 52°

Select a through point
or use dynamic input
to define a point. See Section 2-7.

Figure 2-11

4. Select or define a through point.

An infinitely long line will be drawn through the two designated points.

Specify through point:

Another infinite line will appear through the starting point through the cursor.

5. Press Enter.

This ends the Construction Line command sequence. The sequence may be reactivated and another construction line drawn by pressing the Enter key a second time.

Other Construction Line commands: Hor/Ver/Ang

The lines shown in Figure 2-12 were created using the Hor (horizontal), Ver (vertical), and Ang (angular) options. A grid was created and the Snap option was turned on so the lines could be drawn through known points. Figure 2-12 was created as follows:

1. Set up the drawing screen with Grid and Snap spacings of .5.

2. Select the Construction Line tool in the Draw toolbar.

Command:_ xline Specify a point or [Hor/Ver/Ang/ Bisect/Offset]:

3. Type H; press Enter.

A horizontal line will appear through the cursor.

Specify through point:

4. Select or define a point on the drawing screen.

A horizontal line will appear through the point. As you move the mouse another horizontal line will appear through the cursor.

Specify through point:

5. Select or define a second point.

Specify through point:

6. Select or define a third point.

Specify through point:

7. Double-click the right mouse button and select the Repeat Construction Line option from the dialog box that appears on the screen.

Figure 2-12

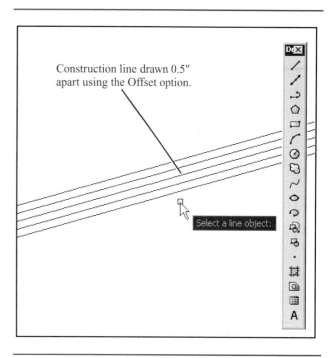

Figure 2-13

Command:_ xline Specify a point or [Hor/Ver/Ang/Bisect/Offset]:

8. Type V; press Enter.

Specify through point:

9. Draw vertical lines, then double-click the Enter key and select the Repeat Construction Line option.

Command:_ xline Specify a point or [Hor/Ver/Ang/Bisect/Offset]:

10. Type A; press Enter.

Enter angle of xline (0) or [Reference]:

11. Type 45; press Enter.

Specify through point:

An infinite line at 45° will appear through the crosshairs.

12. Draw 45° lines.

Specify through point:

13. Press Enter.

Your drawing should look approximately like Figure 2-12.

Other Construction Line command: Offset

The Offset option allows you to draw a line parallel to an existing line, regardless of the line's orientation, at a pre-defined distance. See Figure 2-13.

1. Select the Construction Line tool in the Draw toolbar.

Command:_ xline Specify a point or [Hor/Ver/Ang/Bisect/Offset]:

2. Draw a line approximately 15° to the horizontal.

Specify through point:

3. Double-click the Enter key to restart the Construction Line command sequence.

Command:_ xline Specify a point or [Hor/Ver/Ang/Bisect/Offset]:

4. Type O; press Enter.

The O will appear in the dynamic input box.

Offset distance or through <Through>:

5. Type .5; press Enter.

Select a line object:

6. Select the line.

Select side to offset:

7. Select a point above the line.

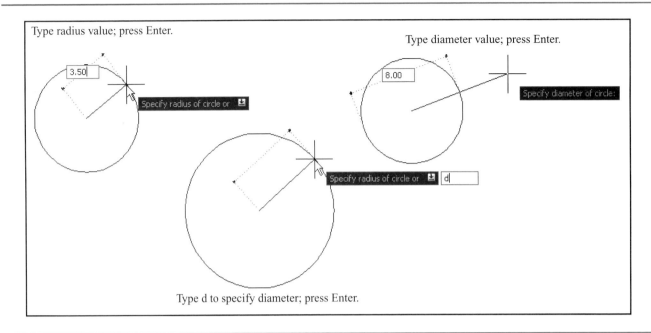

Figure 2-14

Select a line object:

8. Select the line just created by the offset option.

    Select side to offset:

9. Again select a point above the selected line.

    Select a line object:

10. Draw several more lines below the original line.

    Select a line object:

11. Press the right mouse button.

    This will end the Offset command sequence and return a Command prompt to the Command prompt line.

2-8 CIRCLE

The Circle tool is on the Draw toolbar. Circles may be defined by a center point and either a radius or diameter; by two or three points on the diameter; or by the tangents to two existing lines or arcs and a radius value.

To draw a circle—radius (See Figure 2-14.)

1. Select the Circle tool from the Draw toolbar.

    Command: _circle Specify a center point for circle or [3P/2P/Ttr (tan tan radius)]:

2. Select or use dynamic input to define a center point.

    Specify radius of circle or [Diameter]:

3. Type 3.50; press Enter.

    The radius value will appear in the Dynamic Input box.

To draw a circle—diameter (See Figure 2-14.)

1. Select the Circle tool from the Draw toolbar.

    Command: _circle Specify a center point for circle or [3P/2P/Ttr (tan tan radius)]:

2. Select or define a center point.

    Specify radius of circle or [Diameter]:

3. Type d; press Enter.

    Specify diameter of circle <value>:

4. Type 8.00; press Enter.

To draw a circle—2 points (See Figure 2-15.)

1. Select the Circle tool from the Draw toolbar.

    Command: _circle Specify a center point for circle or [3P/2P/Ttr (tan tan radius)]:

2. Type 2p; press Enter.

    Specify first end point of circle's diameter:

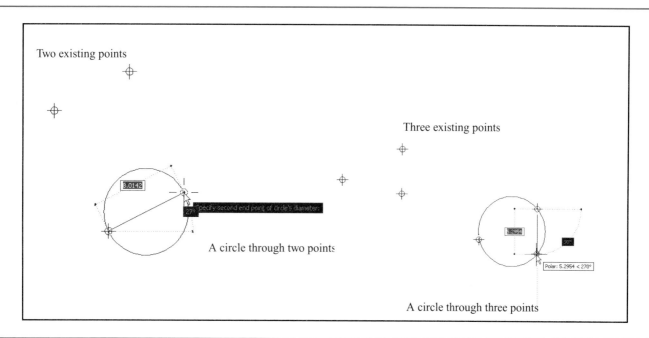

Two existing points

Three existing points

A circle through two points

A circle through three points

Figure 2-15

3. Select or define a first point.

    Select second end point of circle's diameter:

4. Select or define a second point.

    The circle will automatically be drawn through the first and second points.

To draw a circle—3 points (See Figure 2-15.)

1. Select the Circle tool from the Draw toolbar.

    Command: _circle Specify a center point for circle or [3P/2P/Ttr (tan tan radius)]:

2. Type 3p; press Enter.

    Specify first point on circle:

3. Select or define a first point.

    Specify second point on circle:

4. Select or define a second point.

    Specify third point on circle:

5. Select or define a third point.

To draw a circle—tangent tangent radius

    The Tangent Tangent Radius option allows you to draw a circle tangent to two other entities. Figure 2-16 shows a circle drawn tangent to two lines.

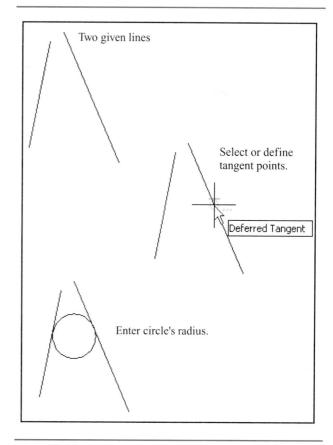

Two given lines

Select or define tangent points.

Deferred Tangent

Enter circle's radius.

Figure 2-16

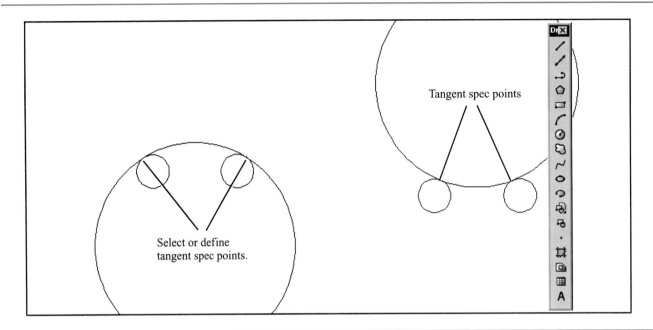

Tangent spec points

Select or define
tangent spec points.

Figure 2-17

1. Select the Circle tool from the Draw toolbar.

   Command: _circle Specify a center point for circle or [3P/2P/Ttr (tan tan radius)]:

2. Type ttr; press Enter.

   Specify point on object for first tangent of circle:

3. Select an entity.

   Specify point on object for second tangent of circle:

4. Select the other entity.

   Specify radius of circle <value>:

5. Type a radius value; press Enter.

Quadrant-sensitive applications

The circle TTR option is quadrant-sensitive, that is, the final location of the tangent circle will depend on the location of the tangent spec points. In Figure 2-17 the TTR option was applied to two circles, and in both examples the tangent circle was created using the same radius. Note the difference in results depending on the circle's quadrants selected.

2-9 CIRCLE CENTERLINES

It is standard drawing convention to include centerlines with all circles. Circles usually represent holes. The circle's center point is used to locate the circle and, during manufac-

ture, serves as the location point for a drill. There are two ways to set up AutoCAD to add centerlines easily to a given circle: redefine the Dimcen system variable, or use the Center Mark option found on the Dimension toolbar.

To change the Dimcen system variable

There are no icons for Dimcen; the change is made using keyboard input entirely.

1. Type setvar next to the Command prompt; press Enter.

   Enter variable name or? <variable>:

2. Type dimcen; press Enter.

   New value for DIMCEN <0.09>:

3. Type −.1 for inch units or −2 for metric units; press Enter.

   Command:

   The system variable is now changed but must be applied to the circle.

4. Type dim; press Enter.

   Dim:

5. Type center; press Enter.

   Select arc or circle:

6. Select the given circle.

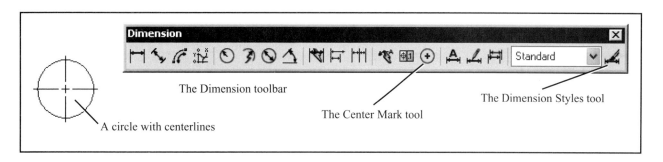

Figure 2-18

A centerline and center point will be added as shown in Figure 2-18.

To use the Center Mark tool

1. Access the Dimension toolbar by locating the cursor on an existing toolbar and right-clicking the mouse.
2. Select the Dimension Styles tool from the Dimension toolbar.

The Dimension Style Manager dialog box will appear. See Figure 2-19.

3. Select the Modify box.

The Override Current Style: Standard dialog box will appear.

4. Select the Symbols and Arrows tab, then the Center Marks option, then Line.

The preview screen will display centerlines.

5. Select OK and return to the drawing screen.

Change the size value to create a clear center point and lines.

6. Click the Center Mark tool on the Dimension toolbar, then the given circle.

Centerlines will appear on the circle.

The Dimension Style Manager dialog box

The Override Current Style: Standard dialog box

Figure 2-19

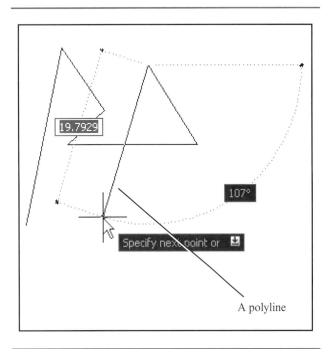

A polyline

Figure 2-20

2-10 POLYLINE

A *polyline* is a line made from a series of individual, connected line segments that act as a single entity. Polylines are used to generate curves and splines and can be used in three-dimensional applications to produce solid objects.

Polylines can be entered using dynamic input. See Section 2-7.

To draw a polyline (See Figure 2-20.)

1. Select the Polyline tool from the Draw toolbar.

   Command: _pline
   Specify start point:

2. Select or define a start point.

   Specify next point or [Arc/Close/Halfwidth/ Length/Undo/Width]:

3. Select or define a second point.

   Specify next point or [Arc/Close/Halfwidth/ Length/Undo/Width]:

4. Select or define several more points.

   Specify next point or [Arc/Close/Halfwidth/ Length/Undo/Width]:

5. Press the right mouse button, then select Enter.

To verify that a polyline is a single entity

Figure 2-20 shows a polyline.

1. Select the Erase tool from the Modify toolbar or type the word erase.

   Select objects:

2. Select any one of the line segments in the polyline.

   Select objects:

   The entire polyline, not just the individual line segment, will be selected, because in AutoCAD the polyline is a single entity.

3. Press Enter.

   The entire polyline will disappear.

4. Select the Undo tool from the Standard toolbar.

   The object will reappear.

To draw a polyline: Arc (See Figure 2-21.)

1. Select the Polyline tool from the Draw toolbar.

   From point:

2. Select or define a start point.

   Specify next point or [Arc/Close/Halfwidth/ Length/Undo/Width]:

3. Type A; press Enter.

   Specify endpoint of arc or [Angle/CEnter/ CLose/Direction/Halfwidth/Line/Radius/Second pt/Undo/Width]:

4. Select or define another point.

   Specify endpoint of arc or [Angle/CEnter/ CLose/Direction/Halfwidth/Line/Radius/Second pt/Undo/Width]:

5. Select or define another point.
6. Press the right mouse button, then select Enter.

Other options with a polyline arc

The example shown in Figure 2-22 includes a background grid with .5 spacing.

1. Select the Polyline tool from the Draw toolbar.

   Command: _pline
   Specify start point:

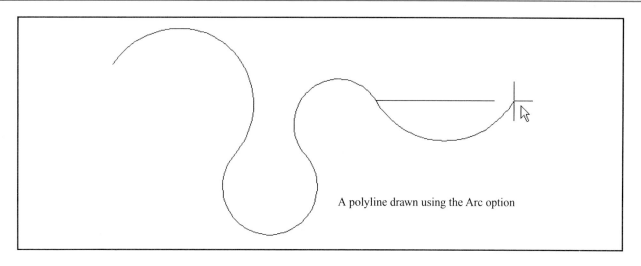

A polyline drawn using the Arc option

Figure 2-21

2. Select or define a start point.

    Specify next point or [Arc/Close/Halfwidth/ Length/Undo/Width]:

3. Draw a short horizontal line segment.

    Specify next point or [Arc/Close/Halfwidth/ Length/Undo/Width]:

4. Type A; press Enter.

    Specify endpoint of arc or [Angle/CEnter/ CLose/Direction/Halfwidth/Line/Radius/Second pt/ Undo/Width]:

5. Type CE; press Enter.

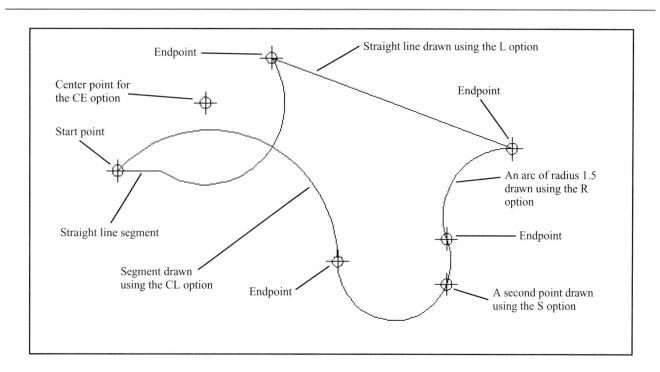

Figure 2-22

CE activates the Center option. You can now define an arc that will be part of the polyline by defining the arc's center point and its angle, chord length, or endpoint.

Specify center point of arc:

6. Select or define a center point.

   Specify endpoint of arc or [Angle/Width]:

7. Select or define an endpoint.

   Specify endpoint of arc or [Angle/CEnter/ CLose/Direction/Halfwidth/Line/Radius/Second pt/ Undo/Width]:

8. Type L; press Enter.

   The Line option is used to draw straight-line segments.

   Specify next point or [Arc/Close/Halfwidth/ Length/Undo/Width]:

9. Select or define an endpoint.

   Specify next point or [Arc/Close/Halfwidth/ Length/Undo/Width]:

10. Type A; press Enter.

    Specify endpoint of arc or [Angle/CEnter/ CLose/Direction/Halfwidth/Line/Radius/Second pt/ Undo/Width]:

11. Type R; press Enter.

    Specify radius of arc:

12. Type 1.5 or other value; press Enter.

    Specify endpoint of arc or [Angle]:

13. Select or define an endpoint.

    Specify endpoint of arc or [Angle/CEnter/ CLose/Direction/Halfwidth/Line/Radius/Second pt/ Undo/Width]:

14. Type S; press Enter.

    Specify second point on arc:

15. Select or define a point.

    Specify endpoint of arc:

16. Select or define an endpoint.

    Specify endpoint of arc or [Angle/CEnter/ CLose/Direction/Halfwidth/Line/Radius/Second pt/ Undo/Width]:

17. Type CL; press Enter.

    The CL (close) option will join the last point drawn to the first point of the polyline using an arc.

To draw different line thicknesses (See Figure 2-23.)

1. Select the Polyline tool from the Draw toolbar.

   Specify start point:

2. Select or define a start point.

   Specify next point or [Arc/Close/Halfwidth/ Length/Undo/Width]:

3. Type W; press Enter.

   The Width option is used to define the width of a line. The Halfwidth option is used to define half the width of a line.

   Specify starting width <0.0000>:

4. Type 1.00; press Enter.

   Specify ending width <1.0000>:

5. Press Enter.

   Specify next point or [Arc/Close/Halfwidth/ Length/Undo/Width]:

6. Draw several line segments.

2-11 SPLINE

A *spline* is a curved line created through a series of predefined points. If the curve forms an enclosed area, it is called a *closed spline*. Curved lines that do not enclose an area are called *open splines*. See Figure 2-24.

1. Select the Spline tool from the Draw toolbar.

   Command: _spline
   Specify first point or [Object]:

2. Select or define a start point.

   Specify next point:

3. Select or define a second point.

   Specify next point or [Close/Fit tolerance] <start tangent>:

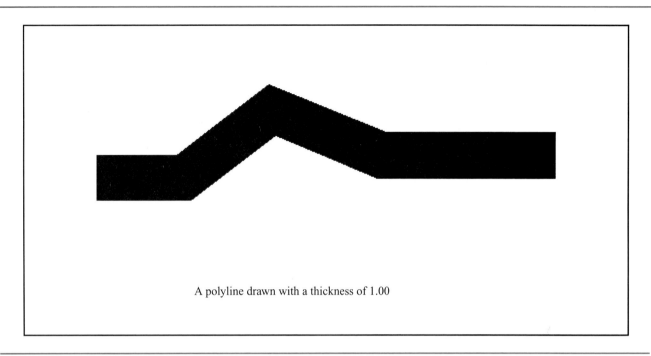

A polyline drawn with a thickness of 1.00

Figure 2-23

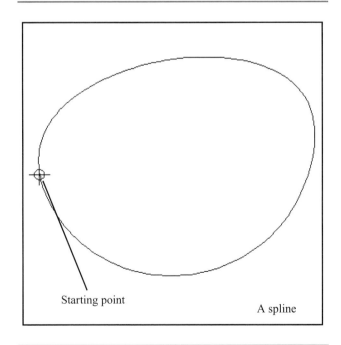

Starting point

A spline

Figure 2-24

4. Select or define two more points.

   Specify next point or [Arc/Close/Halfwidth/ Length/Undo/Width]:

5. Type C; press Enter.

   Specify tangent.

6. Select or define a point.

   Note how the shape of the spline changes as you move the cursor to locate the tangent point. These changes are based on your selection of a tangent point, which, in turn, affects the mathematical calculations used to create the curve.

2-12 ELLIPSE

There are three options associated with the Ellipse tool. These three options allow you to define an ellipse using the lengths of its major and minor axes, an included angle, or an angle of rotation about the major axis.

Figure 2-25

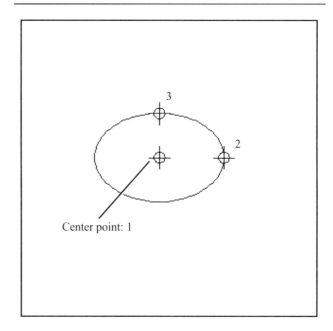

Figure 2-26

To draw an ellipse—axis endpoint (See Figure 2-25.)

1. Select the Ellipse tool from the Draw toolbar.

   Specify axis endpoint of ellipse or [Arc/Center]:

2. Select or define a start point for one of the axes.

   Specify other endpoint of axis:

3. Select or define an endpoint that defines the length of the axis.

   Specify distance to other axis or [Rotation]:

4. Select or define a point that defines half the length of the other axis.

   This distance is the radius of the axis. In the example shown, points 1 and 2 were used to define the major axes, and point 3 defines the minor axis. The bottom figure in Figure 2-25 shows an object in which points 1 and 2 were used to define the minor axes, and point 3 the major axis.

To draw an ellipse—center (See Figure 2-26.)

1. Select the Ellipse tool from the Draw toolbar.

   Specify axis endpoint of ellipse or [Arc/Center]:

2. Type C: press Enter.

   Specify center of ellipse:

3. Select or define the center point of the ellipse.

   Specify axis endpoint:

4. Select or define one of the endpoints of one of the axes.

   The distance between the center point and the endpoint is equal to the radius of the axis.

   Specify distance to other axis or [Rotation]:

5. Select or define a point that defines half the length of the other axis.

To draw an ellipse—arc (See Figure 2-27.)

1. Select the Ellipse tool from the Draw toolbar.

   Specify axis endpoint of ellipse or [Arc/Center]:

2. Type A; press Enter.

   Specify axis endpoint of elliptical arc or [Center]:

3. Select or define a point.

   Specify other endpoint of axis:

4. Select or define a point.

Figure 2-27

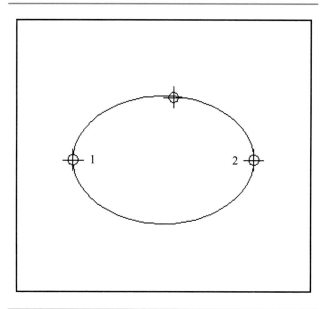

Figure 2-29

The distance between points 1 and 2 defines the length of the major axis.

Specify distance to other axis or [Rotation]:

5. Select or define a point that defines the minor axis.

Specify start angle or [Parameter]:

6. Type 0; press Enter.

Specify end angle or [Parameter/Included angle]:

7. Type 237; press Enter.

An ellipse may also be defined in terms of its angle of rotation about the major axis. An ellipse with 0° rotation is a circle, an ellipse of constant radius. An ellipse with 90° rotation is a straight line, an end view of an ellipse. See Figure 2-28.

To draw an ellipse by defining its angle of rotation about the major axis (See Figure 2-29.)

1. Select the Ellipse tool from the Draw toolbar.

Specify axis endpoint of ellipse or [Arc/Center]:

2. Select or define an endpoint of the major axis.

Specify other endpoint of axis:

3. Select or define the other endpoint of the major axis.

Specify distance to other axis or [Rotation]:

4. Type R; press Enter.

Specify rotation around major axis:

5. Type 47; press Enter.

Figure 2-28

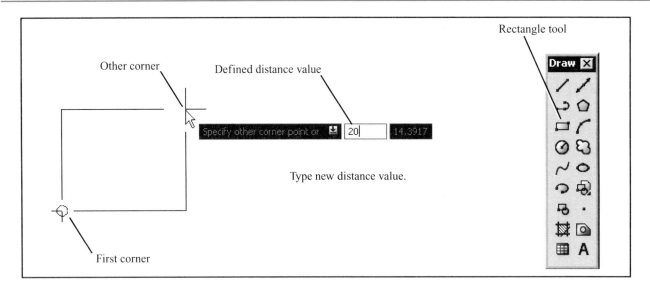

Figure 2-30

The same sequence of commands could have been applied using the Ellipse Center tool option. The distance between points 1 and 2 with the Center option is half the distance of the major axis.

2-13 RECTANGLE

The Rectangle command is used to draw rectangles. The rectangles generated are *blocks*, that is, they are considered to be one entity, not four straight lines. If you try to erase one of the lines that the rectangle comprises, all lines in the rectangle will be erased. The Explode command, whose tool is located on the Modify toolbar, may be applied to any block to reduce it to its individual elements. If Explode is applied to a rectangle, it will be changed from a single entity to four individual straight lines.

To draw a rectangle (See Figure 2-30.)

1. Select the Rectangle tool from the Draw toolbar.

    Specify first corner point or [Chamfer/Elevation/ Fillet/Thickness/Width]:

2. Select or define a starting point.

    Specify other corner point:

3. Select or define a point.

The distance between the two points is the diagonal distance across the rectangle's corners. In this example a distance of 20 was defined using dynamic input.

To explode a rectangle (See Figure 2-30.)

1. Select the Explode tool from the Modify toolbar.

    Select object:

2. Select the rectangle.

    Select object:

3. Press Enter.

There is no visible change in the rectangle, but it is no longer composed of four individual straight lines.

2-14 POLYGON

A *polygon* is a closed figure bounded by straight lines. The Polygon command will draw only regular polygons, in which all sides are equal. A regular polygon with four equal sides is a square. A six-sided polygon or hexagon will be drawn in this example.

To draw a polygon center point (See Figure 2-31.)

1. Select the Polygon tool from the Draw toolbar.

    Command: _polygon
    Enter number of sides <4>:

2. Type 6; press Enter.

    Edge/<Center of polygon>:

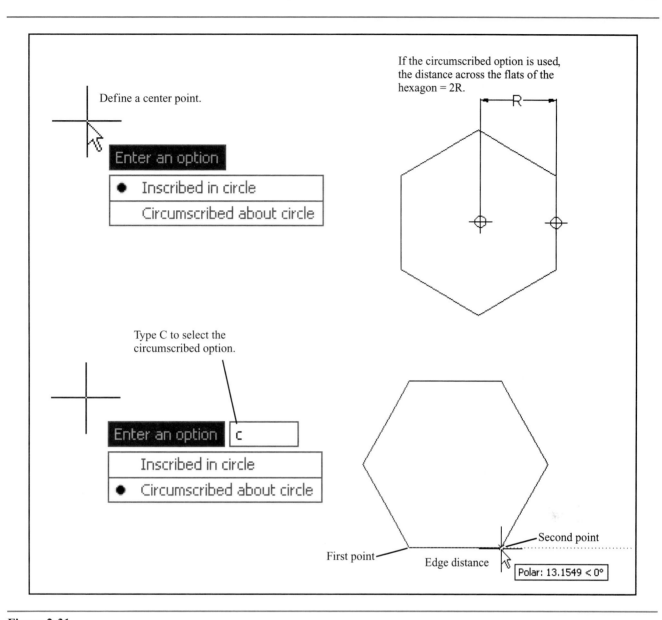

Figure 2-31

3. Select or define a center point.

Enter an option [Inscribed in circle/Circumscribed about a circle] <I>:

4. Type C; press Enter.

Specify radius of circle:

5. Type a value; press Enter.

The Circumscribe option was selected because the diameter of the designated circle will equal the distance across the flats of the hexagon. The distance across the flats is often used to specify hexagon head bolt sizes and the wrench sizes used to fit them. The Inscribe option is used in a similar manner.

To draw a polygon edge distance (See Figure 2-31.)

1. Select the Polygon tool from the Draw toolbar.

Command: _polygn
Enter number of sides <4>:

2. Type 6; press Enter.

Specify center of polygon or [Edge]:

3. Type E; press Enter.

Specify first endpoint of edge:

4. Select or define a point.

Specify second endpoint of edge:

5. Select or define a point.

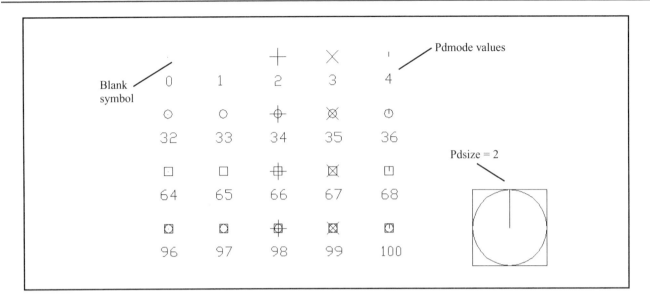

Figure 2-32

2-15 POINT

The Point command is used to draw points on a drawing. The default setting for a point's shape is a small dot, the kind used to display background grids. Other point shapes are available. See Figure 2-32. The default small dot point shape is listed as 0. Note that shape 1 is a void. The five available shapes can be enhanced by adding the numbers 32, 64, and 96 to the point's assigned value. For example, shape 2 is crossed horizontal and vertical lines. Shape 34 is shape 2 with a circle around it; shape 66 is shape 2 with a square overlay; and shape 98 is shape 2 with both a circle and a square around it.

To change the shape of a point (See Figure 2-32.)

Start with a Command prompt.

1. Type pdmode and press Enter in response to a Command prompt.

   Command: _pdmode
   Enter new value for PDMODE<0>:

2. Type 2; press Enter.

   Command: _point POINT

3. Select several points to verify that the shape has been changed.

An Enter command should end the command sequence. If it does not, draw a line and use Enter to return to a Command prompt. Erase the line and continue working.

To change the size of a point (See Figure 2-32.)

1. Type pdsize in response to a Command prompt.

   Command: _pdsize
   Enter new value for PDSIZE<0.0000>:

2. Type 2; press Enter.

   The default value is 0.0000.

2-16 TEXT

There are two ways to apply text to an AutoCAD drawing: use the Multiline Text command or use the Single Line Text command. The Single Line Text command is accessed through the Draw pull-down menu, then selecting the Text option. The Single Line Text command is most useful when entering small amounts of text.

To use the Single Line Text command (See Figure 2-33.)

1. Select the Single Line Text command from the Text option on the Draw pull-down menu.

   Current text style: Standard
   Text height: 0.200
   Specify start point of text or [Justify/Style]:

2. Select or define a start point.

   The text will start at the selected point and run left to right.

This text was created using the
Single Line Text command.

This is sample text.

Figure 2-33

Specify height <0.2000>:

3. Type .25; press Enter.

This changes the text height from .2000 to .2500.

Specify rotation angle of text <0>:

4. Press Enter.

A bracket will appear with its lower left corner at the start point.

Enter text:

5. Type: This is sample text; press Enter.

Enter text:

6. Press Enter.

The Single Line Text command always assumes you will be typing another line of text regardless of how many lines you type. An Enter response signals that you are done entering text.

To use the Multiline Text tool (See Figures 2-34 through 2-39.)

The Multiline Text command is used to enter a large amount of text. First, define the area in which the text is to be entered; the Text Formatting dialog box will appear on the screen. Text is typed into the dialog box, just as with word processing programs, then transferred back to the drawing screen. Text can be moved to different locations on the drawing screen using the Move command.

1. Select the Text tool from the Draw toolbar.

Command:_mtext
Current text style: Standard
Text height: 0.2000
Specify first corner:

2. Select or define a point.

The area you are about to define is for the entire text entry. See Figure 2-34.

Specify opposite corner or [Height/Justify/Line spacing/Rotation/Style/Width]:

3. Define the other corner of the area.

Figure 2-34

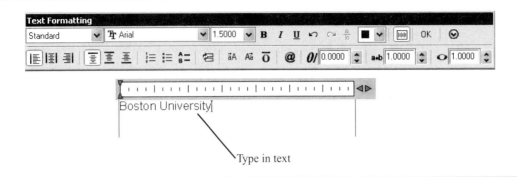

Type in text

Figure 2-35

The Text Formatting dialog box will appear. See Figure 2-35.

4. Type in your text, then select the OK box.

The text will be located on the drawing screen within the specified area.

The Text Formatting dialog box options

The Text Formatting dialog box can be used to change text height, color, font style, and text style. The default justification is top left. The text will start in the upper left corner of the text area and proceed to the right and down, line by line, from the top to the bottom. Other justifications are available.

To change the text font

1. Select the Text tool from the Draw toolbar.
2. Designate a text area as specified in the previous section.

The Text Formatting dialog box will appear.

3. Select the scroll arrow to the right of the Font box.
4. Scroll down the available text listing.
5. Select the Arial Black option. (See Figure 2-36.)

Figure 2-37 shows the new text font. Compare the Arial Black text font shown in Figure 2-37 with the Arial text font shown in Figure 2-35.

To justify text

1. Select the Text tool from the Draw toolbar.
2. Select the first corner; do not select the other corner.

   Specify opposite corner or [Height/Justify/Line spacing/Rotation/Style/Width]:

3. Type J; press Enter.

A listing of justification options will appear. Figure 2-38 shows the meaning of the available options.

4. Select an option, then locate the other corner.

The font options

Figure 2-36

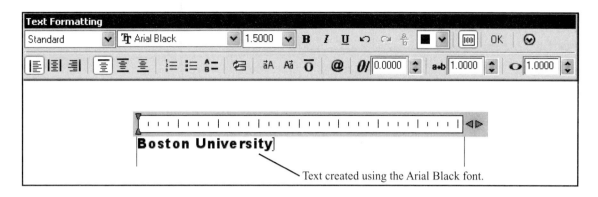

Text created using the Arial Black font.

Figure 2-37

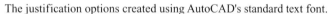

The justification options created using AutoCAD's standard text font.

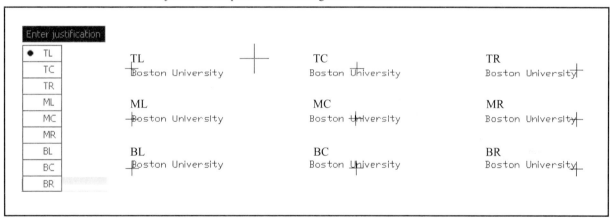

Figure 2-38

The Text Formatting dialog box will appear. Text may be entered as described before.

The symbol options

AutoCAD has three symbol commands:

%%C = ∅
%%P = ±
%%D = °

A symbol will initally appear in the %% form in the Text Formatting dialog box but will change to the equivalent symbol when the text is transferred to the drawing.

Symbols may also be created using the Windows Character chart as follows:

ALT + 0216 = ∅
ALT + 0177 = ±
ALT + 0176 = °

Text color

The color of a text input may be changed using the Color option located on the Text Formatting dialog box. See Figure 2-39. Select the scroll arrow to the right of the Color box, and a listing of available colors will scroll down.

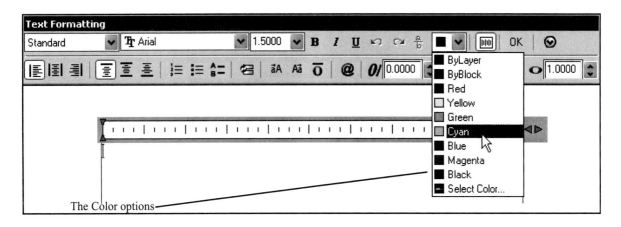

The Color options

Figure 2-39

2-17 MOVE

The Move command is used to move a line or object to a new location on the drawing. See Figure 2-40.

To move an object

1. Select the Move tool from the Modify toolbar.

    Select objects:

2. Window the entire object.

    Select objects:

3. Press Enter.

    Specify base point or displacement:

4. Select or define a base point.

    Any point may be selected. Snap points are usually used as base points because they can define precise displacement distances and accurate new locations.

    Specify second point of displacement or <use first point of displacement>:

5. Select or define a second displacement point.

    The object will now be located relative to the second displacement point.

2-18 COPY

The Copy command is used to make an exact copy of an existing line or object. The Copy command can also be used to create more than one copy without reactivating the command. See Figure 2-41.

To copy an object

1. Select the Copy tool from the Modify toolbar.

    Select objects:

2. Window the entire object.

    Select objects:

3. Press Enter or right-click the mouse.

    Specify base point:

4. Select or define a base point.

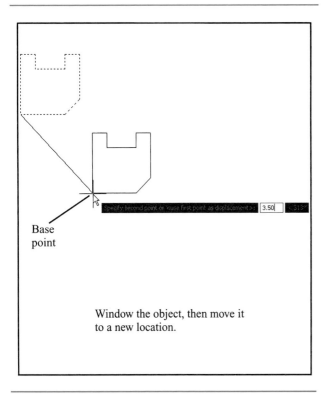

Base point

Window the object, then move it to a new location.

Figure 2-40

Figure 2-41

Figure 2-42

In the example shown in Figure 2-40 the lower left corner of the object was selected as the base point.

Specify second point of displacement or <use first point as displacement>:

5. Select or define a second displacement point.

The original object will remain in its original location, and a new object will appear at the second displacement point.

6. Right-click the mouse to enter the copied object.

To draw multiple copies

(See Figure 2-42.)
AutoCAD will continue to make copies of a selected object until all the copied objects are entered. After each copy appears the prompt

Select a second displacement point:

Move the cursor to a new base point, or right-click the mouse to enter the objects.

2-19 OFFSET

See Figure 2-43.

1. Select the Offset tool from the Modify toolbar.

Specify offset distance or [Through]<Through>:

Figure 2-43

Figure 2-44

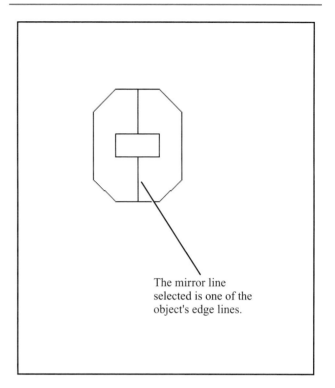

Figure 2-45

2. Specify the offset distance by typing a value.

In this example, a distance of .25 was selected.

Select object to offset or <exit>:

3. Select a line.

Specify point on side to offset:

4. Select a point to the right of the line.

Select object to offset or <exit>:

The process may be repeated by double-clicking the right mouse button and selecting the Repeat Offset option.

2-20 MIRROR (See Figure 2-44.)

1. Select the Mirror tool from the Modify toolbar.

Select objects:

2. Window the object.

Select objects:

3. Press Enter.

Specify first point of mirror line:

4. Select a point on the mirror line.

Specify second point of mirror line:

5. Select a second point on the mirror line.

Delete source object? [Yes/No]<N>:

6. Press Enter.

Any line may be used as a mirror line, including lines within the object. Figure 2-45 shows an object mirrored about one of its edge lines. The Mirror command is very useful when drawing symmetrical objects. Only half of the object need be drawn. The second half can be created using the Mirror command.

2-21 ARRAY

Objects may be arrayed using either the Rectangular or the Polar option. The Rectangular option is demonstrated in Figure 2-46.

1. Select the Array tool from the Modify toolbar.

The Array dialog box will appear.

2. Set Rows for 2, Columns for 3, Row offset for 3.50, and Column offset for 4.00.

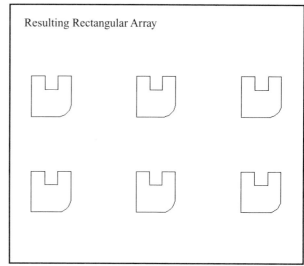

Figure 2-46

3. Click the Select objects box and select the object to be arrayed.

   The Array dialog box will appear.

4. Select OK.

To use the Polar Array option

Objects may also be arrayed using the Polar Array option. The Polar Array option will array objects about a defined center point at a given radius. See Figure 2-47.

1. Select the Array icon from the Modify toolbar.

   The Array dialog box will appear.

2. Select the Polar Array option.
3. Set the Total number of items to 8 and the Angle to fill to 360, and turn off the Rotate items as copied box.
4. Select the Center point, and select the array's centerpoint.

   The Array dialog box will appear.

Figure 2-47

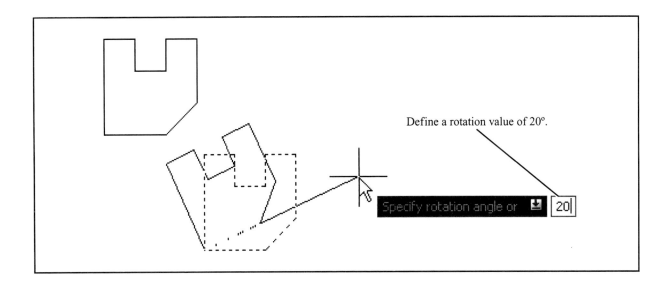

Define a rotation value of 20°.

Specify rotation angle or   20|

Figure 2-48

5. Select the Select objects box and select the figure.
6. Select OK.

2-22 ROTATE

The Rotate tool is used to rotate an object about a specified base point. The 3D Rotate command will be covered later in the book. See Figure 2-48.

AutoCAD defines a horizontal line to the right as 0°. Angles in the counterclockwise direction are positive angles.

To rotate an object (See Figure 2-48.)

1. Select the Rotate tool from the Modify toolbar.

   Select objects:

2. Window the object.

   Select objects:

3. Press Enter.

   Specify base point:

4. Select or define a base point.

The base point may be anywhere on the screen. In the example shown, the lower left corner of the object was selected as the base point.

   Specify rotation angle or [Reference]:

5. Type 20; press Enter.

The object will rotate about the base point 20° in the counterclockwise direction.

2-23 TRIM

The Trim tool is used to cut away excessively long lines. It is a very important AutoCAD command and is used frequently.

To use the Trim command (See Figure 2-49.)

1. Select the Trim tool from the Modify toolbar.

   Select cutting edges:
   Select objects:

2. Select the circle.

   Select objects:

3. Press Enter.

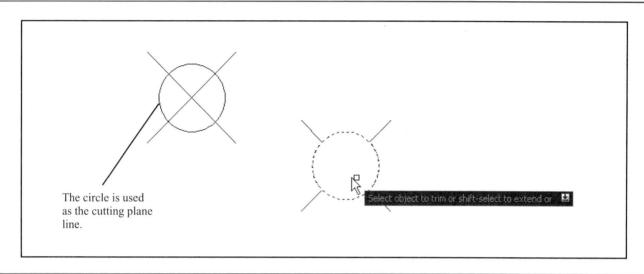

Figure 2-49

Select object to trim or [Project/Edge/Undo]:

4. Select the center portions of the lines within the circle.
5. Press Enter.

The lines within the circle disappear. Figure 2-50 shows an example similar to that presented in Figure 2-49, but in this example the lines were selected as the cutting edges, and portions of the circle were trimmed.

2-24 EXTEND

The Extend command allows given lines to be extended to new lengths. See Figure 2-51.

1. Select the Extend tool from the Modify toolbar.

   Select boundary edges:
   Select objects:

2. Select a line that can be used as a boundary edge.

Figure 2-50

Figure 2-51

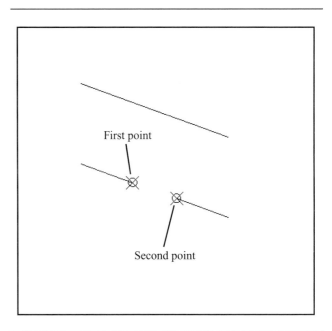

Figure 2-52

A boundary line must be positioned so that all the lines to be extended will intersect it. If you have an object that you want to make longer, draw a boundary line, or use the Move command and move one of the object's edge lines to the new position and use it as a boundary line.

Select object to extend or [Project/Edge/Undo]:

3. Select the lines to be extended.

Select object to extend or [Project/Edge/Undo]:

4. Press the right mouse button and select the Enter option.

2-25 BREAK

The Break command is used to remove portions of an object. It is similar to the Trim command but does not require cutting edges. Break distances are defined between points. See Figure 2-52.

To use the Break command

1. Select the Break tool from the Modify toolbar.

Select object:

2. Select a point on the line.

If needed, press the Shift key and right mouse button simultaneously to access the Object Snap screen menu. Select the None option to eliminate the default snap function.

Specify second break point or [First point]:

3. Select a second point.

The length of the break will be equal to the distance between the two selected points.

To use the First-point option

The F or First-point option allows you to first select the line and then define the size of the break. This means that unlike the original Break command sequence, as just described, the first selection selects only the line, not the line and the first break point.

1. Select the Break tool from the Modify toolbar.

Select object:

2. Select the line.

Specify second break point or [First point]:

Figure 2-53

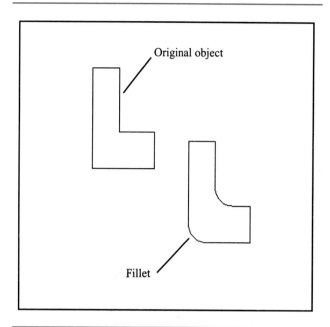

Figure 2-54

3. Type F; press Enter.

   Specify first break point:

4. Select or define the first point of the break.

   Specify second break point:

5. Select or define the second point of the break.

2-26 CHAMFER

A *chamfer* is a straight-line corner cut, usually cut at 45°. Other angles may be used. See Figure 2-53.

To create a chamfer

1. Select the Chamfer tool from the Modify toolbar.

   (TRIM mode) Current chamfer Dist1 = 0.0000, Dist2 = 0.5000
   Select first line or [Polyline/Distance/Angle/Trim/ Method]<Select first line>:

2. Type D; press Enter.

   Specify first chamfer distance <0.0000>:

3. Type .75; press Enter.

   Specify second chamfer distance <0.7500>:

   AutoCAD assumes that the chamfer will be at 45° and automatically sets the second distance equal to the first.

4. Press Enter.

   Command:

   The chamfer has now been set for a 45° chamfer of length .75. The chamfer is now applied to the rectangular figure in Figure 2-53.

5. Again, select the Chamfer tool on the Modify toolbar or press the Enter key and select the Repeat Chamfer option.

   (TRIM mode) Current chamfer Dist1 = 0.7500, Dist2 = 0.7500
   Select first line or [Polyline/Distance/Angle/Trim/ Method]<Select first line>:

6. Select a line.

   Select a second line:

7. Select a second line.

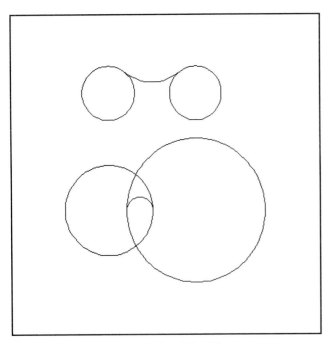

Some examples of the Fillet
command applied to circles

Figure 2-55

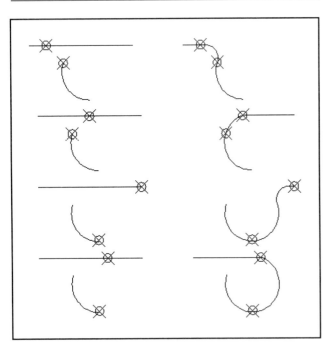

The Fillet command is location sensitive. The final shape
of the fillet will depend on the location of your selection
points. Here are four examples of fillets drawn from the
same initial arc line setup.

Figure 2-56

2-27 FILLET

A *fillet* is a rounded corner. See Figure 2-54.

To draw a fillet

1. Select the Fillet tool from the Modify toolbar.

    Current settings: Mode = Trim, Radius = 0.5000
    Select first object or [Polyline/Radius/Trim]:

2. Type R; press Enter.

    Specify fillet radius <0.0000>:

3. Type 1.25; press Enter.

    Command:

4. Again, select the Fillet tool from the Modify
    toolbar or press the right mouse button and select
    the Repeat Fillet option.

    (TRIM mode) Current fillet radius = 1.2500
    Select first object or [Polyline/Radius/Trim]:

5. Select a line.

    Select second object:

6. Select a second line.

    Fillets can also be drawn between circles. See Figure
2-55. The Fillet command is location sensitive, meaning that
the location of the selection points will affect the shape of
the resulting fillet. Figure 2-56 shows how selection points
can be used to create different fillet shapes.

2-28 TABLE

    The Table command is used to create tables such as the
one shown in Figure 2-57. Tables are used on drawings to
define multiple hole dimensions, to define coordinate data,
and to create parts lists, among other uses.

To create a table

1. Click the Table command tool on the Draw toolbar.

    The Insert Table dialog box will appear. See Figure 2-58.

2. Click the Table Style dialog box.

    The Table Style dialog box will appear. See Figure 2-59.

3. Click the Modify box.

    The Modify Table Style: Standard dialog box will ap-
pear. See Figure 2-60.

Hole Table			
LOCATION	X-DIM	Y-DIM	Ø
A1	15.00	85.00	20.00
A2	15.00	15.00	20.00
A3	145	85.00	20.00
A4	145	15.00	20.00
B1	55	70.00	30.00
B2	110	70.00	30.00
C1	80	30.00	40.00

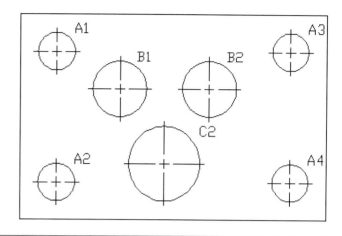

Figure 2-57

4. Click the box to the right of the Text Style heading.

   The Text Style dialog box will appear. See Figure 2-61.

5. Set the text font to Arial and the text height to 0.25, then click Apply, then Close.
6. Click the Title tab on the Modify Table Styles dialog box.
7. Set the text font to Arial and the text height to 0.375, then click Apply, then Close.

   The Column Heads tab is used to control the font and height of the column headings in the table. The Modify Table Style: standard dialog box may also be used to define borders around and within the table.

8. Return to the Insert Table dialog box and set the number of data rows and columns and size of boxes, then click OK. See Figure 2-58.

   Note that the number of data rows does not include the column headings.
   A blank table will appear on the screen. See Figure 2-62.

9. Click on the appropriate box and type in the required data.

   The arrow keys may be used to move from one box to another. Figure 2-57 shows the resulting table.

Figure 2-58

Figure 2-59

Click here.

Figure 2-60

Figure 2-61

Type here.

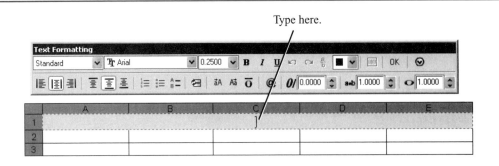

Figure 2-62

2-29 EXERCISE PROBLEMS

Redraw the following figures. Do not include dimensions. Dimensional values are as indicated.

EX2-1 INCHES

GUIDE PLATE

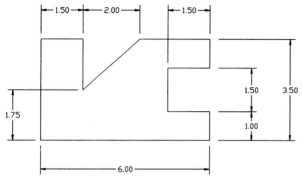

EX2-3 MILLIMETERS

BASE PLATE

EX2-2 INCHES

TOP GASKET

EX2-4 MILLIMETERS

GASKET

EX2-5 INCHES

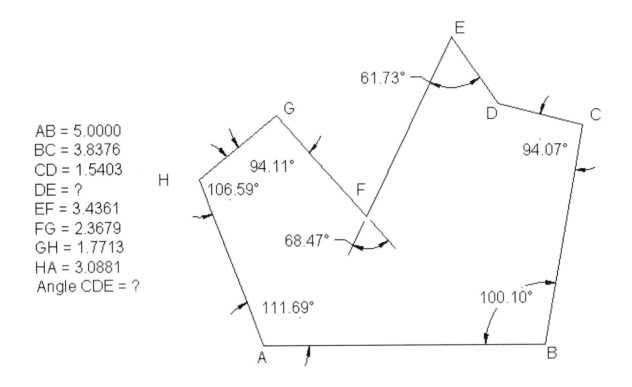

AB = 5.0000
BC = 3.8376
CD = 1.5403
DE = ?
EF = 3.4361
FG = 2.3679
GH = 1.7713
HA = 3.0881
Angle CDE = ?

EX2-6 MILLIMETERS

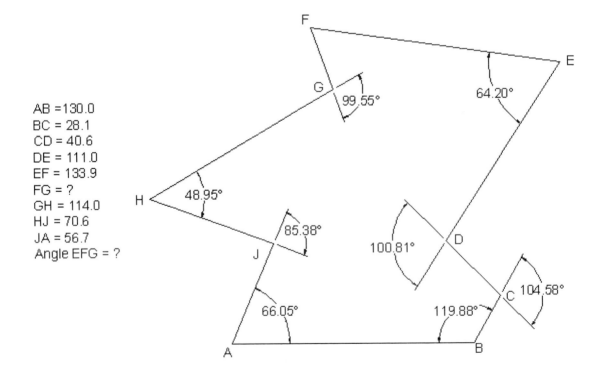

AB =130.0
BC = 28.1
CD = 40.6
DE = 111.0
EF = 133.9
FG = ?
GH = 114.0
HJ = 70.6
JA = 56.7
Angle EFG = ?

EX2-7 INCHES

SIDE BRACKET

EX2-9 MILLIMETERS

FILTER PLATE

EX2-8 INCHES

FILTER PLATE

EX2-10 INCHES

EX2-11 INCHES

FILTER
GUSSET

ALL FILLETS AND
ROUNDS = R.25
UNLESS OTHERWISE
STATED.

4.00
3.00
2.00
1.00

1.50

.75

2.00

4.00

1.50

1.50   2.00

5.00

R.25
2 PLACES

EX2-13 MILLIMETERS

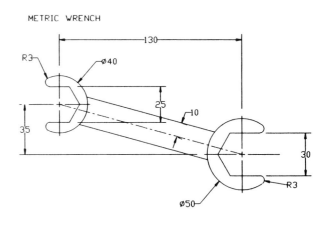

METRIC WRENCH

R3

Ø40

130

25

10

35

30

Ø50

R3

EX2-12 MILLIMETERS

DISTANCE PLATE

50

35

Ø 12-4 HOLES

SYMBOL FOR
SYMMETRY

50

35

20

10

20

R10-8 CORNERS

10

EX2-14 INCHES

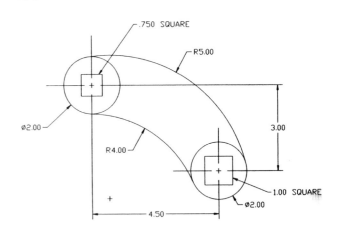

.750 SQUARE

R5.00

Ø2.00

3.00

R4.00

+

4.50

1.00 SQUARE

Ø2.00

EX2-15 MILLIMETERS

TOP FILTER

Ø20 - 8 HOLES EQUALLY SPACED

Ø120

40 SQ

180

EX2-17 INCHES

GUIDE GASKET

2.50 0.75

0.75

Ø0.50-2 HOLES

2.50

1.00

1.50

2.50

4.00

EX2-16 MILLIMETERS

ELLIPTICAL SPACER

65 65

20 20 20

20 30 40

100

30

70

55

20 20

10

40 40

5

15

OBJECT IS SYMMETRICAL ABOUT THIS AXIS.

EX2-18 MILLIMETERS

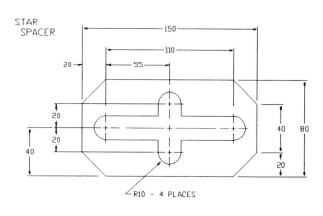

STAR SPACER

150

110

55

20

20

20

20

40

40 80

20

R10 - 4 PLACES

EX2-19 INCHES

CHESS
BOARD

7.00 SQ
.20
.20
.20 ALL AROUND
.60 SQ
.40
.40

EX2-20 MILLIMETERS

STRAP
PLATE

All fillets and rounds=R8 unless
otherwise specified.

60
30
Ø30
20
30
R50
20
110
30
7 X Ø12
30
30
20
6 X 20 (120)
15
155

EX2-21 INCHES

EX2-23 MILLIMETERS

EX2-22 MILLIMETERS

EX2-24 INCHES

EX2-25 MILLIMETERS

EX2-26 MILLIMETERS

EX2-27 MILLIMETERS

EX2-28 INCHES

MATL .25 STEEL

EX2-29 MILLIMETERS

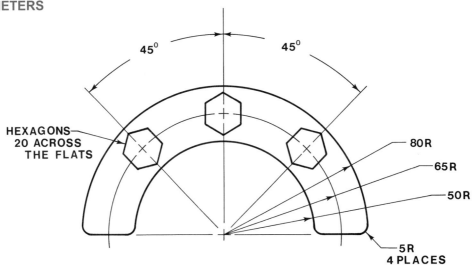

HEXAGONS 20 ACROSS THE FLATS

45°   45°

80R
65R
50R
5R 4 PLACES

EX2-30 MILLIMETERS

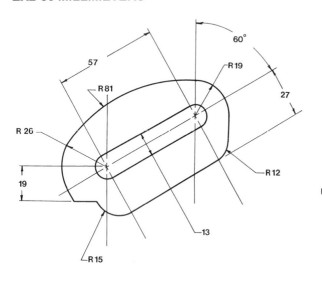

60°
57
R 19
R 81
27
R 26
R 12
19
13
R 15

EX2-31 MILLIMETERS

30
R
13
25 4 PLACES
35
120
17.5
35
R 10−4 PLACES
30
R 10−4 PLACES
R 15−2 PLACES
Ø 7−4 HOLES
10
20

EX2-32 INCHES

Redraw the Hole Plate shown below. Do not include the dimensions. Draw and complete the hole table outlined below. Set the text style for Arial. The data text is .18 high, the heading text is .25 high, and the title text is .375 high.

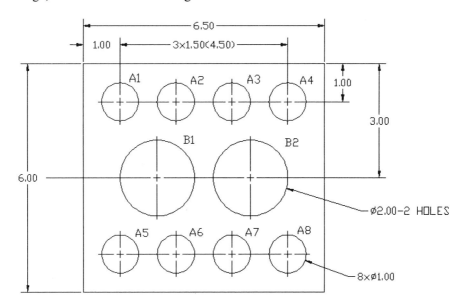

Hole Table			
Location	X-dim	Y-dim	Ø
A1			

EX2-33 MILLIMETERS

Redraw the Hole Plate shown below. Do not include the dimensions. Draw and complete the hole table outlined below. Set the text style for Arial. The data text is 5 high, the heading text is 10 high, and the title text is 15 high.

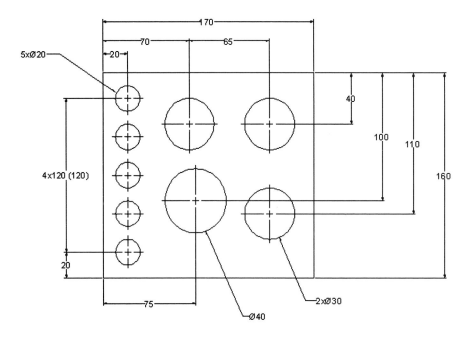

Hole Table			
Location	X-dim	Y-dim	Ø
A1			

CHAPTER 3

More Advanced Commands

3-1 INTRODUCTION

This chapter explains how to use some of the more advanced AutoCAD commands. Included are the Osnap toolbar, Grips, Layer, Block, and Attribute commands, and some of the commands on the Modify II toolbar.

3-2 OSNAP

The Object Snap command allows you to snap to entities on the drawing screen rather than just to points, as does the Snap command. Osnap can snap to the endpoint of a line, to the intersection of two lines, or to the center point of a circle, as well as to other items. The Osnap toolbar allows you to access all Osnap commands. See Figure 3-1.

To access the Osnap toolbar

1. Locate the cursor on an existing toolbar and right-click the mouse.
2. Select the Osnap toolbar and close the dialog box.
3. Dock the Osnap toolbar at a convenient location on the drawing screen.

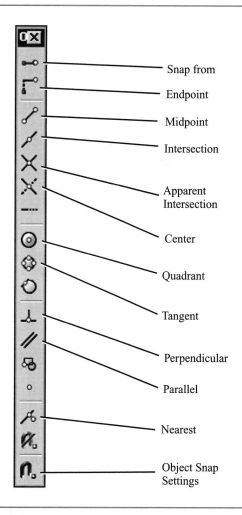

Snap from
Endpoint
Midpoint
Intersection
Apparent Intersection
Center
Quadrant
Tangent
Perpendicular
Parallel
Nearest
Object Snap Settings

Figure 3-1

This dialog box can be accessed by simultaneously pressing the Control key and the right mouse button.

Figure 3-2

Osnap can also be accessed by holding down the Control key and pressing the right mouse button. This feature can be activated during any command sequence. A dialog box appears on the screen listing the Osnap options. See Figure 3-2.

The Osnap Settings tool allows you to access the Osnap Settings dialog box. See Figure 3-2. The Osnap

Settings dialog box may also be accessed using the Tools pull-down menu. The Osnap Settings dialog box can be used to turn an Osnap option on permanently; that is, the option will remain on until you turn it off. If the Endpoint option is on, the cursor will snap to the nearest endpoint every time a point selection is made. Turning an Osnap option on is very helpful when you know you are going to select several points of the same type; however, in most cases, it is more practical to activate an Osnap option as needed using the Osnap toolbar or the Osnap menu.

To turn Osnap on

1. Select the Tools pull-down menu, then Drafting Settings, then select the Object Snap tab.

   The Drafting Settings dialog box will appear. See Figure 3-3.

2. Click the box to the left of the command you wish to activate.

   A check mark will appear, indicating that the command is active.

3. Close the Drafting Settings dialog box.

   The Options box on the Drafting Settings dialog box allows you to access the Options dialog box, which can be used to change the color of the cursor box used to identify Osnap points.

A check mark indicates that the option is active.

Click here to change the cursor box color.

Figure 3-3

To change the size of the Osnap cursor box

The Options dialog box also contains an Aperture Size option. This option allows you to change the size of the rectangular box on the cursor. A larger box makes it easier to grab objects, but too large a box may grab more than one object, or the wrong object.

3-3 OSNAP—Endpoint

The Endpoint option is used to snap to the endpoint of an existing entity. Figure 3-4 shows an existing line.

To snap to the endpoint of a line

1. Select the Line tool from the Draw toolbar.

   Command: _line Specify first point:

2. Select the Endpoint tool from the Object Snap toolbar.

   Specify next point or [Undo]: _endp of

Most of the Osnap options do not work independently but in conjunction with other commands. In this example, the Line command must be activated first, then the Osnap command. Note that a box will appear around the endpoint of the line, indicating that the Osnap endpoint command has selected the line's endpoint. The Endpoint command also works with arcs, mlines, and 3D applications.

The Endpoint option will snap to the end of a given line.

Figure 3-4

3-4 OSNAP—Snap From

The Snap From option allows you to grab the line directly, without having to enter another command. See Section 3-15, Grips.

If you first click the Snap From option, then select a line, the endpoints and midpoint of the line are defined by boxes. See Figure 3-5. The points selected in Figure 3-5 are selected at random locations.

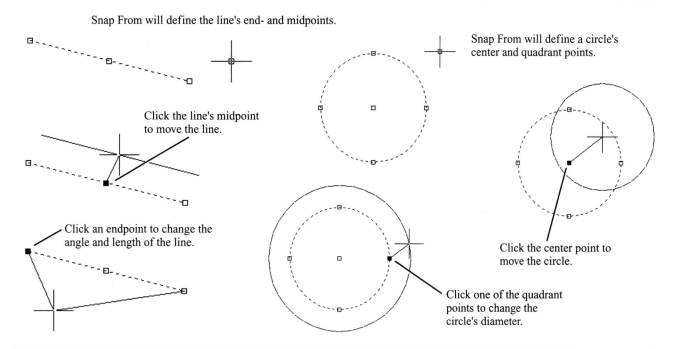

Snap From will define the line's end- and midpoints.

Click the line's midpoint to move the line.

Click an endpoint to change the angle and length of the line.

Snap From will define a circle's center and quadrant points.

Click the center point to move the circle.

Click one of the quadrant points to change the circle's diameter.

Figure 3-5

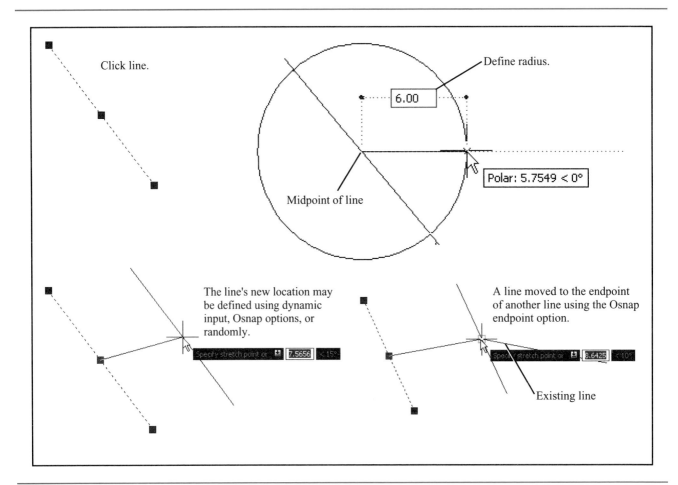

Figure 3-6

To move a line

1. Select the line's midpoint box.

   The box will change to a filled red box.

2. Move the cursor, and the line moves with the cursor.
3. Select a new location for the line.

To change the angle and length of a line

1. Select one of the designated endpoint boxes created using the Snap From option.

   The box will change to a filled red box.

2. Move the cursor, and the line's endpoint will move with the cursor.
3. Select a new angle and length for the line.

To apply the Snap From option to a circle

1. Select the Snap From option, then the circle.

   The four quadrant points and the circle's midpoint are defined by boxes. See Figure 3-5.

2. Select the circle's center point to move the circle, or select one of the quadrant points to change the circle's diameter.

3-5 OSNAP—Midpoint

The Midpoint option is used to snap to the midpoint of an existing entity. In the example presented in Figure 3-6, a circle is to be drawn with its center point at the midpoint of the line.

To draw a circle about the midpoint of a line

1. Select the Circle tool from the Draw toolbar.

   Command:_circle Specify center point for circle or [3P/2P/Ttr (tan tan radius)]:

2. Select the Snap to Midpoint tool from the Object Snap toolbar.

   Command:_circle Specify center point for circle or [3P/2P/Ttr (tan tan radius)]:_mid of

The Intersection option snaps to the intersection of any two or more entities.

Figure 3-7

3. Select the line.

    Specify radius of circle or [Diameter]:

4. Select a radius value.

3-6 OSNAP—Intersection

The Intersection option is used to snap to the intersection of two or more entities. Figure 3-7 shows a set of projection lines that are to be used to define an ellipse.

To use the Osnap Intersection command to define an ellipse

1. Select the Ellipse tool from the Draw toolbar.

    Specify axis endpoint of ellipse or [Arc/Center]:

2. Select the Intersection tool from the Object Snap toolbar.

    Specify axis endpoint of ellipse or [Arc/Center]: _int of

3. Select the first point for the ellipse.

    Specify other endpoint of axis:_int of

4. Select the Intersection option and then select the second point.

    Select the intersection that defines the length of one of the axes from the ellipse centerpoint. In this example the

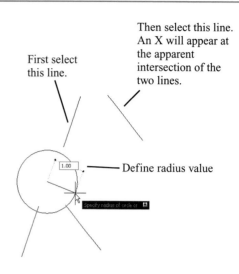

Then select this line. An X will appear at the apparent intersection of the two lines.

First select this line.

Define radius value

The circle's center point will be located on the apparent intersection of the two lines.

Figure 3-8

distance between the two points selected equals the length of the major axis of the ellipse.

Specify distance to other axis or [Rotation]:_int of

5. Select the Intersection tool from the Object Snap toolbar and select the intersection that defines the other axis length.

3-7 OSNAP—Apparent Intersection

The Apparent Intersection option is used to snap to an intersection that would be created if the two entities were extended to create an intersection. Figure 3-8 shows two lines that do not intersect but, if continued, would intersect.

To draw a circle centered about an apparent intersection

1. Select the Circle tool from the Draw toolbar.

    Command: _circle Specify center point for circle or [3P/2P/Ttr (tan tan radius)]:

2. Select the Apparent Intersection tool from the Object Snap toolbar.

    Command: _circle Specify center point for circle or [3P/2P/Ttr (tan tan radius)]: _appint of

3. Select one of the lines.

    Command: _circle Specify center point for circle or [3P/2P/Ttr (tan tan radius)]: _appint of

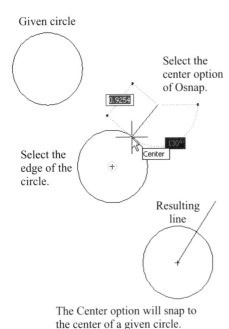

The Center option will snap to
the center of a given circle.

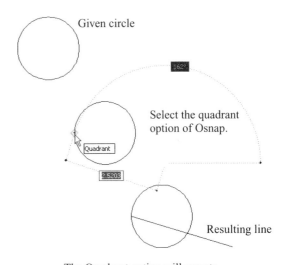

The Quadrant option will snap to
one of the four designated quadrant
points.

Figure 3-9

Figure 3-10

4. Select the other line.

   Specify radius of circle or [Diameter]:

5. Define a radius value for the circle.

3-8 OSNAP—Center

The Center option is used to draw a line from a given point directly to the center point of a circle. See Figure 3-9.

To draw a line to the center point of a circle

1. Select the Line tool from the Draw toolbar.

   Command: _line Specify first point:

2. Select the start point for the line.

   Specify next point or [Undo]:

3. Select the Center tool from the Object Snap toolbar.

   Specify next point or [Undo]: _cen of

4. Select any point on the circle.

   Do *not* try to select the center point directly. Select any point on the edge of the circle or arc; the center point will be calculated automatically.

3-9 OSNAP—Quadrant

The Quadrant option is used to snap directly to one of the quadrant points of an arc or circle. Figure 3-10 shows the quadrant points for an arc and a circle.

To draw a line to one of a circle's quadrant points

1. Select the Line tool from the Draw toolbar.

   Command: _line Specify first point:

2. Select a start point for the line.

   Specify next point or [Undo]:

3. Select the Quadrant tool from the Osnap toolbar.

   Specify next point or [Undo]: _qua of

4. Select a point on the circle near the desired quadrant point.

3-10 OSNAP—Perpendicular

The Perpendicular option is used to draw a line perpendicular to an existing entity. See Figure 3-11.

To draw a line perpendicular to a line

1. Select the Line tool from the Draw toolbar.

   Command: _line Specify first point:

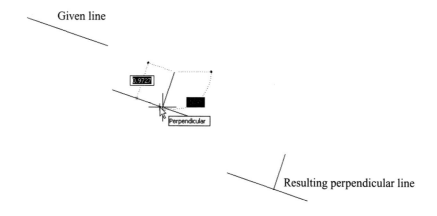

The Perpendicular option can be used to
draw a line perpendicular to another line.

Figure 3-11

2. Select a start point for the line.

   Specify next point or [Undo]:

3. Select the Perpendicular tool on the Osnap
   toolbar.

   Specify next point or [Undo]: _per to

4. Select the line or entity that will be perpendicular
   to the drawn line.

3-11 OSNAP—Tangent

The Tangent option is used to draw lines tangent to
existing circles and arcs. See Figure 3-12.

To draw a line tangent to a circle

1. Select the Line tool from the Draw toolbar.

   Command: _line Specify first point:

2. Select the start point for the line.

   Specify next point or [Undo]:

3. Select the Tangent tool from the Osnap toolbar.

   Specify next point or [Undo]: _tan to

4. Select the circle.

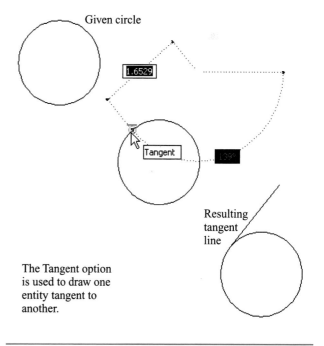

The Tangent option
is used to draw one
entity tangent to
another.

Figure 3-12

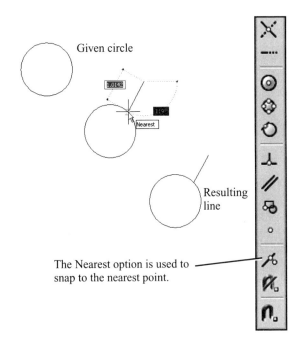

Figure 3-13

3-12 OSNAP—Nearest

The Nearest option is used to snap to the nearest available point on an existing entity. See Figure 3-13.

To draw a line from a point to the nearest selected point on an existing line

1. Select the Line tool from the Draw toolbar.

    Command: _line Specify first point:

2. Select a start point for the line.

    Specify next point or [Undo]:

3. Select the Nearest tool from the Osnap toolbar.

    Specify next point or [Undo]: _nea to

4. Select the existing line.

    The existing line need be only within the rectangular box on the cursor. The line endpoint will be snapped to the nearest available point on the line.

3-13 SAMPLE PROBLEM SP3-1

Redraw the object shown in Figure 3-14. Do *not* include dimensions. Use Osnap commands whenever possible.

Figure 3-14

1. Create a new drawing called SP3-1.
2. Drawing setup:

    Limits: lower left = <0.0000,0.0000>
    Limits: upper right = 297,210
    Zoom All
    Grid = 10
    Snap = 5

3. Draw an 83.3 × 52.7 rectangle starting at point 40,40. Use dynamic input values to draw the rectangle's edge lines. See Figure 3-15.

Figure 3-15

Figure 3-16

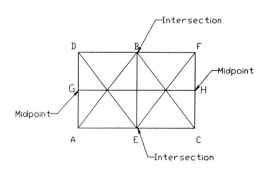

Figure 3-17

4. Draw line A-B-C. Point A is a Grid Snap point, so it may be selected directly. Point B is selected using Osnap Midpoint, and Point C is selected using Osnap Endpoint (or Intersection). See Figure 3-16.
5. Draw line D-E-F using Endpoint, Midpoint, and Endpoint, respectively.
6. Draw line B-E using Intersection. See Figure 3-17.
7. Draw line G-H using Midpoint.
8. Save the drawing if desired.

3-14 SAMPLE PROBLEM—SP3-2

Redraw the object shown in Figure 3-18. Do not include dimensions.

1. Create a new drawing called SP3-2.
2. Drawing setup:

   Limits: accept the default values
   Grid = .50
   Snap = .25

Figure 3-18

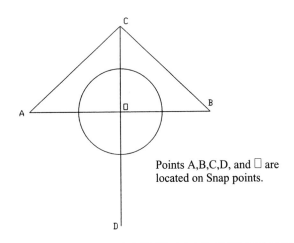

Points A,B,C,D, and ▯ are located on Snap points.

Figure 3-19

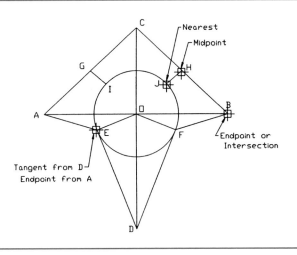

Figure 3-20

3. Draw lines A-B, C-D, A-C, and C-B. The endpoint of each of these lines is located on a Grid Snap point, so the points may be selected directly.
4. Draw circle O. See Figure 3-19. Respond to the center point prompt by selecting Intersection from the Osnap pop-up menu.
5. Draw lines G-I and H-J using Midpoint and Nearest. See Figure 3-20.
6. Draw lines D-E and D-F using Tangent. Draw lines A-E and A-F using Endpoint. Points A, B, and D are Grid Snap points and also are endpoints.
7. Save the drawing if desired.

3-15 GRIPS

The Grips function is used to quickly identify and lock onto convenient points on entities such as the endpoints of lines or the center point of a circle. Figure 3-21 shows some examples of grip points.

Grips are helpful when using some Modify commands. For example, if a line is to be rotated about its center point, a grip can be used to first identify the line's center point (pickbox) and then lock onto it as the center point (basepoint) for the rotation. The center point of a circle can be used to move the circle to a new location.

To turn the Grips function off

By default, the Grips command is automatically on. The Grips command may be turned off as follows.

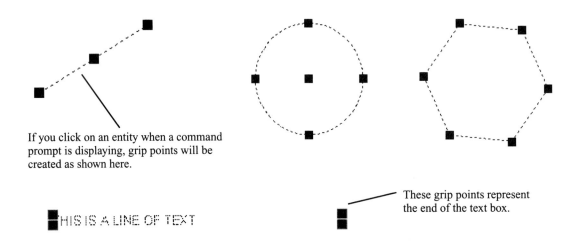

If you click on an entity when a command prompt is displaying, grip points will be created as shown here.

These grip points represent the end of the text box.

Figure 3-21

THE DEFAULT GRIPS VALUE IS 1.

1 = GRIPS ON

0 = GRIPS OFF

Figure 3-22

1. Type Grips in response to a command prompt.

   Enter new value for GRIPS <1>:

   There are two possible values: 1 and 0. The 1 value turns the Grips command on. The 0 value turns the Grips command off. See Figure 3-22.

2. *Type 0; press Enter.*

   The Grips command is now off.

To access the Grips dialog box

1. Grip a line; that is, place the cursor on the line and press the left mouse button.

   A line is gripped when a command prompt is displayed and no other command sequence is active.

2. Click on one of the grip points.

   In this example, the lower endpoint was selected.

   <Stretch to point>/Base point/Copy/Undo/eXit:

3. Press the right mouse button.

   The Grips dialog box appears. See Figure 3-23.

3-16   GRIPS—Extend

To extend the length of a line (See Figure 3-24.)

   Given a line, extend it 1.25 inches.

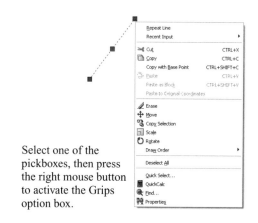

Select one of the pickboxes, then press the right mouse button to activate the Grips option box.

Figure 3-23

1. Draw an angled line as shown, then draw a circle of radius 1.25 centered on one of the line's endpoints.
2. Press the Escape key to ensure a command prompt.
3. Select the line.

   Blue pickboxes should appear at the two endpoints and at the midpoint.

4. Select the endpoint that also serves as the circle's center point.

   The blue pickbox should change to a solid red square box.

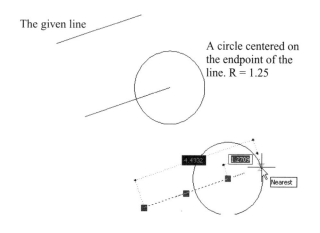

The given line

A circle centered on the endpoint of the line. R = 1.25

Figure 3-24

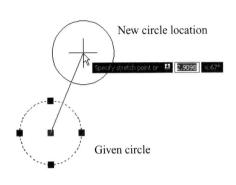

New circle location

Given circle

Figure 3-25

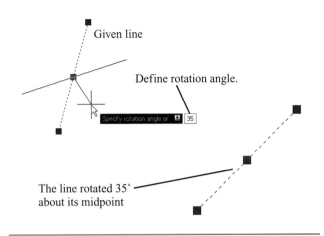

Given line

Define rotation angle.

The line rotated 35°
about its midpoint

Figure 3-26

5. Press the right mouse button and select the Stretch option from the Grips menu.

STRETCH
Specify stretch point or [Base point/Copy/Undo/ eXit]:

Stretch the endpoint of the line to the edge of the 1.25 circle by accessing the Osnap menu (press the Control key and right mouse button) and selecting the Nearest option.

6. Select a point on the circle that aligns the line through the three grip points, then press the left button.
7. Erase the circle.

3-17 GRIPS—Move

To move an object using Grips (See Figure 3-25.)

Move the given circle to a new location on the drawing.

1. Press the Escape key to ensure a command prompt.
2. Select any point on the circle.

Blue pickboxes should appear at circle O's center point and at each of the quadrant points.

3. Select the circle's center point.

The center point pickbox should change to a red solid square box.

STRETCH
Specify stretch point or [Base_point/Copy/ Undo/eXit]:

4. Move the circle to a new location and press the left mouse button.

The circle's new location can be located using dynamic input.

3-18 GRIPS—Rotate

To rotate an object using Grips (See Figure 3-26.)

Given a line, rotate it 35° about its midpoint.

1. Press the Escape key to ensure a command prompt.
2. Select the line.

Blue pickboxes should appear at the line's two endpoints and at its midpoint.

3. Select the line's midpoint.

The blue pickbox at the midpoint should change to a solid red square box.

4. Press the right mouse button, then select Rotate from the Grips dialog box.

Figure 3-27

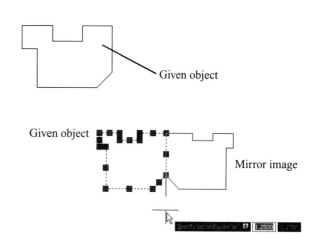

Figure 3-28

ROTATE
Specify rotation angle or [Base point/Copy/ Undo/eXit]:

5. Type 35; press Enter.

The value 35 will appear in the dynamic input box.

3-19 GRIPS—Scale

To change the scale of an object (See Figure 3-27.)

Given an object, reduce it to half its original size.

1. Press the Escape key to ensure a command prompt.
2. Select the object by first windowing it, then pressing the left mouse button.

Blue pickboxes should appear all around the object.

3. Select any one of the pickboxes.

The selected pickbox should change to a red solid square box.

4. Press the right mouse button to activate the Grips dialog box.
5. Select Scale from the menu.

SCALE
Specify scale factor or [Base point/Copy/Undo/ Reference/eXit]:

6. Type .5; press Enter.

Figure 3-27 also shows the same object scaled to twice its original size, that is, a scale factor of 2.

3-20 GRIPS—Mirror

To mirror an object (See Figure 3-28.)

Given an object, draw a mirror image of the object.

1. Press the Escape key to ensure a command prompt.
2. Window the object, then press the left mouse button.

Blue pickboxes should appear at each corner intersection of the hexagon.

3. Select the upper right pickbox.

The selected pickbox should change to a red solid square box.

4. Press the right mouse button to activate the Grips option box.
5. Select the Mirror option.

MIRROR
Specify second point or [Base point/Copy/ Undo/eXit]:

6. Select the pickbox vertically below the selected right upper pickbox.
7. Press the Escape key twice to fix the mirrored object.

Figure 3-29

3-21 BLOCKS

Blocks are groups of entities saved as a single unit. Blocks are used to save shapes and groups of shapes that are used frequently when creating drawings. Once created, blocks can be inserted into the drawings, thereby saving drawing time.

The Block tool is located on the Draw pull-down menu and on the Draw toolbar. See Figure 3-29. The Insert Block tool is associated with the Insert pull-down menu and the Draw toolbar.

To create a block

Figure 3-30 shows an object. A block can be made from this existing drawing as follows.

1. Select the Make Block tool from the Draw toolbar.

The Block Definition dialog box appears. See Figure 3-30.

2. Click the Select Objects box.

    Select objects:

3. Window the object; press Enter.

    The Block Definition dialog box will reappear.

4. Type SHAPE in the Block name box.

    Block names may contain up to 31 characters.

5. Click the Pick point box.
6. Define the insertion base point for the block.

    The Block Definition dialog box will reappear. Osnap may be used to locate an insertion point. The values listed in the Block Definition dialog box are XYZ values relative to the current origin.

    The insertion base point will be a point on the object that will align with the screen cursor during the block insertion process.

7. Select the OK box.

Type block name here.

Click here to define the block's base point.

Save this object as a block named SHAPE.

Figure 3-30

Figure 3-31

To insert a block

1. Select Insert Block from the Draw toolbar.

   The Insert dialog box appears. See Figure 3-31.

2. Select the Name box.

   A cascade menu will appear. See Figure 3-32.

3. Select Shape.

   The word SHAPE appears in the Name box.

4. Select OK.

   The Insert dialog box reappears with the word SHAPE in the Name box.

5. Select OK.

   The Shape block will appear on the screen with its insertion point aligned with the cursor. The shape will move as you move the crosshairs.

   Specify insertion point or [Scale/X/Y/Z/Rotate/ PScale/PX/PY/PZ/PRotate]:

6. Select an insertion point for the shape.

   The default scale factor is 1. This means that if you accept the default value by pressing Enter, the shape will be redrawn at its original size. The shape of the object may be changed by using the options available at the Insert prompt.

To change the scale of a block

1. Select Insert Block from the Draw toolbar.

2. Select the SHAPE block.

   Specify insertion point or [Scale/X/Y/Z/Rotate/ PScale/PX/PY/PZ/PRotate]:

3. Type S; press Enter.

   Specify scale factor for XYZ axes:

4. Type 2; press Enter.

   Specify insertion point:

5. Select a point.

   The Rotation option is used to rotate a block about its insertion point. AutoCAD assumes that a horizontal line to the right of the insertion point is 0° and that counterclockwise is the positive angular direction.

   The block is now part of the drawing; however, the block in its present form may not be edited. Blocks are treated as a single entity and not as individual lines. You can verify this by trying to erase any one of the lines in the block. The entire object will be erased. The object can be returned to the screen by clicking the Undo tool. A block must first be exploded before it can be edited.

To explode a block

1. Select the Explode tool from the Modify toolbar.

   Command: _explode
   Select objects:

2. Window the entire object.

   Select objects:

3. Press Enter.

   The object is now exploded and can be edited. There is no visible change in the screen, but there will be a short blink after the Explode command is executed.

Figure 3-32

Figure 3-33

3-22 WORKING WITH BLOCKS

Figure 3-33 shows a resistor circuit. It was created from an existing block called RESISTOR. The drawing used Decimal units with a Grid set to .5 and a Snap set to .25. The default drawing limits were accepted. The procedure is as follows.

To insert blocks at different angles

1. Select Insert Block from the Draw toolbar.

   The Insert dialog box will appear.

2. Select the cascade menu on the right side of the Name box.
3. Figure 3-34 shows RESISTOR in the Name box. Select the RESISTOR block.

4. Select OK to return to the drawing screen.

   The RESISTOR block will appear attached to the crosshairs at the predefined insertion point. See Figure 3-35.
   The resistor is too large for the drawing, so a reduced scale will be used to generate the appropriate size.

   Specify insertion point or [Scale/X/Y/Z/Rotate/ PScale/PX/PY/PZ/PRotate]:

5. Type S; press Enter.

   Specify scale factor for XYZ axes:

6. Type .50; press Enter.

   Specify insertion point:

Figure 3-34

Dynamic input

The base point of the block will be attached to the crosshairs until a screen location is defined.

Figure 3-35

The RESISTOR block was inserted at an angle of 90°.

Figure 3-36

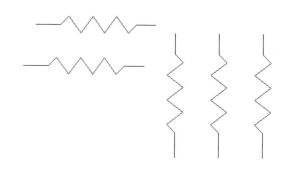

Draw enough resistors for the complete diagram.

Figure 3-37

Locate the resistor on the screen.

7. Press the right mouse button and select the Repeat Insert Block option.
8. Select the RESISTOR block again and set the X Y Z scale factors for 0.50.

Specify insertion point or [Scale/X/Y/Z/Rotate/ PScale/PX/PY/PZ/PRotate]:

9. Type R; press Enter.

Specify rotation angle:

10. Type 90; press Enter.

Specify insertion point:

11. Select an insertion point as shown in Figure 3-36.

Your screen should look like Figure 3-36.

12. Use the Copy command (Modify toolbar) to add the additional required resistors.

See Figure 3-37.

13. Use the Line command (Draw toolbar) to draw the required lines.
14. Select the Circle command (Draw toolbar) and draw a circle of diameter .250.
15. Use the Copy command (Modify toolbar) to create a second circle.
16. Use the Move command to position the circles so that they touch the edges of the two open circles.
17. Use the Dtext command to add the appropriate text.

The drawing should now look like the diagram presented in Figure 3-33.

To insert blocks with different scale factors

Figure 3-38 shows four different-sized threads, all created from the same block. The block labeled A used the default scale factor of 1, so it is exactly the same size as the original drawing used to create the block. The block labeled B was created with an X scale factor equal to 1, and a Y scale factor equal to 2. The procedure is as follows.

1. Select the Insert Block tool from the Draw toolbar.
2. Select the THREAD block.

The THREAD block is not an AutoCAD creation. THREAD was created specifically for this example.

Specify insertion point or [Scale/X/Y/Z/Rotate/ PScale/PX/PY/PZ/PRotate]:

3. Type X; press Enter.

Specify X scale factor:

4. Type 1; press Enter.

Specify insertion point:

5. Type Y; press Enter.

Specify Y scale factor:

6. Type 2; press Enter.

Specify insertion point:

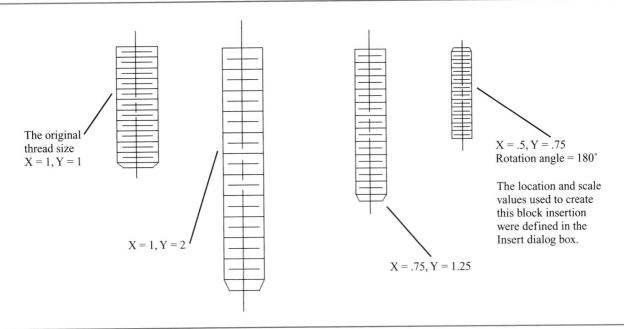

The original thread size
X = 1, Y = 1

X = 1, Y = 2

X = .5, Y = .75
Rotation angle = 180°

The location and scale values used to create this block insertion were defined in the Insert dialog box.

X = .75, Y = 1.25

Figure 3-38

7. Specify a point.

The thread labeled C has an X scale factor of .75 and a Y scale factor of 1.25. The thread labeled D has an X scale factor of .5, a Y scale factor of .75, and a rotation angle of 180°.

To use the insert dialog box to change the shape of a block

The D thread scale factors and rotation angle were defined using the Insert dialog box. The procedure is as follows.

1. Select the Insert block.

The Insert dialog box will appear. See Figure 3-39.

2. Click the box to the left of the words Specify On-screen.

The click should remove the check mark in the box, indicating that the option has been turned off. When the check mark is removed, the options labeled Insertion Point, Scale, and Rotation should change from gray to black in the dialog box.

3. Place the cursor arrow inside the X Scale box, backspace to remove the existing value, and type .50.
4. Change the Y scale factor to .75.
5. Change the Angle to 180.

See Figure 3-39. The insertion point was also defined using the Insert dialog box. In this example, the thread

will appear on the screen with its insertion point at the 11.2500,7.5000 point. These values are unique to the example presented.

To combine blocks

Figure 3-40 shows a hex head screw that was created from two blocks. The threaded portion of the screw was created first, then the head portion was added. Note in Figure 3-40 that when the hex head block was created, the insertion point was deliberately selected so that it could

Turn this option off before entering insertion point, scale, and rotation values.

Figure 3-39

The THREAD block

The two blocks combined

The HEXHEAD block

HEXHEAD insertion point is the bottom line's midpoint.

Figure 3-40

Figure 3-41

easily be aligned with the centerline and the top surface of the thread block.

3-23 WBlock

Wblocks are blocks that can be entered into any drawing. When a block is created, it is unique to the drawing on which it was defined. This means that if you create a block on a drawing, then save and exit the drawing, the block is saved with the drawing but cannot be used on another drawing. If you start a new drawing, the saved block will not be available.

Any block can be defined and saved, however, as a wblock. Wblocks are saved as individual drawing files and can be inserted into any drawing.

To create a wblock

This section shows how to create a wblock for the block called SHAPE shown in Figure 3-30. A wblock may be created directly from an object shown on the screen.

1. At a command prompt, type wblock and press Enter.

    The Write Block dialog box appears. See Figure 3-41. There is no wblock tool.

2. Click the Block radio button under Source.
3. Select the SHAPE file from the listed blocks.

A listing of available blocks is accessed by clicking the arrow on the upper right side of the dialog box.

4. Select OK.

To verify that a wblock has been created

1. Select the Insert block tool from the Draw toolbar.

    The Insert dialog box will appear. See Figure 3-42.

Click here to access the drawing files.

Figure 3-42

Figure 3-43

2. Click the Browse box.

   The Select Drawing File dialog box will appear.

3. Scroll down the file listing to locate the SHAPE file, then click it.

   See Figure 3-43.

4. Click the Open box, then the OK box.

   The wblock will appear on the screen.

To change the size of a wblock.

1. Select the Insert block tool from the Draw toolbar.

   The Insert dialog box will appear. See Figure 3-44.

2. Select the Browse option.
3. Select the SHAPE wblock file, then click the Open box.

   The Insert dialog box will appear.

4. Set the Scale values.
5. Select OK.

   See Figure 3-45.

Set scale values here.

Figure 3-44

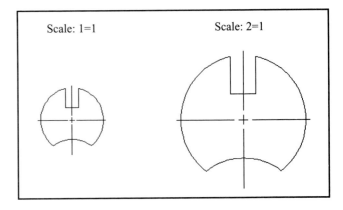

Figure 3-45

Name new block RECT.

Figure 3-46

3-24 DYNAMIC BLOCKS

Dynamic blocks are blocks that can be changed in real time. For example, a dynamic block can be stretched by locating a point and moving the cursor to a new position. In the following example a 4 × 3 rectangular block is changed into a 7 × 3 block.

To create a dynamic block—stretch option

Figure 3-46 shows a 4 × 3 rectangle. It was created using four line segments.

1. Access the Make Block command and define the rectangle as a block. Name the block RECT.
2. Click the Block Editor tool on the Standard toolbar.

The Edit Definition dialog box will appear. See Figure 3-47.

3. Select the RECT block and click OK.

Figure 3-47

The Block Authoring Palettes - All Palettes dialog box will appear. See Figure 3-48.

4. Click the Parameters tab and then click the Linear Parameter option.

    Specify start point or [Name/Label/Chain/ Description/Base/Palette/Value Set]:

5. Select the top left corner of the rectangle.

    See Figure 3-49.

    Specify endpoint:

6. Select the top right corner.

    Specify label location:

7. Move the word Distance away from the rectangle and press the left mouse button, then press the right button.

    This defines the block's parameter. Now define the related actions.

8. Click the Actions tab on the Block Authoring Palettes - All Palettes dialog box and select the Stretch Action option.

    See Figure 3-50.

    Select parameter:

9. Select the word Distance.

    Specify parameter point to associate with action or enter [sTart point/Second point] <Start>:

10. Select the upper left corner of the rectangle.

    Specify first corner of the stretch frame or [CPolygon]:

11. Pick a point above and to the left of the rectangle.

    Specify opposite corner:

12. Window approximately the left half of the rectangle. Do not include the right vertical line in the window.

    Select objects:

13. Select the two horizontal lines and the left vertical line. Do not select the right vertical line.

    See Figure 3-51.

14. Press the right mouse button.

    Specify action location [Multiplier/Offset]:

    The word Stretch will appear on the screen.

15. Select the upper left corner of the rectangle.

    See Figure 3-52.

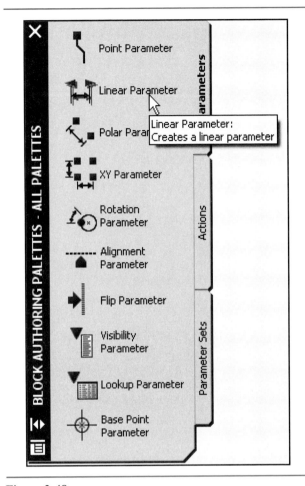

Figure 3-48

16. Select the Save Block Definition and save the block edits, then select the Close Block Editor option on the Block Editor toolbar.

    A dialog box will appear.

    Save changes to RECT:

17. Click yes.

    The RECT block will appear on the screen.

18. Left-click the RECT block.

    See Figure 3-53. Two arrowheads and a filled square will appear. These are the dynamic block indicators.

19. Locate the cursor on the upper left corner and, holding down the left mouse button, move the arrow to the left creating a 7 × 3 rectangle. Use the dynamic input boxes to define the new size.

    See Figures 3-54 and 3-55.

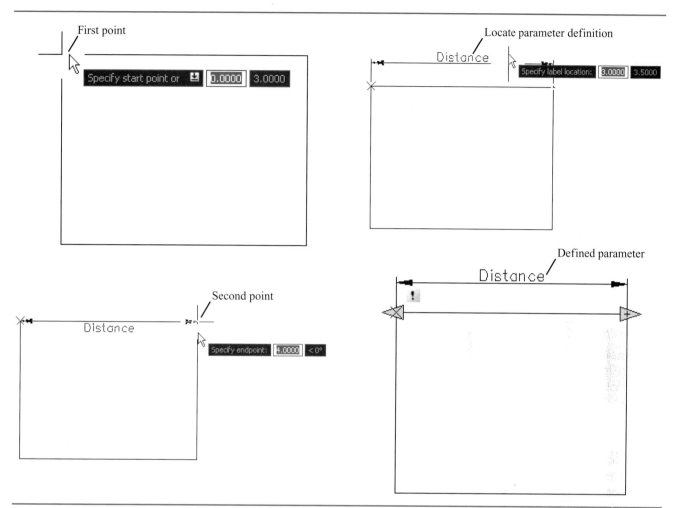

First point

Specify start point or   0.0000   3.0000

Locate parameter definition

Distance

Specify label location: 3.0000   3.5000

Second point

Distance

Specify endpoint: 4.0000   < 0°

Defined parameter

Distance

Figure 3-49

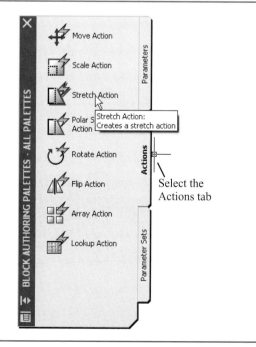

BLOCK AUTHORING PALETTES - ALL PALETTES

Move Action

Scale Action

Stretch Action

Stretch Action:
Creates a stretch action

Polar S
Action

Rotate Action

Flip Action

Array Action

Lookup Action

Parameters

Actions

Parameter Sets

Select the
Actions tab

Figure 3-50

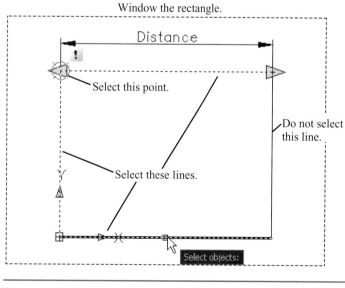

Window the rectangle.

Distance

Select this point.

Do not select
this line.

Select these lines.

Select objects:

Figure 3-51

Figure 3-52

Figure 3-53

Figure 3-54

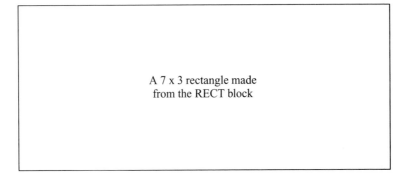

Figure 3-55

To add a second parameter and action

Figure 3-56 shows the RECT block with a stretch action applied to the horizontal direction. This allows dynamic applications in the horizontal direction. A second action will be added to allow dynamic applications in the vertical direction.

1. Add a linear parameter to the right side of the block.
2. Add a stretch action to the vertical linear parameter.

Figure 3-56

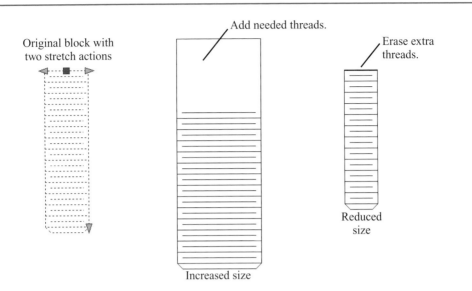

Figure 3-57

3. Save the revised block and close the Block Editor.
4. Left-click the block to reveal the dynamic arrow indicators.
5. Stretch the block in both the horizontal and vertical directions.

Figure 3-57 shows horizontal and vertical stretch actions applied to a thread representation. These actions allow the thread to be sized as needed for different applications.

To create a dynamic block—scale and rotation options

Figure 3-58 shows a block named Thread. A scale and rotation action option will be added to the block.

1. Define a distance parameter along the horizontal section of the block.

2. Select the Scale Action.

   Select parameter:

3. Select the Distance Parameter.

   Select the objects:

4. Window the block; press the right mouse button.

   Specify action location or [Base type]:

5. Select the upper left corner of the block.

   This completes the Scale definition.

6. Select the Rotation Parameter.

   Specify base point or [Name/Label/Chain/Description/Palette/Value Set]:

7. Select the upper left corner of the block.

   Specify radius of parameter:

8. Define a radius.

   Specify default rotation angle or [Base angle]<0>:

9. Press Enter.

   Specify label location:

10. Define a location for the label.
11. Access the Rotation Action option.

    Select parameter:

12. Select the Angle Parameter.

    Select object:

13. Window the block.

    Specify action location or [Base type]:

14. Select the upper left corner.
15. Save and close the Block Editor.

    Figure 3-58 shows the effects of the Scale and Rotation actions on the block.

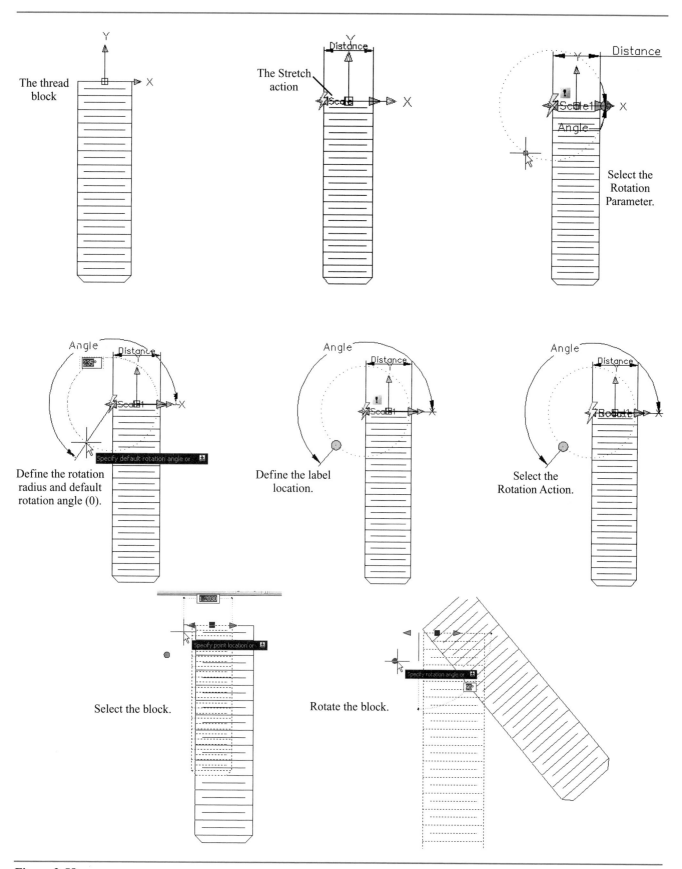

The thread block

The Stretch action

Select the Rotation Parameter.

Define the rotation radius and default rotation angle (0).

Define the label location.

Select the Rotation Action.

Select the block.

Rotate the block.

Figure 3-58

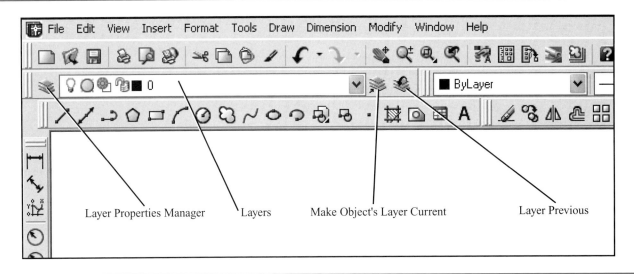

Figure 3-59

3-25 LAYERS

A *layer* is like a clear piece of paper you can lay directly over the drawing. You can draw on the layer and see through it to the original drawing. Layers can be made invisible, and information can be transferred between layers.

In the example shown, a series of layers will be created, then a group of lines will be moved from the initial 0 layer to the other layers.

The Layer tool is located just below the Standard toolbar and includes six associated tools and headings. See Figure 3-59. The associated tools are not command tools but indicators of the status of the Layer options. For example, the open padlock shown indicates that the layer is not locked. If it were locked, the Padlock tool would change to the closed position.

To create new layers

This exercise will create two new layers: Hidden and Center.

1. Select the Layer Properties Manager Tool.

The Layer Properties Manager dialog box will appear. See Figure 3-60.

2. Click the New box.

A new layer listing will appear with the name Layer1. See Figure 3-61.

3. Type Hidden in place of the Layer1 name.

The name Hidden should appear under the 0 layer heading in the Name column.

Click here to create a new layer.

Figure 3-60

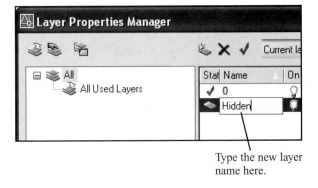

Type the new layer name here.

Figure 3-61

Figure 3-62

4. Click the New box again, and add another new layer named Center.

The name Center will appear in the Name column. There are now three layers associated with the drawing. See Figure 3-62. The 0 layer is the current layer, as indicated by the 0 to the right of the Current Layer box.

To change the color and linetype of a layer

1. Click the Hidden layer line on the Layer Properties Manager dialog box.
2. Click the word white on the Hidden layer line.

See Figure 3-63. The Select Color dialog box will appear. See Figure 3-64. The Select Color dialog box can also be accessed by clicking the Show details box, then scrolling down the options given in the Color box.

3. Select the color blue, then click OK.

All lines drawn on the Hidden layer will be blue.

4. Select the word Continuous on the Hidden layer line under the Linetype heading.

The Select Linetype dialog box will change. See Figure 3-65.

5. Click the Load button.

The Load or Reload Linetypes dialog box will appear. See Figure 3-66.

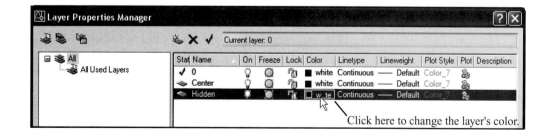

Click here to change the layer's color.

Figure 3-63

The selected color will appear here.

Blue

Figure 3-64

Click here to load new linetypes.

Figure 3-65

Select the desired linetype from the list.

Figure 3-66

Figure 3-67

6. Scroll down the Linetype list and select the Hidden pattern by clicking on the pattern preview, then click OK.

The Select Linetype dialog box will appear with the Hidden linetype listed. See Figure 3-67.

7. Click OK.
8. Select the Center layer line.

The line will be highlighted.

9. Change the Hidden layer's line color to Red and its linetype to Center.

The Layer Properties Manager dialog box should look like Figure 3-68.

Figure 3-68

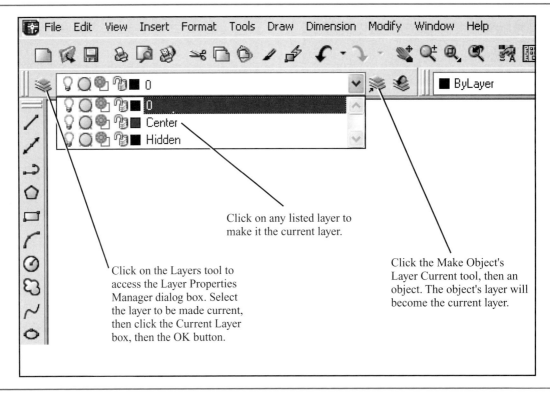

Click on any listed layer to
make it the current layer.

Click the Make Object's
Layer Current tool, then an
object. The object's layer will
become the current layer.

Click on the Layers tool to
access the Layer Properties
Manager dialog box. Select
the layer to be made current,
then click the Current Layer
box, then the OK button.

Figure 3-69

To draw on different layers

Only the layer designated as the current layer may be worked on, even though other layers may be visible. There are three ways to make a layer the current layer. See Figure 3-69.

1. Use the Layer control tool and click the layer name. The layer will become the current layer. The current layer is the name displayed in the Layer control box after the cascade disappears.
2. Use the Layers tool to access the Layer Properties Manager dialog box. Click on a layer name, then click the current box, then OK. The layer name will appear in the Layer control box, indicating that it is the current layer.
3. Use the Make Object's Layer Current tool, by clicking an entity on the screen. The entity's layer will become the current layer.

Once a current layer has been established, objects may be drawn and modified.

To change layers

An object may be drawn on one layer, then moved to another layer. This feature is helpful when designing; for example, an original layout may be created in a single layer, then lines may be transferred to different layers as needed. As a line changes layers, it assumes the color and linetype of the new layer. Figure 3-70 shows a circle and a line drawn on the 0 layer. Change the line to a centerline and the circle to a hidden line by moving the objects to the appropriate layer.

1. Select the circle.

   The grip points will appear.

2. Use the Layer control tool and select the Hidden layer, making it the current layer.
3. Double-click the Escape key.

   The circle will be moved to the Hidden layer and will appear as a blue hidden line.

4. Move the line to the Center layer using the same procedure.

   Figure 3-71 shows the resulting changes.

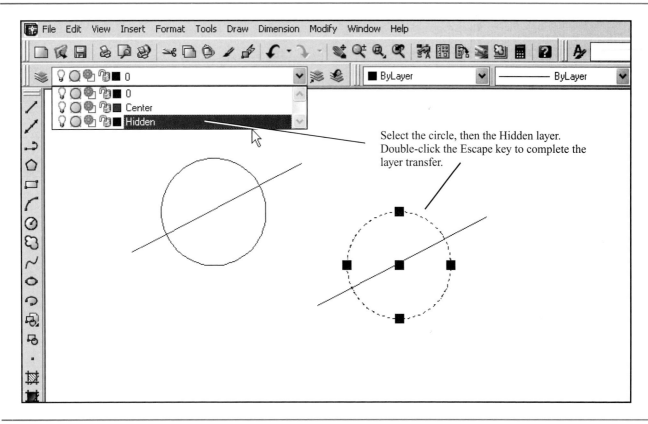

The following text appears within the figure:

Select the circle, then the Hidden layer.
Double-click the Escape key to complete the
layer transfer.

Figure 3-70

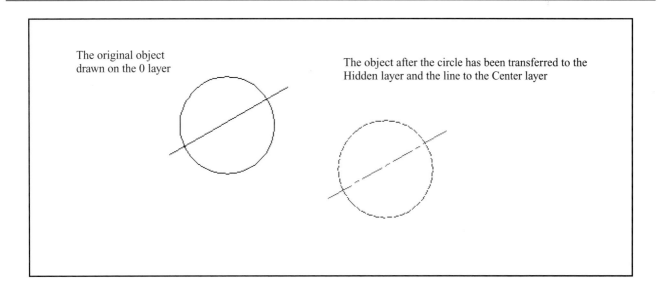

The original object
drawn on the 0 layer

The object after the circle has been transferred to the
Hidden layer and the line to the Center layer

Figure 3-71

Figure 3-72

Figure 3-73

To change the scale of a linetype

Figure 3-72 shows two parallel lines drawn on the Hidden layer.

1. Select the Modify pull-down menu, then Properties, or click the Properties tool on the Standard toolbar.

The Properties dialog box will appear. See Figure 3-73.

2. Select the Linetype scale and change the value from 1.0000 to 3.0000.
3. Select the Exit button on the dialog box and return to the screen.
4. Draw two more lines.

Figure 3-74 shows the resulting change. The new lines have a different linetype scale and therefore different spacing.

To use the Global Linetype scale factor

All line patterns may be modified by the same scale factor using the Global Linetype scale factor.

1. Select the Format pull-down menu, then Linetype, then click the Show Details box.

The Linetype Manager dialog box will appear. See Figure 3-75. The current global scale is 1.0000 and the current object scale, the one set for the Hidden layer, equals 3.0000.

Figure 3-74

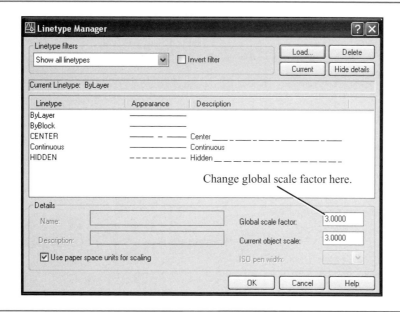

Figure 3-75

2. Change the Global scale factor to 3.000; select OK.

Figure 3-76 shows the resulting changes. All lines were changed by a factor of 3. The difference between the line scales is still 3.

To use the Match Properties tool

1. Select the Match Properties tool from the Standard toolbar.

Select source object:

2. Select one of the lines with the smaller spacing.

Select destination object(s) or[Settings]:

3. Select one of the lines with the larger spacing.

Figure 3-77 shows the resulting changes as applied to the line presented in Figure 3-74. The destination line now has the same properties as the source line.

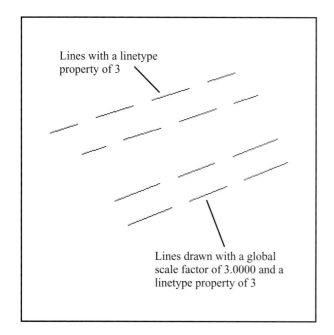

Lines with a linetype property of 3

Lines drawn with a global scale factor of 3.0000 and a linetype property of 3

Figure 3-76

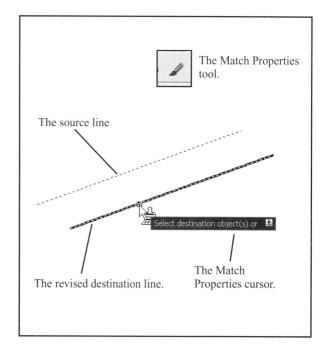

The Match Properties tool.

The source line

Select destination object(s) or

The revised destination line.

The Match Properties cursor.

Figure 3-77

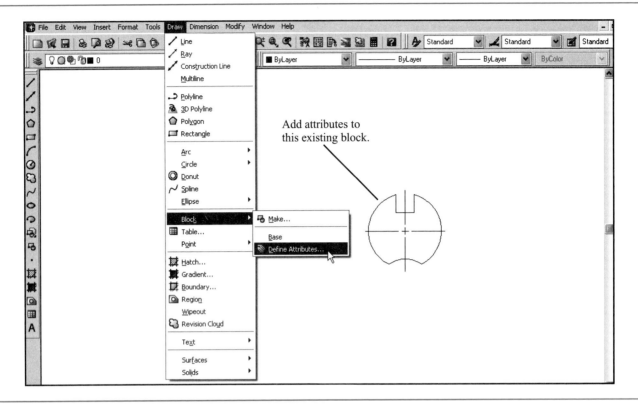

Figure 3-78

To turn layers off

1. Select the Layer control tool.

    A list of current layers will cascade from the box.

2. Click the lightbulb icon on the CENTER layer.

    The lightbulb icon will change from yellow to blue, indicating that the layer is off.

3-26 ATTRIBUTES

Attributes are sections of text added to a block that prompt the drawer to add information to the drawing. For example, a title block may have an attribute that prompts the illustrator to add the date to the title block as it is inserted into a drawing. Attributes have their own toolbar.

To add an attribute to a block

Figure 3-78 shows a block. This example will add attributes that request information about the product's part number, material, quantity, and finish.

1. Select the Draw pull-down menu, then Block, then Define Attributes.

    The Attribute Definition dialog box appears. See Figure 3-79.

2. Select the Tag box and type NUMBER.

A *tag* is the name of an attribute and is used for filing and reference purposes. Tag names must be one word with no spaces.

3. Select the Prompt box and type: Define the part number.

    The prompt line will eventually appear at the bottom of the screen when a block containing an attribute is

Figure 3-79

Figure 3-80

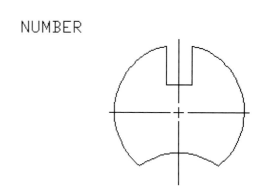

Figure 3-81

inserted into a drawing. If you do not define a prompt, the tag name will be used as a prompt.

4. Leave the Value box empty.

The Value box entry will be the default value if none is entered when the prompt appears. Based on the defined prompt and value inputs, the following prompt line will appear when the attribute is combined with a block:

Define the part number <>:

5. Select Specify On-screen.

The drawing will appear with crosshairs. Select a location for the attribute tag by moving the crosshairs, then press the left mouse button.

The Attribute Definition dialog box will reappear with the X,Y coordinate values of the selected point listed in the Insertion Point box. See Figure 3-80.

6. Select OK.

Figure 3-81 shows the attribute tag applied to a drawing. Figures 3-82, 3-83, and 3-84 show three more Attribute Definition dialog boxes. Note that the Align below previous attribute definition box has a check mark, indicating it has been turned on. The option is turned on by clicking the box. Figure 3-85 shows the resulting drawing.

Figure 3-82

Figure 3-83

Figure 3-84

Figure 3-85

To create a new block that includes attributes

1. Select the Make Block tool from the Draw toolbar.

   The Block Definition toolbar will appear.

2. Name the new block Shape-1.
3. Select a base point.
4. Select the object by windowing the block and all the attribute tags.
5. Select OK.
6. The Edit Attributes dialog box will appear. If all entries are correct, select OK.

   Figure 3-86 shows the resulting block.

To insert an exisiting block with attributes

1. Select the Insert Block tool on the Draw toolbar.

   The Insert dialog box will appear. See Figure 3-87.

2. Select SHAPE-1, then click OK.

   Specify the insertion point or [Scale/X/Y/Z/Rotate/PScale/PX/PY/PZ/PRotate]:

3. Select an insertion point.

   Enter attribute values
   What material is needed? <Steel>:

4. Press Enter.

   What color do you want? <Black>:

Figure 3-86

Figure 3-87

Figure 3-88

5. Select a different color by typing Blue; press Enter.

How many are needed?

6. Type 4; press Enter.

Define the part number <>:

7. Type BU-AM311; press Enter.

Figure 3-88 shows the resulting drawing.

To edit an existing attribute

Once a block has been created that includes attributes, it may be edited using the Edit Attributes command. The procedure is as follows. The block to be edited must be on the drawing screen.

1. Select the Edit Attribute tool from the Modify II toolbar, or select the Modify pull-down menu, then Object, then Attribute, then Single. See Figure 3-89.

   Command: _attedit
   Select block reference:

Figure 3-89

Figure 3-90

Figure 3-91

2. Select the word Steel.

The Enhanced Attribute Editor dialog box will appear. See Figure 3-89. In this example, the material will be changed from Steel to Aluminum. Note that the attribute prompt, tag, and value lines originally entered in the Attribute Definition dialog box are listed on the Enhanced Attribute Editor dialog box.

3. Locate the cursor to the right of the word Steel, backspace to remove Steel, then type Aluminum.

Figure 3-90 shows the resulting changes.

To use the Edit Global command

The Edit Global command is used to change information in a block independent of the block's definitions. The block to be edited must be on the screen.

1. Select the Modify pull-down menu, then Object, then Attribute, then Global.

Command: _-attedit
Edit attributes one at a time? [Yes/No] <Y>:

2. Press Enter.

Block name specification<>:*

3. Press Enter.

Enter attribute tag specification <>:*

4. Press Enter.

Enter attribute value specification <>:*

5. Press Enter.

Select attributes:

6. Select the number 4 associated with the Shape-1 block on the screen; press Enter.

The value 4 will change to a hidden pattern, and a large X will appear on the screen. See Figure 3-91.

Enter an option [Value/Position/Height/Angle/ Style/Layer/Color/Next] <N>:

7. Type V; press Enter.

Enter type of value modification [Change/ Replace?] <R>:

The Change option is used to modify a few characters of the existing value. The Replace option is used to create an entirely new value. The Replace option is the default option.

The quantity value has been changed independently of the block's attributes.

BU–AM311
Aluminum
12
Blue

Figure 3-92

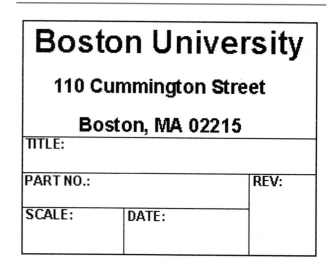

Figure 3-93

8. Press Enter.

   Enter new attribute value:

9. Type 12; press Enter.

   Enter an option [Value/Position/Height/Angle/ Style/Layer/Color/Next]<N>:

10. Press Enter.

The new value will replace the former value. See Figure 3-92.

3-27 TITLE BLOCKS WITH ATTRIBUTES

Figure 3-93 shows a title block that has been saved as a block. It would be helpful to add attributes to the block so that when it is called up to a drawing, the drawer will be prompted to enter the required information.

Note that text may be added to an AutoCAD template using the Mtext command. Create the desired text and use the Move command to position it within the title block. The title block shown in Figure 3-93 was custom drawn for a special application.

Figures 3-94, 3-95, 3-96, 3-97, and Figure 3-98 show the five Attribute Definition dialog boxes used to define the

Figure 3-94

Figure 3-95

Figure 3-96

Figure 3-98

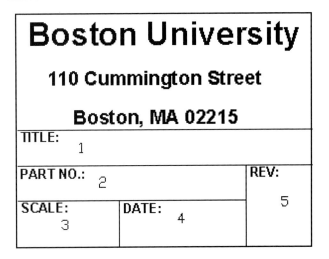

Figure 3-99

title block attributes. Note that the text height in Figures 3-94 through 3-98 may be varied if desired. Also note that no attribute values were assigned. This means that the space on the drawing will be left blank if no prompt value is entered. Figure 3-99 shows the resulting title block with the attribute tags in place.

The new block with attributes was saved as TITLE-A, using the Block command. It can now be saved as a wblock and used on future drawings. Figure 3-100 shows a possible title block created from the TITLE-A block.

A sample use of the block attributes

Figure 3-97

Figure 3-100

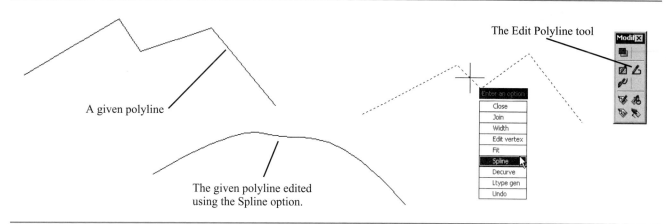

A given polyline

The given polyline edited
using the Spline option.

The Edit Polyline tool

Figure 3-101

3-28 EDIT POLYLINE

The Edit Polyline tool, found on the Modify II toolbar, is used to change the shape of a given polyline. In the example shown in Figure 3-101 the Edit Polyline command was used to create a spline from a given polyline. The Edit Polyline tool is discussed further in Section 16-17.

To create a spline from a given polyline

1. Select the Edit Polyline tool from the Modify II toolbar.

   Command: _pedit Select polyline:

2. Select the polyline.

   Select an option [Close/Join/Width/Edit vertex/Fit/ Spline/Decurve/Ltype gen/Undo]:

3. Select the Spline option; press Enter.

   Figure 3-101 shows the edited polyline.

3-29 EDIT SPLINE

The Edit Spline tool, found on the Modify II toolbar, is used to change the shape of a given spline.

To edit a spline

1. Select the Edit Spline tool from the Modify II toolbar.

   Command: _splinedit Select spline:

2. Select the given spline.

   A series of squares will appear on the screen. See Figure 3-102. These squares are the original data points used to define the spline. In this example one of the points will be moved.

3. Select the Move vertex option; press Enter.

   Specify new location or [Next/Previous/Select point/eXit] <N>:

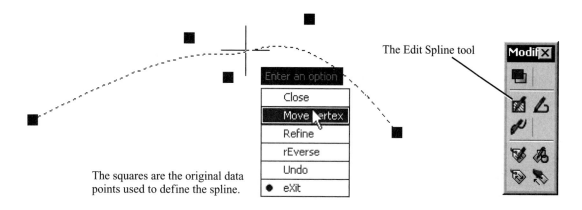

The squares are the original data points used to define the spline.

The Edit Spline tool

Figure 3-102

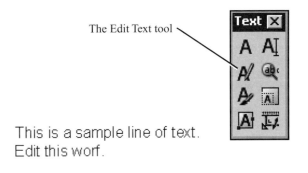

The crosshairs indicate the
new location for the filled point.
Press Enter to advance to the next point.

The first square will change colors.

The Edit Text tool

Figure 3-103

Figure 3-105

The first square will change colors, and a rubber-band–type line with a large + will appear. See Figure 3-103.

advance to the next point. Every time the Enter key is pressed, the Edit command will advance to the next point. Only the X option will allow you to exit the command sequence.

4. Move the first square to a new location, then type X; press Enter.

Figure 3-104 shows the edited spline. The chosen location will become the new location for the first point. If a point other than the first point needs to be moved, press Enter when the X appears, and the Edit command will

3-30 EDIT TEXT

The Edit Text tool is used to change existing text. Figure 3-105 shows a sample of existing text.

To change existing text

1. Select the Edit Text tool from the Modify II toolbar.

    Command: _ddedit
    Select an annotated object or [Undo]:

2. Select the existing text.

    The Text Formatting dialog box will appear (see Figure 3-106) with the selected text.

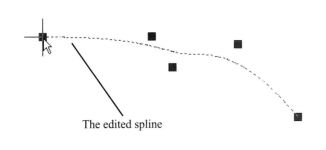

The edited spline

Figure 3-104

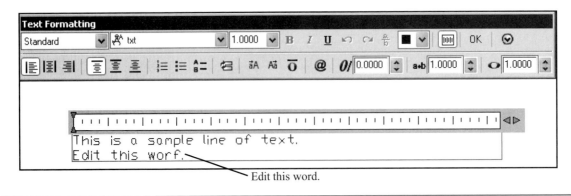

Edit this word.

Figure 3-106

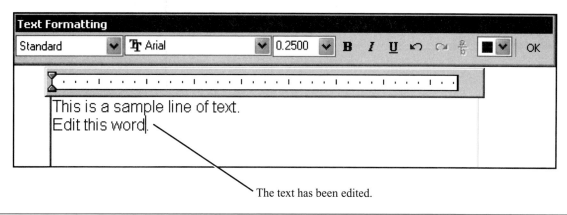

The text has been edited.

Figure 3-107

3. Edit the text shown in the dialog box.

   See Figure 3-107.

4. Select OK.

   The edited text will replace the previous text.

3-31 CONSTRUCTING THE BISECTOR OF AN ANGLE— METHOD I

Given angle A-O-B, bisect it. See Figure 3-108.

1. Select Draw, Circle.
2. Draw a circle with a center point located at point O. The circle may be of any radius. This is an excellent place to take advantage of AutoCAD's Drag mode. Move the cursor until the circle appears to be approximately the same size as that shown.
3. Select Copy, Multiple to draw two more circles equal in radius to the one drawn in step 1. Locate the circles' center points on intersections of the first circle and angle A-O-B. Use Osnap, Intersection to ensure accuracy.
4. Draw a line from point O to intersection C as shown. Use Osnap, Intersection to ensure accuracy.

Figure 3-108

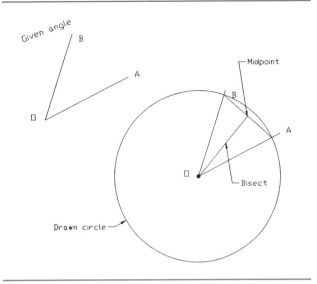

Figure 3-109

3-32 CONSTRUCTING THE BISECTOR OF AN ANGLE— METHOD II

Given angle A-O-B, bisect it. See Figure 3-109.

1. Draw a circle with a center point located at point O. The circle may be of any radius. This is an excellent place to take advantage of AutoCAD's Drag mode. Move the cursor until the circle appears to be approximately the same size as that shown.
2. Draw a line between the intersection point created by the circle and angle A-O-B. Use Osnap, Intersection to ensure accuracy.
3. Draw a Line between point O and the midpoint of the line. Use Osnap, Midpoint to ensure accuracy.

3-33 CONSTRUCTING AN OGEE CURVE (S-CURVE) WITH EQUAL ARCS

Given points B and C, construct an ogee curve between them. See Figure 3-110.

1. Draw a straight line between points B and C. Use Osnap, Endpoint to ensure accuracy.
2. Draw lines perpendicular to lines A-B and C-D as shown.

Use Osnap, Endpoint to accurately start the lines on points B and C, respectively. Use relative coordinates to draw the lines. The lines may be of any length greater than the perpendicular distance between lines A-B and C-D.

3. Construct a perpendicular bisector of line B-C.
4. Define the intersections of the perpendicular lines drawn in step 2 with the perpendicular bisector of B-C at points F and G.
5. Draw a circle centered at point F that passes points B and E. Trim the circle using line B-C.
6. Draw a circle centered at point G that passes points C and E. Trim the circle using line B-C.

Figure 3-110

Figure 3-111

Figure 3-112

The two arcs of steps 5 and 6 define an ogee curve using equal arcs. Figure 3-111 shows the construction of an ogee curve with unequal arcs. The construction techniques are similar to those presented above.

3-34 CONSTRUCTING A PARABOLA

Definition: A *parabola* is the loci of points such that the distances between a fixed point, the *focus*, and a fixed line, the *directrix*, are always equal.

Given a focus point A and a directrix B-C, construct a parabola. See Figure 3-112.

1. Draw a line parallel to B-C so that it intersects the midpoint between line B-C and point A. Use Offset.
2. Draw a circle centered about point A whose radius is equal to half the distance between line B-C and point A.
3. Offset lines and a circle 0.2 inch from the parallel line and the circle created in steps 1 and 2.
4. Identify the intersections of the lines and circles created in step 3. In this example filled circles were used to identify the points.
5. Draw a polyline connecting all the intersection points.
6. Use Edit Polyline, Fit option to change the polyline to a parabolic curve.

3-35 CONSTRUCTING A HYPERBOLA

Definition: A *hyperbola* is the loci of points equidistant between two fixed foci.

Given foci points F1 and F2 equidistant from a vertical line and two other vertical lines drawn through points A and B, draw a hyperbola. See Figures 3-113, 3-114, and 3-115.

1. Draw a circle of arbitrary radius using point F2 as the center. If possible, set the drawing up so that both points F1 and F2 are on snap points. If this is not possible, draw a vertical line through point F2 so that the Osnap, Intersection option may be used to locate the center accurately.

Figure 3-113

Figure 3-114

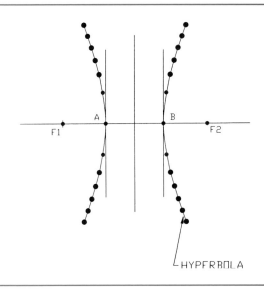

Figure 3-115

2. Draw a circle centered about F2 of radius equal to the radius of the circle drawn in step 1, plus the distance between points A and B. See Figure 3-114.
3. Draw concentric circles about the circles centered about F1 and F2. The distance between all the circles should be equal. Use Offset.

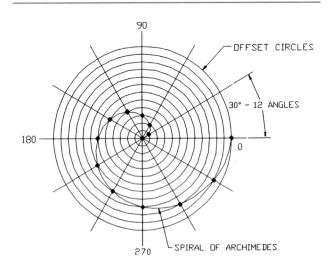

Figure 3-116

4. Mark the intersections between the smaller and larger circles as shown in Figure 3-114. Use filled circles to define the points.
5. Draw a polyline connecting points 1 through 12.
6. Use the Edit Polyline and Fit options to draw the hyperbola.
7. Use Mirror to create the opposing hyperbola. See Figure 3-115.

3-36 CONSTRUCTING A SPIRAL

Construct a Spiral of Archimedes. See Figure 3-116.

1. Draw a set of perpendicular centerlines as shown.
2. Draw 12 concentric circles about center point O. Use Offset to draw circles.
3. Draw 12 equally spaced ray lines as shown. Array either the horizontal or vertical line using the Polar Array command. Use point O as the center of rotation.
4. Draw a polyline starting at point O. The second point is the intersection of the 30° ray with the first circle. Point 2 is the intersection of the 60° ray and the second circle. Continue through all 12 rays and circles.
5. Use the Edit, Polyline, and Fit options to change the polyline to a spiral.

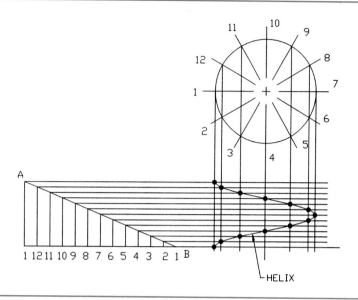

Figure 3-117

3-37 CONSTRUCTING A HELIX

Construct a helix that advances 1.875 inches every 360°. See Figure 3-117.

1. Draw a vertical line 1.875 inches long and a horizontal line as shown.
2. Draw a horizontal line that can easily be divided into 12 equal spaces. The length of the horizontal line is arbitrary. Set up a grid so that the 12 equal spaces can easily be identified.
3. Draw a circle as shown. Use Array and divide the circle using 12 equally spaced rays. Use the Polar Array command with the circle's center point as the center of rotation.
4. Draw line A-B as shown. Draw 12 vertical, equally spaced lines between the horizontal line and line A-B.
5. Label both the circle and horizontal line as shown. The number of divisions must be the same for both the circle and the horizontal line.
6. Draw vertical lines from the intersections of the 12 equally spaced rays and the circle's circumfer-

ence as shown in Figure 3-116. Use the Osnap, Intersection option to ensure accuracy.
7. Draw horizontal lines from the intersections on line A-B so that they intersect the vertical lines from step 5. Use the Osnap, Intersection option to ensure accuracy.
8. Mark the intersections of the lines from steps 5 and 6 as shown.
9. Use a polyline to connect the horizontal and vertical intersections as shown.
10. Use the Edit, Polyline, and Fit options to draw the helix.

3-38 DESIGNING USING SHAPE PARAMETERS

An elementary design problem often faced by beginning designers is to create a shape based on a given set of parameters. This section presents two examples of this type of design problem.

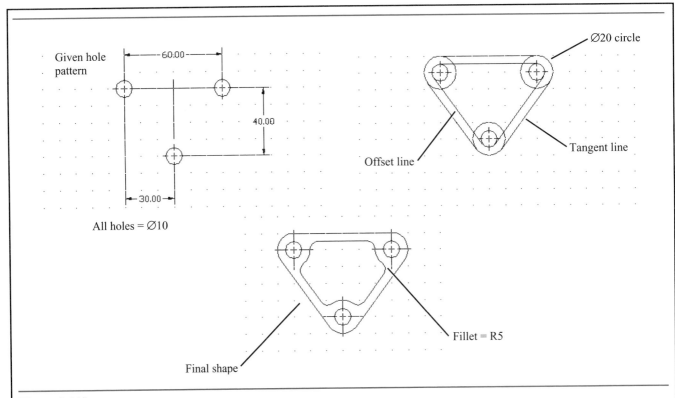

Figure 3-118

Design Problem DP3-1

Design a shape that will support the hole pattern shown in Figure 3-118 subject to the following parameters. Design for the minimum amount of material. All dimensions are in millimeters.

1. The edge of the material may be no closer to the center of a hole than a distance equivalent to the radius of the hole.
2. The minimum distance from any cutout to the edge of the part may not be less than the smallest distance calculated in step 1.
3. The minimum inside radius for a cutout is R = 5 millimeters.

The solution is as follows.

1. Calculate the minimum edge distances for the holes.

In this problem the three holes are all the same diameter: 10 millimeters. Given the parameter that an edge may be no closer to the center of the hole than a distance equivalent to the size of the hole's diameter, the distance from the outside edge of the hole to the edge of the part must be no less than 5 millimeters, or a circular shape of diameter 20 millimeters.

2. Draw Ø20 circles using the existing circle's center point as shown in Figure 3-118.
3. Draw outside tangent lines between the Ø20 circles.

The second parameter limits the minimum edge distance to the minimum edge distance calculated in step 1, or 5 millimeters.

4. Use the Offset command to draw lines 5 millimeters from the outside tangent lines drawn in step 3 to define the internal cutout.
5. Use the inside radius parameter of 5 millimeters and add fillets to the internal cutout.
6. Erase any excess lines.

Figure 3-118 shows the final shape.

Design Problem DP3-2

Design a shape that will support the hole pattern shown in Figure 3-119. Support the center hole with four perpendicular webs. All dimensions are in inches.

1. The edge of the material may be no closer to the center of a hole than a distance equivalent to the radius of the hole.

Given hole pattern

Figure 3-119

Tangent lines   Offset lines

Figure 3-120

2. The minimum distance from any cutout to the edge of the part may not be less than the smallest distance calculated in step 1.
3. The minimum inside radius for a cutout is R = .125 inch.

The solution is as follows.

1. Calculate the minimum edge distances for the holes.

In this example, the hole diameters are 1.00 and 1.50 inches.

2. Add circles of radius 2.00 and 3.00 as shown. See Figure 3-120.

The minimum edge distance based on the Ø1.00 of the smaller hole equals .50 inch.

3. Use the minimum edge distance and define the inside edge of the internal cutouts.
4. Use the minimum edge distance to define the four supporting webs for the center hole.
5. Add the inside bend radii.

The inside bend radii were added using the Fillet command. This will cause a portion of the internal edge to disappear. Use the Offset command again to replace the line defining the edge of the internal cutout. See Figure 3-121.

6. Remove all excess lines.

See Figure 3-122.

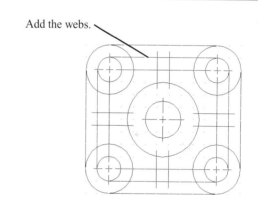

Add the webs.

Figure 3-121

Final shape

Figure 3-122

3-39 EXERCISE PROBLEMS

Redraw the following figures to scale using the given dimensions. Do not include dimensions on the drawing.

EX3-1 INCHES (Hint: Use Osnap)

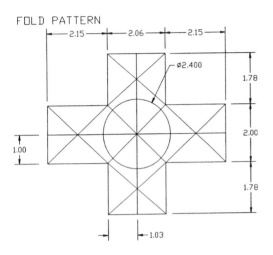

EX3-3 MILLIMETERS (Hint: Use Osnap)

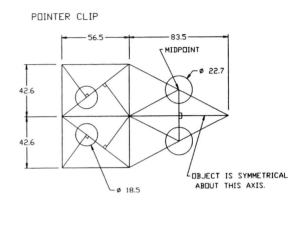

EX3-2 MILLIMETERS (Hint: Use Osnap)

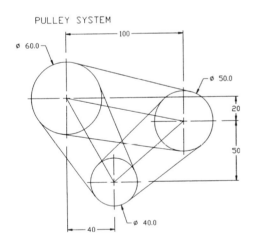

EX3-4 MILLIMETERS (Hint: Use Osnap)

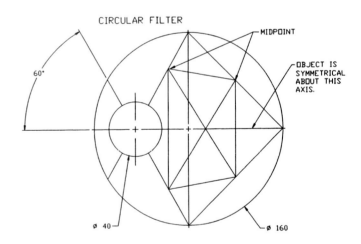

EX3-5

Draw a 54° angle; construct the bisector.

EX3-6

Draw an 89.33° angle; construct the bisector.

EX3-7 INCHES

Given points A and B as shown below, construct an ogee curve of equal arcs.

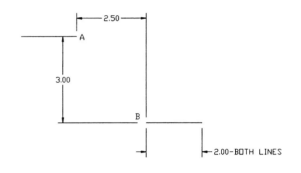

EX3-8 MILLIMETERS

Given points A, B, C, as shown below, construct an ogee curve that starts at point A, passes through point C, and ends at point B.

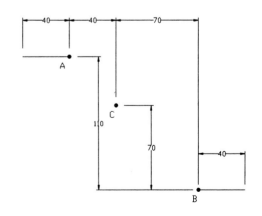

EX3-9

Construct a hexagon inscribed within a 3.63-inch diameter circle.

EX3-10

Construct a hexagon inscribed within a 120-millimeter diameter circle.

EX3-11 INCHES

Given point A and directrix B-C as shown below, construct a parabola.

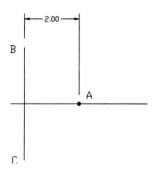

EX3-12 MILLIMETERS

Given point A and directrix B-C as shown below, construct a parabola.

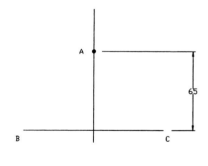

EX3-13 INCHES

Given foci F1 and F2 as shown below, draw a hyperbola.

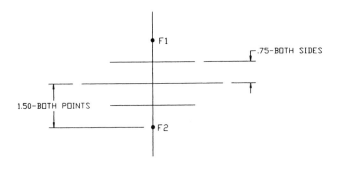

EX3-15 INCHES

Given the concentric circles and rays shown below, construct a spiral.

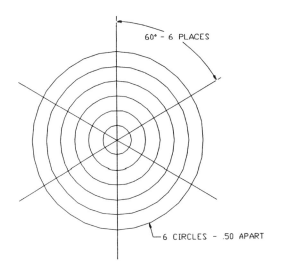

EX3-14 MILLIMETERS

Given foci F1 and F2 as shown below, draw a hyperbola.

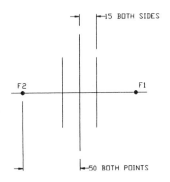

EX3-16 MILLIMETERS

Given the concentric circles and rays shown below, construct a spiral.

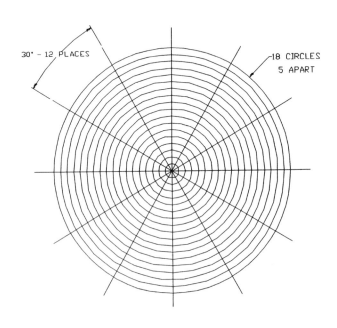

EX3-17 INCHES

Given the setup shown below, construct a helix.

Redraw the following objects based on the given dimensions.

EX3-19 MILLIMETERS

EX3-18 MILLIMETERS

Given the setup shown below, construct a helix.

EX3-20 MILLIMETERS

EX3-21 INCHES

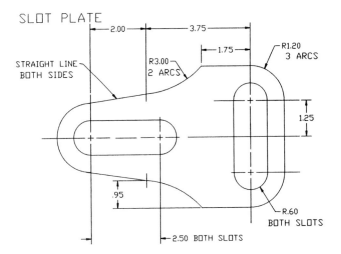

SLOT PLATE

STRAIGHT LINE BOTH SIDES

2.00

3.75

1.75

R3.00 2 ARCS

R1.20 3 ARCS

1.25

.95

R.60 BOTH SLOTS

2.50 BOTH SLOTS

EX3-22 INCHES

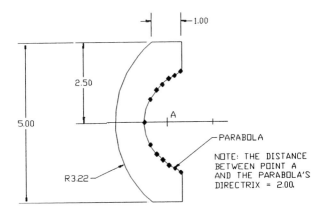

1.00

2.50

5.00

A

R3.22

PARABOLA

NOTE: THE DISTANCE BETWEEN POINT A AND THE PARABOLA'S DIRECTRIX = 2.00.

EX3-23 MILLIMETERS

25

COMBINATION WRENCH

110

R3 – 4 FILLETS

OGEE CURVE

50   30

R29 2 ARCS

70

20 – 4 PLACES

30   40

R10 – 4 FILLETS

10

R20.6 2 ARCS

EX3-24 MILLIMETERS

EX3-25 MILLIMETERS

EX3-26 MILLIMETERS

EX3-27 MILLIMETERS

EX3-29 INCHES

EX3-28 MILLIMETERS

EX3-30 INCHES

EX3-31 MILLIMETERS

EX3-33 MILLIMETERS

EX3-32 MILLIMETERS

EX3-34 MILLIMETERS

EX3-35 INCHES

HOLE	A	B
DIA	.328	.500

EX3-36 INCHES

EX3-37 INCHES

EX3-38 MILLIMETERS

EX3-39 CENTIMETERS

EX3-40 INCHES

EX3-41 MILLIMETERS

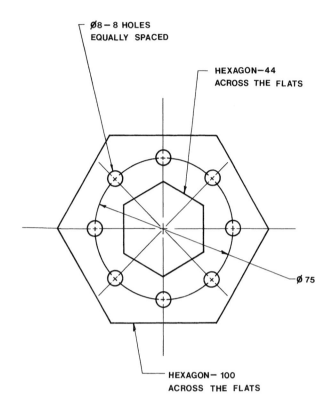

Ø8 – 8 HOLES
EQUALLY SPACED

HEXAGON–44
ACROSS THE FLATS

Ø 75

HEXAGON– 100
ACROSS THE FLATS

EX3-42 MILLIMETERS

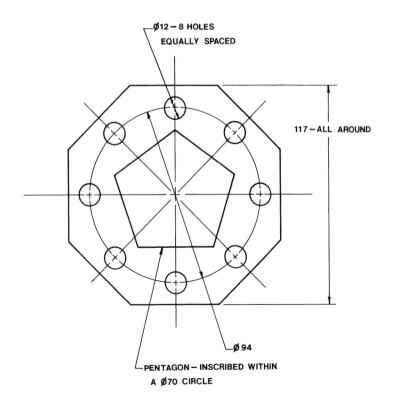

Ø12 – 8 HOLES
EQUALLY SPACED

117 – ALL AROUND

Ø 94

PENTAGON – INSCRIBED WITHIN
A Ø70 CIRCLE

EX3-43

Draw a circle, mark off 24 equally spaced points, then connect each point with every other point using only straight lines.

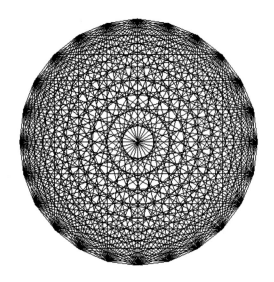

EX3-44 MILLIMETERS

A. Create a block of the following drawing layout. All dimensions are in millimeters.
B. Add the following attributes:

Tag = DATE
Prompt = Enter today's date
Value = (leave blank)

Tag = DRAWING
Prompt = Enter the drawing number
Value = (leave blank)

Tag = NAME
Prompt = Enter your name
Value = (leave blank)

Align the attribute tags on the drawing.

DRAWING LAYOUT − 2(MILLIMETERS)

NOTE: MAKE ALL LETTERING 6 HIGH
UNLESS OTHERWISE STATED.

EX3-45 MILLIMETERS

EX3-46 MILLIMETERS

EX3-47 MILLIMETERS

EX3-48 INCHES

Create a block for the following standard tolerance blocks shown.

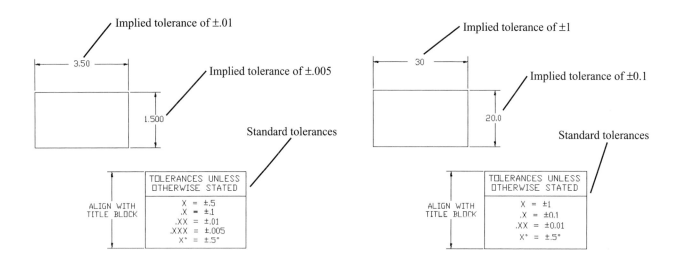

EX3-49 INCHES

A. Create a block for one of the title blocks shown. A sample completed title block is also shown.
B. Add attributes that will help the user complete the title block satisfactorily.

EX3-50

Create a block of the following release block. All dimensions are in inches.

EX3-52

Create blocks for the following revision block formats. The dimensions within the dimension lines are inches; the dimensions within the brackets are millimeters.

EX3-51

Create blocks for the following parts list formats. All dimensions are in inches. Add the appropriate attributes.

Design a shape that will support the hole patterns shown in Exercises EX3-53 through EX3-57. Design for a minimum amount of material and to satisfy the following parameters.

1. The edge distance of the material may be no closer to the center of a hole than a distance equal to the radius of the hole.
2. The minimum edge distance from any internal cutout to the edge of the part may be no less than the distance calculated in Step 1.
3. The minimum inside radius for a cutout is 5 millimeters, or 0.125 inch.

EX3-53 INCHES

EX3-54 MILLIMETERS

EX3-55 MILLIMETERS

EX3-56 MILLIMETERS

THE OBJECT IS SYMMETRICAL
ABOUT BOTH X AND Y AXES

EX3-57 MILLIMETERS

C H A P T E R 4

Sketching

4-1 INTRODUCTION

The ability to create freehand sketches is an important skill for engineers and designers to acquire. The old joke about engineers and designers not being able to talk without a pencil in their hands is not far from the truth. Many design concepts and ideas are very difficult to express verbally, so they must be expressed visually. Sketches can be created quickly and used as a powerful aid in communicating technical ideas.

This chapter presents the fundamentals of freehand sketching as applied to technical situations. It includes both two-dimensional and three-dimensional sketching. Like any skill, freehand sketching is best learned by lots of practice.

4-2 ESTABLISHING YOUR OWN STYLE

As you learn and practice how to sketch, you will find that you develop your own way of doing things, your own style. This is very acceptable, as there is no absolutely correct method for sketching, but only recommendations.

The most important requirement of freehand sketching is that you be comfortable. As you practice and experiment

you may find that you prefer a certain pencil lead hardness, a certain angle for your paper, and a certain way to make your lines, both straight and curved. You may find that you prefer to use oblique sketches rather than isometric sketches when sketching three-dimensional objects. Eventually you will develop a style that is comfortable for you and that you can consistently use to create good-quality sketches.

It is recommended that you try all the types of sketches presented in the chapter. Only after you have tried and practiced all the different types will you be able to settle on a technique and style that works best for you.

4-3 GRAPH PAPER

Graph paper is very helpful when preparing freehand sketches. It helps you sketch straight lines, allows you to set up guide points for curved lines, and can be used to establish proportions. It is recommended that you start by doing all two-dimensional sketches on graph paper. As your sketching becomes more proficient you may sketch on plain paper, but because most technical sketching requires some attention to correct proportions, grid paper will always be helpful.

Graph paper is available in many different scales and in both inch and metric units. Some graph paper is printed

Figure 4-1

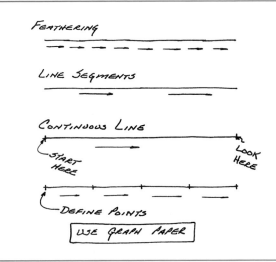

Figure 4-2

using light blue lines, since many copying machines cannot easily reproduce blue lines. This means that copies of the sketches done on light-blue guidelines will appear to have been drawn on plain paper and will include only the sketch.

4-4 PENCILS

Pencils are made with many grades of lead hardness. See Figure 4-1. Hard leads can produce thin, light lines and are well suited for the accuracy requirements of board-type drawings, but are usually too light for sketching. The soft leads produce broad, dark lines but tend to smudge easily if handled too much.

The choice of lead hardness is a personal one. Some designers use 3H leads very successfully; others use HB leads with equal results. You are probably used to a 2H lead, as this is the most commonly available. Start sketching with a 2H lead, and if the lines are too light, try a softer lead; if they are too dark, try a harder lead until you are satisfied with your work. Pencils with different grades of lead hardness are available at most stationery and art supply stores.

Most sketching is done in pencil because it can easily be erased and modified. If you want the very dark lines that inked lines produce, it is recommended that you first prepare the drawing in pencil, then use a pen to trace over the lines you want to emphasize.

4-5 LINES

Straight lines are sketched using one of two methods: by drawing a series of short lines—called *feathering*—or by a series of line segments. The line segments should be about 1 to 2 inches or 25 to 50 millimeters long. It is very difficult to keep the line segments reasonably straight if they are much longer. As you practice you will develop a comfortable line segment distance. See Figure 4-2.

Lines may also be sketched as long, continuous lines. First locate the pencil at the line's starting point, then look at the endpoint as you sketch. This will help develop straighter long lines. Continuous lines are best sketched on graph paper because the graph lines will serve as an additional guide for keeping the line straight.

Long lines can be created by a series of shorter lines, and very long lines can be sketched by first defining a series of points, then using short segments to connect the points.

It is usually more comfortable to turn the paper slightly when sketching, as shown in Figure 4-3. Right-handers turn the paper counterclockwise and left-handers, clockwise.

It is also easier to sketch all lines in the same direction, that is, with your hand motion always the same. Rather than change your hand position for lines of different angles, simply change the position of the paper and sketch the lines as before. Horizontal and vertical lines are sketched using exactly the same motion; the paper is just turned 90°. Straight lines of any angle can be sketched in the same manner.

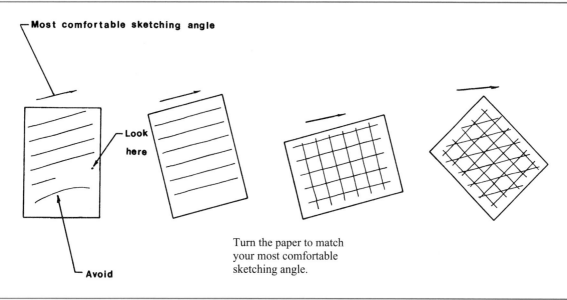

Most comfortable sketching angle

Look here

Avoid

Turn the paper to match
your most comfortable
sketching angle.

Figure 4-3

Sketch lines using a gentle, easy motion. Don't squeeze the pencil too hard. Sketch lines with more of an arm motion than a wrist motion. If too much wrist motion is used, the lines will tend to curve down at the ends and look more like arcs than straight lines.

4-6 PROPORTIONS

Sketches should be proportional. A square should look like a square, and a rectangle like a rectangle. Graph paper is very helpful in sketching proportionally, but it is still sometimes difficult to be accurate even with graph paper. Start by first sketching very lightly and then checking the proportionality of the work. See Figure 4-4. Go back over the lines, making corrections if necessary, then darken in the lines. The technique of first sketching lightly, checking the proportions, making corrections, and then going over the lines is useful regardless of the type of paper used.

It is often helpful to sketch a light grid background based on the unit values of the object being sketched. This is true even if you are working on graph paper because it helps to emphasize the unit values you need. See Figure 4-5.

The exact proportions of an object are not always known. A simple technique to approximately measure an object is to use the sketching pencil. See Figure 4-6. Hold the pencil at arm's length and sight the object. Move your thumb up the pencil so that the distance between the end of

ESTABLISH PROPORTIONS

ADD DETAIL

DARKEN LINES,
ERASE AS NECESSARY

Figure 4-4

Figure 4-5

Figure 4-6

the pencil and your thumb represents a distance on the object. Transfer the distance to the sketch. Continue taking measurements and transferring them to the sketch until reasonable proportions have been created.

4-7 CURVES

Curved shapes are best sketched by first defining points along the curve, then lightly sketching the curve between the points. See Figure 4-7. Evaluate the accuracy and smoothness of the curve, make any corrections necessary, then darken in the curve.

Circles can be sketched by sketching perpendicular centerlines and marking off four points equally spaced from the center point along the centerlines. The distance between the center point and the points on the centerlines should be approximately equal to the circle's radius. See Figure 4-8.

Draw a second set of perpendicular centerlines approximately 45° to the first. Again mark four points approximately equal to the radius of the circle. Sketch a light curve through the eight points, and check the curve for accuracy and smoothness. Make any corrections necessary and darken in the circle.

An ellipse can be sketched by first sketching a perpendicular axis, then locating four marks on the centerlines that are approximately equal to major and minor axis distances. Sketch a light curve, make any corrections necessary, and darken in the elliptical shape. See Figure 4-9.

Figure 4-10 shows how to sketch a slot. To sketch the slot, centerlines for the two end semicircles are located and sketched. Two additional radius points are added, then the overall shape of the slot is lightly sketched. Corrections are made and the final lines are darkened.

The triangular object is first sketched as a triangle, guidelines and axis are added for the curved sections, and the final shape of the object is sketched.

Figure 4-7

Figure 4-8

Figure 4-9

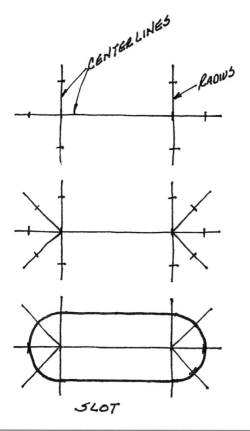

Figure 4-10

4-8 SAMPLE PROBLEM SP4-1

Sketch the object shown in Figure 4-11.

1. Sketch the overall rectangular shape of the object. See Figure 4-12.
2. Add proportional guidelines for the outside shape of the object and lightly sketch the outside shape.
3. Locate and sketch guidelines and axis lines for the other features.
4. Lightly sketch the object and make any corrections necessary.
5. Darken the final lines.

Figure 4-11

Figure 4-12

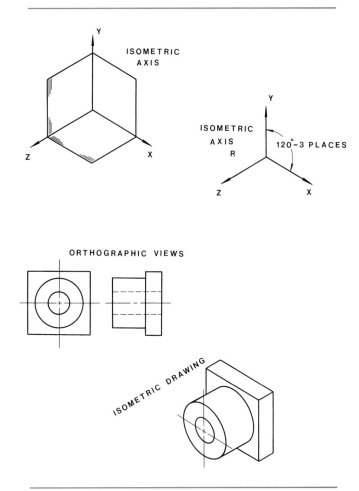

Figure 4-13

4-9 ISOMETRIC SKETCHES

Isometric sketches are based on an isometric axis that contains three lines, 120° apart. See Figure 4-13. The isometric axis can also be drawn in a modified form that contains a vertical line and two 30° lines. The modified axis is more convenient for sketching and is the more commonly used form. See Figure 4-14.

The receding lines of an isometric sketch are parallel. This is not visually correct, as the human eye naturally sees objects farther away as smaller than those closer. Railroad tracks appear to converge; however, it is easier to draw objects with parallel receding lines, and if the object is not too big, the slight visual distortion is acceptable. See Section 4-12 for an explanation of perspective drawings whose receding lines are not parallel but convergent.

The three planes of an isometric axis are defined as the left, right, and top planes, respectively. See Figure 4-14. When creating isometric sketches, it is best to start with the three planes drawn as if the object were a rectangular prism or cube. Think of creating the sketch from these

Figure 4-14

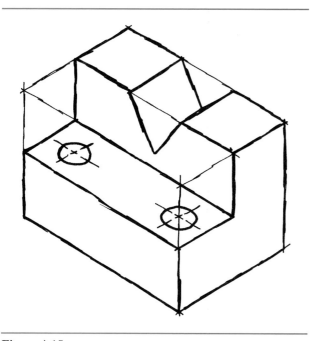

Figure 4-15

planes as working with a piece of wood, and trim away the unnecessary areas. Figure 4-15 shows an example of an isometric sketch. In the example, the overall proportions of the object were used to define the boundaries of the object, then other surfaces were added as necessary.

Isometric sketches may be sketched in different orientations. Figure 4-16 shows six possible orientations. Note how orientation 1 makes the object look as if it is below you, and orientation 6 makes it look as if it is above you. Orientation can also serve to show features that would otherwise be hidden from view. The small cutout in the rear of the object is visible in only four of the orientations. Always try to orient the isometric sketch so that it shows as many of the object's features as possible.

Figure 4-17 shows an isometric drawing of a cube that has a hole in the top plane. The hole must be sketched as an ellipse to appear visually correct in the isometric drawing. The axis lines for the ellipse are parallel to the edge lines of the plane. The proportions of the ellipse are defined by four points equidistant from the ellipse center point along the axis lines. The ellipse is then sketched lightly, checked for accuracy, then darkened.

Figure 4-16

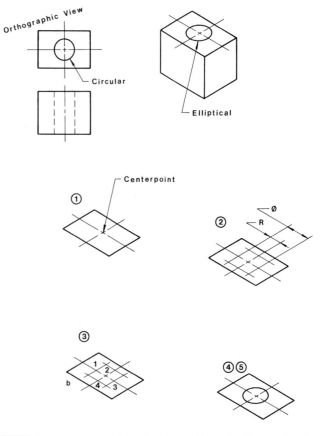

Figure 4-17

4-10 SAMPLE PROBLEM SP4-2

Sketch the object shown in Figure 4-18. Do not include dimensions, but keep the object proportional.

1. Use the overall dimensions of the object to sketch a rectangular prism of the correct proportions. This is a critical step. If the first attempt is not proportionally correct, erase it, and sketch again until a satisfactory result is achieved. See Figure 4-19.
2. Sketch the cutout.
3. Sketch the rounded surfaces. Note how axis lines are sketched and the elliptical shape added. Tangency lines are added, and visually incorrect lines are erased.
4. Sketch the holes. The holes are located by locating their centerlines and then sketching the required ellipses.

Figure 4-18

Figure 4-19

Figure 4-20

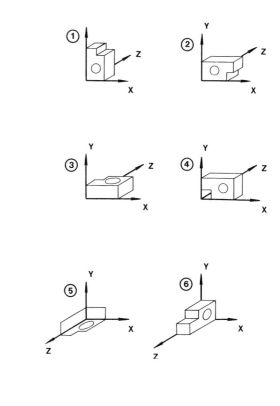

Figure 4-21

4-11 OBLIQUE SKETCHES

Oblique sketches are based on an axis system that contains one perpendicular set of axis lines and one receding line. See Figure 4-20. The front plane of an oblique axis is perpendicular, so the front face of a cube will appear as a square and the front face of a cylinder as a circle. The receding lines can be at any angle, but 30° is most common.

The receding lines of oblique sketches are parallel. As with isometric sketches this causes some visual distortions, but unless the object is very large, these distortions are acceptable.

Holes in the front plane of an oblique sketch may be sketched as circles, but holes in the other two planes are sketched as ellipses. See Figure 4-21. The axis lines for the ellipse are parallel to the edge lines of the plane. The proportions of the ellipses are determined by points equidistant from the center point along the axis.

Figure 4-22 shows an example of a circular object sketched as an oblique sketch. Oblique sketches are particularly useful in sketching circular objects because they allow

Figure 4-22

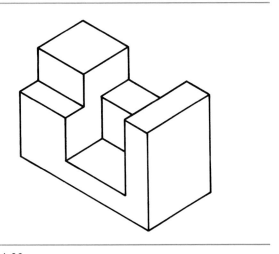

Figure 4-23

circles in the frontal planes to be sketched as circles rather than the elliptical shapes required by isometric sketches.

Figure 4-23 shows an object. Figure 4-24 shows how an oblique sketch of the object was developed.

4-12　PERSPECTIVE SKETCHES

Perspective sketches are sketches whose receding lines converge to a vanishing point. Perspective sketches are visually accurate in that they look like what we see: objects farther away appear smaller than those that are closer.

Figure 4-25 shows a comparison among the axis systems used for oblique, isometric, and two-point perspective drawings. The receding lines of the perspective drawings converge to vanishing points that are located on a theoretical

Figure 4-24

Figure 4-25

Figure 4-26

Figure 4-27

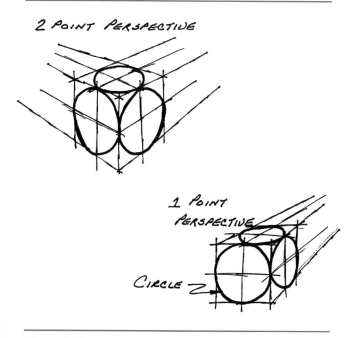

Figure 4-28

horizon. The horizon line is always located at eye level. Objects above the horizon line appear to be above, and objects below the horizon appear to be below.

Perspective drawings are often referred to as *pictorial drawings*. Figure 4-26 shows an object drawn twice: once as an isometric drawing, and again as a pictorial or two-point perspective. Note how much more lifelike the pictorial drawing looks in comparison with the isometric drawing.

Figure 4-27 shows a perspective sketch based on only one vanishing point. One-point perspective sketches are similar to oblique sketches. The front surface plane is sketched using a 90° axis, and then receding lines are sketched from the front plane to a vanishing point. As you practice sketching, eventually you will not need to include a vanishing point, but will imply its location.

Figure 4-28 shows how to sketch circular shapes in one- and two-point perspective sketches. In each style the axis lines consist of a vertical line and a line that is aligned with the receding edge lines. Circular shapes in perspective drawings are not elliptical, but are irregular splines. Each surface will require a slightly different shape depending on the angle of the receding lines to produce a visually accurate circular shape.

4-13 WORKING IN DIFFERENT ORIENTATIONS

It is important for designers to be able to sketch an object in different orientations to present a clear representation of all the design's different facets.

Figure 4-29 shows three different objects sketched in three different orientations. Each sketch was done using an isometric format. Proportions for each object were determined by using the dot grid background.

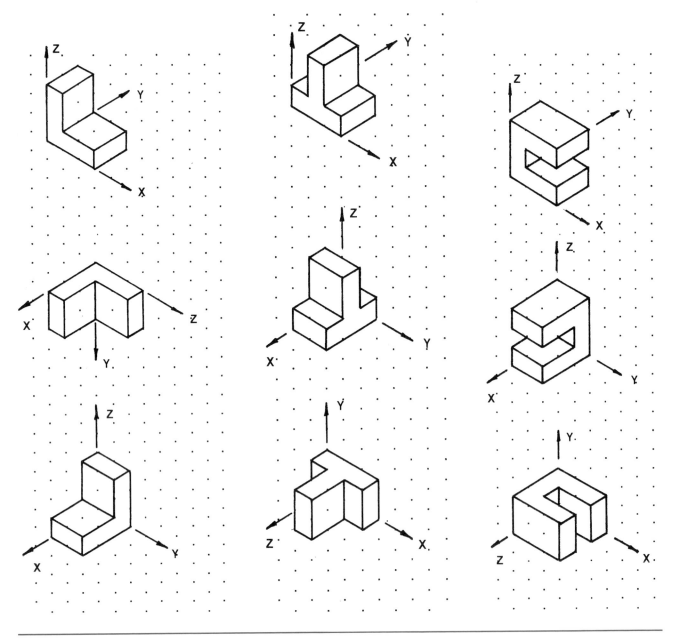

Figure 4-29

4-14 EXERCISE PROBLEMS

Sketch the shapes in Exercise Problems EX4-1 to EX4-6. Measure the shapes to determine their dimensions.

EX4-1

EX4-2

EX4-3

EX4-4

EX4-5

EX4-6

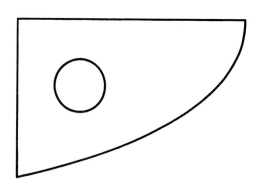

Prepare isometric or perspective sketches of the objects shown in Exercise Problems EX4-7 to EX4-18. Measure the objects to determine their dimensions.

EX4-7

EX4-9

EX4-8

EX4-10

EX4-11

EX4-13

30^0

EX4-12

EX4-14

EX4-15

EX4-17

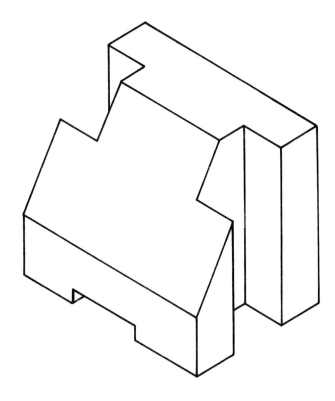

EX4-16

EX4-18

.75R

Prepare oblique or perspective sketches of the objects shown in Exercise Problems EX4-19 to EX4-22. Measure the objects to determine their dimensions.

EX4-19

EX4-21

EX4-20

EX4-22

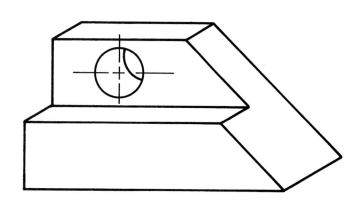

Prepare isometric sketches of the following shapes in the given orientation, then sketch the objects in the three different orientations defined by the X,Y,Z axes. Assume that the spacing between dots in the background grid is approximately .25 inch, or 10 millimeters.

EX4-23

EX4-25

EX4-24

EX4-26

EX4-27

EX4-29

EX4-28

EX4-30

EX4-31

EX4-33

EX4-32

EX4-34

24

EX4-35

EX4-37

EX4-36

EX4-38

EX4-39

EX4-41

EX4-40

EX4-42

EX4-43

EX4-45

EX4-44

EX4-46

EX4-47

EX4-49

EX4-48

EX4-50

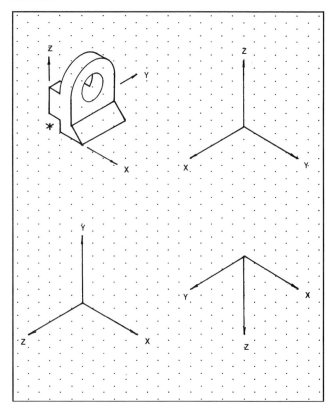

C H A P T E R 5

Orthographic Views

5-1 INTRODUCTION

This chapter introduces orthographic views. *Orthographic views* are two-dimensional views of three-dimensional objects. Orthographic views are created by projecting a view of an object onto a plane that is usually positioned so it is parallel to one of the planes of the object. See Figure 5-1.

Orthographic projection planes may be positioned at any angle relative to an object, but in general the six views parallel to the six sides of a rectangular object are used. See Figure 5-2. Technical drawings usually include only the front, top, and right-side orthographic views because together they are considered sufficient to completely define an object's shape.

5-2 THREE VIEWS OF AN OBJECT

Orthographic views are positioned on a technical drawing so that the top view is located directly over the front view, and the side view is directly to the right side of the front view. See Figure 5-2.

The location of the front, top, and right-side views relative to each other is critical. Correct relative positioning of views allows information to be projected between the views. Vertical lines are used to project information between the front and top views, and horizontal lines are used to project information between the front and right-side views.

Orthographic views are two-dimensional, so they cannot show depth. In Figure 5-2 plane A-B-C-D appears as a straight line in both the front and top orthographic views. Edge A-B appears as a vertical line in the top view, as a horizontal line in the side view, and as point AB in the front view. The end view of a plane is a straight line, and the end view of a line is a point. See Figure 5-3.

Figure 5-1

163

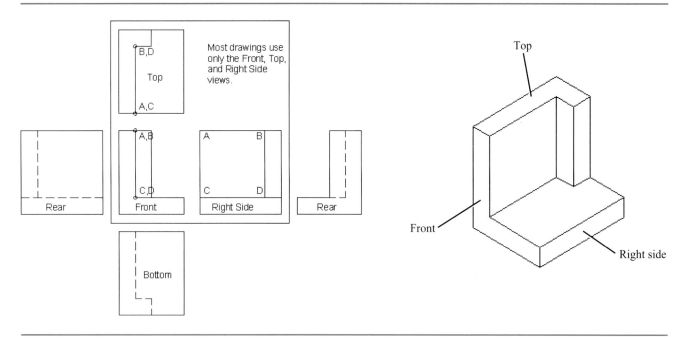

Figure 5-2

Figure 5-4 shows an object and the front, top, and right-side orthographic views of the object. Plane A-B-C-D appears as a rectangle in the front view and as a line in both the top and right-side views.

To help you better understand the relationship between orthographic views and in particular the front, top, and side views of an object, place a book on a table as shown in Figure 5-5. Note how the front, top, and side views were projected and then arranged to create a technical drawing of the book.

5-3 VISUALIZATION

Visualization is the ability to look at a three-dimensional object and mentally see the appropriate three orthographic views.

It is an important skill for a designer and an engineer to develop. Visualization also includes the ability to look at two-dimensional orthographic views and mentally picture the three-dimensional object the views represent.

Figure 5-3

Figure 5-4

Figure 5-5

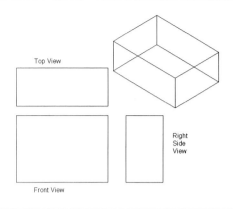

Figure 5-6

Figure 5-6 shows a 5 × 3.5 × 2-inch box and three orthographic views of the box. The creation of three-dimensional objects is explained in detail in Chapters 14, 15, and 16. This section presents a short exercise to help you better understand how orthographic views are related to three-dimensional objects.

To draw a three-dimensional box

1. Set the screen for inches, then select the 3D View command from the View pull-down menu, then SE Isometric.

    The origin axis reference icon will change to the 3D alignment.

2. Type the word box to a Command: prompt.

    Specify corner of box or [Center] <0,0,0>:

3. Press Enter.

    Specify corner or [Cube/Length]:

4. Type L; press Enter.

    Specify length:

5. Type 5; press Enter.

    Specify width:

6. Type 3.5; press Enter.

    Specify height:

7. Type 2; press Enter.

    A box will appear on the screen.

8. Select the 3D Orbit command from the View pull-down menu. Move the cursor around the drawing screen holding the left mouse button down. Position the box so as to create each of the three orthographic views shown in Figure 5-6.

    Figures 5-7 and 5-8 show two additional objects and their orthographic views.

Figure 5-7

Figure 5-8

Figure 5-9

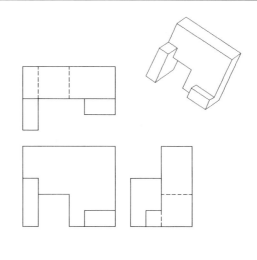

Figure 5-10

5-4 HIDDEN LINES

Hidden lines are used to represent surfaces that are not directly visible in an orthographic view. Figure 5-9 shows an object that contains a surface A-B-C-D that is not directly visible in the side view. A hidden line is used to represent the end view of plane A-B-C-D in the side view.

Figure 5-10 shows an object and three views of the object. The top and side views of the object contain hidden lines.

Figure 5-11 shows an object that contains an edge line A-B. In the top view of the object, line A-B is partially hidden and partially visible. When the line is directly visible through the square hole it is drawn as a continuous line; when it is not directly visible it is drawn as a hidden line.

5-5 HIDDEN LINE CONVENTIONS

Figure 5-12 shows several conventions associated with drawing hidden lines. Whenever possible, show intersections of hidden lines as touching lines, not as open gaps. Corners should also be shown as touching lines.

The Linetype Scale option on the Properties dialog box can be used to change the spacing of hidden lines. Figure 5-13 shows two hidden lines and a continuous line that are aligned. A small gap should be included between the two types of lines to prevent confusion as to where one type of line ends and the other begins. A visual distinction can also be created by selecting a different color for hidden lines. If continuous and hidden lines are drawn using different colors, then gaps are not necessary.

Figure 5-11

Figure 5-12

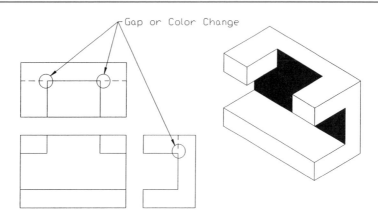

Figure 5-13

5-6 DRAWING HIDDEN LINES

There are three ways to draw hidden lines: modify the line from a continuous line to a hidden line, transfer the continuous line to a special layer created specifically for hidden lines, or use the Properties dialog box. In this example both the linetype and the line's color are changed.

To change a continuous line to a hidden line

1. Select the line.

The grip points appear.

2. Right-click the mouse and select the Properties option.

The Properties dialog box will appear. See Figure 5-14.

3. Select Linetype, then Hidden.

See Figure 5-15. The selected line will be changed to a hidden line. If the linetype is not listed, return to the drawing screen and click the Format pull-down menu. Select the Linetype option. The Linetype Manager dialog box will appear. Select the Load option, and the Load or

Figure 5-14

Figure 5-15

Figure 5-16

Reload Linetypes dialog box will appear. See Figure 5-16. Scroll down and select the Hidden line option. Select OK and return to the drawing screen. Access the Modify Line dialog box as explained above. This time the Hidden line pattern will be listed as an option.

4. Select the the Color option in the Properties dialog box, then the scroll arrow.

Figure 5-17

The color options will cascade down. See Figure 5-17.

5. Select Blue and exit the Properties dialog box.

If the line changes color but the broken-line pattern does not appear, or if the line segments are too short or too long, use the Linetype Scale option found in the Properties dialog box to change the length of the hidden line segments. See Figure 5-14. It may be necessary to use a trial-and-error process to obtain the most appropriate hidden line pattern.

To use Layer to create a hidden line

Linetype can be changed by creating a layer specifically set up for hidden lines. Both the line pattern and color can be preset on the layer. This procedure may seem a bit lengthy when compared with the Modify Properties procedure outlined above, but it is very efficient if there are many lines to change.

1. Select the Layer tool from the Object Properties toolbar.

The Layer Properties Manager dialog box will appear. See Figure 5-18. Create a new layer called Hidden.

2. Select the New option.
3. Create a layer named Hidden using the hidden line pattern and the color blue, then return to the drawing screen.

Figure 5-18

A more detailed discussion of layers is presented in Section 3-25.

4. Select the line.

The grip points will appear.

5. Select the Layer control tool.

See Figure 5-19. The available layer options will cascade down.

6. Select the Hidden layer, then double-click the Escape key.

To use the Properties dialog box

1. Select the line.

The grip points will appear.

2. Right-click the mouse and select the Properties option.

The Properties dialog box will appear.

3. Select the Layer option and change the layer to the Hidden layer.

See Figure 5-20.

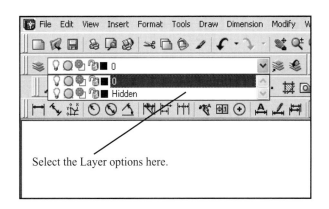

Select the Layer options here.

Figure 5-19

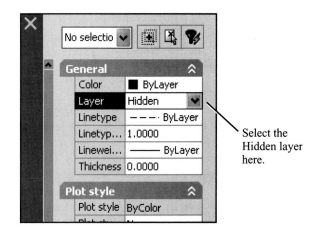

Select the Hidden layer here.

Figure 5-20

Figure 5-21

Figure 5-22

Figure 5-23

Figure 5-24

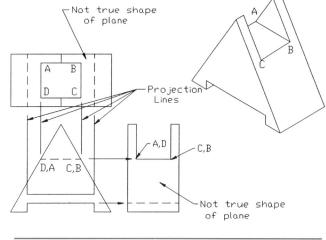

Figure 5-25

Figures 5-21 and 5-22 show an object and three views of that object. There are hidden lines in several of the orthographic views.

5-7 PRECEDENCE OF LINES

When orthographic views are prepared, it is not unusual for one type of line to be drawn over another type: a continuous line over a centerline, for example. See Figure 5-23. Drawing convention has established a precedence of lines: A continuous line takes precedence over a hidden line, and a hidden line takes precedence over a centerline.

If different linetypes are of different lengths, include a gap where the line changes from continuous to either hidden or center to create a visual distinction between the lines. Color changes may also be used to create visual distinctions between lines.

5-8 SLANTED SURFACES

Slanted surfaces are surfaces that are not parallel to either the horizontal or vertical axis. Figure 5-24 shows a slanted surface A-B-C-D. Slanted surface A-B-C-D

appears as a straight line in the side view and as a plane in both the front and top views. It is important to note that neither the front nor top view of surface A-B-C-D is a true representation of the surface. Both orthographic views are actually smaller than the actual surface. Lines B-C and A-D in the top view are true length, but lines A-B and C-D are shorter than the actual edge lengths. The same is true for the front view of the surface. The side view shows the true length of lines A-B and D-C. True lengths of lines and true shapes of planes are discussed again in Chapter 7, Auxiliary Views.

Figure 5-25 shows another object that contains slanted surfaces. Note how projection lines are used between the views. As objects become more complex the shape of a surface or the location of an edge line will not always be obvious, so projecting information between views, and therefore exact, correct relative view location, becomes critical. Information can be projected only between views that are correctly positioned and accurately drawn.

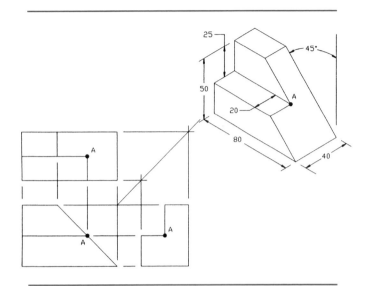

Figure 5-26

5-9 PROJECTION BETWEEN VIEWS

Information is projected between the front and side views using horizontal lines and between the front and top views using vertical lines. Information can be projected between the top and side views using a combination of horizontal and vertical lines that intersect a 45° miter line. See Figure 5-26.

A 45° miter line is constructed between the top and side views. This line allows the project lines to change direction, turn a corner, and change from horizontal to vertical lines. To go from the top view to the side view, construct horizontal projection lines from the top view so that they intersect the miter line. Construct vertical lines from the intersection points on the miter line into the side view. The reverse process is used to go from the side view to the top view.

The following sample problem shows how projection lines can be used to create orthographic views using AutoCAD.

5-10 SAMPLE PROBLEM SP5-1

Draw the front, top, and right-side orthographic views of the object shown in Figure 5-26. Set up the drawing as follows.

1. Create a separate layer for hidden lines.

Limits = 297 × 210 (Metric setup)
Grid　= 10
Snap = 5
Ortho = ON (F8)
Layer　= HIDDEN (LType = HIDDEN, Color = Green)

2. Use the overall dimensions (length = 80, height = 50, and depth = 40) to define the overall size requirements of the three orthographic views. See Figure 5-27. The 20 spacing between the views is arbitrary. The distance between the front and top views does not have to equal the distance between the front and side views. In this example the two distances are equal.

3. Draw a 45° miter line starting from the upper right corner of the front view. This step is possible only if the distances between the views are equal. If the distances are not equal, draw the front and top views, add the miter line, and project the overall size of the side view from the front and top views.

3a. (Optional) Trim away the excess lines to clearly define the areas of the front, top, and side views.

3b. (Optional) The Layer tool may be used to create a layer for construction lines and another layer for final drawing lines. The lines for the final drawing may then be transferred to the final drawing layer and the construction layer turned off. This method eliminates the need for extensive erasing or trimming.

4. Draw the 45° slanted surface in the front view as shown in Figure 5-27. Project the intersection of the slanted surface and the top edge of the front view into the top view. Add a horizontal line across the front and right-side views 25 from the bottom edge line. The 25 value comes from the given dimension. Label the intersection of the slanted line and the horizontal line as point A.

5. Draw a horizontal line in the top view 20 from the top edge as shown in Figure 5-27. Continue the line so that it intersects the miter line. Project the line into the side view. Use Osnap, Intersection with Ortho on to ensure an accurate projection. Label point A in the side view.

6. Project point A in the front view into the top view (vertical line). Label the intersection of the projection line and the horizontal line in the top view as point A.

7. Use Erase and Trim to remove the excess lines.

8. Save the drawing if desired.

Figure 5-28

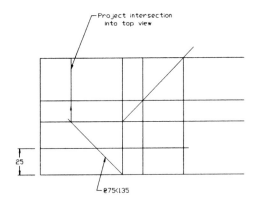

5-11 COMPOUND LINES

A *compound line* is formed when two slanted surfaces intersect. See Figure 5-28. The true length of a compound line is not shown in the front, top, or side views.

Figure 5-29 shows another object that contains compound lines. The three orthographic views of a compound line are sometimes difficult to visualize, making it more important to be able to project information accurately between views. Usually, part of an object can be visualized and part of the orthographic views created. The remainder of the drawing can be added by projecting from the known information.

Figure 5-27

Figure 5-29

Figure 5-30

5-12 SAMPLE PROBLEM SP5-2

Figure 5-30 shows how the front, top, and side views of the object shown in Figure 5-29 were created by projecting information. The procedure is as follows.

1. Set the drawing up as follows.

   Limits = Default
   Grid   = .5
   Snap = .25

2. Use the overall dimensions to define the space and location requirements for the views. Draw the 45° miter line.
3. Use the given dimensions to define the starting and end points on the compound lines in the top and front views. One of the lines has been labeled A-B.
4. Draw the compound line in the top view and then project it into the side view using information from both the top and front views.
5. Add the dovetailed shape using the given dimensions. Draw the appropriate hidden lines for the dovetail.
6. Erase and trim the excess lines.
7. Save the drawing if desired.

Figure 5-31 shows the three orthographic views and pictorial view of another example of an object that includes compound lines. Some of the projection lines have also been included.

Figure 5-31

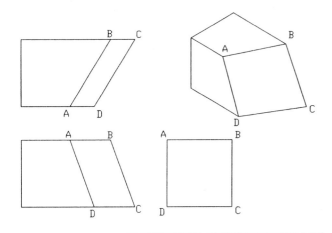

Figure 5-32

5-13 OBLIQUE SURFACES

Oblique surfaces are surfaces that do not appear correctly shaped in the front, top, or side views. Figure 5-32 shows an object that contains oblique surface A-B-C-D. Figure 5-32 also shows three views of just surface A-B-C-D. Oblique surfaces are projected by first projecting their corner points and then joining the points with straight lines. The orthographic views of oblique surfaces are sometimes visually abstract. This makes the development of their orthographic views more dependent on projection than other types of surfaces.

Figure 5-33 shows another object that contains an oblique surface. Figure 5-34 shows how the three orthographic views were developed. The oblique surface is defined using only two angles, but this is sufficient to create the three views because the surface is flat. The edge lines are parallel. Lines A-B, C-D, and E-F are parallel to each other, and lines C-B, D-E, and F-A are also parallel to each other. Figure 5-34 also shows three views of just the oblique surface along with the appropriate projection lines.

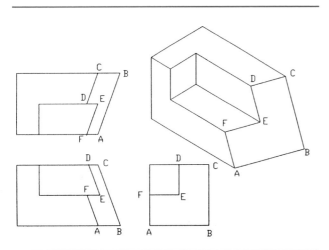

Figure 5-33

Width

Height

Length

Width

Remove rectangular portion from all views.

Line C–D is parallel to line A–B

TRIM LINES beyond line A–B

Lower edge of oblique plane

TRIM excess lines

Parallel to C–B from point D

Parallel to C–B from point A

Figure 5-34

5-14 SAMPLE PROBLEM SP5-3

The three views of the object shown in Figure 5-35A may be drawn as follows. (The given dimensions are in millimeters.)

1. Use the Line and the Offset commands to set up the sizes and locations of the three views. Use Osnap, Intersection to draw the projection lines. See Figure 5-35B.
2. Draw an oblique surface based on the given dimensions. The edge lines of the oblique surface are parallel.
3. Draw the slanted surface in the side view and project the surface into the other views. Use the intersection between the slanted surface and flat sections on the top and side of the object to determine the shape of the oblique surface.
4. Use Erase and Trim to remove any excess lines. Save the drawing if desired.

Figure 5-35A

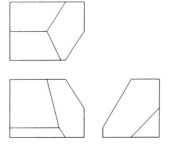

Figure 5-35B

5-15 ROUNDED SURFACES

Rounded surfaces are surfaces that have constant radii such as arcs or circles. Surfaces that do not have constant radii are classified as *irregular surfaces*. See Section 5-24.

Figure 5-36 shows an object with rounded surfaces. Surface A-B-C-D is tangent to both the top and side surfaces of the object, so no edge line is drawn. This means that the top and side orthographic views of the object are ambiguous. If only the top and side views are considered, then other interpretations of the views are possible. Figure 5-36 shows another object that generates the same top and side orthographic views but does not include rounded surface A-B-C-D. The front view is needed to define the rounded surfaces and limit the views to only one interpretation.

Surfaces perpendicular to an orthographic view always produce lines in that orthographic view. The vertical surface shown in the front view of Figure 5-37A requires an edge line in the top view. The vertical line in the front view is perpendicular to the top views.

The object shown in Figure 5-37B has no lines perpendicular to the top view, so no lines are drawn in the top view. Figure 5-37C shows two rounded surfaces that intersect at points tangent to their centerlines. The intersection point is considered sufficient to require an edge line in the top view. No line would be visible on the actual object, but drawing convention prescribes that a line be drawn.

Figure 5-36

Figure 5-37

Figure 5-38

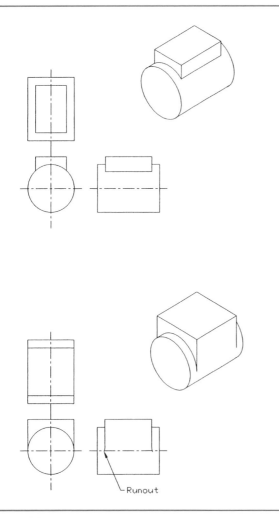

Figure 5-39

Figure 5-38 shows an object that contains two semicircular surfaces. Note how lines representing the widest and deepest point of the surfaces generate lines in the top view. No line would actually appear on the object. Figure 5-39 shows further examples of objects with curved surfaces.

5-16 SAMPLE PROBLEM SP5-4

Figure 5-40 shows an object that includes rounded surfaces, and Figure 5-41 shows how the three views of the object were developed.

The procedure is as follows.

1. Use the given overall dimensions to lay out the size and location of the three views.
2. Draw in the external details, the cutout, and the circular extension in all three views.
3. Add the appropriate hidden lines. Use either the Modify Properties option, or create a layer for hidden lines.
4. Erase and trim any excess lines and save the drawing if desired.

5-17 HOLES

Holes are represented in orthographic views by circles and parallel hidden lines. All views of a hole always include centerlines. See Figure 5-42. It is suggested that a layer entitled Center be added to any drawing being created. Specify the linetype center and the color red.

Holes that go completely through an object are dimensioned using only a diameter. The notation THRU may be added to the diameter specification for clarity.

Figure 5-40

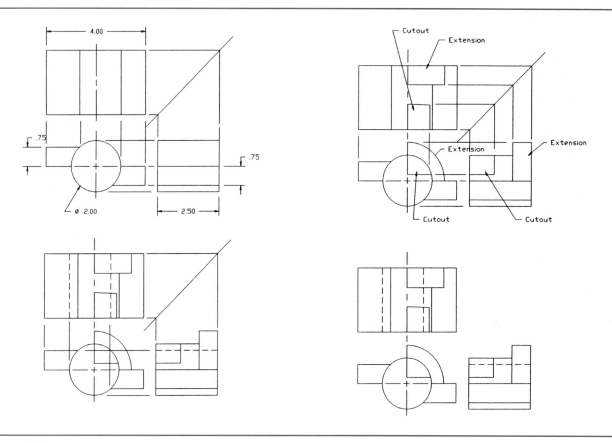

Figure 5-41

Holes that do not go completely through an object include a depth specification in their dimension. The depth specification is interpreted as shown in Figure 5-42. Holes that do not go completely through an object must include a conical point. The conical point is not included in the depth specification. Conical points must be included because most holes are produced using a twist drill with conically shaped cutting edges.

Figure 5-42

Figure 5-43

The cutting angles of twist drills vary, but they are always represented by a 30° angle as shown.

Figure 5-43 shows an object that contains two through holes and one hole with a depth specification. Note how these holes are represented in the orthographic views and how centerlines are used in the different views.

Figure 5-44 is another example of an object that includes a hole. The hole is centered about the edge line between the two normal surfaces. Figure 5-45 shows the same object with the hole's center point offset from the edge line between the two normal surfaces. Compare the differences between Figures 5-44 and 5-45.

Figure 5-44   **Figure 5-45**

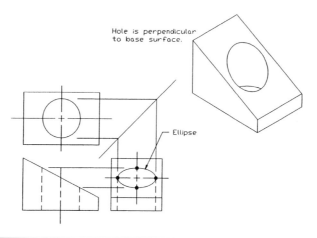

Figure 5-46

5-18 HOLES IN SLANTED SURFACES

Figure 5-46 shows a hole that penetrates a slanted surface. The hole is perpendicular to the bottom surface of the object. The top view of the hole appears as a circle because we are looking straight down into it. The side view shows a distorted view of the circle and is represented using an ellipse.

The shape of the ellipse in the side view is defined by projecting information from the front and top views. Points 1 and 2 are known to be on the vertical centerline, so their location can be projected from the front view to the side view using horizontal lines. Points 3 and 4 are located on the horizontal centerline, so their location can be projected from the top view into the side view using the 45° miter line.

The elliptical shape of the hole in the side view is drawn connecting the projected points using the Ellipse command.

To draw an ellipse representing a projected hole

See Figure 5-47.

1. Define the First Point as one of the points where the major axis intersects one of the centerlines.
2. Define the Second Point as the other point on the major axis that intersects the same centerline.
3. Define the Third Point as one of the points on the minor axis that intersects the centerline perpendicular to the centerline used in steps 1 and 2.

Figure 5-47

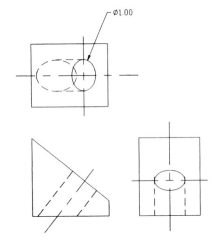

Figure 5-48

To draw three views of a hole in a slanted surface

Figure 5-48 shows an object that includes a hole drilled perpendicular to the slanted surface. The hole is 1.00 in diameter. The hidden lines in the front view that represent the edges of the hole are drawn parallel to the centerline at a distance of .50. The horizontal and vertical centerlines of the hole are located in the top and right views. The intersection of the hole edges with the slanted surface shown in the front view is projected into the top and side views as shown.

The slanted surface shown in Figure 5-48 appears as a straight line in the front view. This means that the hole representations in the top and side views are rotated about only one axis. This in turn means that the hole representation is foreshortened in only one direction. The other direction, the other axis length, remains at the original diameter distance on 1.00. The four points needed to define the projected elliptical shape can be defined by the projection lines and the measured 1.00 distance.

The hole also penetrates the bottom surface, forming a different-sized ellipse. The hole's penetration can be shown in the side view by hidden lines parallel to the given centerline. The elliptical shape in the top view is defined by drawing horizontal parallel lines from the intersection of the hole's projected shape with the vertical centerline, and by projection lines from the front view that define the hole's length.

To draw three views of a hole through an oblique surface

Figure 5-49A shows a hole drilled horizontally through the exact center of an oblique surface of an object. The oblique surface means that both axes in the top and

Figure 5-49A

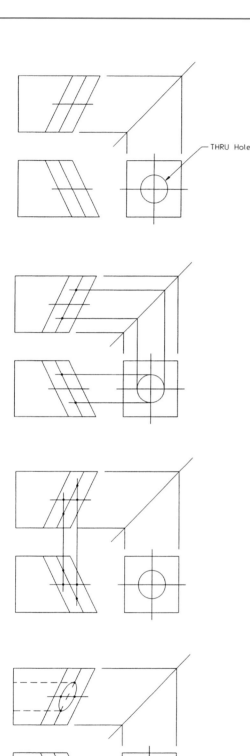

front views will be foreshortened. The procedure used to create the hole's projection in the front and top views is as follows. (See Figure 5-49B.)

1. Draw the hole in the side view. The hole will appear as a circle because it is drilled horizontally.
2. Draw the hole's centerlines in the front and top views. The hole is located exactly in the center of the oblique surface, so lines parallel to the surface's edge lines located midway across the surface may be drawn.
3. Project the intersection of the hole and the horizontal centerline into the top view, and project the intersection of the hole with the vertical centerline into the front view.
4. Project the intersections created in step 3 with the horizontal centerline, represented by the slanted centerline, onto the horizontal centerline in the front view. Likewise, project the intersection points created in step 3 on the horizontal centerline in the front view to the slanted centerline in the top view.
5. Draw the ellipses as required, add the appropriate hidden lines, and erase and trim any excess lines. Save the drawing if desired.

5-19 CYLINDERS

Figure 5-50 shows three views of a cylinder that is cut along the centerline by surface A-B-C-D. Note that each of

Figure 5-49B

Figure 5-50

Figure 5-51

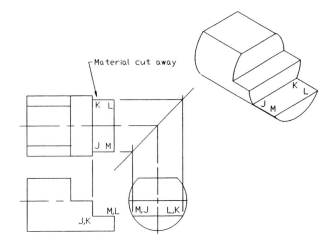

Figure 5-52

the three views includes centerlines. The front and top views of a cylinder are called the *rectangular views,* and the side view (end view) is called the *circular view.* The width of the top view is equal to the diameter of the cylinder.

Figure 5-51 shows a cylinder that has a second surface located above the centerline in the front view. The top view of the cylinder shows the flat surface and the rounded portion of the cylinder. Both the flat surface and the two rounded surfaces appear as rectangles.

Figure 5-52 shows a cylinder with a surface J-K-L-M that is located below the centerline in the front view. The

top view of this surface does not include any rounded surfaces because they have been cut away.

5-20 SAMPLE PROBLEM SP5-5

Figure 5-53 shows a cylindrically shaped object that has three surface cuts: one above the centerline, one below the centerline, and one directly on the centerline. Figure 5-54 shows how the three views of the object were developed. The procedure is as follows.

Figure 5-53

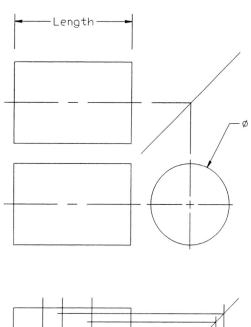

1. Use the given overall length of the cylinder and its diameter to create the two rectangular top and front views and the circular end views.
2. Draw horizontal lines in the side view that define the end views of the three surfaces. Project the size and location of the surfaces into the front and top views. Use Osnap, Intersection, with Ortho on, for accurate projection.
3. Erase and trim the excess lines.
4. Save the drawing if desired.

5-21 CYLINDERS WITH SLANTED AND ROUNDED SURFACES

Figure 5-55 shows a front and side view of a cylindrical object that includes a slanted surface. Slanted surfaces are projected by defining points along their edges in known orthographic views and then projecting the edge points. At least two known views are needed for accurate projection. Sample Problem SP5-6 shows how to define and project a slanted cylindrical surface into the top view given the front and side views.

Top view ?

Figure 5-54

Figure 5-55

5-22 SAMPLE PROBLEM SP5-6

(See Figure 5-56.)

1. Draw the rectangular shape of the top view by projecting the length from the front view and the width from the side view.
2. Project the centerlines, and label points 1, 2, and 3 in the front and side views. The locations of these points are known from the given information.
3. Draw three horizontal lines across the front and side views. The location of the lines is arbitrary. Label the intersections of the horizontal lines with the edge of the slanted surface as shown.
4. The three horizontal lines serve to define point locations along the surface's edge.

A line contains an infinite number of points, so any six can be used.

5. Draw vertical projection lines (Osnap, Intersection) from the six point locations in the front view into the area of the top view.
6. Project the six point locations from the side view into the area of the top view. Use the 45° miter line to make the turn between the two views. The intersection of the vertical projection lines of step 2 and the projection lines from the side view defines the location of the points in the top view. Label the six points.
7. Use Draw, Polyline, Polyedit, Fit Curve to create a smooth line between the six projected points.
8. Remove any excess lines and save the drawing if desired.

Figure 5-56

Figure 5-57

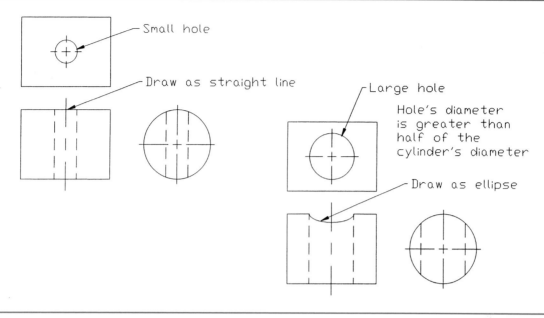

Figure 5-58

Figure 5-57 shows another cylindrical object that contains a slanted surface along with some of the projection lines.

5-23 DRAWING CONVENTIONS AND CYLINDERS

A hole drilled into a cylinder will produce an elliptically shaped edge line in a profile view of the hole. See Figure 5-58. Drawing convention allows a straight line to

be drawn in place of the elliptical shape for small holes. The elliptical shape should be drawn for large holes in cylinders, that is, one whose diameter is greater than half the diameter of the cylinder.

Drawing convention also permits straight lines to be drawn for the profile view of a keyway cut into a cylinder. See Figure 5-59. As with holes, if a keyway is large relative to a cylinder, the correct offset shape should be drawn. A keyway is considered large if its width is greater than half the diameter of the cylinder.

Figure 5-59

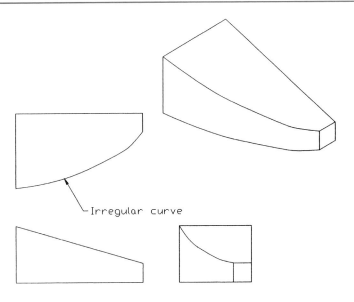

Figure 5-60

5-24 IRREGULAR SURFACES

Irregular surfaces are curved surfaces that do not have constant radii. See Figures 5-60 and 5-61. Irregular surfaces are defined using the X,Y coordinates of points located on the edge of the surface. The points may be dimensioned directly on the view but are often presented in chart form, as shown in Figure 5-61. Figure 5-61 also shows a wing surface defined relative to a given X,Y coordinate system.

Irregular surfaces are projected by defining points along their edges and then projecting the points. At least two known views are needed for accurate projection. The more points used to define the curve, the more accurate the final curve shape will be.

5-25 SAMPLE PROBLEM SP5-7

Figure 5-62 shows an object that includes an irregular surface. The irregular surface is defined by points referenced to an X,Y coordinate system. The point values are listed in a chart. Draw three views of the object shown in Figure 5-62. Your views should look similar to those in Figure 5-63.

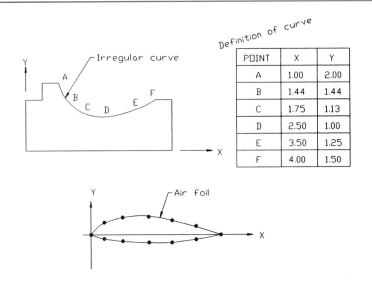

Definition of curve

POINT	X	Y
A	1.00	2.00
B	1.44	1.44
C	1.75	1.13
D	2.50	1.00
E	3.50	1.25
F	4.00	1.50

Figure 5-61

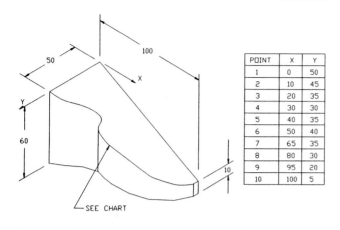

POINT	X	Y
1	0	50
2	10	45
3	20	35
4	30	30
5	40	35
6	50	40
7	65	35
8	80	30
9	95	20
10	100	5

Figure 5-62

1. Draw the front and top views using the given dimensions and chart values. Draw the outline of the side view using the given dimensions.
2. Project the points that define the irregular curve in the top view into the front view. Label the points.
3. Project the points for the curve from both the top and front views into the side view. Label the intersection points.
4. Use Polyline, Polyedit, and Fit Curve to create a curve that represents the side view of the irregular surface.
5. Erase and trim any excess lines. Save the drawing if desired.

Remember, it is possible to use Layer to create a layer for construction lines and for the final drawing. After the initial drawing is laid out, the final drawing lines may be copied onto another layer and the construction layer turned off. This method eliminates the need for extensive erasing and trimming.

Figure 5-63

Figure 5-64

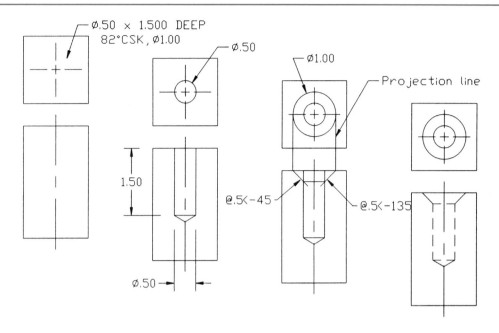

Figure 5-65

5-26 HOLE CALLOUTS

There are four hole-shape manufacturing processes that are used so often that they are defined using a standardized drawing callout: ream, counterbore, countersink, and spotface. See Figure 5-64.

A ream is a process that smooths out the inside of a drilled hole. Holes created using twist drills have spiral-shaped machine marks on their surfaces. Reaming is used to remove the spiral machine marks and to increase the roundness of the hole. Ream callouts generally include a much tighter tolerance than do drill diameter callouts.

A *counterbore* consists of two holes drilled along the same centerline. Counterbores are used to allow fasteners or other objects to be recessed, thus keeping the top surface uniform in height.

A counterbore drawing callout specifies the diameter of the small hole, the diameter of the large hole, and the depth of the large hole.

The information is given in this sequence because it is also the sequence the manufacturer uses. Note that the hidden lines used in the front view of the counterbored hole clearly show the intersection between the two holes.

Figure 5-64 shows an alternative notation for drawing callouts as defined by ISO standards (see Chapter 8) that is intended to remove language from drawings. As parts are often designed in one country and manufactured in another, it is important that drawing callouts be universally understood.

A *countersink* is a conical-shaped hole used primarily for flat-head fasteners. The drawing callout specifies the diameter of the hole, the included angle of the countersink, and the diameter of the countersink as measured on the surface of the object. Almost all countersinks are 82°, but some are drawn at 45°.

To draw a countersunk hole (See Figure 5-65.)

1. Draw a 0.50-diameter hole in the top view. Project the hole's diameter into the front view.
2. Draw a 1.00-diameter hole in the top view and project its diameter into the front view. In the front view draw 45° lines from the intersection of the 1.00-diameter hole and the top surface of the front view so that the lines intersect the 0.50-diameter hole's projection lines. Use Osnap, Intersection to ensure accuracy.
3. Draw a horizontal line between the intersection created in step 2. Again use Osnap, Intersection.
4. Erase and trim the excess lines.

A *spotface* is a very shallow counterbored hole generally used on cast surfaces. Cast surfaces are more porous than machine surfaces. Rather than machine an entire surface flat, it is cheaper to manufacture a spotface because only a small portion of the surface is machined. Spotfaces are usually used for bearing surfaces of fasteners.

Figure 5-66

Figure 5-67

A spotface callout defines the diameter of the hole and the diameter of the spotface. A depth need not be given. When machining was done mostly by hand, the machinist would make the spotface just deep enough to produce a shiny surface (most cast surfaces are more gray in color), so no depth was needed. Automated machines require a spotface depth specification. Usually the depth is very shallow.

5-27 CASTINGS

Casting is one of the oldest manufacturing processes. Metal is heated to liquid form, then poured into molds and allowed to cool. The resulting shapes usually include many rounded edges and surface tangencies because it is very difficult to cast square edges. Concave edges are called *rounds,* and convex edges are called *fillets.* See Figure 5-66. A runout is used to indicate that two rounded surfaces have become tangent to one another. A *runout* is a short arc of arbitrary radius, that is, arbitrary as long as the runout is visually clear.

Cast objects are often partially machined to produce flatter surfaces than can be produced by the casting process. Machined surfaces are defined using machine marks (check marks), as shown in Figure 5-66. The numbers within the machine marks specify the flatness requirements in terms of microinches or micrometers. Machine marks are explained in greater detail in Section 9-26.

A *boss* is a turretlike shape that is often included on castings to localize and minimize machining. A boss is defined by its diameter and its height. The sides of a boss

Figure 5-68

Figure 5-69

are rounded and defined by a radius usually equal to the height of the boss. See Figure 5-67.

Spotfacing is a machine process often associated with castings. As with bosses, spotfaces help localize and minimize machining requirements. Spotfaces were defined in Section 5-26.

The direction of runouts is determined by the shape of the two surfaces involved. Flat surfaces intersecting rounded surfaces generate runouts that turn out. Rounded surfaces that intersect rounded surfaces generate runouts that turn in. See Figure 5-68.

The same convention is followed for flat and rounded surfaces that intersect flat surfaces.

The location of a runout is determined by the location of the tangent it represents. See Figure 5-69. The location of a tangency point can be determined by first drawing the top view of the tangency line using Osnap, Tangency. A line can then be drawn from the center point of the circular top view to the end of the tangency line using Osnap, Endpoint. The point of tangency can then be projected from the top view to the front view using Osnap, Intersection with Ortho on.

Use Arc (type the word "arc" in response to a command prompt) to draw runouts. Any convenient radius may be used, providing the runout is clearly visible and visually distinct from the straight line. Figure 5-70 shows some further examples of cast surfaces that include runouts.

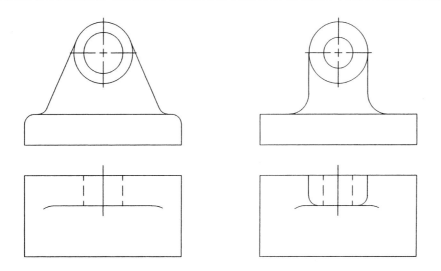

Figure 5-70

5-28 SAMPLE PROBLEM SP5-8

Draw three views of the object shown in Figure 5-71. The solution was drawn as follows:

1. Use the given overall dimensions and draw the outline of the front, top, and side views.
2. Modify the appropriate lines to hidden lines. Draw the fillets and rounds. The Fillet command may erase needed lines. This cannot always be avoided, so simply redraw the needed lines after the fillet or round is complete.
3. Draw the spotface and boss in each of the views. The hole in the boss is .500 deep. Clearly show the bottom of the hole, including the conical point. Draw the hole in the front view and use Copy to copy the hole into the side view.
4. Use Draw, Circle to draw the 1.00-diameter hole in the front view. Draw the appropriate hidden and centerlines in the other views.
5. Save the drawing if desired.

See Figure 5-72.

Figure 5-71

Figure 5-72

Figure 5-73

5-29 THIN-WALLED OBJECTS

Thin-walled objects such as parts made from sheet metal or tubing present some unique drawing problems. For example, the distance between surfaces is usually so small that hidden lines can't be used to define holes, and there isn't enough distance to draw a broken-line pattern. See Figure 5-73.

Hidden lines may be applied to thin-walled objects in one of three ways: draw the lines as continuous lines but use a different color from that used for the actual continuous lines; use an enlarged detail of the area including the hidden lines; or omit the hidden lines and include only a centerline.

Each of these techniques is shown in Figure 5-73. All holes must include a centerline.

Companies often have a drawing manual that states their policy on drawing hidden lines in thin-walled objects. The most important goal is to be consistent in the representation.

Many sheet-metal parts are manufactured by bending. Bending produces an inside bend radius and an outside bend radius. The inside bend radius plus the material thickness should equal the outside bend radius. See Figure 5-74. The same radius should not be used for both the inside and outside bends.

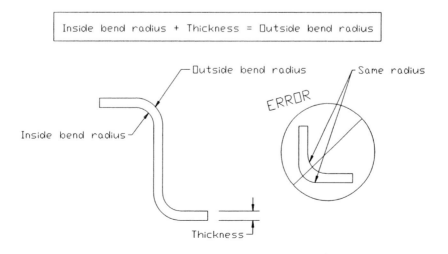

Figure 5-74

5-30 SAMPLE PROBLEM SP5-9

Draw three views of the object shown in Figure 5-75. Figure 5-76 shows how the three views were developed.

1. Use the given overall dimensions to draw the outline of the three views. Draw the object as if all bends are 90°.
2. Use Offset, set to a distance of 3 mm, to draw the thickness of the object. Use Extend and Trim to add or remove lines as needed. The thickness can also be drawn by setting the Snap spacing equal to the material thickness.

    Change the appropriate lines to hidden lines.

3. Draw fillets using a radius of 5 mm for the inside bend radii and 8 mm for the outside bend radii.
4. Use Draw, Circle to draw the holes in the appropriate view and add centerlines as shown.
5. Save the drawing if desired.

Figure 5-75

Figure 5-76

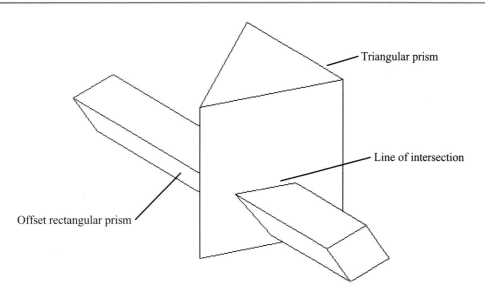

Figure 5-77

5-31 INTERSECTIONS

Intersection drawings are drawings that show the intersection of two objects. Figure 5-77 shows the intersection between two offset squares. A discussion of intersections has been included at this point in the book because they rely heavily on projection of information between views. They require not only a knowledge of the principles of projection but also an understanding about what the various lines represent. Intersections will be discussed again in Chapter 16, Solid Modeling.

Three intersection problems are presented in the following three sample problems.

5-32 SAMPLE PROBLEM SP5-10

Given the side and top views of a smaller circle intersecting a larger circle as shown in Figure 5-78, draw the front view. All dimensions are in inches. Because the object is symmetrical, the intersection for one side will be developed and then mirrored.

1. Draw the outline of the front view by projecting lines from the given top and front views. See Figure 5-79.
2. Define points on the edge of the smaller circle. In this example, 17 points were defined.

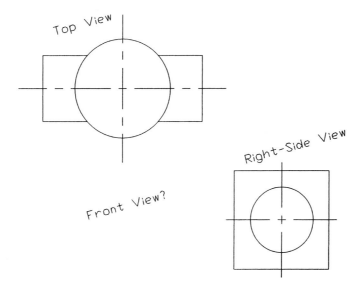

Figure 5-78

3. Extend the horizontal centerline of the smaller circle in the side view into the area of the front view. Use Draw, Offset and add six lines parallel to the horizontal centerline in the side view. Label the intersection of the horizontal lines with the edge of the smaller circle as shown.

4. Project points 5, 6, 7, 8, 9, and 10 into the top view. Use Draw, Line along with Osnap, Intersection to draw vertical lines from the side view so that they intersect the 45° miter line. Then, project the intersections on the miter line

into the top view using horizontal lines. Label the points as shown.

5. Project points 5, 6, 7, 8, 9, and 10 from the top view into the area of the front view so they intersect the horizontal lines from the side view. Label the points as shown. Use Draw, Polyline, Edit Polyline, and Fit Curve to draw the curve that represents the intersection.

6. Add the lines needed to complete the front view, remove all excess lines, and save the drawing if desired.

Figure 5-79

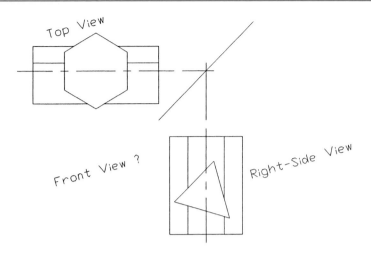

Figure 5-80

5-33 SAMPLE PROBLEM SP5-11

Figure 5-80 shows the top and right-side views of a triangular-shaped piece intersecting a hexagonal-shaped piece. What is the shape of the front view?

Figure 5-81 shows the solution obtained by projecting lines from the two given views into the front view, and shows an enlargement of the intersecting surfaces. Use a straightedge and verify the location of each labeled point by projecting horizontal lines from the front view and vertical lines from the top view into the front view.

5-34 SAMPLE PROBLEM SP5-12

Given the side and top views of a circle intersecting a cone as shown in Figure 5-82, draw the front view.

As in the previous sample problems, the problem is solved by defining intersection points in the given two views and then projecting them into the front view. The cone, however, presents a unique problem because it is both round and tapered. There are few edge lines to work with.

The solution requires that there be a more precise definition of the cone's surface than is presented by the

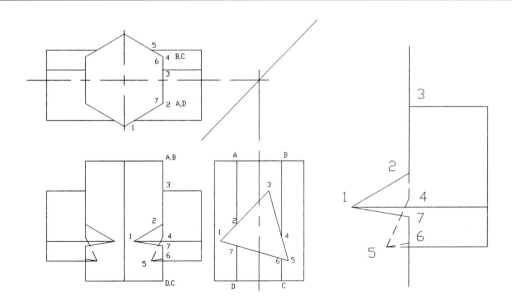

Figure 5-81

circle and centerlines in the top view and the profile front view.

1. Figure 5-83, step 1, shows how points 1 and 3, located on the vertical centerline of the cylinder, are projected from the side view to the front view and then to the top view. The vertical centerline is aligned with the right-side profile line of the cone so that it can be used for projection.

This is not true for points 2 and 4, located on the horizontal centerline in the side view. Currently the location of points 2 and 4 is unknown in both the front and top views, so projection lines cannot be drawn. The location of points 2 and 4 can be determined in the front and top views.

2. Extend the horizontal centerline in the side view so that it intersects the edge lines of the cone. Use Osnap, Intersection, with Ortho on and project the intersection of the extended horizontal centerline and the cone's edge line so that it intersects the vertical centerline in the top view. Draw a circle in the top view using the distance between the intersection with the vertical centerline and the projection line and the center point of the cone as the radius.

The circle in the top view represents a slice of the cone located at exactly the same height as points 2 and 4. Points 2 and 4 must be located somewhere in the slice.

3. Project points 2 and 4 into the top view from the side view so that the projection line intersects the circular slice drawn in step 2. Label the intersections 2 and 4.

4. Project the locations of points 2 and 4 in the top view into the front view using a vertical line. Project the locations of the points from the side view into the front view using a horizontal line. The intersection of the vertical and horizontal projection lines defines the locations of points 2 and 4 in the front view.

5. Expand the procedure explained in steps 2 and 3 by drawing a series of horizontal projection lines between the front and side views as shown. Use Draw for the first line and Offset for the other lines. The location of these additional lines is random.

Use Osnap, Intersection with Ortho on to project the intersections of the horizontal lines with the cone's edge lines in the top view.

6. Draw circles using the distance between the cone's center point and the projection lines' intersections with the vertical centerline as radii. Use Osnap, Intersection to locate the circles' center point and radii distances.

7. Use Draw, Polyline, Edit Polyline, and Fit Curve to draw the required curves in the top and front views. Use Osnap, Intersection to ensure accurate curve point locations. The Move option located on the Edit Polyline command options line can be used to move vertex points on the curves to make them appear smoother and more continuous.

8. Trim and erase all excess lines and save the drawing if desired.

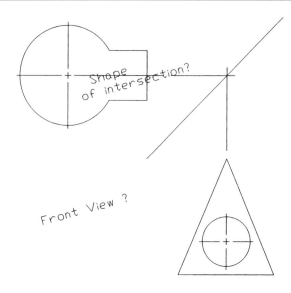

Figure 5-82

Step 1

Step 2

Slice of cone
that contains points
2 and 4.

Project intersection
point into the top
view.

Radius for
circular
cone slice.

EXTEND centerline
to the edge of
the cone.

Step 3

Step 4

Project the location
of points 2 and 4
into the top view.

Project point
from the top to
front view.

Project point location
from the side to the
front view.

Horizontal projection lines

Step 5

Step 6

Figure 5-83

NOTE: ALL FILLETS AND
ROUNDS = R%.

Extend rectangular cutout to
the lower portion of the part,
and add a 10 mm radius to each
internal corner.

Round the external corners
using a 10 mm radius,
4 corners.

Remove circular
cutout.

Change two holes to Δ10.

Figure 5-84

5-35 DESIGNING BY MODIFYING AN EXISTING PART

Many beginning design assignments require that an existing part be modified to meet a new set of requirements. Designers must therefore create something different from the original drawing. This ability to look beyond the drawing is an important design skill.

Figure 5-84 shows a dimensioned part, and Figure 5-85 shows the three orthographic views of the part. The part is to be redesigned as follows.

1. Replace the two Ø7.5 holes with Ø10 holes.
2. Remove the R20 cutout.
3. Modify the horizontal portion of the part so its overall length is 45 millimeters; make the entire part symmetrical about its 90° axis.

Original views

Figure 5-85

4. Round the four external and four internal corners
    using a 10-millimeter radius.

Figure 5-86 shows the resulting three orthographic
views.

Revised views

Figure 5-86

5-36 EXERCISE PROBLEMS

Draw a front, top, and right-side orthographic view of each of the objects in Exercise Problems EX5-1 to EX5-94. Do not include dimensions.

EX5-1 INCHES

EX5-2 MILLIMETERS

EX5-3 MILLIMETERS

EX5-4 INCHES

EX5-5 MILLIMETERS

EX5-6 MILLIMETERS

EX5-7 MILLIMETERS

EX5-10 MILLIMETERS

EX5-8 MILLIMETERS

EX5-11 MILLIMETERS

EX5-9 INCHES

EX5-12 INCHES

EX5-13 MILLIMETERS

EX5-14 MILLIMETERS

EX5-15 MILLIMETERS

EX5-16 MILLIMETERS

EX5-17 MILLIMETERS

EX5-18 MILLIMETERS

EX5-19 MILLIMETERS

EX5-20 MILLIMETERS

EX5-21 INCHES

EX5-22 MILLIMETERS

EX5-23 MILLIMETERS

EX5-24 INCHES

EX5-25 MILLIMETERS

EX5-26 MILLIMETERS

EX5-27 MILLIMETERS

EX5-28 MILLIMETERS

EX5-29 MILLIMETERS

EX5-30 MILLIMETERS

EX5-31 INCHES

EX5-34 MILLIMETERS

EX5-32 MILLIMETERS

EX5-35 MILLIMETERS

EX5-33 INCHES

EX5-36 INCHES

EX5-37 MILLIMETERS

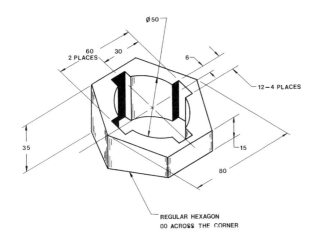

REGULAR HEXAGON
00 ACROSS THE CORNER

EX5-38 MILLIMETERS

EX5-39 MILLIMETERS

EX5-40 MILLIMETERS

EX5-41 INCHES

EX5-42 INCHES

EX5-43 MILLIMETERS

EX5-46 MILLIMETERS

EX5-44 MILLIMETERS

EX5-47 INCHES

EX5-45 MILLIMETERS

EX5-48 INCHES

EX5-49 MILLIMETERS

EX5-50 INCHES

EX5-51 INCHES

EX5-52 MILLIMETERS

EX5-53 INCHES

EX5-54 MILLIMETERS

EX5-55 MILLIMETERS

Ø 25 PERPENDICULAR
TO BACK SURFACE

60°

50

60

7
2 PLACES

23

35

16

18

14
2 HOLES

23 – 2 HOLES

Ø 9 – 2 HOLES

EX5-58 MILLIMETERS

12-4 PLACES

100

20

20

20

14

20

8

70

8

R

21

35

60

10

8

20

40

ALL FILLETS AND
ROUNDS = R5

EX5-56 MILLIMETERS

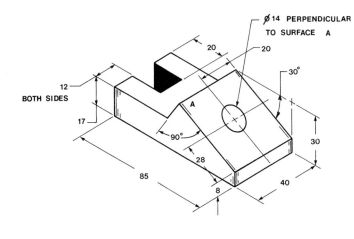

Ø 14 PERPENDICULAR
TO SURFACE A

20

20

30°

12
BOTH SIDES

A

17

90°

30

85

28

40

8

EX5-59 MILLIMETERS

25
BOTH ENDS

20

35 ACROSS THE FLATS
CENTERED ABOUT ℄

90

Ø 100

EX5-57 MILLIMETERS

14

10

15

15°

5

8

30°

R5
4PLACES

10

30°

23

65

40

10

22

40

80

EX5-60 INCHES

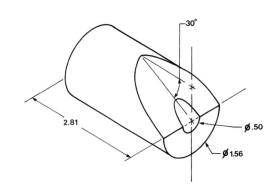

30°

2.81

Ø .50

Ø 1.56

EX5-61 MILLIMETERS

ALL FILLETS AND ROUNDS = R3

EX5-62 MILLIMETERS

EX5-63 MILLIMETERS

EX5-64 MILLIMETERS

EX5-65 MILLIMETERS

EX5-66 MILLIMETERS

EX5-67 MILLIMETERS

EX5-70 MILLIMETERS

EX5-68 MILLIMETERS

EX5-71 MILLIMETERS

EX5-69 MILLIMETERS

EX5-72 MILLIMETERS

EX5-73 MILLIMETERS

EX5-74 INCHES

EX5-75 INCHES

EX5-76 MILLIMETERS

EX5-77 MILLIMETERS

NOTE: ALL FILLET AND ROUNDS=R3

EX5-78 MILLIMETERS

MATL 5 THK

ALL INSIDE BEND RAD 5

EX5-79 MILLIMETERS

10-2 PLACES
70
50
20
10
Ø6-2 PLACES
5
45
50
27.5
Ø10-2 PLACES
7.5-2 PLACES
27.5
32.5
R20
70
R7.5-2 PLACES

ALL FILLETS AND ROUNDS= R5
MATL 5 THK

EX5-80 MILLIMETERS

8-2 PLACES
60
28
25
15
16-2 PLACES
8-2 PLACES
60
Ø12-4 PLACES
Ø8-2 PLACES
5-2 PLACES
R5-2 PLACES
32
20
16-2 PLACES
48
10
28
60
60 REF
8-2 PLACES
Ø6-2 PLACES
MATL 5 THK

EX5-81 MILLIMETERS

35
25
50
12-2 PLACES
15
8-2 PLACES
35
Ø8-4 PLACES
12
10-4 PLACES
12
18
40-2 PLACES
10
45
80
20-4 PLACES

ALL FILLETS AND ROUNDS = R3
MATL 5 THK

EX5-82 MILLIMETERS

50
10
20
15
28
15
Ø10-2 PLACES
R30-2 PLACES
45
15
25
12
20
25
15
70
R5-2 PLACES

ALL FILLETS AND ROUNDS = R3
MATL 12 THK

EX5-83 MILLIMETERS

40
12
20
16
53
10
40
13
30°
50
20
10
15
30°
20
Ø10-2 HOLES
10

EX5-84 INCHES

Ø.375 x .500 DEEP
4 HOLES
1.75
2.25
.75
.50
1.00
.88
.63
1.63
1.13
1.25
30°
.50
.88
60°
.75
.25
Ø.750 x .25 DEEP
2 HOLES - BOTH
BOTTOM DRILLED
2.00
1.75

EX5-85 MILLIMETERS

EX5-87 INCHES

EX5-86 MILLIMETERS

EX5-88 MILLIMETERS

EX5-89 MILLIMETERS

EX5-90 MILLIMETERS

EX5-91 MILLIMETERS

EX5-92 MILLIMETERS

ALL FILLETS AND ROUNDS = R5

EX5-93 MILLIMETERS

EX5-94 MILLIMETERS

For Exercises EX5-95 to EX5-100:

A. Sketch the given orthographic views and add the top view so that the final sketch includes a front, top, and right-side view.
B. Prepare a three-dimensional sketch of the object.

EX5-95   **EX5-98**

EX5-96   **EX5-99**

EX5-97   **EX5-100**

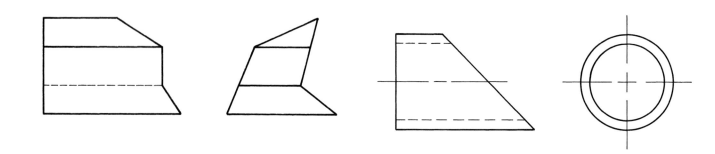

For Exercise Problems EX5-101 to EX5-128:

A. Redraw the given views and draw the third view.
B. Prepare a three-dimensional sketch of the object.

EX5-101 INCHES

EX5-104 INCHES

EX5-102 INCHES

EX5-105 INCHES

EX5-103 INCHES

EX5-106 INCHES

EX5-107 INCHES

EX5-110 INCHES

EX5-108 INCHES

EX5-111 INCHES

EX5-109 INCHES

All fillets and rounds = $\frac{1}{8}$ R

EX5-112 INCHES

All fillets and rounds = $\frac{1}{8}$ R

Each exercise on this page is presented on a 10 × 10–mm grid.

EX5-115

EX5-113

EX5-114

EX5-116

Each exercise on this page is presented on a .50″ × .50″ grid.

EX5-117

EX5-119

EX5-118

EX5-120

NOTE: ALL FILLETS AND
ROUNDS = R%.

Extend rectangular cutout to
the lower portion of the part,
and add a 10 mm radius to each
internal corner.

Round the external corners
using a 10 mm radius,
4 corners.

Ø10–2 HOLES

R7.5–2 PLACES

Ø6–2 HOLES

R20

Remove circular
cutout.

Change two holes to Δ10.

Figure 5-84

5-35 DESIGNING BY MODIFYING AN EXISTING PART

Many beginning design assignments require that an existing part be modified to meet a new set of requirements. Designers must therefore create something different from the original drawing. This ability to look beyond the drawing is an important design skill.

Figure 5-84 shows a dimensioned part, and Figure 5-85 shows the three orthographic views of the part. The part is to be redesigned as follows.

1. Replace the two Ø7.5 holes with Ø10 holes.
2. Remove the R20 cutout.
3. Modify the horizontal portion of the part so its overall length is 45 millimeters; make the entire part symmetrical about its 90° axis.

Original views

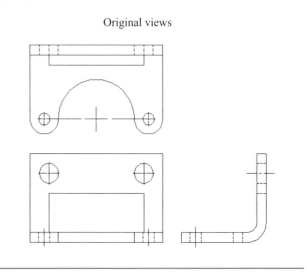

Figure 5-85

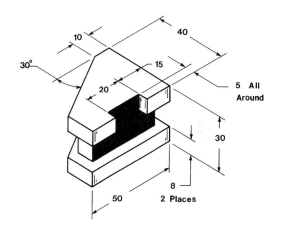

EX5-25 MILLIMETERS

CYLINDRICAL KEY

EX5-26 MILLIMETERS

EX5-27 MILLIMETERS

EX5-28 MILLIMETERS

EX5-29 MILLIMETERS

EX5-30 MILLIMETERS

EX5-89 MILLIMETERS

ALL FILLETS AND ROUNDS = R3

EX5-90 MILLIMETERS

ALL FILLETS AND ROUNDS = R5

Each exercise on this page is presented on a .50″ ×
.50″ grid.

EX5-121

EX5-123

EX5-122

EX5-124

Each exercise on this page is presented on a 10 × 10–mm grid.

EX5-125

EX5-127

EX5-126

EX5-128

Draw the complete front, top, and side views of the two intersecting objects given in Exercise Problems EX5-129 to EX5-134 based on the given complete and partially complete orthographic views.

EX5-129 MILLIMETERS

EX5-131 INCHES

EX5-130 MILLIMETERS

EX5-132 INCHES

EX5-133 MILLIMETERS

Draw the front, top, and side orthographic views of the objects given in Exercise Problems EX5-135 to EX5-138 based on the partially complete isometric drawings.

EX5-135 MILLIMETERS

EX5-134 MILLIMETERS

EX5-136 MILLIMETERS

EX5-137 INCHES

EX5-138 INCHES (SCALE: 5=1)

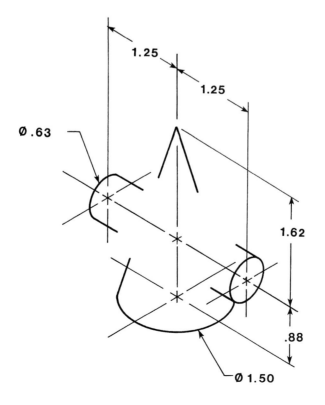

Redesign the existing objects as indicated in Exercise Problems EX5-139 to EX5-142, then prepare a front, top, and right-side view of the object.

EX5-139 MILLIMETERS

1. Replace the four existing 12-wide slots with seven slots 16 wide.
2. Increase the distance between the slots from 20 to 24.
3. Modify the overall length as needed.
4. Increase the size of the 60 slot so that it is 20 from both ends.

Change to 16-7 PLACES.

Modify as needed.

ALL FILLETS AND ROUNDS = R5

Modify as needed.

Maintain at both ends.

EX5-140 MILLIMETERS

Modify to
Ø16-23 DEEP
Ø30-82°CSK.

Modify to
Ø10
Ø16CBORE - 8 DEEP.

Modify to 80.

Modify to 130.

EX5-141 MILLIMETERS

Modify to a ∅20 hole perpendicular to the slanted surface.

Ø 25 PERPENDICULAR
TO BACK SURFACE

60°

50

60

7
2 PLACES

23

35

16

Round the four front corners using R10.

18

14
2 HOLES

23 – 2 HOLES

Ø 9 – 2 HOLES

EX5-142 MILLIMETERS

∅16 THRU

∅30 CBORE
x 3 DEEP

12 R
TYP

∅12 THRU
2 HOLES

130

65

10 TYP

∅ 100

∅ 75 x 5 DEEP

Modify to 15 DEEP.

55

Modify so that there are 6 standoffs equally spaced around the top surface of the object.

∅ 30 CBORE
x 10 DEEP

Modify to ∅30-82°CSK.

C H A P T E R 6

Sectional
Views

6-1 INTRODUCTION

Sectional views are used in technical drawing to expose internal surfaces. They serve to present additional orthographic views of surfaces that appear as hidden lines in the standard front, top, and side orthographic views.

Figure 6-1A shows an object intersected by a cutting plane. Figure 6-1B shows the same object with its right side and the cutting plane removed. Hatch lines are drawn on the surfaces that represent where the cutting plane passed through solid material. Also shown are the front and right-side orthographic views and a sectional view. Note the

SECTION A-A
SCALE 2 : 1

Figure 6-1A

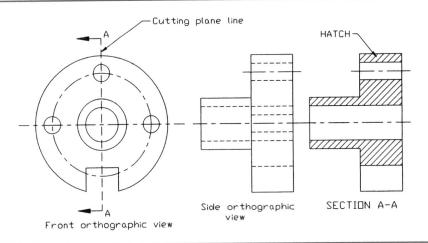

Figure 6-1B

similarity between the sectional view and the cut pictorial view.

Sectional views do not contain hidden lines, so they are used to clarify orthographic views that are difficult to understand because of excessive hidden lines. Figure 6-2 shows an object with a complex internal shape. The standard right view contains many hidden lines and is difficult to follow. Note how much easier it is to understand the object's internal shape when it is presented as a sectional view.

Sectional views *do* include all lines that are directly visible. Figure 6-3 shows an object, a cutting plane line, and a sectional view taken along the cutting plane line. Surfaces that are directly visible are shown in the sectional view. For example, part of the large hole in the back left surface is, from the given sectional view's orientation, blocked by the shorter rectangular surface. The part of the hole that appears above the blocking surface is shown; the part behind the surface is not.

Figure 6-2

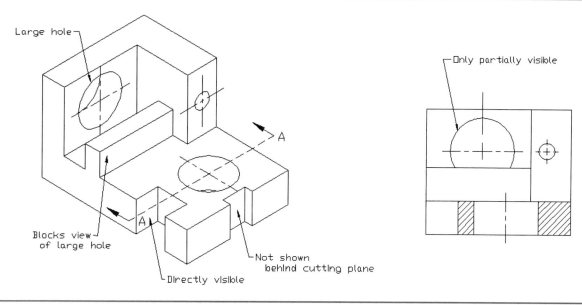

Figure 6-3

Sectional views are always viewed in the direction defined by the cutting plane arrows. Any surface that is behind the cutting plane is not included in the sectional view. Sectional views are aligned and oriented relative to the cutting plane lines as a side orthographic view is to the front view. The orientation of a sectional view may be better understood by placing your right hand on the cutting plane line so that your thumb is pointing up. Move your hand to the right and place it palm down. Your thumb should now be pointing to the left. Your thumb indicates the top of the view.

Drafters and designers often refer to sectional views as "sectional cuts" or simply "cuts." The terminology is helpful in understanding how sectional views are defined and created.

6-2 CUTTING PLANE LINES

Cutting plane lines are used to define the location for the sectional view's cutting plane. An object is "cut" along a cutting plane line.

Figure 6-4 shows two linetype patterns for cutting plane lines. Either pattern is acceptable, although some companies prefer to use only one linetype for all drawings to ensure a uniform appearance in all their drawings. The dashed line pattern will be used throughout this book.

The two patterns shown in Figure 6-4 are included in AutoCAD's linetype library as Dashed and Phantom styles.

The arrow portion of the cutting plane line is created using the Leader command listed within the Dimension toolbar, or by creating a wblock that includes an arrowhead and extension line.

To draw a cutting plane line—Method I

Change a given continuous line, A-A, to a cutting plane line. See Figure 6-5.

1. Select Format (pull-down), Linetype.

   The Linetype Manager dialog box will appear.

2. Select Load.

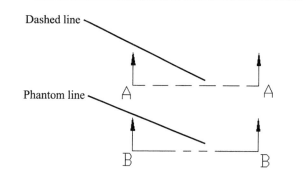

Use Dtext to add the lettering.

Figure 6-4

Figure 6-5

The Load or Reload Linetypes dialog box will appear. See Figure 6-6.

3. Select Dashed or Phantom, then return to the drawing screen.
4. Select Modify (pull-down), Properties.

Select object(s):

5. Select line A-A.

    The Change Properties dialog box will appear.

6. Select Linetype.

    The Linetype Manager dialog box will appear. See Figure 6-7.

7. Select Dashed and return to the drawing screen.

Figure 6-6

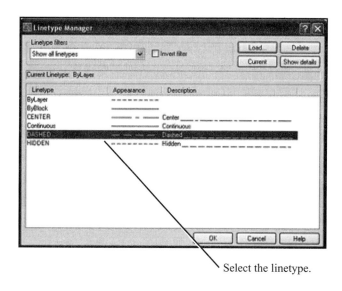

Select the linetype.

Figure 6-7

Arrowhead scale factor

Figure 6-8

To draw an arrowhead

1. Select the Leader tool from the Dimension toolbar.

   Command: _qleader
   Specify first leader point, or [Settings] <Settings>:

2. Select the location for the tip of the arrow.

   Specify next point:

3. Select the end of the line, then right-click the mouse.

   Specify text width <0.000>:

4. Press Enter.

   Enter first line of annotation text <Mtext>:

5. Press Enter.

   The Text Formatting dialog box will appear.

6. Click OK.

   If necessary, use the Rotate command to align the leader line to the horizontal or vertical direction.

To change the size of an arrowhead

Arrowheads used for cutting plane lines are usually drawn larger than arrowheads used for dimension lines. This serves to make them more distinctive and easier to find. The normal arrowhead scale factor is 0.19. In this example, the scale factor is 0.375.

1. Select the Dimension Style tool from the Dimension toolbar.
2. Select Modify.

   The Modify Dimension Style: Standard dialog box will appear. See Figure 6-8.

3. Select the Symbols and Arrows tab and use the Arrow size box within the Arrowheads portion of the dialog box to change the arrowhead's scale factor (change to 0.3750).
4. Return to the drawing screen and use Leader to create the needed arrowheads.

   The arrowhead size can also be changed by typing **dimasz** in response to a command prompt and typing in the new scale factor.

To draw a cutting plane line—Method II

A cutting plane can also be created by first defining a separate layer setup for cutting plane lines. The linetype will be dashed or phantom, and a color can be assigned if desired. Section 3-25 described how to create and work with layers.

To draw cutting plane lines

Cutting plane lines should extend beyond the edges of the object. See Figure 6-9. A cutting plane line should extend far enough beyond the edges of the object so that there is a clear gap between the arrowhead and the edge of the object.

Figure 6-9

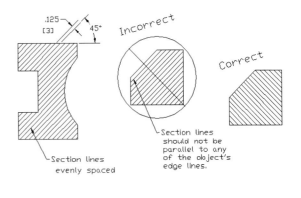

Figure 6-10

If an object is symmetrical about the centerline and only one sectional view is to be taken exactly aligned with the centerline, the cutting plane line may be omitted.

6-3 SECTION LINES

Section lines are used to define areas that represent where solid material has been cut in a sectional view. Section lines are evenly spaced at any inclined angle that is not parallel to any existing edge line and should be visually distinct from the continuous lines that define the boundary of the sectional view.

Figure 6-10 shows an area that includes uniform section lines evenly spaced at 45°. The other area shown in

Figure 6-10 includes a 45° edge line; therefore, the section lines cannot be drawn at 45°. Lines at 135° (0° is horizontal to the right) were drawn instead.

Figure 6-11 shows an object that contains edge lines at both 45° and 135°. The section lines within this area were drawn at 60°.

If two or more parts are included within the same sectional view, each part must have visually different section lines. Figure 6-12 shows a sectional view that contains two parts. Part one's section lines were spaced 3 apart at 45°, and part two's were spaced 5 apart at 135° (−45).

The recommended spacing for sectional lines is 0.125 inch or 3 millimeters, but smaller areas may use section lines spaced closer together than larger areas. See Figure 6-13. Section lines should never be spaced so close together as to

Figure 6-11

Figure 6-12

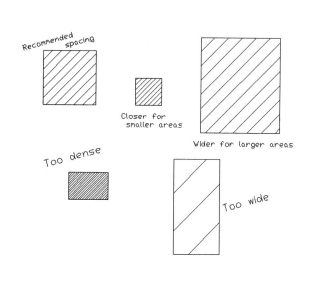

Figure 6-13

look blurry or be so far apart that they are not clearly recognizable as section lines.

Evenly spaced sectional line patterns drawn at 45° are called *general*, or *uniform*, patterns; other patterns are available. Different section line patterns are used to help distinguish different materials. The different patterns allow the drawing reader to see what materials are used in a design without having to refer to the drawing's parts list. It should be noted that not all companies use different patterns to define material differences. When you are in doubt, the general pattern is usually acceptable.

How to draw different section line patterns is explained in Section 6-4.

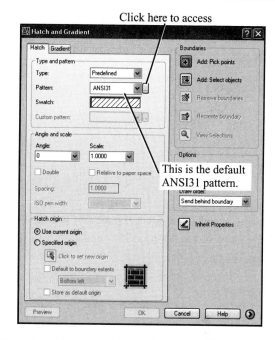

Figure 6-14

6-4 HATCH

Section lines are drawn in AutoCAD using the Hatch tool. The Hatch tool is located on the Draw toolbar. The Hatch tool offers many different hatch patterns and spacings. The general pattern of evenly spaced lines at 45° is defined as pattern ANSI31 and is the default setting for the Hatch tool.

To hatch a given area

Given an area, use Hatch to draw section lines.

1. Select the Hatch tool from the Draw toolbar.

The Hatch and Gradient dialog box will appear. See Figure 6-14. Note that ANSI31 is the default pattern.

2. Select the Pick Points option.

Command: _bhatch
Select internal point:

3. Select a point within the area to be hatched, then right-click the mouse, then select Enter.

The Hatch and Gradient dialog box will reappear.

4. Select the OK option.

The area will be hatched. See Figure 6-15.

To change hatch patterns

1. Select the Hatch tool from the Draw toolbar.

Figure 6-15

Figure 6-16

The Hatch and Gradient dialog box will appear.

2. Click the arrow to the right of the Pattern ANSI31 designation.

A list of available ANSI patterns will appear. See Figure 6-16.

Figure 6-18

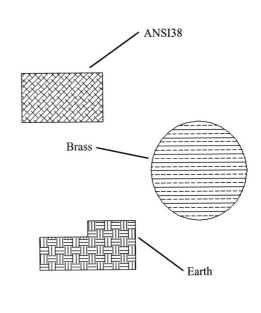

Figure 6-17

3. Select the desired pattern and apply it as described above.

A swatch of the selected pattern will appear on the Hatch and Gradient dialog box. Figure 6-17 shows three areas with three different hatch patterns applied.

To change the spacing and angle of a hatch pattern

1. Select the Hatch tool from the Draw toolbar.

The Hatch and Gradient dialog box will appear. See Figure 6-18. The Angle and Scale option boxes are located just below the Custom pattern box.

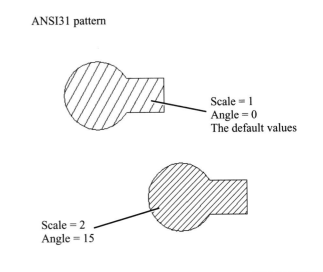

Figure 6-19

2. Change the scale to 2 and the angle to 15.

Figure 6-19 shows a comparison between an ANSI31 pattern created using the default values of 1 and 0°, and the adjusted pattern of 2 and 15°.

6-5 SAMPLE PROBLEM SP6-1

Figure 6-20 shows an object with a cutting plane line. Figure 6-21 shows how a front view and a sectional view of the object are created.

1. Draw the front orthographic view of the object and lay out the height and width of the object based on the given dimensions. Sectional views must be directly aligned with the angle of the cutting plane line. Sectional views are in fact orthographic views that are based on the angle of the cutting plane line. Information is projected to sectional views as it was projected to top and side views. In this example the cutting plane line is a vertical line, so horizontal projection lines are used to draw the sectional view.
2. Draw the object features. No hidden lines are drawn.
3. Use Hatch to draw sectional lines within the appropriate areas.
4. Erase or trim any excess lines.
5. Modify the color of the sectional lines if desired.
6. Save the drawing if desired.

SECTION A-A

Figure 6-20

Figure 6-21

6-6 STYLES OF SECTION LINES

AutoCAD has more than 50 different hatch patterns. The different patterns can be previewed in the Swatch option in the Hatch and Gradient dialog box.

Most of the available options are for architectural use. The patterns can be used to create elevation drawings and to add texture patterns to drawings of houses, buildings, and other structures. Technical drawings usually refer to objects made from steel, aluminum, or a composite material. There are hundreds of variations of each of these materials.

In general, if you decide to assign a particular pattern to a material, clearly state which pattern has been assigned to which material on the drawing. This is best done by including a note on the drawing that includes a picture of the pattern and the material that it is to represent. Figure 6-22 shows a drawing note for a hatch pattern used to represent SAE 1040 steel. The representation is unique for the drawing shown.

6-7 SECTIONAL VIEW LOCATION

Sectional views should be located on a drawing behind the arrows. The arrows represent the viewing direction for the sectional view. See Figure 6-23. If it is impossible to locate sectional views behind the arrows, they may be located above or below, but still behind, the arrowed portion of the cutting plane line. Sectional views should never be located in front of the arrows.

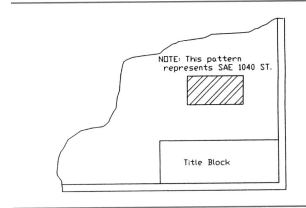

Figure 6-22

Sectional views located on a different drawing sheet than the cutting plane line must be cross-referenced to the appropriate cutting plane line. See Figure 6-24. The boxed notation C/3 SHT2 next to the cutting plane line means that the sectional view may be found in zone C/3 on sheet 2 of the drawing.

The location of the sectional view must be referenced to the cutting plane line if the view's location is not near the cutting plane. The notation C/3 SHT2 defines the location of the cutting plane line for the sectional view.

The reference numbers and letters are based on a drawing area charting system similar to that used for locating

Figure 6-23

Figure 6-24

Figure 6-26

features on maps. A sectional view located at C/3 SHT2 can be found by going to sheet 2 of the drawing, then drawing a vertical line from the box marked 3 at the top or bottom of the drawing and a horizontal line from the box marked C on the left or right edge of the drawing. The sectional view should be located somewhere near the intersection of the two lines.

6-8 HOLES IN SECTIONS

Figure 6-25 shows a sectional view of an object that contains three holes. As with orthographic views, a conical point must be included on holes that do not completely penetrate the object.

A common mistake is to omit the back edge of a hole when drawing a sectional view. Figure 6-25 shows a hole drilled through an object. Note that the sectional view includes a straight line across the top and bottom edges of the view that represents the back edges of the hole.

Figure 6-26 shows a countersunk hole, a counterbored hole, a spotface, and a hole through a boss. Again, any hole that does not completely penetrate the object must include a conical point.

Figure 6-25

Original shape   Shape with gradients added

Figure 6-27

6-9 GRADIENTS

In AutoCAD a *gradient* is shading that varies in intensity. Figure 6-27 shows a rectangular shape with two internal circles. The figure also shows the same shape with various gradients added.

To create a gradient

1. Select the Gradient tool from the Draw toolbar.

The Hatch and Gradient dialog box will appear. See Figure 6-28.

2. Select the Add: Select objects button.

The dialog box will disappear.

3. Select one of the circles by clicking its edge line.

The Hatch and Gradient dialog box will appear.

4. Select a gradient pattern, then click OK.

A gradient will appear within the circle.

Select here to access the Advanced Options dialog box.

Select gradient pattern here.

Figure 6-28

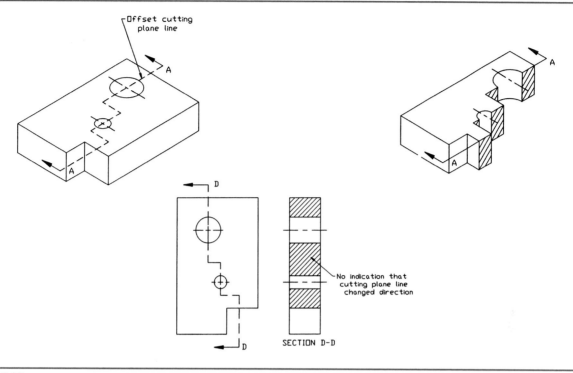

SECTION D-D

Figure 6-29

6-10 OFFSET SECTIONS

Cutting plane lines need not be drawn as straight lines across the surface of an object. They may be stepped so more features can be included in the sectional view. See Figure 6-29. In the object shown in Figure 6-29, the cutting plane line crosses two holes and a directly visible open surface that contains a hole. There is no indication in the sectional view that the cutting plane line has been offset.

Cutting plane lines should be placed to include as many features as possible without causing confusion. The intent of using sectional views is to simplify views and to clarify the drawing. Several features can be included on the same cutting plane line so that fewer views are used, giving the drawing a less cluttered look and making it easier for the reader to understand the shape of the object's features.

Figure 6-30 shows another example of an offset cutting plane line.

SECTION F-F

Figure 6-30

Figure 6-31

6-11 MULTIPLE SECTIONS

More than one sectional view may be taken off the same orthographic view. Figure 6-31 shows a drawing that includes three sectional views, all taken off a front view. Each cutting plane line is labeled with a letter. The letters are in turn used to identify the appropriate sectional view. Identifying letters are also placed at the ends of the cutting plane lines, behind the arrowheads. Identifying letters are also placed below the sectional view and written using the format SECTION A-A, SECTION B-B, and so on. The abbreviation SECT may also be used: SECT A-A, SECT B-B.

The letters I, O, and X are generally not used to identify sectional views because they can easily be misread. If more than 23 sectional views are used, the lettering starts again with double letters: AA-AA, BB-BB, and so on.

6-12 ALIGNED SECTIONS

Cutting plane lines taken at angles on circular shapes may be aligned as shown in Figure 6-32. Aligning the sectional views prevents the foreshortening that would result if the view were projected from the original cutting plane line location. A foreshortened view would not present an accurate picture of the object's surfaces.

6-13 DRAWING CONVENTIONS IN SECTIONS

Slots and small holes that penetrate cylindrical surfaces may be drawn as straight lines, as shown in Figure 6-33. Larger holes, that is, holes whose diameters are greater than the radii of their cylinders, should be drawn showing an elliptical curvature.

Intersecting holes are represented by crossed lines, as shown in Figure 6-34. The crossed lines are drawn from the intersecting corners of the holes.

Figure 6-32

Figure 6-33

6-14 HALF, PARTIAL, AND BROKEN-OUT SECTIONAL VIEWS

Half and partial sectional views allow a designer to show an object using an orthographic view and a sectional view within one view. A half-sectional view is shown in Figure 6-35. Half the view is a sectional view; the other half is a normal orthographic view including hidden lines. The cutting plane line is drawn as shown and includes an arrowhead at only one end of the line.

Figure 6-36 shows a partial sectional view. It is similar to a half sectional view, but the sectional view is taken at a location other than directly on a centerline or one defined by a cutting plane line. A broken line is used to separate the sectional view from the orthographic view. A broken line is a freehand line drawn using the Sketch command.

Figure 6-34

Figure 6-35

Figure 6-36

Figure 6-37

Broken-out sectional views are like small partial views. They are used to show only small internal portions of an object. Figure 6-37 shows a broken-out sectional view. Broken lines are used to separate the broken-out section from the rest of the orthographic views.

To draw a broken line

1. Type Sketch in response to a command prompt.

   Command:_sketch

   Record Increment <0.1000>:

2. Press Enter.

   Sketch. Pen/eXit/Quit/Record/Erase/Connect:

3. Press the left mouse button.

   <Pen down>

4. Move the cursor across the screen. A green freehand line will emerge from the crosshairs as it is moved.

5. Press the left mouse button again.

   <Pen up>

The crosshairs can now be moved without producing a sketched line.

6. Select RECORD from the menu.

   23 lines recorded

The number of lines generated and recorded will depend on the length of the line and the size of the line increment.

7. Select eXit from the menu.

   Command:

Do not use the right mouse button to exit the Sketch command. If the right mouse button is pressed, a line will be drawn from the end of the sketched line to the present location of the crosshairs. Use eXit to end the Sketch command.

6-15 REMOVED SECTIONAL VIEWS

Removed sectional views are used to show how an object's shape changes over its length. Removed sectional views are most often used with long objects whose shape changes continuously over its length. See Figure 6-38. The sectional views are not positioned behind the arrowheads but are positioned across the drawing as shown; however, the view orientation is the same as it would be if the view were projected from the arrowheads; it is simply located in a different position in the drawing.

It is good practice to identify the cutting plane lines and the sectional views in alphabetical order. This will make it easer for the drawing's readers to find the sectional views.

6-16 BREAKS

It is often convenient to break long continuous shapes so that they take up less drawing space. There are two drawing conventions used to show breaks: *freehand lines* used for rectangular shapes, and *S-breaks* used for cylindrical shapes. See Figure 6-39. Freehand break lines are drawn using the Sketch command as explained in Section 6-14. Instructions for drawing S-breaks follow.

SECTION A-A   SECTION B-B   SECTION C-C

Figure 6-38

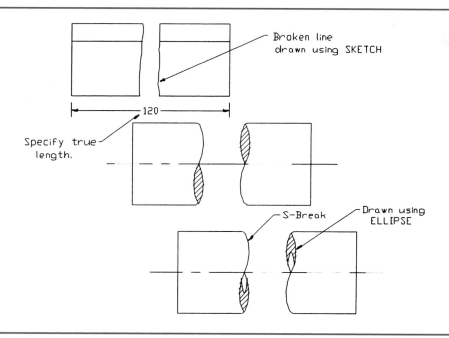

Broken line
drawn using SKETCH

|← 120 →|

Specify true
length.

S-Break

Drawn using
ELLIPSE

Figure 6-39

To draw an S-break (See Figure 6-40.)

1. Draw a rectangular view of the cylindrical object and draw a construction line where the break is to be located. The rectangular view should include a centerline.
2. Draw two 30° lines: one from the intersection of the construction line and the outside edge line of the view, and the other from the intersection of the construction line and the centerline as shown.
3. Draw an arc using the intersection created in step 2 as the center point. Mirror the arc about the centerline and then about the construction line.
4. Use Fillet, set to a small radius, to smooth the corners between the arc and the edge lines. Any small radius may be used for the fillet, provided it produces a smooth visual transition between the arc and the edge lines.
5. Erase and trim any excess lines.
6. Hatch the area created by the two arcs and fillet as shown.

The Copy, Mirror, and Move commands may be used to create the opposing S-break as shown in Figure 6-39. The internal shapes of the tubular S-breaks are created using Ellipse. Position the end of the ellipse according to the thickness specifications, and determine the elliptical shape by eye. Trim the sectional lines from the inside of the inside ellipse.

6-17 SECTIONAL VIEWS OF CASTINGS

Cast objects are usually designed to include a feature called a *rib*. See Figure 6-41. Ribs add strength and rigidity to an object. Sectional views of ribs do not include complete section lines because this is considered misleading to the reader. Ribs are usually narrow, and a large sectioned area gives the impression of a denser and stronger area than is actually on the casting.

There are two conventions used to present sectional views of cast ribs: one that does not draw any section lines on the ribs, and one that puts every other section line on the rib. Sectional views of castings that do not include section lines on ribs are created using Hatch for those areas that are to be hatched.

Figure 6-40

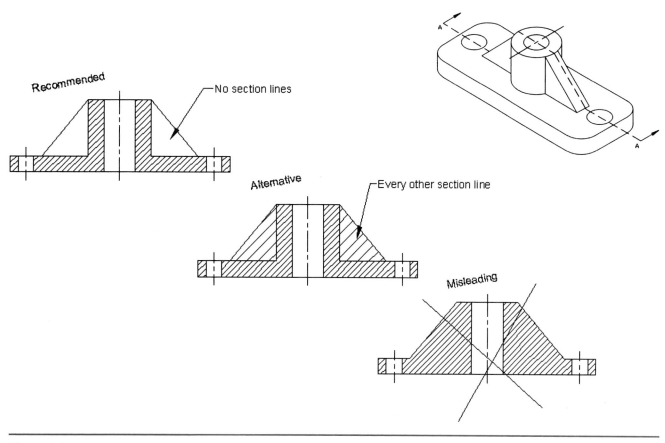

Figure 6-41

6-18 EXERCISE PROBLEMS

Draw a complete front view and a sectional view of the objects in Exercise Problems EX6-1 to EX6-4. The cutting plane line is located on the vertical centerline of the object.

EX6-1 MILLIMETERS

EX6-3 INCHES

EX6-2 MILLIMETERS

EX6-4 MILLIMETERS

NOTE: Taper from Ø80 to Ø68 over 13.

Draw the following sectional views using the given dimensions.

EX6-5

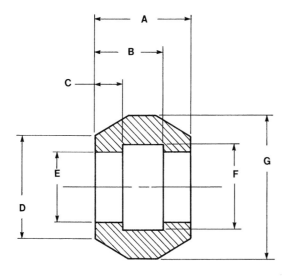

DIMENSIONS	INCHES	mm
A	.50	12
B	1.25	32
C	1.75	44
D	Ø1.75	44
E	Ø 1.25	32
F	Ø1.50	38
G	Ø2.50	64

EX6-6

DIMENSIONS	INCHES	mm
A	3.00	72
B	2.00	48
C	.75	18
D	2.00	48
E	1.00	24
F	1.38	33
G	Ø.25	6
H	Ø .375 X 2.50 DEEP Ø.875 X 82° CSINK	Ø10 X 60 DEEP Ø24 X 82° CSINK

Resketch the given top view and Section A-A, then sketch Sections B-B, C-C, and D-D.

EX6-7

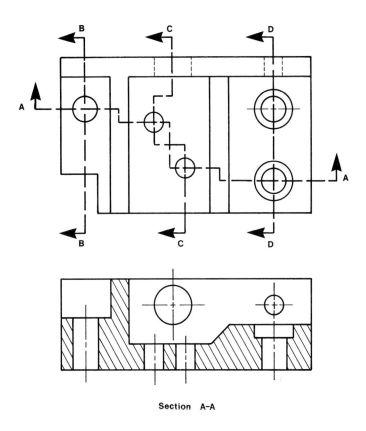

Section A-A

Resketch the given front views in Exercise Problems EX6-8 to EX6-11 and replace the given side orthographic view with the appropriate sectional view.

EX6-9

EX6-8

EX6-10 INCHES

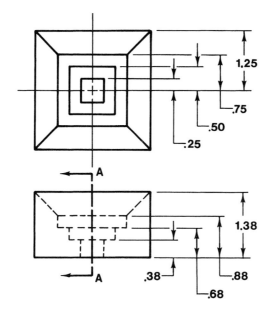

1.25
.75
.50
.25

Object is symmetrical
about both
centerlines

A

A

1.38
.38
.88
.68

EX6-11

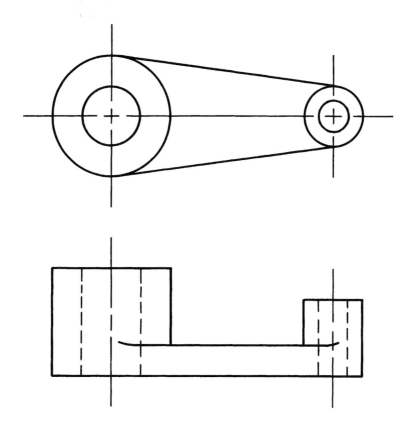

Redraw the given front views in Exercise Problems EX6-12 to EX6-15 and replace the given side orthographic view with the appropriate sectional view. The cutting plane is located on the vertical centerlines of the objects.

EX6-12 INCHES

EX6-14 INCHES

EX6-13 INCHES

EX6-15 MILLIMETERS

Draw the top orthographic view and the indicated sectional view.

EX6-16 MILLIMETERS

EX6-18 MILLIMETERS

EX6-17 INCHES

EX6-19 MILLIMETERS

Redraw the given views and add the specified sectional views in Exercise Problems EX6-20 to EX6-34.

EX6-20 INCHES

ALL FILLETS AND ROUNDS = R.125

EX6-21 INCHES

HOLE	X	Y	DIA
A	1.63	2.00	.44
B	1.13	1.00	.56
C	2.50	2.00 1.00	.63
D	3.88	2.00 1.00	.50

EX6-22 INCHES

EX6-23 INCHES

EX6-24 INCHES

Redraw the given front and top views and add Sections
A-A, B-B, and C-C as indicated.

EX6-25 MILLIMETERS

EX6-26 INCHES

EX6-27 INCHES

EX6-28 INCHES

EX6-30 MILLIMETERS

EX6-29 MILLIMETERS

EX6-31 MILLIMETERS

EX6-32 MILLIMETERS

EX6-33 MILLIMETERS

EX6-34 INCHES

EX6-35

New customer requirements require that the part shown below be redesigned as follows. Draw a front and a sectional view of the redesigned part.

1. The diameters of the Ø9 internal access holes are to be increased to Ø12.
2. The diameter of the internal cavity is to be increased to Ø30.
3. The length of the internal cavity is to be increased from 33 to 50.
4. All other sizes and distances are to be increased to maintain the same wall thickness.

New diameter for access hole is Ø12.

New internal cavity is to be Ø30 x 50 LONG.

Modify the other dimensions so that the wall thicknesses are the same.

NOTE: Taper from Ø80 to Ø68 over 13.

EX6-36

The following object is to be redesigned as follows.

1. Extend the 1.00-inch vertical slot all the way through the object, creating four corner sections.
2. Locate countersunk holes in each of the four corner sections. Note that two of the corner sections presently have Ø.50 holes. The countersink specifications are Ø.50 - 82°, Ø.75.
3. Locate a Ø.625 hole in the center of the object.

Extend this slot across the object.

Change to Ø.500 82° CSK - .75
4 HOLES.

1.00

.50

A

45°
2 PLACES

1.56

.56

.50

1.00

2.00 R

3.00 DIA

.50 DIA

A

Add a Ø.625 here.

C H A P T E R 7

Auxiliary Views

7-1 INTRODUCTION

Auxiliary views are orthographic views used to present true-shaped views of slanted and oblique surfaces. Slanted and oblique surfaces appear foreshortened or as edge views in normal orthographic views. Holes in the surfaces are elliptical, and other features are also distorted.

Figure 7-1 shows an object with a slanted surface that includes a hole drilled perpendicular to that surface. Note how the slanted surface is foreshortened in both the

Figure 7-1

Figure 7-2

normal top and side views and that the hole appears as an ellipse in both of these views. The hole appears as an edge view with hidden lines in the front view, so none of the normal views show the hole as a circle.

Figure 7-2 shows the same object shown in Figure 7-1. The top and side views are the same, but the top view is replaced with an auxiliary view. The auxiliary view shows the true shape of the slanted surface, and the hole appears as a circle.

The auxiliary view in Figure 7-2 shows the true shape of the slanted surface but a foreshortened view of surface A-B-C-D. Positioning the auxiliary view to generate the true shape of the slanted surface foreshortened the other surfaces.

7-2 PROJECTION BETWEEN NORMAL AND AUXILIARY VIEWS

Information about an object's features can be projected between the normal views and any additional auxiliary views by establishing reference planes. A reference plane RPT is located between the top and front views of Figure 7-3. The plane appears as a horizontal line, and its location is arbitrary. In the example shown, the plane was located 10 millimeters from the top view.

A second reference plane, RPA, was established parallel to the slanted surface at a location that prevents the

Figure 7-3

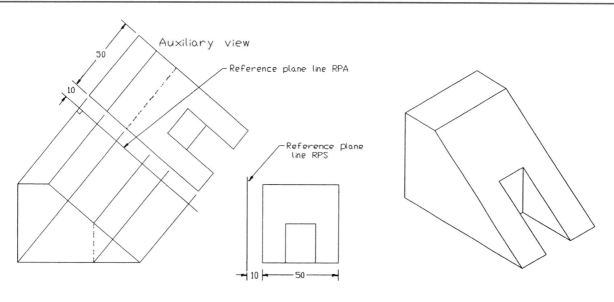

Figure 7-4

auxiliary view from interfering with the top view. The Move command can be used to move the top view farther away from the front view if necessary.

Information was projected from the front view into the auxiliary view by using projection lines perpendicular to reference plane RPA.

The depth of the object was transferred from the top view to the auxiliary view. Figure 7-3 shows the 50-millimeter depth and 15-millimeter slot depth dimensioned in both the top and auxiliary views.

Figure 7-4 shows information projected from given front and side views into an auxiliary view. Reference planes RPS and RPA were located 10 millimeters from and parallel to the side and auxiliary views, and information was projected from the front view into the auxiliary view using lines perpendicular to plane RPA. The depth information was transferred from the side view to the auxiliary view.

Figure 7-5 shows an object that has a slanted surface in the top view. The reference plane line, RPA, for the auxiliary view was located parallel to the slanted surface and

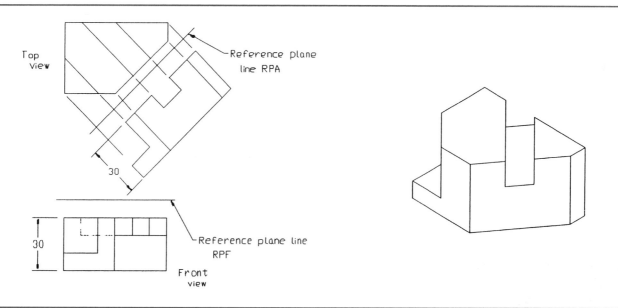

Figure 7-5

another reference plane, RPF (horizontal line), was established between the front and top views. Information was projected from the top view into the auxiliary view using lines perpendicular to RPA. The 30-millimeters height measurement was transferred from the front view into the auxiliary view.

Reference plane lines and projection lines drawn perpendicular to them are best drawn by rotating the drawing's axis system, indicated by the crosshairs, so that it is parallel to the slanted surface. A separate layer may be created for projection lines.

To rotate the drawing's axis system (See Figure 7-6.)

1. Type Snap in response to a Command prompt.

    The command prompts are as follows.

    Command: _snap
    Specify snap spacing or [ON/OFF/Aspect/Rotate/Style/Type]<0.5000>:

2. Type r; press Enter.

    Specify base point <0.0000,0.0000>:

3. Accept the default value by pressing Enter.

    Specify rotation angle <0>:

4. Type 45; press Enter.

    The cursor rotates 45° counterclockwise. Any angle value, including negative values, may be used.

    The grid also is rotated, and the Snap command will limit the crosshairs to spacing aligned with the rotated axis. Ortho will limit lines to horizontal and vertical relative to the rotated axis.

    The angle value entered for Snap, Rotate is always interpreted as an absolute value. For example, if the above procedure is repeated and a value of 60 entered, the crosshairs will advance only 15° from its present location, or 60° from the system's absolute 0° axis system.

7-3 SAMPLE PROBLEM SP7-1

Figure 7-7 shows an object that includes a slanted surface. The front, top, and auxiliary views projected from the slanted surface were developed as follows. See Figure 7-8.

1. Draw the front and top orthographic views as explained in Chapter 5.

    Use the Move command to position the top view so that it will not interfere with the auxiliary view.

2. Establish two reference plane lines: RPT parallel to the top view (horizontal line) and RPA parallel to the slanted surface (45° line).

    In this example the reference plane line for the top view is located along the lower edge of the view.
    Use Snap, Rotate to establish an axis system parallel to the slanted surface. The slanted surface is 45° to the horizontal. Turn Ortho on and draw a line parallel to the slanted surface.
    Option: Create a layer for projection lines.

3. Project lines perpendicular to RPA from the drawing's feature presented in the front view into the area of the auxiliary view. Use Osnap, Intersection to ensure accuracy.

4. Type Dist in response to a command prompt to determine the distance from the reference plane line RPT to the object's features.

Figure 7-6

Figure 7-7

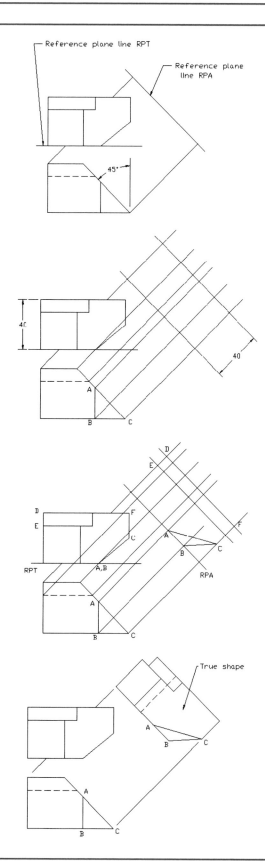

Figure 7-8

5. Use Offset to draw a line parallel to RPA at a distance equal to the distances of the object's features.

6. Erase and trim any excess lines and save the drawing, if desired.

7-4 TRANSFERRING LINES BETWEEN VIEWS

Objects are often dimensioned so that only some of their edge lines are dimensioned. This means that Offset may not be used to transfer distances to auxiliary views until the line length is known. There are three possible methods that can be used to transfer an edge line of unknown length: measure the line length using Dist and then use the determined distance with the Offset command; use Grips, and Rotate and Move the line; or use Copy, Modify, Rotate and relocate the line. The procedures are as follows.

To measure the length of a line

1. Type Dist in response to a command prompt.

The command prompts are as follows:

Command: Dist
Specify first point:

2. Select one end of the line. The Osnap, Endpoint option will help identify the endpoint of the line. The intersection of one of the projection lines with a reference plane is usually used.

Specify second point:

3. Select the other end of the line.

The following style display will appear in the screen's prompt area.

Distance=40, Angle in X-Y Plane=45, Angle from the X-Y Plane=0

Delta X=28.2885, Delta Y=28.2885, Delta Z=0.0000

Figure 7-9 shows the meaning of the displayed distance information.

Record the distance and use it with the Offset command to locate the line's endpoints relative to a reference plane. See Figure 7-9.

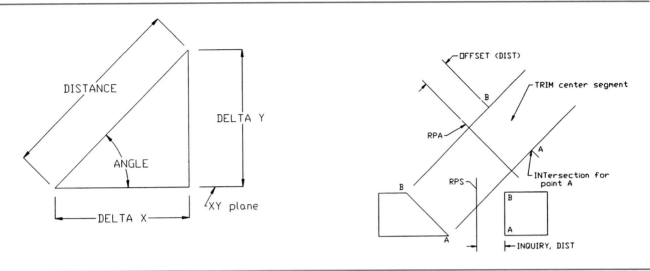

Figure 7-9

To Grip and Move a line (See Figure 7-10.)

1. Copy the line and move the copy to an open area of the drawing.
2. Click the line to highlight its Grip points. See Section 3-15.
3. Select the line's lower endpoint; press the right mouse button.
4. Select the Rotate option from the menu.

   ROTATE
   Specify rotation angle or [Base point/Copy/Undo/ Reference/eXit]:

5. Select the endpoint as the base point.
6. Type 45; press Enter.

   The Dist command can also be used to determine the angle of a slanted surface if it is not known.

7. Select the line's lower endpoint again.
8. Select Move from the menu.
9. Select the lower line point as the base point.
10. Move the line to a new location or use dynamic input to define a new location.

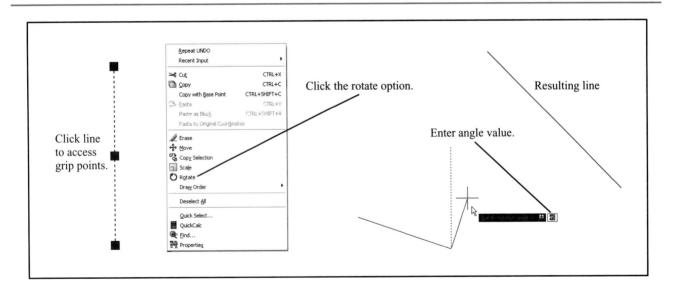

Figure 7-10

To rotate and move a line

1. Copy the line and move the line to an open area of the drawing.
2. Select Modify (pull-down menu), Rotate and rotate the line 45°. See Section 3-15.
3. Select Modify (pull-down menu), Move and relocate the line to the auxiliary view. Use Osnap if necessary to ensure accuracy.

7-5 SAMPLE PROBLEM SP7-2

Figure 7-11 shows an object that contains two slanted surfaces and two cutouts. Draw a front and right-side orthographic view, and an auxiliary view. See Figure 7-12.

1. Draw the front and side orthographic views as described in Chapter 5.
2. Define a reference plane, RPS, between the front and side views.
3. Use Snap, Rotate (37.5) to align the crosshairs with the slanted surface. The 37.5° value was determined using the Dist command.
4. Draw a reference plane line RPA parallel to the slanted surface and project the features of the object into the auxiliary view area.
5. Transfer the distance measurements from RPS and the side view into the auxiliary view.

   Label the various points as needed.

6. Erase and trim any excess lines and save the drawing, if desired.

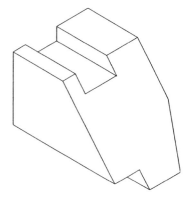

Figure 7-11

Figure 7-12

7-6 PROJECTING ROUNDED SURFACES

Rounded surfaces are projected into auxiliary views as they were projected into the normal orthographic views, as described in Section 5-15. Additional lines are added to one of the normal orthographic views and then projected into the other normal view. The additional lines define a series of points that define the outside shape of the surface. The two views with the added lines are used to project and transfer the points into the auxiliary view.

7-7 SAMPLE PROBLEM SP7-3

Figure 7-13 shows a cylindrical object that includes a slanted surface. Draw the front, side, and auxiliary views.

The procedure is as follows. See Figure 7-14.

1. Draw the front and side orthographic views.
2. Draw a reference plane line, RPS.

In this example the reference plane line was located on the side view's vertical centerline.

3. Draw a reference plane line, RPA, parallel to the slanted surface. The reference plane line will also be used as the centerline for the auxiliary view.

In this example the endpoints of both the major and minor axes of the projected elliptical auxiliary view are

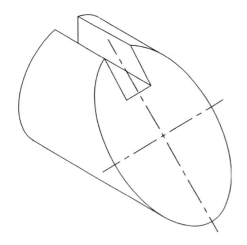

Figure 7-13

Figure 7-14

known, as well as the angle of the auxiliary view. It is therefore not necessary to define points in the circular side view, as was done in Section 5-21. Enough information is present to draw the elliptical shape directly in the auxiliary view.

4. Draw the elliptical surfaces in the auxiliary view as shown.
5. Transfer the width and location of the slot from the side view to the auxiliary view.
6. Erase and trim any excess lines and save the drawing, if desired.

7-8 PROJECTING IRREGULAR SURFACES

Auxiliary views of irregular surfaces are created by projecting information from given normal orthographic views into the auxiliary views in a manner similar to the way information was projected between orthographic views. See Section 5-28. The irregular surface is defined by a series of points along its edge line. The location of the points is random, although more points should be used when the curve's shape is changing sharply than when the curve tends to be smoother.

7-9 SAMPLE PROBLEM SP7-4

Figure 7-15 shows an object that includes an irregular surface. Draw front and side orthographic and auxiliary views of the object. The procedure is described below. See Figure 7-16.

1. Draw the front and side views as defined in Chapter 5.

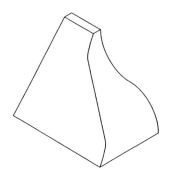

Figure 7-15

2. Draw two reference lines: RPF between the front and side views, and RPA parallel to the slanted surface in the side view.

Use Snap, Rotate to align the crosshairs with the slanted surface.

3. Define points along the irregular surface edge line in the front view and project the points into the side view using horizontal lines.
4. Project the points into the auxiliary view using lines perpendicular to line RPA. Label the points and their projection lines.
5. Transfer the depth measurements from RPS and the object's features and the points defining the irregular curve to the auxiliary view.

Type Dist in response to a command prompt to determine the distance from RPF to the points. Record the distances.

    A = 3.00
    B = 2.91
    C = 2.62
    D = 1.50
    E = 0.30
    F = 0.09
    G = 0

Use Offset to draw lines parallel to RPA.

6. Use Polyline, Edit Polyline, Fit Curve as explained in Section 5-26 to draw the irregular curve required in the auxiliary view. Use Edit Vertex to smooth the curve, if necessary.
7. Project the points defined in the front view to the back surface (far right vertical line) in the side view, and project the points into the auxiliary view.
8. Use Polyline, Edit Polyline, Fit Curve to draw the required irregular curve.
9. Erase and trim any excess lines and save the drawing, if desired.

7-10 SAMPLE PROBLEM SP7-5

Figure 7-17 shows a top view and an auxiliary view of an object. Redraw the given views and add the front and right-side views. The procedure is described below.

1. Draw a reference plane line, RPA, parallel to the auxiliary view and a reference plane line, RPT, a horizontal line.

The object contains a dihedral angle, and the auxiliary view was aligned with the vertex line of the angle.

Figure 7-16

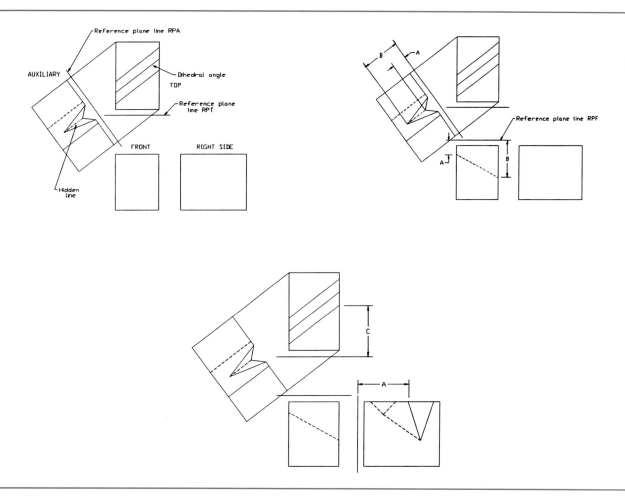

Figure 7-17

Reference plane RPA is perpendicular to the vertex of the di-hedral angle's vertex.

2. Project information from the top view and transfer information from the auxiliary view into the front view.
3. Project information from the front view and transfer information from the top view into the side view.
4. Erase and trim any excess lines and save the drawing, if desired.

7-11 PARTIAL AUXILIARY VIEWS

Auxiliary views help present true-shaped views of slanted and oblique surfaces, but in doing so generate fore-shortened views of other surfaces. It is often clearer to cre-ate an auxiliary view of just the slanted surface and omit the surfaces that would be foreshortened. Auxiliary views that show only one surface of an object are called *partial auxiliary views.*

Figure 7-18 shows a front view and three partial views of the object: a partial top view and two partial auxiliary views. A broken line (see Section 6-14) may be used to show that the partial auxiliary view is part of a larger view that has been omitted. Likewise, hidden lines may or may not be included. Figure 7-19 shows a front, side, and two partial auxiliary views of an object. Both the hidden lines and broken lines were omitted. If you are unsure about the interpretation of a view with hidden lines omit-ted, add a note to the drawing next to the partial views: ALL HIDDEN LINES OMITTED FOR CLARITY.

7-12 SECTIONAL AUXILIARY VIEWS

Sectional views may also be drawn as auxiliary views. Figure 7-20 shows an auxiliary sectional view. The cutting plane line is positioned across the object. A refer-ence plane line is drawn parallel to the cutting plane line, and information is projected into the auxiliary sectional view, using lines perpendicular to the cutting plane line.

Figure 7-18

Figure 7-19

Figure 7-21 shows front, partial auxiliary, and auxiliary sectional views of an object. In this example the partial sectional view was used to help clarify the shape of the object's feature that would appear vague in the normal top or side views.

7-13 AUXILIARY VIEWS OF OBLIQUE SURFACES

The true shape of an oblique surface cannot be determined by a single auxiliary view taken directly from the oblique surface. An auxiliary view shows the true shape of

Figure 7-20

Figure 7-21

Figure 7-22

a surface only when it is taken at exactly 90° to the surface. The auxiliary views taken for Sample Problems 1 through 5 were taken off slanted surfaces.

Slanted surfaces are surfaces that are rotated about only one axis. See Figure 7-22. One of the orthographic views must be an edge view of the surface (the surface appears as a line) for an auxiliary view created by projecting lines perpendicular to that view to show the true shape of the surface.

Oblique surfaces are surfaces rotated about two axes. See Figures 7-22 and 7-23. This means that none of the normal orthographic views will show the oblique surface as an edge view; there is no given end view of the surface. This in turn means that an auxiliary view taken directly from one of the given views will not be perpendicular to the surface and therefore will not show the true shape of the surface. An auxiliary view that shows an edge view of the surface must first be created, then a second auxiliary taken perpendicular to one of the other normal orthographic views is needed to show the true shape of the surface.

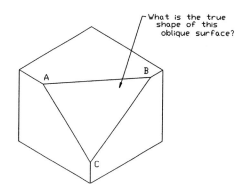

Figure 7-24

7-14 SECONDARY AUXILIARY VIEWS

Consider the object shown in Figure 7-24. What is the true shape of surface A-B-C? An auxiliary view taken perpendicular to the surface will show its true shape, but what is the angle for a plane perpendicular to the surface?

Figure 7-25 shows the normal orthographic views of the object.

Start by choosing an edge line in the plane that is perpendicular to either the X or Y axis. Edge line A-B in the front view is a horizontal line, so it is parallel to the X axis. Take an auxiliary view aligned with the top view of the edge line (you're looking straight down the line). This auxiliary view will be perpendicular to the edge line and will generate an end view of the plane. A second auxiliary view can then be taken perpendicular to the end view that will show the true shape of the surface.

Figure 7-26 shows how a secondary auxiliary view is created for the object shown in Figure 7-24. The specific procedure is as follows.

Figure 7-23

Figure 7-25

Figure 7-26

To draw the first auxiliary view

1. Draw the normal orthographic views of the object.
2. Draw a reference plane, RPT, between the front and top views.
3. Extend a line from the top view of line A-B in the area for the first auxiliary view.

The Extend command can be used by drawing a construction line slightly beyond the expected area of the first auxiliary view, then using the construction line as an Extend boundary line (see Section 2-24), and extending line A-B to the boundary. The construction line can then be erased.

4. Draw a reference plane line, RPA1, perpendicular to the line A-B extension.

Use Snap, Rotate to align the crosshairs with the extension line. The Dist command can be used to determine the line's angle if it is not known.

5. Project the feature of the object into the auxiliary view using lines perpendicular to RPA1.
6. Transfer the distance measurements from RPT and the front view as shown.
7. Erase and trim any excess lines and create the first auxiliary view.

The surface A-B-C should appear as a straight line. This is an edge view of surface A-B-C.

To draw the secondary auxiliary view

1. Use Snap, Rotate and align the crosshairs with the end view of surface A-B-C. Dist can be used to determine the angle of the edge view line.
2. Draw a reference plane line, RPA2, parallel to the edge view of the surface.
3. Project the features of the object into the second auxiliary view using lines perpendicular to RPA2.
4. Transfer the distance measurements from RPA1 and the top view as shown.
5. Erase and trim any excess lines and save the drawing, if desired.

The secondary auxiliary view shows the true shape of surface A-B-C.

Figure 7-27 shows another example of a secondary auxiliary view used to show the true shape of an oblique surface. In this example the first auxiliary view was taken from line F-A in the front view because it is a vertical line in the side view. The distance measurements came from the top view. The procedure used is the same as described above.

The auxiliary view shown in Figure 7-27 includes only the oblique surface. This is a partial auxiliary view. The purpose of the auxiliary view is to determine the true shape of the oblique surface. All the other surfaces would be foreshortened, not their true shape, if included in the auxiliary views.

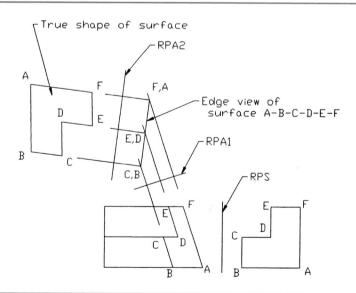

Figure 7-27

7-15 SAMPLE PROBLEM SP7-6

What is the true shape of the plane shown in Figure 7-28?

None of the edge lines are horizontal or vertical lines, so a line must be defined within the plane that is either horizontal or vertical. The added line can then be used to generate the two auxiliary views needed to define the true shape of the plane.

The procedure is as follows. See Figure 7-29.

1. Draw a horizontal line from point A in the front view.

Use Osnap, Intersection with Ortho on and draw the line across the view. Use Trim to remove the excess portion of the line.

2. Define the intersection of the new line with one of the plane's edge lines (D-C) as x.

3. Project line A-x into the top view.

Option: Create a layer for projection lines.
The location of point A is already known in the top view. The location of point x in the top view can be found by drawing a vertical line from point x in the front view so that the line intersects line D-C in the top view. Use Osnap, Intersection, Ortho on to ensure accuracy.

4. Extend line A-x into the area for the first auxiliary view.

Draw a construction line to use as a boundary line for the Extend command.

5. Draw two reference plane lines: RPT between the front and top views, and RPA1 perpendicular to the extension of line A-x.

Use Snap, Rotate to align the crosshairs with the extension of line A-x.

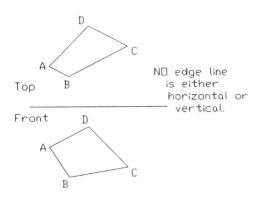

Figure 7-28

Figure 7-29

6. Project the plane's corner points into the area of the first auxiliary view from the top view. Transfer the distance measurements from RPT and the front view.

Use Dist to determine the distance from RPF and the corner points of the surface. Use Offset to transfer the point distance from RPF to RPA1. Use Trim to remove the internal portion of the offset lines. This will help clarify the drawing by removing excess lines from the auxiliary view but will retain intersection points needed to draw lines using Osnap, Intersection.

The plane should appear as a straight line, the end view of the plane.

7. Draw a third reference plane line, RPA2, parallel to the end view of the plane and project the plane's corner points into the secondary auxiliary view area.
8. Transfer the depth distances from RPA1 and the top view to RPA2 and the secondary auxiliary view.
9. Erase and trim any excess lines and save the drawing, if desired.

The secondary auxiliary view shows the true shape of surface A-B-C-D.

7-16 SECONDARY AUXILIARY VIEW OF AN ELLIPSE

Figure 7-30 shows the front and side views of an oblique surface and includes a foreshortened view of a hole, that is, an ellipse. Also included are two auxiliary views, the second of which shows the hole as a circle.

The ellipse is projected by first determining the correct projection angle that will produce an edge view of surface A-B-C-D. In this example, line B-C appears as a vertical line in the side view, so its front view can be used to project the required edge view.

It is known that the secondary view of the surface will show the hole as a circle, so only a radius value need be carried between the views. In this example, point 1 in the front view was projected into the first auxiliary view and then into the second auxiliary view, thereby defining the radius of the circle.

The hole is located at the center of the surface, which means that its centerlines are located on the midpoints of the edge lines in the secondary auxiliary views. If the hole's center point was not in the center of the surface, the intersections of the hole's centerlines with the surface's edge lines would also have to be projected into the secondary auxiliary view to accurately locate the hole.

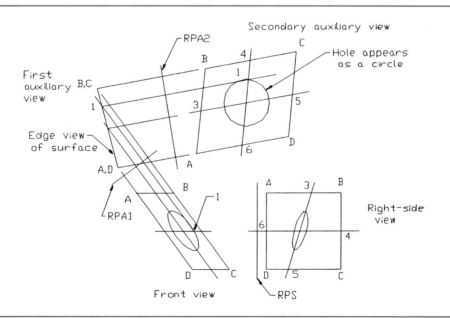

Figure 7-30

7-17 EXERCISE PROBLEMS

Given the outlines for front, side, and auxiliary views as shown, substitute one of the side views shown in Exercise Problems EX7-1A to EX7-1D and complete the front and auxiliary views. All dimensions are in millimeters.

EX7-1A

EX7-1B

NOTE: This surface is 10 from and parallel to the top surface.

EX7-1C

EX7-1D

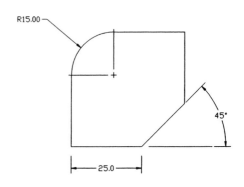

Given the outlines for front, side, and auxiliary views as shown, substitute one of the side views shown in Exercise Problems EX7-2A to EX7-2D and complete the front and auxiliary views. All dimensions are in millimeters.

Draw two orthographic views and an auxiliary view for each of the objects shown.

EX7-2A

EX7-2B

EX7-2C

EX7-2D

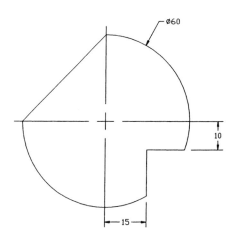

Draw two orthographic views and an auxiliary view for each of the objects in Exercise Problems EX7-3 to EX7-6.

EX7-3 MILLIMETERS

EX7-5 INCHES

EX7-4 MILLIMETERS

EX7-6 MILLIMETERS

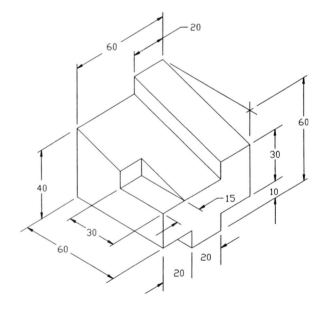

Redraw the given orthographic views in Exercise Problems EX7-7 to EX7-10 and add the appropriate auxiliary view.

EX7-7 MILLIMETERS

EX7-9 INCHES

EX7-8 MILLIMETERS

NOTE: ALL FILLETS AND ROUNDS = R15

EX7-10 MILLIMETERS

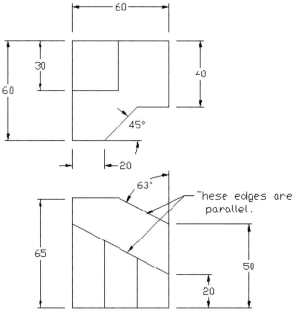

Draw two orthographic views and an auxiliary view for each of the objects in Exercise Problems EX7-11 to EX7-40.

EX7-11 MILLIMETERS

EX7-14 MILLIMETERS

EX7-12 MILLIMETERS

EX7-15 INCHES

EX7-13 MILLIMETERS

EX7-16 INCHES

EX7-17 MILLIMETERS

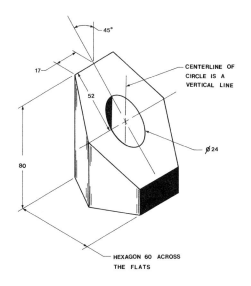

45°
17
52
80
CENTERLINE OF
CIRCLE IS A
VERTICAL LINE
Ø 24
HEXAGON 60 ACROSS
THE FLATS

EX7-20 INCHES

2.69
1.00
1.00
1.94
2 LARGE HOLES -.75 DIA
1 SMALL HOLE -.50 DIA
.75
.88
.38
.75
1.25 2.75
1.50

EX7-18 MILLIMETERS

Ø 13
15
30
70
15
80
1.00
BOTH
SIDES
35
75°
50
15
12
R
10
8
50
15

EX7-21 MILLIMETERS

Ø 50
60
2 PLACES
30
6
12 — 4 PLACES
35
15
80
REGULAR HEXAGON
80 ACROSS THE CORNER

EX7-19 MILLIMETERS

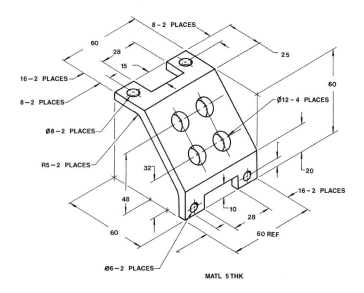

8 — 2 PLACES
60
28
25
15
16 — 2 PLACES
60
8 — 2 PLACES
Ø12 — 4 PLACES
Ø8 — 2 PLACES
R5 — 2 PLACES
32
20
16 — 2 PLACES
48
10
28
60
60 REF
Ø6 — 2 PLACES
MATL 5 THK

EX7-22 MILLIMETERS

EX7-25 INCHES

EX7-23 INCHES

EX7-26 MILLIMETERS

EX7-24 MILLIMETERS

ALL FILLETS AND ROUNDS = R3

EX7-27 MILLIMETERS

EX7-28 MILLIMETERS

EX7-31 INCHES

EX7-29 MILLIMETERS

EX7-32 MILLIMETERS

EX7-30 MILLIMETERS

EX7-33 MILLIMETERS

EX7-34 MILLIMETERS

EX7-35 MILLIMETERS

EX7-36 INCHES

EX7-37 INCHES

EX7-38 INCHES

EX7-39 MILLIMETERS

EX7-40 MILLIMETERS

Draw at least two orthographic views and one auxiliary view for the following objects.

EX7-41 INCHES

EX7-43 INCHES

EX7-42 INCHES

EX7-44 INCHES

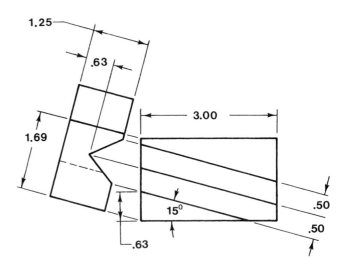

Use a secondary auxiliary view to find the true shape of the planes in Exercise Problems EX7-45 to EX7-50.

EX7-45 MILLIMETERS

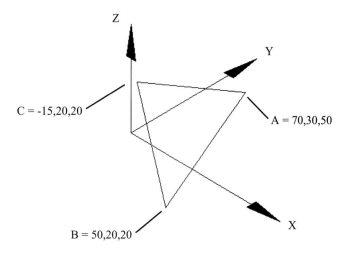

C = -15,20,20
A = 70,30,50
B = 50,20,20

EX7-46 MILLIMETERS

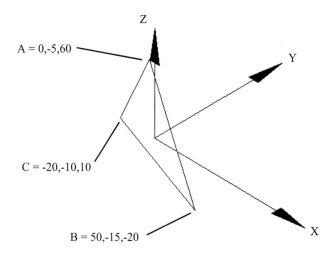

A = 0,-5,60
C = -20,-10,10
B = 50,-15,-20

EX7-47 MILLIMETERS

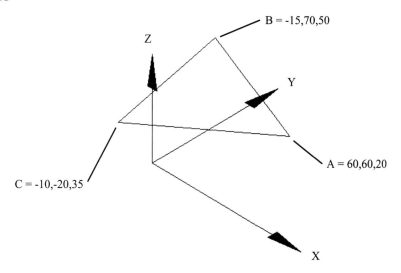

B = -15,70,50
A = 60,60,20
C = -10,-20,35

EX7-48 INCHES (SCALE: 4:1)

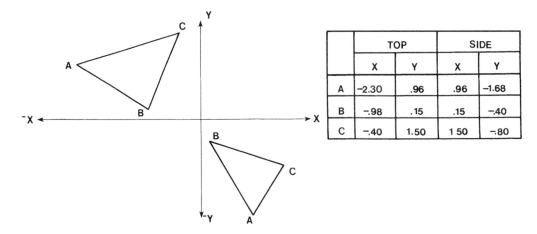

	TOP		SIDE	
	X	Y	X	Y
A	-2.30	.96	.96	-1.68
B	-.98	.15	.15	-.40
C	-.40	1.50	1 50	-.80

EX7-49 MILLIMETERS (SCALE: 2:1)

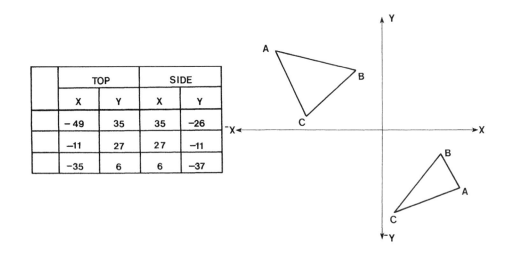

	TOP		SIDE	
	X	Y	X	Y
	− 49	35	35	-26
	−11	27	27	-11
	−35	6	6	-37

EX7-50 INCHES (SCALE: 3:1)

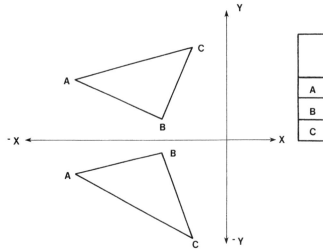

	FRONT		TOP	
	X	Y	X	Y
A	-2.80	-.60	-2.80	1.05
B	-1.17	-20	-1.17	.35
C	-.61	-1.62	-.61	1.62

EX7-51 MILLIMETERS

Redesign the following object to include two Ø10 holes in the slanted surface. The holes should be centered along the longitudinal axis, and spaced so that the distance between the holes' centers equals the distance from the holes' centers to the upper and lower edges of the slanted surface. The holes should be perpendicular to the slanted surface.

Draw the front, top, and side views of the object plus an auxiliary view of the slanted surface.

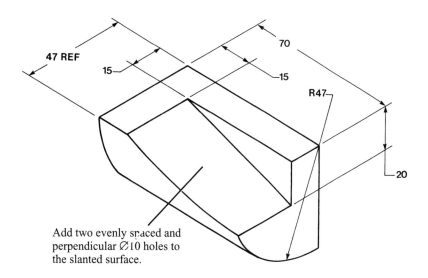

Add two evenly spaced and perpendicular Ø10 holes to the slanted surface.

EX7-52 MILLIMETERS

Redesign the following object so that the outside shape is a regular heptagon (seven-sided polygon) 80 across the flats, and the inside Ø50 hole is intersected by six evenly spaced slots each 12 wide. Draw front and top orthographic views and an auxiliary view of the object.

EX7-53 MILLIMETERS

Calculate the area of the following plane. Redesign the plane so that the new plane is congruent to the original but has an area equal to 1.5 times the original area. Draw and label the true shape of the new plane relative to the X, Y, Z axes.

CHAPTER 8

Dimensioning

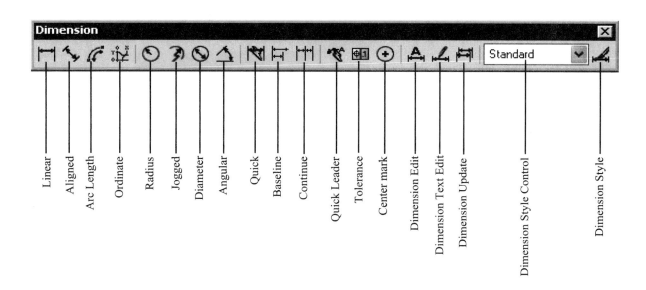

Figure 8-1

8-1 INTRODUCTION

This chapter explains the Dimension toolbar. See Figure 8-1. The chapter first explains dimensioning terminology and conventions, then presents an explanation of each tool within the Dimension toolbar. The chapter also demonstrates how dimensions are applied to drawings and gives examples of standard drawing conventions and practices.

8-2 TERMINOLOGY AND CONVENTIONS

Some common terms (See Figure 8-2.)

Dimension lines: Mechanical drawings contain lines between extension lines that end with arrowheads and include a numerical dimensional value located within the line; architectural drawings contain lines between extension lines that end with tick marks and include a numerical dimensional value above the line.

Extension lines: Lines that extend away from an object and allow dimensions to be located off the surface of an object.

Leader lines: Lines drawn at an angle, not horizontal or vertical, that are used to dimension specific shapes such as holes. The start point of a leader line includes an arrowhead. Numerical values are drawn at the end opposite the arrowhead.

Linear dimensions: Dimensions that define the straight-line distance between two points.

Angular dimensions: Dimensions that define the angular value, measured in degrees, between two straight lines.

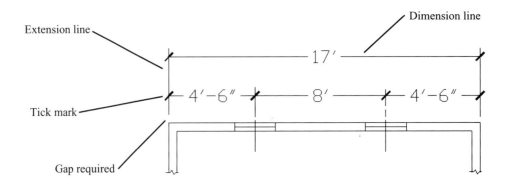

Figure 8-2

Some dimensioning conventions (See Figure 8-3.)

1. Dimension lines are drawn evenly spaced; that is, the distance between dimension lines is uniform. A general rule of thumb is to locate dimension lines about 1/2 inch, or 15 millimeters, apart.
2. There should be a noticeable gap between the edge of a part and the beginning of an extension line. This serves as a visual break between the object and the extension line. The visual difference between the linetypes can be emphasized by using different colors for the two types of lines.
3. Leader lines are used to define the size of holes and should be positioned so that the arrowhead points at the center of the hole.
4. Centerlines may be used as extension lines. No gap is used when a centerline is extended beyond the edge lines of an object.
5. Dimension lines should be aligned whenever possible to give the drawing a neat, organized appearance.

Some common errors (See Figure 8-4.)

1. Avoid crossing extension lines. Place longer dimensions farther away from the object than shorter dimensions.
2. Do not locate dimensions within cutouts; always use extension lines.
3. Do not locate any dimension too close to the object. Dimension lines should be at least 1/2 inch, or 15 millimeters, from the edge of the object.
4. Avoid long extension lines. Locate dimensions in the same general area as the feature being defined.

Figure 8-3

Figure 8-4

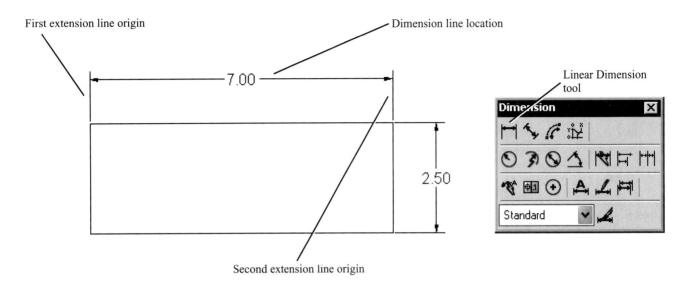

First extension line origin

Dimension line location

Linear Dimension tool

7.00

2.50

Second extension line origin

Figure 8-5

8-3 LINEAR DIMENSION

The Linear Dimension command is used to create horizontal and vertical dimensions.

To create a horizontal dimension by selecting extension lines (See Figure 8-5.)

1. Select the Linear Dimension tool from the Dimension toolbar.

   Command: _dimlinear
   Specify first extension line origin or <select object>:

2. Select the starting point for the first extension line.

   Specify second extension line origin:

3. Select the starting point for the second extension line.

   [MText/Text/Angle/Horizontal/Vertical/Rotated]:

4. Locate the dimension line by moving the crosshairs.
5. Press the left mouse button when the desired dimension line location has been selected.

The dimensional value locations shown in Figure 8-5 are the default settings locations. The location and style may be changed using the Dimension Style command discussed in Section 8-4.

To create a vertical dimension

The vertical dimension shown in Figure 8-5 was created using the same procedure demonstrated for the hori-

zontal dimension, except different extension line origin points were selected. AutoCAD will automatically switch from horizontal to vertical dimension lines as you move the cursor around the object.

If there is confusion between horizontal and vertical lines when adding dimensions, that is, you don't seem to be able to generate a vertical line, type V and press Enter in response to the following prompt:

   [MText/Text/Angle/Horizontal/Vertical/Rotated]:

The system will now draw vertical dimension lines.

To create a horizontal dimension by selecting the object to be dimensioned (See Figure 8-6.)

1. Select the Linear Dimension tool from the Dimension toolbar.

   Command: _dimlinear
   Specify first extension line origin or <select object>:

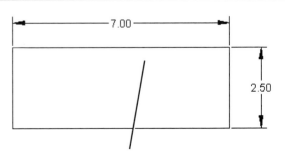

7.00

2.50

Select this line for dimensioning; extension lines will be added automatically.

Figure 8-6

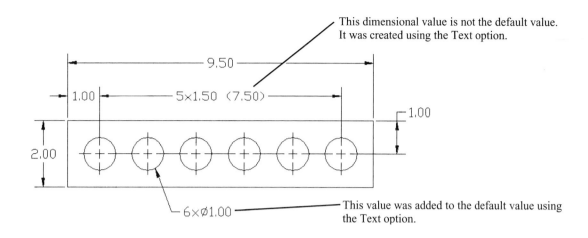

This dimensional value is not the default value.
It was created using the Text option.

This value was added to the default value using
the Text option.

Figure 8-7

2. Press the right mouse button.

   Select object to Dimension:

3. Select the line to be dimensioned.

   This option allows you to select the distance to be dimensioned directly. The option applies only to horizontal and vertical lengths. Aligned dimensions, although linear, are created using the Aligned Dimension tool.

**To change the default dimension text—
Text option**

   AutoCAD will automatically create a text value for a given linear distance. A different value or additional information may be added as follows. See Figure 8-7.

1. Select the Linear Dimension tool from the Dimension toolbar.

   Command: _dimlinear
   Specify first extension line origin or <select object>:

2. Select the starting point for the first extension line.

   Specify second extension line origin:

3. Select the starting point for the second extension line.

   [MText/Text/Angle/Horizontal/Vertical/Rotated]:

4. Type t; press Enter.

   Enter dimension text <7.50>:

The value given will be the linear value of the distance selected. In this example more information is required, so the default distance value must be modified.

5. Type 5 × 1.50 (7.50); press Enter.

   The typed dimension will appear on the screen and can be located by moving the cursor.

**To change the default dimension text—
Mtext option**

1. Select the Linear Dimension tool from the Dimension toolbar.

   Command: _dimlinear
   Specify first extension line origin or <select object>:

2. Select the starting point for the first extension line.

   Specify second extension line origin:

3. Select the starting point for the second extension line.

   [MText/Text/Angle/Horizontal/Vertical/Rotated]:

4. Type m; press Enter.

   The Text Formatting dialog box will appear. See Figure 8-8. The text value will appear in a box below the Text Formatting dialog box. To remove the existing text, highlight the text and press the Delete key. New text can then be typed into the box. In the example shown, the default value of 7.0000 was replaced with a value of 7.00.

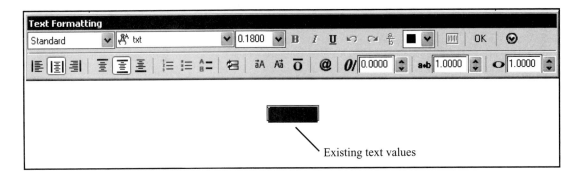

Figure 8-8

Information can be added before or after the default text by placing the cursor in the appropriate place and typing the additional information. For example, placing the cursor to the right of the text value box and typing -2 PLACES would yield a final value of 7.00-2 PLACES on the drawing.

The Text Formatting dialog box can be used to edit the dimension text in the same way as it was used to edit drawing screen text (Section 2-16). Figure 8-9 shows the Font pull-down menu.

Figure 8-10 shows the color pull-down menu that may be used to change the color of a dimension.

To edit an existing dimension

The Dimension Text Edit tool, located on the Dimension toolbar, is used to change the text justification or style. See Figure 8-11. The New option of the Dimension Edit tool located on the Dimension toolbar may be used to edit an existing dimensional value. See Figure 8-12. Figure 8-13 shows a revised dimensional text value.

Figure 8-9

Figure 8-10

Figure 8-11

Figure 8-12

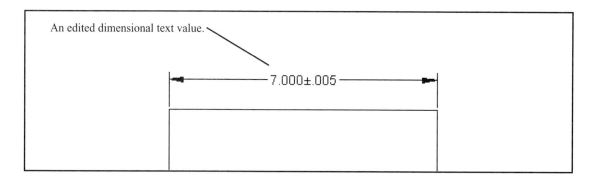

Figure 8-13

8-4 DIMENSION STYLES

The Dimension Style command opens a group of dialog boxes that are used to control the appearance of dimensions. Figure 8-14 shows the Dimension Style tool on the Dimension toolbar.

A great variety of styles are used to create technical drawings. The style difference may be the result of different drawing conventions. For example, architects locate dimensions above the dimension lines, and mechanical engineers locate the dimensions within the dimension lines. AutoCAD works in decimal units for either millimeters or inches, so parameters set for inches would not be usable for millimeter drawings. The Dimension Style command allows you to conveniently choose and set dimension parameters that suit your particular drawing requirements.

Figure 8-15 shows the Dimension Style Manager dialog box. This section will explain how to use the Modify option to change the Standard style settings to suit a specific drawing requirement. The Set Current, New, Override, and Compare options are used to create a new custom dimension style designed to meet specific applications. Figure 8-16 shows the Primary Units option of the Modify Dimension Style: Standard dialog box.

To change the scale of a drawing

Drawings are often drawn to scale because the actual part is either too big to fit on a sheet of drawing paper or too small to be seen. For example, a microchip circuit must be drawn at several thousand times its actual size to be seen.

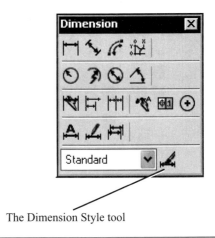

The Dimension Style tool

Figure 8-14

Drawing scales are written using the following formats.

SCALE: 1=1
SCALE: FULL
SCALE: 1000=1
SCALE: .25=1

In each example the value on the left indicates the scale factor. A value greater than 1 indicates that the drawing is larger than actual size. A value less than 1 indicates that the drawing is smaller than actual size.

Regardless of the drawing scale selected, the dimension values must be true size. Figure 8-17 shows the same rectangle drawn at two different scales. The top rectangle is drawn at a scale of 1=1, or its true size. The bottom

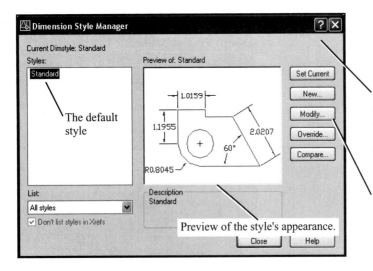

The Dimension Style Manager dialog box can be used to create and modify custom dimension styles designed to meet specific applications.

The Modify box is used to make changes to the existing standard values.

Preview of the style's appearance.

The default style

Figure 8-15

Change this value to change the scale of the drawing.

Figure 8-16

rectangle is drawn at a scale of 2=1, or twice its true size. In both examples the 3.00 dimension remains the same.

The Measurement scale box on the Primary Units option on the Modify Dimension Style: Standard dialog box is used to change the dimension values to match different drawing scales. Figure 8-18 shows the measurement scale set to a factor of 0.5000. If the drawing scale is 2=1,

as shown in Figure 8-17, then the scale factor for the Measurement scale must be 0.5000. Compare the preview in Figure 8-16 with the preview in Figure 8-18, where the scale factor has been changed.

To use the Text option

Figure 8-19 shows the Text option on the Modify Dimension Style: Standard dialog box. This option can be used to

Figure 8-17

Figure 8-18

Figure 8-19

New text height

Resulting changes

Figure 8-20

change the height of dimension text or the text placement. In Figure 8-20 the text height was changed from the default value of 0.1800 to a value of 0.3500. The preview box shows the resulting changes in both the text and how it will be positioned on the drawing.

Figure 8-21 shows text located above the dimension lines and positioned nearer the first extension line. These changes were created using the Vertical and Horizontal options within the Text placement box.

Figure 8-22 shows text aligned with the direction of the dimension lines in accordance with ISO standards. This change was created using the ISO standard radio button within the Text alignment box.

Resulting changes

Changes in text placement

Figure 8-21

Resulting changes

Change in text alignment—use ISO Standard.

Figure 8-22

Figure 8-23

Figure 8-25

8-5 UNITS

It is important to understand that dimensional values are not the same as mathematical units. Dimensional values are manufacturing instructions and always include a tolerance, even if the tolerance value is not stated. Manufacturers use a predefined set of standard dimensions that are applied to any dimensional value that does not include a written tolerance. Standard tolerance values differ from organization to organization. Figure 8-23 shows a chart of standard tolerances.

In Figure 8-24 a distance is dimensioned twice: once as 5.50 and a second time as 5.5000. Mathematically these two values are equal, but they are not the same manufacturing instruction. The 5.50 value could, for example, have a standard tolerance of ±0.01, whereas the 5.5000 value could have a standard tolerance of ±0.0005. A tolerance of ±0.0005 is more difficult and therefore more expensive to manufacture than a tolerance of ±0.01.

Figure 8-24

Figure 8-25 shows examples of units expressed in millimeters, decimal inches, and architectural units. A zero is not required to the left of the decimal point for decimal inch values less than one. Millimeter values do not require zeros to the right of the decimal point. Architectural units should always include the feet (′) and inch (″) symbols. Millimeter and decimal inch values never include symbols; the units will be defined in the title block of the drawing.

To prevent a 0 from appearing to the left of the decimal point

1. Select the Dimension Style tool.

   The Dimension Style dialog box will appear.

2. Select Modify.

   The Modify Dimension Style: Standard dialog box will appear.

3. Select the Primary Units option.

   The Primary Units dialog box will appear. See Figure 8-26.

4. Click the box to the left of the word Leading within the Zero suppression box.

   A check mark will appear in the box indicating that the function is on.

5. Select OK to return to the drawing.

   Save the change, if desired. You can now dimension using any of the dimension commands; no zeros will appear to the left of the decimal point. Figure 8-27 shows the results.

Turn the Leading option on to prevent zeros to the left of the decimal point.

Turn the Trailing option on to prevent zeros to the right of the decimal point.

Figure 8-26

To change the number of decimal places in a dimension value

1. Select the Dimension Style tool.

    The Dimension Style Manager dialog box will appear.

2. Select Modify.

    The Modify Dimension Style: Standard dialog box will appear.

3. Select the Primary Units option.
4. Select the arrow to the right of the Precision box.

    A list of precision options will cascade down. See Figure 8-28.

5. Select the desired value.

    Save the changes, if desired. You can now dimension using any of the dimension commands, and the resulting values will be expressed using the selected precision.

Figure 8-27

Figure 8-28

8-6 ALIGNED DIMENSIONS (See Figures 8-29 and 8-30.)

To create an aligned dimension

1. Select the Aligned Dimension tool.

   Command: _dimaligned
   Specify first extension line origin or <select object>:

2. Select the first extension line origin point.

   Specify second extension line origin:

3. Select the second extension line origin point.

   [Mtext/ Text/ Angle]:

4. Select the location for the dimension line.

The Select Object option

1. Select the Aligned Dimension tool.

   Command: _dimaligned
   Specify first extension line origin or <select object>:

2. Press the Return key.

   Select object to dimension:

3. Select the line.

   [Mtext/ Text/ Angle]:

4. Select the dimension line location.

A response of M to the last prompt line will activate the Multiline Text option. The Text Formatting dialog box will appear. The Text option can be used to replace or supplement the default text generated by AutoCAD. The Multiline Text option is discussed in Section 2-16.

A dimension aligned using the Aligned with Dimension line option on the Modify Dimension Style: Standard dialog box.

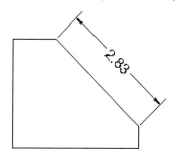

This format can also be achieved using the Angle option within the Aligned Dimension command.

Figure 8-29

A response of A to the prompt will activate the Angle option. The Angle option allows you to change the angle of the text within the dimension line. See Figure 8-30. The default angle value is 0 degrees, or horizontal. The example shown in Figure 8-29 used an angle of $-45°$. The prompt responses are as follows.

Specify angle of dimension text:
[MTExt/ Text/ Angle]:

1. Type -45; press Enter.
2. Select the location for the dimension.

8-7 RADIUS AND DIAMETER DIMENSIONS

Figure 8-31 shows an object that includes both arcs and circles. The general rule is to dimension arcs using a radius dimension, and circles using diameter dimensions.

A dimension aligned with the Horizontal option on the Modify Dimension Styles on the aligned dimension tool.

Figure 8-30

Figure 8-31

Radius
Dimension
tool

R.50

Figure 8-32

This convention is consistent with the tooling required to produce the feature shape. Any arc greater than 180° is considered a circle and is dimensioned using a diameter.

To create a radius dimension

1. Select the Radius Dimension tool.

   Command: _dimradius
   Select arc or circle:

2. Select the arc to be dimensioned.

   Specify dimension line location or [Mtext/Text/Angle]:

3. Position the radius dimension so that its leader line is not horizontal or vertical.

   Figure 8-32 shows the resulting dimension. The dimension text and the angle of the text can be altered using the (MText/Text/Angle) options in the last prompt. In the example shown, it would be better to add the words 4 PLACES to the radius dimension than to include four radius dimensions.

R.50 - 4 PLACES

Figure 8-34

To alter the default dimensions

1. Select the Radius Dimension tool.

   Command: _dimradius
   Select arc or circle:

2. Select the arc to be dimensioned.

   Specify dimension line location or [Mtext/Text/Angle]:

3. Type M; press Enter.

   The Text Formatting dialog box will appear.

4. Place the flashing cursor just to the right of the dimension value box and type - 4 PLACES.

   See Figure 8-33.

5. Select OK.

   Figure 8-34 shows the resulting dimension. The Radius Dimension command will automatically include a center point with the dimension. The center point can be excluded from the dimension as follows.

Type -4 places to the right of the dimension value.

Figure 8-33

Figure 8-35

To remove the center mark from a radius dimension

1. Select the Dimension Style tool.

   The Dimension Style Manager dialog box will appear.

2. Select Modify.

   The Modify Dimension Style: Standard dialog box will appear.

3. Select the Symbols and Arrows option.
4. Select the None radio button in the Center marks area.

   A solid circle will appear in the preview box, indicating that it is on. See Figure 8-35.

5. Select OK to return to the drawing.

   You will have to redimension the arc, including the text alteration. Figure 8-36 shows the results.

To create a diameter dimension

   Circles require three dimensions: a diameter value plus two linear dimensions used to locate the circle's center point. AutoCAD can be configured to automatically add horizontal and vertical centerlines as follows.

1. Select the Dimension Style tool.

   The Dimension Style Manager dialog box will appear.

2. Select Modify.

   The Modify Dimension Style: Standard dialog box will appear.

3. Select the Symbols and Arrows option.
4. Select the Line option from the Center marks box.
5. Select OK to return to the drawing.

   Centerlines will be added to the existing radius dimension.

6. Explode the radius dimension, then erase the radius centerlines.
7. Select the Diameter Dimension tool.

   Command: _dimdiameter
   Select arc or circle:

Figure 8-36

Figure 8-37

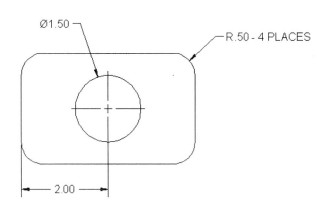

Figure 8-38

8. Select the circle.

   Specify dimension line location or [MText/Text/Angle]:

9. Locate the dimension away from the object so that the leader line is neither horizontal nor vertical.

   Figure 8-37 shows the results.

To add linear dimensions to given centerlines

1. Select the Linear Dimension tool.

   Command: _dimlinear
   Specify first extension line origin or <select object>:

2. Select the lower endpoint of the circle's vertical centerline.

   Specify second extension line origin:

3. Select the endpoint of the vertical edge line (the endpoint that joins with the corner arc).

   Figure 8-38 shows the results.

4. Repeat the above procedure to add the vertical dimension needed to locate the circle's center point.

5. Add the overall dimensions using the Linear Dimension command.

   Figure 8-39 shows the results. Radius and diameter dimensions are usually added to a drawing after the linear dimensions because they are less restricted in their locations. Linear dimensions are located close to the distance they are defining, whereas radius and diameter dimensions can be located farther away and use leader lines to identify the appropriate arc or circle.

   Avoid crossing extension and dimension lines with leader lines. See Figure 8-40.

Figure 8-39

Figure 8-40

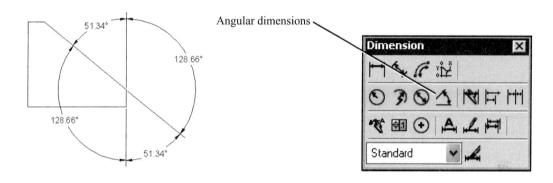

Figure 8-41

NOTE:

The diameter symbol can be added when using the Text Formatting dialog box by typing %%c or by using the Symbols option. See Figure 8-40. The characters %%c will appear on the Text Formatting screen but will be converted to the diameter symbol ∅ when the text is applied to the drawing.

8-8 ANGULAR DIMENSIONS

Figure 8-41 shows four possible angular dimensions that can be created using the Angular Dimension command. The extension lines and degree symbol will be added automatically.

To create an angular dimension (See Figure 8-42.)

1. Select the Angular Dimension tool.

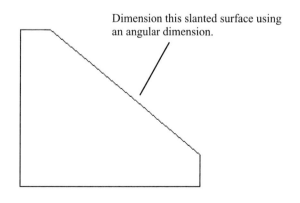

Figure 8-42

Command: _dimangular
Select arc, circle, line, or <specify vertex>:

2. Select the short vertical line on the lower right side of the object.

   Select second line:

3. Select the slanted line.

   Specify dimension arc line location [MText/Text/ Angle]:

4. Locate the text away from the object.

Figure 8-43 shows the results. It is considered better to use two extension lines for angular dimensions and to not have an arrowhead touch the surface of the part.

> **NOTE:**
>
> The degree symbol can be added when using the Text Formatting dialog box by using the Symbols option or by typing %%d. The characters %%d will appear on the Text Formatting screen, but will be converted to ° when the text is applied to the drawing.

Avoid overdimensioning

Figure 8-44 shows a shape dimensioned using an angular dimension. The shape is completely defined. Any additional dimension would be an error. It is tempting, in an effort to make sure a shape is completely defined, to add more dimensions, such as a horizontal dimension for the short horizontal edge at the top of the shape. This dimension is not needed and is considered double dimensioning.

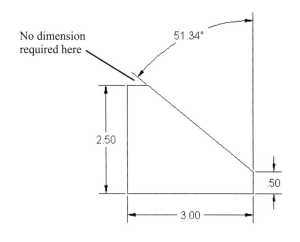

Figure 8-44

8-9 ORDINATE DIMENSIONS

Ordinate dimensions are dimensions based on an X,Y coordinate system. Ordinate dimensions do not include extension, or dimension lines, or arrowheads but simply horizontal and vertical leader lines drawn directly from the features of the object. Ordinate dimensions are particularly useful when dimensioning an object that includes many small holes.

Figure 8-45 shows an object that is to be dimensioned using ordinate dimensions. Ordinate dimensions are automatically calculated from the X, Y origin, or in this example, the lower left corner of the screen. If the object had been drawn with its lower left corner on the origin, you could proceed directly to the Ordinate Dimension command; however, the lower left corner of the object is currently located at X=3, Y=4. First move the origin to the corner of the object, then use the Ordinate Dimension command.

Figure 8-43

Figure 8-45

Select here to relocate the screen origin.

Figure 8-46

To move the origin

1. Select the Tools pull-down menu.

The Tools pull-down menu will cascade.

2. Select New UCS.

The New UCS menu will appear next to the Tools pull-down menu. See Figure 8-46.

3. Select Origin.

Specify new origin point <0,0,0>:

4. Select the lower left corner of the object.

The origin (0,0) is now located at the lower left corner of the object. This can be verified by looking at the coordinate display at the lower left corner of the screen.

The origin icon may move to the lower left corner as shown in Figure 8-47, depending on your computer's settings. The tool can be moved back to the original screen location as follows.

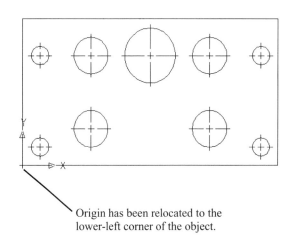

Origin has been relocated to the lower-left corner of the object.

Figure 8-47

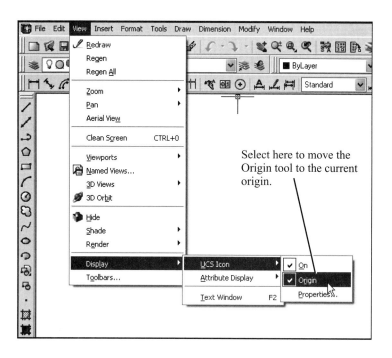

Select here to move the Origin tool to the current origin.

Figure 8-48

To move the Origin tool

1. Select the View pull-down menu, then Display.

The Display menu will appear next to the View pull-down menu. See Figure 8-48.

2. Select the UCS icon, then Origin.

The Origin tool will go to the current origin.

To add ordinate dimensions to an object

The following procedure assumes that you have already used the Dimension Style command (Section 8-4) to set the desired dimension style and that you have moved the origin to the lower left corner of the object as shown.

1. Turn the Ortho command on (click the ORTHO box at the bottom of the screen).
2. Select the Ordinate Dimension tool from the Dimension toolbar.

   Command: _dimordinate
   Select feature location:

3. Select the lower endpoint of the first circle's vertical centerline.

Specify leader endpoint or [Xdatum/Ydatum/MText/Text/Angle]:

4. Select a point along the X axis directly below the vertical centerline of the circle.

The ordinate value of the point will be added to the drawing. This point should have a 0.50 value. The text value may be modified using either the MText or Text option, or by using the Dimension Style Manager dialog box to define the precision of the text.

5. Press the right mouse button to restart the command and dimension the object's other features.
6. Extend the centerlines across the object and add the diameter dimensions for the holes.

Figure 8-49 shows the completed drawing. The Text option of the prompt shown in step 3 can be used to modify or remove the default text value.

8-10 BASELINE DIMENSIONS

Baseline dimensions are a series of dimensions that originate from a common baseline or datum line. Baseline dimensions are very useful because they help eliminate tolerance buildup associated with chain-type dimensions.

Ordinate dimensions

Figure 8-49

Baseline dimensions

The first line extension of this dimension, created using the Linear Dimension command, will become the baseline for the other dimensions.

Figure 8-50

The Baseline command can be used only after an initial dimension has been drawn. AutoCAD will define the first extension line origin of the initial dimension selected as the baseline for all baseline dimensions.

To use the Baseline Dimension command (See Figure 8-50.)

1. Select the Linear Dimension tool.

   Command: _dimlinear
   Specify first extension line origin or <select object>:

2. Select the upper left corner of the object.

   This selection determines the baseline.

   Specify second extension line origin:

3. Select the endpoint of the first circle's vertical centerline.

   Specify dimension line location or [Text/Angle/Horizontal/Vertical/Rotated]:

4. Select a location for the dimension line.

   Command:

5. Select the Baseline Dimension tool.

   Specify a second extension line origin or [Undo/Select] <Select>:

6. Select the endpoint of the next circle's vertical centerline.

   Specify a second extension line origin or [Undo/Select] <Select>:

7. Continue to select the circle centerlines until all circles are located.

   Specify a second extension line origin or [Undo/Select] <Select>:

8. Select the upper right corner of the object.
9. Press the right mouse button, then select Enter.

   This will end the Baseline Dimension command.

10. Repeat the preceding procedure for the vertical baseline dimensions.
11. Add the circles' diameter values.

   The Baseline Dimension option can also be used with the Angular Dimension command.

The second extension line of the previous dimension becomes the first extension line of the next dimension.

Figure 8-51

8-11 CONTINUE DIMENSION

The Continue Dimension command is used to create chain dimensions based on an initial linear, angular, or ordinate dimension. The second extension line's origin becomes the first extension line origin for the continued dimension.

To use the Continue Dimension command (See Figure 8-51.)

1. Select the Linear Dimension tool.

   Command: dimcontinue
   Specify first extension line origin or <select object>:

2. Select the upper left corner of the object.

   Specify second extension line origin:

3. Select the right endpoint of the uppermost horizontal line.

   Dimension line location (Text/Angle/Horizontal/Vertical/Rotated):

4. Select a dimension line location.

   Command:

5. Select the Continue Dimension tool.

   Command: _dimcontinue

Continue Dimension tool

Figure 8-52

Specify a second extension line origin or [Undo/ Select] <Select>:

6. Select the next linear distance to be dimensioned.

Specify a second extension line origin or [Undo/ Select] <Select>:

7. Continue until the object's horizontal edges are completely dimensioned.

AutoCAD will automatically align the dimensions. Figure 8-52 shows how the Continue Dimension command dimensions distances that are too small for both the arrowhead and dimension value to fit within the extension lines.

8-12 QUICK DIMENSION

The Quick Dimension tool is used to add a series of dimensions. See Figure 8-53.

To use the Quick Dimension command

1. Select the Quick Dimension tool from the Dimension toolbar.

   Command: _qdim
   Select geometry to dimension:

2. Select the left vertical edge line of the object to be dimensioned; press Enter.

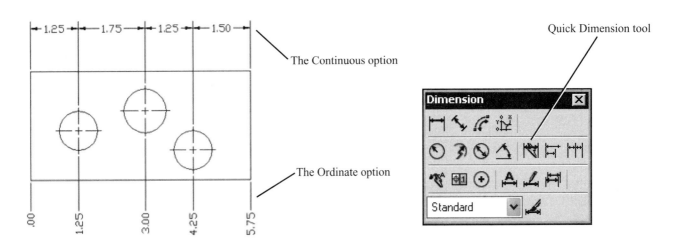

The Continuous option

Quick Dimension tool

The Ordinate option

Figure 8-53

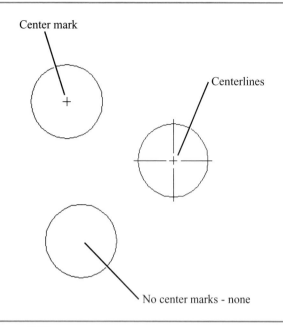

Center mark

Centerlines

No center marks - none

Figure 8-54

Specify dimension line position, or [Continuous/ Staggered/Baseline/Ordinate/Radius/Diameter/ datumPoint/Edit]<Baseline>:

3. Select the vertical centerline of the first hole.

   Select geometry to dimension:

4. Select the vertical centerline of the second hole.

   Select geometry to dimension:

5. Select the vertical centerline of the third hole.
6. Press the right mouse button.

   Specify dimension line position, or [Continuous/ Staggered/Baseline/Ordinate/Radius/Diameter/ datumPoint/Edit]<Baseline>:

7. Type c; press Enter.
8. Position the dimension lines, press the right mouse button, and enter the position.

The ordinate dimensions along the bottom of the object in Figure 8-53 were created by typing o rather than c in step 7.

8-13 CENTER MARK

When AutoCAD first draws a circle or arc, a center mark appears on the drawing; however, these marks will disappear when the Redraw View or Redraw All command is applied. See Figure 8-54.

To add centerlines to a given circle

1. Select the Dimension Style tool.

   The Dimension Style dialog box appears.

2. Select Modify, then the Symbols and Arrows option.

   The Modify Dimension Style: Standard dialog box will appear. See Figure 8-35.

3. Select the Line option.

   The preview display will show a horizontal and a vertical centerline.

4. Select OK to return to the drawing.
5. Select the Center Mark tool.

   Select arc or circle:

6. Select the circle.

Horizontal and vertical centerlines will appear. The size of the center mark can be controlled using the Size box in the Center marks box. If the centerline's size appears unacceptable, try different sizes until you get an acceptable size.

8-14 QUICK LEADER

Quick Leader lines are slanted lines that extend from notes or dimensions to a specific feature or location on the surface of a drawing. They usually end with an arrowhead or dot. The Radius and Diameter Dimension commands automatically create a leader line. The Quick Leader command can be used to add leader lines not associated with radius and diameter dimensions.

To create a leader line with text

1. Select the Leader tool.

   Command: _qleader
   Specify first leader point, or [Settings]<Settings>:

2. Select the starting point for the leader line.

   This is the point where the arrowhead will appear. In the example shown in Figure 8-55 the upper right corner of the object was selected.

   Specify next point:

3. Select the location of the endpoint of the slanted line segment.

   Specify next point:

Figure 8-55

4. Draw a short horizontal line segment; press Enter.

   Specify text width <0.0000>:

5. Press Enter.

   Enter first line of annotation text <MText>:

6. Press Enter.

   The Text Formatting dialog box will appear.

7. Use the cursor and extend the text box as needed.
8. Type the desired text. See Figure 8–56.
9. Click the OK button.

   The text will appear next to the horizontal line segment of the leader line.

To draw a leader line to the edge of a circle

The Quick Leader command automatically activates the Endpoint, Center, Intersection, and Extension Osnap commands. To point a leader at the ouside edge of a circle, these commands must be deactivated.

1. Select the Tools pull-down menu, then Drafting Settings, or the Object Snap Settings tool from the Object Snap toolbar.
2. Select the Object Snap option.

   The Drafting Settings dialog box will appear.

3. Select the Clear all box, then OK.
4. Select the Quick Leader tool.

   Command: _qleader
   Specify first leader point, or [Settings] <Settings>:

5. Select the edge of the circle being dimensioned and proceed as explained previously for drawing a leader line with text.

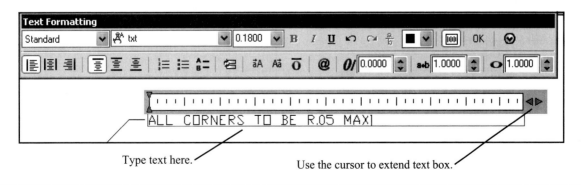

Type text here. Use the cursor to extend text box.

Figure 8-56

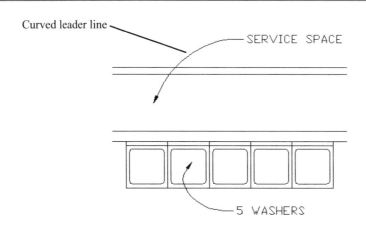

Curved leader line

SERVICE SPACE

5 WASHERS

Figure 8-57

To draw a curved leader line

The Leader command can be used to draw curved leader lines and leader lines that end with dots. See Figure 8-57.

1. Select the Leader tool.

   Command: _qleader
   Specify first leader point, or [Settings] <Settings>:

2. Type s; press Enter.
3. Select the Leader Line & Arrow option.

   The Leader Settings dialog box will appear. See Figure 8-58.

4. Select the Spline option in the Leader Line box, then OK.

Figure 8-58

Specify first leader point, or [Settings] <Settings>:

5. Select the starting point for the leader line.

   This is the point where the arrowhead will appear.

   Specify next point:

6. Select the next point.

   Select next point:

   AutoCAD will shift to the Drag mode, which allows you to move the cursor around and watch the changes in shapes of the leader line. More than one point may be selected to define the shape.

7. Complete the leader line as explained previously.

To draw a leader line with a dot at its end

1. Select the Leader tool.

   Command: _qleader
   Specify first leader point, or [Settings] <Settings>:

2. Type s; press Enter.
3. Select the Leader Line & Arrow option.

   The Leader Settings dialog box will appear. See Figure 8-59.

4. Select the arrow to the right of the Arrowhead box.

   A list of arrowhead options will appear.

5. Select the Dot small option.
6. Select OK to return to the drawing.
7. Use the Leader tool to create leader lines as described previously.

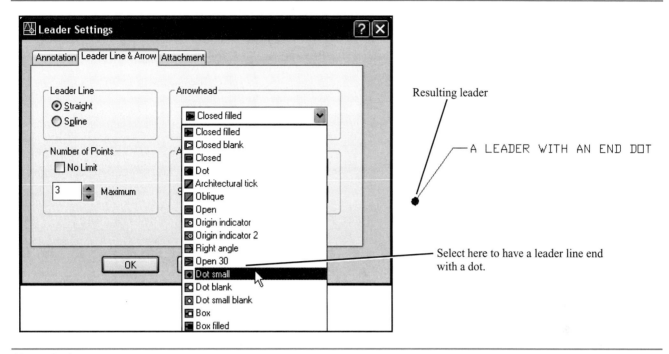

Figure 8-59

8-15 DIMENSION EDIT

The Dimension Edit command is used to edit existing dimensioning text. Existing text can be moved or rotated, or the text value can be changed. See Figure 8-60.

To use the Dimension Edit option to change a text value

1. Select the Dimension Edit tool.

   Command: _dimtedit
   Enter type of dimension editing [Home/New/ Rotate/Oblique] <Home>:

2. Select the New option or type n; press Enter.

The Text Formatting dialog box will appear. See Section 2-16 for a more complete explanation of the Text Formatting dialog box.

3. Delete the existing text value and type in a new value; click OK.
4. Select the dimension to be edited.
5. Press the right mouse button to enter the new text value.

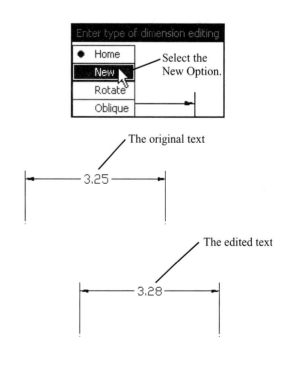

Figure 8-60

To change the angle of existing dimension text

1. Select the Dimension Edit tool.

    Command: _dimtedit
    Enter type of dimension editing [Home/New/
    Rotate/Oblique] <Home>:

2. Select the Rotate option or type R; press Enter.

    Specify angle for dimension text:

3. Type 90; press Enter.

    Select objects:

4. Select the dimension to be rotated; press Enter.

    Figure 8-61 shows the results.

8-16 TOLERANCES

Tolerances are numerical values assigned with the dimensions that define the limits of manufacturing acceptability for a distance. AutoCAD can create four types of tolerances: symmetrical, deviation, limits, and basic. See Figure 8-62. Many companies also use a group of standard tolerances that are applied to any dimensional value that is not assigned a specific tolerance. See Figure 8-23. Tolerances for numerical values expressed in millimeters are applied using a different convention than that used for inches. Tolerances are discussed in Chapters 9 and 10. The discussion of the appropriate dimensioning tools will be covered in those chapters.

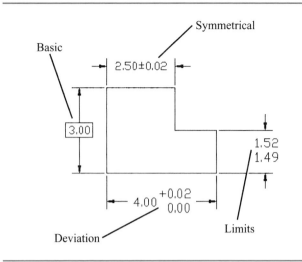

Figure 8-62

8-17 DIMENSIONING HOLES

Holes are dimensioned by stating their diameter and depth, if any. The symbol Ø is used to represent diameter. It is considered good practice to dimension a hole using a diameter value because the tooling used to produce the hole is also defined in terms of diameter values. A notation like 12 DRILL is considered less desirable because it specifies a machining process. Manufacturing processes should be left, whenever possible, to the discretion of the shop.

To dimension individual holes

Figure 8-63 shows three different methods that can be used to dimension a hole that does not go completely

Figure 8-61

Figure 8-63

Figure 8-64

Figure 8-66

through an object. If the hole goes completely through, only the diameter need be specified. The Radius and Diameter Dimension commands were covered in Section 8-7. Depth values may be added using the Text Formatting dialog box or by using the Text option of any of the dimension commands.

Figure 8-64 shows two methods of dimensioning holes in sectional views. The single-line note version is the preferred method.

To dimension hole patterns

Figure 8-65 shows two different hole patterns dimensioned. The circular pattern includes the note Ø10-4 HOLES. This note serves to define all four holes within the object.

Figure 8-65 also shows a rectangular object that contains five holes of equal diameter, equally spaced from one another. The notation 5 × Ø10 specifies five holes of 10 diameter. The notation 4 × 20 (=80) means 4 equal spaces of 20. The notation (=80) is a reference dimension and is included for convenience. Reference dimensions are explained in Chapter 9.

Figure 8-66 shows two additional methods for dimensioning repeating hole patterns. Figure 8-67 shows a circular hole pattern that includes two different hole diameters. The hole diameters are not noticeably different and could be confused. One group is defined by indicating letter (A); the other is dimensioned in a normal manner.

Figure 8-65

Figure 8-67

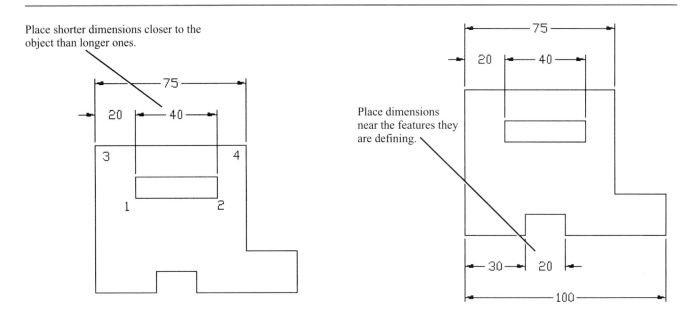

Place shorter dimensions closer to the object than longer ones.

Place dimensions near the features they are defining.

DO NOT PLACE DIMENSIONS ON THE SURFACE OF THE OBJECT.

Use the Explode, Erase, and Move commands to reconstruct and relocate inappropriate dimensions.

Align groups of dimensions.

Place overall dimensions the farthest away from the object.

Figure 8-68

8-18 PLACING DIMENSIONS

There are several general rules concerning the placement of dimensions. See Figure 8-68.

1. Place dimensions near the features they are defining.
2. Do not place dimensions on the surface of the object.
3. Align and group dimensions so that they are neat and easy to understand.
4. Avoid crossing extension lines.

Sometimes it is impossible not to cross extension lines because of the complex shape of the object, but whenever possible, avoid crossing extension lines.

5. Place shorter dimensions closer to the object than longer ones.
6. Always place overall dimensions the farthest away from the object.
7. Do not dimension the same distance twice. This is called double dimensioning and will be discussed in Chapter 9.

8-19 FILLETS AND ROUNDS

Fillets and rounds may be dimensioned individually or by a note. In many design situations all the fillets and rounds are the same size, so a note as shown in Figure 8-69 is used. Any fillets or rounds that have a different radius from that specified by the note are dimensioned individually.

See Chapter 2 for an explanation of how to draw fillets and rounds using the Fillet command.

8-20 ROUNDED SHAPES (INTERNAL)

Internal rounded shapes are called *slots*. Figure 8-70 shows three different methods for dimensioning slots. The end radii are indicated by the note R - 2 PLACES, but no numerical value is given. The width of the slot is dimensioned, and it is assumed that the radius of the rounded ends is exactly half of the stated width.

Figure 8-69

Figure 8-70

Figure 8-71

8-21 ROUNDED SHAPES (EXTERNAL)

Figure 8-71 shows two example shapes with external rounded ends. As with internal rounded shapes, the end radii are indicated but no value is given. The width of the object is given, and the radius of the rounded end is assumed to be exactly half of the stated width.

The second example shown in Figure 8-72 shows an object dimensioned using the object's centerline. This type of dimensioning is used when the distance between the hole is more important than the overall length of the object; that is, the tolerance for the distance between the holes is more exact than the tolerance for the overall length of the object.

The overall length of the object is given as a reference dimension (100). This means the object will be manufactured based on the other dimensions, and the 100 value will be used only for reference.

Objects with partially rounded edges should be dimensioned as shown in Figure 8-72. The radii of the end features are dimensioned. The center point of the radii is implied to be on the object centerline. The overall dimension is given; it is not referenced unless specific radii values are included.

8-22 IRREGULAR SURFACES

There are three different methods for dimensioning irregular surfaces: tabular, baseline, and baseline with oblique extension lines. Figure 8-72 shows an irregular surface dimensioned using the tabular method. The X,Y axes are defined using the edges of the object. Points are then defined relative to the X,Y axes. The points are assigned reference numbers, and the reference numbers and X,Y coordinate values are listed in chart form as shown.

Figure 8-73 shows an irregular curve dimensioned using baseline dimensions. The baseline method references all dimensions back to specified baselines. Usually there are two baselines, one horizontal and one vertical.

It is considered poor practice to use a centerline as a baseline. Centerlines are imaginary lines that do not exist on the object and would make it more difficult to manufacture and inspect the finished objects.

Baseline dimensioning is very common because it helps eliminate tolerance buildup (see Section 9-12) and is easily adaptable to many manufacturing processes. AutoCAD has a special Baseline Dimension command for creating baseline dimensions.

Station	1	2	3	4	5	6
X	0	20	40	55	62	70
Y	40	38	30	16	10	0

Figure 8-72

Figure 8-73

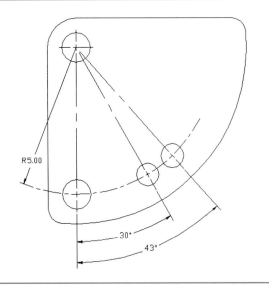

Figure 8-74

Figure 8-75

8-23 POLAR DIMENSIONS

Polar dimensions are similar to polar coordinates. A location is defined by a radius (distance) and an angle. Figure 8-74 shows an object that includes polar dimensions. The holes are located on a circular centerline, and their positions from the vertical centerline are specified using angles.

Figure 8-75 shows an example of a hole pattern dimensioned using polar dimensions.

8-24 CHAMFERS

Chamfers are angular cuts made on the edges of objects. They are usually used to make it easier to fit two parts together. They are most often made at 45° angles but may be made at any angle. Figure 8-76 shows two objects with chamfers between surfaces 90° apart and two examples between surfaces that are not 90° apart. Either of the two types of dimensions shown for the 45° dimension may be used. If an angle other than 45° is used, the angle and setback distance must be specified.

Figure 8-77 shows two examples of internal chamfers. Both define the knurl using an angle and diameter. Internal chamfers are very similar to countersunk holes. See Section 5-26.

Figure 8-76

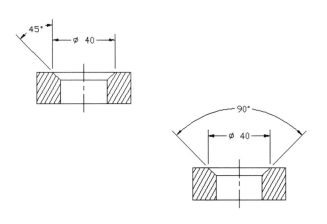

Figure 8-77

8-25 KNURLING

There are two types of knurls: diamond and straight. Knurls are used to make it easier to grip a shaft, or to roughen a surface before it is used in a press fit.

Knurls are defined by their pitch and diameter. See Figure 8-78. The *pitch* of a knurl is the ratio of the number of grooves on the circumference to the diameter. Standard knurling tools sized to a variety of pitch sizes are used to manufacture knurls for both English and metric units.

Diamond knurls may be represented by a double hatched pattern or by an open area with notes. The Hatch command is used to draw the double-hatched lines. See Section 6-4.

Straight knurls may be represented by straight lines in the pattern shown or by an open area with notes. The straight-line pattern is created by projecting lines from a construction circle. The construction points are evenly spaced on the circle. Once drawn, the straight-line knurl pattern can be saved as a wblock for use on other drawings. See Section 3-23 for an explanation of wblock.

Figure 8-78

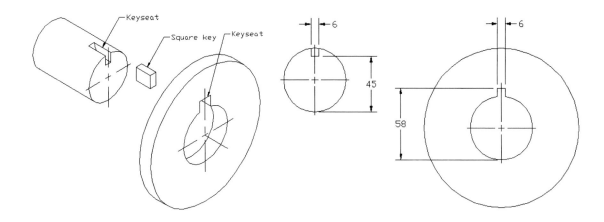

Figure 8-79

8-26 KEYS AND KEYSEATS

Keys are small pieces of material used to transmit power. For example, Figure 8-79 shows how a key can be fitted between a shaft and a gear so that the rotary motion of the shaft can be transmitted to the gear.

There are many different styles of keys. The key shown in Figure 8-79 has a rectangular cross section and is called a square key. Keys fit into grooves called *keyseats,* or *keyways*.

Keyways are dimensioned from the bottom of the shaft or hole as shown.

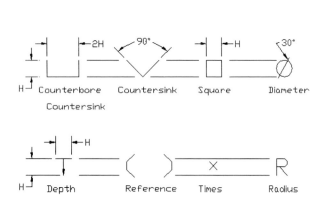

Figure 8-80

AL	= Aluminum
C'BORE	= Counterbore
CRS	= Cold Rolled Steel
CSK	= Countersink
DIA	= Diameter
EQ	= Equal
HEX	= Hexagon
MAT'L	= Material
R	= Radius
SAE	= Society of Automotive Engineers
SFACE	= Spotface
ST	= Steel
SQ	= Square
REQD	= Required

Figure 8-81

Figure 8-82

Figure 8-83

8-27 SYMBOLS AND ABBREVIATIONS

Symbols are used in dimensioning to help accurately display the meaning of the dimension. Symbols also help eliminate language barriers when reading drawings. Figure 8-80 shows a list of dimensioning symbols and their meanings. The height of a symbol should be the same as the text height.

Abbreviations should be used very carefully on drawings. Whenever possible, write out the full word including correct punctuation. Figure 8-81 shows several standard abbreviations used on technical drawings.

8-28 SYMMETRY AND CENTERLINE

An object is symmetrical about an axis when one side is an exact mirror image of the other. Figure 8-82 shows a symmetrical object. The two short parallel lines symbol or the note OBJECT IS SYMMETRICAL ABOUT THIS AXIS (centerline) may be used to designate symmetry.

If an object is symmetrical, only half the object need be dimensioned. The other dimensions are implied by the symmetry note or symbol.

Centerlines are slightly different from the axis of symmetry. An object may or may not be symmetrical about its centerline. See Figure 8-82. Centerlines are used to define the center of both individual features and entire objects. Use the centerline symbol when a line is a centerline, but do not use it in place of the symmetry symbol.

8-29 DIMENSIONING TO POINTS

Curved surfaces can be dimensioned using theoretical points. See Figure 8-83. There should be a small gap between the surface of the object and the lines used to define the theoretical point. The point should be defined by the intersection of at least two lines.

There should also be a small gap between the extension lines and the theoretical point used to locate the point.

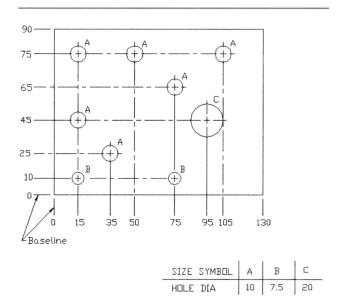

SIZE SYMBOL	A	B	C
HOLE DIA	10	7.5	20

Figure 8-84

8-30 COORDINATE DIMENSIONS

Coordinate dimensions are used for objects that contain many holes. Baseline dimensions can also be used, but when there are many holes, baseline dimensions can create a confusing appearance and will require a large area on the drawing. Coordinate dimensions use charts that simplify the appearance, use far less space on the drawing, and are easy to understand.

Figure 8-84 shows an object that has been dimensioned using coordinate dimensions without dimension lines. Holes are identified on the drawing using letters. Holes of equal diameter use the same letter. The hole diameters are presented in chart form.

Hole locations are defined using a series of centerlines referenced to baselines. The distance from the baseline to the centerline is written below the centerline as shown.

Figure 8-85 shows an object that has been dimensioned using coordinate dimensions in tabular form. Each hole is assigned both a letter and a number. Holes of equal diameter are assigned the same letter. A chart is used to define the diameter values for each hole letter.

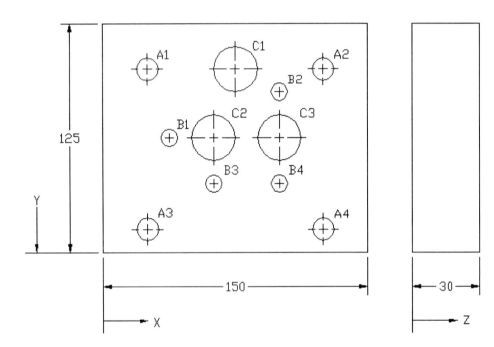

HOLE	FROM	X	Y	Z
A1	XY	15	65	THRU
A2	XY	80	65	THRU
A3	XY	15	10	THRU
A4	XY	80	10	THRU
B1	XY	25	40	12
B2	XY	65	56	12
B3	XY	40	25	12
B4	XY	65	25	12
C1	XY	48	65	THRU
C2	XY	40	40	THRU
C3	XY	65	40	THRU

HOLE	DESCRIPTION	QTY
A	Ø8	4
B	Ø5	4
C	Ø16	3

Figure 8-85

Figure 8-86

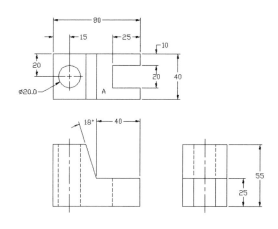

Figure 8-87

Hole locations are defined relative to X,Y axes. A Z axis is used for depth dimensions. A chart lists each hole by its letter–number designation and specifies its distance from the X, Y, or Z axis. The overall dimensions are given using extension and dimension lines.

The side view does not show any hidden lines because if all the lines were shown, it would be too confusing to understand. A note THIS VIEW LEFT BLANK FOR CLARITY may be added to the drawing.

8-31 SECTIONAL VIEWS

Sectional views are dimensioned, as are orthographic views. See Figure 8-86. The sectional lines should be drawn at an angle that allows the viewer to clearly distinguish between the sectional lines and the extension lines.

8-32 ORTHOGRAPHIC VIEWS

Dimensions should be added to orthographic views where the features appear in contour. Holes should be dimensioned in their circular views. Figure 8-87 shows three views of an object that has been dimensioned.

The hole dimensions are added to the top view where the hole appears circular. The slot is also dimensioned in the top view because it appears in contour. The slanted surface is dimensioned in the front view.

The height of surface A is given in the side view rather than run along extension lines across the front view. The length of surface A is given in the front view. This is a contour view of the surface.

It is considered good practice to keep dimensions in groups. This makes it easier for the viewer to find dimensions.

Be careful not to double-dimension a distance. A distance should be dimensioned only once per view. If a 30 dimension were added above the 25 dimension on the right-side view, it would be an error. The distance would be double-dimensioned: once with the 25 + 30 dimension and again with the 55 overall dimension. The 25 + 30 dimensions are mathematically equal to the 55 overall dimension, but there is a distinct difference in how they affect the manufacturing tolerances. Double dimensions are explained more fully in Chapter 9.

Figure 8-88 shows an object dimensioned from its centerline. This type of dimensioning is used when the distance between the holes relative to each other are critical.

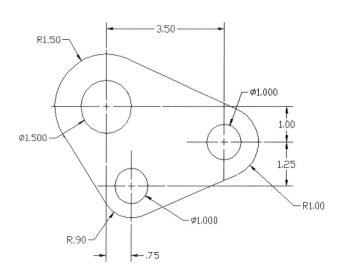

Figure 8-88

8-33 VERY LARGE RADII

Some radii are so large that it is not practical to draw the leader for radius dimension at full size. Figure 8-89 shows an example of an object that uses foreshortened leader lines.

To create a radius dimension for large radii

1. Select the Quick Leader tool from the Dimension toolbar.

   Command: _leader
   Specify first leader point, or [Settings] <Settings>:

2. Type s; press Enter.

The Leader Settings dialog box will appear. See Figure 8-90.

3. Select the Leader Line and Arrow option.
4. Select the upper arrow to the right of the Maximum box in the Number of Points box and set the maximum number of points to 4. Select OK.
5. Select a point on the large arc.

   Specify next point:

6. Specify points 1, 2, and 3 as shown in Figure 8-89.
7. Complete the leader dimension by typing in the appropriate text value in the Text Formatting dialog box.
8. Explode the leader line.
9. Use the Break command and create an opening in the leader line for the text value.
10. Use the Move command and locate the text value within the opening.
11. Erase any excess lines.

Figure 8-89

Figure 8-90

8-34 EXERCISE PROBLEMS

Redraw the shapes shown in Exercise Problems EX8-1 to EX8-6. Locate the dimensions and tolerances as shown.

EX8-1 INCHES

1. 3.00±.01
2. 1.56±.01
3. 46.50°
   45.50°
4. 750±.005
5. 2.75
   2.70
6. 3.625±.010
7. 45°±.5
8. 2.250±.005°

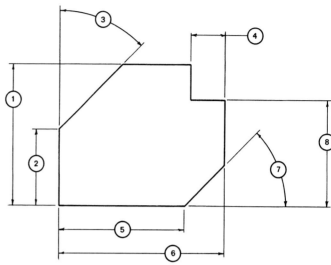

EX8-2 MILLIMETERS

1. 38±0.05
2. 10±0.1
3. 5±0.05
4. 45.50°
   44.50°
5. 40±0.1
6. 22±0.1
7. 12 $^{+0}_{-0.1}$
8. 25 $^{+0.05}_{-0}$
9. 51.50
   50.75
10. 76±0.1

EX8-3 MILLIMETERS

1. 34±0.25
2. 17±0.25
3. 25±0.05
4. 15.00
   14.80
5. 50±0.05
6. 80±0.1
7. R5±0.1 - 8 PLACES
8. 45±0.25
9. 60±0.1
10. Ø14 - 3 HOLES
11. 15.00
    14.80
12. 30.00
    29.80

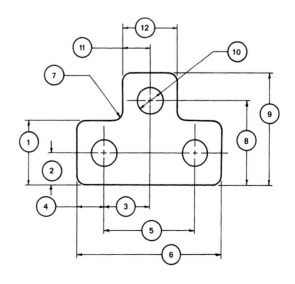

EX8-4 INCHES

1. 1.50±.02

2. 1.50±.03

3. .625±.001

4. .754
    .749

5. .625±.001

6. 2.253
    2.249

7. ⌀ .502
    .500

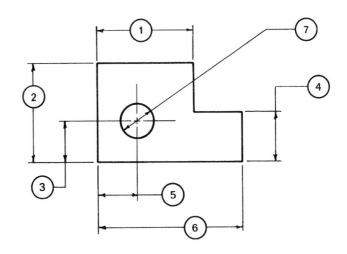

EX8-5 MILLIMETERS

Note : ⑨

1. ⌀30±0.5

2. ⌀ 15.04
      15.00

3. 10±1

4. 20±1

5. 66.50
    65.03

6. 15±0.3

7. 35±0.02

8. 70±0.2

    NOTE: ALL FILLETS AND
    ROUNDS = R5 UNLESS
    OTHERWISE STATED

EX8-6 MILLIMETERS

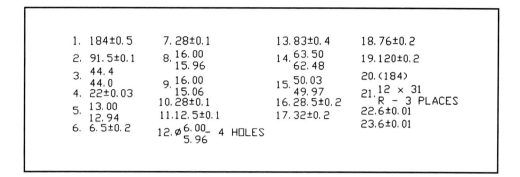

1. 184±0.5
2. 91.5±0.1
3. 44.4 / 44.0
4. 22±0.03
5. 13.00 / 12.94
6. 6.5±0.2
7. 28±0.1
8. 16.00 / 15.96
9. 16.00 / 15.06
10. 28±0.1
11. 12.5±0.1
12. ⌀ 6.00 / 5.96 4 HOLES
13. 83±0.4
14. 63.50 / 62.48
15. 50.03 / 49.97
16. 28.5±0.2
17. 32±0.2
18. 76±0.2
19. 120±0.2
20. (184)
21. 12 × 31 / R − 3 PLACES
22. 6±0.01
23. 6±0.01

Measure and redraw the shapes in Exercise Problems EX8-7 through EX8-49. Add the appropriate dimensions. Specify the units and scale of the drawing. The dotted grid background has either .50-inch or 10-millimeter spacing.

EX8-7

EX8-9

EX8-8

EX8-10

EX8-11

EX8-13

EX8-12

EX8-14

EX8-15

EX8-17

EX8-16

EX8-18

EX8-19

EX8-21

EX8-20

EX8-22

EX8-23

EX8-24

EX8-25

EX8-26

EX8-28

EX8-27

EX8-29

EX8-30

EX8-32

EX8-31

EX8-33

EX8-34

EX8-36

EX8-35

EX8-37

EX8-38

EX8-39

EX8-40

EX8-41

EX8-42A

EX8-43A

EX8-42B

EX8-43B

EX8-42C

EX8-43C

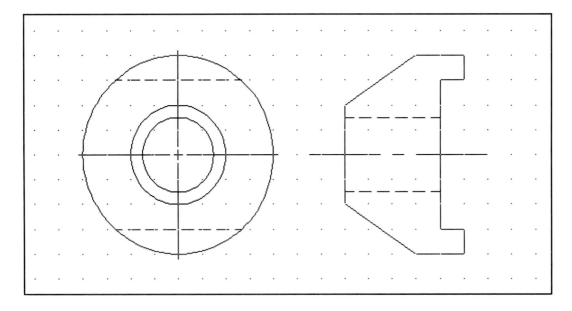

Front View   Right Side View

EX8-44

EX8-45

EX8-46

EX8-48

EX8-47

EX8-49

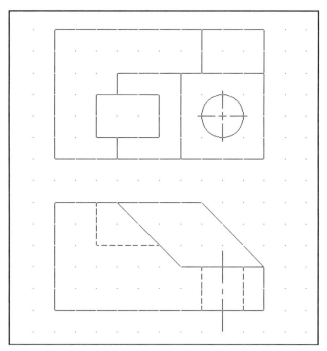

CHAPTER 9
Tolerancing

9-1 INTRODUCTION

Tolerances define the manufacturing limits for dimensions. All dimensions have tolerances either written directly on the drawing as part of the dimension or implied by a predefined set of standard tolerances that apply to any dimension that does not have a stated tolerance.

This chapter explains general tolerance conventions and how they are applied using AutoCAD. It includes a sample tolerance study and an explanation of standard fits and surface finishes.

Chapter 10 explains geometric tolerances.

9-2 DIRECT TOLERANCE METHODS

There are two methods used to include tolerances as part of a dimension: plus and minus, and limits. Plus and minus tolerances can be expressed in either bilateral or unilateral forms.

A bilateral tolerance has both a plus and a minus value. A unilateral tolerance has either the plus or minus value equal to 0. Figure 9-1 shows a horizontal dimension of 60 millimeters that includes a bilateral tolerance of plus or minus 0.1 and another dimension of 60 millimeters that

includes a bilateral tolerance of plus 0.20 or minus 0.10. Figure 9-1 also shows a dimension of 65 millimeters that includes a unilateral tolerance of plus 1 or minus 0.

Plus or minus tolerances define a range for manufacturing. If inspection shows that all dimensioned distances on an object fall within their specified tolerance range, the object is considered acceptable; that is, it has been manufactured correctly.

Figure 9-1

359

Figure 9-2

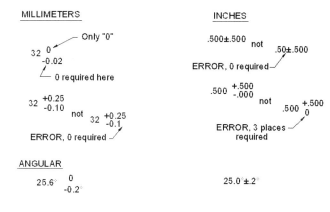

Figure 9-3

The dimension and tolerance 60 ±0.1 means that the distance must be manufactured within a range no greater than 60.1 nor less than 59.9. The dimension and tolerance 65 + 1, −0 defines the tolerance range as 65.0 to 66.0.

Figure 9-2 shows some bilateral and unilateral tolerances applied using decimal inch values. Inch dimensions and tolerances are written using a slightly different format from that used for millimeter dimensions and tolerances, but they also define manufacturing ranges for dimension values. The horizontal bilateral dimension and tolerance 2.50 ±.02 defines the longest acceptable distance as 2.52 inches and the shortest as 2.48. The unilateral dimension 2.50 +.02, −.00 defines the longest acceptable distance as 2.52 and the shortest as 2.50.

9-3 TOLERANCE EXPRESSIONS

Dimension and tolerance values are written differently for inch and millimeter values. See Figure 9-3. Unilateral dimensions for millimeter values specify a zero limit with a single 0. A zero limit for inch values must include the same number of decimal places given for the dimension value. In the example shown in Figure 9-3, the dimension value .500 has a unilateral tolerance with minus zero tolerance. The zero limit is written as .000, three decimal places for both the dimension and the tolerance.

Both values in a bilateral tolerance must contain the same number of decimal places, although for millimeter values the tolerance values need not include the same number of decimal places as the dimension value. In Figure 9-3

the dimension value 32 is accompanied by tolerances of +0.25 and −0.10. This form is not acceptable for inch dimensions and tolerances. An equivalent inch dimension and tolerance would be written 32.00 +.25/−.10.

Degree values must include the same number of decimal places in both the dimension value and the tolerance values for bilateral tolerances. A single 0 may be used for a unilateral tolerance.

9-4 UNDERSTANDING PLUS AND MINUS TOLERANCES

A millimeter dimension and tolerance of 12.0 +0.2/−0.1 means the longest acceptable distance is 12.2000...0, and the shortest, 11.9000...0. The total range is .3000...0.

After an object is manufactured, it is inspected to ensure that the object has been manufactured correctly. Each dimensioned distance is measured and, if it is within the specified tolerance, is accepted. If the measured distance is not within the specified tolerance, the part is rejected. Some rejected objects may be reworked to bring them into the specified tolerance range, whereas others are simply scrapped.

Figure 9-4 shows a dimension with a tolerance. Assume that five objects were manufactured using the same 12 +0.2/−0.1 dimension and tolerance. The objects were then inspected and the results were as listed. Inspected measurements are usually at least one more decimal place than that specified in the tolerance. Which

GIVEN (mm)
12 +0.2 −0.1

MEANS

TOL MAX = 12.2
TOL MIN = 11.9
TOTAL TOL = 0.3

OBJECT	AS MEASURED	ACCEPTABLE?
1	12.160	OK
2	12.020	OK
3	12.203	TOO LONG
4	11.920	OK
5	11.895	TOO SHORT

Figure 9-4

GIVEN (inches)
3.50±.02

MEANS

TOL MAX = 3.52
TOL MIN = 3.48
TOTAL TOL = .04

OBJECT	AS MEASURED	ACCEPTABLE?
1	3.520	OK
2	3.486	OK
3	3.470	TOO SHORT
4	3.521	TOO LONG
5	3.515	OK

Figure 9-5

objects are acceptable and which are not? Object 3 is too long, and object 5 is too short because their measured distances are not within the specified tolerances.

Figure 9-5 shows a dimension and tolerance of 3.50 ±.02 inches. Object 3 is not acceptable because it is too short, and object 4 is too long.

9-5 CREATING PLUS AND MINUS TOLERANCES USING AUTOCAD

Plus and minus tolerances may be created using AutoCAD in four ways: using the Text option, the Mtext option, typing the tolerances directly using Dtext, or by setting the plus and minus values using the Dimension Style tool.

To create plus and minus tolerances using the Text option

The example given is for a horizontal dimension, but the procedure is the same for any linear or radial dimension.

1. Select the Linear Dimension tool from the Dimension toolbar.
2. Select the extension line origins as explained in Section 8-3 and locate the dimension line.

   Specify dimension line location or [Mtext/Text/Angle/Horizontal/Vertical/Rotated]:

3. Type t; press Enter.

Dimension text <x.xxxx>:

4. Type the appropriate text value; press Enter.

Type the dimension value, then %%p, then the tolerance value.

Dimension text <x.xxxx>:5.00%%p.02.

In this example, the resulting dimension will be 5.00±.02.

To create plus and minus tolerances using the Mtext option

1. Select the Linear Dimension tool from the Dimension toolbar.
2. Select the extension line origins as explained in Section 8-3 and locate the dimension line.

   Specify dimension line location or [Mtext/Text/Angle/Horizontal/Vertical/Rotated]:

3. Type M; press Enter.

The Text Formatting dialog box will appear. See Figure 9-6. The existing dimension value will appear in a box. The value may be changed by deleting the existing values, and then typing in a new value.

4. Place the flashing cursor to the right of the dimension value.
5. Type %%p or press the ALT key and type 0177.
6. Type in the tolerance value; select OK.

Type either %%p or hold the ALT key and type 0177 to produce the ± symbol.

Figure 9-6

The modified dimension will appear on the drawing screen and can be located by moving the mouse.

The Dimension Style tool on the Dimension toolbar can be used to change the precision of the inital AutoCAD select dimension values. (The default value is four places; 1.0000.) If, for example, two decimal places are desired, use the Precision box in the Primary Units tab on the Modify Dimension Style: Standard dialog box to reset the system for two decimal places. See Section 8-5.

To use Dtext to create a plus and minus tolerance

1. Type Dtext in response to a command prompt.
2. Place the starting point for the text, then define the appropriate height and angle.
3. Type the desired dimension.

    Text: 5.00%%p.02

4. Press Enter.

In the example shown, the resulting dimension will be 5.00±.02. The symbol will initially appear on the screen as %%p, but will change to ± when the last text line is entered. The symbol ± can also be created using the Windows character map by holding down the ALT key and typing 0177.

To use the Dimension Style tool

1. Select the Dimension Style tool from the Dimension toolbar.
2. Select the Modify option, then the Tolerances tab.

3. Select the arrow to the right of the Method box.

A list of available tolerancing methods will cascade. See Figure 9-7. AutoCAD offers two options for plus and minus tolerancing: Symmetrical and Deviation.

The symmetrical method

4a. Select the symmetrical method.

The Tolerance format box within the Modify Dimension Style: Standard dialog box is used to create a symmetrical tolerance by entering a value in the Upper value box. See Figure 9-8.

5a. Type a value.

In this example, a value of 0.0300 was entered. Only an upper value needed to be entered, as the tolerance value is symmetrical.

6a. Return to the drawing screen.

Dimensions created using the Dimension toolbar will now automatically include a ±0.03000 tolerance.

The deviation method

4b. Select the Deviation method.

The Tolerance Format dialog box is used to create a deviation tolerance by entering values in the Upper value and Lower value boxes. See Figure 9-9.

5b. Type in values.

Select the tolerance method here.

Figure 9-7

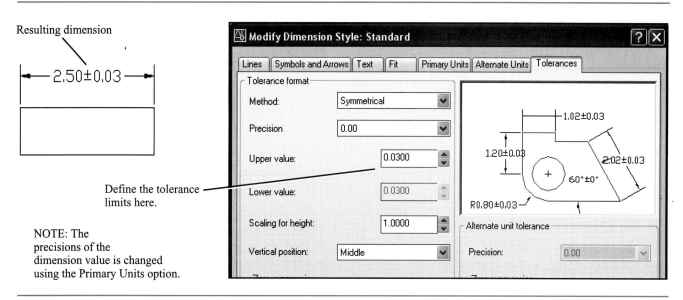

Resulting dimension

Define the tolerance limits here.

NOTE: The precisions of the dimension value is changed using the Primary Units option.

Figure 9-8

In this example values of 0.0100 and 0.0200 were entered.

6b.   Return to the drawing screen.

Dimensions created using the Dimension toolbar will now automatically include a +0.0100, −0.0200 tolerance.

The Dimension Style tool on the Dimension toolbar can also be used to change the precision of the initial AutoCAD selected dimension values. (The default value is four places: 1.0000.) If, for example, two decimal places are desired, use the Precision box on the Primary Units tab on the Dimension Style Manager dialog box to reset the system for two decimal places. See Section 8-5.

9-6   LIMIT TOLERANCES

Figure 9-10 shows examples of limit tolerances. Limit tolerances replace dimension values. Two values are given: the upper and lower limits for the dimension value. The limit tolerance of 62.1 and 59.9 is mathematically equal to 62 ± 0.1, but the stated limit tolerance is considered easier to read and understand.

Limit tolerances define a range for manufacture. Final distances on an object must fall within the specified range to be acceptable.

Resulting dimension

Define values here.

Figure 9-9

Figure 9-10

9-7 CREATING LIMIT TOLERANCES USING AUTOCAD

Limit tolerances may be created using AutoCAD in two ways: by using the Dimension Style tool, or by modifying a given dimension using the Dimension Edit tool.

To create a limit tolerance using the Dimension Style tool

1. Select the Dimension Style tool from the Dimension toolbar.

    The Dimension Style Manager dialog box will appear.

2. Select the Modify option, then the Tolerances tab.

    The Modify Dimension Style: Standard dialog box will appear.

3. Select the arrow to the right of the Method option box.

    A list of available tolerance methods will cascade. See Figure 9-7.

4. Select the Limits option.

    The Annotation dialog box will reappear with the headings Upper value and Lower value now in black letters, meaning that they can be accessed.

5. Type in the upper and lower values.

    In this example values of 0.1000 and 0.3000 were chosen. See Figure 9-11.

6. Return to the drawing screen.

    Every dimension created using the Linear Dimension tool will now automatically create a limit tolerance based on the selected distance and the selected upper and lower values. Figure 9-11 shows the results of the Linear Dimension tool applied to a distance of 3.2500. The upper limit is 3.2500 + 0.1000 and the lower limit is 3.2500 − 0.3000.

    If only a few limit-type tolerances are to be used on a drawing, it is sometimes easier simply to modify an existing dimension rather than to change the Tolerance settings.

To modify an existing dimension into a limit tolerance

1. Select the Dimension Edit tool from the Dimension toolbar.

    Enter type of dimension editing [Home/New/ Rotate/Oblique] <Home>:

2. Select the New option or type n; press Enter.

Figure 9-11

Figure 9-12

The Text Formatting dialog box will appear. See Figure 9-12.

3. Delete the existing dimension value and type in the new limit tolerance value.
4. Type 3.3700, press Enter, then type 2.9000; select OK.

Select objects:

5. Select the dimension to be changed; press Enter.

Figure 9-12 shows the resulting changed dimension.

9-8 ANGULAR TOLERANCES

Figure 9-13 shows an example of an angular dimension with a tolerance. The procedure explained for plus and minus tolerances applies to angular as well as to linear dimensions and tolerances.

The precision of angular dimensions is set using the Primary Units dialog box. In the following example, a deviation tolerance of $+0.10$, -0.30 was also specified.

To set the precision for angular dimensions and tolerances

1. Select the Dimension Style tool, then the Modify option, then the Primary Units option.
2. Select the arrow to the right of the Precision box.

Figure 9-13

Standard Tolerances

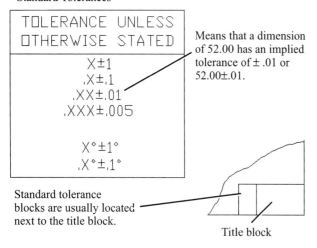

Figure 9-14

A list of available precision factors will cascade. See Figure 9-13.

3. Select two significant figures for both Dimension and Tolerance and return to the drawing screen.

The precision for the angular value can be changed using the Dimension Precision option.

To create an angular dimension and tolerance

1. Select the Angular tool from the Dimension toolbar.

   Select arc, circle, line, or <specify vertex>:

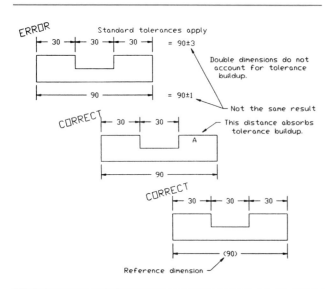

Figure 9-15

2. Select one of the lines that defines the angle.

   Select second line:

3. Select the second line.

   Specify dimension arc line location or [Mtext/ Text/Angle]:

4. Select a location for the dimension; press Enter.

The Mtext and Text options are used as explained for linear dimensions and tolerance in Section 9-5. Symmetrical, deviation, and limit tolerances can be applied to angular tolerances in the same way they were to linear tolerances.

9-9 STANDARD TOLERANCES

Most manufacturers establish a set of standard tolerances that are applied to any dimension that does not include a specific tolerance. Figure 9-14 shows some possible standard tolerances. Standard tolerances vary from company to company. Standard tolerances are usually listed on the first page of a drawing to the left of the title block, but this location may vary.

The X value used when specifying standard tolerances means any X stated in that format. A dimension value of 52.00 will have an implied tolerance of ±.01 because the stated standard tolerance is .XX ±.01, so any dimension value with two decimal places will have a standard implied tolerance of ±.01. A dimension value of 52.000 will have an implied tolerance of ±.005.

9-10 DOUBLE DIMENSIONING

It is an error, called *double dimensioning*, to dimension the same distance twice. Double dimensioning is an error because it does not allow for tolerance buildup across a distance.

Figure 9-15 shows an object that has been dimensioned twice across its horizontal length; once using three 30-millimeter dimensions and a second time using the 90-millimeter overall dimension. The two dimensions are mathematically equal but are not equal when tolerances are considered. Assume that each dimension has a standard tolerance of ±1 millimeter. The three 30-millimeter dimensions could create an acceptable distance of 90±3 millimeters, or a maximum distance of 93 and a minimum distance of 87. The overall dimension of 90 millimeters allows a maximum distance of 91 and a minimum distance of 89. The two dimensions yield different results when tolerances are considered.

The size and location of a tolerance depends on the design objectives of the object, how it will be manufactured, and how it will be inspected. Even objects that have similar shapes may be dimensioned and toleranced very differently.

One possible solution to the double dimensioning shown in Figure 9-15 is to remove one of the 30-millimeter dimensions and to allow that distance to "float," that is, absorb the cumulated tolerances. The choice of which 30-millimeter dimension to eliminate depends on the design objectives of the part. For this example the far-right dimension was eliminated to remove the double-dimensioning error.

Another possible solution to the double-dimensioning error is to retain the three 30-millimeter dimensions and to change the 90-millimeter overall dimension to a reference dimension. A reference dimension is used only for mathematical convenience. It is not used during the manufacturing or inspection process. A reference dimension is designated on a drawing with parentheses (90).

If the 90-millimeter dimension were referenced, then only the three 30-millimeter dimensions would be used to manufacture and inspect the object. This would eliminate the double-dimensioning error.

9-11 CHAIN DIMENSIONS AND BASELINE DIMENSIONS

There are two systems used to apply dimensions and tolerances to a drawing: *chain* and *baseline*. Figure 9-16 shows examples of both systems. Chain dimensions relate each feature to the feature next to it; baseline dimensions relate all features to a single baseline or datum

Chain and baseline dimensions may be used together. Figure 9-16 also shows two objects with repetitive features: one object includes two slots, and the other three sets of three holes. In each example, the center of the repetitive feature is dimensioned to the left side of the object, which serves as a baseline. The sizes of the individual features are dimensioned using chain dimensions referenced to centerlines.

Baseline dimensions eliminate tolerance buildup and can be related directly to the reference axis of many machines. They tend to take up much more area on a drawing than do chain dimensions.

Figure 9-16

Figure 9-17

Chain dimensions are useful in relating one feature to another, such as the repetitive hole pattern shown in Figure 9-16. In this example the distance between the holes is more important than the distance of the individual hole from the baseline.

Figure 9-17 shows the same object dimensioned twice, once using chain dimensions and once using baseline dimensions. All distances are assigned a tolerance range of 2 millimeters stated using limit tolerances. The maximum distance for surface A is 28 millimeters using the chain system and 27 millimeters using the baseline system. The 1-millimeter difference comes from the elimination of the first 26–24 limit dimension found on the chain example but not on the baseline.

The total tolerance difference is 6 millimeters for the chain and 4 millimeters for the baseline. The baseline reduces the tolerance variations for the object simply because it applies the tolerances and dimensions differently. So why not always use baseline dimensions? For most applications, the baseline system is probably better, but if the distance between the individual features is more critical than the distance from the feature to the baseline, use the chain system.

To create baseline dimensions using AutoCAD

The Baseline tool can be applied only after a linear dimension has been created. The object shown in Figure 9-18 was dimensioned by first creating the 1.00 dimension using the Linear Dimension tool, then using the Baseline tool as follows.

1. Create a linear dimension using the Linear Dimension tool.

The point selected as the origin for the first extension line will become the origin of the baseline.

2. Select the Baseline Dimension tool from the Dimension toolbar.

Specify a second extension line origin or [Undo/ <Select>]:

3. Select the origin for the second extension line of the baseline dimension.

Specify a second extension line origin or [Undo/ Select] <Select>:

4. Repeat the process until the baseline dimensioning is complete.

5. Press the right mouse button and Enter the dimensions.

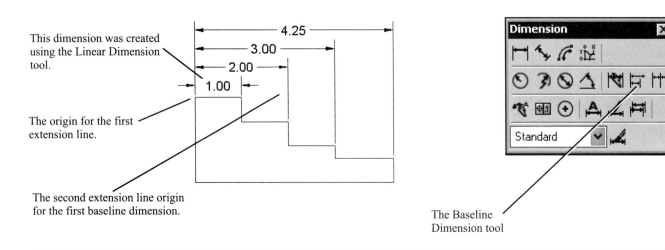

This dimension was created using the Linear Dimension tool.

The origin for the first extension line.

The second extension line origin for the first baseline dimension.

The Baseline Dimension tool

Figure 9-18

Figure 9-19

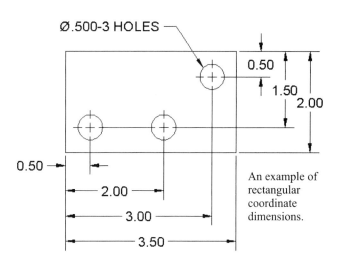

An example of rectangular coordinate dimensions.

Figure 9-20

9-12 TOLERANCE STUDIES

The term *tolerance study* is used when analyzing the effects of a group of tolerances on each other and on an object. Figure 9-19 shows an object with two horizontal dimensions. The horizontal distance A is not dimensioned. Its length depends on the tolerances of the two horizontal dimensions.

To calculate A's maximum length

Distance A will be longest when the overall distance is at its longest and the other distance is at its shortest:

$$\begin{array}{r} 65.2 \\ -29.8 \\ \hline 35.4 \end{array}$$

To calculate A's minimum length

Distance A will be shortest when the overall length is at its shortest and the other length is at its longest:

$$\begin{array}{r} 64.9 \\ -30.1 \\ \hline 34.8 \end{array}$$

Figure 9-19 also shows an object that includes three horizontal dimensions. Surface A is at its maximum length when the overall dimension is at its longest and the other dimensions are at their shortest. Surface A is at its minimum when the overall length is at its shortest and the other dimensions are at their longest.

9-13 RECTANGULAR DIMENSIONS

Figure 9-20 shows an example of rectangular dimensions referenced to baselines. Figure 9-21 shows a circular object for which dimensions are referenced to a circle's centerlines. Dimensioning to a circle's centerline is critical to accurate hole location.

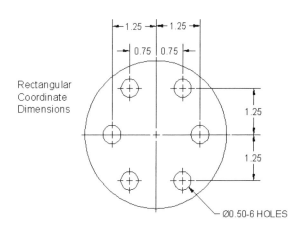

Rectangular Coordinate Dimensions

Figure 9-21

Figure 9-22

9-14 HOLE LOCATIONS

When rectangular dimensions are used, the location of a hole's center point is defined by two linear dimensions. The result is a rectangular tolerance zone whose size is based on the linear dimension's tolerances. The shape of the center point's tolerance zone may be changed to circular using positional tolerancing, as described in Section 10-16.

Figure 9-22 shows the location and size dimensions for a hole. Also shown is the resulting tolerance zone and the overall possible hole shape. The center point's tolerance is 0.2 by 0.3, based on the given linear locating tolerances.

The hole diameter has a tolerance of ±0.05. This value must be added to the center point location tolerances to define the maximum overall possible shape of the hole. The maximum possible hole shape is determined by drawing the maximum radius from the four corner points of the tolerance zone.

This means that the left edge of the hole could be as close to the vertical baseline as 12.75 or as far as 13.25. The 12.75 value was derived by subtracting the maximum hole diameter value, 12.05, from the minimum linear distance, 24.80 (24.80 − 12.05 = 12.75). The 13.25 value was derived by subtracting the minimum hole diameter, 11.95, from the maximum linear distance, 25.20 (25.20 − 11.95 = 13.25).

Figure 9-23 shows a hole's tolerance zone based on polar dimensions. The zone has a sector shape, and the possible hole shape is determined by locating the maximum radius at the four corner points of the tolerance zone.

9-15 CHOOSING A SHAFT FOR A TOLERANCED HOLE

Given the hole location and size shown in Figure 9-23, what is the largest diameter shaft that will always fit into the hole?

Figure 9-24 shows the hole's center point tolerance zone based on the given linear locating tolerances. Four circles have been drawn centered at the four corners of the linear tolerance zone that represent the smallest possible hole diameter. The circles define an area that represents the maximum shaft size that will always fit into the hole, regardless of how the given dimensions are applied.

Figure 9-23

Figure 9-24   **Figure 9-25**

The diameter of this circular area can be calculated by subtracting the maximum diagonal distance across the linear tolerance zone (corner to corner) from the minimum hole diameter.

The results can be expressed as a formula.

For linear dimensions and tolerances

$$S_{max} = H_{min} - DTZ$$

where

S_{max} = Maximum shaft diameter

H_{min} = Minimum hole diameter

DTZ = Diagonal distance across the tolerance zone

In the example shown the diagonal distance is determined using the Pythagorean theorem.

$$DTZ = \sqrt{(.4)^2 + (.6)^2}$$

$$= \sqrt{.16 + .36}$$

$$DTZ = .72$$

This means that the maximum shaft diameter that will always fit into the given hole is 11.23.

$$S_{max} = H_{min} - DTZ$$

$$= 11.95 - .72$$

$$S_{max} = 11.23$$

This procedure represents a restricted application of the general formula presented in Chapter 10 for positional tolerances. For a more complete discussion see Section 10-16.

Once the maximum shaft size has been established, a tolerance can be applied to the shaft. If the shaft had a total tolerance of .25, the minimum shaft diameter would be 11.23 – .25, or 10.98. Figure 9-24 shows a shaft dimensioned and toleranced using these values.

The formula presented is based on the assumption that the shaft is perfectly placed on the hole's center point. This assumption is reasonable if two objects are joined by a fastener and both objects are free to move. When both objects are free to move about a common fastener, they are called *floating objects*.

9-16   SAMPLE PROBLEM SP9-1

Parts A and B in Figure 9-25 are to be joined by a common shaft. The total tolerance for the shaft is to be 0.05. What are the maximum and minimum shaft diameters?

Both objects have the same dimensions and tolerances and are floating relative to each other.

$$S_{max} = H_{min} - DTZ$$

$$= 15.93 - .85$$

$$S_{max} = 15.08$$

The shaft's minimum diameter is found by subtracting the total tolerance requirement from the calculated maximum diameter.

$$15.08 - .05 = 15.03$$

Therefore,

Shaft max = 15.08
Shaft min = 15.03

$$DZT = \sqrt{(.007)^2 + (.007)^2}$$
$$= .010$$

Figure 9-26

9-17 SAMPLE PROBLEM SP9-2

The procedure presented in Sample Problem SP9-1 can be worked in reverse to determine the maximum and minimum hole size based on a given shaft size.

Objects AA and BB as shown in Figure 9-26 are to be joined using a bolt whose maximum diameter is .248. What is the minimum hole size for the objects that will always accept the bolt? What is the maximum hole size if the total hole tolerance is .007?

$$S_{max} = H_{min} - DZT$$

In this example the H_{min} is the unknown factor, so the equation is rewritten.

$$H_{min} = S_{max} + DZT$$
$$= .248 + .010$$
$$H_{min} = .258$$

This is the minimum hole diameter, so the total tolerance requirement is added to this value:

$$.258 + .007 = .265$$

Therefore,

Hole max = .265
Hole min = .258

9-18 STANDARD FITS (METRIC VALUES)

Calculating tolerances between holes and shafts that fit together is so common in engineering design that a group of standard values and notations has been established. These values are listed in tables in the appendix.

There are three possible types of fits between a shaft and a hole: clearance, transition, and interference. See Figure 9-27. There are several subclassifications within each of these categories.

A *clearance fit* always defines the maximum shaft diameter as smaller than the minimum hole diameter. The difference between the two diameters is the amount of clearance. It is possible for a clearance fit to be defined with zero clearance; that is, the maximum shaft diameter is equal to the minimum hole diameter.

An *interference fit* always defines the minimum shaft diameter as larger than the maximum hole diameter, or more simply said, the shaft is always bigger than the hole. This definition means that an interference fit is the converse of a clearance fit. The difference between the diameter of the shaft and the hole is the amount of interference.

An interference fit is primarily used to assemble objects together. Interference fits eliminate the need for threads, welds, or other joining methods. Using an interference for joining two objects is generally limited to light-load applications.

It is sometimes difficult to visualize how a shaft can be assembled into a hole with a diameter smaller than that of the shaft. It is sometimes done using a hydraulic press that slowly forces the two parts together. The joining process can be augmented by the use of lubricants or heat. The hole is heated, causing it to expand, the shaft is inserted, and the hole is allowed to cool and shrink around the shaft.

A *transition fit* may be either a clearance or an interference fit. It may have a clearance between the shaft and the hole or an interference.

Figure 9-27 shows two graphic representations of 20 different standard hole/shaft tolerance ranges. The figure shows ranges for hole tolerances, shaft tolerances, and the amount of clearance or interference for each classification. The notations are based on Standard International Tolerance values. A specific description for each category of fit is as follows.

Clearance Fits

H11/c11 or C11/h11 = Loose running fit
H9/d9 or D9/h9 = Free running fit
H8/f7 or F8/h7 = Close running fit
H7/g6 or G7/h6 = Sliding fit
H7/h6 = Locational clearance fit

Transition Fits

H7/k6 or K7/h6 = Locational transition fit
H7/n6 or N7/h6 = Locational transition fit

Figure 9-27

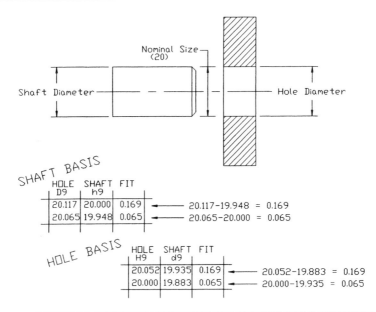

Figure 9-28

Interference Fits

H7/p6 or P7/h6 = Locational transition fit
H7/s6 or S7/h6 = Medium drive fit
H7/u6 or U7/h6 = Force fit

Not all possible sizes are listed in the tables in the appendix. Only preferred sizes are listed. Tolerances for sizes between the stated sizes are derived by going to the next nearest given size. The values are not interpolated. A basic size of 27 would use the tolerance values listed for 25. Sizes that are exactly halfway between two stated sizes may use either set of values depending on the design requirements.

9-19 NOMINAL SIZES

The term *nominal* refers to the approximate size of an object that matches a common fraction or whole number. A shaft with a dimension of $1.500\pm.003$ is said to have a nominal size of "one and a half inches." A dimension of $1.500 +.000/-0.005$ is still said to have a nominal size of one and a half inches. In both examples, 1.5 is the closest common fraction.

9-20 HOLE AND SHAFT BASIS

One of the charts shown in Figure 9-27 applies tolerances starting with the nominal hole sizes, called *hole basis tolerances*; the other applies tolerances starting with the

shaft nominal sizes, called *shaft basis tolerances*. The choice of which set of values to use depends on the design application. In general, hole basis numbers are used more often because it is more difficult to vary hole diameters manufactured using specific drill sizes than shaft sizes manufactured using a lathe. Shaft sizes may be used when a specific fastener diameter is used to assemble several objects.

Figure 9-28 shows a hole, a shaft, and a set of sample values taken from the tables found in the appendix. One set of values is for hole basis tolerance and the other for shaft

Figure 9-29

Figure 9-30

Figure 9-31

basis tolerance. The fit values are the same for both sets of values. The hole basis values were derived starting with a nominal hole size of 20.000, whereas the shaft basis values were derived starting with a shaft nominal size of 20.000. The letters used to identify holes are always written using capital letters, and the letters for shaft values use lowercase.

9-21 SAMPLE PROBLEM SP9-3

Dimension a hole and a shaft that are to fit together using a preferred clearance fit. Use hole basis values based on a nominal size of 12 mm.

Figure 9-29 shows values taken from the appropriate table in the appendix. The values may be applied directly to the shaft and hole as shown.

9-22 STANDARD FITS (INCH VALUES)

The appendix also includes tables of standard fit tolerances for inch values. The tables for inches are presented for a range of nominal values and are not for specific values, as are the metric value tables. The values may be hole or shaft basis.

Fits defined using inch values are classified as follows:

    RC = Running and sliding fits
    LC = Clearance locational fits

    LT = Transitional locational fits
    LN = Interference fits
    FN = Force fits

Each of these general categories has several subclassifications within it defined by a number, for example, Class RC1, Class RC2, through Class RC9. The letter designations are based on International Tolerance Standards, as are metric designations.

The values are listed in thousandths of an inch. A table value of 1.1 means .0011 inch. A table value of .5 means .0005 inch.

Figure 9-30 shows a set of values for a Class RC3 clearance fit hole basis taken from the appendix. If the values are applied to a nominal size of .5 inch, the resulting hole and shaft sizes will be as shown. Plus table values are added to the nominal value; minus values are subtracted from the nominal value.

Nominal values that are common to two nominal ranges (0.71) may use values from either range.

9-23 SAMPLE PROBLEM SP9-4

Dimension a hole and shaft for a Class LN1 Interference fit based on a nominal diameter of .25 in. Use hole basis values.

Figure 9-31 shows the values for the 0.24 − 0.40 nominal range as listed in the appendix. The values are in thousandths of an inch. Plus values are added to the nominal size. The resulting shaft and hole dimensions are as shown. The diameter of the shaft is larger than that of the hole because this example calls for an interference fit.

PREFERRED SIZES (mm)

First Choice	Second Choice	First Choice	Second Choice
1	1.1	12	14
1.2	1.4	16	18
1.6	1.8	20	22
2	2.2	25	28
2.5	2.8	30	35
3	3.5	40	45
4	4.5	50	55
5	5.5	60	70
6	7	80	90
8	9	100	110
10	11	120	140

Figure 9-32

Fraction	Decimal Equivalent	Fraction	Decimal Equivalent	Fraction	Decimal Equivalent
7/64	.1094	21/64	.3281	11/16	.6875
1/8	.1250	11/32	.3438	3/4	.7500
9/64	.1406	23/64	.3594	13/16	.8125
5/32	.1562	3/8	.3750	7/8	.8750
11/64	.1719	25/64	.3906	15/16	.9375
3/16	.1875	13/32	.4062	1	1.0000
13/64	.2031	27/64	.4219		
7/32	.2188	7/16	.4375	PARTIAL LIST	
1/4	.2500	29/64	.4531	of standard	
17/64	.2656	15/32	.4688	Twist Drill Sizes	
9/32	.2812	1/2	.5000	(Fractional	
19/64	.2969	9/16	.5625	Sizes)	
5/16	.3125	5/8	.6250		

Figure 9-33

9-24 PREFERRED AND STANDARD SIZES

It is important that designers always consider preferred and standard sizes when selecting sizes for designs. Most tooling is set up to match these sizes, so manufacturing is greatly simplified when preferred and standard sizes are specified. Figure 9-32 shows a list of preferred sizes for metric values.

Consider the case of design calculations that call for a 42-mm diameter hole. A 42-mm diameter hole is not a preferred size. A diameter of 40 mm is the closest preferred size, and a 45-mm diameter is a second choice. A 42-mm hole could be manufactured but would require an unusual drill size that may not be available. It would be wise to reconsider the design to see if a 40-mm diameter hole could be used, and if not, possibly a 45-mm diameter hole.

A very large quantity production run could possibly justify the cost of special tooling, but for smaller runs it is probably better to use preferred sizes. Machinists will have the required drills, and maintenance people will have the appropriate tools for these sizes.

Figure 9-33 shows a list of standard fractional drill sizes. Most companies now specify metric units or decimal inches; however, many standard items are still available in fractional sizes, and many older objects may still require fractional-sized tools and replacement parts. A more complete listing is available in the appendix.

9-25 SURFACE FINISHES

The term *surface finish* refers to the accuracy (flatness) of a surface. Metric values are measured using micrometers (μm), and inch values are measured in microinches (μin.).

The accuracy of a surface depends on the manufacturing process used to produce the surface. Figure 9-34 shows a list of several manufacturing processes and the quality of the surface finish they can be expected to produce.

Surface finishes have several design applications. *Datum surfaces,* or surfaces used for baseline dimensioning, should have fairly accurate surface finishes to help assure accurate measurements; bearing surfaces should have good-quality surface finishes for better load distribution, and parts that operate at high speeds should have smooth finishes to help reduce friction.

Figure 9-35 shows a screw head sitting on a very wavy surface. Note that the head of the screw is in contact with only two wave peaks, meaning all the bearing load is concentrated on the two peaks. This situation could cause stress

Surface Roughness Average Obtained by Common Production Methods

Process	Roughness Height Rating Micrometers, Microinches (μm) 50 25 12.5 6.3 3.2 1.6 0.8 0.4 0.2 0.1 0.05 0.025 (μin) 2000 1000 500 250 125 63 32 16 8 4 2 1
Flame Cutting	
Snagging	
Sawing	
Planning, Shaping	
Drilling	
Chemical Milling	
Elect Discharge Machine	
Milling	
Broaching	
Reaming	
Electron Beam	
Laser	

Surface Roughness Average Obtained by Common Production Methods

Process	Roughness Height Rating Micrometers, Microinches (μm) 50 25 12.5 6.3 3.2 1.6 0.8 0.4 0.2 0.1 0.05 0.025 (μin) 2000 1000 500 250 125 63 32 16 8 4 2 1
Electrochemical	
Boring, Turning	
Barrel Finishing	
Electronic Grinding	
Roller Burnishing	
Grinding	
Honing	
Electropolishing	
Polishing	
Lapping	
Superfinish	

Surface Roughness Average Obtained by Common Production Methods

Process	Roughness Height Rating Micrometers, Microinches (μm) 50 25 12.5 6.3 3.2 1.6 0.8 0.4 0.2 0.1 0.05 0.025 (μin) 2000 1000 500 250 125 63 32 16 8 4 2 1
Sand Casting	
Hot Rolling	
Forging	
Perm Mold Casting	
Investment Casting	
Extruding	
Cold Rolling, Drawing	
Die Casting	

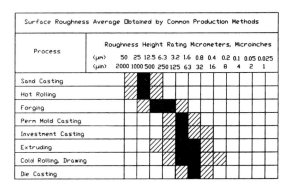

■ Average Application   ▨ Less Frequent Application

Figure 9-34

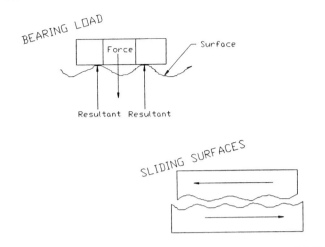

Figure 9-35

Figure 9-36

cracks and greatly weaken the surface. A better-quality surface finish would increase the bearing contact area.

Figure 9-35 also shows two very rough surfaces moving in contact with each other. The result will be excess wear to both surfaces because the surfaces touch only on the peaks, and these peaks will tend to wear faster than flatter areas. Excess vibration can also result when interfacing surfaces are too rough.

Surface finishes are classified into three categories: surface texture, roughness, and lay. *Surface texture* is a general term that refers to the overall quality and accuracy of a surface.

Roughness is a measure of the average deviation of a surface's peaks and valleys. See Figure 9-36.

Lay refers to the direction of machine marks on a surface. See Figure 9-37. The lay of a surface is particularly

Figure 9-37

Figure 9-38

Figure 9-39

important when two moving objects are in contact with each other, especially at high speeds.

9-26 SURFACE CONTROL SYMBOLS

Surface finishes are indicated on a drawing with surface control symbols. See Figure 9-38. The general surface control symbol looks like a check mark. Roughness values may be included with the symbol to specify the required accuracy. Surface control symbols can also be used to specify the manufacturing process that may or may not be used to produce a surface.

Figure 9-39 shows two applications of surface control symbols. In the first example, a 0.8-μm (32-μin.) surface finish is specified on the surface that serves as a datum for several horizontal dimensions. A 0.8-μm surface finish is generally considered the minimum acceptable finish for datums.

A second finish mark with a value of 0.4 μm is located on an extension line that refers to a surface that will be in contact with a moving object. The extra flatness will help prevent wear between the two surfaces.

It is suggested that a general finish mark be drawn and saved as a wblock so it can be inserted as needed on future drawings. Add the machine mark wblock to any prototype drawings created.

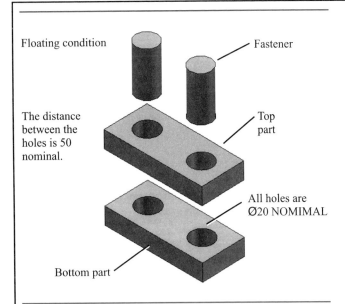

Floating condition

Fastener

The distance between the holes is 50 nominal.

Top part

All holes are Ø20 NOMIMAL

Bottom part

Figure 9-40

Tolerance zones for the center points of the holes using linear tolerances 50±.01

NOT TO SCALE

.02

.02

.028

.02

.02

.028

50

Figure 9-41

9-27 DESIGN PROBLEMS

Figure 9-40 shows two objects that are to be fitted together using a fastener such as a screw-and-nut combination. For this example a cylinder will be used to represent a fastener. Only two nominal dimensions are given. The dimensions and tolerances were derived as follows.

The distance between the centers of the holes is given as 50 NOMINAL. The term *nominal* means that the stated value is only a starting point. The final dimensions will be close to the given value, but do not have to equal it.

Assigning tolerances is an iteration process; that is, a tolerance is selected and other tolerance values are calculated from the selected initial values. If the results are not satisfactory, go back and modify the initial value and calculate the other values again. As your experience grows, you will become better at selecting realistic initial values.

In the example shown in Figure 9-40, start by assigning a tolerance of ±0.01 to both the TOP and BOTTOM parts for both the horizontal and vertical dimensions used to locate the holes. This means that there is a possible center point variation of 0.02 for both parts. The parts must always fit together, so tolerances must be assigned based on the worst-case condition, or when the parts are made at the extreme ends of the assigned tolerances.

Figure 9-41 shows a greatly enlarged picture of the worst-case condition created by a tolerance of ±0.01. The center points of the two holes could be as much as 0.028 apart if they were located at opposite corners of the tolerance zones. This means that the minimum hole diameter must always be at least 0.028 larger than the maximum stud diameter. See Section 9-15. In addition, there should be a

clearance tolerance assigned so that the hole and stud are never exactly the same size. Figure 9-42 shows the resulting tolerances.

Floating condition

The TOP and BOTTOM parts shown in Figure 9-40 are to be joined by two independent fasteners; that is, the location of one fastener does not depend on the location of the other. This is called a *floating condition*. This means

FASTENER (top view)

The 19.96 value includes a .01 clearance allowance, and the 19.94 value is the result of an assigned feature tolerance of .02.

Ø19.96
Ø19.94

Ø20 +.02/0

HOLE for both parts

Figure 9-42

that the tolerance zones for both the TOP and BOTTOM parts can be assigned the same values, and that a fastener diameter selected to fit one part will also fit the other part.

The final tolerances were developed by first defining a minimum hole size of 20.00. An arbitrary tolerance of .02 was assigned to the hole and was expressed as 20.00 +.02/−0, so that the hole can never be any smaller than 20.00.

The 20.00 minimum hole diameter dictates that the maximum fastener diameter can be no greater than 19.97, or .03 (the rounded-off diagonal distance across the tolerance zone −.028) less than the minimum hole diameter. A .01 clearance was assigned. The clearance ensures that the hole and fastener are never exactly the same diameter. The resulting maximum allowable diameter for the fastener is 19.96. Again, an arbitrary tolerance of .02 was assigned to the fastener. The final fastener dimensions are therefore 19.96 to 19.94.

The assigned tolerances ensure that there will always be at least .01 clearance between the fastener and the hole. The other extreme condition occurs when the hole is at its largest possible size (10.02) and the fastener is at its smallest (19.94). This means that there could be as much as .08 clearance between the parts. If this much clearance is not acceptable, then the assigned tolerances will have to be re-evaluated.

Figure 9-43 shows the TOP and BOTTOM parts dimensioned and toleranced. Any dimensions that do not have assigned tolerances are assumed to have standard tolerances. See Figure 9-14.

Note, in Figure 9-43, that the top edge of each part was assigned a surface finish. This was done to help ensure the accuracy of the 20±.01 dimension. If this edge surface were rough, it could affect the tolerance measurements.

This example will be repeated in Chapter 10 using geometric tolerances. Geometric tolerance zones are circular rather than rectangular.

Fixed condition

Figure 9-44 shows the same nominal conditions presented in Figure 9-40, but the fasteners are now fixed to the TOP part. This is called the *fixed condition*. In analyzing the tolerance zones for the fixed condition, one must consider two positional tolerances: the positional tolerances for the holes in the BOTTOM part and the positional tolerances for the fixed fasteners in the TOP part. This may be expressed in an equation as follows:

$$S_{max} + DTSZ = H_{min} - DTZ$$

where

S_{max} = Maximum shaft (fastener) diameter

H_{min} = Minimum hole diameter

$DTSZ$ = Diagonal distance across the shaft's center point tolerance zone

DTZ = Diagonal distance across the hole's center point tolerance zone

---

FASTENER

Surface finish

Holes in both parts

⌀ 19.96 / 19.94

20 — 50±.01

⌀20.00 +.02/−0

32√

20±.01

40

90

TOP and BOTTOM

All dimensions not assigned a tolerance will be assumed to have a standard tolerance. See Figure 9-14.

Figure 9-43

Fixed condition

Fasteners are fixed to TOP part.

The distance between the holes is 50 nominal.

All holes are ⌀20 NOMINAL.

Figure 9-44

If a dimension and tolerance of 50±.01 and 20±.01 are assigned to both the center distance between the holes and the center distance between the fixed fasteners, the values for DTSZ and DTZ will be equal. The formula can then be simplified as follows:

$$S_{max} = H_{min} - 2(DTZ)$$

where DTZ equals the diagonal distance across the tolerance zone. If a hole tolerance of 20.00 +.02/−0 is also defined, the resulting maximum shaft size can be determined, assuming that the calculated distance of .028 is rounded off to .03. See Figure 9-45.

$$\begin{aligned} S_{max} &= 20.00 - 2(.03) \\ &= 19.94 \end{aligned}$$

This means that the largest possible shaft diameter that will just fit equals 19.94. If a clearance tolerance of .01 is assumed to ensure that the shaft and hole are never exactly the same size, the maximum shaft diameter becomes 19.93. See Figure 9-46.

A feature tolerance of .02 on the shaft will result in a minimum shaft diameter of 19.91. Note that the .01 clearance tolerance and the .02 feature tolerance were arbitrarily chosen. Other possible values could have been used.

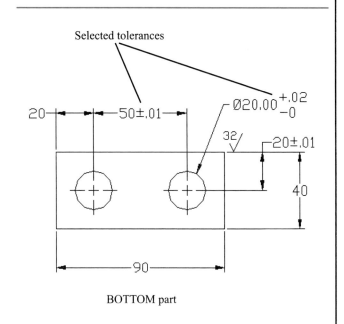

BOTTOM part

Figure 9-45

The shaft values were derived as follows.

20.00	The selected value for the minimum hole diameter
−.03	The rounded-off value for the hole positional tolerance
−.03	The rounded-off value for the shaft positional tolerance
−.01	The selected clearance value
19.93	The maximum shaft value
−.02	The selected tolerance value
19.91	The minimum shaft diameter

TOP part

Figure 9-46

To design given a fastener size

The previous two examples started by selecting a minimum hole diameter and then calculating the resulting fastener size. Figure 9-47 shows a situation in which the fastener size is defined, and the problem is to determine the appropriate hole sizes. Figure 9-48 shows the dimensions and tolerances for both top and bottom parts.

Requirements:
Clearance, minimum = .003
Hole tolerances = .005
Positional tolerance = .002

Ø.500/.499 BOTH FASTENERS

The distance between the holes is 2.50 nominal.

Figure 9-47

Given fastener tolerances

Selected positional tolerances

Resulting hole tolerances

Results include
.003 clearance
.005 tolerance

ø .500
.499

1.00   2.500±.001

ø .511
.506

32

1.000±.002

2.00

4.50

.500 Maximum fastener diameter
+.003 Rounded-off diagonal distance of tolerance zone
+.003 Defined clearance
.506 Minumum hole diameter
+.005 Defined hole tolerance
.511 Maximum hole diameter

Figure 9-48

9-28 EXERCISE PROBLEMS

Redraw the objects shown in Exercise Problems EX9-1 to EX9-4 using the given dimensions. Include the listed tolerances.

EX9-1 MILLIMETERS

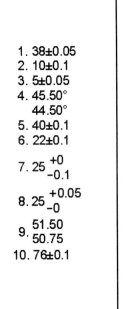

1. 38±0.05
2. 10±0.1
3. 5±0.05
4. 45.50°
   44.50°
5. 40±0.1
6. 22±0.1
7. $25^{+0}_{-0.1}$
8. $25^{+0.05}_{-0}$
9. 51.50
   50.75
10. 76±0.1

EX9-2 MILLIMETERS

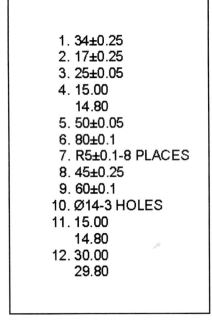

1. 34±0.25
2. 17±0.25
3. 25±0.05
4. 15.00
   14.80
5. 50±0.05
6. 80±0.1
7. R5±0.1-8 PLACES
8. 45±0.25
9. 60±0.1
10. Ø14-3 HOLES
11. 15.00
    14.80
12. 30.00
    29.80

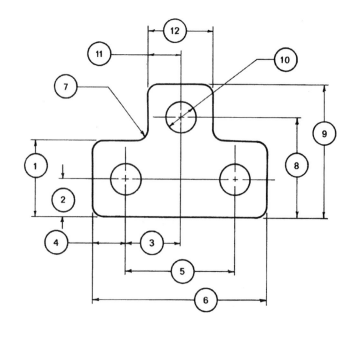

EX9-3 INCHES

1. 3.00±.01
2. 1.56±.01
3. 46.50
   45.50
4. .750±.005
5. 2.75
   2.70
6. 3.625±.010
7. 45°±.5°
8. 2.250±.005

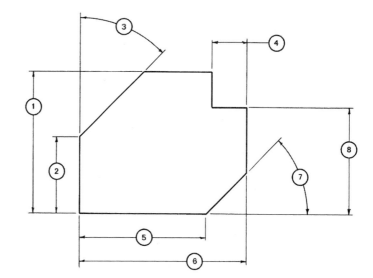

EX9-4 INCHES

1. $50^{+.2}_{\ 0}$
2. R45±.1-2 PLACES
3. $63.5^{\ 0}_{\ 0.2}$
4. 76±.1
5. 38±.1
6. $\varnothing 12.00^{+.05}_{\ 0}$ -3 HOLES
7. 30±.03
8. 30±.03
9. $100^{+.4}_{\ 0}$

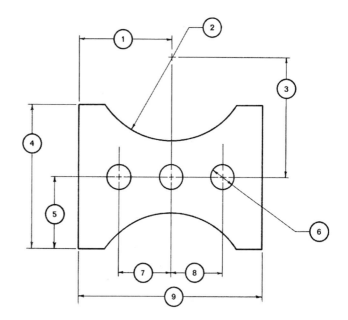

EX9-5 MILLIMETERS

Redraw the following object, including the given dimensions and tolerances. Calculate and list the maximum and minimum distances for surface A.

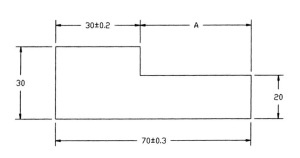

EX9-7 MILLIMETERS

Redraw the following object, including the dimensions and tolerances. Calculate and list the maximum and minimum distances for surfaces D and E.

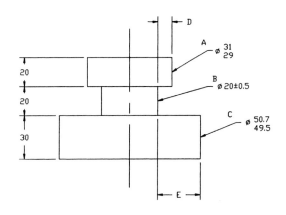

EX9-6 INCHES

A. Redraw the following object, including the dimensions and tolerances. Calculate and list the maximum and minimum distances for surface A.
B. Redraw the given object and dimension it using baseline dimensions. Calculate and list the maximum and minimum distances for surface A.

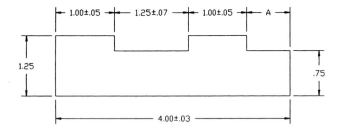

EX9-8 MILLIMETERS

Dimension the following object twice: once using chain dimensions and once using baseline dimensions. Calculate and list the maximum and minimum distances for surface D for both chain and baseline dimensions. Compare the results.

EX9-9 INCHES

Redraw the following shapes, including the dimensions and tolerances. Also list the required minimum and maximum values for the specified distances.

B_{min} = _____
B_{max} = _____

C_{min} = _____
C_{max} = _____

C_{min} = _____
C_{max} = _____

C_{min} = _____
C_{max} = _____

EX9-10

Redraw and complete the following inspection report. Under the Results column classify each "AS MEASURED" value as OK if the value is within the stated tolerances, REWORK if the value indicates that the measured value is beyond the stated tolerance but can be reworked to bring it into the acceptable range, or SCRAP if the value is not within the tolerance range and cannot be reworked to make it acceptable.

INSPECTION REPORT				
PART NAME AND NO: 10755002				
INSPECTOR:				
DATE:				
BASE DIMENSION	TOLERANCES		AS MEASURED	RESULTS
	MAX	MIN		
① 100 ± 0.5			99.8	
② $\phi {}^{57}_{56}$			57.01	
③ 22 ± 0.3			21.72	
④ ${}^{40.05}_{39.95}$			39.98	
⑤ 22 ± 0.3			21.68	
⑥ $R52 {}^{+0}_{-0.2}$			51.99	
⑦ $35 {}^{+0.2}_{-0.3}$			35.20	
⑧ $30 {}^{+0.4}_{0}$			30.27	
⑨ $6.0 {}^{+.1}_{-.2}$			5.85	
⑩ 12.0 ± 0.2			11.90	

1.00 3 PLACES

.50 —10 PLACES

EX9-11 MILLIMETERS

Redraw the following charts and complete them based on the following information. All values are in millimeters.

A. Nominal=16, Fit=H9/d9
B. Nominal=30, Fit=H11/c11
C. Nominal=22, Fit=H7/g6
D. Nominal=10, Fit=C11/h11
E. Nominal=25, Fit=F8/h7
F. Nominal=12, Fit=H7/k6
G. Nominal=3, Fit=H7/p6
H. Nominal=19, Fit=H7/s6
I. Nominal=27, Fit=H7/u6
J. Nominal=30, Fit=N7/h6

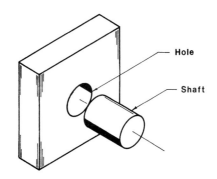

half space

NOMINAL	HOLE		SHAFT		CLEARANCE	
	MAX	MIN	MAX	MIN	MAX	MIN
A						
B						
C						
D						
E						

3.75
6 equal
spaces

1.5 — 6.0 - 6 equal spaces

NOMINAL	HOLE		SHAFT		INTERFERENCE	
	MAX	MIN	MAX	MIN	MAX	MIN
F						
G						
H						
I						
J						

Use the same dimensions given above

EX9-12

Redraw the following charts and complete them based on the following information. All values are in inches.

A. Nominal=0.25, Fit=Class LC5
B. Nominal=1.00, Fit=Class LC7
C. Nominal=1.50, Fit=Class LC10
D. Nominal=0.75, Fit=Class RC3
E. Nominal=2.50, Fit=Class RC6
F. Nominal=.500, Fit=Class LT2
G. Nominal=1.25, Fit=Class LT5
H. Nominal=3.00, Fit=Class LN3
I. Nominal=1.625, Fit=Class FN1
J. Nominal=2.00, Fit=Class FN4

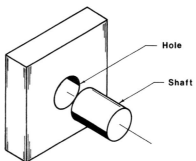

Hole

Shaft

half space

3.75
6 equal
spaces

NOMINAL	HOLE		SHAFT		CLEARANCE	
	MAX	MIN	MAX	MIN	MAX	MIN
A						
B						
C						
D						
E						

1.5   6.0 – 6 equal spaces

NOMINAL	HOLE		SHAFT		INTERFERENCE	
	MAX	MIN	MAX	MIN	MAX	MIN
F						
G						
H						
I						
J						

Use the same dimensions given above

Draw the chart shown and add the appropriate values based on the dimensions and tolerances given in Exercise Problems EX9-13 to EX9-16.

EX9-13 MILLIMETERS

```
PART NO: 9-M53A
    A.  20±0.1
    B.  30±0.2
    C.  Ø20±0.05
    D.  40
    E.  60
```

MAXIMUM SHAFT DIAMETER
THAT WILL ALWAYS FIT
= _____ ?

PART NO:									
A		B		C		D		E	
MAX	MIN	MAX	MIN	MAX	MIN	MAX	MIN	MAX	MIN

20 – 10 PLACES

EX9-15 MILLIMETERS

```
PART NO: 9-M53B
    A.  32.02
        31.97
    B.  47.52
        47.50
    C.  Ø18  +0.05
              0
    D.  64±0.05
    E.  100±0.05
```

EX9-14 MILLIMETERS

```
PART NO: 9-M53B
    A.  32.02
        31.97
    B.  47.52
        47.50
    C.  Ø18  +0.05
              0
    D.  64±0.05
    E.  100±0.05
```

EX9-16 MILLIMETERS

```
PART NO: 9-E47B
    A.  18    +0
              -0.02
    B.  26    +0
              -0.04
    C.  Ø    24.03
             23.99
    D.  52±0.04
    E.  36±0.02
```

EX9-17 MILLIMETERS

Prepare front and top views of Parts 4A and 4B based on the given dimensions. Add tolerances to produce the stated clearances.

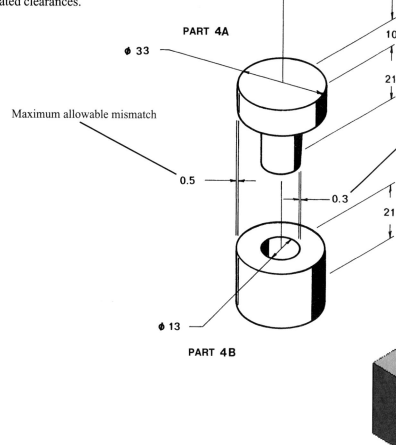

PART 4A

φ 33

10

21

Maximum allowable mismatch

Maximum allowable clearance

0.5

0.3

21

φ 13

PART 4B

EX9-18 INCHES

Redraw parts A and B and add dimensions and tolerances to meet the "UPON ASSEMBLED" requirements.

Material is 1.00 thick.

Nominal sizes

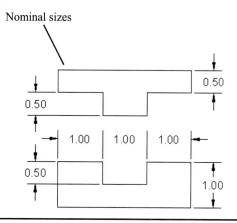

0.50

0.50

1.00   1.00   1.00

0.50

1.00

The Upon Assembled requirements.

1.50±.04

.02
.06

EX9-19 MILLIMETERS

Draw a front and a top view of both given objects. Add dimensions and tolerances to meet the "FINAL CONDITION" requirements.

FINAL CONDITION

MAX = 0.03
MIN = 0.01

MIN = 0.00
MAX = 0.04

EX9-20 INCHES

Given the following nominal sizes, dimension tolerance parts AM311 and AM312 so that they always fit together regardless of orientation. Further, dimension the overall lengths of each part so that, in the assembled condition, they will always pass through a clearance gage with an opening of 90.00±.02.

In the assembled condition, both parts must always pass through the clearance gage.

All given dimensions, except for the clearance gage, are nominal.

EX9-21 MILLIMETERS

Design a bracket that will support the three Ø100 wheels shown. The wheels will utilize three Ø5.00±0.01 shafts attached to the bracket. The bottom of the bracket must have a minimum of 10 millimeters from the ground. The wall thickness of the bracket must always be at least 5 millimeters, and the minimum bracket opening must be at least 15 millimeters.

1. Prepare a front and a side view of the bracket.
2. Draw the wheels in their relative positions using phantom lines.
3. Add all appropriate dimensions and tolerances.

ALL SIZES ARE NOMINAL, UNLESS
OTHERWISE STATED.

SHAFT Ø = 5.00±.01
3 REQUIRED

ROLLER BLADE ASSEMBLY
PART NUMBER BU110-44

Given a TOP and BOTTOM part in the floating condition as shown in Figure EX9-22 add dimensions and tolerances to satisfy the following conditions. Size the TOP and BOTTOM parts and FASTENER length as needed.

EX9-22 INCHES–CLEARANCE FIT

A. The distance between the holes is 2.00 nominal.
B. The diameter of the fasteners is Ø.375 nominal.
C. The fasteners have a total tolerance of .001.
D. The holes have a tolerance of .002.
E. The minimum allowable clearance between the fastener and the holes is .003.
F. The material is .375 inch thick.

EX9-23 MILLIMETERS–CLEARANCE FIT

A. The distance between the holes is 80 nominal.
B. The nominal diameter of the fasteners is Ø12.
C. The fasteners have a total tolerance of .05.
D. The holes have a tolerance of .03.
E. The minimum allowable clearance between the fastener and the holes is .02.
F. The material is 12 millimeters thick.

EX9-24 INCHES–CLEARANCE FIT

A. The distance between the holes is 3.50 nominal.
B. The diameter of the fasteners is Ø.625.
C. The fasteners have a total tolerance of .005.
D. The holes have a tolerance of .003.
E. The minimum allowable clearance between the fastener and the holes is .002.
F. The material is .500 inch thick.

EX9-25 MILLIMETERS–CLEARANCE FIT

A. The distance between the holes is 120 nominal.
B. The diameter of the fasteners is Ø24 nominal.
C. The fasteners have a total tolerance of .01.
D. The holes have a tolerance of .02.
E. The minimum allowable clearance between the fastener and the holes is .04.
F. The material is 20 millimeters thick.

EX9-26 INCHES–INTERFERENCE FIT

A. The distance between the holes is 2.00 nominal.
B. The diameter of the fasteners is Ø.250 nominal.
C. The fasteners have a total tolerance of .001.
D. The holes have a tolerance of .002.
E. The maximum allowable interference between the fastener and the holes is .0065.
F. The material is .438 inch thick.

Figure EX9-22

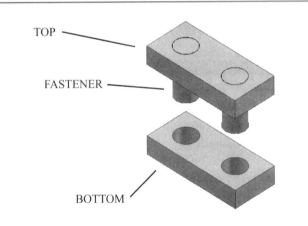

Figure EX9-23

EX9-27 MILLIMETERS–INTERFERENCE FIT

A. The distance between the holes is 80 nominal.
B. The diameter of the fasteners is Ø10 nominal.
C. The fasteners have a total tolerance of .01.
D. The holes have a tolerance of .02.
E. The maximum allowable interference between the fastener and the holes is .032.
F. The material is 14 millimeters thick.

EX9-28 INCHES–LOCATIONAL FIT

A. The distance between the holes is 2.25 nominal.
B. The diameter of the fasteners is Ø.50 nominal.

C. The fasteners have a total tolerance of .001.
D. The holes have a tolerance of .002.
E. The minimum allowable clearance between the fastener and the holes is .0010.
F. The material is .370 inch thick.

EX9-29 MILLIMETERS–TRANSITIONAL FIT

A. The distance between the holes is 100 nominal.
B. The diameter of the fasteners is Ø16 nominal.
C. The fasteners have a total tolerance of .01.
D. The holes are to have a tolerance of .02.
E. The minimum allowable clearance between the fastener and the holes is .01.
F. The material is 20 millimeters thick.

Given a TOP and BOTTOM part in the fixed condition as shown in Figure EX9-23 add dimensions and tolerances to satisfy the following conditions. Size the TOP and BOTTOM parts and FASTENER length as needed.

EX9-30 INCHES–CLEARANCE FIT

A. The distance between the holes is 2.00 nominal.
B. The diameter of the fasteners is Ø.375 nominal.
C. The fasteners have a total tolerance of .001.
D. The holes have a tolerance of .002.
E. The minimum allowable clearance between the fastener and the holes is .003.
F. The material is .375 inch thick.

EX9-31 MILLIMETERS–CLEARANCE FIT

A. The distance between the holes is 80 nominal.
B. The nominal diameter of the fasteners is Ø12.
C. The fasteners have a total tolerance of .05.
D. The holes have a tolerance of .03.
E. The minimum allowable clearance between the fastener and the holes is .02.
F. The material is 12 millimeters thick.

EX9-32 INCHES–CLEARANCE FIT

A. The distance between the holes is 3.50 nominal.
B. The diameter of the fasteners is Ø.625.
C. The fasteners have a total tolerance of .005.
D. The holes have a tolerance of .003.
E. The minimum allowable clearance between the fastener and the holes is .002.
F. The material is .500 inch thick.

EX9-33 MILLIMETERS–CLEARANCE FIT

A. The distance between the holes is 120 nominal.
B. The diameter of the fasteners is Ø24 nominal.
C. The fasteners have a total tolerance of .01.
D. The holes have a tolerance of .02.
E. The minimum allowable clearance between the fastener and the holes is .04.
F. The material is 20 millimeters thick.

EX9-34 INCHES–INTERFERENCE FIT

A. The distance between the holes is 2.00 nominal.
B. The diameter of the fasteners is Ø.250 nominal.
C. The fasteners have a total tolerance of .001.
D. The holes have a tolerance of .002.
E. The maximum allowable interference between the fastener and the holes is .0065.
F. The material is .438 inch thick.

EX9-35 MILLIMETERS–INTERFERENCE FIT

A. The distance between the holes is 80 nominal.
B. The diameter of the fasteners is Ø10 nominal.
C. The fasteners have a total tolerance of 0.01.
D. The holes have a tolerance of 0.02.
E. The maximum allowable interference between the fastener and the holes is 0.032.
F. The material is 14 millimeters thick

EX9-36 INCHES–LOCATIONAL FIT

A. The distance between the holes is 2.25 nominal.
B. The diameter of the fasteners is Ø.50 nominal.
C. The fasteners have a total tolerance of .001.
D. The holes have a tolerance of .002.
E. The minimum allowable clearance between the fastener and the holes is .0010.
F. The material is .370 inch thick.

EX9-37 MILLIMETERS–TRANSITIONAL FIT

A. The distance between the holes is 100 nominal.
B. The diameter of the fasteners is Ø16 nominal.
C. The fasteners have a total tolerance of .01.
D. The holes are to have a tolerance of .02.
E. The minimum allowable clearance between the fastener and the holes is .01.
F. The material is 20 millimeters thick.

DESIGN

EX9-38 MILLIMETERS

Given the following two assemblies, size the individual parts so that they always fit together. Create a drawing for each part including dimensions and tolerances.

BLOCK ASSEMBLY

BLOCK, BASE

BLOCK, TOP

PEG

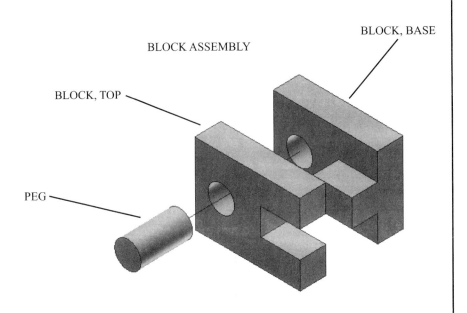

SUPPORT ASSEMBLY

BRACKET, END
2 REQD

PLATE, 4 HOLE
2 REQD

PEG

Geometric Tolerances

10-1 INTRODUCTION

Geometric tolerancing is a dimensioning and tolerancing system based on the geometric shape of an object. Surfaces may be defined in terms of their flatness or roundness, or in terms of how perpendicular or parallel they are to other surfaces.

Geometric tolerances allow a more exact definition of the shape of an object than do conventional coordinate-type tolerances. Objects can be toleranced in a manner more closely related to their design function, or so that their features and surfaces are more directly related to each other.

Figure 10-1 shows a square shape dimensioned and toleranced using plus and minus tolerances. The resulting tolerance zone has an outside length of 51 and an inside length of 49 square. The defined tolerance zone allows any shape that falls within in it to be deemed acceptable, or correctly manufactured. Figure 10-1 shows an exaggerated shape that fits within the defined tolerance zone and is not square yet would be acceptable under the specified dimensions and tolerances. Geometric tolerancing can be used to more precisely define the tolerance zone when a more nearly square shape is required.

It should be pointed out that geometric tolerancing is not a panacea for all dimensioning and tolerancing problems. In many cases coordinate tolerancing, as presented in

Chapter 9, is sufficient to accurately define an object. Unnecessary or excessive use of geometric tolerances can increase production costs. Most objects are toleranced using a combination of coordinate and geometric tolerances, depending on the design function of the object.

The key to using tolerances and types of tolerances may be simply stated as "decimal points cost money." Every tolerance should be made as loose as possible while

Figure 10-1

Figure 10-2

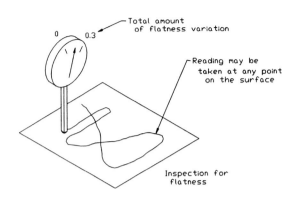

Figure 10-3

still maintaining the design integrity of the object. If a surface flatness is critical to the correct functioning of the object, then, of course, it will require a very close tolerance. But every tolerance should be considered individually and loosened wherever possible to make the object's manufacture easier and therefore less expensive.

10-2 TOLERANCES OF FORM

Tolerances of form are used to define the shape of a surface relative to itself. There are four classifications: flatness, straightness, roundness and cylindricity. Tolerances of form are not related to other surfaces but apply only to an individual surface.

10-3 FLATNESS

Flatness tolerances are used to define the amount of variation permitted in an individual surface. The surface is thought of as a plane not related to the rest of the object.

Figure 10-2 shows a rectangular object. How flat is the top surface? The given plus or minus tolerances allow a variation of ±0.5 across the surface. Without additional tolerances the surface could look like a series of waves that vary between 30.5 and 29.5.

If the example in Figure 10-2 is assigned a flatness tolerance of 0.3, the height of the object, the feature tolerance could continue to vary based on the 30 ±0.5 tolerance, but the surface itself could not vary by more than 0.3. In the most extreme condition, one end of the surface could be 30.5 above the bottom surface and the other end 29.5, but the surface would still be limited to within two parallel planes 0.3 apart as shown.

To better understand the meaning of flatness, consider how the surface would be inspected. The surface would be acceptable if a gage could be moved all around the surface and never varied by more than 0.3. See Figure 10-3. Every point in the plane must be within the specified tolerance.

10-4 STRAIGHTNESS

Straightness tolerances are used to measure the variation of an individual feature along a straight line in a specified direction. Figure 10-4 shows an object with a straightness tolerance applied to its top surface. Straightness differs from flatness because straightness measurements are checked by moving a gage directly across the surface in a single direction. The gage is not moved randomly about the surface, as is required by flatness.

Figure 10-4

Figure 10-5

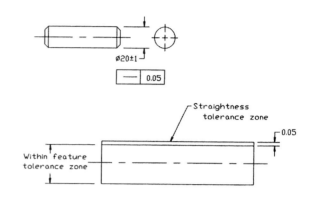

Figure 10-6

Straightness tolerances are most often applied to circular or matching objects to help ensure that the parts are not barreled or warped within the given feature tolerance range and therefore not fit together well. Figure 10-5 shows a cylindrical object dimensioned and toleranced using a standard feature tolerance. The surface of the cylinder may vary within the specified tolerance range as shown.

Figure 10-6 shows the same object shown in Figure 10-5 dimensioned and toleranced using the same feature tolerance, but also including a 0.05 straightness tolerance. The straightness tolerance limits the surface variation to 0.05 as shown.

10-5 STRAIGHTNESS (RFS AND MMC)

Figure 10-7 again shows the same cylinder shown in Figures 10-5 and 10-6. This time the straightness tolerance is applied about the cylinder's centerline. This type of tolerance permits the feature tolerance and geometric tolerance to be used together to define a virtual condition. A *virtual condition* is used to determine the maximum possible size variation of the cylinder or the smallest diameter hole that will always accept the cylinder. See Section 10-17.

The geometric tolerance specified in Figure 10-7 is applied to any circular segment along the cylinder, regardless of the cylinder's diameter. This means that the 0.05 tolerance is applied equally when the cylinder's diameter measures 19 or when it measures 21. This application is called *RFS, regardless of feature size*. RFS conditions are specified in a tolerance either by an S with a circle around

it or implied tacitly when no other symbol is used. In Figure 10-7 no symbol is listed after the 0.05 value, so it is assumed to be applied RFS.

Figure 10-8 shows the cylinder dimensioned with an *MMC* condition applied to the straightness tolerance. MMC stands for *maximum material condition* and means that the specified straightness tolerance (0.05) is applied only at the MMC condition or when the cylinder is at its maximum diameter size (21).

A shaft is an external feature, so its largest possible size or MMC occurs when it is at its maximum diameter. A hole is an internal feature. A hole's MMC condition occurs when it is at its smallest diameter. The MMC condition for holes will be discussed later in the chapter along with positional tolerances.

Figure 10-7

Measured Size	Allowable Tolerance Zone	Virtual Condition
21.0	0.05	21.05
20.9	0.15	21.15
20.8	0.25	21.25
.	.	.
.	.	.
20.0	1.05	22.05
.	.	.
.	.	.
19.0	2.05	23.05

Figure 10-8

Applying a straightness tolerance at MMC allows for a variation in the resulting tolerance zone. Because the 0.05 flatness tolerance is applied at MMC, the virtual condition is still 21.05, the same as with the RFS condition; however, the tolerance is applied only at MMC. As the cylinder's diameter varies within the specified feature tolerance range the acceptable tolerance zone may vary to maintain the same virtual condition.

Figure 10-8 lists how the tolerance zone varies as the cylinder's diameter varies. When the cylinder is at its largest size, or MMC, the tolerance zone equals 0.05, or the specified flatness variation. When the cylinder is at its smallest diameter the tolerance zone equals 2.05, or the

total feature size plus the total flatness size. In all variations the virtual size remains the same, so at any given cylinder diameter value, the size of the tolerance zone can be determined by subtracting the cylinder's diameter value from the virtual condition.

Figure 10-9 shows a comparison between different methods used to dimension and tolerance a .750 shaft. The first example uses only a feature tolerance. This tolerance sets an upper limit of .755 and a lower limit of .745. Any variations within that range are acceptable.

The second example in Figure 10-9 sets a straightness tolerance of .003 about the cylinder's centerline. No conditions are defined, so the tolerance is applied RFS.

The RFS condition does not allow the tolerance zone to grow, as does the same tolerance applied as MMC.

Figure 10-9

Figure 10-10

Figure 10-11

This limits the variations in straightness to .003 at all feature sizes. For example, when the shaft is at its smallest possible feature size, .745, the .003 still applies. This means that a shaft measuring .745 that had a straightness variation greater than .003 would be rejected. If the tolerance has been applied at MMC, the part would be accepted. This does not mean that straightness tolerances should always be applied at MMC. If straightness is critical to the design integrity or function of the part, then straightness should be applied in the RFS condition.

The third example in Figure 10-9 applies the straightness tolerance about the centerline at MMC. This tolerance creates a virtual condition of .758. The MMC condition allows the tolerance to vary as the feature tolerance varies, so when the shaft is at its smallest feature size, .745, a straightness tolerance of .013 is acceptable (.010 feature tolerance +.003 straightness tolerance).

If the tolerance specification for the cylinder shown in Figure 10-9 were to have a 0.000 tolerance applied at MMC, it would mean that the shaft would have to be perfectly straight at MMC, or when the shaft was at its maximum value (.755); however, the straightness tolerance could vary as the feature size varied, as discussed for the other tolerance conditions. A 0.000 tolerance means that the MMC and the virtual conditions are equal.

Figure 10-10 shows a very long .750-diameter shaft. Its straightness tolerance includes a length qualifier that serves to limit the straightness variations over each inch of the shaft length and prevents excess waviness over the full length. The tolerance Ø.002/1.000 means that the total straightness may vary over the entire length of the shaft by .003 but that the variation is limited to .002 per 1.000 of shaft length.

10-6 CIRCULARITY

Circularity tolerances are used to limit the amount of variation in the roundness of a surface of revolution and are measured at individual cross sections along the length of the object. The measurements are limited to the individual cross sections and are not related to other cross sections. This means that in extreme conditions the shaft shown in Figure 10-11 could actually taper from a diameter of 21 to a diameter of 19 and never violate the circularity requirement. It also means that qualifications such as MMC cannot be applied.

Figure 10-11 shows a shaft that includes a feature tolerance and a circularity tolerance of 0.07. To understand circularity tolerances, consider an individual cross section, or

Figure 10-12

Figure 10-13

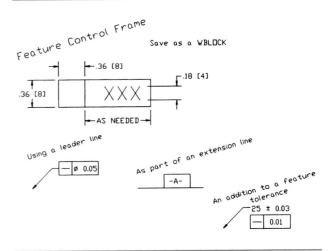

Figure 10-14

slice of the cylinder. The shape of the outside edge of the slice varies around the slice. The difference between the maximum diameter and the minimum diameter of the slice can never exceed the stated circularity tolerance.

Circularity tolerances can be applied to tapered sections and spheres, as shown in Figure 10-12. In both applications, circularity is measured around individual cross sections, as it was for the shaft shown in Figure 10-11.

10-7 CYLINDRICITY

Cylindricity tolerances are used to define a tolerance zone both around individual circular cross sections of an object and also along its length. The resulting tolerance zone looks like two concentric cylinders.

Figure 10-13 shows a shaft that includes a cylindricity tolerance that establishes a tolerance zone of .007. This means that if the maximum measured diameter is determined to be .755, the minimum diameter cannot be less than .748 anywhere on the cylindrical surface. Figure 10-14 shows how to draw the feature control frames that surround the tolerance symbol and size specifications.

Cylindricity and circularity are somewhat analogous to flatness and straightness. Flatness and cylindricity are concerned with variations across an entire surface or plane. In the case of cylindricity, the plane is shaped like a cylinder. Straightness and circularity are concerned with variations of a single element of a surface, that is, a straight line across the plane in a specified direction for straightness, and a path around a single cross section for circularity.

	TYPE OF TOLERANCE	CHARACTERISTIC	SYMBOL
FOR INDIVIDUAL FEATURES	FORM	STRAIGHTNESS	—
		FLATNESS	▱
		CIRCULARITY	○
		CYLINDRICITY	⌭
INDIVIDUAL OR RELATED FEATURES	PROFILE	PROFILE OF A LINE	⌒
		PROFILE OF A SURFACE	⌓
RELATED FEATURES	ORIENTATION	ANGULARITY	∠
		PERPENDICULARITY	⊥
		PARALLELISM	//
	LOCATION	POSITION	⊕
		CONCENTRICITY	◎
	RUNOUT	CIRCULAR RUNOUT	↗
		TOTAL RUNOUT	↗↗

TERM	SYMBOL
AT MAXIMUM MATERIAL CONDITION	Ⓜ
REGARDLESS OF FEATURE SIZE	Ⓢ
AT LEAST MATERIAL CONDITION	Ⓛ
PROJECTED TOLERANCE ZONE	Ⓟ
DIAMETER	⌀
SPHERICAL DIAMETER	S⌀
RADIUS	R
SPHERICAL RADIUS	SR
REFERENCE	( )
ARC LENGTH	⌒

Figure 10-15

Figure 10-16

10-8 GEOMETRIC TOLERANCES USING AUTOCAD

Geometric tolerances are tolerances that limit dimensional variations based on the geometric properties of an object. Figure 10-15 shows a list of geometric tolerance symbols. Figure 10-16 shows an object dimensioned using geometric tolerances. The geometric tolerances were created as follows.

To define a datum

1. Select the Tolerance tool from the Dimension toolbar.

The Geometric Tolerance dialog box will appear. See Figure 10-17.

2. Click the Datum Identifier box and type -A-, click OK.

   Command: _tolerance
   Enter tolerance location:

3. Position the datum identifier and press the left mouse button. See Figure 10-16.

To define a straightness value

1. Select the Tolerance tool from the Dimension toolbar.

Figure 10-17

Straightness symbol

Straightness value

Straightness symbol on Symbol dialog box

Figure 10-18

The Geometric Tolerance dialog box will appear.

2. Select the top open box under the heading Sym.

The Symbol dialog box will reappear. See Figure 10-18.

3. Select the straightness symbol, then OK.

The Geometric Tolerance dialog box will reappear with the straightness symbol in the first box under the heading Sym.

4. Click the open box in the Tolerance 1 box and type .003; click OK.

Command: _tolerance
Enter tolerance location:

5. Position the straightness tolerance and press the left mouse button

See Figure 10-19. Use the Move and Osnap tools if necessary to reposition the tolerance box. See Figure 10-16.

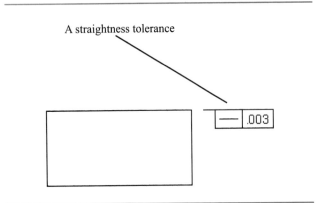

A straightness tolerance

Figure 10-19

To create a positional tolerance

A *positional tolerance* is used to locate and tolerance a hole in an object. Positional tolerances require base locating dimensions for the hole's center point. Positional tolerances also require a feature tolerance to define the diameter tolerances of the hole, and a geometric tolerance to define the position tolerance for the hole's center point.

To create a basic dimension

See the two 1.50 dimensions in Figure 10-16 used to locate the center position of the hole.

1. Select the Dimension Style tool or type DDIM in response to a Command: prompt.

The Dimension Style Manager dialog box will appear.

2. Select Modify.

The Modify Dimension Style: Standard dialog box will appear. See Figure 9-7.

3. Select the Basic option next to the heading Method in the Tolerance box.
4. Return to the drawing screen.
5. Use the Linear Dimension tool from the Dimension toolbar and add the appropriate dimensions.

See Figure 10-16.

To create basic dimensions from existing dimensions

Figure 10-20 shows a shape that includes dimensions. It has been decided to change two of the dimensions to base dimensions. The procedure is as follows.

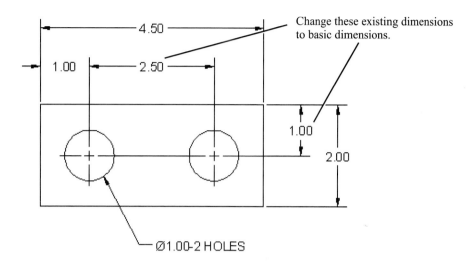

Change these existing dimensions to basic dimensions.

Ø1.00-2 HOLES

Figure 10-20

1. Click on the 2.50 dimension.

   Blue squares will appear on the dimension.

2. Right-click the mouse.

   A dialog box will appear.

3. Select the Properties option.

   The Properties dialog box will appear. See Figure 10-21.

Locate the Tolerance option and click to the right of the word None.

Scroll arrow

Figure 10-21

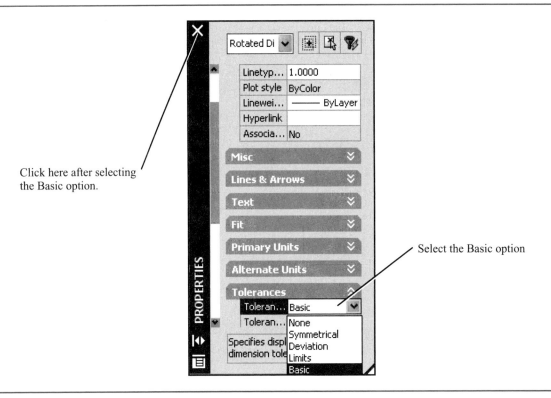

Figure 10-22

4. Use the scroll arrow next to the P in Properties and locate the Tolerances option.
5. Click the open space next to the word None and scroll down to the Basic option.

   See Figure 10-22.

6. Select the Basic option, then click the return X, then press the Esc key.
7. Repeat the procedure for the vertical 1.00 dimension.

   Figure 10-23 shows the final results.

Figure 10-23

Figure 10-24

To add a limit feature tolerance to a hole

1. Select the Dimension Style tool or type DDIM in response to a command prompt.

   The Dimension Style Manager dialog box will appear.

2. Select Modify, then the Tolerance tab.

   The Modify Dimension Style: Standard dialog box will appear.

3. Select the Limits option in the Method box located in the Tolerance format box.

   See Figure 10-24.

4. Change the upper value to 0.0020 by placing the cursor within the Upper value box, backspacing out the existing value, and typing in the new value.

5. Change the lower value to 0.0010 by placing the cursor within the Lower value box, backspacing out the existing value, and typing in the new value.

6. Select the arrow to the right of the Precision box.

   The Precision options will cascade down.

7. Change the precision for both Dimension and Tolerance boxes to three decimal places (0.000).

   See Figure 10-24. AutoCAD will truncate any input according to the number of decimal places allowed by the precision settings. If the precision settings had been two decimal places (0.00), the resulting limit dimensions would have both been 1.50. The values defined in the third decimal place would have been ignored.

8. Return to the drawing screen.
9. Select the Diameter Dimension tool.

   Select arc or circle:

10. Select the hole.

    Dimension line location (Text/Angle):

11. Locate the diameter dimension.

The position tolerance symbol.

Figure 10-25

Maximum material condition symbol

Figure 10-26

To add a positional tolerance to the hole's feature tolerance

1. Select the Tolerance tool.

   The Geometric Tolerance dialog box will appear.

2. Select the top open box under the heading Sym.

   The Symbol dialog box will appear with the positioning symbol highlighted. See Figure 10-25.

3. Select the top left open box under the heading Tolerance 1.

   A diameter symbol will appear.

4. Select the Value box and type 0.0005.

   The numbers will appear in the box.

5. Select the top far right open box under the heading Tolerance 1.

   The Material Condition dialog box will appear. See Figure 10-26.

6. Select the maximum material condition symbol (the circle with an M in it).

7. Select OK.

   The MMC symbol will appear in the MC box in the Geometric Tolerance dialog box.

8. Select OK.

   Enter tolerance location:

9. Locate the tolerance box.

   Use the Move and Osnap commands to position the box, if necessary.

Define the tolerance here.

Select the Tolerance option.

Resulting dimension.

// 0.0010 A

Figure 10-27

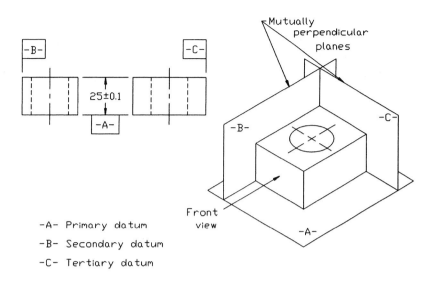

Figure 10-28

To add a geometric tolerance with a leader line

1. Select the Quick Leader tool from the Dimension toolbar.

   Specify first leader point, or [Settings] <Settings>:

2. Select Settings by pressing the Enter key.

   The Leader Settings dialog box will appear. See Figure 10-27.

3. Select the Tolerance option in the Annotation Type box, then OK.

   Specify first leader point, or [Settings] <Settings>:

4. Select a starting point for the leader line.

   Specify next point:

5. Draw a short horizontal segment.

   The Geometric Tolerance dialog box will appear. See Figure 10-27.

6. Select the top Sym box.

   The Symbol dialog box will appear.

7. Select the parallel symbol.
8. Select the open box under the heading Tolerance 1 and type 0.0010.
9. Select the open box under the heading Datum 1, type A, then OK.

   See Figure 10-27.

10-9 TOLERANCES OF ORIENTATION

Tolerances of orientation are used to relate a feature or surface to another feature or surface. Tolerances of orientation include perpendicularity, parallelism, and angularity. They may be applied using RFS or MMC conditions, but they cannot be applied to individual features by themselves. To define a surface as parallel to another surface is very much like assigning a flatness value to the surface. The difference is that flatness applies only within the surface; every point on the surface is related to a defined set of limiting parallel planes. Parallelism defines every point in the surface relative to another surface. The two surfaces are therefore directly related to each other, and the condition of one affects the other.

Orientation tolerances are used with locational tolerances. A feature is first located, then it is oriented within the locational tolerances. This means that the orientation tolerance must always be less than the locational tolerances. The next four sections will further explain this requirement.

10-10 DATUMS

A *datum* is a point, axis, or surface used as a starting reference point for dimensions and tolerances. Figure 10-28 shows a rectangular object with three datum planes labeled –A–, –B–, and –C–. The three datum planes are called the primary, secondary, and tertiary datums, respectively. The three datum planes are, by definition, oriented exactly 90° to one another.

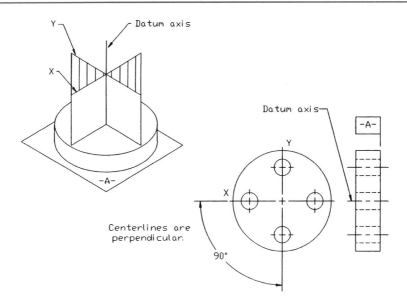

Figure 10-29

Figure 10-29 shows a cylindrical datum frame that includes three datum planes. The X and Y planes are perpendicular to each other, and the base A plane is perpendicular to the datum axis between the X and Y planes.

Datums are defined on a drawing by using letters enclosed in rectangular boxes, as shown. The defining letters are written between dash lines: –A– , –B– , and –C–.

Datum planes are assumed to be perfectly flat. When assigning a datum status to a surface, be sure that the surface is reasonably flat. This means that datum surfaces should be toleranced using surface finishes, or created using machine techniques that produce flat surfaces.

10-11 PERPENDICULARITY

Perpendicularity tolerances are used to limit the amount of variation for a surface or feature within two planes perpendicular to a specified datum. Figure 10-30 shows a rectangular object. The bottom surface is assigned as datum A, and the right vertical edge is toleranced so that it must be perpendicular within a limit of 0.05 to datum A. The perpendicularity tolerance defines a tolerance zone 0.05 wide between two parallel planes that are perpendicular to datum A.

The object also includes a horizontal dimension and tolerance of 40 ± 1. This tolerance is called a *locational tol-*

erance because it serves to locate the right edge of the object. As with rectangular coordinate tolerances discussed in Chapter 9, the 40 ± 1 controls the location of the edge, how far away or how close it can be to the left edge, but does not directly control the shape of the edge. Any shape that falls within the specified tolerance range is acceptable. This may, in fact, be sufficient for a given design, but if a more controlled shape is required, a perpendicularity tolerance must be added. The perpendicularity tolerance works

Figure 10-30

Figure 10-31

Figure 10-32

Figure 10-33

within the locational tolerance to ensure that the edge is not only within the locational tolerance but is also perpendicular to datum A.

Figure 10-30 shows the two extreme conditions for the 40 ± 1 locational tolerance. The perpendicularity tolerance is applied by first measuring the surface and determining its maximum and minimum lengths. The difference between these two measurements must be less than 0.05. Thus, if the measured maximum distance is 41, then no other part of the surface may be less than 41 − 0.05 = 40.95.

Tolerances of perpendicularity serve to complement locational tolerances, to make the shape more exact, so tolerances of perpendicularity must always be smaller than tolerances of location. It would be of little use, for example, to assign a perpendicularity tolerance of 1.5 for the object shown in Figure 10-30. The locational tolerance would prevent the variation from ever reaching the limits specified by such a large perpendicularity tolerance.

Figure 10-31 shows a perpendicularity tolerance applied to cylindrical features: a shaft and a hole. The figure includes examples of both RFS and MMC applications. As with straightness tolerances applied at MMC, perpen-dicularity tolerances applied about a hole or shaft's centerline allow the tolerance zone to vary as the feature size varies.

The inclusion of the Ø symbol in a geometric tolerance is critical to its interpretation. See Figure 10-32. If the Ø symbol is not included, the tolerance applies only to the view in which it is written. This means that the tolerance zone is shaped like a rectangular slice, not a cylinder, as would be the case if the Ø symbol were included. In general, it is better always to include the Ø symbol for cylindrical features because it generates a tolerance zone more like that used in positional tolerancing.

Figure 10-33 shows a perpendicularity tolerance applied to a slot, a noncylindrical feature. Again, the MMC specification is always for variations in the tolerance zone.

10-12 PARALLELISM

Parallelism is used to ensure that all points within a plane are within two parallel planes that are parallel to a referenced datum plane. Figure 10-34 shows a rectangular object that is toleranced so that its top surface is parallel to the bottom surface within 0.02. This means that every point on the top surface must be within a set of parallel planes 0.02 apart. These parallel tolerancing planes are located by determining the maximum and minimum distances from the datum surface. The difference between the maximum and minimum values may not exceed the stated 0.02 tolerance.

In the extreme condition of maximum feature size, the top surface is located 40.5 above the datum plane. The parallelism tolerance is then applied, meaning that no point on the surface may be closer than 40.3 to the datum. This is an RFS condition. The MMC condition may also be applied, thereby allowing the tolerance zone to vary as the feature size varies.

10-13 ANGULARISM

Angularism tolerances are used to limit the variance of surfaces and axes that are at an angle relative to a datum. Angularism tolerances are applied like perpendicularity and parallelism tolerances as a way to better control the shape of locational tolerances.

Figure 10-35 shows an angularism tolerance and several ways in which it is interpreted at extreme conditions.

Figure 10-34

10-14 PROFILES

Profile tolerances are used to limit the variations of irregular surfaces. They may be assigned as either bilateral or unilateral tolerances. There are two types of profile tolerances: surface and line. *Surface profile tolerances* limit the variation of an entire surface, whereas a *line profile tolerance* limits the variations along a single line across a surface.

Figure 10-36 shows an object that includes a surface profile tolerance referenced to an irregular surface. The tolerance is considered a bilateral tolerance because no other specification is given. This means that all points on the surface must be located between two parallel planes 0.08 apart that are centered about the irregular surface. The measurements are taken perpendicular to the surface.

Figure 10-35

Figure 10-36

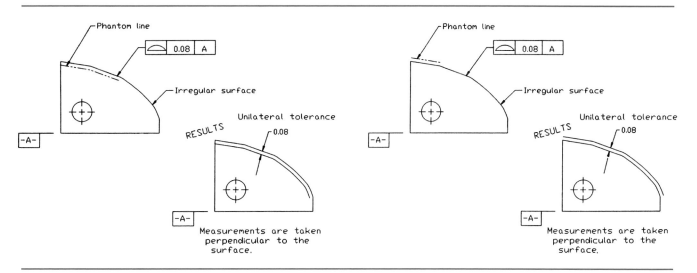

Figure 10-37

Unilateral applications of surface profile tolerances must be indicated on the drawing using phantom lines. The phantom line indicates on which side of the true profile line of the irregular surface the tolerance is to be applied. A phantom line above the irregular surface indicates that the tolerance is to be applied using the true profile line as 0 and then adding a specified tolerance range above that line. See Figures 10-37 and 10-38.

Profiles of line tolerances are applied to irregular surfaces, as shown in Figure 10-37. Profiles of line toler-

ances are particularly helpful for tolerancing an irregular surface that is constantly changing, such as the surface of an airplane wing.

Surface and line profile tolerances are somewhat analogous to flatness and straightness tolerances. Flatness and surface profile tolerances are applied across an entire surface; straightness and line profile tolerances are applied only along a single line across the surface.

Figure 10-38

Figure 10-39

10-15 RUNOUTS

A *runout tolerance* is used to limit the variations between features of an object and a datum. More specifically, runout tolerances are applied to surfaces around a datum axis such as a cylinder or to a surface constructed perpendicular to a datum axis. There are two types of runout tolerances: circular and total.

Figure 10-39 shows a cylinder that includes a circular runout tolerance. The runout requirements are checked by rotating the object about its longitudinal axis or datum axis while holding an indicator gage in a fixed position on the surface of the object.

Runout tolerances may be either bilateral or unilateral. A runout tolerance is assumed to be bilateral unless otherwise indicated. If a runout tolerance is to be unilateral, a phantom line is used to indicate to which side of the object's true surface the tolerance is to be applied. See Figure 10-40.

Figure 10-40

Figure 10-41

Figure 10-42

Runout tolerances may be applied to tapered areas of cylindrical objects, as shown in Figure 10-41. The tolerance is checked by rotating the object about a datum axis while holding an indicator gage in place.

A total runout tolerance limits the variation across an entire surface. See Figure 10-42. An indicator gage is not held in place while the object is rotated, as it is for circular runout tolerances, but is moved about the rotating surface.

Figure 10-43 shows a circular runout tolerance that references two datums. The two datums serve as one datum. The object can then be rotated about both datums simultaneously as the runout tolerances are checked.

10-16 POSITIONAL TOLERANCES

Positional tolerances are used to locate and tolerance holes. Positional tolerances create a circular tolerance zone for hole center point locations that differs from the rectangular-shaped tolerance zone created by linear coordinate dimensions. See Figure 10-44. The circular tolerance zone allows for an increase in acceptable tolerance variation without compromising the design integrity of the object. Note that some of the possible hole center points fall in an area outside the rectangular tolerance zone but are still within the circular tolerance zone. If the hole had been located using linear coordinate dimensions, center points located beyond

Figure 10-43

Figure 10-44

Figure 10-45

the rectangular tolerance zone would have been rejected as beyond tolerance, and yet holes produced using these locations would function correctly from a design standpoint. The center point locations would be acceptable if positional tolerances had been specified. The finished hole is round, so a round tolerance zone is appropriate. The rectangular tolerance zone rejects some holes unnecessarily.

Holes are dimensioned and toleranced using geometric tolerances by a combination of locating dimensions, feature dimensions and tolerances, and positional tolerances. See Figure 10-45. The locating dimensions are

enclosed in rectangular boxes and are called *basic dimensions*. Basic dimensions are assumed to be exact.

The feature tolerances for the hole are as presented in Chapter 9. They can be presented using plus or minus or limit-type tolerances. In the example shown in Figure 10-45 the diameter of the hole is toleranced using a plus and minus 0.05 tolerance.

The basic locating dimensions of 45 and 50 are assumed to be exact. The tolerances that would normally accompany linear locational dimensions are replaced by the positional tolerance. The positional tolerance also specifies that the tolerance be applied at the centerline at maximum material condition. The resulting tolerance zones are as shown in Figure 10-45.

Figure 10-46 shows an object containing two holes that are dimensioned and toleranced using positional tolerances. There are two consecutive horizontal basic dimensions. Because basic dimensions are exact, they do not have tolerances that accumulate; that is, there is no tolerance buildup.

10-17 VIRTUAL CONDITION

Virtual condition is a combination of a feature's MMC and its geometric tolerance. For external features (shafts) it is the MMC plus the geometric tolerance; for internal features (holes) it is the MMC minus the geometric tolerance.

The following calculations are based on the dimensions shown in Figure 10-47.

Figure 10-46

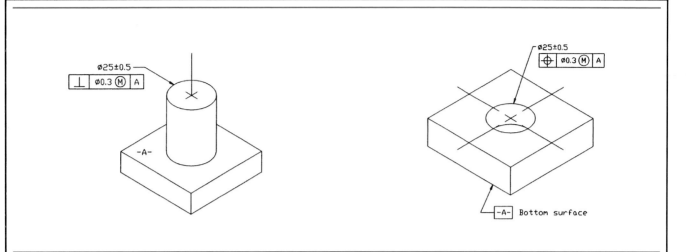

Figure 10-47

To calculate the virtual condition for a shaft

    25.5 MMC for shaft—maximum diameter
    +0.3 Geometric tolerance
    25.8 Virtual condition

To calculate the virtual condition for a hole

    24.5 MMC for hole—minimum diameter
    −0.3 Geometric tolerance
    24.2 Virtual condition

10-18 FLOATING FASTENERS

Positional tolerances are particularly helpful when dimensioning matching parts. Because basic locating dimensions are considered exact, the sizing of mating parts is dependent only on the MMC of the hole and shaft and the geometric tolerance between them.

The relationship for floating fasteners and holes in objects may be expressed as a formula:

$$H - T = F$$

Figure 10-48

where

> H = Hole at MMC
> T = Geometric tolerance
> F = Shaft at MMC

A *floating fastener* is one that is free to move in either object. It is not attached to either object and it does not screw into either object. Figure 10-48 shows two objects that are to be joined by a common floating shaft, such as a bolt or screw. The feature size and tolerance and the positional geometric tolerance are both given. The minimum size hole that will always just fit is determined using the preceding formula:

$$H - T = F$$
$$11.97 - .02 = 11.95$$

Therefore, the shaft's diameter at MMC, the shaft's maximum diameter, equals 11.95. Any required tolerance would have to be subtracted from this shaft size.

The 0.02 geometric tolerance is applied at the hole's MMC. Thus, as the hole's size expands within its feature tolerance, the tolerance zone for the acceptable matching parts also expands. See the table in Figure 10-48.

10-19 SAMPLE PROBLEM SP10-1

The situation presented in Figure 10-48 can be worked in reverse; that is, hole sizes can be derived from given shaft sizes.

The two objects shown in Figure 10-49 are to be joined by a .250-inch bolt. The parts are floating; that is,

Figure 10-49

Figure 10-50

they are both free to move, and the fastener is not joined to either object. What is the MMC of the holes if the positional tolerance is to be .030?

A manufacturer's catalog specifies that the tolerance for a .250 bolt is .2500 to .2600.

Rewriting the formula

$$H - T = F$$

to isolate the H, we have

$$H = F + T$$
$$= .260 + .030$$
$$= .290$$

The .290 value represents the minimum hole diameter, MMC, for all four holes that will always accept the .250 bolt. Figure 10-50 shows the resulting drawing callout.

Any clearance requirements or tolerances for the hole would have to be added to the .290 value.

10-20 SAMPLE PROBLEM SP10-2

Repeat the problem presented in SP10-1 but be sure that there is always a minimum clearance of .002 between the hole and the shaft and assign a hole tolerance of .0010.

Sample Problem SP10-1 determined that the maximum hole diameter that would always accept the .250 bolt was .290 based on the .030 positional tolerance. If the minimum clearance is to be .002, the maximum hole diameter is found as follows:

Figure 10-51

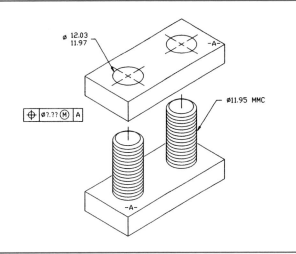

Figure 10-53

.290 Minimum hole diameter that will always
accept the bolt (0 clearance at MMC)
+.002 Mininum clearance
.292 Minimum hole diameter including clearance

Now assign the tolerance to the hole.

.292 Minimum hole diameter
+.001 Tolerance
.293 Minimum hole diameter

See Figure 10-51 for the appropriate drawing callout. The choice of clearance size and hole tolerance varies with the design requirements for the objects.

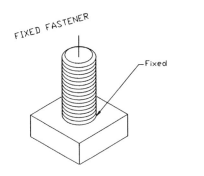

Figure 10-52

10-21   FIXED FASTENERS

A *fixed fastener* is one that is attached to one of the mating objects. See Figure 10-52. Because the fastener is fixed to one of the objects, the geometric tolerance zone must be smaller than that used for floating fasteners. The fixed fastener cannot move without moving the object it is attached to. The relationship between fixed fasteners and holes in mating objects is defined by the formula

$$H - 2T = F$$

The tolerance zone is cut in half, as can be demonstrated by the objects shown in Figure 10-53. The same feature sizes that were used in Figure 10-48 are assigned, but in this example the fasteners are fixed. Solving for the geometric tolerance, we obtain the following value:

$$H - F = 2T$$
$$11.97 - 11.95 = 2T$$
$$.02 = 2T$$
$$.01 = T$$

The resulting positional tolerance is half of that obtained for floating fasteners.

Figure 10-54

10-22 SAMPLE PROBLEM SP10-3

This problem is similar to Sample Problem SP10-1, but the given conditions are applied to fixed fasteners rather than to floating fasteners. Compare the resulting shaft diameters for the two problems. See Figure 10-54.

A. What is the minimum diameter hole that will always accept the fixed fasteners?
B. If the minimum clearance is .005 and the hole is to have a tolerance of .002, what are the maximum and minimum diameters of the hole?

$$H - 2T = F$$
$$H = F + 2T$$
$$= .260 + 2(.030)$$
$$= .260 + .060$$
$$= .320 \quad \text{Minimum diameter that will always accept the fixed fastener}$$

If the minimum clearance = .005 and the hole tolerance is .002,

.320	Virtual condition
+.005	Clearance
.325	Minimum hole diameter

.325	Minimum hole diameter
+.002	Tolerance
.327	Maximum hole diameter

The maximum and minimum values for the hole's diameter can then be added to the drawing of the object that fits over the fixed fasteners. See Figure 10-55.

.320	Virtual condition
.005	Clearance
.325	MMC
.002	Tolerance
.327	LMC

Figure 10-55

10-23 DESIGN PROBLEMS

This problem was originally done in Section 9-27 using rectangular tolerances. It is done in this section using positional geometric tolerances so that the two systems can be compared. It is suggested that you review Section 9-27 before reading this section.

Figure 10-56 shows top and bottom parts that are to be joined in the floating condition. A nominal distance of 50 between hole centers and 20 for the holes has been assigned. In Section 9-27 a rectangular tolerance of ±.01 was selected and there was a minimum hole diameter of 20.00. Figure 10-57 shows the resulting tolerance zones.

The diagonal distance across the rectangular tolerance zone is .028 and was rounded off to .03 to yield a maximum possible fastener diameter of 19.97. If the same .03 value is used to calculate the fastener diameter using positional tolerance, the results will be as follows:

$$H - T = F$$
$$20.00 - .03 = 19.97$$

The results seem to be the same, but because of the circular shape of the positional tolerance zone, the manufactured results are not the same. The minimum distance between the inside edges of the rectangular zones is 49.98, or .01 from the center point of each hole. The minimum distance from the innermost points of the circular tolerance zones is 49.97, or .015 (half of the rounded-off .03 value)

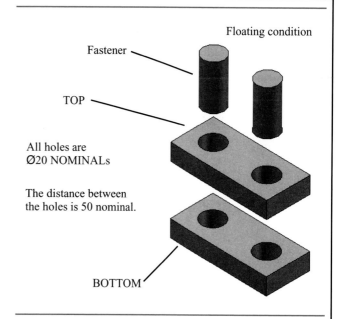

All holes are
Ø20 NOMINALs

The distance between
the holes is 50 nominal.

Figure 10-56

from the center point of each hole. The same value difference also occurs for the maximum distance between center points, where 50.02 is the maximum distance for the rectangular tolerances, and 50.03 is the maximum distance for the circular tolerances. The size of the circular tolerance zone increased more because the hole tolerances are assigned at

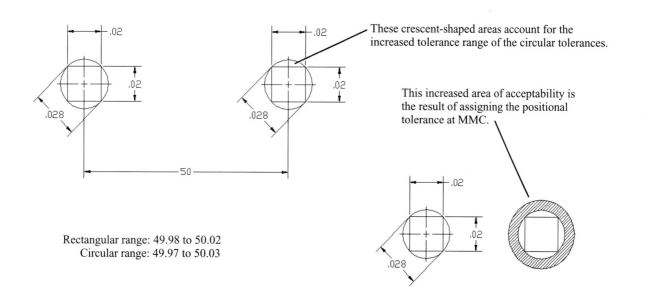

Rectangular range: 49.98 to 50.02
Circular range: 49.97 to 50.03

These crescent-shaped areas account for the increased tolerance range of the circular tolerances.

This increased area of acceptability is the result of assigning the positional tolerance at MMC.

Figure 10-57

Figure 10-58

All holes are Ø20 NOMINALs.
The distance between the holes is 50 nominal.

Figure 10-59

MMC. Figure 10-57 shows a comparison between the tolerance zones, and Figure 10-58 shows how the positional tolerances would be presented on a drawing of either the top or bottom part.

Figure 10-59 shows the same top and bottom parts joined together in the fixed condition. The initial nominal values are the same. If the same .03 diagonal value is assigned as a positional tolerance, the results are as follows:

$$H - 2T = F$$
$$20.00 - .06 = 19.94$$

These results appear to be the same as those generated by the rectangular tolerance zone, but the circular tolerance zone allows a greater variance in acceptable manufactured parts. Figure 10-60 shows how the positional tolerance would be presented on a drawing.

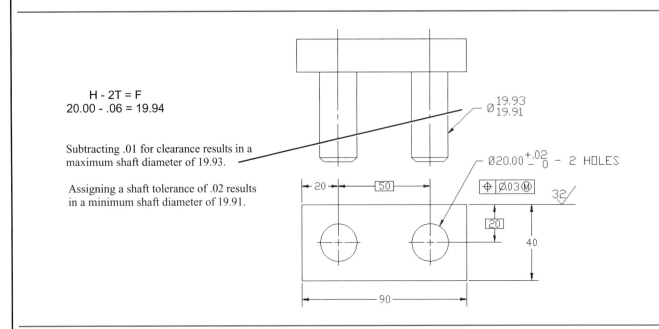

$$H - 2T = F$$
$$20.00 - .06 = 19.94$$

Subtracting .01 for clearance results in a maximum shaft diameter of 19.93.

Assigning a shaft tolerance of .02 results in a minimum shaft diameter of 19.91.

Figure 10-60

10-24 EXERCISE PROBLEMS

EX10-1

Redraw the object shown. Include all dimensions and tolerances.

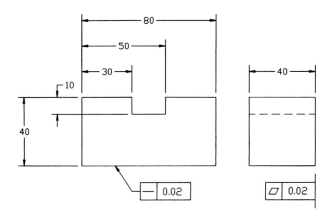

EX10-2

Redraw the following shaft and add a feature dimension and tolerance of 36 ± 0.1 and a straightness tolerance of 0.07 about the centerline at MMC.

EX10-3

A. Given the shaft shown, what is the minimum hole diameter that will always accept the shaft?
B. If the minimum clearance between the shaft and a hole is equal to 0.02, and the tolerance on the hole is to be 0.6, what are the maximum and minimum diameters for the hole?

EX10-4

A. Given the shaft shown, what is the minimum hole diameter that will always accept the shaft?
B. If the minimum clearance between the shaft and a hole is equal to .005, and the tolerance on the hole is to be .007, what are the maximum and minimum diameters for the hole?

EX10-5

Draw a front and a right-side view of the object shown in Figure EX10-5 and add the appropriate dimensions and tolerances based on the following information. Numbers located next to an edge line indicate the length of the edge.

A. Define surfaces A, B, and C as primary, secondary, and tertiary datums, respectively.
B. Assign a tolerance of ± 0.5 to all linear dimensions.
C. Assign a feature tolerance of 12.07 − 12.00 to the protruding shaft.
D. Assign a flatness tolerance of 0.01 to surface A.
E. Assign a straightness tolerance of 0.03 to the protruding shaft.
F. Assign a perpendicularity tolerance to the centerline of the protruding shaft of 0.02 at MMC relative to datum A.

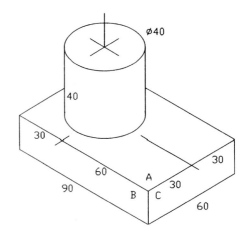

Figure EX10-5

EX10-6

Draw a front and right-side view of the object shown in Figure EX10-6 and add the following dimensions and tolerances.

A. Define the bottom surface as datum A.
B. Assign a perpendicularity tolerance of 0.4 to both sides of the slot relative to datum A.
C. Assign a perpendicularity tolerance of 0.2 to the centerline of the 30-diameter hole centerline at MMC relative to datum A.
D. Assign a feature tolerance of ±0.8 to all three holes.
E. Assign a parallelism tolerance of 0.2 to the common centerline between the two 20-diameter holes relative to datum A.
F. Assign a tolerance of ±0.5 to all linear dimensions.

Figure EX10-6

EX10-7

Draw a circular front and the appropriate right-side view of the object shown in Figure EX10-7 and add the following dimensions and tolerances.

A. Assign datum A as indicated.
B. Assign the object's longitudinal axis as datum B.
C. Assign the object's centerline through the slot as datum C.
D. Assign a tolerance of ±0.5 to all linear tolerances.
E. Assign a tolerance of ±0.5 to all circular-shaped features.
F   Assign a parallelism tolerance of 0.01 to both edges of the slot.
G. Assign a perpendicularity tolerance of 0.01 to the outside edge of the protruding shaft.

Figure EX10-7

EX10-8

Given the two objects shown in Figure EX10-8, draw a front and a side view of each. Assign a tolerance of ±0.5 to all linear dimensions. Assign a feature tolerance of ±0.4 to the shaft, and also assign a straightness tolerance of 0.2 to the shaft's centerline at MMC.

Tolerance the hole so that it will always accept the shaft with a minimum clearance of 0.1 and a feature tolerance of 0.2. Assign a perpendicularity tolerance of 0.05 to the centerline of the hole at MMC.

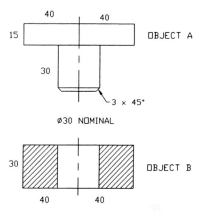

Figure EX10-8

EX10-9

Given the two objects shown in Figure EX10-9, draw a front and a side view of each. Assign a tolerance of ±.005 to all linear dimensions. Assign a feature tolerance of ±.004 to the shaft, and also assign a straightness tolerance of .002 to the shaft's centerline at MMC.

Tolerance the hole so that it will always accept the shaft with a minimum clearance of .001 and a feature tolerance of .002.

Figure EX10-9

EX10-10

Refer to parts A through G for this exercise problem. Use the format shown in Figure EX10-10 and redraw the given geometric tolerance symbols and frame as shown in the sample. Express in words (Dtext) the meaning of each tolerance callout.

Figure EX10-10

A.   B.

EX10-10, continued

C.

① | ↗ | .015 | A | B |

② | ⌒ | .008 | A | B Ⓜ |

③ | — | ⌀ 0.000 Ⓜ | ⌀ 0.002 MAX |

④ | ◎ | ⌀ 0.005 | A |

⑤ | ↗↗ | .004 | A - B |
　　　TOTAL

F.

① | ∠ | 0.04 Ⓜ | C | A Ⓜ | B Ⓜ |

② | ↗ | 0.02 | A |

③ | ⊥ | 0.03 | A | B |

④ | // | ⌀ 0.01 | A | B Ⓜ |

⑤ | ⌒ | 0.03 | A | B |
　　　ALL AROUND

D.

① | ⊕ | 0.25 Ⓜ | A | B | C |

② | ⊕ | 0.8 Ⓜ | A | B Ⓜ |

③ | ⊕ | ⌀ 0.4 Ⓜ | A | B | C |

④ | ⊕ | ⌀ 0.3 Ⓜ | A | B Ⓜ | C Ⓜ |

⑤ | ⊕ | ⌀ 0.1 Ⓜ |

G.

① | ⊕ | ⌀ .002 Ⓜ |

② | ⊕ | .005 Ⓜ | A | B | C |

③ | ⊕ | .002 | A | B Ⓜ |

④ | ⊕ | ⌀ .003 Ⓜ | A | B Ⓜ | C Ⓜ |

⑤ | ⊕ | ⌀ .015 Ⓜ | A | B |

E.

① | ⊕ | ⌀ 0.06 Ⓜ | A Ⓜ |

② | — | ⌀ 0.02 Ⓜ | ⌀ 0.05 MAX |

③ | ⊕ | ⌀ 0.0 Ⓜ | A | ⌀ .05 MAX |

④ | ↗↗ | .002 | A | B |
　　　TOTAL

⑤ | ⌒ | .003 | A | B | C |
　　　ALL AROUND

EX10-11 MILLIMETERS

Draw front, top, and right-side views of the object in Figure EX10-11, including dimensions. Add the following tolerances and specifications to the drawing.

A. Surface 1 is datum A.
B. Surface 2 is datum B and is perpendicular to datum A within 0.1 millimeter.
C. Surface 3 is datum C and is parallel to datum A within 0.3 millimeter.
D. Locate a 16-millimeter-diameter hole in the center of the front surface that goes completely through the object. Use positional tolerances to locate the hole. Assign a positional tolerance of 0.02 at MMC perpendicular to datum A.

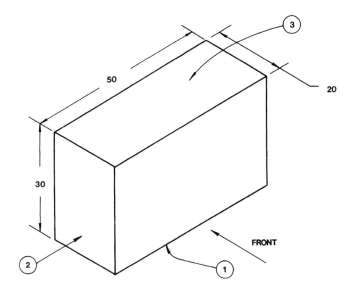

Figure EX10-11

EX10-12

Draw front, top, and right-side views of the object in Figure EX10-12, including dimensions. Add the following tolerances and specifications to the drawing.

A. Surface 1 is datum A.
B. Surface 2 is datum B and is perpendicular to datum A within .003 inch.
C. Surface 3 is parallel to datum A within .005 inch.
D. The cylinder's longitudinal centerline is to be straight within .001 inch at MMC.
E. Surface 2 is to have circular accuracy within .002 inch.

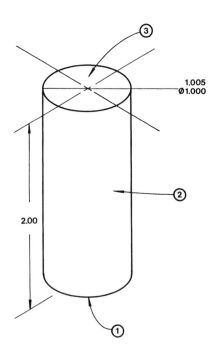

Figure EX10-12

EX10-13

Draw front, top, and right-side views of the object in Figure EX10-13, including dimensions. Add the following tolerances and specifications to the drawing.

A. Surface 1 is datum A.
B. Surface 4 is datum B and is perpendicular to datum A within 0.08 millimeter.
C. Surface 3 is flat within 0.03 millimeter.
D. Surface 5 is parallel to datum A within 0.01 millimeter.
E. Surface 2 has a runout tolerance of 0.2 millimeter relative to surface 4.
F. Surface 1 is flat within 0.02 millimeter.
G. The longitudinal centerline is to be straight within 0.02 millimeter at MMC and perpendicular to datum A.

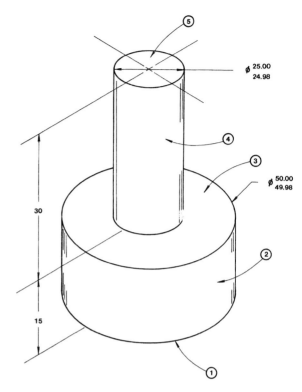

Figure EX10-13

EX10-14

Draw front, top, and right-side views of the object in Figure EX10-14, including dimensions. Add the following tolerances and specifications to the drawing.

A. Surface 2 is datum A.
B. Surface 6 is perpendicular to datum A with 0.000 allowable variance at MMC but with a .002 inch MAX variance limit beyond MMC.
C. Surface 1 is parallel to datum A within .005 inch.
D. Surface 4 is perpendicular to datum A within .004 inch.

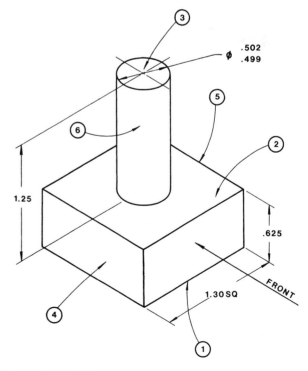

Figure EX10-14

EX10-15

Draw front, top, and right-side views of the object in Figure EX10-15, including dimensions. Add the following tolerances and specifications to the drawing.

A. Surface 1 is datum A.
B. Surface 2 is datum B.
C. The hole is located using a true position tolerance value of 0.13 millimeter at MMC. The true position tolerance is referenced to datums A and B.
D. Surface 1 is to be straight within 0.02 millimeter.
E. The bottom surface is to be parallel to datum A within 0.03 millimeter.

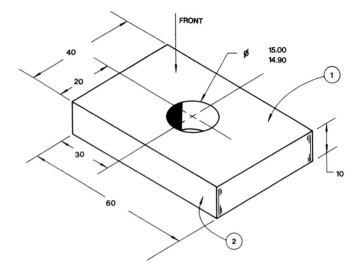

Figure EX10-15

EX10-16

Draw front, top, and right-side views of the object in Figure EX10-16, including dimensions. Add the following tolerances and specifications to the drawing.

A. Surface 1 is datum A.
B. Surface 2 is datum B.
C. Surface 3 is perpendicular to surface 2 within 0.02 millimeter.
D. The four holes are to be located using a positional tolerance of 0.07 millimeter at MMC referenced to datums A and B.
E. The centerlines of the holes are to be straight within 0.01 millimeter at MMC.

Figure EX10-16

EX10-17

Draw front, top, and right-side views of the object in Figure EX10-17, including dimensions. Add the following tolerances and specifications to the drawing.

A. Surface 1 has a dimension of .378−.375 inch and is datum A. The surface has a dual primary runout with datum B to within .005 inch. The runout is total.
B. Surface 2 has a dimension of 1.505−1.495 inch. Its runout relative to the dual primary datums A and B is .008 inch. The runout is total.
C. Surface 3 has a dimension of 1.000 ±.005 and has no geometric tolerance.
D. Surface 4 has no circular dimension but has a total runout tolerance of .006 inch relative to the dual datums A and B.
E. Surface 5 has a dimension of .500−.495 inch and is datum B. It has a dual primary runout with datum A within .005 inch. The runout is total.

Figure EX10-17

EX10-18

Draw front, top, and right-side views of the object in Figure EX10-18, including dimensions. Add the following tolerances and specifications to the drawing.

A. Hole 1 is datum A.
B. Hole 2 is to have its circular centerline parallel to datum A within 0.2 millimeter at MMC when datum A is at MMC.
C. Assign a positional tolerance of 0.01 to each hole's centerline at MMC.

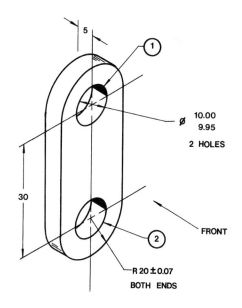

Figure EX10-18

EX10-19

Draw front, top, and right-side views of the object in Figure EX10-19, including dimensions. Add the following tolerances and specifications to the drawing.

A. Surface 1 is datum A.
B. Surface 2 is datum B.
C. The six holes have a diameter range of .502—.499 inch and are to be located using positional tolerances so that their centerlines are within .005 inch at MMC relative to datums A and B.
D. The back surface is to be parallel to datum A within .002 inch.

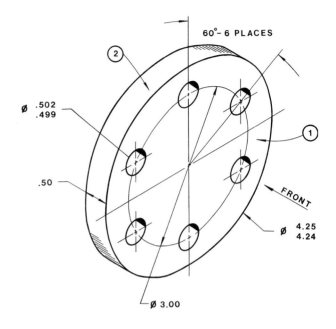

Figure EX10-19

EX10-20

Draw front, top, and right-side views of the object in Figure EX10-20, including dimensions. Add the following tolerances and specifications to the drawing.

A. Surface 1 is datum A.
B. Hole 2 is datum B.
C. The eight holes labeled 3 have diameters of 8.4–8.3 millimeters with a positional tolerance of 0.15 millimeter at MMC relative to datums A and B. Also, the eight holes are to be counterbored to a diameter of 14.6–14.4 millimeters and to a depth of 5.0 millimeters.
D. The large center hole is to have a straightness tolerance of 0.2 at MMC about its centerline.

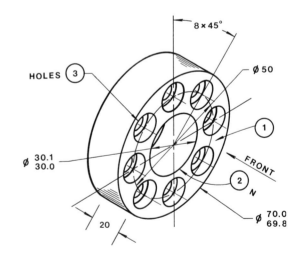

Figure EX10-20

EX10-21

Draw front, top, and right-side views of the object in Figure EX10-21, including dimensions. Add the following tolerances and specifications to the drawing.

A. Surface 1 is datum A.
B. Surface 2 is datum B.
C. Surface 3 is datum C.
D. The four holes labeled 4 have a dimension and tolerance of 8 +0.3,−0 millimeters. The holes are to be located using a positional tolerance of 0.05 millimeter at MMC relative to datums A, B, and C.
E. The six holes labeled 5 have a dimension and tolerance of 6 +0.2,−0 millimeters. The holes are to be located using a positional tolerance of 0.01 millimeter at MMC relative to datums A, B, and C.

EX10-22

The objects on page 434 labeled A and B, are to be toleranced using four different tolerances as shown. Redraw the charts shown in Figure EX10-22 and list the appropriate allowable tolerance for "as measured" increments of 0.1 millimeter or .001 inch. Also include the appropriate geometric tolerance drawing called out above each chart.

Figure EX10-21

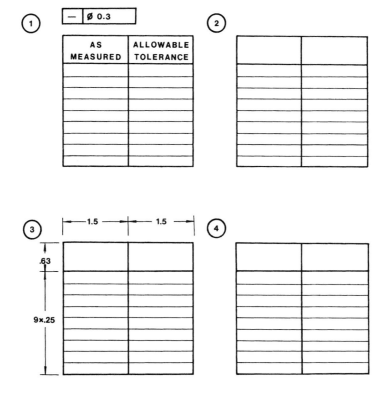

Figure EX10-22

EX10-22, CONTINUED

A.

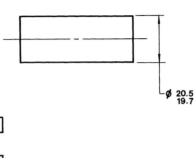

Ø 20.5
19.7

① ⬜ — | Ø 0.3

② ⬜ — | Ø 0.3 Ⓜ

③ ⬜ — | Ø 0.0 Ⓜ

④ ⬜ — | Ø 0.0 Ⓜ | Ø0.04 MAX

B.

1.50

Ø 1.005
.997

FEATURE SIZE	ALLOWABLE TOL ZONE
1.005	
1.004	
1.003	
1.002	
1.001	
1.000	
.999	
.998	
.997	

○ | Ø .003

○ | Ø .003 Ⓜ

○ | Ø .000 Ⓜ

○ | Ø .000 Ⓜ   .004 MAX

EX10-23

Dimension and tolerance parts 1 and 2 of Figure EX10-23 so that part 1 always fits into part 2 with a minimum clearance of .005 inch. The tolerance for part 1's outer matching surface is .006 inch.

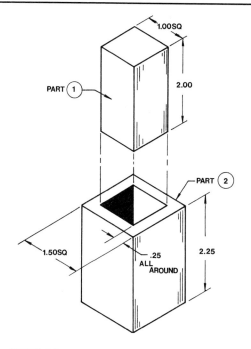

Figure EX10-23

EX10-24

Dimension and tolerance parts 1 and 2 of Figure EX10-24 so that part 1 always fits into part 2 with a minimum clearance of 0.03 millimeter. The tolerance for part 1's diameter is 0.05 millimeter. Take into account the fact that the interface is long relative to the diameters.

Figure EX10-24

EX10-25

Prepare front and top views of parts 4A and 4B of Figure EX10-25 based on the given dimensions. Add geometric tolerances to produce the stated maximum clearance and mismatch.

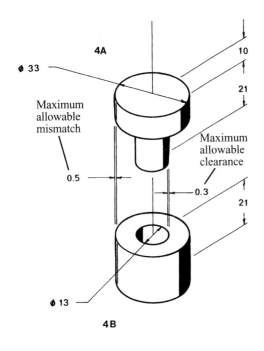

Figure EX10-25

EX10-26

Redraw parts A and B of Figure EX10-26 and add dimensions and tolerances to meet the "UPON ASSEMBLY" requirements.

The UPON ASSEMBLY condition.

Nominal sizes

Figure EX10-26

EX10-27

Draw front and top views of both objects in Figure EX10-27. Add dimensions and geometric tolerances to meet the "FINAL CONDITION" requirements.

FINAL CONDITION

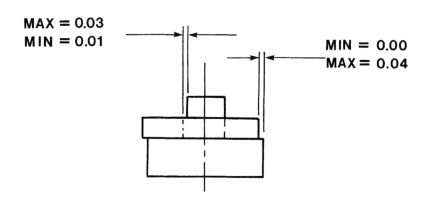

Figure EX10-27

Given a TOP and BOTTOM part in the floating condition as shown in Figure EX10-28 add dimensions and tolerances to satisfy the following conditions. Size the TOP and BOTTOM parts and FASTENER length as needed. Use geometric and positional tolerances.

EX10-28 INCHES–CLEARANCE FIT

A. The distance between the holes is 2.00 nominal.
B. The diameter of the fasteners is Ø.375 nominal.
C. The fasteners have a total tolerance of .001.
D. The holes have a tolerance of .002.
E. The minimum allowable clearance between the fastener and the holes is .003.
F. The material is .375 inch thick.

EX10-29 MILLIMETERS–CLEARANCE FIT

A. The distance between the holes is 80 nominal.
B. The nominal diameter of the fasteners is Ø12.
C. The fasteners have a total tolerance of .05.
D. The holes have a tolerance of .03.
E. The minimum allowable clearance between the fastener and the holes is .02.
F. The material is 12 millimeters thick.

EX10-30 INCHES–CLEARANCE FIT

A. The distance between the holes is 3.50 nominal.
B. The diameter of the fasteners is Ø.625.
C. The fasteners have a total tolerance of .005.
D. The holes have a tolerance of .003.
E. The minimum allowable clearance between the fastener and the holes is .002.
F. The material is .500 inch thick.

EX10-31 MILLIMETERS–CLEARANCE FIT

A. The distance between the holes is 120 nominal.
B. The diameter of the fasteners is Ø24 nominal.
C. The fasteners have a total tolerance of .01.
D. The holes have a tolerance of .02.
E. The minimum allowable clearance between the fastener and the holes is .04.
F. The material is 20 millimeters thick.

EX10-32 INCHES–INTERFERENCE FIT

A. The distance between the holes is 2.00 nominal.
B. The diameter of the fasteners is Ø.250 nominal.
C. The fasteners have a total tolerance of .001.
D. The holes have a tolerance of .002.

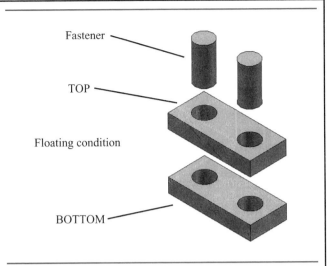

Fastener
TOP
Floating condition
BOTTOM

Figure EX10-28

E. The maximum allowable interference between the fastener and the holes is .0065.
F. The material is .438 inch thick.

EX10-33 MILLIMETERS–INTERFERENCE FIT

A. The distance between the holes is 80 nominal.
B. The diameter of the fasteners is Ø10 nominal.
C. The fasteners have a total tolerance of .01.
D. The holes have a tolerance of .02.
E. The maximum allowable interference between the fastener and the holes is .032.
F. The material is 14 millimeters thick.

EX10-34 INCHES–LOCATIONAL FIT

A. The distance between the holes is 2.25 nominal.
B. The diameter of the fasteners is Ø.50 nominal.
C. The fasteners have a total tolerance of .001.
D. The holes have a tolerance of .002.
E. The minimum allowable clearance between the fastener and the holes is .0010.
F. The material is .370 inch thick.

EX10-35 MILLIMETERS–TRANSITIONAL FIT

A. The distance between the holes is 100 nominal.
B. The diameter of the fasteners is Ø16 nominal.
C. The fasteners have a total tolerance of .01.
D. The holes are to have a tolerance of .02.
E. The minimum allowable clearance between the fastener and the holes is .01.
F. The material is 20 millimeters thick.

Given a TOP and BOTTOM part in the fixed condition as shown in Figure EX10-36 add dimensions and tolerances to satisfy the following conditions. Size the TOP and BOTTOM parts and FASTENERlength as needed. Use geometric and positional tolerances.

EX10-36 INCHES–CLEARANCE FIT

A. The distance between the holes is 2.00 nominal.
B. The diameter of the fasteners is Ø.375 nominal.
C. The fasteners have a total tolerance of .001.
D. The holes have a tolerance of .002.
E. The minimum allowable clearance between the fastener and the holes is .003.
F. The material is .375 inch thick.

EX10-37 MILLIMETERS–CLEARANCE FIT

A. The distance between the holes is 80 nominal.
B. The nominal diameter of the fasteners is Ø12.
C. The fasteners have a total tolerance of 0.05.
D. The holes have a tolerance of 0.03.
E. The minimum allowable clearance between the fastener and the holes is 0.02.
F. The material is 12 millimeters thick.

EX10-38 INCHES–CLEARANCE FIT

A. The distance between the holes is 3.50 nominal.
B. The diameter of the fasteners is Ø.625.
C. The fasteners have a total tolerance of .005.
D. The holes have a tolerance of .003.
E. The minimum allowable clearance between the fastener and the holes is .002.
F. The material is .500 inch thick.

EX10-39 MILLIMETERS–CLEARANCE FIT

A. The distance between the holes is 120 nominal.
B. The diameter of the fasteners is Ø24 nominal.
C. The fasteners have a total tolerance of .01.
D. The holes have a tolerance of .02.
E. The minimum allowable clearance between the fastener and the holes is .04.
F. The material is 20 millimeters thick.

EX10-40 INCHES–INTERFERENCE FIT

A. The distance between the holes is 2.00 nominal.
B. The diameter of the fasteners is Ø.250 nominal.
C. The fasteners have a total tolerance of .001.
D. The holes have a tolerance of .002.

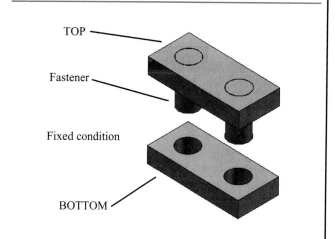

Figure EX10-36

E. The maximum allowable interference between the fastener and the holes is .0065.
F. The material is .438 inch thick.

EX10-41 MILLIMETERS–INTERFERENCE FIT

A. The distance between the holes is 80 nominal.
B. The diameter of the fasteners is Ø10 nominal.
C. The fasteners have a total tolerance of .01.
D. The holes have a tolerance of .02.
E. The maximum allowable interference between the fastener and the holes is .032.
F. The material is 14 millimeters thick.

EX10-42 INCHES–LOCATIONAL FIT

A. The distance between the holes is 2.25 nominal.
B. The diameter of the fasteners is Ø.50 nominal.
C. The fasteners have a total tolerance of .001.
D. The holes have a tolerance of .002.
E. The minimum allowable clearance between the fastener and the holes is .0010.
F. The material is .370 inch thick.

EX10-43 MILLIMETERS–TRANSITIONAL FIT

A. The distance between the holes is 100 nominal.
B. The diameter of the fasteners is Ø16 nominal.
C. The fasteners have a total tolerance of .01.
D. The holes are to have a tolerance of .02.
E. The minimum allowable clearance between the fastener and the holes is .001.
F. The material is 20 millimeters thick.

EX10-44

Given the following two assemblies, size the parts so that they always fit together. Create individual drawings of each part including dimensions and tolerances. Use geometric and positional tolerances.

SUPPORT ASSEMBLY

BRACKET, END
2 REQD

PLATE, 4 HOLE
2 REQD

PEG
4 REQD

EX10-45

   Assume that there are two copies of the part in Figure EX10-45 and that these parts are to be joined together using four fasteners in the floating condition. Draw front and top views of the object, including dimensions and tolerances. Add the following tolerances and specifications to the drawing, then draw front and top views of a shaft that can be used to join the two objects. The shaft should be able to fit into any of the four holes.

A. Surface 1 is datum A.
B. Surface 2 is datum B.
C. Surface 3 is perpendicular to surface 2 within 0.02 millimeter.
D. Specify the positional tolerance for the four holes applied at MMC.
E. The centerlines of the holes are to be straight within 0.01 millimeter at MMC.
F. The clearance between the shafts and the holes is to be 0.05 minimum and 0.10 maximum.

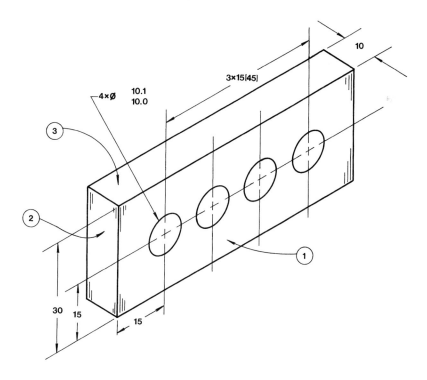

Figure EX10-45

EX10-46

Assume that there are two copies of the part in Figure EX10-46 and that these parts are to be joined together using six fasteners in the floating condition. Draw front and top views of the object, including dimensions and tolerances. Add the following tolerances and specifications to the drawing, then draw front and top views of a shaft that can be used to join the two objects. The shaft should be able to fit into any of the six holes.

A. Surface 1 is datum A.
B. Surface 2 is round within .003.
C. Specify the positional tolerance for the six holes applied at MMC.
D. The clearance between the shafts and the holes is to be .001 minimum and .003 maximum.

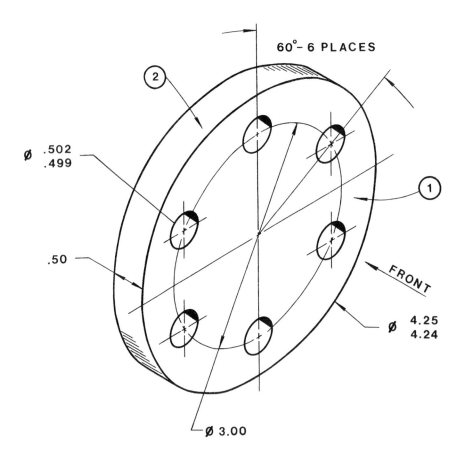

Figure EX10-46

C H A P T E R 11

Threads and Fasteners

11-1 INTRODUCTION

This chapter explains how to draw threads, washers, keys, and springs. It explains how to use fasteners to join parts together and design uses for washers, keys, and springs.

Throughout the chapter it will be suggested that blocks and wblocks be created of the various thread and fastener shapes. Thread representations, fastener head shapes, set screws, and both internal and external thread representations for orthographic views and sectional views are so common in technical drawings that it is good practice to create a set of wblocks that can be used on future drawings to prevent having to redraw a thread shape every time it is needed.

See Chapter 3 for an explanation of the Block command.

11-2 THREAD TERMINOLOGY

Figure 11-1 shows a thread. The peak of a thread is called the *crest*, and the valley portion is called the *root*. The *major diameter* of a thread is the distance across the thread from crest to crest. The *minor diameter* is the distance across the thread from root to root.

The *pitch* of a thread is the linear distance along the thread from crest to crest. Thread pitch is usually referred

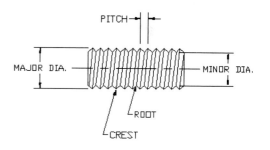

Detailed representation

Figure 11-1

to in terms of a unit of length such as 20 threads per inch or 1.5 threads per millimeter.

11-3 THREAD CALLOUTS (METRIC UNITS)

Threads are specified on a drawing using drawing callouts. See Figure 11-2. The M preceding a drawing callout specifies that the callout is for a metric thread. Holes that are not threaded use the Ø symbol.

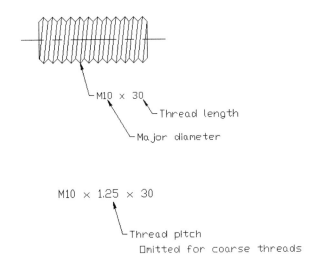

Figure 11-2

Major Dia	Coarse		Fine	
	Pitch	Tap Drill Dia	Pitch	Tap Drill Dia
1.6	0.35	1.25		
2	0.4	1.6		
2.5	0.45	2.05		
3	0.5	2.5		
4	.7	3.3		
5	0.8	4.2		
6	1	5.0		
8	1.25	6.7	1	7.0
10	1.5	8.5	1.25	8.7
12	1.75	10.2	1.25	10.8
16	2	14	1.5	14.5
20	2.5	17.5	1.5	18.5
24	3	21	2	22
30	3.5	26.5	2	28
36	4	32	3	33
42	4.5	37.5	3	39
48	5	43	3	45

Figure 11-3

The number following the M is the major diameter of the thread; for example, an M10 thread has a major diameter of 10 millimeters. The pitch of a metric thread is assumed to be a coarse thread unless otherwise stated. The callout M10 × 30 assumes a coarse thread, or 1.5 threads per millimeter. The number 30 is the thread length in millimeters. The "×" is read as "by," so the thread is called a "ten by thirty."

The callout M10 × 1.25 × 30 specifies a pitch of 1.25 threads per millimeter. This is not a standard coarse thread size, so the pitch must be specified.

Figure 11-3 shows a list of preferred thread sizes. These sizes are similar to the standard sizes shown in Figure 9-32. A list of other metric thread sizes is included in the appendix.

Whenever possible use preferred thread sizes for designing. Preferred thread sizes are readily available and are usually cheaper than nonstandard sizes. In addition, tooling such as wrenches is also readily available for preferred sizes.

11-4 THREAD CALLOUTS (ENGLISH UNITS)

English unit threads always include a thread form specification. Thread form specifications are designated by capital letters, as shown in Figure 11-4, and are defined as follows:

UNC—Unified National Coarse
UNF—Unified National Fine
UNEF—Unified National Extra Fine
UN—Unified National, or constant pitch threads

An English unit thread callout starts by defining the major diameter of the thread followed by the pitch specification. The callout .500 –13 UNC means a thread whose major diameter is .500 inch with 13 threads per inch and is manufactured to the Unified National Coarse standards.

There are three possible classes of fit for a thread: 1, 2, and 3. The different class specifications specify a set of manufacturing tolerances. A class 1 thread is the loosest and a class 3, the most exact. A class 2 fit is the most common.

The letter A designates an external thread, B an internal thread. The symbol × means "by" as in 2 × 4, "two by four." The thread length (3.00) may be followed by the word LONG to prevent confusion about which value represents the length.

Drawing callouts for English unit threads are sometimes shortened, as in Figure 11-4. The callout .500–13UNC–2A × 3.00 LONG is shortened to .500–13 × 3.00. Only a coarse thread has 13 threads per inch, and it should be obvious whether a thread is internal or external, so these specifications may be dropped. Most threads are class 2, so it is tacitly accepted that all threads are class 2 unless otherwise specified. The shortened callout form is not universally accepted. When in doubt, use a complete thread callout.

A partial list of standard English unit threads is shown in Figure 11-5. A more complete list is included in the appendix. Some of the drill sizes listed use numbers and letters. The decimal equivalents to the numbers and letters are listed in the appendix.

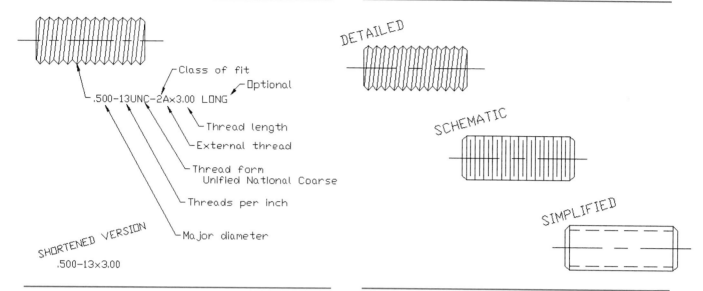

Figure 11-4

Figure 11-6

11-5 THREAD REPRESENTATIONS

There are three ways to graphically represent threads on a drawing: detailed, schematic, and simplified. Figure 11-6 shows the three representations.

Detailed representations look the most like actual threads but are time-consuming to draw. Creating a wblock of a detailed shape will help eliminate this time constraint.

Schematic and simplified thread representations are created using a series of straight lines. The simplified rep-

resentation uses only two hidden lines and can be mistaken for an internal hole if it is not accompanied by a thread specification callout. The choice of which representation to use depends on individual preferences. The resulting drawing should be clear and easy to understand. All three representations may be used on the same drawing, but in general, only very large threads (those over 1.00 in. or 25 mm) are drawn using the detailed representation.

Ideally, thread representations should be drawn with each thread equal to the actual pitch size. This is not practical

Major Dia	Decimal	UNC		UNF		UNEF	
		Thread/in	Tap drill Dia.	Thread/in	Tap drill Dia.	Thread/in	Tap drill Dia.
#6	.138	40	#38	44	#37		
#8	.164	32	#29	36	#29		
#10	.190	24	#25	32	#21		
1/4	.250	20	7	28	3	32	.219
5/16	.312	18	F	24	1	32	.281
3/8	.375	16	.312	24	Q	32	.344
7/16	.438	14	U	20	.391	28	Y
1/2	.500	13	.422	20	.453	28	.469
9/16	.562	12	.484	18	.516	24	.516
5/8	.625	11	.531	18	.578	24	.578
3/4	.750	10	.656	16	.688	20	.703
7/8	.875	9	.766	14	.812	20	.828
1	1.000	8	.875	12	.922	20	.953
1 1/4	1.250	7	1.109	12	1.172	18	1.188
1 1/2	1.500	6	1.344	12	1.422	18	1.438

UNC = Unified National Coarse

UNF = Unified National Fine

UNEF = Unified National Extra Fine

Figure 11-5

for smaller threads and not necessary for larger ones. Thread representations are not meant to be exact duplications of the threads but representations, so convenient drawing distances are acceptable.

To draw a detailed thread representation

Draw a detailed thread representation for a 1.00-inch-diameter thread that is 3.00 inches long. See Figure 11-7.

1. Set Grid = .5 and Snap = .125.
2. Draw a 4.00-inch centerline near the center of the screen.
3. Zoom the area around the centerline.
4. Draw a zigzag pattern .375 above the centerline using the .125 snap points. Start the zigzag line .50 from the left end of the centerline.
5. Access the Array command.

   The Array dialog box will appear.

6. Select the Rectangular option.
7. Click the Select objects button, then select the zigzag pattern.
8. Set the Row value for 1 and the column value for 12.
9. Set the Row offset for 0.0000
10. Set the Column offset for 0.25, then select the OK button.
11. Mirror the arrayed zigzag line about the centerline.
12. Draw vertical lines at both ends of the thread and two slanted lines between the thread's roots and crests as shown.
13. Array both slanted lines using the same array parameters used for the zigzag line: 12 columns .25 apart.
14. Save the thread representation as a block and wblock named DETLIN. Define the insertion point as shown.

   Creating blocks is explained in Chapter 3.
   Another technique for drawing a detailed thread representation is to draw a single thread completely and then use the Copy or Array command to generate as many additional threads as is necessary.

Figure 11-7

Figure 11-8

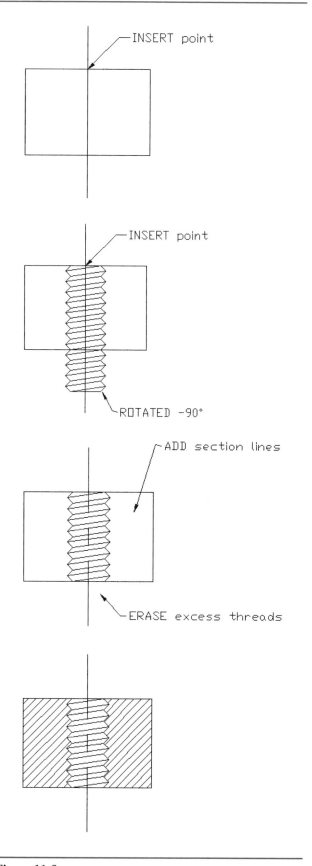

It is recommended that you save all thread wblocks on a separate disk. This disk will become a reference disk that you can use when creating other drawings that require threads.

Figure 11-8 shows a metric unit detailed thread representation. It was created using the procedure outlined. Grid was set at 10, Snap was set at 2.5, and the distance from the centerline to the zigzag pattern was 10. Draw and save the metric detailed thread representation shown in Figure 11-8 as a wblock named DETLMM.

To create an internal detailed thread representation in a sectional view

Figure 11-9 shows how to create a 1.00-inch internal detailed thread representation from the wblock DETLIN of the external detailed thread created above.

1. Use Block, Insert and locate the detailed wblock on the drawing screen at the indicated insert point. In this example the thread is to be drawn in a vertical orientation, so the block is rotated 90° when it is inserted. The same scale size is used for the wblock as was drawn for a 1.00-inch diameter thread.
2. The thread created from wblock DETLIN is longer than needed, so explode the block and then erase the excess lines.
3. Define the hatch pattern as ANSI31 and apply hatching to the areas outside the thread as shown.

Figure 11-9

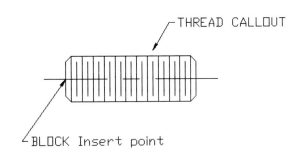

Figure 11-10

To create a schematic thread representation

Draw a schematic representation of a 1.00-inch-diameter thread. See Figure 11-10.

1. Set Grid to .50 and Snap to .125.
2. Draw a 4.00-inch centerline near the middle of the drawing screen.
3. Draw the outline of the thread, including a chamfer, using the dimensions shown.

The chamfer was drawn in this example using the .125 snap points, but the Chamfer command could also have been used.

The 1.00 diameter was chosen because it will make it easier to determine scale factors for the wblock when inserting the representation into other drawings.

4. Draw three vertical lines as shown.
5. Use the Rectangular Array command to draw 11 vertical lines across the thread. The distance between the 11 lines (COLUMNS) is .25.

A distance of −.25 would create lines to the left of the original line.

6. Save the representation as a wblock named SCHMINCH. Define the insertion point as shown.

Figure 11-11 shows a metric unit version of a schematic thread representation in a sectional view. The procedure used to create the representation is the same as explained previously but with different drawing limits and different values. The major diameter is 20, and the spacing between lines is 2.5 and 5 as shown. Draw and save the representation as a wblock named SCHMMM.

To create an internal schematic thread representation

Figure 11-12 shows a 36-millimeter-diameter internal schematic thread representation. It was developed from the wblock SCHMMM created previously.

1. Set Grid = 10
   Snap = 5
   Limits = 297,210
   Zoom = ALL

2. Insert the wblock SCHMMM at the indicated insert point.

The required thread diameter is 36 millimeters. The wblock SCHMMM was drawn using a diameter of 20 mil-

Figure 11-11

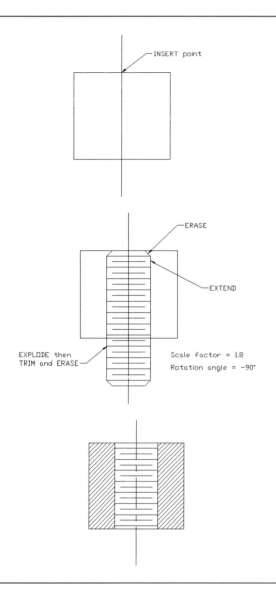

Figure 11-12

limeters. This means that the block must be enlarged by using a scale factor. The scale factor is determined by dividing the desired diameter by the wblock's diameter.

36/20 = 1.8

The wblock must also be rotated 90° to give it the correct orientation.

3. The inserted thread shape is longer than desired, so first explode the wblock and then use the Erase, Trim, and Extend commands as needed.
4. Draw the sectional lines using Hatch ANSI31.
5. Save the drawing as a wblock if desired.

To create a simplified thread representation

The simplified representation looks very similar to the orthographic view of an internal hole, so it is important to always include a thread callout with the representation. In the example shown, a leader line was included with the representation. See Figure 11-13. The leader serves as a reminder to add the appropriate drawing callout. If the leader line is in an inconvenient location when the wblock is inserted into a drawing, the leader line can be moved or simply erased.

1. Set Grid = .5
   Snap = .125
2. Draw a 4.00 centerline near the center of the screen.
3. Draw the thread outline using the given dimensions.
4. Draw the hidden lines using the given dimensions.
5. Save the thread representation as a wblock named SIMPIN. Define the insertion point as shown.

Figure 11-14 shows an internal simplified thread representation in a sectional view. Note how hidden lines that cross over the sectional lines are used. The hatch must be drawn first and the hidden lines added over the pattern. If the hidden lines are drawn first, the Hatch command may not add section lines to the portion between the hidden line and the solid line that represents the edge of the threaded hole.

Figure 11-13

Figure 11-14

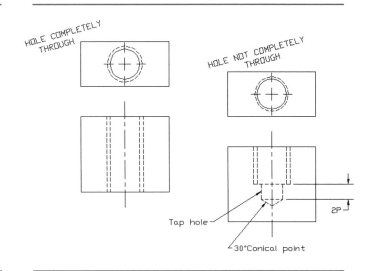

Figure 11-15

11-6 ORTHOGRAPHIC VIEWS OF INTERNAL THREADS

Figure 11-15 shows top and front orthographic views of internal threads. One thread goes completely through the object, the other only partially.

Internal threads are represented in orthographic views using parallel hidden lines. The distance between the lines should be large enough so that there is a clear distinction between the lines; that is, the lines should not appear to blend together or become a single, very thick line.

Circular orthographic views of threaded holes are represented by two circles: one drawn using a continuous line and the other drawn using a hidden line. The distance between the circles should be large enough to be visually distinctive. The two circles shown should both be clearly visible.

Threaded holes are created by first drilling a tap hole and then tapping (cutting) the threads using a tapping bit. Tapping bits have cutting surfaces on their side surfaces, not on the bottom. This means that if the tapping bit were forced all the way to the bottom of the tap hole, the bit could be damaged or broken. It is good design practice to make the tap hole deep enough so that a distance equivalent to at least two thread lengths (2P) extends beyond the tapped portion of the hole.

Threaded holes that do not go completely through an object must always show the unused portion of the tap hole. The unused portion should also include the conical point. See Chapter 5.

If an internal .500–13 UNC thread does not go completely through an object, the length of the unused portion of the tap hole is determined as follows:

Inches/Thread
= Pitch length = 1.00/13
= .077 inch

so

$$2P = 2(.077) = .15 \text{ inch}$$

The distance .15 represents a minimum. It would be acceptable to specify a pilot hole depth greater than .15 depending on the specific design requirements.

If an internal M12 × 1.75 thread does not go completely through an object, the length of the unused portion of the tap hole is determined as follows:

$$2(\text{Pitch length}) = 2(1.75) = 3.50 \text{ mm}$$

11-7 SECTIONAL VIEWS OF INTERNAL THREAD REPRESENTATIONS

Figure 11-16 shows sectional views of internal threads that do not go completely through an object. Each example was created from wblocks of the representations. The hatch pattern used was ANSI32. Each example includes both a threaded portion and an untapped pilot hole that extends approximately 2P beyond the end of the tapped portion of the hole.

When drawing a simplified representation in a sectional view, draw the hidden lines that represent the outside edges of the threads after the section lines have been added. If the lines are drawn before the section lines are added, the section lines will stop at the outside line. Section lines should be drawn up to the solid line, as shown.

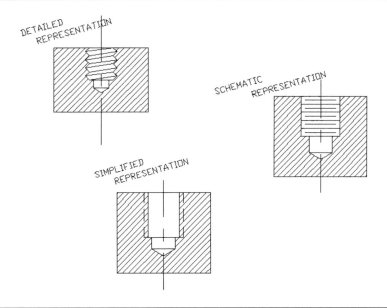

Figure 11-16

11-8 TYPES OF THREADS

Figure 11-17 shows the profiles of four different types of thread: American National, square, acme, and knuckle. There are many other types of threads. In general, square and acme threads are used when heavy loading is involved. A knuckle thread can be manufactured from sheet metal and is most commonly found on a lightbulb.

The American National thread is the thread shape most often used in mechanical design work. All threads in this chapter are assumed to be American National threads unless otherwise stated.

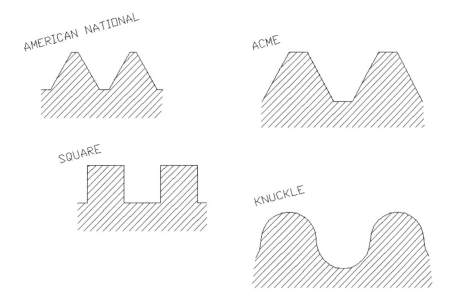

Figure 11-17

11-9 HOW TO DRAW AN EXTERNAL SQUARE THREAD

Figure 11-18 shows how to draw a 4.00-inch long external square thread that has a major diameter of 5.25 and 2 threads per inch. The procedure is as follows.

1. Set Grid = .50
     Snap = .125
2. Draw two 5.00 long horizontal lines 2.00 apart and a 4.50 centerline between them.
3. Draw a rhomboid center about the centerline using the given dimensions.

    In this example $P = .5$, so $.5P = .25$.

4. Use the Array, Rectangular command to create eight columns (2 threads per inch) .50 apart.
5. Draw slanted lines 1-2 and 3-4.
6. Zoom the upper right portion of the thread as needed.
7. Draw a horizontal line .25 (.5P) from the outside edge of the thread as shown.
8. Draw line 5-6 from the intersection of the horizontal line drawn in step 7 with line 1-2, labeled point 5, to the intersection of the toothline 1-6 and the thread's centerline.
9. Trim the horizontal line to create line 5-7, and trim line 1-2 below point 5.
10. Array lines 1-5, 5-6, and 5-7 using Rectangular Array with eight columns −.25 apart.

    The minus sign will generate a right-to-left array.

11. Repeat steps 7 through 10 for the lower portion of the thread. Array eight columns, +.25 apart. The plus sign generates a left-to-right array.
12. Erase any excess lines and add any necessary shaft information to the drawing.
13. Save the drawing as a wblock named SQIN using the indicated insertion point.

Figure 11-18

11-10 HOW TO DRAW AN INTERNAL SQUARE THREAD

Figure 11-19 shows an external 2.25 × 2 square thread. The drawing was developed from wblock SQIN created in Section 11-9. The wblock was rotated to the correct orientation. Erase and Trim were used to fit the thread within the required depth. No scale factor was needed.

11-11 HOW TO DRAW AN EXTERNAL ACME THREAD

Draw a 2.25 × 2 × 4.00–long external acme thread. The procedure is as follows. See Figure 11-20.

1. Set Grid = .5
   Snap = .125
2. Draw a 5.00-long horizontal centerline.
3. Draw two .5-long horizontal lines 1.125 above and below.

These lines establish the major diameter of the thread.

4. Draw a single acme thread using the given dimensions. Use Zoom to help create an enlarged working area. The first thread should start at the right end of the short horizontal line above the centerline.

The width dimensions are taken along the horizontal centerline of the individual thread. Each side of the thread is slanted at 14.5° [.5(29)]. In this example $P = .5$, so $.5P = .25$, and $.25P = .125$.

5. Use the Array command and draw eight columns (two threads per inch) .5 apart to develop the top portion of the thread.
6. Copy and Move the top portion of the thread to create the lower portion.

Do not use Mirror. The lower portion of the thread is not a mirror image of the upper portion.

7. Erase and extend lines as necessary along the lower left portion of the thread to blend the thread into the shaft.

Figure 11-19

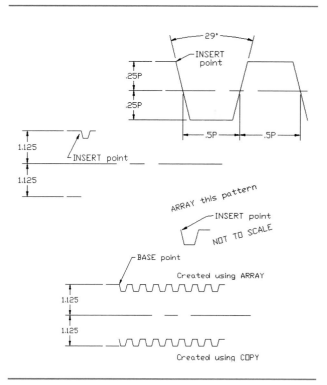

Figure 11-20, Part 1

8. Draw two slanted lines between the thread's root lines at the left end of the thread.
9. Array the lines drawn in step 8 so that there are eight columns, .5 apart.
10. Draw two slanted lines across the thread's crest lines at the left end of the thread.
11. Array the lines drawn in step 10 so that there are eight columns, .5 apart.

12. Draw a vertical line at each end of the thread, establishing the thread's 4.00-inch length.
13. Erase and trim the excess lines from the left end of the thread.
14. Copy and trim a crest-to-crest line to complete the left end of the thread.
15. Save the drawing as a wblock named ACMEIN using the indicated insertion point.

Figure 11-20, Part 2

Figure 11-21

Figure 11-22

11-12 BOLTS AND NUTS

A *bolt* is a fastener that passes through a clearance hole in an object and is joined to a nut. There are no threads in the objects. See Figure 11-21. Note that there are no hidden lines within the nut to indicate that the bolt is passing through. Drawing convention allows for nuts to be drawn without hidden lines.

Threads on a bolt are usually made just long enough to correctly accept a nut. This is done to minimize the amount of contact between the edges of threads and the inside surfaces of the clearance holes. The sharp, knife-like thread edges could cut into the object, particularly if the application involves vibrations.

It is considered good design practice to specify a bolt length long enough to allow at least two threads to extend beyond the end of the nut. This ensures that the nut is fully attached to the bolt.

Bolt drawings can be created from wblocks of threads. Remember that a block must be exploded before it can be edited.

11-13 SCREWS

A *screw* is a fastener that assembles into an object. It does not use a nut. The joining threads are cut into the assembling object. See Figure 11-22.

Screws may or may not be threaded over their entire length. If a screw passes through a clearance hole in an object before it assembles into another object, it is good design practice to minimize the number of threads that contact the sides of the clearance hole.

It is also considered good design practice to allow a few unused threads in the threaded hole beyond the end of an assembled screw. If a screw was forced to the bottom of a tapped hole, it might not assemble correctly or could possibly be damaged.

It is good design practice to allow at least two unused threads beyond the end of the screw. Figure 11-22 shows a schematic thread representation of a screw mounted in a threaded hole.

There is a distance of $2P$ (two threads) between the end of the screw and the end of the threaded portion of the hole. There should also be a $2P$ distance between the end of the threaded hole and the end of the pilot hole, plus the conical point of the tap hole, as described in Section 11-6.

Threads are usually not drawn in a threaded hole beyond the end of an assembling screw. This makes it easier to visually distinguish the end of the screw.

Figure 11-23 shows a screw assembled into a hole drawn using the detailed, schematic, and simplified representations in a sectional view. An orthographic view of a screw in a threaded hole is also shown.

The top view shown in Figure 11-23 applies to all three representations and the orthographic view.

11-14 STUDS

A *stud* is a threaded fastener that both screws into an object and accepts a nut. See Figure 11-24. The thread callouts and representations for studs are the same as they are for bolts and screws.

Figure 11-23

11-15 HEAD SHAPES

Bolts and screws are manufactured with a variety of different head shapes, but hexagon (hex) and square head shapes are the most common. There are many different head sizes available for different applications. Extra-thick heads are used for heavy-load applications, and very thin heads are used for applications where space is limited. The exact head size specifications are available from fastener manufacturers.

This section shows how to draw hex and square heads based on accepted average sizes that are functions of the major diameters of both the bolt and the screw. It is suggested that hexagon and square head drawings be saved as wblocks for both inch and millimeter values so that they can be combined with the thread wblocks to form fasteners.

Figure 11-24

To draw a hexagon (hex) shaped head

Draw front and top orthographic views of a hex head based on a thread with an M24 major diameter. See Figure 11-25.

1. Set Limits = 297,210
        Grid = 10
        Snap = 5
2. Draw a vertical line and two horizontal lines using the given dimensions.

The two horizontal lines are used to locate the center of the head in the top view and the bottom of the head in the front view.

3. Use Polygon and draw a hexagon distance across the flats equal to 1.5*D*, where *D* is the major diameter of the thread.

In this example a radius of 18 was used to draw the hexagon. $1.5D = 1.5(24) = 36$ is the distance across the flats of the hexagon. Use the Polygon command to circumscribe a six-sided polygon around a circle of radius 18.

4. Offset a line .67*D* from the lower horizontal.

This line defines the thickness of the head. The head thickness is .67*D*, where *D* is the major diameter of the thread. In this example $D = 24$, so $.67D = .67(24) = 16.08$, which can be rounded off to 16.

5. Draw projection lines from the corners of the hexagon in the top view into the front view.
6. Zoom the front view portion of the drawing if necessary. Draw two 60° lines from the corners of the front view as shown so that they intersect on the vertical centerline.

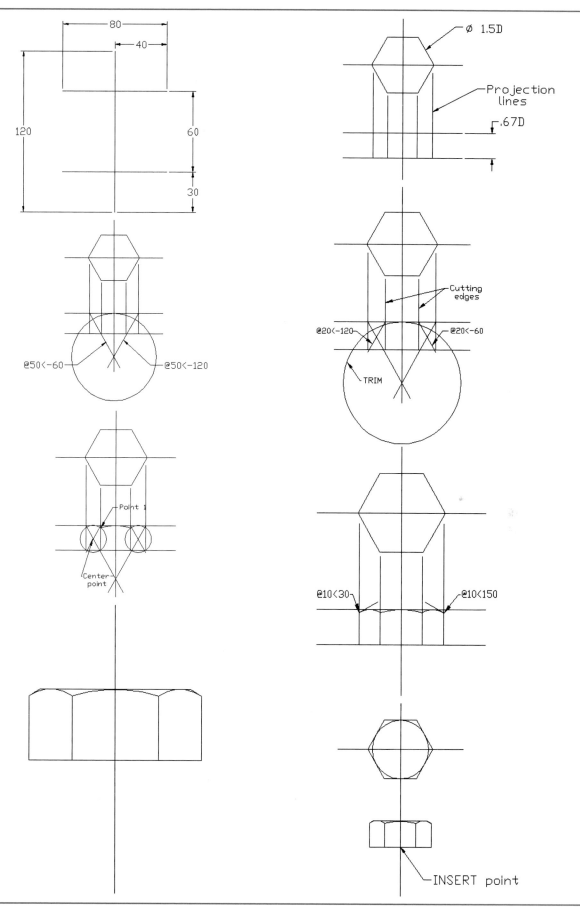

Figure 11-25

Use Osnap, Intersection to accurately locate the corner points. The line from the left corner uses an input of @50<−60; the line from the right corner uses the input @50<−120.

7. Draw a circle whose center point is the intersection of the two 60° lines drawn in step 6 and the vertical centerline, and whose radius equals the distance from the center point to the line at the top of the front view.
8. Trim the circle so that only the arc between the inside projection lines remains.
9. Draw two 60° lines as shown using the inputs @20<−120 and @20<−60.
10. Draw two circles centered about the intersection of the slanted lines drawn in steps 6 and 8. The radius of each circle equals the distance from the center point to the intersection of the circle drawn in step 7 and the inside projection lines labeled point 1.
11. Trim and erase as needed.
12. Draw two lines from the intersections of the smaller arcs with the outside edge of the head. The input for the lines is @10<30 and @10<150.

These lines could have been generated using the Chamfer command.

13. Trim the chamfer lines to the top of the head.
14. Zoom All and draw a circle that is circumscribed within the hexagon as shown.
15. Save the drawing as a wblock named HEXHEAD, using the indicated insertion point.

To draw a square-shaped head

Draw front and top orthographic views of a hex head based on a thread with a 1.00-inch major diameter. See Figure 11-26.

1. Set Grid = .50
   Snap = .25
2. Draw two horizontal lines and a vertical line using the given dimensions.

The intersection of the top horizontal line and the vertical line will be the center point of the top view, and the lower horizontal line will be the bottom edge of the head.

3. Use Draw, Polygon and Modify, Rotate (45°) to create a square oriented as shown.

The distance across the square equals 1.50D or 1.50 inches. This means that the radius for the polygon is .75.

Figure 11-26, Part 1

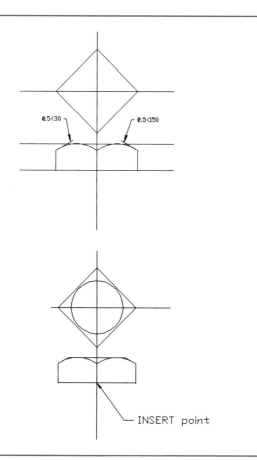

Figure 11-26, Part 2

4. Offset a line .67 (.67*D*) from the lower horizontal line.

The offset distance is equal to the thickness of the head.

5. Project the corners of the square in the top view into the front view.
6. Zoom the front view and draw four 60° lines from the head's upper corners and intersection of the centerline and the top surface of the head as shown. The inputs for the lines are @1.5<−120 and @1.5<−60. Use Osnap, Intersection to ensure accuracy.
7. Use Draw, Circle, Center, Radius and draw two circles about the center points created in step 6. Trim the excess portions of the circle.
8. Trim and erase any excess lines.
9. Add the 30° chamfer lines as shown. The line inputs are @.5<150 and @.5<30. Use Osnap, Intersection to accurately locate the intersection

between the arc and the vertical side line of the head.
10. Trim any excess lines.
11. Zoom the drawing back to its original size and draw a circle in the top view tangent to the inside edges of the square.
12. Save the drawing as a wblock named SQHEAD using the insertion point indicated.

11-16 NUTS

This section explains how to draw hexagon- and square-shaped nuts. Both construction methods are based on the head shape wblocks created in Section 11-15.

There are many different styles of nuts. A finished nut has a flat surface on one side that acts as a bearing surface when the nut is tightened against an object. A finished nut has a thickness equal to .88*D*, where *D* is the major diameter of the nut's thread size.

A locknut is symmetrical, with the top and bottom surfaces identical. A locknut has a thickness equal to .5*D*, where *D* is the major diameter of the nut's thread size.

To draw a hexagon-shaped finished nut

Draw a hexagon-shaped finished nut for an M36 thread. See Figure 11-27.

1. Set Limits = 297,210
       Grid = 10
       Snap = 2.5
2. Construct a vertical line that is intersected by two horizontal lines 32 millimeters apart.

The thickness of a finished nut is .88*D*. In this example, .88(36) = 31.68, or 32.

3. Use Block, Insert and insert the HEXHEAD wblock created in Section 11-15.

The wblock HEXHEAD was created for an M24 thread, so the X and Y scale factors must be increased to accommodate the larger thread size. The scale factor is determined by dividing the desired size by the wblock size. In this example, 36/24 = 1.5. The scale factor is 1.5. Respond to the command prompts as follows.

Command: INSERT

The Insert dialog box will appear.

4. Type or select HEXHEAD; press Enter.

5. Select the indicated insertion point.
6. Specify an X and Y scale of 1.5 and a 0 rotation angle; select OK.

   Specify insertion point or [Scale/X/Y/Z/Rotate/ PScale/PX/PY/PZ/PRotate]:

7. Press Enter.

   If you have not created a wblock, refer to Section 11-15 and draw a hexagon-shaped head.

8. Explode the wblock.

9. Move the front view of the nut so that the top surface aligns with the top parallel horizontal line.
10. Erase the bottom line of the front view of the nut and extend the vertical line to the lower horizontal line. Erase the top horizontal line in the front view.
11. Use Offset to draw a horizontal line 2 millimeters below the bottom of the nut.

    This line defines the shoulder surface of the nut. Any offset distance may be used as long as the line is clearly

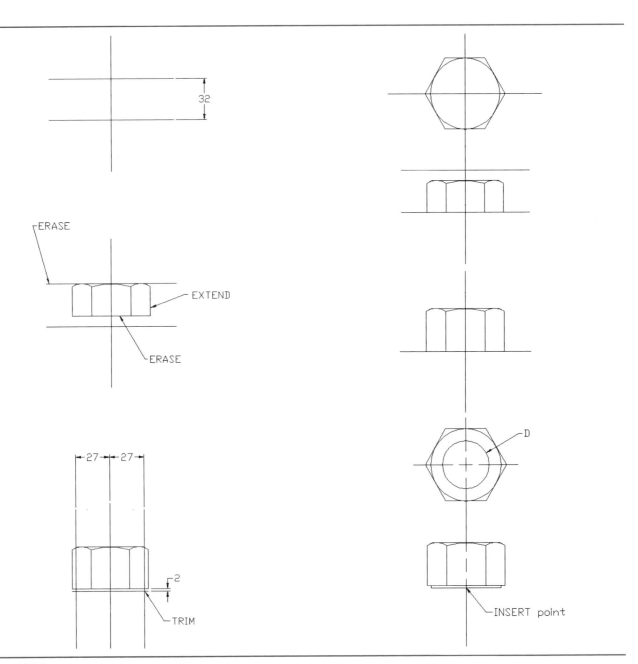

Figure 11-27

visible. The actual shoulder surface is less than 1 millimeter deep and would not appear clearly on the drawing.

The shoulder surface has a diameter equal to 1.5D [1.5(36) = 54] or, in this example, 54.

12. Offset the centerline 27 (half of 54) to each side and trim the excess lines.
13. Save the drawing as a wblock named FNUTHEX. Define the insertion point as shown.

To draw a locking nut

Draw a locking nut for an M24 thread. See Figure 11-28. The HEXHEAD wblock was originally drawn for an M24 thread, so no scale factor is needed.

1. Set Limits = 297,210
      Grid = 10
      Snap = 5
2. Draw a vertical line and two horizontal lines using the given dimensions.

The 6 distance is half the .5D [.5(24) = 12] thickness distance recommended for locknuts. Locknuts are symmetrical, so half the nut will be drawn and then mirrored.

3. Insert the HEXHEAD wblock at the indicated insert point.
4. Explode the wblock.
5. Move the front view of the hex head so that it aligns with the horizontal line as shown.
6. Trim and erase the lines that extend beyond the lower horizontal line.
7. Mirror the remaining portion of the front view about the lower horizontal line, then erase the horizontal line.
8. Draw a circle of diameter D in the top view as shown.
9. Save the drawing as a wblock named LNUTHEX using the indicated insertion point.

The procedure explained previously for hexagon-shaped finish nuts and locknuts is the same for square-shaped nuts. Use the wblock SQHEAD in place of the HEXHEAD wblock.

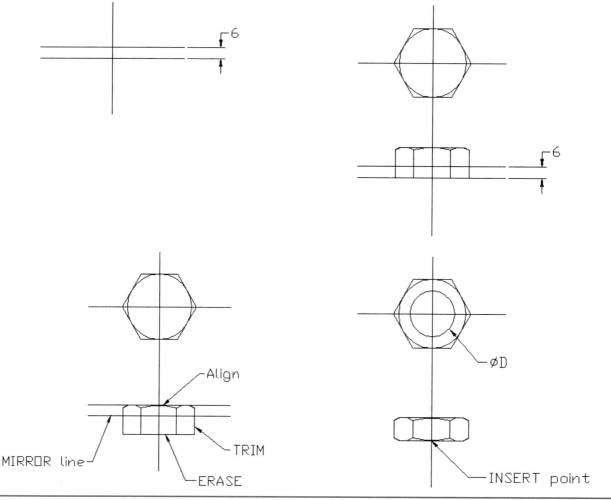

Figure 11-28

11-17 SAMPLE PROBLEM SP11-1

Draw and specify the mimimum threaded hole depth and pilot hole depth for an M12 × 1.75 × 50 hex head screw. Assemble the screw into the object shown in Figure 11-29. Use the schematic thread representation and a sectional view.

The SCHMMM wblock was originally drawn for an M20 thread, so a scale factor is needed. The scale factor to reduce an M20 diameter to an M12 is 12/20 = .6.

1. Insert the SCHMMM wblock and insert it at the indicated point. Use a .6 X and Y scale factor.
2. Explode the block and trim any excess threads.
3. Insert the HEXHEAD wblock as indicated. The HEXHEAD wblock was also created for an M20 thread, so the scale factor is again .6.

The thread pitch equals 1.75, so $2P = 3.5$. This means that the threaded hole should be at least 50 + 3.5, or 53.5, deep to allow for two unused threads beyond the end of the screw.

The unused portion of the pilot hole should also extend $2P$ beyond the end of the threaded portion of the hole, so the minimum pilot hole depth equals 53.5 + 3.5 = 57.

The diameter of the tap hole for the thread is given in a table in the appendix as 10.3. For this example a diameter of 10 was used for drawing purposes. If required, the 10.3 value would be given in the hole's drawing callout.

4. Draw the unused portion of the thread hole and pilot hole as shown. Omit the thread representation in the portion of the threaded hole beyond the end of the screw for clarity.

Figure 11-29

1. Insert the SCHMINCH wblock at the indicated point. Use an X and Y scale factor of .75. Rotate the block −90° to the correct orientation.

The wblock SCHMINCH is not long enough to go completely through the objects, so a second wblock is inserted below the first.

2. Insert the SQHEAD wblock at the indicated point. Use an X and Y scale factor of .75.

11-18 SAMPLE PROBLEM SP11-2

Determine the length of a .750–10UNC square head bolt needed to pass through objects 1 and 2 shown in Figure 11-30. Include a hexagon-shaped locknut on the end of the bolt. Allow at least two threads beyond the end of the nut. Use the closest standard bolt length and draw a schematic representation as a sectional view.

This construction is based on the wblocks SCHMINCH, HEXHEAD, and LNUTHEX created in Sections 11-5, 11-15, and 11-16. If no wblocks are available, refer to these sections for an explanation of how to create the required shapes.

The wblocks SCHMINCH, HEXHEAD, and LNUTHEX were created for a major diameter of 1.00 inch, so the scale factor needed to create a major diameter of .750 is .75.

Figure 11-30

3. Insert the wblock LNUTHEX at the indicated point. Use an X and Y scale factor of .75.
4. Explode the wblocks.
5. Trim the excess lines within the nut.
6. Calculate the minimum length for the bolt.

The total depth of objects 1 and 2 equals $1.250 + 1.625 = 2.875$.

The thickness of the nut equals $.88D$ or $.88(.75) = .375$.

The pitch length of the thread equals $1.00/10 = .1$, so $2P = .2$.

The minimum bolt length equals $2.875 + .375 + .200 = 3.450$.

From the table of standard bolt lengths in the appendix, the standard bolt length that is greater than 3.45 is 3.50, so the bolt callout can now be completed:

.750 − 10UNC − 2A × 3.50 LONG

The completed drawing with the appropriate bolt callout is shown in Figure 11-30.

11-19 STANDARD SCREWS

Figure 11-31 shows a group of standard screw shapes. The proportions given in Figure 11-30 are acceptable for general drawing purposes and represent average values. The exact dimensions for specific screws are available from manufacturers' catalogs. A partial listing of standard screw sizes is included in the appendix.

The given head shape dimensions are all in terms of D, the major diameter of the screw's thread. Information about the available standard major diameters and lengths is included in the appendix.

The choice of head shape is determined by the specific design requirements. For example, a flat head mounted flush with the top surface is a good choice when space is critical, when two parts butt against each other, or when aerodynamic considerations are involved. A round head can be assembled using a common blade screwdriver, but it is more susceptible to damage than a hex head. The hex head, however, requires a specific wrench for assembly.

Figure 11-31

11-20 SET SCREWS

Set screws are fasteners used to hold parts like gears and pulleys to rotating shafts or other objects to prevent slippage between the two objects. See Figure 11-32.

Most set screws have recessed heads to help prevent interference with other parts. Many different head styles and point styles are available. See Figure 11-33.

Set screws are referenced on a drawing using the following format.

THREAD SPECIFICATION
HEAD SPECIFICATION POINT SPECIFICA-
    TION
SET SCREW

.250 – 20UNC – 2A 1.00 LONG
SLOT HEAD FLAT POINT
SET SCREW

The words LONG, HEAD, and POINT are optional.

Figure 11-32

Figure 11-33

Figure 11-34

Figure 11-36

11-21 WASHERS

There are many different styles of washers available for different design applications. The three most common types of washers are plain, lock, and star. Plain washers can be used to help distribute the bearing load of a fastener or used as a spacer to help align and assemble objects. Lock and star washers help absorb vibrations and prevent fasteners from loosening prematurely. All washers are identified as follows:

Inside diameter × Outside diameter × Thickness

Examples of plain washers and their callouts are shown in Figure 11-34. A listing of standard washer sizes is included in the appendix.

To draw a plain washer (See Figure 11-35.)

1. Draw concentric circles for the inside and outside diameters.
2. Project lines from the circular view and draw a line that defines the width of the washer.
3. Use Offset to define the thickness.

Figure 11-36 shows two views of a lock washer. As the lock washer is compressed during assembly it tends to flatten, so the slanted end portions are not usually included on the drawing. The drawing callout should include the words LOCK WASHER.

Figure 11-37 shows an internal and an external tooth lock-type washer. They may also be called *star washers*.

Figure 11-35

TOOTH LOCK TYPE

EXTERNAL   INTERNAL

Figure 11-37

They are best drawn by first drawing an individual tooth, then using Array to draw a total of 12 teeth. Because there are 12 teeth, each tooth and the space between the tooth and the next tooth require a total of 30° − 15° for the tooth and 15° for the space between.

11-22 KEYS

Keys are used to help prevent slippage in power transmission between parts, for example, a gear and a drive shaft. Grooves called *keyways* are cut into both the gear and the drive shaft and a key is inserted between, as shown in Figure 11-38.

There are four common types of keys: square, Pratt & Whitney, Woodruff, and gib head. Each has design advantages and disadvantages. See Figure 11-39. A list of standard key sizes is included in the appendix.

Square keys are called out on a drawing by specifying the length of one side of the square cross section and the overall length; Pratt & Whitney and Woodruff keys are specified by numbers; and gib head keys are defined by a group of dimensions. See the appendix for the appropriate tables and charts of standard key sizes.

Keyways are dimensioned as shown in Figure 8-46. Note that the depth of a keyway in a shaft is dimensioned from the bottom of the shaft. Because material has been cut away, the intersection between the shaft's centerline and top

outside edge does not exist. It is better to dimension from a real surface than from a theoretical one. The same dimensioning technique also applies to the gear.

11-23 RIVETS

Rivets are fasteners that hold adjoining or overlapping objects together. A rivet starts with a head at one end and a straight shaft at the other. The rivet is then inserted into the object, and the headless end is "bucked" or otherwise forced into place. A force is applied to the headless end that changes its shape so that another head is formed holding the objects together.

There are many different shapes and styles of rivets. Figure 11-40 shows five common head shapes for rivets. Aircraft use hollow rivets because they are very lightweight. A design advantage for using rivets is that they can be drilled out and removed or replaced without damaging the objects they hold together.

Rivet types are represented on technical drawings using a coding system. See Figure 11-41. The lines used to code a rivet must be clearly visible on the drawing. Because rivets are sometimes so small and the material they hold together so thin that it is difficult to clearly draw the rivets, companies draw only the rivet's centerline in the side view and identify the rivet using a drawing callout.

Figure 11-38

Figure 11-39

Figure 11-40

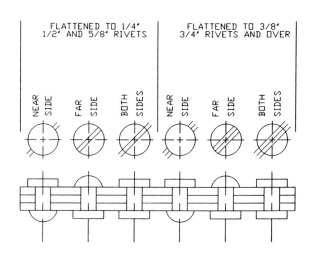

Figure 11-41

11-24 SPRINGS

The most common types of springs used on technical drawings are compression, extension, and torsional. This section explains how to draw detailed and schematic representations of springs. Springs are drawn in their relaxed position (not expanded or compressed). Phantom lines may be used to show several different positions for springs as they are expanded or compressed.

Springs are defined by the diameter of their wire, the direction of their coils, their outside diameter, their total number of coils, and their total relaxed length. Information about their loading properties may also be included. The pitch of a spring equals the distance from the center of one coil to the center of the next coil.

As with threads, the detailed representations are difficult and time consuming to draw, but the Array command shortens the drawing time considerably. Saving the representation as a wblock also helps avoid having to redraw the representation for each new drawing.

Ideally, the distance between coils should be exactly equal to the pitch of the spring, but this is not always practical for smaller springs. Any convenient distance between coils may be used that presents a clear, easy-to-understand representation of the spring.

Figure 11-42

To draw a detailed representation of an extension spring

Draw an extension spring 2.00 inches in diameter with right-hand coils made from .250-inch wire. The spring's pitch equals .25, and the total length of the coils is 3.00 inches. See Figure 11-42.

Because the pitch of the spring equals the wire diameter, the coils will touch each other.

1. Set Grid = .5
   Snap = .25
2. Draw the rounded shape of one of the coils.

The distance between the lines equals the diameter of the spring wire. The diameter of the rounded ends also equals the diameter of the wire. The coil's offset equals the spring's pitch.

3. Array the coil shape.

The Array used was a Rectangular Array with 1 row, and 12 columns .25 apart.

4. Draw two concentric circles at the left end of the spring so that the larger circle's diameter equals the spring's diameter. The vertical centerline of the circles is tangent to the left edge of the first coil.
5. Draw a line across the thread offset a distance equal to one pitch. The endpoints of the line are on snap points.
6. Trim the excess portion of the circles and fillet the circles as shown.
7. Trim the excess portion of the slanted line and cut back the end of the circles so that there is a noticeable gap between the first coil and the end of the circles. The gap distance is determined by eye.
8. Copy, Rotate, and Move the circular end portion to the right end of the spring.
9. Draw a slanted line across the farthest right coil as shown.
10. Trim and extend the lines as necessary and add the FILLET .25R as shown.
11. Save the drawing as a wblock named EXTSPRNG.

To draw a detailed representation of a compression spring

Draw a compression spring with six right-hand coils made from .25-inch-diameter wire. The pitch of the spring equals .50 inch. The diameter of the spring is 2.00 inches. See Figure 11-43.

1. Set Grid = .50
   Snap = .25

2. Draw the rounded shape of the first left coil as shown. The diameter of the rounded ends of the coil equals the diameter of the spring's wire.
3. Array the coil shape.

In this example a Rectangular Array was used to draw 1 row, and 6 columns .50 inch apart.

Figure 11-43

4. Draw two slanted lines as shown.

These lines represent the back portion of the coil. They are most easily drawn from a snap point next to the rounded portion of the coil shape (this point would be the corner point of the coil if the coil were not rounded) to a point tangent to the opposite rounded end of the coil.

5. Trim and array the slanted lines as shown.

Use rectangular array with 1 row, and 6 columns .50 inch apart.

6. Draw the right end of the spring so that it appears to end just short of the spring's centerline. Any convenient distance may be used.

7. Draw the left end of the spring using Copy, and copy one of the existing slanted lines. Use Zoom, if necessary, to align the copied line with the coil. Draw the left end of the spring so that it appears to end just short of the centerline.

8. Save the drawing as a wblock named COMP-SPNG.

Figure 11-44 shows schematic representations of a compression and an extension spring. The distance between the peaks of the slanted lines should equal the pitch of the spring.

11-25 DESIGNCENTER

AutoCAD includes a DesignCenter that includes, among other things, a set of fastener blocks. (See Section 3-21 for an explanation of blocks.) The DesignCenter is accessed using the DesignCenter tool located on the Standard toolbar.

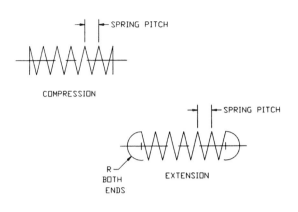

Figure 11-44

To access U.S. fastener blocks

1. Click the DesignCenter tool on the Standard toolbar.

The DesignCenter dialog box will appear. See Figure 11-45.

2. Scroll down the Folder List and select the Fasteners - U.S.dwg heading, then Blocks.

A grouping of available blocks will appear in the dialog box.

3. Double-click the Hex Bolt 1/2in. -side option.

Figure 11-45

Figure 11-46

The Insert dialog box will appear. See Figure 11-46.

4. Accept the default scale values and click OK.

A side view of a hex bolt will appear on the screen. See Figure 11-47.

To change the size of a fastener block

The available blocks are common sizes and can easily be modified to different sizes using the Scale options on the Insert dialog box. Figure 11-48 shows the dimension values for the Hex Bolt block. The dimensions were created using the Linear Dimension tool. The dimensions for any block can be determined by first inserting a drawing of the block and then using the Dimension tool.

To create a hex bolt that has a .75-inch diameter and a length of 2.00 inches

1. Select the Hex Bolt 1/2in. -side block from the DesignCenter.

Hex Bolt 1/2 in - side

Figure 11-47

Figure 11-48

The Insert dialog box will appear. See Figure 11-49.

2. Set the X scale factor for 2.0000 and the Y scale factor for 1.5000, then click OK.

Figure 11-50 shows the resulting fastener drawing. The dimensions were added for demonstration purposes. Dimensions will not appear on the initial drawing.

To access metric fasteners

1. Click the DesignCenter tool on the Standard toolbar.

The DesignCenter dialog box will appear. See Figure 11-51.

2. Scroll down the Folder List and select the Fasteners - Metric.dwg heading, then Blocks.

Most of the available fasteners are based on 10-millimeter sizes. This allows for easier scale-factor determination.

Figure 11-49

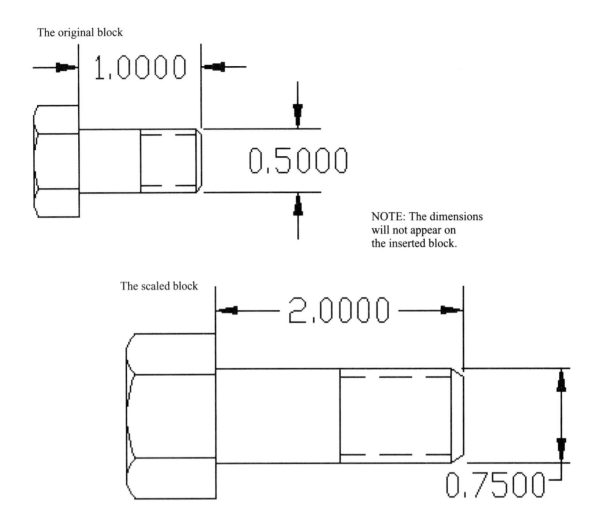

The original block

1.0000

0.5000

NOTE: The dimensions will not appear on the inserted block.

The scaled block

2.0000

0.7500

Figure 11-50

Figure 11-51

To draw a detailed representation of an extension spring

Draw an extension spring 2.00 inches in diameter with right-hand coils made from .250-inch wire. The spring's pitch equals .25, and the total length of the coils is 3.00 inches. See Figure 11-42.

Because the pitch of the spring equals the wire diameter, the coils will touch each other.

1. Set Grid = .5
    Snap = .25
2. Draw the rounded shape of one of the coils.

The distance between the lines equals the diameter of the spring wire. The diameter of the rounded ends also equals the diameter of the wire. The coil's offset equals the spring's pitch.

3. Array the coil shape.

The Array used was a Rectangular Array with 1 row, and 12 columns .25 apart.

4. Draw two concentric circles at the left end of the spring so that the larger circle's diameter equals the spring's diameter. The vertical centerline of the circles is tangent to the left edge of the first coil.
5. Draw a line across the thread offset a distance equal to one pitch. The endpoints of the line are on snap points.
6. Trim the excess portion of the circles and fillet the circles as shown.
7. Trim the excess portion of the slanted line and cut back the end of the circles so that there is a noticeable gap between the first coil and the end of the circles. The gap distance is determined by eye.
8. Copy, Rotate, and Move the circular end portion to the right end of the spring.
9. Draw a slanted line across the farthest right coil as shown.
10. Trim and extend the lines as necessary and add the FILLET .25R as shown.
11. Save the drawing as a wblock named EXTSPRNG.

To draw a detailed representation of a compression spring

Draw a compression spring with six right-hand coils made from .25-inch-diameter wire. The pitch of the spring equals .50 inch. The diameter of the spring is 2.00 inches. See Figure 11-43.

1. Set Grid = .50
    Snap = .25

2. Draw the rounded shape of the first left coil as shown. The diameter of the rounded ends of the coil equals the diameter of the spring's wire.
3. Array the coil shape.

In this example a Rectangular Array was used to draw 1 row, and 6 columns .50 inch apart.

Figure 11-43

4. Draw two slanted lines as shown.

These lines represent the back portion of the coil. They are most easily drawn from a snap point next to the rounded portion of the coil shape (this point would be the corner point of the coil if the coil were not rounded) to a point tangent to the opposite rounded end of the coil.

5. Trim and array the slanted lines as shown.

Use rectangular array with 1 row, and 6 columns .50 inch apart.

6. Draw the right end of the spring so that it appears to end just short of the spring's centerline. Any convenient distance may be used.
7. Draw the left end of the spring using Copy, and copy one of the existing slanted lines. Use Zoom, if necessary, to align the copied line with the coil. Draw the left end of the spring so that it appears to end just short of the centerline.
8. Save the drawing as a wblock named COMP-SPNG.

Figure 11-44 shows schematic representations of a compression and an extension spring. The distance between the peaks of the slanted lines should equal the pitch of the spring.

11-25 DESIGNCENTER

AutoCAD includes a DesignCenter that includes, among other things, a set of fastener blocks. (See Section 3-21 for an explanation of blocks.) The DesignCenter is accessed using the DesignCenter tool located on the Standard toolbar.

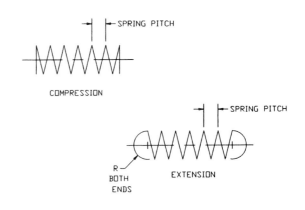

Figure 11-44

To access U.S. fastener blocks

1. Click the DesignCenter tool on the Standard toolbar.

The DesignCenter dialog box will appear. See Figure 11-45.

2. Scroll down the Folder List and select the Fasteners - U.S.dwg heading, then Blocks.

A grouping of available blocks will appear in the dialog box.

3. Double-click the Hex Bolt 1/2in. -side option.

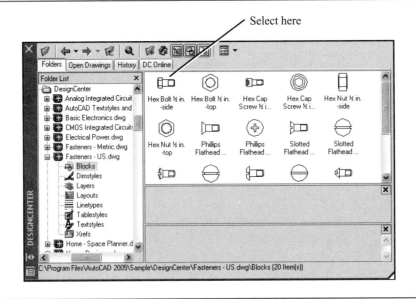

Figure 11-45

Figure 11-46

Figure 11-48

The Insert dialog box will appear. See Figure 11-46.

4. Accept the default scale values and click OK.

A side view of a hex bolt will appear on the screen. See Figure 11-47.

To change the size of a fastener block

The available blocks are common sizes and can easily be modified to different sizes using the Scale options on the Insert dialog box. Figure 11-48 shows the dimension values for the Hex Bolt block. The dimensions were created using the Linear Dimension tool. The dimensions for any block can be determined by first inserting a drawing of the block and then using the Dimension tool.

To create a hex bolt that has a .75-inch diameter and a length of 2.00 inches

1. Select the Hex Bolt 1/2in. -side block from the DesignCenter.

The Insert dialog box will appear. See Figure 11-49.

2. Set the X scale factor for 2.0000 and the Y scale factor for 1.5000, then click OK.

Figure 11-50 shows the resulting fastener drawing. The dimensions were added for demonstration purposes. Dimensions will not appear on the initial drawing.

To access metric fasteners

1. Click the DesignCenter tool on the Standard toolbar.

The DesignCenter dialog box will appear. See Figure 11-51.

2. Scroll down the Folder List and select the Fasteners - Metric.dwg heading, then Blocks.

Most of the available fasteners are based on 10-millimeter sizes. This allows for easier scale-factor determination.

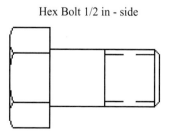

Hex Bolt 1/2 in - side

Figure 11-47

Figure 11-49

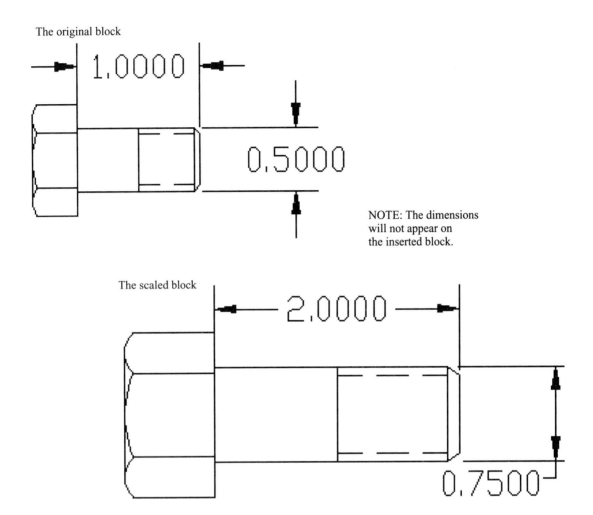

The original block

1.0000

0.5000

NOTE: The dimensions
will not appear on
the inserted block.

The scaled block

2.0000

0.7500

Figure 11-50

Figure 11-51

11-26 EXERCISE PROBLEMS

EX11-1

Create wblocks for the following thread major diameters.

A. 1.00-in. detailed representation
B. 1.00-in. schematic thread representation
C. 1.00-in. simplified thread representation
D. 100-mm detailed representation
E. 100-mm schematic thread representation
F. 100-mm simplified thread representation

EX11-2

Draw a .750–10UNC–2_ × ___ LONG thread. Include the thread callout.

A. External −3.00 LONG.
B. Internal to fit into the object shown in Figure EX11-2.
C. Use a detailed representation.
D. Use a schematic representation.
E. Use a simplified representation.

EX11-3

Draw a .250 − 28UNF − 2_ × ___ LONG thread. Include the thread callout.

A. External−1.50 LONG.
B. Internal to fit into the object shown in Figure EX11-2.
C. Use a detailed representation.
D. Use a schematic representation.
E. Use a simplified representation.

EX11-4

Draw an M36 × 4 × ___ LONG thread. Include the thread callout.

A. External −100 LONG.
B. Internal to fit into the object shown in Figure EX11-2.
C. Use a detailed representation.
D. Use a schematic representation.
E. Use a simplified representation.

EX11-5

Draw an M12 × 1.75 × ___ LONG thread. Include the thread callout.

A. External −40 LONG.
B. Internal to fit into the object shown in Figure EX11-2.
C. Use a detailed representation.
D. Use a schematic representation.
E. Use a simplified representation.

EX11-6

Draw a 2.75 × 2 × 5.00 inch–long external square thread.

EX11-7

Draw a 50 × 2 × 100 millimeter–long external square thread.

EX11-8

Draw a 3 × 1.5 × 6 inch–long external acme thread.

EX11-9

Draw an 80 × 1.5 × 200 millimeter–long external acme thread.

Figure EX11-2

Draw the bolts, nuts, and screws in Exercise Problems EX11-10 to EX11-13 assembled into the object shown in Figure EX11-2. If not given, determine the length of the fasteners using the tables given in this chapter or in the appendix. Include the appropriate drawing callout.

EX11-10

A. .500–13UNC × ____ LONG HEX HEAD BOLT. Include a finished nut on the end of the bolt.
B. 5/8(.625)–18UNF × 1.5 LONG HEX HEAD SCREW. Specify the diameter and length of the tap hole.
C. Draw a detailed representation.
D. Draw a schematic representation.
E. Draw a simplified representation.
F. Draw an orthographic view.
G. Draw a sectional view.

EX11-11

A. M24–____ LONG HEX HEAD BOLT. Include a finished nut on the end of the bolt.
B. M16–30 LONG HEX HEAD SCREW. Specify the diameter and length of the tap hole.
C. Draw a detailed representation.
D. Draw a schematic representation.
E. Draw a simplified representation.
F. Draw an orthographic view.
G. Draw a sectional view.

EX11-12

A. M30 × ____ LONG SQUARE HEAD BOLT. Include two locknuts on the end of the bolt.
B. M12 × 1.4 × 24 LONG SQUARE HEAD SCREW. Specify the diameter and length of the tap hole.
C. Draw a detailed representation.
D. Draw a schematic representation.
E. Draw a simplified representation.
F. Draw an orthographic view.
G. Draw a sectional view.

EX11-13

A. 1.25–7UNC × ____ LONG SQUARE HEAD BOLT. Include two locknuts on the end of the bolt.
B. .375–32UNEF × 1.5 LONG SQUARE HEAD SCREW. Specify the diameter and length of the tap hole.
C. Draw a detailed representation.
D. Draw a schematic representation.
E. Draw a simplified representation.
F. Draw an orthographic view.
G. Draw a sectional view.

Figure EX11-14

EX11-14

Redraw the sectional view shown in Figure EX11-14. Include a drawing callout that defines the threads as M12. Specify the depth of the threaded hole and the diameter and depth of the tap hole.

EX11-15

Redraw the drawing shown in Figure EX11-15. Add a drawing callout for the bolt and nut based on the following thread major diameters. Use only standard bolt lengths as defined in the appendix.

A. .375–24UNF–2A × _____ LONG
B. M16 × 2 × _____ LONG

Figure EX11-15

EX11-16

Draw a front sectional view and a top orthographic view based on the following drawing and table information. Include the following set screws in the indicated holes. Include the appropriate drawing callout for each set screw.

FOR INCH VALUES:
1. .250–20UNC–2A × 1.00
   SLOT HEAD, FLAT POINT
   SET SCREW
2. .375–24UNF–2A × .750
   HEX SOCKET, FULL DOG
   SET SCREW
3. #10–28UNF–2A × .625
   SQUARE, OVAL
   SET SCREW

4. #6–32UNC–2A × .50
   SLOT, CONE POINT
   SET SCREW

FOR MILLIMETER VALUES:
1. M12 × 20
   SLOT HEAD, FLAT POINT
   SET SCREW
2. M16 × 2 × 30
   SQUARE HEAD, HALF DOG
   SET SCREW
3. M6 × 20
   HEX SOCKET, CONE
   SET SCREW
4. M10 × 1.5 × 20
   CUP, SLOT
   SET SCREW

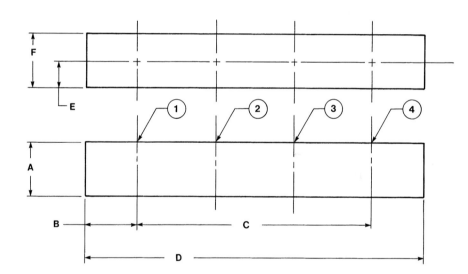

DIMENSION	INCHES	mm
A	2.00	50
B	1.00	25
C	3 X 1.00	3 X 40
D	6.5	170
E	.75	20
F	1.50	40

EX11-17

Draw a front sectional view and a top orthographic view based on the following drawing and table information.

A. Use inch values.
B. Use millimeter values.

OBJECT IS SYMMETRICAL
ABOUT THIS CENTERLINE

FRONT

DIMENSION	INCHES	mm
A	1.00	26
B	.50	13
C	1.00	26
D	.50	13
E	.38	10
F	.190–32 UNF	M8X1
G	2.38	60
H	1.38	34
J	.164–36 UNF	M6
K	Ø1.25	Ø30
L	1.00	26
M	2.00	52

EX11-18

Redraw the following drawing as a sectional view. Select and include the drawing callouts for the nut and washer based on the following bolts. Specify the bolt lengths based on standard lengths listed in the appendix.

A. .625–11UNC–2A × _____ LONG HEX HEAD BOLT
B. M16 × 2 × _____ LONG HEX HEAD

C. .500-20 UNF × _____ LONG SQUARE HEAD
D. M20 × _____ SQUARE HEAD
E. .438-28 UNEF × _____ LONG HEX HEAD
F. M12 × 1.25 × _____ LONG HEX HEAD
G. .750-10 UNC × _____ LONG HEX HEAD
H. M24 × 3 × _____ LONG HEX HEAD

DIMENSION	INCHES	mm
A	3.00	76
B	1.50	38
C	2.50	64
D	.50	13
E	.75	19
F	1.50	38

EX11-19

Draw a front sectional view and a top orthographic view based on the following drawing and table information. Add fasteners to the labeled holes based on the following information. Include the appropriate drawing callouts. Use only standard sizes as listed in the appendix.

FOR INCH VALUES:
1. Nominal diameter = .250, UNC
   Square head bolt and nut
   A washer between the bolt head and part 23
   A washer between the nut and part 24
2. .375–24UNF–2A × 1.00
   SLOT, OVAL
   SETSCREW
3. Nominal diameter =.375, UNF
   Flat head screw, 1.25 LONG

FOR MILLIMETER VALUES:
1. Nominal diameter = 12, coarse
   Square head bolt and nut
   A washer between the bolt head and part 23
   A washer between the nut and part 24
2. M10 × .5 × 20
   SQUARE HEAD, FULL DOG
   SET SCREW
3. Nominal diameter = 12, fine
   Flat head screw, 20 LONG

NOTE: HOLES IN PART 24
ALIGN WITH THOSE IN
PART 23.

FRONT

DIMENSION	INCHES	mm
A	1.25	32
B	.63	16
C	.50	13
D	.38	10
E	.25	7
F	.63	16

EX11-20

Redraw the following sectional view and include the appropriate bolts and nuts at locations W, X, Y, and Z so that the selected bolt heads sit flat on their bearing surfaces. Select the bolts from the standard sizes listed in the appendix.

(W)(X)(Y)(Z)   INDICATES FASTENER LOCATIONS

DIMENSION	INCHES	mm
A	1.00	50
B	1.63	41
C	.38	10
D	2.00	50
E	.75	19
F	1.50	38
G	1.00	25
H	.25	6
J	.38	10
K	2.00	50
L	3.63	92
M	4.00	100
N	R.13	3

EX11-21

Redraw the following drawing based on the following information. Include all bolt, nut, washer, and spring callouts. Use only standard sizes as listed in the appendix.

FOR INCH VALUES:
A. Major diameter of bolt = .375 coarse thread.
B. Add the appropriate nut.
C. Washer is .125 thick and allows a minimum clearance from the bolt of at least .125.
D. Compression springs are made from .125-diameter wire and are 1.00 long. They have an inside diameter that always clears the bolt by at least .125.
E. Parts 1 and 2 are 1.00 high and 4.00 wide.
F. Locate the bolts at least 1.00 from each end.

FOR MILLIMETER VALUES:
A. Major diameter of bolt = 12 coarse thread.
B. Add the appropriate nut.
C. Washer is 3 thick and allows a minimum clearance from the bolt of at least 2.
D. Compression springs are made from 4-diameter wire and are 24 long. They have an inside diameter that always clears the bolt by at least 3.
E. Parts 1 and 2 are 25 high and 100 wide.
F. Locate the bolts at least 25 from each end.

EX11-22

Figure EX11-22 shows two identical blocks that are to be held together using a bolt and a nut. Two washers are also used. Specify the appropriate fastener, nut, and washer for the following block sizes.

Block and nominal hole sizes:
A. 1.50 × 1.50 × 0.75 inches: Ø.375 inch
B. 20 × 20 × 12 mm; Ø8 mm
C. 2.00 × 2.00 × 0.625 inches; Ø.500 inch
D. 30 × 30 × 15 mm; Ø10 mm

Figure EX11-22

EX11-23

Figure EX11-23 shows three parts that are to be held together using six screws. Given the part sizes, specify the six fasteners needed to assemble the parts.

Figure EX11-23

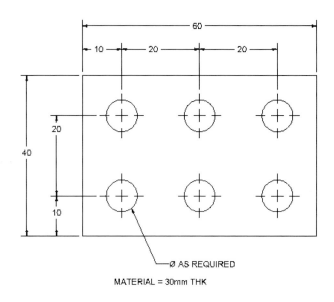

Ø AS REQUIRED

MATERIAL = 30mm THK

A.

B.

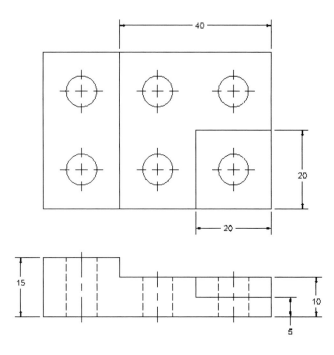

C.

C H A P T E R 12

Working Drawings

12-1 INTRODUCTION

This chapter explains how to create assembly drawings, parts lists, and detail drawings. It includes guidelines for titles, revisions, tolerances, and release blocks. The chapter shows how to create a design layout, then use the layout to create assembly and detail drawings using the Layer command.

Figure 12-1

Figure 12-2

12-2 ASSEMBLY DRAWINGS

Assembly drawings show how objects fit together. See Figure 12-1. All information necessary to complete the assembly must be included on the drawing. This information may include specific assembly dimensions, torque require-ments for bolts, finishing and shipping instructions, and any other appropriate company or customer specifications.

Assembly drawings are sometimes called *top draw-ings* because they are the first of a series of drawings used to define a group of parts that are to be assembled together. The group of drawings, referred to as a *family of drawings*, may include subassemblies, modification drawings, detail drawings, and a parts list. See Figure 12-2.

Assembly drawings do *not* contain hidden lines. A sectional view may be used to show internal areas critical to the assembly. Specific information about the internal surfaces of objects that make up the assembly can be found on the detail drawings of the individual objects. See Figure 12-3.

Each part of an assembly is identified by an assem-bly, or item, number. Assembly numbers are enclosed in a circle or ellipse, and a leader line is drawn between the assembly number and the part. Assembly numbers are unique to each assembly drawing; that is, a part that is used in several different assemblies may have a different assem-bly number on each assembly drawing.

If several of the same part are used in the same assembly, each part should be assigned the same assembly number. A leader line should be used to identify each part

Figure 12-3

Figure 12-4

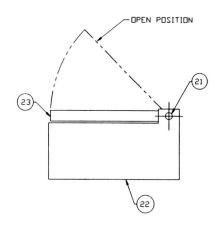

Figure 12-6

unless the differences between the parts are obvious. In Figure 12-4 the difference between head sizes for the fasteners is obvious, so all parts need not be identified.

Assemblies should be shown in their natural or neutral positions. Figure 12-5 shows a clamp in a slightly open position. It is best to show the clamp jaws partially open,

not fully closed or fully open. In general, a drawing should show an assembly in its most common position.

The range of motion for an assembly is shown using phantom lines. See Figure 12-6. Note how the range of motion for the hinged top piece is displayed using phantom lines.

Figure 12-5

Figure 12-7

12-3 DRAWING FORMATS (TEMPLATES)

Figure 12-7 shows a general format for an assembly drawing. The format varies from company to company and with the size of the drawing paper. Figure 12-8 shows two different possible formats for A-size drawings. Each of the blocks of the drawing is explained in the following sections.

AutoCAD includes many different drawing templates that conform to ANSI and ISO standards. Templates automatically include a drawing border, title block, revision block, and a partial release block.

Figure 12-8

Figure 12-9

To add a drawing template

1. Click the New tool.

The Select template dialog box will appear. See Figure 12-9.

2. Select the ANSI A -Named Plot Styles template, click the OPEN box.

The template will appear on the screen. See Figure 12-10. Drawings may be created on the template just as they are with a blank, no template, drawing screen.

The letter A in the template name refers to the drawing sheet size. A listing of standard drawing sheet sizes is included in Section 1-8, Drawing Limits. An A-size

Figure 12-10

Figure 12-11

drawing sheet is 8.5 × 11 inches. If an A-size template is selected, the screen units will automatically be fitted to the sheet size and will be in inches.

Standard metric drawing sheet sizes are also listed in Section 1-8. The closest equivalent to an A-size inch draw-

ing is an A4-size drawing, which is 210 × 297 millimeters. Figure 12-11 shows the Select template dialog box set to select an ISO A3 -Named Plot Styles template. An A3 sheet is 297 × 420 millimeters. Figure 12-12 shows the resulting template. The screen units will be in millimeters for all ISO templates.

Figure 12-12

12-4 TITLE BLOCK

Title blocks are located in the lower right corner of a drawing and include, at a minimum, the drawing's name and number, the company's name, the drawing scale, the release date of the drawing, and the sheet number of the drawing. Other information may be included. Figure 12-13 shows a sample title block created from an ANSI Layout template. The text was added using the Multiline text tool and positioned using the Move tool.

Figure 12-14 shows an ISO A4 -Color Dependent Plot. The title block will appear with a series of XXX inputs. Use the Explode command and explode the title block.

The XXX inputs will be replaced with words. Erase the unwanted words and replace them with the appropriate names and numbers.

Drawing titles (names)

Drawing titles should be chosen so that they clearly define the function of the part. They should be presented in the following word sequence:

Noun, modifier, modifying phrase

For example,

SHAFT, HIGH SPEED, LEFT HAND
GASKET, LOWER

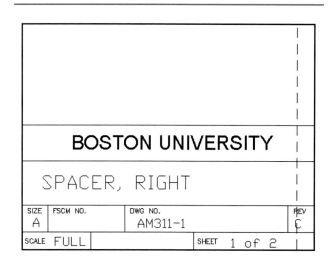

Figure 12-13

Noun names may be two words if normal usage includes the two words.

GEAR BOX, COMPOSITE
SHOCK ABSORBER, LEFT

Drawing numbers

Drawing numbers are assigned by companies according to their usage requirement. The numbering system

Erase unwanted text, use Mtext to add new text, use Move to position new text.

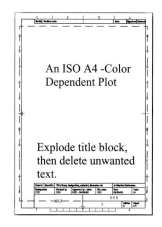

An ISO A4 -Color Dependent Plot

Explode title block, then delete unwanted text.

Figure 12-14

varies greatly. Usually, drawing numbers are recorded in a log book to prevent duplication of numbers.

Company name

The company's name and logo are preprinted on drawing paper or are included as a wblock so that they can be inserted on each drawing.

Scale

Define the scale of the drawing.

SCALE: FULL, or 1 = 1

The drawing size is the same as the object size.

SCALE: 2 = 1

The drawing size is twice as large as the object size.

SCALE: 1 = 2

The drawing size is half as large as the object size.

Release date

A drawing is released only after all persons required by the company's policy have reviewed it and added their signatures to the release block. Once released, a drawing becomes a legal document. Drawings that have not been officially released are often stamped with statements such as "NOT RELEASED" or "FOR REFERENCE ONLY."

Sheet

The number of the sheet relative to the total number of sheets that make up the drawing should be stated clearly.

SHEET 2 OF 3

or

SH 2 OF 3

12-5 REVISION BLOCK

Drawings used in industry are constantly being changed. Products are improved or corrected, and drawings must be changed to reflect and document these changes. Figure 12-15 shows a sample revision block.

Drawing changes are listed in the revision block by letter. Revision blocks are located in the upper right corner of the drawing. See Figure 12-7. Figure 12-16 shows a revision block from an ISO A4 -Color Dependent Plot. The text was added using Mtext, and the chart lines using Line.

Each drawing revision is listed by letter in the revision block. A brief description of the change is also

Figure 12-15

included. It is important that the description be as accurate and complete as possible. Revisions are often used to check drawing requirements on parts manufactured before the revisions were introduced.

The revision letter is also added to the field of the drawing in the area where the change was made. The letter is located within a "flag" to distinguish it from dimensions and drawing notes. The flag serves to notify anyone reading the drawing that revisions have been made.

Most companies have systems in place that allow engineers and designers to make quick changes to drawings. These change orders are called engineering change orders (ECOs), change orders (COs), or engineering orders (EOs), depending on the company's preference. Change orders are documented on special drawing sheets that are usually stapled to a print of the drawing. Figure 12-17 shows a change order attached to a drawing.

After a group of change orders accumulate, they are incorporated into the drawing. This process is called a drawing revision, which is different from a revision to the drawing. Drawing revisions are usually indicated by a letter located somewhere in the title block. The revision letters may be included as part of the drawing number or in a separate box in the title block. Whenever you are working on a drawing, make sure you have the latest revision and all

Figure 12-16

Figure 12-17

Figure 12-19

appropriate change orders. Companies have recording and referencing systems for listing all drawing revisions and drawing changes.

12-6 TOLERANCE BLOCK

Most drawings include a tolerance block next to the title block that lists the standard tolerances that apply to the dimensions on the drawing. A dimension that does not include a specific tolerance is assumed to have the appropriate standard tolerance.

Figure 12-18 shows a sample tolerance block for inch values, and Figure 12-19 shows a sample tolerance

block for millimeter values. In Figure 12-18 the dimension 2.00 has an implied tolerance of ±.01. In Figure 12-19 the 20 dimension has an implied tolerance of ±1.

12-7 RELEASE BLOCK

A release block contains a list of approval signatures or initials required before a drawing can be released for production. See Figure 12-20. The required signatures are generally as follows.

Drawn

Person that created the drawing.

Figure 12-18

Figure 12-20

Checked

Drawings are checked for errors and compliance with company procedures and conventions. Some large companies have checking departments, whereas smaller companies have drawings checked by a senior person or the drafting supervisor.

Design

The engineer in charge of the design project. The designer and the drafter may be the same person.

Stress/Wts

The department or person responsible for the stress analysis of the design.

Materials

Usually, a person in the production department checks the design and makes sure that the necessary materials and the machine times for the design are available. This person may also schedule production time.

Customer

The customer for the design may have a representative on site at the production facility to check that its design requirements are being met. For example, it is not unusual for the Air Force to assign an officer to a plant that manufactures its fighter aircraft.

12-8 PARTS LIST (BILL OF MATERIALS)

A *parts list* is a listing of all parts used on an assembly. See Figure 12-21. The parts list was created using the Table tool. See Section 2-28. Parts lists may be located on an assembly drawing above the title block or on a separate sheet of paper. Assembly drawings done using AutoCAD often include the parts list on a separate layer within the drawing. Use only capital letters on a parts list.

Figure 12-22 shows two sample parts list formats, including dimensions. Parts list formats vary greatly from company to company. The dimensions are given in inches. They may be converted to millimeters using the conversion factor 1.00 inch = 25.4 millimeters.

A parts list serves as a way to cross-reference detail drawing numbers to assembly item numbers. It also provides a list of the materials needed for production and is very helpful for scheduling and materials purchasing.

Parts purchased from a vendor and used exactly as they are supplied, without any modification, will not have detail drawings but are included on the parts list. The washers, bolts, and screws listed on the parts list shown in Figure 12-21 would not have detail drawings. This means that the information on the parts list must be sufficient for a purchaser to know exactly what size washers, bolts, and screws to buy. The information used to define an object on the drawing, the drawing callout, is also used on the parts list. See Chapter 11 for an explanation of drawing callouts for fasteners.

PARTS LIST					
NO.	DESCRIPTION	PART NO.	MATL	NOTE	QTY
1	BLOCK, TOP	BU311S1	SAE 1020		1
2	BLOCK, BOTTOM	BU311S2	SAE 1020		1
3	M16×24 HEX HEAD BOLT	SPM16H	STEEL	2	1
4	20×40×3 PLAIN WASHER		STEEL		3
5	M16 HEX NUT	2PM16N	STEEL		1
6	M16×20 HEX HEAD SCREW		STEEL		1

Figure 12-21

Figure 12-22

12-9 DETAIL DRAWINGS

A *detail drawing* is a drawing of a single part. The drawing should include all the information necessary to accurately manufacture the part, including orthographic views with all appropriate hidden lines, dimensions, toler-ances, material requirements, and any special manufacturing requirements. Figure 12-23 shows a sample detail drawing.

Detail drawings include title, release, tolerance, and revision blocks located on the drawing in the same places as they are found on assembly drawings.

Figure 12-23

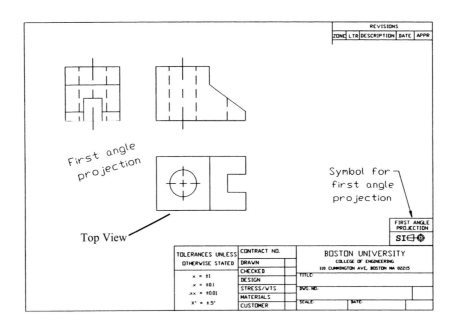

Figure 12-24

12-10 FIRST-ANGLE PROJECTION

The instructions for the creation of orthographic views as presented in this book are based on third-angle projection. See Chapter 5. Third-angle projection is used in the United States, Canada, and Great Britain, among other countries. Many other countries such as Japan use first-angle projection to create orthographic views.

Figure 12-24 shows an object and the orthographic views of the object created in first-angle projection. Note that the top view in the first-angle projection is the same as the top view in the third-angle projection, but it is located below the front view, not above the front view, as in the third-angle projection. Right-side views are also the same but are located to the left of the front view in first-angle projections and to the right in third-angle projections.

Many companies now do business internationally. They can have manufacturing plants in one country and assembly plants in another. Drawings can be prepared in several different countries. It is important to indicate on a drawing whether first-angle or third-angle projections are being used. Figure 12-25 shows the SI (International System of Units) symbols for first-angle projections. The SI symbol is included on a drawing in the lower right corner above the title block, as shown in Figure 12-24.

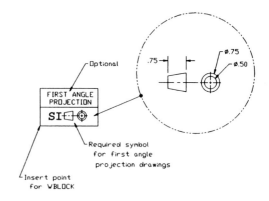

Figure 12-25

12-11 DRAWING NOTES

Drawing notes are used to provide manufacturing information that is not visual, for example, finishing instructions, torque requirements for bolts, and shipping instructions.

Drawing notes are usually located above the title block on the right side of the drawing. See Figure 12-26. Drawing notes are listed by number. If a note applies to a specific part of the drawing, the note number is enclosed in a triangle. The note numbers enclosed in triangles are also drawn next to the corresponding areas of the drawing.

12-12 DESIGN LAYOUTS

A design layout is not a drawing. It is like a visual calculation sheet used to size and locate parts as a design is developed. A design layout allows you to "build the assembly" on paper.

When drawings are created on a drawing board an initial layout is made locating and sizing the parts. Then the individual detail drawings and the assembly drawing are traced from the layout.

The same procedure can be followed using AutoCAD. First, create a design layout on one layer, then either transfer the individual parts and assembly drawing to other layers or create a new drawing from the layout drawing using the Save As command.

The sample problem in the next section demonstrates how to create a design layout and then use the layout to create the required detail and assembly drawings.

Figure 12-26

Figure 12-27

12-13 SAMPLE PROBLEM SP12-1

Figure 12-27 shows an engineer's sketch for a design problem. Prepare an assembly drawing and a detail drawing of the PN123 BASE and PN124 CENTER PLATE based on the following information.

1. Parts PM107S END BRACKET are existing parts and can be used as is. Figure 12-28 shows a detail drawing of the part.
2. Place the mounting holes for the two END BRACKETS 200 millimeters apart, as shown in the engineer's sketch.
3. Establish the size of the BASE so that it aligns with the END BRACKETS and is 40 millimeters thick.

4. Determine the sizes for the CENTER BRACKET so that it just fits between the end plates and has a 25-millimeter-diameter hole centered in its top surface. The CENTER BRACKET should extend 10 millimeters above the END BRACKETS and 5 millimeters above the BASE. The CENTER BRACKET should be 10 millimeters thick all around.
5. Mount the END BRACKETS to the BASE using M12 FLAT HEAD screws, and attach the END BRACKETS to the CENTER PLATE using M20 bolts with appropriate nuts.
6. Use only standard length fasteners.

To create the design layout (See Figure 12-29.)

1. Draw horizontal and vertical lines that define the top of the BASE and the distance between the mounting holes in the END BRACKETS.
2. Draw front and top views of the END BRACKETS using the vertical lines drawn in step 1. The vertical lines should align with the centerlines of the mounting holes.
3. Draw the BASE 40 millimeters thick.
4. Size the CENTER BRACKET.

Note that at this stage of the layout all lines are drawn using the same pattern. Lines can be changed to hidden lines or centerlines when the detail and assembly drawings are created.

Figure 12-28

5. Add the M12 FLAT HEAD screws. A length of 20 millimeters was chosen from the tables in the appendix. The threaded holes in the BASE are M12 to match the screws. The tap drill size is included on the layout for reference.

6. Add the M20 × 60 bolts and nuts.

The bolt length is determined by adding 25 (END BRACKET) + 10 (CENTER BRACKET) + 15 (nut thickness = .75D) + 2 thread pitches = 52 millimeters. The next largest standard bolt length, as listed in the appendix, is 60, so an M20 × 60 bolt is specified.

7. The diameter of the clearance holes was chosen as 14 and 22 and is listed on the layout.

The design layout is complete. It may be used to create the required assembly drawing and detail drawings in one of two ways: using the Layer command and including all the drawings under one file name, or by using the Save As command to create separate drawings.

Figure 12-29

To create a drawing using layers

When lines are moved from one layer to another the lines will disappear from the original layer. This will, in essence, erase the layout drawing because all the lines will have been moved to other layers. The layout may be preserved by first making a copy of the layout, or that part of the layout you wish to transfer, then using the copy for the transfers.

To make a copy of the layout, use the Copy command. Select the entire screen and select a base point. Select the exact same point as the second point of displacement, and AutoCAD will copy the layout exactly over itself. You can then move the appropriate lines to different layers.

Note: Explode all blocks before transferring them between layers. A block cannot be edited once it is moved from its original layer.

Create a detail drawing of the BASE by transferring the BASE from the design layout. Respond to the prompts as follows.

1. Copy the layout onto itself.

   COMMAND:_Copy
   Select objects:

2. Window the entire layout, press Enter.

   <Base point or displacement>/Multiple:

3. Select a point on the screen.

   Second point of displacement:

4. Select exactly the same point as that used in the previous step.
5. Create the following layers. See Section 3-24.

   ASSEMBLY
   END
   END-DIM
   BASE
   BASE-DIM
   CENTER
   CENTER-DIM
   PARTSLIST

The "DIM" layers will be used for the dimensions for the detail drawings. This will allow the dimensions to be shut off if they are not needed.

6. Transfer the BASE to a layer called BASE. See Section 3-24. Turn off all the other layers. The resulting transfer should look like Figure 12-30.

Figure 12-30

It will be difficult to make a perfectly clean transfer, that is, only the lines of the BASE. If other lines appear on the transferred BASE, erase and trim them as necessary.

7. Move the views closer together, if necessary.
8. Turn on the BASE-DIM layer and make it the current layer. Add the appropriate dimensions, tolerances, and callouts.
9. Create the drawing format and add the necessary information (drawing title, etc.).

The title block, and so forth, may be saved as a block or as part of a prototype drawing. Figure 12-31 shows the resulting drawing.

Figure 12-31

NOTES:
1. ASSEMBLE ITEM
   5 BEFORE ITEM
   4.

TOLERACES UNLESS OTHERVISE STATED	CONTRACT NO.		BOSTON UNIVERSITY
x = ±1	DRAWN		COLLEGE OF ENGINEERING
.x = ±0.1	CHECKED		110 CUMMINGTON AVE. BOSTON MA 02215
.xx = ±0.01	DESIGN		TITLE: ASSEMBLY, BRACKET
X° = ±.5°	STRESS/VTS		DWG NO.
	MATERIALS		
	CUSTOMER		SCALE: .5=1 DATE:

REVISIONS
ZONE	LTR	DESCRIPTION	DATE	APPR

Figure 12-32

To create a drawing from a layout

Figure 12-32 shows an assembly drawing that was created from the design layout. The procedure is as follows.

1. Save the design layout.
2. Create the assembly drawing from the layout drawing, but use the Save As command to save it under a different drawing name.
3. Add the appropriate drawing format and notes.
4. Save the assembly drawing using its new name.

Figure 12-33 shows a parts list for the assembly.

PARTS LIST			
ITEM NO	DESCRIPTION	MATL	QTY
1	BASE	STEEL	1
2	END BRACKET - PM107S	STEEL	2
3	CENTER PLATE	STEEL	1
4	M20×60 HEX HEAD BOLT	STEEL	2
5	M12×36 FLAT HEAD SCREW	STEEL	2
6	M20 NUT	STEEL	2

Figure 12-33

12-14 EXERCISE PROBLEMS

EX12-1

A. Draw an assembly drawing of the given objects.
B. Draw detail drawings for all nonstandard parts.
C. Prepare a parts list. Specify the length for the M10 hex head screw.

EX12-2

A. Draw an assembly drawing of the given objects.
B. Draw detail drawings for all nonstandard parts. Include positional tolerances for all holes.
C. Prepare a parts list. Specify the diameter, thread specification, and length for the hex head screw.

EX12-3

A. Draw an assembly drawing of the given objects.
B. Draw detail drawings for all nonstandard parts.
C. Prepare a parts list.

EX12-4

A. Draw an assembly drawing of the given objects.
B. Draw detail drawings for all nonstandard parts.
C. Prepare a parts list.

EX12-5

A. Draw an assembly drawing of the given objects.
B. Draw detail drawings for all nonstandard parts.
C. Prepare a parts list.

DESIGN

D. Replace part 3 with a bolt and appropriate nut. Add four washers.

EX12-6

A. Draw an assembly drawing of the given objects.
B. Draw detail drawings for all nonstandard parts.
C. Prepare a parts list.

EX12-7

A. Draw an assembly drawing of the given objects.
B. Draw detail drawings for all nonstandard parts.
C. Prepare a parts list.

EX12-8

A. Draw an assembly drawing of the given objects.
B. Draw detail drawings for all nonstandard parts.
C. Prepare a parts list.

DESIGN

D. Replace the rivets with the appropriate screws and nuts.

EX12-9

A. Draw an assembly drawing of the given object.
B. Prepare a parts list.

SIMPLIFIED INTERFACE GAUGE

NOTE: ALL PARTS MADE
FROM SAE 1020 STEEL

EX12-10

Redraw the given objects as an assembly drawing and add two slot head, full dog set screws in the holes indicated. Add either a .625-inch or 16-millimeter bolt with the appropriate nut in the hole indicated. Add callouts for the fasteners. Specify a standard bolt length.

A. Use inch values.
B. Use millimeter values.
C. Draw the front assembly view using a sectional view.
D. Draw the fasteners using schematic representations.
E. Draw the fasteners using simplified representations.
F. Prepare a parts list.
G. Prepare detail drawings for each part.

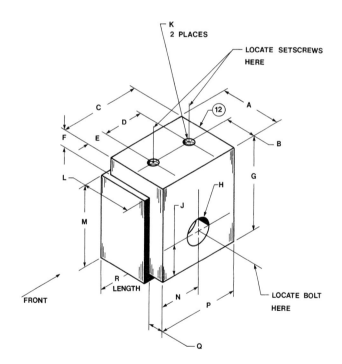

DIMENSION	INCHES	mm
A	1.50	38
B	.75	16
C	2.00	50
D	1.00	25
E	.50	12.5
F	.38	9
G	2.25	57
H	Ø.66	Ø17
J	.75	19
K	.250–20 UNC	M6
L	1.25	32
M	2.00	50
N	1.00	25
P	2.00	50
Q	.38	9
R	2.00	50

EX12-11

Redraw the given objects as an assembly drawing and add bolts with the appropriate nuts at the L and H holes. Add the appropriate drawing callouts. Specify standard bolt lengths.

A. Use inch values.
B. Use millimeter values.
C. Draw the front assembly view using a sectional view.
D. Draw the fasteners using schematic representations.
E. Draw the fasteners using simplified representations.
F. Prepare a parts list.
G. Prepare detail drawings for each part.

DIMENSION	INCHES	mm
A	.25	6
B	2.00	50
C	1.00	25
D	.50	13
E	1.75	45
F	2.00	50
G	4.00	100
H	Ø.438	Ø11
J	.50	12.5
K	1.00	25
L	Ø.781	Ø19
M	.63	16
N	.88	22
P	2.00	50
Q	.25	6

EX12-12

Redraw the given views and add the appropriate hex head machine screws at M and N. Use standard length screws and allow at least two unused threads at the bottom of each threaded hole. Add a bolt with the appropriate nut at hole P.

A. Use inch values.
B. Use millimeter values.
C. Draw the front assembly view using a sectional view.
D. Draw the fasteners using schematic representations.
E. Draw the fasteners using simplified representations.
F. Prepare a parts list.
G. Prepare detail drawings for each part.

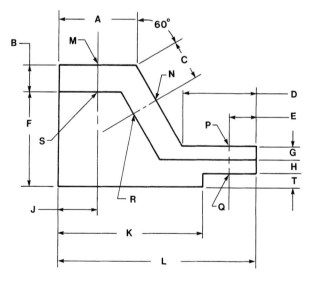

DIMENSION	INCHES	mm
A	1.50	38
B	.50	13
C	.75	19
D	1.38	35
E	.50	13
F	1.75	44
G	.25	6
H	.25	6
J	.75	19
K	2.75	70
L	3.75	96
M	Ø.31	Ø8
N	Ø.25	Ø6
P	Ø.41	Ø12
Q	Ø.41	Ø12
R	.164–32 UNF X .50 DEEP	M4 X 14 DEEP
S	.250–20 UNC X 1.63 DEEP	M6 X 14 DEEP
T	.25	6

EX12-13

Redraw the given objects as an assembly drawing and add the appropriate hex head bolts and nuts. Use only standard length bolts and include callouts for the bolts and nuts on the drawing.

A. Use inch values.
B. Use millimeter values.
C. Draw the front assembly view using a sectional view.
D. Draw the fasteners using schematic representations.

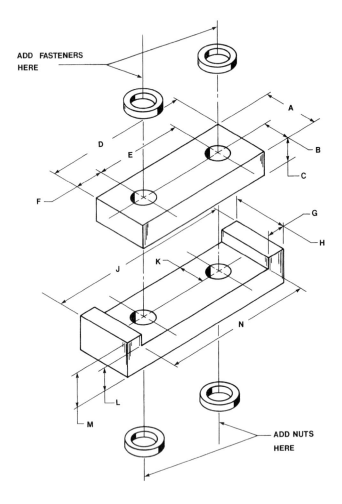

ADD FASTENERS HERE

ADD NUTS HERE

DIMENSION	INCHES	mm
A	1.25	32
B	.63	16
C	.50	13
D	3.25	82
E	2.00	50
F	.63	16
G	.38	10
H	1.25	32
J	4.13	106
K	.63	16
L	.50	13
M	.75	10
N	3.38	86

EX12-14

The given objects are to be assembled as shown. Select sizes for the parts that make the assembly possible. (Choose dimensions for the top and bottom blocks and then determine the screw and stud lengths.) The hex head screws (5) have a major diameter of either .375 inch or M10. The studs (3) are to have the same thread sizes as the screws and are to be screwed into the top part (2). The holes in the lower part (1) that accept the studs are to be clearance holes.

A. Draw an assembly drawing.
B. Draw detail drawings of each nonstandard part. Include positional tolerances for all holes.
C. Prepare a parts list.

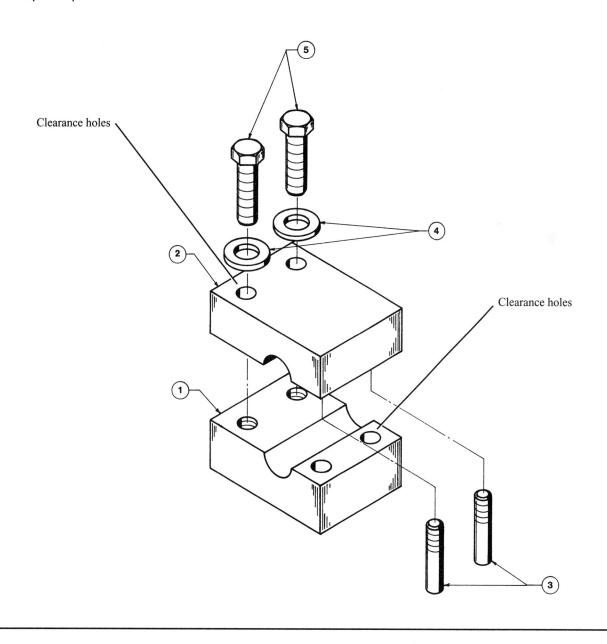

EX12-15

Select values for the dimensions indicated in A through J. Use either inches or millimeters. Use either .375 inch or M10 as the major diameter of the screws. Assemble the parts using three identical screws.

The holes in Part 1 are clearance holes, and the holes in Part 2 are threaded.

A. Draw an assembly drawing.
B. Draw detail drawings of each nonstandard part. Include positional tolerances for all holes.
C. Prepare a parts list.

EX12-16

A. Draw an assembly drawing of the given object.
B. Prepare a parts list
C. Replace the pegs used in the current assembly and select appropriate fasteners to hold the object together.
D. Add the appropriate tolerances.

Add a spacer between the FLYLINK and the SUPPORT PLATE.

FLY ASSEMBLY

3

FLYLINK
Part Number: BU200A
SAE 1040 STEEL

60
Ø5-2 HOLES

R2.5
40
10
R5 BOTH ENDS

54

23

10

12
28
Ø5-2 HOLES

NOTE: ALL FILLETS AND ROUNDS = R2 UNLESS OTHERWISE SPECIFIED.

WEDGE PLATE
Part Number: BU200B
STEEL

Ø10
Ø5

27

10   3.6

16

43

27

3

2

4

8

EX12-17

Design a hand-operated grinding wheel specifically for sharpening a chisel. The chisel is to be located on an adjustable rest while it is being sharpened. The mechanism should be able to be clamped to a table during operation using two thumbscrews.

A standard grinding wheel is Ø6.00 inch and 1/2 inch thick, and has an internal mounting hole with a 50.00±.03 bore.

Prepare the following drawings.

A. Draw an assembly drawing.
B. Draw detail drawings of each nonstandard part. Include positional tolerances for all holes.
C. Prepare a parts list.

EX12-18

A. Draw an assembly drawing of the given object.
B. Prepare a parts list.
C. Select appropriate fasteners to hold the object together.
D. Define the appropriate tolerances.
E. Define an assembly sequence considering the size of any screw heads and nuts, and the tooling required for assembly.

BRACKET ASSEMBLY

C-BRACKET, SAE1020 STEEL, 2 REQD
Part Number: AM311-1

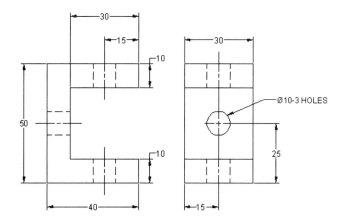

QUAD SPACER, SAE 1020 STEEL
2 REQD, Part Number: AM311-2

EX12-19

A. Draw an assembly drawing of the given object.
B. Prepare a parts list.
C. Select appropriate fasteners to hold the object together.
D. Define the appropriate tolerances.
E. Define an assembly sequence considering the size of any screw heads and nuts, and the tooling required for assembly.

CLIP ASSEMBLY

SUPPORT PLATE
SAE 1040 STEEL, 2 REQD
Part Number: AM312-3

L-CLIP
SAE 1040 STEEL, 2 REQD
Part Number: AM312-4

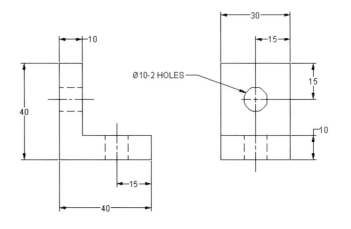

EX12-20

A. Draw an assembly drawing of the given object.
B. Prepare a parts list.
C. Select appropriate fasteners to hold the object together.
D. Define the appropriate tolerances.
E. Define an assembly sequence considering the size of any screw heads and nuts, and the tooling required for assembly.

C-BRACKET
SAE 1020 STEEL, 4 REQD
Part Number: AM311-1

GUIDE ASSEMBLY

L-CLIP
SAE 1040 STEEL, 2 REQD
Part Number: AM312-4

SUPPORT PLATE
SAE 1040 STEEL, 2 REQD
Part Number: AM312-3

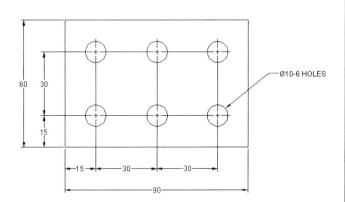

EX12-21

A. Draw an assembly drawing of the given object.
B. Prepare a parts list.
C. Replace the pegs used in the current assembly and select appropriate fasteners to hold the object together.
D. Define the appropriate tolerances.
E. Use phantom lines and define the motion of the CROSSLINK if both LINK-L and LINK-R rotate 360°.
F. Add spacers as necessary.

Add spacers

Add spacers

ROTATOR ASSEMBLY

LINK-L and LINK-R
Part Number: AM311-21A
SAE 1020 STEEL

CROSSLINK
Part Number: AM312-21B
SAE 1020 STEEL

PLATE, BASE
Part Number: AM311-21C
SAE 1020 STEEL

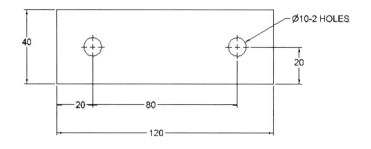

EX12-22

ROCKER ASSEMBLY

A. Draw an assembly drawing of the given object.
B. Prepare a parts list.
C. Select appropriate fasteners to hold the object together. Note that the fastener used to join the CENTER LINK and the DRIVE LINK passes over the WEB PLATE as the DRIVE LINK rotates.
D. Define the appropriate tolerances.
E. Use phantom lines and define the motion of the CENTER LINK and the ROCKER LINK if the DRIVE LINK rotates 360°.

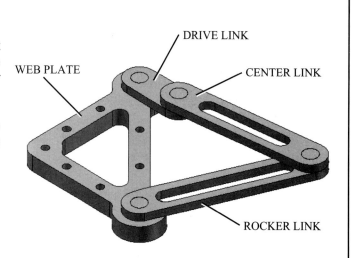

DRIVE LINK
WEB PLATE
CENTER LINK
ROCKER LINK

DRIVE LINK
Part Number:
AM311-22A

SAE 1040 STEEL
5mm THK

30
R10 BOTH ENDS
Ø10-2 HOLES

Ø10
R15
ALL FILLETS AND ROUNDS = R3
40
Ø5-7 HOLES
30
26
6 TYP
12 TYP
40
80
R15
4
R15
R10
Ø10
20
26
30
80

ROCKER LINK
Part Number: AM311-2C
SAE 1040 STEEL
5mm THK

Ø10 BOTH HOLES
R10 BOTH ENDS
10
100
70
15

WEB PLATE
Part Number: AM311-22B
SAE 1040 STEEL
10mm THK

CENTER LINK
Part Number: AM311-22D
SAE 1040 STEEL
5mm THK

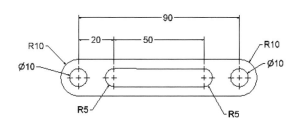

90
20
50
R10
R10
Ø10
Ø10
R5
R5

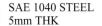

EX12-23

A. Draw an assembly drawing of the given object.
B. Prepare a parts list.
C. Select appropriate fasteners to hold the object together. Note that the fasteners used to join the SIDE LINKS to the HOLDER ARM pass over the HOLDER BASE.
D. Define the appropriate tolerances. Use an H7/p6 tolerance between BUSHING-A and the HOLDER BASE.
E. Use phantom lines to define the motion of the HOLDER ARM, SIDE LINKs, and CROSS LINK if the HOLDER ARM rotates between +30° and −30°.

LINK ASSEMBLY

ALL FILLETS AND ROUNDS = R3

HOLDER ARM, BU100-2, 7075-T6, AL, 5mm THK

SIDE LINK
BU100-4
7075-T6 AL
5mm THK
2 REQD

CROSS LINK, BU100-3, 7075-T6, AL, 5mm THK

BUSHING-A
A/M CORP - B20-AD
TEFLON

EX12-24

A. Draw an assembly drawing of the Minivise.
B. Prepare a parts list.
C. Select the appropriate fasteners to hold the vise together.

D. Redesign the interface between the Drive Screw and the Holder Plate.

MINIVISE

Minivise

1. BASE
SAE 1040 STEEL

2. DRIVE SCREW
SAE 1040 STEEL

3. END PLATE
SAE 1040 STEEL

4. SLIDER
SAE 1040 STEEL

5. HOLDER PLATE
   SAE 1040 STEEL

6. FACE PLATE
   SAE 1040 STEEL

7. HANDLE
   SAE 1040 STEEL

8. END CAP
   SAE 1040 STEEL

9. DRIVE PLATE
   SAE 1040 STEEL

10. M5×10 RECESSED COUNTERSUNIT HEAD-STEEL
11. M5×22 RECESSED COUNTERSUNIT HEAD-STEEL

Gears, Bearings, and Cams

13-1 INTRODUCTION

This chapter explains how to draw and design with gears and bearings. The chapter does not discuss how to design specific gears and bearings but how to design using existing parts selected from manufacturers' catalogs. Various gear terms are defined, and design applications demonstrated.

The chapter also discusses how to design and draw a cam based on a displacement diagram. Different types of follower motion are explained as well as different types of followers.

13-2 TYPES OF GEARS

There are many types of gears, including spur, bevel, worm, helical, and rack. See Figure 13-1. Each type has its own terminology, drawing requirements, and design considerations.

13-3 GEAR TERMINOLOGY—SPUR

Following is a list of common spur gear terms and their meanings. Figure 13-2 illustrates the terms, and Figure 13-3 shows a listing of relative formulas.

For spur gears using English units

Pitch diameter (PD)—The diameter used to define the spacing of gears.

Diametral pitch (DP)—The number of teeth per inch or millimeter.

Circular pitch (CP)—The circular distance from a fixed point on one tooth to the same position on the next tooth as measured along the pitch circle. The circumference of the pitch circle divided by the number of teeth.

Preferred pitches—The standard sizes available from gear manufacturers. Whenever possible, use preferred gear sizes.

Center distance (CD)—The distance between the center points of two meshing gears.

Backlash—The difference between a tooth width and the engaging space on a meshing gear.

Addendum (a)—The height of a tooth above the pitch diameter.

Dedendum (d)—The depth of a tooth below the pitch diameter.

Whole depth—The total depth of a tooth. The addendum plus the dedendum.

Working depth—The depth of engagement of one gear into another. Equal to the sum of the two gear addendums.

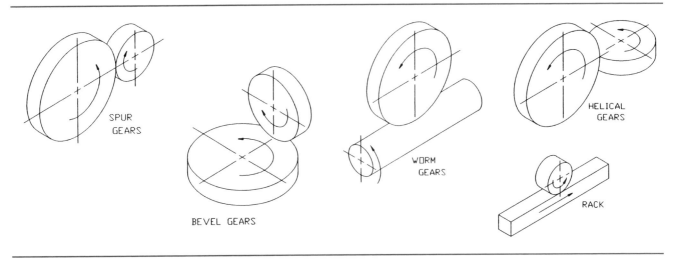

Figure 13-1

Circular thickness—The distance across a tooth as measured along the pitch circle.

Face width (FW)—The distance from front to back along a tooth as measured perpendicular to the pitch circle.

Outside diameter (OD)—The largest diameter of the gear. Equals the pitch diameter plus the addendum.

Root diameter (RD)—The diameter of the base of the teeth. The pitch circle minus the dedendum.

Clearance—The distance between the addendum of a meshing gear and the dedendum of the mating gears.

Pressure angle—The angle between the line of action and a line tangent to the pitch circle. Most gears have pressure angles of either 14.5° or 20°.

Figure 13-2

Pitch Diameter (PD)	See catalogs
Circular Pitch (CP)	$CP = \dfrac{\pi}{DP}$
Diametral Pitch (DP)	$DP = \dfrac{\pi}{CP}$
Number of Teeth (N)	$N = (PD)(DP)$
Outside Diameter (OD)	See catalogs
Addendum (a)	$a = \dfrac{1}{DP}$
Dedendum (d)	$d = a + .125$ (for drawing purposes ONLY)
Root Diameter (RD)	$RD = PD - d$
Circular Thickness (CT)	$CT = \dfrac{PD}{2N}$
Face Width (F)	See catalogs

Figure 13-3

For English units

$$Pitch = \frac{Number\ of\ Teeth\ (N)}{Pitch\ Diameter\ (PD)} = \frac{N}{PD}$$

For metric units

$$Module = \frac{Pitch\ Diameter\ (PD)}{Number\ of\ Teeth\ (N)} = \frac{PD}{N}$$

Figure 13-4

For spur gears using metric units

The preceding definitions apply to both English unit and metric unit spur gears with the exception of pitch. For English unit gears, pitch is defined as the number of teeth per inch relative to the pitch diameter and is expressed by the formula shown in Figure 13-4. Gears made to metric specifications are defined in terms of the amount of pitch diameter per tooth, called the gear's *module*. Figure 13-4 shows the formula for calculating a gear's module. Metric gears also have a slightly different tooth shape that makes them incompatible with English unit gears.

13-4 SPUR GEAR DRAWINGS

Figure 13-5 shows a representation of spur gears. The individual teeth are not included in the front view but are represented by three phantom lines. The diameters of the three lines represent the outside diameter, the pitch diameter, and the root diameter.

The outside diameter and the pitch circle are usually given in manufacturers' catalogs. The root circle can be calculated from the pitch circle using the formula presented in Figure 13-3.

Figure 13-5

Figure 13-6

Figure 13-7

The side view of the gear is drawn as a sectional view taken along the vertical centerline. The gear size is defined using the manufacturer's stock number, dimensions, and a list of appropriate design information.

Figure 13-6 shows the front representation view of three meshing gears. The gears are positioned so that the pitch circle diameters are tangent. Ideally, mating gears always mesh exactly tangent to their pitch circles.

Gear representations were developed because it was both difficult and time consuming to accurately draw individual teeth when creating drawings on a drawing board. AutoCAD can be used to create detailed gear drawings that include all teeth by using the Array and Block commands, among others; however, it is usually sufficient to show a few meshing teeth and use the representative centerlines for the remaining portions of both gears. See Figure 13-7.

Most gear tooth shapes are based on an involute curve. Involute-based teeth fit together well, transfer forces smoothly, and can use one cutter to generate all gear tooth variations within the same pitch. Standards for tooth proportions have been established by the American National Standards Institute (ANSI) and the American Gear Manufacturers Association (AGMA).

13-5 SAMPLE PROBLEM SP13-1

Draw a front view of a spur gear that has an outside diameter of 6.50 inches, a pitch diameter of 6.00 inches, and a root diameter of 5.25 inches. The gear has 12 teeth.

The method presented is a simplified method and is an acceptable representation for most drawing applications. See Figure 13-8.

1. Draw three concentric circles of diameter 6.50, 6.00, and 5.25. Use the Center Mark command modified to draw a centerline for the circles.
2. Use the Array command and create 48 ray lines as shown. Label three rays on each side of the top vertical centerline as shown. Zoom the labeled area.

The number of rays should equal four times the number of teeth to be drawn. Two adjoining sectors are used to define the width of the tooth, and the next two adjacent sectors are used to define the space between teeth.

3. Draw a circle whose center point is at the intersection of the pitch circle and the ray labeled 2, and whose radius is determined by the distance from the center point to the intersection of the pitch circle and the ray labeled −1.
4. Repeat step 3 using the intersection of the pitch circle and the point labeled −2 as the center point.
5. Use the Fillet command to draw a radius at the base of the tooth. Select the side of the tooth as one of the lines for the fillet, and the root circle as the other line.

Both the circle and ray line will be within the selected cursor, but AutoCAD will select the last entity drawn, so the circle will be selected.

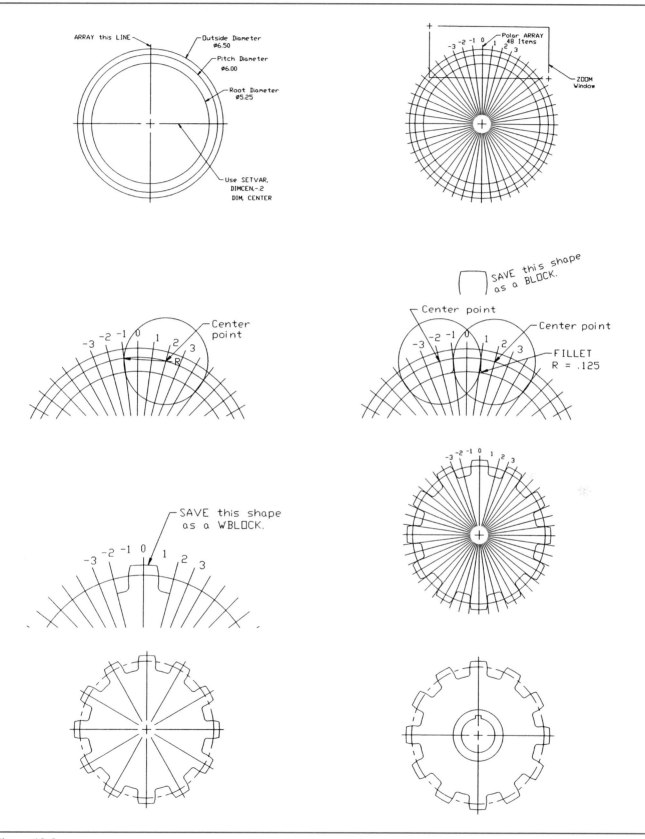

Figure 13-8

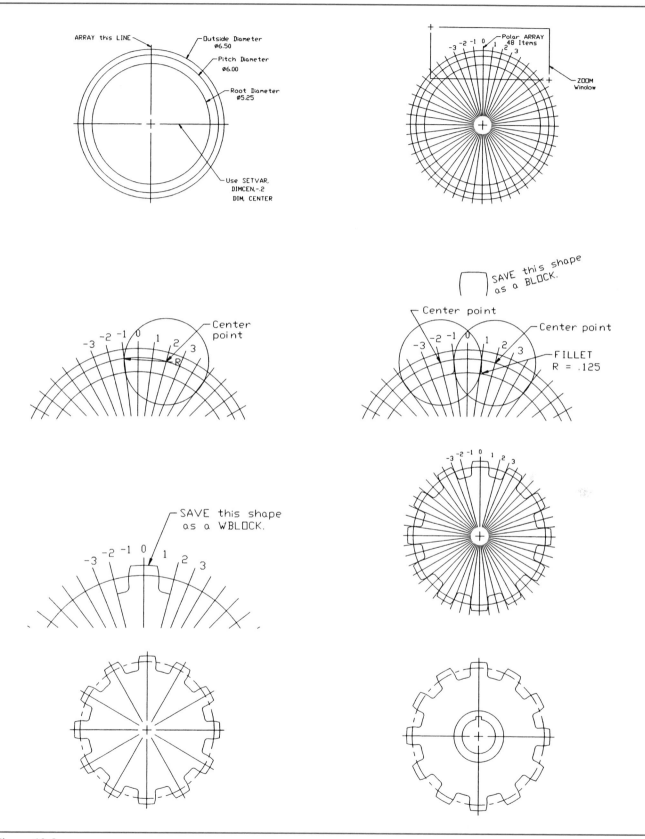

Figure 13-8

The tooth shape can be saved as a wblock named TOOTH and used when drawing other gears. Only the lines that represent the top of the gear and the two side sections need to be saved. A different size gear will have a different root diameter, and new fillets can be drawn that align with the new root circle.

6. Use the Trim and Erase commands to remove excess lines and create the tooth shape between rays −2 and 2 as shown.

This tooth shape may be saved as a wblock and used when drawing other gears.

7. Array the tooth shape about the gear's center point.
8. Erase the excess ray lines and change the pitch circle to a centerline.
9. Draw the gear's bore hole or center hole and hub as required.

13-6 SAMPLE PROBLEM SP13-2

Figure 13-9A shows two meshing gears. In the example shown, the larger gear has a diameter of 6.00 inches with 24 teeth; the smaller gear has a diameter of 3.00 inches and 12 teeth. The drawing utilizes the wblock created in Sample Problem SP13-1 as follows.

The circular thickness of the wblock tooth as measured along the pitch diameter equals $\frac{1}{12}$ the circumference of the pitch diameter.

$(\frac{1}{12})(P\ PD)$

For the gear in SP13-1, where PD = 6

$(\frac{1}{12})(P\ 6) = P/2$
$\qquad\qquad = 1.57$ inches

The large gear requires 24 teeth on a pitch diameter of 6, or twice as many teeth as the gear used to create the wblock. The teeth on the 24-tooth gear must be half the size of the tooth created in the wblock. The teeth on the smaller gear must be the same size as the teeth on the larger gear.

Figure 13-9A

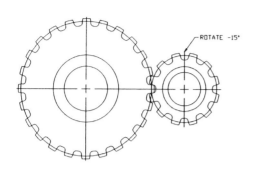

Figure 13-9B

To draw meshing spur gears (See Figure 13-9B.)

1. Draw two circles of diameter 6.00 and 3.00 inches. Include the circles' centerlines. Use Setvar, Dimcen, set to −.2, or use a modified Center Mark tool.

   The gears will be drawn separately, then meshed.

2. Insert the TOOTH wblock on both gears as shown on the pitch diameter. Use an X and Y scale factor of .5. Explode the wblock.

3. Use the Array command to create the required 24 and 12 teeth.

4. Draw a line between the roots of two of the teeth as shown. Use the Array command to create the root circle. Add the fillet to each tooth base.

   The line in this example is a straight line acceptable for smaller gears. If more accuracy of shape is required, draw a complete root circle, then trim all of it away except the portion between two tooth roots. Array this sector between all the other teeth.

5. Use the Rotate command to orient the small gear with the large gear.

   Each tooth on the large gear requires 360/24 = 15°. Rotate the smaller gear 15°.

6. Use the Move command to position the small gear.

   The pitch circles of the two gears should be tangent.

7. Rotate the smaller gear's centerline −15°.

8. Add the center hubs to both gears as shown.

Figure 13-10

13-7 SAMPLE PROBLEM SP13-3

Figure 13-10 shows a gear that has a pitch diameter of 4.00 with 18 teeth. The TOOTH wblock can be used as follows.

The wblock is first reduced to accommodate the smaller diameter.

1. Draw a circle with a 4.00-inch diameter. Include centerlines.
2. Insert the wblock using an X and Y scale factor of .4445.

The scale factor was derived by first considering the ratio between the number of teeth on the gear used to create the TOOTH wblock (12) and the number of teeth on the desired gear, 18, or 12/18 = .6667. The ratio between the diameters is also considered: 4.00/6.00 = .6667. The two ratios are multiplied together: (.6667)(.6667) = .4445.

3. Use the Array command to create the required 18 teeth.
4. Draw a line between the end lines of two of the teeth, then array the line 18 times around the gear.

The line may be drawn as a straight line for small gears or as an arc for larger gears. The arc may be created by drawing a circle, then using the Trim command to create the desired length.

5. Add the center hub as required.

The same wblock can be used for metric gears using the conversion factor 1.00 inch = 25.4 millimeters. It is probably easier to create a separate wblock for a metric tooth.

13-8 SELECTING SPUR GEARS

When two spur gears are engaged, the smaller gear is called the *pinion gear* and the larger gear is called simply the *gear*. The relationship between the relative speed of two mating gears is directly proportional to the gears' pitch diameters. Also, the number of teeth on a gear is proportional to the gear's pitch diameter. This means that the ratio of speed between two meshing gears is equal to the ratio of the number of teeth on the two gears. If one gear has 40 teeth and the other 20, the speed ratio between the two gears is 2:1.

For gears to mesh properly, they must have the same pitch and pressure angle. Gear manufacturers present their gears in charts that include a selection of gears with common pitches and pressure angles. Figure 13-11 shows a sample spur gear listing from Berg's *B92 Precision Mechanical Components Catalog*. The charts also include dimensional values for the outside diameter of the gear, the pitch diameter, and the face width; information about the bore; center hub, if appropriate; and the gear's material. The list is set up to give the designer a wide choice in selecting gears. For example, the chart shows 12 different combinations of gears that could be used to create a 2:1 ratio between gears.

13-9 CENTER DISTANCE BETWEEN GEARS

The center distance between meshing spur gears is needed to align the gears properly. Ideally, gears mesh exactly on their pitch diameters, so the ideal center distance between two meshing gears is equal to the sum of the two pitch radii, or the sum of the two diameters divided by 2:

CD1 = (PD1 + PD2)/2

If two gears were chosen from the chart in Figure 13-11, and one had 30 teeth and a pitch diameter of .9375, and the other had 60 teeth and a pitch diameter of 1.8750, the center distance between the gears would be

CD1 = (.9375 + 1.8750)/2 = 2.8125

The center distance of gears is dependent on the tolerance of the gears' bores, the tolerance of the supporting shafts, and the feature and positional tolerance of the holes in the shaft's supporting structure. The following sample problem shows how these tolerances are considered and applied when matching two spur gears.

13-10 SAMPLE PROBLEM SP13-4

An electric motor generates power at 1750 rpm. Reduce this speed by a factor of 2 using steel metric gears with a module of 1.5 and a pressure angle of 20°. Figure 13-12 shows a list of gears. Determine the center distance between the gears, and specify the shaft sizes required for both gears.

Gear number A 1C22MYKW150 50A and number A 1C22MKYW150 100A were selected from the chart shown in Figure 13-12. The pinion gear has 50 teeth, and the large gear has 100, so if the pinion gear is mounted on

| Pin Hub Style | Precision Spur Gears | 32 PITCH
3/8″ Bore
3/8″ Face |

20° Pressure Angle   AGMA Quality 10

303 STAINLESS STEEL STOCK NUMBER	BRONZE ALLOY 464 STOCK NUMBER	BERG QUALITY #10 OR BETTER PER AGMA STANDARD 2000-A88 (FORMERLY 390.03)		
		NO. OF TEETH	PITCH DIAMETER	OUTSIDE DIAMETER
P32S34-20	P32B34-20	20	.6250	.687
P32S34-24	P32B34-24	24	.7500	.812
P32S34-28	P32B34-28	28	.8750	.937
P32S34-30	P32B34-30	30	.9375	1.000
P32S34-32	P32B34-32	32	1.0000	1.062
P32S34-36	P32B34-36	36	1.1250	1.187
P32S34-40	P32B34-40	40	1.2500	1.312
P32S34-48	P32B34-48	48	1.5000	1.562
P32S34-56	P32B34-56	56	1.7500	1.812
P32S34-60	P32B34-60	60	1.8750	1.937
P32S34X-64	P32B34X-64	64	2.0000	2.062
P32S34X-72	P32B34X-72	72	2.2500	2.312
P32S34X-80	P32B34X-80	80	2.5000	2.562
P32S34X-96	P32B34X-96	96	3.0000	3.062
P32S34X-112	P32B34X-112	112	3.5000	3.562
P32S34X-128	P32B34X-128	128	4.0000	4.062
P32S34X-160	P32B34X-160	160	5.0000	5.062

An X in a number indicates two-piece construction (some dimensions may vary).
W.M. Berg, Inc., 499 Ocean Avenue, East Rockaway, New York, 11518
Telephone 516-596-1700

NOTE: See www.wmberg.com

Figure 13-11

Stock Drive Products   Metric   Spur Gears - Module 1.5
   2101 Jericho Turnpike   20° Pressure Angle
     Box 5416
   New Hyde Park, NY 11042-5416
      (516) 328-3300

FIG. 1   FIG. 2

Catalog Number	Fig No.	No. of Teeth	P.D.	O.D.	B* Bore (H7)	F Face Width	C Hub Dia	D Hub Proj	A Dia	W Dim	K Dim
A 1C22MYKW150 20A		20	30	33	14		25			5	2.3
A 1C22MYKW150 24A		24	36	39	16		30				
A 1C22MYKW150 25A		25	37.5	40.5	18	18	32				
A 1C22MYKW150 28A		28	42	45			36				
A 1C22MYKW150 30A		30	45	48							
A 1C22MYKW150 32A	1	32	48	51						6	2.8
A 1C22MYKW150 36A		36	54	57							
A 1C22MYKW150 40A		40	60	63				14			
A 1C22MYKW150 48A		48	72	75							
A 1C22MYKW150 50A		50	75	78	20		40				
A 1C22MYKW150 56A		56	84	87		16					
A 1C22MYKW150 60A		60	90	93					76		
A 1C22MYKW150 64A		64	96	99					82		
A 1C22MYKW150 70A		70	105	108					91		
A 1C22MYKW150 72A	2	72	108	111					94		
A 1C22MYKW150 80A		80	120	123	25		50		106	8	3.3
A 1C22MYKW150 100A		100	150	153					136		

* Gears with 14, 16, and 18mm bores have a tolerance of +.018, +.000.

   20 and 25mm bores have a tolerance of +0.021/- 0

Figure 13-12

the motor shaft, the larger gear will turn at 875 rpm, or half the 1750 motor speed.

½ = x/1750
x = 1750/2 = 875 rpm

The specific design information for the selected gears is as follows:

PINION GEAR
    PD = 75
    OD = 78
    N = 50
    Bore = 20 +.021/−.000
    Tolerance = H7

LARGE GEAR
    PD = 150
    OD = 153
    N = 100
    Bore = 25 +.021/−.000
    Tolerance = H7

The center distance between the gears is equal to the sum of the two pitch diameters divided by 2:

(PD1 + PD2)/2 =
(75 + 150)/2 = 112.5

The manufacturer's catalog lists the bore tolerance as an H7. One gear has a nominal bore diameter of 20 and the other one of 25. Standard fit tolerances for metric values are discussed in Chapter 9, and appropriate tables are included in the appendix.

Tolerance values for a sliding fit (H7/g6) hole basis were selected for this design application. This means that the shaft tolerances are 19.993 and 19.980 for the pinion gear and 24.993 and 24.980 for the large gear.

13-11 COMBINING SPUR GEARS

Gears may be mounted on the same shaft. Gears on a common shaft have the same turning speed. Combining gears on the same shaft enables the designer to develop larger gear ratios within a smaller space.

Combining gears can also be used to help reduce the size of gear ratios between individual gears and the amount of space needed to create the reductions. Figure 13-13 shows a four-gear setup. Gears B and C are mounted on the same shaft. Gear A is the driver gear and is turning at a speed of 1750 rpm. The speed of gear D is determined as follows.

The ratio between gears A and B is

48/72 = .6667

The speed of gear B is therefore

1750 × .6667 = 1166.7 rpm

Gears B and C are on the same shaft, so they have the same speed. Gear C is turning at 1166.7 rpm.

The ratio between gears C and D is

24/48 = .5000

The speed of gear D is therefore

1166.7 × .5000 = 583 rpm

The ratio between gears A and D is 3:1.

Figure 13-13

Figure 13-14

Stock Drive Products

Metric Bevel Gears

20° Pressure Angle

Module 1.5, 2.0, 2.5, 3.0

Material: Steel

Catalog Number	Module	No. of Teeth	Ratio	PD	OD	B* Bore (H8)	F Face Width	E Length	C Hub Dia	D Hub Proj	MD Dim
A 1C 3MYK 15018	1:5	18		27	29.7	8	9.8	23	22	12.5	40.74
A 1C 3MYK 15036		36		54	55.4	10		18.5	30	10	26.75
A 1C 3MYK 20018	2:0	18		36	39.6	9	12.6	29	28	15	53.12
A 1C 3MYK 20036		36	1:2	72	73.8	12		24	36	13	35.21
A 1C 3MYK 25018	2.5	18		45	49.5	12	16.7	35	36	17	64.29
A 1C 3MYK 25036H		36		90	92.2	14		29	50	15	42.55
A 1C 3MYK 30018	3.0	18		54	59.4	12	20	40	41	18	75.27
A 1C 3MYK 30036H		36		108	110.7	16		36	60	19	52.32

* Gears with: 8, 9, 10mm bores have a tolerance of +0.022/-0
12, 14, 16mm bores have a tolerance of +0.027/-0

Figure 13-15

13-12 GEAR TERMINOLOGY— BEVEL

Bevel gears align at an angle with each other. An angle of 90° is most common. Bevel gears use much of the same terminology as spur gears but with the addition of several terms related to the angles between the gears and the shape and position of the teeth. Figure 13-14 defines the related terminology.

Bevel gears must have the same pitch or module value and have the same pressure angle for them to mesh properly. Manufacturers' catalogs usually list bevel gears in matched sets designated by ratios that have been predetermined to fit together correctly. Figure 13-15 shows a sample list of matched set bevel gears using millimeter values, and Figure 13-16 shows a list for inch values.

Catalog Number	Ratio	No. of Teeth	PD	A	Material
S1346Z-48S30A030	1:1	30 / 30	.625	.687	St Steel / Aluminum
S1346Z-48S30S030	1:1	30 / 30	.625	.687	St Steel
S1346Z-48A30A030	1:1	30 / 30	.625	.687	Aluminum
S1346Z-48S30A045	1:1-1/2	30 / 45	.625 / .937	.812	St Steel / Aluminum
S1346Z-48S30S045	1:1-1/2	30 / 45	.625 / .937	.812	St Steel
S1346Z-48A30A045	1:1-1/2	30 / 45	.625 / .937	.812	Aluminum
S1346Z-48S30A060	1:2	30 / 60	.625 / 1.250	.937	St Steel / Aluminum
S1346Z-48S30S060	1:2	30 / 60	.625 / 1.250	.937	St Steel
S1346Z-48A30A060	1:2	30 / 60	.625 / 1.250	.937	Aluminum
S1346Z-48S30A090	1:3	30 / 90	.625 / 1.875	1.250	St Steel / Aluminum
S1346Z-48S30S090	1:3	30 / 90	.625 / 1.875	1.250	St Steel
S1346Z-48S30A090	1:3	30 / 90	.625 / 1.875	1.250	Aluminum
S1346Z-48S30A120	1:4	30 / 120	.625 / 2.500	1.531	St Steel / Aluminum
S1346Z-48S30S120	1:4	30 / 120	.625 / 2.500	1.531	St Steel
S1346Z-48A30A120	1:4	30 / 120	.625 / 2.500	1.531	Aluminum

Figure 13-16

13-13 HOW TO DRAW BEVEL GEARS

Bevel gears are usually drawn by working from dimensions listed in manufacturers' catalogs for specific matching sets. The gears are drawn using either a sectional view or a half-sectional view that shows the profiles of the two gears. Figure 13-17 shows a matching set of bevel gears that were drawn from the information given in Figure 13-15.

The procedure used to draw the gears, based on information given in manufacturers' catalogs, is as follows.

To draw a matched set of beveled gears

1. Draw a perpendicular centerline pattern and use the Offset command to define the pitch diameters of the pinion and gear.
2. Extend the pitch diameter lines and draw lines from the center point to the intersections as shown.

These lines are called the *face angle lines*. The ends of beveled gears are drawn perpendicular to the face angle lines. Gear manufacturers do not always include the outside

Figure 13-17

diameter values with matching sets of gears. The values are sometimes listed with data for the individual gears elsewhere in the catalog. If the outside diameter values are not given, they can be conservatively estimated by drawing the addendum angle approximately −5.0° from the face angle and the dedendum 6.0° from the face angle.

The perpendicular end lines may be constructed using the Copy and Rotate commands. Copy the existing face angle line directly over the existing line, then rotate the line 90° from the face angle line.

Use the Extend command to extend the rotated lines as needed. Add a construction line to help define an intersection between the dedendum ray line and the face line perpendicular to the face angle line. Trim and erase any excess lines.

3. Use the Copy and Rotate commands to copy the face shape and rotate it into the two other positions shown.
4. Use the given dimensions to complete the profiles. Erase and trim lines as necessary.
5. Draw the bore holes and holes for the set screws based on the manufacturer's specifications.
6. Use the Hatch command to draw the appropriate hatch lines.

The two gears should have hatch patterns at different angles. In this example the hatch pattern on the pinion is at 90° to the pattern on the gear.

13-14 WORM GEARS

A worm gear setup is created using a cylindrical gear called a *worm*, and a circular matching gear called a *worm gear*. See Figure 13-18. As with other types of gears, worm gears must have the same pitch and pressure angle to mesh correctly. Manufacturers list matching worms and worm gears together in their catalogs. Figure 13-20 shows a gear manufacturer's listing for a worm gear and the appropriate worms.

Worm gears are drawn using the representation shown in Figure 13-20 or using sectional views as shown in Figure 13-19. The worm teeth shown can be drawn using the procedure explained in Chapter 11 for acme threads.

Figure 13-18

Figure 13-19

BERG Precision Worm Gears

$$Ratio = \frac{No.\ of\ Teeth}{Worm\ Threads}$$

		FOR SINGLE THREAD WORM			FOR DOUBLE THREAD WORM		NO. OF TEETH	PITCH DIA
CIRCULAR PITCH		.0982	CIRCULAR PITCH		.1963			
HELIX ANGLE		4° – 5′	HELIX ANGLE		8° – 8′			
PRESSURE ANGLE		14-1/2°	PRESSURE ANGLE		20°			
STOCK NUMBER			STOCK NUMBER					
W32B29-S20			W32B29-D20				20	.625
W32B29-S30			W32B29-D30				30	.938
W32B29-S40			W32B29-D40				40	1.250
W32B29-S50			W32B29-D50				50	1.562
W32B29-S60			W32B29-D60				60	1.875
W32B29-S80			W32B29-D80				80	2.500
W32B29-S96			W32B29-D96				96	3.000
W32B29-S100			W32B29-D100				100	3.125
W32B29-S120			W32B29-D120				120	3.750
W32B29-S180			W32B29-D180				180	5.625

Precision Worms

STOCK NUMBER	THREAD	LEAD	LEAD ANGLE	PRESSURE ANGLE
W32S-3S	SINGLE	.0982	4°-5′	14-1/2°
W32S-3D	DOUBLE	.1963	8°-8′	20°

Figure 13-20

The relationship between worm gears is determined by the *lead* of the worm thread. The lead of a worm thread is similar to the pitch of a thread discussed in Chapter 11. Worm threads may be single, double, or quadruple. If a worm has a double thread, it will advance the gear twice as fast as a worm with a single thread.

13-15 HELICAL GEARS

Helical gears are drawn as shown in Figure 13-21. The two gears are called the *driver* and the *driven*, as indicated. Figure 13-22 shows a manufacturer's listing of compatible helical gears.

Helical gears may be manufactured with either left- or right-hand threads. Left- and right-hand threads are used to determine the relative rotation direction of the gears.

Figure 13-21

STOCK NUMBER		NO. OF TEETH	PITCH DIAMETER	OUTSIDE DIAMETER
RIGHT-HAND	LEFT-HAND			
H16S38-R12	H16S38-L12	12	1.060	1.185
H16S38-R16	H16S38-L16	16	1.4142	1.539
H16S38-R20	H16S38-L20	20	1.7677	1.892
H16S38-R24	H16S38-L24	24	2.1213	2.246
H16S38-R32	H16S38-L32	32	2.8284	2.953
H16S38-R40	H16S38-L40	40	3.5355	3.660
H16S38-R48	H16S38-L48	48	4.2426	4.367

Figure 13-22

13-16 RACKS

Racks are gears whose teeth are in a straight row. Racks are used to change rotary motion into linear motion. See Figure 13-23. Racks are usually driven by a spur gear called a *pinion*.

One of the most common applications of gear racks is the steering mechanism of an automobile. Rack-and-pinion steering helps create a more positive relationship between the rotation of the steering wheel and the linear input to the car's wheel than did the mechanical linkages used on older-model cars.

Figure 13-24 shows a manufacturer's list for racks. The rack and pinions must have the same pitch and pressure angle to mesh correctly.

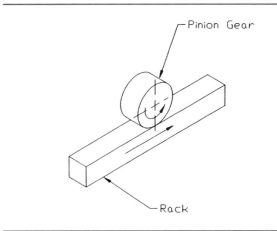

Figure 13-23

Berg Precision Racks

416 ST. Steel &
2024T4 Aluminum
Anodized

24 to 120 Pitch
20° Pressure Angle
AGMA Quality 10

.156 (72, 80, and 120 Pitch)
.218 (24, 48, and 64 Pitch)

#26 Dr (4 Holes) on 24, 32 48, and 64 Pitch
#31 Dr (4 Holes) On 72, 80, 96, and 120 Pitch

STOCK NUMBER	MATERIAL	PITCH	A	P	W	F	C
R4-5 R4-6	STAINLESS ST ALUMINUM	24	10″	.4383	.480	.230	3.208
R4-9 R4-10	STAINLESS ST ALUMINUM	32	10″	.4487	.480	.230	3.208
R4-11 R4-12	STAINLESS ST ALUMINUM	48	9″	.4592	.480	.230	2.879
R4-15 R4-16	STAINLESS ST ALUMINUM	64	7″	.4644	.480	.230	2.208
R4-17 R4-18	STAINLESS ST ALUMINUM	72	5″	.3411	.355	.167	1.541
R4-19 R4-20	STAINLESS ST ALUMINUM	80	5″	.3425	.355	.167	1.541
R4-21 R4-22	STAINLESS ST ALUMINUM	96	3″	.3446	.355	.167	.875
R4-23 R4-24	STAINLESS ST ALUMINUM	120	3″	.3467	.355	.167	.875

Figure 13-24

Figure 13-25

13-17 BALL BEARINGS

Ball bearings are used to help eliminate friction between moving and stationary parts. The moving and stationary parts are separated by a series of balls that ride in a *race*.

Figure 13-25 shows a manufacturer's list for ball bearings that includes applicable dimensions and tolerances. There are many other types and sizes of ball bearings available.

Ball bearings may be drawn as shown in Figure 13-25 or by using one of the representations shown in Figure 13-26. It is recommended that the representations be drawn and saved as wblocks for use on future drawings.

The outside diameter of the bearings listed in Figure 13-25 has a tolerance of +.0000/−.0002. The same tolerance range applies to the center hole. These tight tolerances are manufactured because this type of ball bearing is usually assembled using a force fit. See Chapter 9 for an explanation of fits. Ball bearings are available that do not assemble using force fits.

The following sample problem shows how ball bearings can be used to support the gear's shafts.

13-18 SAMPLE PROBLEM SP13-5

Figure 13-27 shows two spur gears and a dimensioned drawing of a shaft used to support both gears. Design a support plate for the shafts. Use ball bearings to support the shafts. Specify dimensions and tolerances for the support plate and assume that the bearings are to be fitted into the support plate using an LN2 medium press fit. The tolerance for the center distance between the gears is to be +.001, −.000.

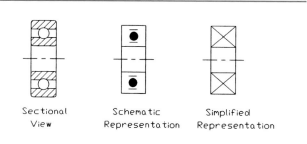

Figure 13-26

The maximum interference permitted for an LN2 medium press fit is .0011. See the fits tables in the appendix. For purposes of calculation, the bearing is considered to be the shaft and the holes in the support plate.

Maximum interference occurs when the shaft (bearing) is at its maximum diameter and the hole (support plate) is at its minimum. The maximum shaft diameter, the maximum diameter of the bearing, is .5000, as defined in the manufacturer's listing. This means that the minimum hole diameter should be .5000−.0011 = .4989. An LN2 fit has a hole tolerance of +.0007, so the maximum hole size should be .4989 + .0007 = .4996.

The minimum interference, or the difference between the minimum shaft diameter and the maximum hole diameter, is .4998−.4996 = .0002. There will always be at least .0002 interference between the ball bearing and the hole.

The bore of the selected bearing, listed in Figure 13-25, has a limit tolerance of .2500−.2498. The shafts specified in Figure 13-27 have a limit tolerance of .2497−.2495. This means that there will always be a slight clearance between the shaft and the bore hole.

The nominal center distance between the two gears is 3.000 inches. The given tolerance for the center distance is +.001, −.000. This tolerance can be ensured by assigning a positional tolerance of .0005 to each of the two holes applied at maximum material condition at the centerline. The base distance between the two holes is defined as 3.0000. The maximum center distance, including the positional tolerance, is 3.0000 + .0005 = 3.0005, and the minimum is 3.0000−.0005 = 2.9995, or a total maximum tolerance of .001.

Figure 13-28 shows a detail drawing of the support plate.

Figure 13-27

Figure 13-28

13-19 BUSHINGS

A *bushing* is a cylindrically shaped bearing that helps reduce friction between a moving part and a stationary part. Bushings, unlike ball bearings, have no moving parts. Bushings are usually made from oil-impregnated bronze or Teflon. Figure 13-29 shows a manufacturer's list of bronze bushings, and Figure 13-30 shows a list for Teflon bushings.

Bushings are cheaper than ball bearings but they wear over time, particularly if the application is high speed or one with heavy loading. Bushings are usually pressed into a supporting plate. Gear shafts must always have clearance from the inside diameters of bushings.

PLAIN STYLE	FLANGED STYLE					FLANGED ONLY	
STOCK NUMBER	STOCK NUMBER	SHAFT SIZE	d +.001	D −.001	B ±.005	C ±.005	E ±.003
B6-2	B7-31	1/8	.126	.252	.250	.375	.047
B6-7	B7-35	3/16	.188	.314	.500	.375	.047
B6-11	B7-11	1/4	.251	.377	.500	.562	.047
B6-15	B7-40	5-16	.313	.439	.625	.562	.062
B6-18	B7-44	3/8	.376	.502	.625	.625	.062
B6-23	B7-49	1/2	.501	.627	.750	.875	.062

Figure 13-29

PLAIN STYLE	FLANGED STYLE					FLANGED ONLY	
STOCK NUMBER	STOCK NUMBER	SHAFT SIZE	d +.001	D −.001	B ±.005	C ±.005	E ±.003
	B9-3	1/8	.126	.252	.250	.312	.047
B8-5	B9-6	3/16	.188	.315	.250	.375	.047
B8-11	B9-11	1/4	.251	.377	.500	.500	.047
B8-14	B9-15	5/16	.313	.439	.500	.562	.093
B8-19	B9-19	3/8	.376	.502	.625	.687	.093
B8-23	B8-29	1/2	.501	.628	.750	.875	.125

Figure 13-30

13-20 SAMPLE PROBLEM SP13-6

Figure 13-31 shows two support plates used to support and align a matched set of bevel gears. The gears selected are numbered S1346Z–48S30S60 in the Berg listings presented in Figure 13-16. The calculations are similar to those presented earlier for Sample Problem SP13-5 but with the addition of tolerances for the holes and machine screws used to join the two perpendicular support plates together.

Figure 13-31 shows an assembly drawing of the two gears along with appropriate bushings, stock number B6-11 from Figure 13-29, and shafts and supporting parts 1 and 2. The figure also shows detailed drawings of the two support plates with appropriate dimensions and tolerances.

The bushings are fitted into the support plates using an FN1 fit. The fit tables in the appendix define the maximum interference for an FN1 fit as .0075 and the minimum interference as .0001. The outside diameter of the bushing has a tolerance of .3770 − .3760, per Figure 13-29. The feature tolerances for the holes in the support parts are found as follows:

Shaft max − hole min = interference max

Shaft min − hole max = interference min

The feature tolerance for the hole is therefore .3750 − .3695.

The positional tolerance is determined as described in SP13-5 and is based on a tolerance of .001 between gear centers.

Figure 13-31

13-21 CAM DISPLACEMENT DIAGRAMS

A *displacement diagram* is used to define the motion of a cam follower. Displacement diagrams are set up as shown in Figure 13-32. The horizontal axis is marked off in 12 equal spaces that represent 30° on the cam. The vertical axis is used to define the linear displacement of the follower and is defined using either inches or millimeters.

The vertical axis of a displacement diagram must be drawn to scale because, once defined, the vertical distances are transferred to the cam's base circle to define the cam's shape. Figure 13-32 shows distances A, B, and C on both the displacement diagram and cam. The distances define the follower displacement at the 30°, 60°, and 90° marks, respectively.

The horizontal axis may use any equal spacing to indicate the angle because the vertical distances will be transferred to the cam along ray lines. The lower horizontal line represents the circumference of the base circle.

Figure 13-33 shows a second displacement diagram. Note how the distance between the 60° and 90° lines has been further subdivided. The additional lines are used to more accurately define the cam motion. Additional degree lines are often added when the follower is undergoing a rapid change of motion.

The term *dwell* means the cam follower does not move either up or down as the cam turns. Dwells are drawn as straight horizontal lines on a displacement diagram. Note the horizontal line between the 90° and 210° lines on the displacement diagram shown in Figure 13-33. Dwells are drawn as sectors of constant radius on the cam.

Figure 13-33

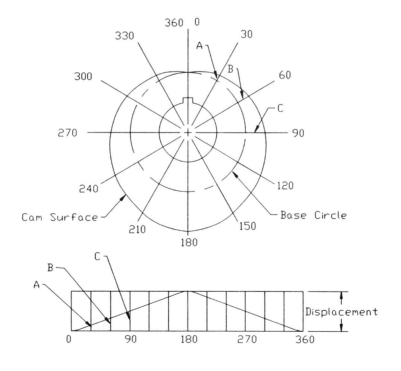

Figure 13-32

To set up a displacement diagram

See Figure 13-34. The given dimensions are in inches. The values in the brackets, [ ], are in millimeters.

1. Set Grid = .5 [10]
   Snap = .25 [5]
2. Draw a horizontal line 6 [120] long.
3. Draw a vertical line 2 [40] from the left end of the horizontal line as shown.

The length 2 [40] was chosen arbitrarily for this example. The vertical distance should be equal to the total displacement of the follower.

4. Use the Array command to create a rectangular array with 12 columns .5 [10] apart. Draw a horizontal line across the top of the diagram.
5. Label the horizontal axis in degrees, with each vertical line representing 30°, and the vertical axis in inches [millimeters] of displacement.

13-22 CAM MOTIONS

The shape of a cam surface is designed to move a follower through a specific distance. The surface also determines the acceleration, deceleration, and smoothness of motion of the follower. It is important that a cam surface be shaped to maintain continuous contact with the follower. Several standard cam motions are defined next.

Uniform motion

Uniform motion is drawn as a straight line on a displacement diagram. See Figure 13-35. The follower rises the same distance for each degree of rotation by the cam.

Modified uniform motion

Modified uniform motion is similar to uniform motion but has a curved radius shape added to each end of the line to facilitate a smooth transition from the uniform motion to another type of motion or to a dwell section.

Figure 13-36 shows how to create a modified uniform motion on a displacement diagram. The procedure is as follows.

1. Set up a displacement diagram as presented in Section 13-21.
2. Draw two arcs or circles of radius no greater than half the required displacement.

Figure 13-34

Figure 13-35

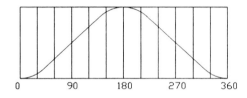

Figure 13-36

Any radius value can be used. In general, the larger the radius, the smoother the transition. In the example shown, a radius equal to half the total displacement was used.

3. Use Osnap, Tangent, and draw a line between the two arcs.
4. Erase and trim any excess lines.

Harmonic motion

Figure 13-37 shows how to create a harmonic cam motion. The procedure is as follows.

1. Set up a displacement diagram as presented in Section 13-21.
2. Draw a semicircle aligned with the left side of the displacement diagram. The diameter of the semicircle equals the total height of the displacement.

3. Use the Array command or the Line command with relative coordinate inputs, and draw rays every 30° on the circle as shown. Label the rays from 0° to 180° in 30° segments.
4. Use Osnap, Intersection with Ortho on (F8), and draw projection lines from the intersections of the rays with the circumference of the circle across the displacement diagram.
5. Draw a polyline starting at the lower left corner of the diagram and connecting the intersections of like angle lines.

For this example, the horizontal line from the circle's 30° increment intersects with the vertical line from the 30° mark on the displacement diagram.

6. Use Edit Polyline, Fit option, to change the straight polyline into a smooth curved line.
7. Project the same lines to the far side of the diagram to define the deceleration harmonic motion path.

Harmonic Motion

Use OSNAP, INTERSECTION, ORTHO ON

Use PLINE, PEDIT, FIT CURVE

Figure 13-37

Uniform acceleration and deceleration

Uniform acceleration and deceleration are based on the knowledge that acceleration is related to distance by the square of the distance. Acceleration is measured in distance per second squared. Distances of units 1, 2, and 3 may be expressed as 1, 4, and 9, respectively.

Uniform acceleration and deceleration motions create smooth transitions between various displacement heights and are often used in high-speed applications.

Figure 13-38 shows how to create a uniform acceleration cam motion. The procedure is as follows.

1. Set up a displacement diagram as presented in Section 13-21.
2. Draw a horizontal construction line to the left and align it with the bottom horizontal line of the displacement diagram.
3. Use the Array command and create 1 column and 19 rows, .1111 apart.

The 19 rows create 18 spaces. The uniform motion shape is created by combining six horizontal steps (30°, 60°, 90°, 120°, 150°, 180°) and the squares of six vertical steps (1, 4, 9, 4, 1, 0).

The vertical spacing is symmetrical about the centerline of the displacement diagram, so the original spacing is 1, 2, 3, 2, 1. The square of these values is used to create the uniform acceleration and deceleration.

The .1111 value was derived by dividing the displacement distance by the number of spaces, 2.00/18 = .1111.

4. Label the stack of vertical construction lines as shown.
5. Use the Extend command to extend the horizontal construction lines so that they intersect with the appropriate vertical degree line.
6. Use the Edit Polyline command's Fit option to create a smooth, continuous curve between the 0° and 180° lines.

The same line may be used to create a deceleration curve as shown.

Figure 13-39

Figure 13-38

13-23 CAM FOLLOWERS

There are two basic types of cam followers: those that roll as they follow the cam's surface, and those that have a fixed surface that slides in contact with the cam surface. Figure 13-39 shows an example of a roller follower and a fixed- or flat-surface follower. The flat-surface-type followers are limited to slow-moving cams with low force requirements.

Followers are usually spring loaded to keep them in contact with the cam surface during operation. Springs were discussed in Section 11-24.

13-24 SAMPLE PROBLEM SP13-7

Design a cam that rises 2.00 inches over 180° using harmonic motion, dwells for 60°, descends 2.00 inches in 90° using modified uniform motion, and dwells the remaining 30°. The base circle for the cam is 3.00 inches in diameter, and the follower is a roller type with a 1.00-inch diameter. The cam will rotate in a counterclockwise direction. The center hole is .75 inch in diameter with a .125 × .875 keyway. See Figures 13-40 and 13-41.

1. Set up a displacement diagram as described in Section 13-21.
2. Define a path between the 0° and 180° vertical lines using the method described for harmonic motion. Draw the required circle on the left end of the diagram as shown.
3. Draw a horizontal line from the 180° to the 240° line.

This line defines the follower's dwell.

4. Draw two arcs of .50 radius, one tangent to the top horizontal line of the displacement diagram and the second tangent to the bottom line.

Draw one arc on the 240° line and the other on the 330° line as shown. In this example the arcs have a radius equal to .25 of the total displacement. Any convenient radius value may be used.

5. Use the Osnap, Tangent command and draw a line tangent to the two arcs.
6. Erase and trim any excess lines and constructions.

This completes the displacement diagram. The follower distances are now transferred to the cam's base circle to define the surface shape. See Figure 13-41.

7. Draw two concentric circles of 3.00 and 8.00 diameter, respectively.

The 3.00 diameter is the base circle. The 8.00-diameter-circle value is derived from the radius of the base circle plus the maximum displacement plus the radius of the follower: 1.50 + 2 + .5 = 4.00 radius, or 8.00 diameter.

8. Use the Setvar, Dimcen, −.2, Dim, Center commands, or a modified Center Mark tool to draw the centerlines for the 8.00 circle.
9. Use the Array command, and polar array the top portion of the vertical centerline 12 times around the full 360°.
10. Label the ray lines as shown.

Note that the top vertical ray line is labeled both as 0 and 360.

11. Transfer the follower distances from the displacement diagram to the cam drawing.

Several different techniques can be used to transfer the distances: use the Linear Dimension tool, the Distance command found under the Tools pull-down menu, or the Inquiry command. Use the Osnap, Intersection command to ensure accuracy. In this example the measured distance values are listed below the displacement diagram in Figure 13-40. The .50 addition to the bottom of the diagram is to account for the .50 follower radius. Note how the distance of 2.1000 was measured.

The distance values can be used to draw lines from the base circle along the appropriate ray line on the cam drawing using relative coordinate values. The values for this example are as follows:

.5000-(0)	@.5000<90
.6340-(30)	@.6340<60
1.0000-(60)	@1.0000<30
1.5000-(90)	@1.5000<0
2.0000-(120)	@2.0000<−30
2.3660-(150)	@2.3660<−60

Figure 13-40

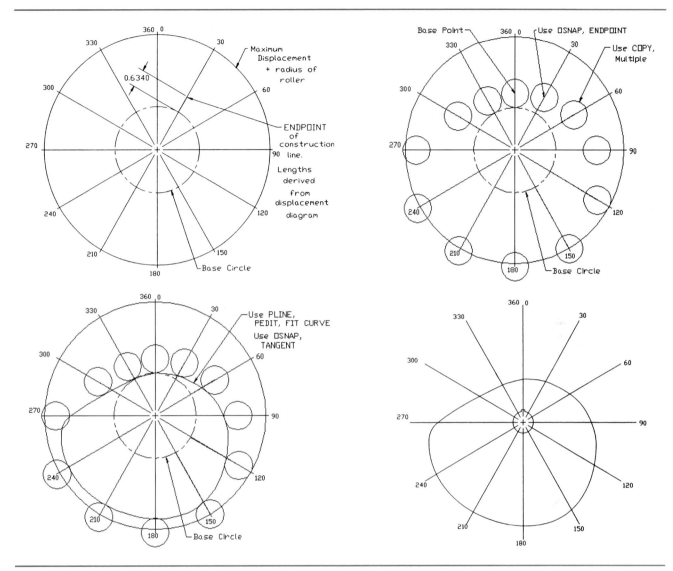

Figure 13-41

2.5000-(180) @2.5000<−90
2.5000-(210) @2.5000<−120
2.5000-(240) @2.5000<−150
2.1000-(270) @2.1000<180
.9000-(300) @.9000<150
.5000-(330) @.5000<120

Lines can be drawn over the existing vertical lines between the base line and the displacement path on the displacement diagram. The Move, Rotate or Grips, Rotate command can be used to transfer the lines to the base circle and appropriate ray line.

12. Draw circles of diameter .50, representing the roller follower, with their center points on the ends of the lines created in step 11.

Note that these lines and their endpoints are not visible on the screen because they are drawn directly over the existing ray lines. The Osnap, Endpoint command should be used to locate the circle's center point.

13. Use the Draw, Polyline command and draw a line tangent to the follower at each ray line.

The tangent point for each ray may not be exactly on the ray line.

14. Use the Edit Polyline, Spline command to create the cam surface.
15. Draw the center hole and keyway using the given dimensions.
16. Save the drawings, if desired.

13-25 EXERCISE PROBLEMS

EX13-1 INCHES

Draw a spur gear with 24 teeth on a 4.00-pitch circle. The fillets at the base of each tooth have a radius of .0625. Locate a 1.00-diameter mounting hole in the center of the gear.

EX13-2 MILLIMETERS

Draw a spur gear with 36 teeth on a 100-pitch circle. The fillets at the base of each tooth have a radius of 3. Locate a 20-diameter mounting hole in the center of the gear.

EX13-3

Use the information presented in Figure 13-11 and draw front and side sectional views of gear number P32S34-60.

EX13-4

Use the information presented in Figure 13-12 and draw front and side sectional views of gear number A 1C22MYKW150 64A.

EX13-5

Use the information presented in Figure 13-15 and draw a sectional view of bevel gears A 1C 3MYK 30018 and A 1C 3MYK 30036H.

EX13-6

Use the information presented in Figure 13-16 and draw a sectional view of the matched set of bevel gears S1346Z-48S30A120.

EX13-7

Use the information presented in Figure 13-19 and draw front and side views of a set of worm gears.

EX13-8

Use the information presented in Figure 13-22 and draw a front view of a matched set of helical gears.

EX13-9

Use the information presented in Figure 13-24 and draw a front view of a set of rack-and-pinion gears.

EX13-10 INCHES

Draw a displacement diagram and appropriate cam based on the following information.

Dwell for 60°, rise 1.00 inch using harmonic motion over 180°, dwell for 30°, then descend 1.00 inch using harmonic motion over 90°.

The cam's base circle is 4.00 inches in diameter. Include a 1.25-inch center mounting hole.

EX13-11 MILLIMETERS

Draw a displacement diagram and appropriate cam based on the following information.

Dwell for 60°, rise 30 millimeters using harmonic motion over 180°, dwell for 30°, then descend 30 millimeters using harmonic motion over 90°.

The cam's base circle is 120 millimeters in diameter. Include a 20-millimeter center mounting hole.

EX13-12 INCHES

Draw a displacement diagram and appropriate cam based on the following information.

Rise 1.25 inches over 180° using uniform acceleration motion, dwell for 60°, descend 1.25 inches over 90° using modified uniform motion, dwell for 30°.

The cam's base circle is 3.25 inches in diameter. Include a .75-inch-diameter center mounting hole.

EX13-13 MILLIMETERS

Draw a displacement diagram and appropriate cam based on the following information.

Rise 20 millimeters over 180° using uniform acceleration motion, dwell for 60°, descend 20 millimeters over 90° using modified uniform motion, dwell for 30°.

The cam's base circle is 80 millimeters in diameter. Include a 16-millimeter-diameter center mounting hole.

EX13-14 INCHES

Draw a displacement diagram and appropriate cam based on the following information.

Rise .60 inch in 90° using harmonic motion, dwell for 30°, rise .60 inch in 60° using modified uniform motion, dwell 60°, descend 1.20 inches using uniform deceleration in 120°.

The cam's base circle is 3.20 inches in diameter. Include a 1.75-inch-diameter center mounting hole.

EX13-15 MILLIMETERS

Draw a displacement diagram and appropriate cam based on the following information.

Rise 16 millimeters in 90° using harmonic motion, dwell for 30°, rise 16 millimeters in 60° using modified uniform motion, dwell 60°, descend 32 millimeters using uniform deceleration in 120°.

The cam's base circle is 84 millimeters in diameter. Include a 20-millimeter-diameter center mounting hole.

EX13-16

.50" [12mm]

An electrical motor operates at 1750 rpm. Design a gear system that includes at least four spur gears and reduces the motor speed by a ratio of 100:1.

Draw the gear setups. Assume that the center distances have a tolerance of $+.001, -.000$, and the support shafts have tolerances of $+.0000, -.0002$, or their metric equivalents.

A. Draw an assembly drawing showing the gears in their assembled positions.
B. Support the gear shafts with either bushings or ball bearings press fitted into the support plate. The support plate is to be 0.50 inch or 12 millimeters thick. The length and width dimensions are arbitrary.
C. Draw detail drawings of the required support plates. Include dimensions and tolerances. Locate all support holes using positional tolerances.
D. The figure below shows a four-gear setup made from "Eitech" construction kit parts. If available, build a four-gear setup as shown and measure the speed of the final gear. Use the gear ratios to determine the motor speed.

SUPPORT PLATE
Define the length and width

The gear setup shown represents one of many possible setups.
Consider mounting two gears on the same shaft to save space.

Made from Eitech parts

See the tables in Chapter 13 and in the appendix for gear, shaft, bearing, and tolerance selections. Also see www.wmberg.com and www.bostgear.com for components.

EX13-17

An electric motor operates at 3600 rpm. Design a gear that includes at least four spur gears (more may be used if needed) and reduces the motor speed to 200 rpm. Select gears and bearings from the tables in this book or from manufacturers' web sites. Design each shaft as needed.

Enclose the gears in a box made from .50-inch [12-millimeter] plates, assembled using flat-head screws. There should be at least three screws per edge on the box.

Extend the shafts for the input and output at least .50[12] outside the box. The other shafts should end at the edge of the box. Mount each shaft using two ball bearings, one mounted in each support plate.

Assume that the center distances have a tolerance of +.001, −.000 and the support shafts have tolerances of +.0000, −.0002, or their metric equivalent.

A. Draw an assembly drawing showing the gears in their assembled positions.
B. Support the gear shafts with ball bearings press fitted into the support plate. The support plate is to be .50 inch or 12 millimeters thick. The length and width dimensions are arbitrary, but there should be at least .25 [6] clearance between the gears and the support plate.
C. Draw detail drawings of the required support plates and shafts. Include dimensions and tolerances. Locate all support holes using positional tolerances.

Suggested Web sites:

www.wmberg.com
www.bostgear.com
www.newmantools.com

Do your own search for gears and bearings.

Top and end pieces omitted for clarity

Plate, Side
Shaft
Bearing
Gear
Bearing
Shaft
Plate, Base

EX13-18

The following figure shows a general setup for matched bevel gears. Complete the design for a gear box with a ratio of 3:1 between the two gears. Select appropriate bearings and fasteners. Dimension and tolerance the shaft sizes and each of the six supporting plates. Extend the input and output shafts at least 1.00 inch [24 millimeters] beyond the surface of the box.

Assume that the center distances have a tolerance of +.001, −.000 and the support shafts have a tolerance of +.0000, −.0002, or their metric equivalent.

The figure shown represents half the gear box. The other half includes another three plates without the holes for the shafts. There should be at least three screws in each edge of the box.

A. Draw an assembly drawing showing the gears in their assembled positions.
B. Support the gear shafts with ball bearings press fitted into the support plate. The support plate is to be .50 inch or 12 millimeters thick. The length and width dimensions are arbitrary, but there should be at least .375 [10] clearance between the gears and the support plates.
C. Draw detail drawings of the required support plates. Include dimensions and tolerances. Locate all support holes using positional tolerances.

EX13-19

An electrical motor operates at 1750 rpm. Design a gear system that includes at least six spur gears and reduces the motor speed to 20 rpm.

Draw the gear setups. Assume that the center distances have a tolerance of +.001, −.000, and the support shafts have tolerances of +.0000, −.0002 or their metric equivalents.

A. Draw an assembly drawing showing the gears in their assembled positions.
B. Support the gear shafts with either bushings or ball bearings press fitted into the support plate. The support plate is to be .50 inch or 12 millimeters thick. The length and width dimensions are arbitrary.
C. Draw detail drawings of the required support plates. Include dimensions and tolerances. Locate all support holes using positional tolerances.
D. Sketch several different gear configurations that generate the required 20 rpm. Consider a worm gear.

EX13-20

Objective

Design and build a cam and its supporting structure that lifts a dial indicator gage 10 millimeters and holds it there for 3 seconds. The cam should rotate at 10 rpm.

Design parameters

1. The device must include at least three gears.
2. The device may include a potentiometer, but the potentiometer many be used only to fine-tune the device. The potentiometer many not be the principal controlling device.
3. The support structure for the device must be an original design. Kit parts, such as Lego, Eitech, Errectors, and the like, may be used, but their configuration must be original.

Procurement

Parts may be derived from any source. Search the Web for kits, gears, and motors.

Suggested Web site: www.constructiontoys.com

Drawing requirements

1. A displacement diagram and a detailed final drawing of the cam.
2. An assembly drawing of the final device including a parts list.

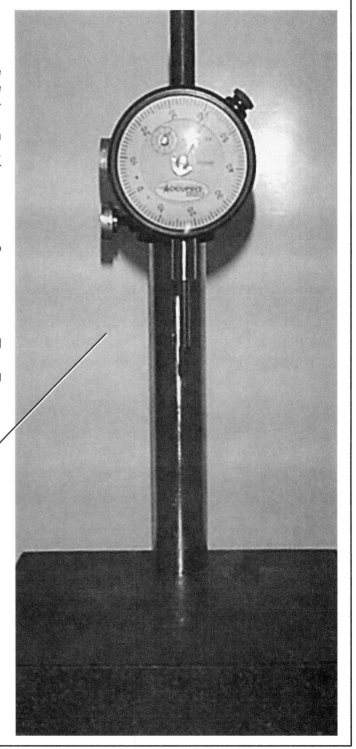

A dial indicator

EX13-21

Create the following for the slider assembly shown below.

1. Select the appropriate fasteners.
2. Create an assembly drawing.
3. Create a parts list.
4. Specify the tolerance for the Guide Shaft/Bearings interface.

Hole Plate

Guide Shaft-1

Lock Plate-2

RACK ASSEMBLY

Rack Assembly - 1

Ø7-4 HOLES

1.25 MODULE, 20° PRESSURE ANGLE

17.17

282.8

4 — 50 — 75 — 75 — 50 — 4

10

M5x0.8 - 6H ∇ 8
6 HOLES

VIEW C-C
SCALE 1 : 1

5

BASED ON: PRECISION RACK R1M-2
BERG MANUFACTURING CO.

Rack

M2.5x0.45 - 6H ∇ 6
6 HOLES

5

2.5

SIDE PLATE

Ø16
Ø10 THRU
M3.5x0.6 - 6H ∇ 4

10 — 10

PITCH Ø = 20.00
1.25 MODULE

PRECISION SPUR GEAR
BERG MANUFACTURING CO.
PART NUMBER: PBS86-16

GEAR 16

Ø19

Ø10

5

0.5X0.5 CHAMFER

BALL BEARING
BERG MANUFACTURING CO.
PART NUMBER: B11M-11

BEARING

BASE SLIDER

THUMB NUT

KNURLED THUMB NUT
BERG MANUFACTURING CO.
STOCK NUMBER: PD1M-15

LOCK PLATE - 2

GUIDE SHAFT - 1

HOLE PLATE

C H A P T E R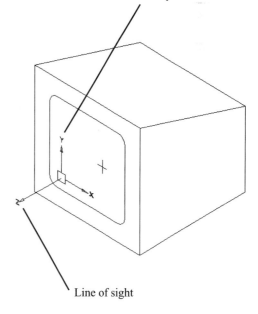

Fundamentals of 3-D Drawing

14-1 INTRODUCTION

This chapter introduces the fundamental concepts needed to produce 3-D drawings using AutoCAD. The chapter shows how to change viewpoints and how to create, save, and work with user-defined coordinate systems called *user coordinate systems,* or UCSs.

The chapter demonstrates how to use both the Viewports and UCS toolbars. It also shows how to create orthographic views from given 3-D objects using the View toolbar.

14-2 THE WORLD COORDINATE SYSTEM

AutoCAD's absolute coordinate system is called the *world coordinate system* (WCS). The default setting for the WCS is a viewing position located so that you are looking at the system 90° to its X,Y plane. See Figure 14-1. The Z axis is also perpendicular to the X,Y plane, or directly aligned with your viewpoint. This setup is ideal for 2-D drawings and is called a *plan view.* All your drawings up to now have been done in this orientation.

The World Coordinate System icon--WCS.

Line of sight

Figure 14-1

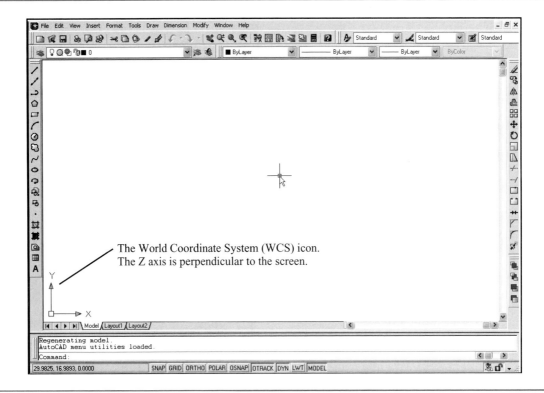

The World Coordinate System (WCS) icon.
The Z axis is perpendicular to the screen.

Figure 14-2

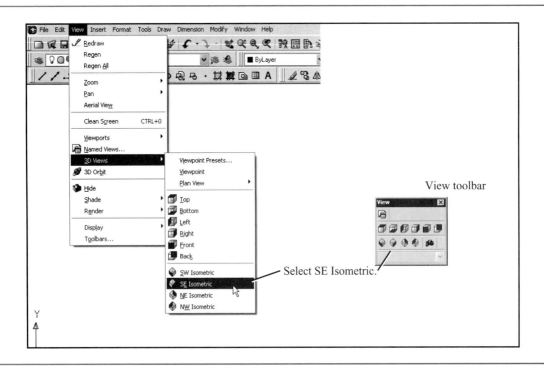

View toolbar

Select SE Isometric.

Figure 14-3

Figure 14-4

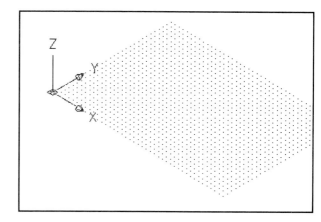

Figure 14-5

Figure 14-2 shows a standard drawing screen setup oriented so that you are looking directly down on the X,Y plane of the world coordinate system. Note the icon in the lower left corner of the screen. The box around the icon's origin indicates that it is the WCS, and the X and Y indicate the orientation of these axes. The WCS icon will always be present when you are in the world coordinate system.

14-3 VIEWPOINTS

The orientation of the WCS may be changed by changing the drawing's viewpoint. There are three ways to change the viewpoint: use the View pull-down menu, type the word *view,* or use the View toolbar.

To change the viewpoint using the View pull-down menu

This exercise assumes that the screen includes a grid. The grid serves to help define a visual orientation.

1. Select the View pull-down menu.
2. Select 3D Views.

See Figure 14-3. The current WCS orientation is the Plan View setting.

3. Select SE Isometric.

To change the viewpoint using the View command

1. Type the word *view* in response to a command prompt.

The View dialog box will appear. See Figure 14-4.

2. Select the Orthographic & Isometric Views tab, then select Southeast Isometric, then select OK.

The drawing will now be oriented as shown in Figure 14-5. Note the change in the WCS icon. It is important to remember that you are still in the WCS but are merely looking at it from a different perspective. This concept may be verified by drawing some simple shapes. Figure 14-6 shows a rectangular shape created using the Line command, and a circle created using the Circle command. These shapes are 2-D shapes drawn in the WCS.

Figure 14-6

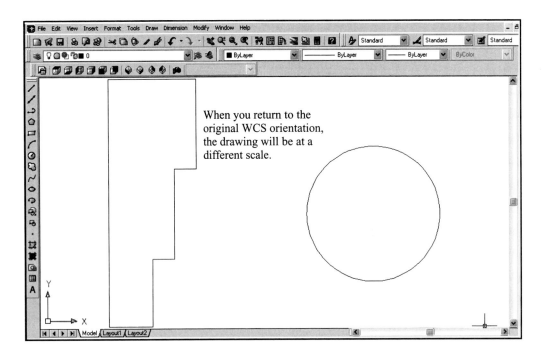

When you return to the original WCS orientation, the drawing will be at a different scale.

Figure 14-7

To return to the original WCS orientation

1. Select the View pull-down menu.
2. Select 3D Views, Plan View, World UCS.

See Figure 14-7. The drawing will reappear on the screen at a different scale than was originally defined.

3. Type zoom; press Enter.

   [All/Center/Dynamic/Extents/Previous/Scale/Window/] <real time>:

4. Type .75; press Enter.

   Figure 14-8 shows the resulting screen scale.

To change the viewpoint using the View toolbar

1. Locate the cursor on an existing toolbar and right click the mouse.
2. Select the View toolbar.

The View toolbar will appear on the screen. It can be moved and reshaped as described in Chapter 1. Figure 14-9 shows both the View toolbar and the View, 3D Views, Viewpoint Presets menus. The same commands are included in both.

3. Select the SE Isometric tool.

   The View dialog box will appear. See Figure 14-4.

Figure 14-8

Figure 14-9

4. Set the Southeast Isometric view as the current view; select OK.

The screen will return to the same orientation as was achieved using the SE Isometric command listed on the View pull-down menu, Figure 14-4. The scale will be larger, so use the Zoom command to achieve a smaller scale.

5. Type zoom; press Enter.

    All/Center/Dynamic/Extents/Left/Previous/Vmax/ Window/<Scale(X/XP)>:

6. Type .75; press Enter.

To return to the original WCS orientation

1. Select the Top tool from the View toolbar.

The original plan view orientation will return to the screen. Use the Zoom command to reduce the drawing's scale size if necessary. In Figure 14-10 a Zoom scale factor of .50 was used.

It is suggested that you try several of the View toolbar commands and watch how the WCS icon and grid pattern change. Remember that the Top View command will return the plan view in WCS orientation.

Drawing with a Zoom scale factor of .50

Figure 14-10

14-4 USER COORDINATE SYSTEMS (UCSs)

User coordinate systems are coordinate systems that you define relative to the WCS. Drawings often contain several UCSs. UCSs can be saved and recalled.

Figure 14-11 shows a wedge oriented using the SE Isometric View icon. This section assumes that a wedge shape already exists on the screen and will create a UCS aligned with the slanted surface of the wedge.

To create a UCS

1. Locate the cursor on an existing toolbar and right click the mouse.
2. Select the UCS toolbar.

The UCS toolbar will appear on the screen. As with viewpoints, UCS-related commands can be accessed through a toolbar or through pull-down menus. Figure 14-12 shows the UCS toolbar, the UCS tool, and the UCS pull-down menus. When the UCS tool is used, the available options are listed in the prompt on the command line.

Figure 14-11

Figure 14-12

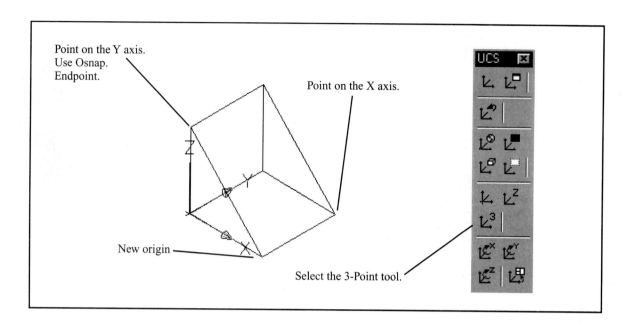

Point on the Y axis.
Use Osnap.
Endpoint.

Point on the X axis.

New origin

Select the 3-Point tool.

Figure 14-13

3. Select the 3-Point UCS tool.

   Specify new origin point <0,0,0>:

4. Select the lower corner of the wedge as shown in Figure 14-13.

   Specify point on positive portion of the X-axis <5.0000,0.0000,0.0000>:

   The given coordinate values are the coordinate values of the new origin point relative to the WCS.

5. Select the lower right corner of the wedge.

   Specify point on the positive-Y portion of the UCS XY plane <3.0000,0.0000,0.00000>:

6. Select the upper left corner of the wedge.

   It is imperative that the Endpoint option of the Object Snap command be used to locate the point. If the Object Snap option is not on, the crosshair will move only in the current coordinate plane. In this exercise we are still in the WCS because the new UCS has not been completely defined yet. If you were to try to select the upper corner of the wedge visually, that is, by moving the crosshairs so that they appeared to be located on the corner, you would get an incorrect result. The selected point would actually be a point on the WCS directly behind the corner point. Figure 14-14 shows the reoriented coordinate system.

The new UCS is aligned with the slanted surface.

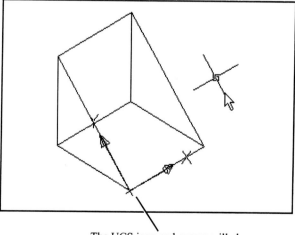

The UCS icon and cursor will change orientation to align with the new UCS.

Figure 14-14

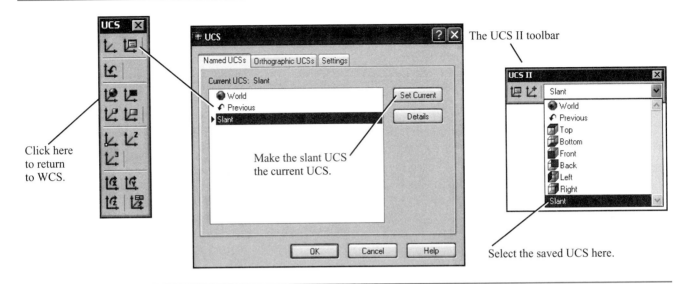

Figure 14-15

To save a UCS

It is helpful to save defined UCSs so that if they are needed again during the preparation of the drawing, they will not have to be redefined.

1. Select the UCS from the UCS toolbar.

    Enter an option [New/Move/orthoGraphic/Prev/ Restore/Save/Del/Apply/?/World]<World>:

2. Type s; press Enter.

    Enter name to save current UCS or [?]:

3. Type slant; press Enter.

The new UCS named Slant has been saved and can be retrieved using the Display UCS Dialog tool on the UCS toolbar and selecting the Slant UCS listed on the UCS dialog box or by selecting directly from the listing on the UCS II toolbar. See Figure 14-15.

To return to the WCS

There are several ways to return to the WCS: select the World option on the UCS II toolbar, select the World option from the UCS dialog box, select the World UCS from the 3D Views. Plan View options under the View pull-down menu, or click on the World UCS tool on the UCS toolbar.

14-5 WORKING WITH UCSs

Drawing with AutoCAD in 3-D is limited to the UCS orientation. You can draw only in the current UCS, as shown in Figure 14-16. You cannot draw a circle on the slanted surface of the wedge or on the side or back surfaces of the wedge using the current UCS orientation. You must draw on a surface oriented to the surface you wish to work on.

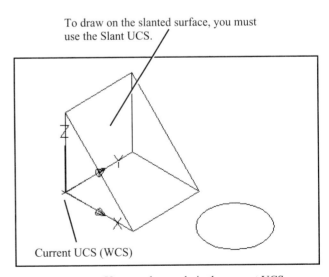

You can draw only in the current UCS, in this example, the WCS.

Figure 14-16

To draw on a slanted surface

To draw on the slanted surface shown in Figure 14-16, you must first move to a UCS oriented to the slanted surface. A UCS named Slant was created in the previous section, so we will return to that UCS and then draw a circle. The procedure is as follows.

1. Select the Slant UCS from the UCS II toolbar.

   The screen is reoriented to the Slant UCS settings.

2. Use the Circle tool to draw the circle.

   See Figure 14-17.

3. Select the World UCS icon to return to the original drawing orientation.

To draw on a surface perpendicular to the WCS X,Y axes—X axis rotation

The side surface of the wedge is perpendicular to the WCS X,Y axes. To draw on the side surface we must reorient the current surface UCS to be aligned with the side surface. In addition, we must also align the origin of the axis with the side surface.

1. Select the X Axis Rotate UCS tool from the UCS toolbar.

   Specify rotation angle about X axis <90>:

2. Press Enter.

In the example shown, the corner of the wedge was drawn directly on the WCS origin. If it were not, the origin of the new UCS would have to be moved to the side surface.

3. Use the Circle tool to draw a circle on the side surface of the wedge.

   See Figure 14-18.

4. Select the World tool on the UCS toolbar to return the drawing to its original WCS orientation.

To draw on a surface perpendicular to the WCS X,Y axes—preset UCSs

AutoCAD includes a group of preset UCS orientations. Figure 14-19 shows the Orthographic UCSs option in the UCS dialog box. The preset orientations are set up to help generate standard orthographic views. The icons in the dialog box can also be used to return to the last UCS you were working on, or to return to the WCS.

1. Select Name UCS from the UCS toolbar.
2. Select the Orthographic UCSs option.
3. Select Front UCS.
4. Select Set Current, then OK.

The drawing icon will shift positions, because the drawing is no longer in the WCS.

The preset UCSs can also be accessed using the UCS II toolbar.

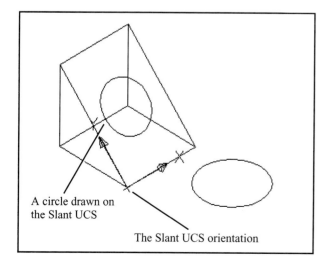

A circle drawn on the Slant UCS

The Slant UCS orientation

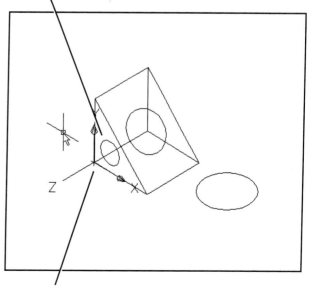

A circle drawn in the current UCS.

The UCS rotated 90° about the current WCS X axis

Figure 14-17

Figure 14-18

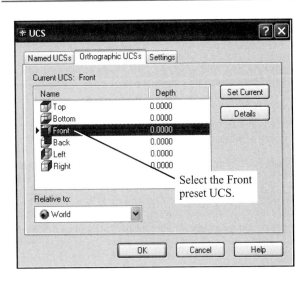

Figure 14-19

5. Go to the UCS II toolbar and select the Front preset UCS from the list.

See Figure 14-20.

To move a UCS origin

1. Select the Origin tool from the UCS toolbar.

   Specify new origin point<0,0,0>:

2. Select the new origin point.

The origin can also be moved using the Move UCS option under the Tools pull-down menu.

Figure 14-21

Select the Front preset UCS.

Figure 14-20

14-6 SAMPLE PROBLEM SP14-1

Figure 14-21 shows an L-shaped object. This section assumes that a 3-D L-shaped object, as shown in Figure 14-21, already exists on the screen. The toolbars shown in Figures 14-9 and 14-12 show that the commands listed in the View and New UCS menus under the View and Tool pull-down menus, respectively, are directly equivalent to the View and UCS toolbars.

To avoid visual errors

When working in 3-D, it is important to remember that you cannot rely on visual inputs to locate shapes. What you see may be misleading. For example, Figure 14-22

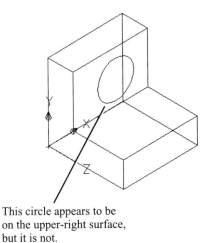

This circle appears to be on the upper-right surface, but it is not.

Figure 14-22

shows a circle that appears to be drawn on the upper right surface of an L-shaped object. In fact, the circle is not located on the surface. Figure 14-23 shows a 3-D view and a top view of the same drawing. The circle appears to be located on the surface because of the line of sight of the current viewpoint orientation, but it is actually drawn behind the surface and off the object. This visual distortion can be avoided by ensuring that the origin for the current UCS is located on the plane where you are working.

To locate the screen icon on the current origin

To help avoid visual errors based on an incorrectly located origin, it is best to set the screen icon so that it is located directly on the current origin.

1. Select the View pull-down menu.

See Figure 14-24.

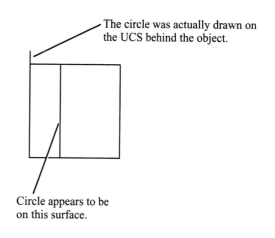

The circle was actually drawn on the UCS behind the object.

Circle appears to be on this surface.

Figure 14-23

2. Select Display, then UCS Icon.
3. Select Origin.

There should be a check mark to the left of the word *On*. After Origin has been selected, there should be check marks next to both the words *On* and *Origin*. The screen icon should move to the current origin: 0,0,0 on the WCS. See Figure 14-25.

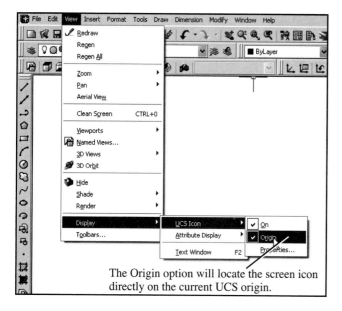

The Origin option will locate the screen icon directly on the current UCS origin.

Figure 14-24

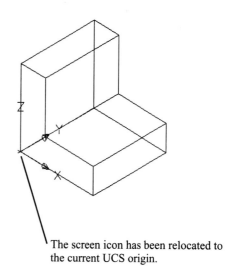

The screen icon has been relocated to the current UCS origin.

Figure 14-25

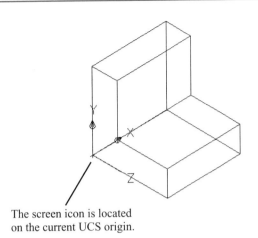

The screen icon is located on the current UCS origin.

Figure 14-26

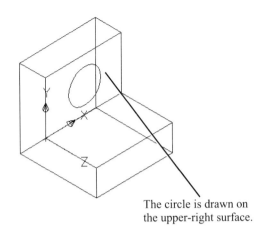

The circle is drawn on the upper-right surface.

Figure 14-28

To draw in the right plane of an object using preset UCSs

This section will draw a circle on the inside right plane of the object shown in Figure 14-21.

1. Select the Right tool from the UCS II toolbar.

The screen icon and grid pattern will change as shown in Figure 14-26. It is important to note that the origin of the current Right UCS is still located at the 0,0,0 point on the WCS. If you try to draw now, the shapes will be located on a plane aligned with the 0,0,0 origin. The origin must be moved before you can draw on the inside right surface of the object.

2. Select the Origin UCS tool from the UCS toolbar.

   Specify new origin point<0,0,0>:

3. Use Osnap, Endpoint (Shift key, right mouse button) and select the lower left corner of the inside right surface.

The origin of the Right UCS is now located at the lower left corner of the inside right surface of the object. The screen icon will move to this new origin location. See Figure 14-27. The new UCS will be listed as an unnamed UCS until a name is entered.

4. Use the Circle tool to draw a circle as shown in Figure 14-28.

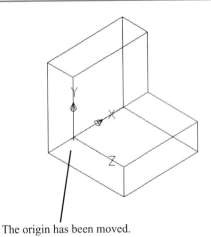

The origin has been moved.

Figure 14-27

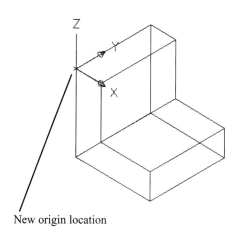

New origin location

Figure 14-29

To draw more complex shapes on UCSs

In this section, a slot shape will be drawn on the upper top surface of the object shown in Figure 14-28. The shape can be drawn directly on the surface once a UCS has been established, but in this exercise we will change the view orientation to create a 2-D drawing surface.

1. Select World from the UCS II toolbar.
2. Select Origin from the UCS toolbar.

   Origin point<0,0,0>:

3. Use Osnap, Endpoint (Shift key, right mouse button) and select the lower left corner of the upper top surface.

The screen icon will shift to the designated origin corner. See Figure 14-29.

4. Select Top View from the View toolbar.

   The View dialog box will appear.

5. Make the Top view the current view.

   The View dialog box can also be accessed using Named Views on the View pull-down menu.

6. Type Zoom; press Enter.

   All/Center/Dynamic/Extents/Left/Previous/Vmax/Window/<Scale(X/XP)>:

7. Type .75; press Enter.

   A top view of the object appears on the screen, as shown in Figure 14-30. Note that AutoCAD color codes the view and UCS icons to prevent confusion. The preset UCSs designates the orientation using red, and the named views uses cyan.

8. Use the Line, Circle, and Trim tools to create the slot shape shown in Figure 14-31.
9. Select the SE Isometric View tool.

   The object will appear oversized. Use the Zoom command to reduce its appearance and size.

10. Type Zoom; press Enter.

   All/Center/Dynamic/Extents/Left/Previous/Vmax/Window/<Scale(X/XP)>:

11. Type .75; press Enter.

   Your screen should look like Figure 14-32.

12. Select the World command to return to the original WCS orientation.

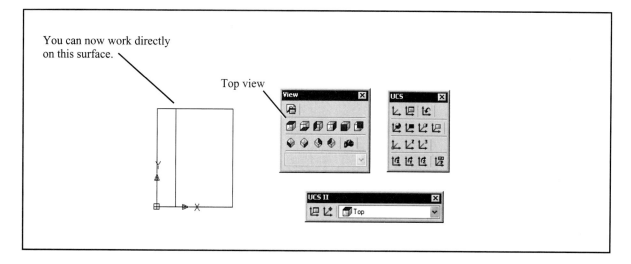

You can now work directly on this surface.

Top view

Figure 14-30

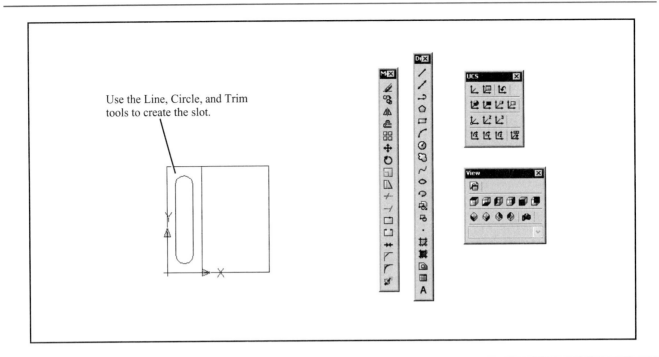

Use the Line, Circle, and Trim tools to create the slot.

Figure 14-31

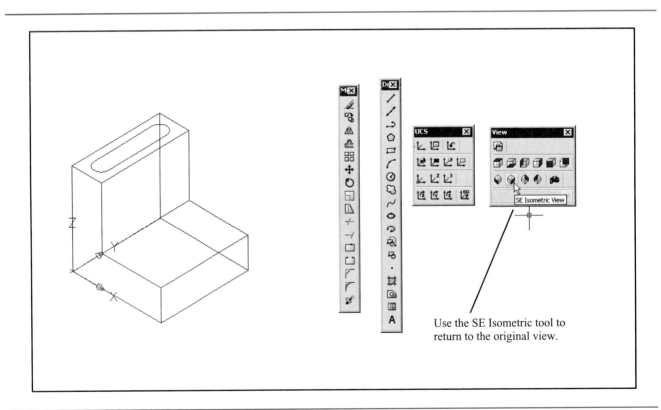

Use the SE Isometric tool to return to the original view.

Figure 14-32

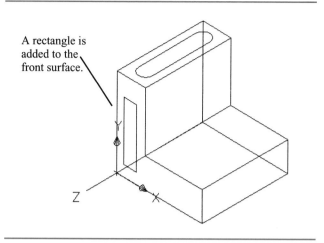

A rectangle is added to the front surface.

Z

Figure 14-33

To draw on the front surface

1. Select the Front tool from the UCS II toolbar.

The screen icon will appear at the lower left corner of the front surface because this corner of the object was originally located on the origin of the WCS. It is not necessary to relocate the origin.

2. Use the Line tool to draw a rectangular shape on the Front surface as shown in Figure 14-33.

The rectangular shape may appear to be out of visual perspective as you draw it, but it will be drawn in the correct orientation after the corner points are defined.

3. Use the World command to return to the original WCS orientation.

14-7 ORTHOGRAPHIC VIEWS

Once a 3-D object has been created, orthographic views may be taken directly from the object. The screen is first split into four ports, each showing the 3-D object. The viewpoint of three of the ports will be changed to create the front, top, and right-side views of the object.

To create four viewports

1. Select the View pull-down menu.

   See Figure 14-34.

2. Select Viewports, 4 Viewports.

Select 4 Viewports

Figure 14-34

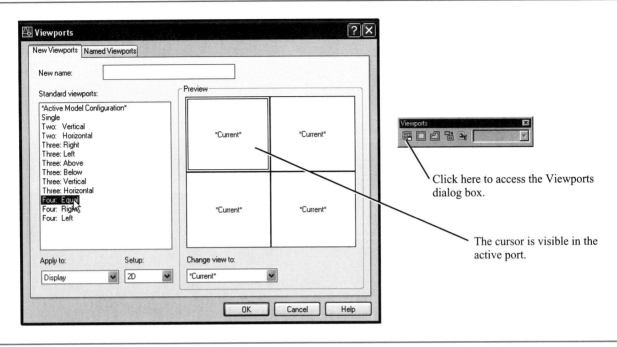

Figure 14-35

The four viewports can also be created using the Viewports toolbar.

3. Select from the Viewports toolbar.

The Viewports dialog box will appear. See Figure 14-35.

4. Select Four: Equal, then OK.

See Figure 14-36. Note that the crosshairs are visible only in the active viewport. An arrow will appear if the cursor is moved into any other port.

To create orthographic views

1. Move the cursor into the top left port and press the left mouse button.

This will make this viewport the current viewport, and the crosshairs will appear in the port.

Figure 14-36

Figure 14-37

2. Select the Top tool from the View toolbar.

    The View dialog box will appear.

3. Make the Top view the current view.

    An oversized top view of the object will appear in the port.

4. Type Zoom; press Enter.

All/Center/Dynamic/Extents/Left/Previous/Vmax/ Window/<Scale(X/XP)>:

5. Type 1; press Enter.

    See Figure 14-37. Repeat the proceedure and make the lower left port the front view and the lower right port the right view. Figure 14-38 shows the completed orthographic views.

Figure 14-38

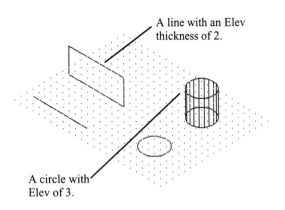

A line with an Elev thickness of 2.

A circle with Elev of 3.

Figure 14-39

14-8 ELEV

The Elev (elevation) command is used to create surfaces from 2-D drawing commands. Figure 14-39 shows a line and a circle drawn as normal 2-D entities and then drawn a second time with the Elev command thickness set for 2 and 3, respectively. The Line command generates a plane perpendicular to the plane of the original line, and the Circle command generates a cylinder perpendicular to the plane of the base circle.

To use the Elev command

There is no icon for the Elev command. It is accessed by typing Elev in response to a command prompt. In the following example, Grid and Snap have .5 spacing using decimal units, and there is an SE Isometric viewpoint.

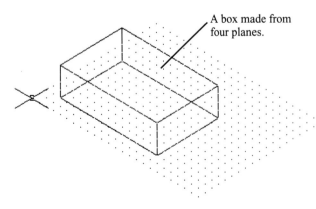

A box made from four planes.

Figure 14-40

Command:

1. Type Elev; press Enter.

    Specify new default elevation <0.0000>:

    The current elevation is the base plane for the constructions. In this example the base plane is the current X,Y (WCS) plane, that is, the plane with the grid.

2. Press Enter.

    Specify new default thickness <0.0000>:

    The thickness defines the height of the generated planes. It is currently set at 0.0000, so any shapes drawn have no thickness; that is, they are two dimensional.

3. Type 2; press Enter.

    The height of the elevation is now set for 2 units.

4. Select the Line tool.

    Command: _line
    From point:

5. Draw the box shape shown in Figure 14-40.

    The shape shown in the figure is not a box, but is four perpendicular planes. There is no top or bottom surface.

    The default thickness value may also be defined using the Properties command on the Modify pull-down menu. The Properties dialog box will appear. See Figure 14-41. Change the thickness value to 2.0000.

Specify the default thickness value here.

Figure 14-41

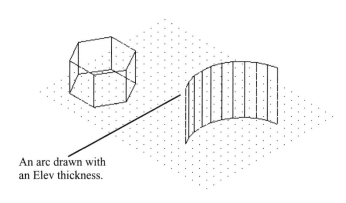

An arc drawn with
an Elev thickness.

Figure 14-42

Figure 14-42 shows a hexagon and an arc drawn with the Elev command set at thickness values of 2 and 4, respectively.

To draw a curve using Elev (See Figure 14-43.)

1. Type Elev; press Enter.

   Specify new default elevation <0.0000>:

2. Press Enter.

   Specify new default thickness <0.0000>:

3. Type 3.5; press Enter.
4. Select the Polyline tool from the Draw toolbar.

   Command: _pline
   Specify start point:

5. Draw a polyline approximately like the one shown in Figure 14-43.
6. Select the Edit Polyline tool from the Modify II toolbar.

   Command: _pedit
   Select polyline:

7. Select the Polyline.

   Enter an option [Close/Join/Width/Edit vertex/Fit/ Spline Decurve/Ltype gen/Undo]:

8. Type f; press Enter twice.

   See Figure 14-44.

14-9 USING THE ELEV COMMAND TO CREATE OBJECTS

The Elev command can be used with different UCSs to create simulated 3-D objects. The objects will actually be open-ended plane structures. The following procedure shows how to create the object shown in Figure 14-45. The drawing was created with Grid and Snap set to .5 using decimal units and with an SE Isometric viewpoint.

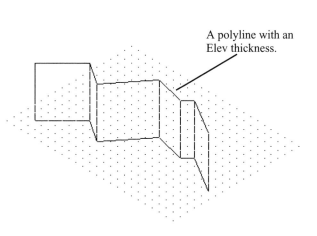

A polyline with an
Elev thickness.

Figure 14-43

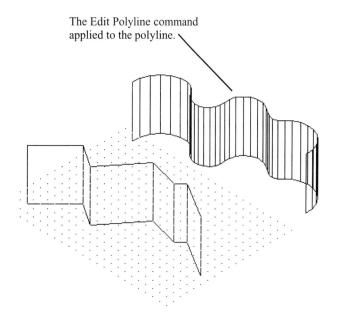

The Edit Polyline command
applied to the polyline.

Figure 14-44

Figure 14-45

The box is drawn so that its corner
is on the origin of the WCS.

Figure 14-46

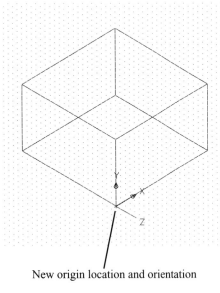

New origin location and orientation

Figure 14-47

To draw the box

1. Type Elev; press Enter.

    New current elevation <0.0000>:

2. Press Enter.

    New current thickness <0.0000>:

3. Type 6; press Enter.

    Command:

4. Select the Line tool and draw a 10 x 10 box as shown in Figure 14-46.

To create a new UCS

1. Select the Right tool from the UCS II toolbar.
2. Select the Origin command from the UCS toolbar.

    Specify new origin point <0,0,0>:

3. Select the lower right corner as shown in Figure 14-47.

To draw the right cylinder

This cylinder will be 6 units long, so there is no need to change the Elev thickness setting.

1. Select the Circle tool and draw a cylinder centered on the right face of the box.

    The coordinate value for the cylinder's center point is 5,3 and the radius value is 2.00. See Figure 14-48.

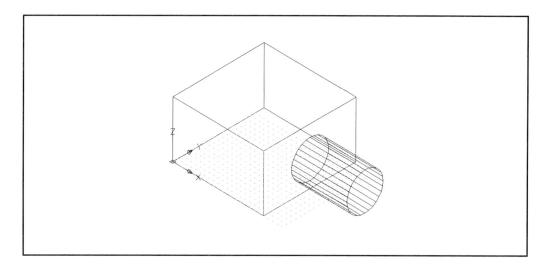

Figure 14-48

To draw the top cylinder

First return the drawing to the original WCS X,Y axes, then change the location of the X,Y plane so the top cylinder can be drawn in the correct position.

1. Select the World tool from the UCS toolbar.
2. Type Elev; press Enter.

   Specify new default elevation <0.0000>:

3. Type 6; press Enter.

The value 6 is used because this is the thickness of the box.

Specify new default thickness <6.0000>:

4. Type 4; press Enter.

Note the shift in the grid pattern. The WCS origin icon is still located at the same place, but the grid origin is on the top surface. See Figure 14-49. Positions on the top surface may be located using the displayed coordinate values.

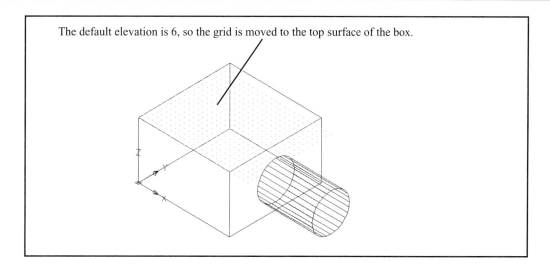

The default elevation is 6, so the grid is moved to the top surface of the box.

Figure 14-49

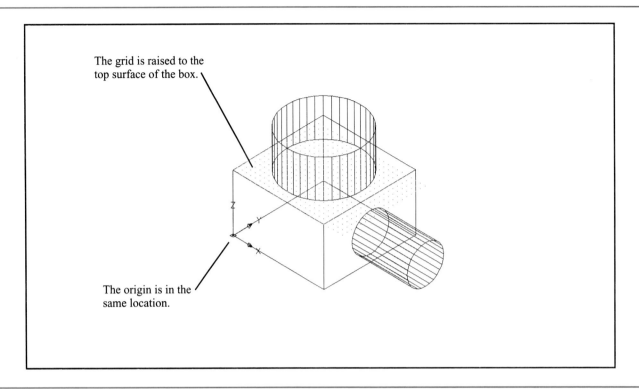

The grid is raised to the top surface of the box.

The origin is in the same location.

Figure 14-50

5. Select the Circle tool and draw the cylinder as shown in Figure 14-50.

   The cylinder's center point is at 5,5 and its radius = 2.

To return the drawing to its original settings

1. Type Elev; press Enter.

   New current elevation <6.0000>:

2. Type 0; press Enter.

   New current thickness <4.0000>:

3. Type 0; press Enter.

   The object should look like the one shown in Figure 14-50.

14-10 EXERCISE PROBLEMS

Exercise problems EX14-1 to EX14-4 require you to draw 2-D shapes on various surfaces of 3-D objects created using the Elev command. All 2-D shapes should be drawn at the center of the surfaces on which they appear.

A. Draw the 2-D shapes as shown.
B. Divide the screen into four viewports, and create front, top, and right-side orthographic views for each object.

EX14-1 INCHES

EX14-2 MILLIMETERS

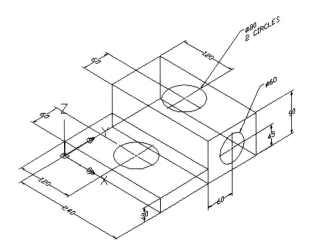

EX14-3 MILLIMETERS

Both cylinders are centered on the top surfaces as shown.

EX14-4 MILLIMETERS

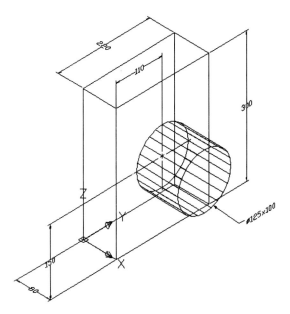

Redraw the figures presented in Exercise Problems EX14-5 to EX14-17 as wire frame models using the Elev command. Divide the screen into four viewports and create front, top, and right-side orthographic views and one isometric view as shown in Figure 14-38.

EX14-5 INCHES

Box a: X = 6, Y = 5, Z = 2
Box b: X = 4, Y = 4, Z = 4
Box c: X = 5, Y = 2, Z = 1

Hint: Consider a modified version of the NE Isometric viewpoint.

EX14-6 INCHES

Box a: X = 8, Y = 8, Z = 1
Box b: X = 6, Y = 6, Z = 2
Box c: X = 2, Y = 2, Z = 6

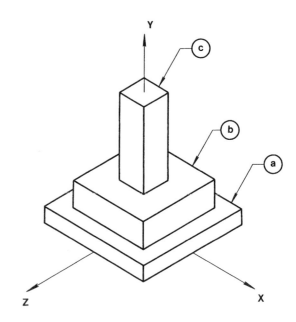

EX14-7 MILLIMETERS

Each box is 2 × 2 × 5.

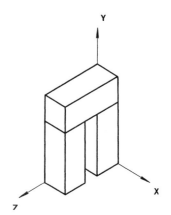

EX14-8 MILLIMETERS

Cylinder a: Ø10 × 30 LONG
Cylinder b: Ø20 × 8 LONG
Cylinder c: Ø35 × 18 LONG

EX14-10 MILLIMETERS

EX14-9 MILLIMETERS

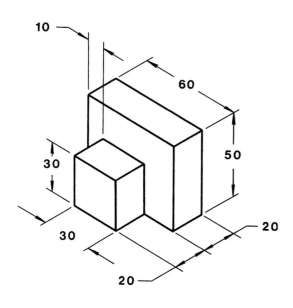

EX14-11 MILLIMETERS

Cylinders are 30 LONG.

EX14-12 MILLIMETERS

EX14-14 MILLIMETERS

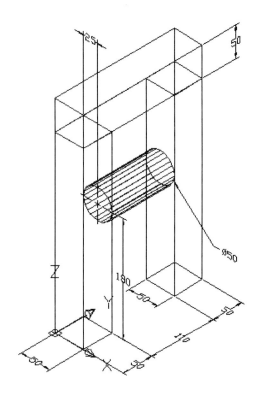

EX14-13 MILLIMETERS

The Ø12 cylinder is 20 LONG.
The Ø20 cylinder is 12 LONG.

EX14-15 MILLIMETERS

EX14-16 MILLIMETERS

EX14-17 MILLIMETERS

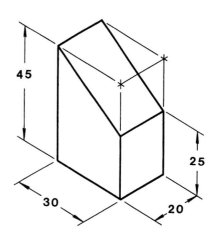

CHAPTER 15

Surface Modeling

15-1 INTRODUCTION

This chapter introduces surface modeling. Surface modeling creates 3-D objects by joining surfaces together. The Surface commands are accessed using the Surfaces toolbar (see Figure 15-1) or by using the Draw pull-down menu, then selecting Surfaces, then 3D Surfaces. See Figure 15-2. AutoCAD's surface commands generate what AutoCAD calls "faceted surfaces using a polygonal mesh." This means that the curved surfaces generated are only mathematical approximations and not true, smooth surfaces. The approximations are, however, very accurate and present minimal visual distortion.

Surface modeling is different from solid modeling. Surface modeling deals only with individual surfaces, whereas solid modeling deals with entire solid shapes. A box created as a surface model comprises six surfaces. A box created using solid modeling is a solid object with six sides. Surface models cannot be unioned or subtracted as can solid models.

Surface modeling is particularly well suited for drawing complex 3-D meshes, such as might be found on a surface profile map, or for the transition area between an airfoil and the fuselage on an aircraft.

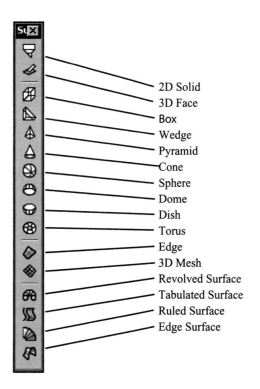

2D Solid
3D Face
Box
Wedge
Pyramid
Cone
Sphere
Dome
Dish
Torus
Edge
3D Mesh
Revolved Surface
Tabulated Surface
Ruled Surface
Edge Surface

Figure 15-1

Figure 15-2

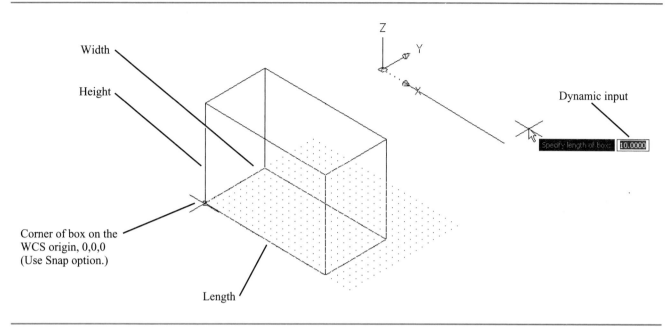

Figure 15-3

15-2 BOX

The Box command is used to draw a box comprising six surfaces. See Figure 15-3. The command sequence is as follows.

To draw a box

1. Select the Box tool from the Surfaces toolbar.

    Command: ai_box
    Specify corner point of box:

2. Select a corner location for the box.

    In the example shown, the coordinate display was used to locate the corner point on the 0,0,0 WCS origin. The Snap option was on. The corner could have been defined using a 3-D coordinate value (X, Y, Z).

3. Move the cursor until the cursor display reads 0,0,0; press the left mouse button.

    Specify length of box:

4. Type 10; press Enter or use dynamic input to define the length.

    The length can also be determined by moving the crosshairs and then picking a random point, using Osnap to align with an existing entity, or using the values displayed in the coordinate display box.

    Specify width of box or [cube]:

5. Type 5; press Enter.

If the box is a cube, enter a C response instead of a width value. AutoCAD will automatically take the length value and apply it to the width and height, skipping the width and height prompts in the sequence.

Specify height of box:

6. Type 7; press Enter.

    Specify rotation angle of box about the Z axis or [Reference]:

    AutoCAD is now in a dynamic mode, meaning that as you move the crosshairs, the box will rotate about a Z axis projected out of the original corner point.

7. Type 0; press Enter.

15-3 WEDGE

The wedge in this example will be drawn aligned with the box drawn in Section 15-2. See Figure 15-4.

To draw a wedge

1. Select the wedge tool from the Surfaces toolbar.

    Command: ai_wedge
    Specify corner point of wedge:

2. Use Osnap, Endpoint (press the Shift key and right mouse button simultaneously) and select the lower right corner of the box.

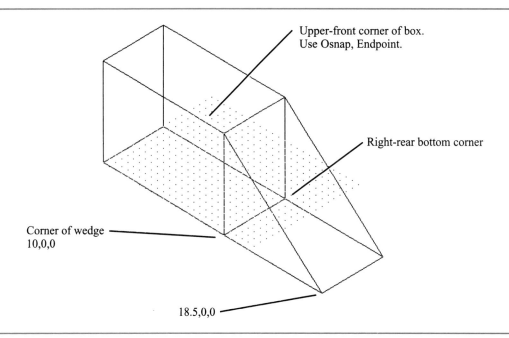

Upper-front corner of box.
Use Osnap, Endpoint.

Right-rear bottom corner

Corner of wedge
10,0,0

18.5,0,0

Figure 15-4

Specify length of wedge:

3. Move the crosshair away from the corner until the dynamic input reads 18.5,0,0; press the left mouse button.

Specify width of wedge:

4. Use Osnap, Endpoint and select the right-rear bottom corner of the box.

Specify height of wedge:

5. Use Osnap, Endpoint and select the upper front corner of the box as shown in Figure 15-4.

Specify rotation angle of wedge about the Z axis:

6. Type 0; press Enter.

The box and the wedge are not joined objects. Each has a surface that occupies the same space, but they are still two individual entities.

7. Clear the screen using the Erase tool.

15-4 PYRAMID

There are several different types of pyramids. Pyramids may have triangular, rectangular, or square bases. Any polygon can be used as the base of a pyramid, but the

Surfaces toolbar commands are limited to triangular and rectangular bases. Polygons with more points can be used with the solid modeling options.

A tetrahedron is a pyramid made from three triangles. Pyramids whose apexes are located directly over the center point of their base polygons are called *right pyramids. Pyramids* whose apexes are not located directly over the center point of their base polygons are called *oblique pyramids.* Pyramids with their top sections removed are called *truncated pyramids,* and pyramids whose tops are edges and not point apexes are called *ridged pyramids.*

To draw a rectangular pyramid (See Figure 15-5.)

1. Select the Pyramid tool from the Surfaces toolbar.

Command: ai_pyramid
Specify first corner point for base pyramid:

2. Type 0,0; press Enter.

Specify second corner point for base of pyramid:

3. Press F8 to turn the Ortho command on.
4. Move the crosshairs to the 8,0 point, and press the left mouse button.

Specify third corner point for base of pyramid:

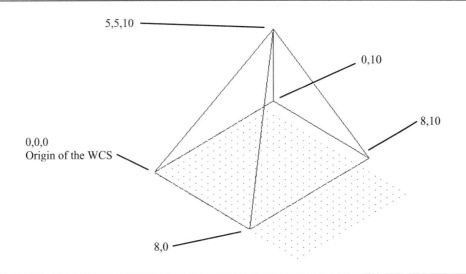

5,5,10
0,10
8,10
0,0,0
Origin of the WCS
8,0

Figure 15-5

5. Move the crosshairs to the 8,10 point and press the left mouse button.

    Specify fourth corner point for base of pyramid or [Tetrahedron]:

6. Move the crosshairs to the 0,10 point and press the left mouse button.

    Specify apex point of pyramid or [Right/Top]:

    The apex point location requires a Z component. All the previous points have been in the X, Y plane, so only X

and Y coordinates were necessary. The apex point can be located randomly; that is, you can simply move the crosshairs and select a point, but this procedure can be visually misleading. It is better to use either coordinate values or the Osnap command to locate a pyramid's apex.

7. Type 5,5,10; press Enter.

    A negative Z value could have been entered.

To draw a tetrahedron (See Figure 15-6.)

1. Select the Pyramid tool from the Surfaces toolbar.

    Command: ai_pyramid
    Specify first corner point for base of pyramid:

2. Type 0,0; press Enter.

    Specify second corner point for base of pyramid:

3. Type 8,2; press Enter.

    Specify third corner point for base of pyramid:

4. Type 2,8; press Enter.

    Specify fourth corner point for base of pyramid or [Tetrahedron]:

5. Type T; press Enter.

    Specify apex point of tetrahedron or [Top]:

6. Type 3,3,10; press Enter.

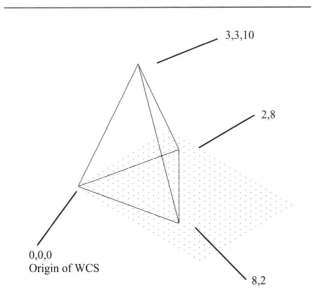

3,3,10
2,8
0,0,0
Origin of WCS
8,2

Figure 15-6

A truncated pyramid

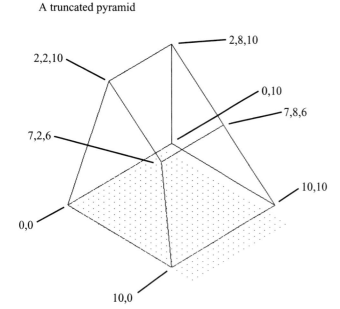

Figure 15-7

An oblique pyramid

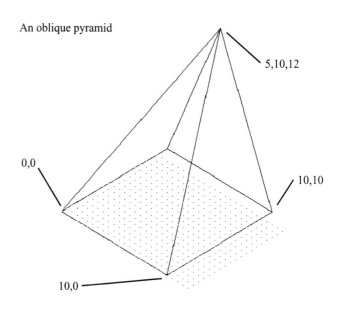

Figure 15-8

To draw a truncated pyramid (See Figure 15-7.)

1. Select the Pyramid tool from the Surfaces toolbar.

   Command: ai_pyramid
   Specify first corner point for pyramid:

2. Type 0,0; press Enter.

   Specify second corner point for the base of pyramid:

3. Type 10,0; press Enter.

   Specify third corner point for base of pyramid:

4. Type 10,10; press Enter.

   Specify fourth corner point for base of pyramid or [Tetrahedron]:

5. Type 0,10; press Enter.

   Specify apex point of pyramid or [Ridge/Top]:

6. Type t; press Enter.

   Specify first corner point for top of pyramid:

7. Type 2,2,10; press Enter.

   Remember that top points are not in the base plane and therefore their coordinate values require a Z component. Also note that a line will appear from the crosshairs to the corner point whose top point is being defined.

Specify second corner point for top of pyramid:

8. Type 7,2,6; press Enter.

   Specify third corner point for top of pyramid:

9. Type 7,8,6; press Enter.

   Specify fourth corner point for top of pyramid:

10. Type 2,8,10; press Enter.

To draw an oblique pyramid (See Figure 15-8.)

1. Select the Pyramid tool from the Surfaces toolbar.

   Command: ai_pyramid
   Specify first corner point for base of pyramid:

2. Type 0,0; press Enter.

   Specify second corner point for base of pyramid:

3. Type 10,0; press Enter.

   Specify third corner point for base of pyramid:

4. Type 10,10; press Enter.

   Specify fourth corner point for base of pyramid or [Tetrahedron]:

5. Type 0,10; press Enter.

   Specify apex point of pyramid or [Ridge/Top]:

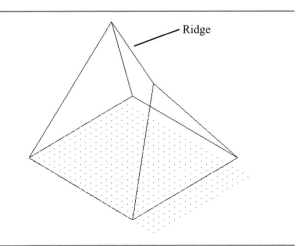

Figure 15-9

6. Type 5,10,12; press Enter.

This apex point is located over the center point of the rear line in the base polygon. Because the apex is not located over the base polygon's center point, the figure is classified as an oblique pyramid.

To draw a ridged pyramid (See Figure 15-9.)

1. Select the Pyramid tool from the Surfaces toolbar.

   Command: ai_pyramid
   Specify first corner point for base of pyramid:

2. Type 0,0; press Enter.

   Specify second corner point for base of pyramid:

3. Type 10,0; press Enter.

   Specify third corner point for base of pyramid:

4. Type 10,10; press Enter.

   Specify fourth corner point for base of pyramid or [Tetrahedron]:

5. Type 0,10; press Enter.

   Specify apex point of pyramid or [Ridge/Top]:

6. Type r; press Enter.

   Specify first ridge end point of pyramid:

7. Type 3,5,10; press Enter.

   Specify second ridge end point of pyramid:

8. Type 7,5,7; press Enter.

15-5 CONE (See Figure 15-10.)

To draw a cone

1. Select the Cone command

   Command: ai_cone
   Specify center point for base of cone:

2. Type 5,5; press Enter.

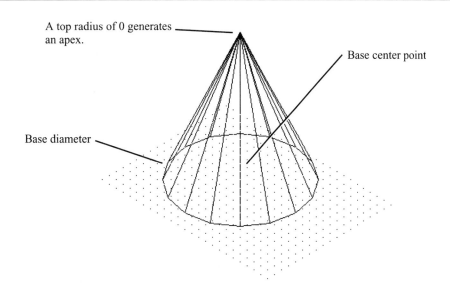

Figure 15-10

The cone's center point could also have been selected by locating a point using the crosshairs, then pressing the left mouse button.

Specify radius for base of cone or [Diameter]:

3. Type 4; press Enter.

Specify radius for top of cone or [Diameter]<0>:

A top radius of 0 will create a cone with an apex. A radius value other than 0 will create a truncated cone.

4. Press Enter.

Specify height of cone:

5. Type 9; press Enter.

Enter number of segments for surface of cone <16>:

The number of segments defines the number of facets used to show the cone. The more segments, the smaller each segment will be, and the resulting cone will appear smoother; however, a large number of segments will use more memory and will require more time to process. The default value of 16 is a good compromise between visual accuracy and drawing speed.

6. Press Enter.

To draw a truncated cone (See Figure 15-11.)

1. Select the Cone tool from the Surfaces toolbar.

   Command: ai_cone
   Specify center point for base of cone:

2. Type 5,5; press Enter.

Specify radius for base of cone or [Diameter]:

3. Type 6; press Enter.

Specify radius for top of cone or [Diameter]<0>:

4. Type 3; press Enter.

Specify height of cone:

5. Type 8; press Enter.

Enter number of segments for surface of cone <16>:

6. Press Enter.

15-6 SPHERE (See Figure 15-12.)

To draw a sphere

In this example, the sphere will be drawn above the X, Y plane.

1. Select the Sphere tool from the Surfaces toolbar.

   Command: ai_sphere
   Specify center point of sphere:

2. Type 5,5,5; press Enter.

   Specify radius of sphere or [Diameter]:

3. Type 5; press Enter.

   Specify number of longitudinal segments for surface of sphere <16>:

4. Press Enter.

Figure 15-11

Figure 15-12

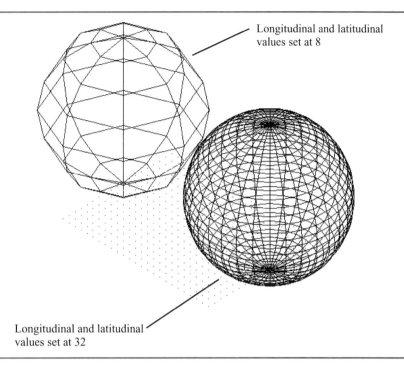

Longitudinal and latitudinal values set at 8

Longitudinal and latitudinal values set at 32

Figure 15-13

Specify number of latitudinal segments for surface of sphere <16>:

5. Press Enter.

The number of longitudinal and latitudinal segments controls the number of facets that will show on the sphere. Longitudinal lines are equivalent to vertical lines. Latitudinal lines are equivalent to horizontal lines. The more segments defined, the smoother the resulting sphere, but more line segments increase the drawing time needed to generate the sphere.

Figure 15-13 shows two spheres: one drawn with 8 longitudinal and latitudinal segments, and one drawn with 32 longitudinal and latitudinal segments. Note the differences in the overall smoothness of the visual presentation.

15-7 DOME

A *dome* is a hemisphere, or the top half of a sphere. (See Figure 15-14.)

To draw a dome

1. Select the Dome tool from the Surfaces toolbar.

   Command: ai_dome
   Specify center point of dome:

2. Type 5,5; press Enter.

   Specify radius of dome or [Diameter]:

3. Type 8; press Enter.

   Enter number of longitudinal segments for surface of dome <16>:

4. Press Enter.

   Enter number of latitudinal segments for surface of dome <8>:

5. Press Enter.

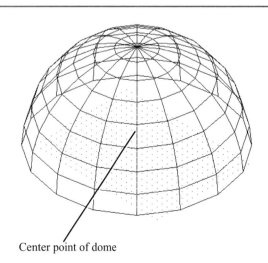

Center point of dome

Figure 15-14

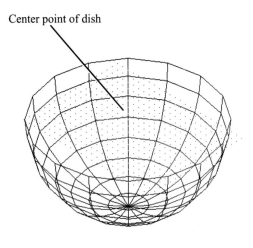

Center point of dish

Figure 15-15

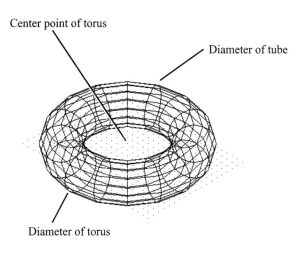

Center point of torus

Diameter of tube

Diameter of torus

Figure 15-16

15-8 DISH

A *dish* is a semisphere, or the bottom half of a sphere. (See Figure 15-15.)

To draw a dish

1. Select the Dish tool from the Surfaces toolbar.

   Command: ai_dish
   Specify center point of dish:

2. Type 5,5; press Enter.

   Specify radius or dish or [Diameter]:

3. Type 7; press Enter.

   Enter number of longitudinal segments for surface of dish <16>:

4. Press Enter.

   Enter number of latitudinal segments for surface of dish <8>:

5. Press Enter.

15-9 TORUS

A *torus* is a donutlike shape. See Figure 15-16.

To draw a torus

1. Select the Torus tool from the Surfaces toolbar.

   Command: ai_torus
   Specify center point of torus:

2. Type 5,5; press Enter.

   Specify radius of torus or [Diameter]:

3. Type 6; press Enter.

   Specify radius of tube or [Diameter]:

4. Type 1.5; press Enter.

   The radius of a torus is the distance from the center point to the outside edge of the torus, as measured along the center plane.

   Enter number of segments around the tube circumference <16>:

5. Press Enter.

   Enter number of segments around the torus circumference <16>:

6. Press Enter.

A surface created using 3-D Face

Figure 15-17

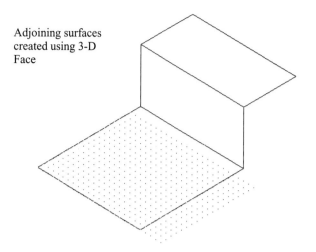

Adjoining surfaces created using 3-D Face

Figure 15-18

15-10 3-D FACE

A 3-D face is a plane. 3-D faces may be created as individual planes or as adjoining groups of planes. A 3-D face can be added to an existing 3-D object to close an open area or to create a transition between existing objects.

To draw a single 3-D face

In this example we will select points on a grid. Coordinate values can also be used to define the 3-D face's corner points. See Figure 15-17.

1. Select the 3D Face tool from the Surfaces toolbar.

   Command: _3dface
   Specify first point or [Invisible]:

2. Select the 0,0 point on the grid.

   Use the coordinate display at the lower left of the screen to verify the point location.

   Specify second point or [Invisible]:

3. Select 10,0.

   Specify third point or [Invisible]<exit>:

4. Select 10,10.

   Specify fourth point or [Invisible]<create three-sided face>:

5. Select 0,10.

   Specify third point or [Invisible]:

   This point assumes that you will also be creating an adjacent plane, but because you are not, enter a null value.

6. Press Enter.

To draw adjoining 3-D faces

In this example we will draw three adjoining planes, each 90° to the others. See Figure 15-18.

1. Select the 3D Face tool from the Surfaces toolbar.

   Command: _3dface
   Specify first point or [Invisible]:

2. Select the 0,0 point on the grid.

   Specify second point or [Invisible]:

3. Select 10,0.

   Specify third point or [Invisible]<exit>:

4. Select 10,10.

   Specify fourth point or [Invisible]<create three-sided face>:

5. Select 0,10.

   The adjoining plane will be perpendicular to the line on the Y axis.

   Specify third point or [Invisible] <exit>:

6. Type 0,10,5; press Enter.

Figure 15-19

Specify fourth point or [Invisible] <create three-sided face>:

7. Type 10,10,5; press Enter.

Specify third point or [Invisible] <exit>:

8. Type 10,15,5; press Enter.

Specify fourth point or [Invisible] <create three-sided face>:

9. Type 0,15,5; press Enter.

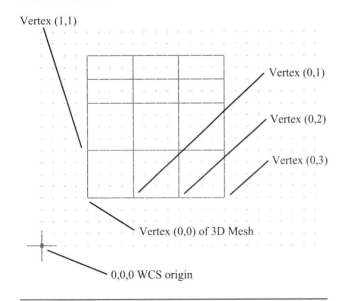

Figure 15-20

Specify third point or [Invisible] <exit>:

10. Press Enter.

15-11 3-D MESH

The 3D Mesh command defines a surface by defining a series of points on the surface. Mesh surfaces are usually irregular surfaces, that is, not flat. (See Figure 15-19.)

The points used to define a mesh surface are located in terms of M,N axes. First, the number of points in both the M and N directions is defined, then each point is automatically assigned a vertex notation. The vertex notation 0,2 means first row, that is, the first line in the M direction, and the third column, third line in the N direction. The first line in both the M and N directions is labeled 0. Figure 15-20 is a top view of the finished 3-D mesh.

Coordinate values for each mesh point are expressed in terms of their X, Y, Z values relative to the existing X, Y plane.

To draw a 3-D mesh

1. Select the 3D Mesh command.

   Command: _3dmesh
   Enter size of mesh in M direction:

2. Type 5; press Enter.

   Enter size of mesh in N direction:

3. Type 4; press Enter.

Specify location for vertex (0,0):

This prompt is asking for the first point value on the M,N axes. It is not a numerical input, but rather a point location definition relative to the M,N axis. Note that the numbers are enclosed by ( ), which means that they are not default values.

4.   Type 2,2,0; press Enter.

This input establishes the corner of the mesh surface at the 2,2,0 point on the current X, Y, Z axes.

Specify location for vertex (0,1):

5.   Type 4,2,.5; press Enter.

Specify location for vertex (0,1):

6.   Type 6,2,1; press Enter.

Specify location for vertex (0,2):

7.   Type 8,2,.5; press Enter.

Specify location for vertex (1,0):

8.   Type 2,4,.5; press Enter.

Specify location for vertex (1,1):

9.   Type 4,4,1; press Enter.

Specify location for vertex (1,2):

10. Type 6,4,1.2; press Enter.

Specify location for vertex (1,3):

11. Type 8,4,1.5; press Enter.

Specify location for vertex (2,0):

12. Type 2,6,.75.

Specify location for vertex (2,1):

13. Type 4,6,1.2; press Enter.

Specify location for vertex (2,2):

14. Type 6,6,.5; press Enter.

Specify location for vertex (2,3):

15. Type 8,6,1.7; press Enter.

Specify location for vertex (3,0):

16. Type 2,7,.7; press Enter.

Specify location for vertex (3,1):

17. Type 4,7,.1; press Enter.

Specify location for vertex (3,2):

18. Type 6,7,1.3; press Enter.

Specify location for vertex (3,3):

19. Type 8,7,1.5; press Enter.

Specify location for vertex (4,0):

20. Type 2,8,0; press Enter.

Specify location for vertex (4,1):

21. Type 4,8,.5; press Enter.

Specify location for vertex (4,2):

22. Type 6,8,1; press Enter.

Specify location for vertex (4,3):

23. Type 8,8,.5; press Enter.

15-12 REVOLVED SURFACE

A revolved surface is created by revolving a given shape about an axis of revolution. Cones, cylinders, spheres, toruses, and ellipsoids are all shapes that can be created as revolved surfaces. AutoCAD can also create unusual shapes by revolving polylines.

To create a cylinder

A cylinder can be created by revolving a line around another line. The resulting cylinder is not a solid cylinder but a cylindrical shape with open ends. It is analogous to a rolled sheet of paper. Figure 15-21 shows two lines that will be used to construct a cylinder.

1.   Select the Revolved Surface tool from the Surfaces toolbar.

     Command: _revsurf
     Current wire frame density: SURFTAB1 = 16,
     SURFTAB2 = 16
     Select object to revolve:

Figure 15-21

Figure 15-22

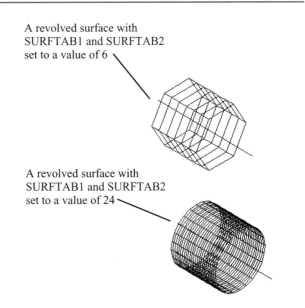

A revolved surface with SURFTAB1 and SURFTAB2 set to a value of 6

A revolved surface with SURFTAB1 and SURFTAB2 set to a value of 24

Figure 15-23

In this example the shorter of the two lines will be revolved about the longer line.

2. Select the shorter line.

Select object that defines the axis of revolution:

3. Select the longer line.

Specify start angle <0>:

Revolved shapes need not be 360°. They can be started at and ended at any angle.

4. Press Enter.

Specify included angle (+=ccw, -=cw) <360>:

This prompt reminds you that the counterclockwise direction is the positive direction. Either positive or negative values may be entered. The default value is a full circle, or 360°.

5. Press Enter.

See Figure 15-22. If the resulting cylinder doesn't look like a cylinder it is because the default system variables Surftab1 and Surftab2 are set too small for the example. Their values must be increased to produce a smooth-looking cylinder.

To change SURFTAB1 and SURFTAB2

1. Type SURFTAB1; press Enter in response to a command prompt.

Command: surftab1
Enter new value for SURFTAB1 <16>:

2. Type 24; press Enter.

Command:

3. Type SURFTAB2; press Enter.

Command: surftab2
Enter new value for SURFTAB2 <16>:

4. Type 24; press Enter.

The Surftab variables are now reset from a value of 16 to a value of 24. Figure 15-23 shows the resulting cylinder created using the Revolved Surface command.

Figure 15-24 shows a cylinder drawn perpendicular to the X, Y plane. The lines used to define the surface of revolution were defined using the X, Y, Z values of the line's endpoints. For example, the shorter vertical line was drawn between points 0,0,0 and 0,0,5.

Figure 15-24 also shows an example of a partial cylinder that was created by not revolving the line a full 360°. The partial cylinder shown was created by revolving a line 120°.

Figure 15-25 shows an object that was created by first drawing a polyline, then revolving the polyline around an axis of revolution. Any curved shape can be used to create a surface of revolution. A torus, for example, can be created by revolving a circle around an axis of revolution.

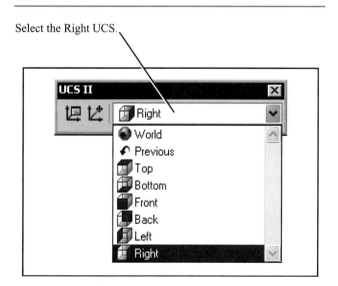

Figure 15-24

Figure 15-25

15-13 TABULATED SURFACE

A *tabulated surface* creates an object by tracking a given shape along a direction vector. Only straight lines can be used as direction vectors. A curved line may be specified as a direction vector, but AutoCAD will draw a straight line from the first point to the last point on the curve and use that straight line as the direction vector.

Tabulated surfaces often involve objects drawn in two different planes. The following example will create a cylinder by extruding a circle along a straight line. The circle will be drawn in a plane perpendicular to the plane of the line.

Figure 15-26

To draw a tabulated surface

1. Use the Line tool from the Draw toolbar to draw a line in the current X, Y plane (WCS).
2. Select Right UCS from the Modify II toolbar.

See Figure 15-26. The screen grid pattern will shift to the new UCS orientation.

3. Select the Origin tool from the UCS toolbar.
4. If necessary, use the Osnap, Endpoint commands to define the start point of the line as the new origin for the Right UCS.

See Figure 15-27.

5. Use the Circle tool from the Draw toolbar to draw a circle about the start point of the line.

See Figure 15-28.

6. Return to the WCS by selecting the World tool from the Modify II or UCS toolbar.
7. Select the Tabulated Surface tool from the Surfaces toolbar.

Command: _tabsurf
Select object for path curve:

8. Select the circle.

Select object for direction vector:

9. Select the line.

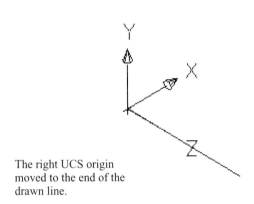

The right UCS origin moved to the end of the drawn line.

Figure 15-27

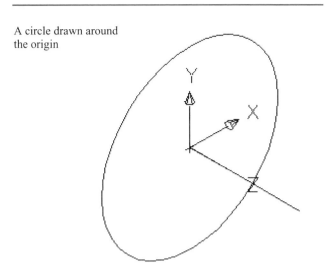

A circle drawn around the origin

Figure 15-28

Figure 15-29 shows the resulting extruded surface. The circle has been extended in the direction and length of the line. The cylinder is drawn perpendicular to the base plane, which was established as the Right UCS with its origin at the start point of the line. Had the same procedure been followed, but the other end of the line selected as the origin, the cylinder would have covered the line.

Figure 15-30 shows a polyline that was edited to form a curve. The Tabulated Surface command was then applied using a line perpendicular to the plane of the polyline as a direction vector.

15-14 RULED SURFACE

A ruled surface is created between two existing curves or between a point and a curve.

To draw a ruled surface between two curves (See Figure 15-31.)

1. Select the Ruled Surface command.

    Command: _rulesurf
    Current wire frame density: SURFTAB1=16
    Select first defining curve:

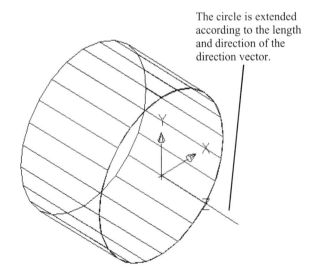

The circle is extended according to the length and direction of the direction vector.

Figure 15-29

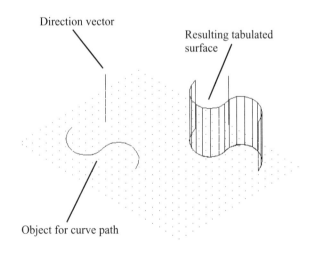

Direction vector

Resulting tabulated surface

Object for curve path

Figure 15-30

Defining curve

Resulting ruled surface

Defining curve

Figure 15-31

2. Select the straight line.

Select second defining line:

Ruled surfaces are selection-sequence dependent. Figure 15-32 shows two ruled surfaces created from the same defining curves. The differences between the resulting surfaces are the result of different selection point locations. The selection points for the defining curves for the lower left surface were the left end of each line. The selection points for the upper surface were the left end of the curved line and the right end of the straight line.

Figure 15-33 shows a ruled surface drawn between curves drawn in different planes. The left curve was drawn in the preset Right UCS, and the right curve was drawn in the WCS.

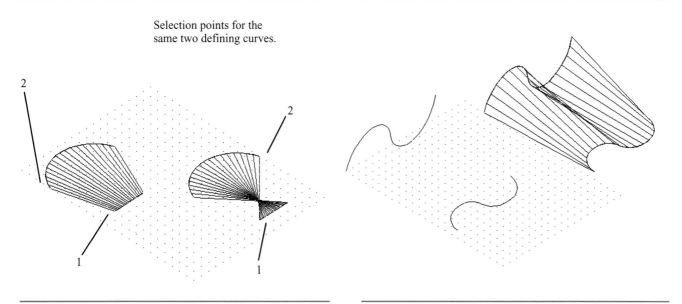

Selection points for the same two defining curves.

2

2

1

1

Figure 15-32

Figure 15-33

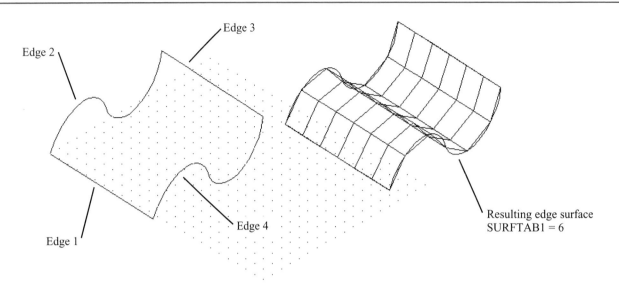

Figure 15-34

15-15 EDGE SURFACE

The Edge Surface command is used to create a surface among four existing adjoining lines. See Figure 15-34.

1. Select the Edge Surface tool from the Surfaces toolbar.

   Command: _edgesurf
   Current wire frame density: SURFTAB1=16
   Select object 1 for surface edge:

2. Select one of the lines.

   Select object 2 for surface edge:

3. Select a second line.

Select object 3 for surface edge:

4. Select a third line.

   Select object 4 for surface edge:

5. Select a fourth line.

The edge surface shown in Figure 15-34 was created with a Surftab setting of 6. Note that the surface contains a 6 × 6 pattern of rectangles. Figure 15-35 shows an edge surface created on the same four lines, but with Surftab1 and Surftab2 both set to 18. Note the difference in visual appearance.

Figure 15-36 shows an edge surface created among three 3-D polylines edited to form splines and a single straight line. Both Surftabs were set at 18.

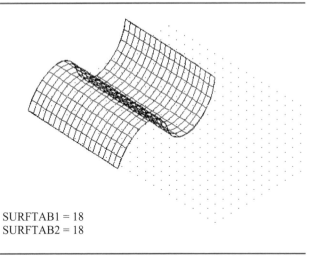

SURFTAB1 = 18
SURFTAB2 = 18

Figure 15-35

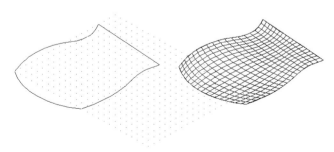

An example of an edge surface

Figure 15-36

15-16 COMBINING SURFACES

Figure 15-37 shows an object created by combining two surfaces: a cylinder and a truncated cone. The procedure is as follows. The object will be centered around the 0,0 point on the X, Y axes.

To draw the truncated cone

1. Set the Grid and Snap spacing for 0.50.
2. Select the SE Isometric View tool from the View toolbar.
3. Select the Zoom Window tool and create a zoom window around the 0,0,0 point.
4. Select the Cone tool from the Surfaces toolbar.

   Specify center point for base of cone:

5. Select 0,0,0; press Enter.

   Specify radius for base of cone or [Diameter]:

6. Type d; press Enter.

   Specify diameter for base of cone:

7. Type 1.38; press Enter.

   Specify radius for top of cone or [Diameter] <0>:

8. Type d; press Enter.

   Specify diameter for top of cone <0>:

9. Type .62; press Enter.

   Specify height of cone:

10. Type .75; press Enter.

    Enter number of segments for surface of cone <16>:

11. Press Enter.

See Figure 15-38. Use the Zoom Window tool again, if necessary, to approximate the screen size shown.

The problem now requires that a cylinder be joined to the top of the truncated cone. The Elev command can be used to create a cylinder located on top of the cone, but in this example, two circles will be drawn, then joined, using the Ruled Surface command. The cone was created using a Surface command and has no top surface. The Ruled Surface command requires an edge, and the top of the cone does not constitute an edge, so a circle must be added at the top of the cone.

Figure 15-37

A cone drawn using the Cone tool from the Surfaces toolbar.

Base = Ø1.38
Top = Ø0.62

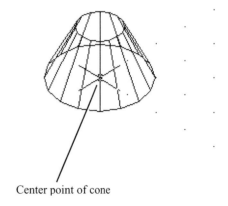

Center point of cone

Figure 15-38

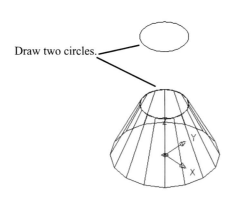

Draw two circles.

Figure 15-39

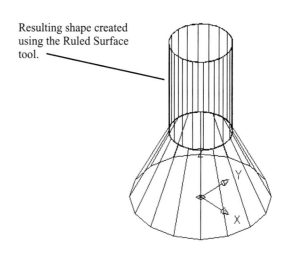

Resulting shape created using the Ruled Surface tool.

Figure 15-40

To add the cylinder to the top of the cone

1. Select the Circle tool.

   Command: _circle
   Specify center point for circle or [3P/2P/Ttr/(tan tan radius)]:

2. Type 0,0,.75; press Enter.

   Specify radius of circle or [diameter] <0.3100>:

3. Press Enter.

   There is no visual change in the object, although a tick mark may appear at the center point of the circle. The circle and the top of the cone occupy the same space.

4. Press Enter again to restart the Circle command sequence.

   Command: _circle
   Specify center point for circle or [3P/2P/Ttr/(tan tan radius)]:

5. Type 0,0,1.75; press Enter.

   Specify radius of circle or [diameter] <0.3100>:

6. Press Enter.

   See Figure 15-39.

To create the cylinder

1. Select the Ruled Surface tool from the Surfaces toolbar.

   Select the first defining curve:

2. Select the top circle.

Select the second defining curve:

3. Select the circle drawn on the top surface of the cone.

   See Figure 15-40. Use the Zoom Window tool to enlarge the top surface of the cone, if necessary, to select the Ø.62 circle. The density of line segments in the cylinder results because the Surftab settings are at 18.

15-17 USING SURFACES WITH A UCS

Figure 15-41 shows a dimensioned object. The following section shows how the object was created as a surface model.

To draw the box portion

1. Set the Grid and Snap spacing for .5, and select Decimal Units.
2. Select the SE Isometric tool from the View toolbar.
3. Select the Zoom tool and create a zoom window around the 0,0,0 point.
4. Select the Box tool.

   Specify corner point of box:

5. Select 0,0,0.

   Specify length of box:

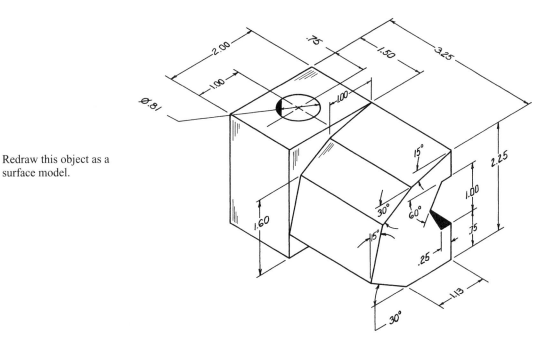

Redraw this object as a
surface model.

Figure 15-41

6. Type 1.50; press Enter or use dynamic input.

   Specify width of box or [Cube]:

7. Type 2.00; press Enter.

   Specify height of box:

8. Type 2.25; press Enter.

   *Specify rotation angle of box about the Z axis or
   [Reference]:*

9. Type 0; press Enter.

See Figure 15-42. The size values for the box were
taken from the dimensions given in Figure 15-41. Use the
Zoom command again, if necessary, to approximate the size
shown in Figure 15-41.

To add the hole to the object

The hole can be created using the Elev command, but
in this example, the Ruled Surface command will be used.

1. Select the Circle tool.

   *Command: _circle
   Specify center point for circle or [3P/2P/Ttr/(tan
   tan radius)]:*

A surface model created using the Box tool.

Figure 15-42

The hole was created using two circles and the Ruled Surface tool.

Figure 15-43

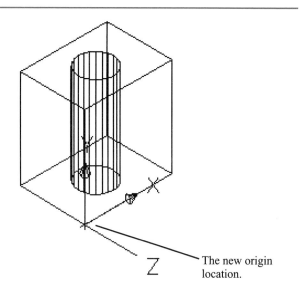

The new origin location.

Figure 15-44

2. Type .75,1.00,0; press Enter.

The hole location came from the given dimensions.

Specify radius of circle or [Diameter]:

3. Type .405; press Enter.
4. Press Enter again to restart the Circle command sequence.

Command: _circle
Specify center point for circle or [3P/2P/Ttr/(tan tan radius)]:

5. Type .75,1.00, 2.25; press Enter.

This will locate the second circle on the top surface of the box.

Specify radius of circle or [Diameter] <0.4050>:

6. Press Enter.
7. Select the Ruled Surface tool.

Select first defining curve:

8. Select the lower circle.

Select second defining curve:

9. Select the upper circle.

See Figure 15-43.

To create the extended portion of the object

The procedure presented is one of several different approaches that can be used to create the object. The procedure presented was selected to help demonstrate and teach different AutoCAD commands.

1. Select the Right tool from the UCS II toolbar.
2. Select Move UCS Origin tool from the UCS II toolbar.

Specify new origin point:

3. Use Osnap, Endpoint and select the lower corner of the box as shown.

See Figure 15-44. The screen icon is on the new origin.

4. Select the UCS tool from the UCS toolbar.

Enter an option [New/Move/orthoGraphic/Prev/ Restore/Save/Del/Apply/?/World]<World>:

5. Type s: press Enter.

Enter name to save current UCS or [?]:

6. Type box; press Enter.
7. Select the Top view from the View toolbar.

The View dialog box will appear. Remember that we are working in the new UCS defined as Box, so the top view is required. If we were working relative to the WCS, the right view would be used.

8. Make the Top view the current view and set the Relative to option to the Box UCS.
9. Type zoom; press Enter.

[All/Center/Dynamic/Extents/Previous/Scale/ Window]<real time>:

10. Type 1; press Enter.

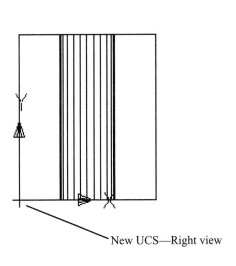

Figure 15-45

See Figure 15-45. Use the Zoom Window tool on the Standard toolbar to increase the size of the view, if necessary.

Figure 15-45 is a two-dimensional view of the right surface of the box. The required extension shape can be created in this 2-D view and then extended to the required length using the Tabsurface tool.

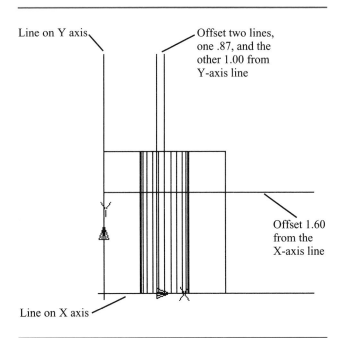

Figure 15-46

To draw the end shape of the object

Many angular dimensions are used to define the object's shape, so several construction lines will be needed to define the angular intersection points.

1. Select the line tool from the Draw toolbar and the Offset tool from the Modify toolbar and draw the construction lines shown in Figure 15-46. Figure 15-47 is a more detailed illustration of the required lines.

Figure 15-47

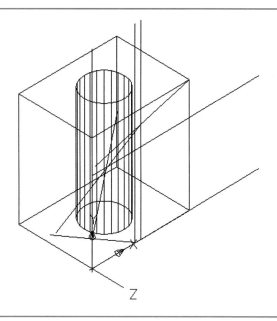

Figure 15-48

Figure 15-47 shows the untrimmed construction of the extension shape. The length value of 2 was an arbitrary selection. Remember, you are working in the new UCS. The lines for the box may not be used for the extension shape. New lines must be added.

Figure 15-48 shows the construction from the SE Isometric viewpoint. A new layer was created, and the box and cylinder shape was moved to the new layer to prevent visual confusion. The layer was created using the Layer tool, and the box was moved using the Properties command on the Modify pull-down menu.

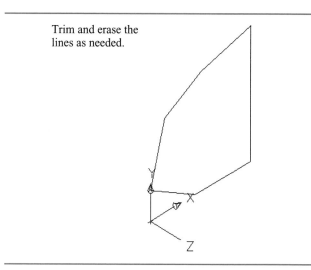

Trim and erase the lines as needed.

Figure 15-49

Figure 15-49 shows the final trimmed shape with the construction lines erased. Figure 15-50 shows the completed shape with the internal cutout added.

2. Use the Edit Polyline tool from the Modify II toolbar and change the shape into a polyline.
3. Select Tabulated Surface tool from the Surfaces toolbar and use the polyline as the object, and the line from 0,0,0 to 0,0,1.75 as the direction vector.
4. Use the Move tool from the Modify toolbar to align the extended shape with the appropriate surface of the box.
5. Turn the Box's layer on.

If necessary, set the SURFTABs to a value of 6. Also use the Zoom command to help select the correct lines. Figure 15-51 shows the finished drawing of the object oriented to the WCS.

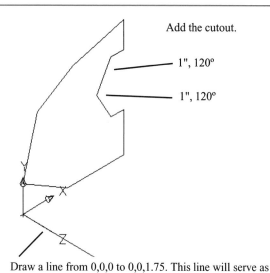

Add the cutout.

1", 120°

1", 120°

Draw a line from 0,0,0 to 0,0,1.75. This line will serve as the directional vector for the Tabulated Surface command.

Figure 15-50

Figure 15-51

Figure 15-52

15-18 SAMPLE PROBLEM SP15-1

The following section explains in detail how to draw the pulley assembly shown in Figure 15-52. When creating a complex design or drawing of an object, it is best to start with a freehand sketch and locate all the important assembly and insertion points. A sketch is not required, but it provides a quick and easy way to become familiar with the drawing requirements, resulting in a more efficient drawing approach. Figure 15-53 shows a design layout for the pulley assembly. Note how the sizes and shapes are defined. Center point locations for the pulleys are given in terms of coordinate values, shaft sizes and locations are defined, and assembly points use coordinate values.

It is also good practice to draw each part on its own layer. This allows individual parts to be shown or not shown as needed during the construction. The following layers are recommended. See Chapter 3 for an explanation of the Layer command.

Figure 15-53

Select the Layer tool from the Object Properties tool-bar to access the Layer Properties Manager dialog box and create the following layers. See Figure 15-54.

LAYER - COLOR - LINETYPE
CONSTRUCTION - white - continuous
CENTERLINES - white - centerlines
PLATE - white - continuous
A-PULLEY - blue - continuous
B-PULLEY - cyan - continuous
SHAFT - red - continuous
BELT - yellow - continuous

To draw the support plate

See Figure 15-55. The drawing uses decimal units.

1. Set Grid and = 1, and the viewpoint for SE Isometric.
2. Select the Layer Control tool from the Standard toolbar.
3. Select the Plate layer and make it the current layer.
4. Select Box from the Surfaces toolbar and draw a 1 x 18 x 10 box with its lower front corner on the 0,0,0 origin of the WCS.

To draw the pulley centerlines (See Figure 15-56.)

1. Select the Layer Control tool.
2. Select the Centerlines layer.
3. Select the Line tool from the Draw toolbar.

Draw the three pulley centerlines using coordinate values based on the values given in Figure 15-53. Each shaft is to be 4 inches long, so the centerlines should be longer than 4 inches. A length of 6 inches was chosen. The centerlines should start at a point 1 inch beyond the end of the shaft and end 1 inch beyond the other end.

The centerline coordinate points are as follows:

1. From point: –2,3,7 to point: 4,3,7
2. From point: –2,7.5,3 to point: 4,7.5,3
3. From point: –2,14,4 to point: 4,14,4

To draw the A-and-B pulley profiles

The profiles of the pulleys will be drawn on the Construction layer and from a top viewpoint. The top view will give the drawing a 2-D appearance and make it visually easier to draw the profiles. The Elev command will be used to position the working planes for the profiles at the correct height above the WCS X, Y plane.

1. Select the Top tool from the View toolbar and make it the current view.

Define the needed layers

Figure 15-54

A box of size 1,18,10

Figure 15-55

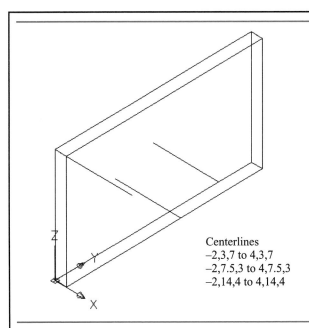

Centerlines
–2,3,7 to 4,3,7
–2,7.5,3 to 4,7.5,3
–2,14,4 to 4,14,4

Figure 15-56

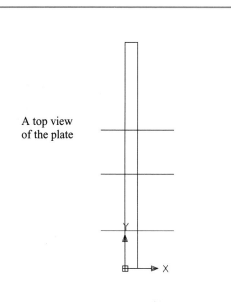

A top view
of the plate

Figure 15-57

The view will change to a top view of the plate. See Figure 15-57.

2. Select the Tools pull-down menu, then Drafting Settings, then the Snap and Grid folder.
3. Change the Snap setting to .125.

The .125 value was chosen because it is the length of the smallest distance on the pulley profile.

4. Select the Zoom Window tool from the Standard toolbar and zoom the plate and pulley centerlines.
5. Select the Layer Control tool, then select the Construction layer.

At this time you may also turn off any layers that you find visually confusing.

The profiles of the pulleys will be drawn using Polyline, then the Revolved Surface command will be used to generate the final pulley shapes. The Polyline construction will be done on the Construction layer, and the Revolved Surface command will be applied to the profiles on the A-pulley and B-pulley layers.

6. Type Elev and set the new current elevation to 7 and the new current thickness to 0.0000.

The value of 7 was derived from the centerline location of the first A-pulley which, according to the sketch in Figure 15-53, has a Y component of 7. The chosen orientation on the WCS changes the component value to the Z axis.

7. Select Polyline from the Draw toolbar and draw the A-pulley profile.

The new current elevation of 7 has raised the working plane of the drawing so that it is aligned with the pulley's centerline. This means you can draw the pulley directly. Turn on the Ortho command (F8), if desired, to help produce the required horizontal and vertical lines of the profile. See Figure 15-57.

8. Type Elev and change the new current elevation to 4.
9. Use the Zoom All tool to return the drawing to its original size, then use the Zoom Window tool to enlarge the area for the B-pulley.
10. Select the Layer Control tool and select the B-pulley layer.
11. Use Polyline to draw the B-pulley profile.
12. Type Elev and change the new current elevation to 0.

Turn off the Ortho command, if it was turned on. See Figure 15-58.

To copy the A-pulley profile

The assembly requires two A-pulleys, so it is easier to copy the existing profile than to redraw it. The pulleys are located on two different Z planes so you cannot make the copy directly. The displacement points must be defined in terms of their X, Y, Z component values relative to the WCS.

1. Select the Copy tool from the Modify toolbar.

   Select objects:

2. Select the A-pulley profile.

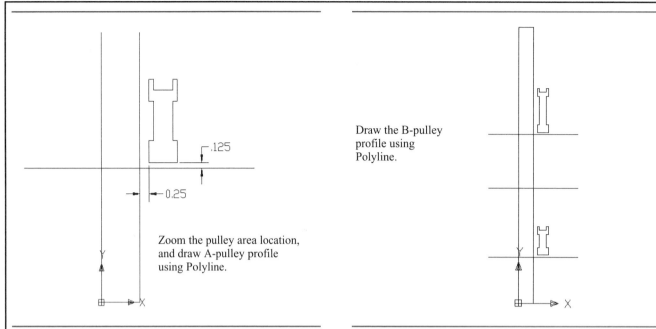

Figure 15-58

<Base point of displacement>/Multiple/:

3. Type 1.25,3,7; press Enter.

   Second point of displacement:

4. Type 1.25,7.5,3; Press Enter.

   See Figures 15-59 and 15-60.

Figure 15-59

To create the A- and B-pulleys

1. Select SE Isometric from the View toolbar and make it the current view.

   See Figure 15-61.

2. Select the Layer Control tool, then select the A-pulley layer.

Figure 15-60

Figure 15-61

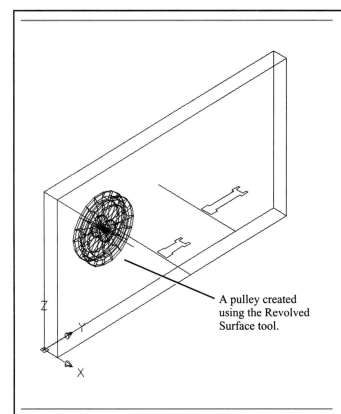

A pulley created using the Revolved Surface tool.

Figure 15-62

Turn off any layers that are not needed or that cause visual confusion.

3. Type Surftab1 and set the value to 18.
4. Type Surftab2 and set the value to 18.
5. Select the Revolved Surface tool from the Surfaces toolbar.
6. Select the first A-pulley profile, use the centerline as an axis of revolution, and rotate the profile 360°.

See Figure 15-62.

7. Press Enter and repeat the sequence for the second A-pulley.
8. Select the Layer tool, then select the B-pulley layer.
9. Again use the Revolved Surface tool on the Surfaces toolbar to rotate the B-pulley profile 360° around its centerline.

See Figure 15-63.

To draw the shafts

The three shafts are each 4 inches long, perpendicular to the face of the support plate. The right view will be used to create a viewpoint perpendicular to the face of the support plate. The Elev command can then be used to draw the shafts.

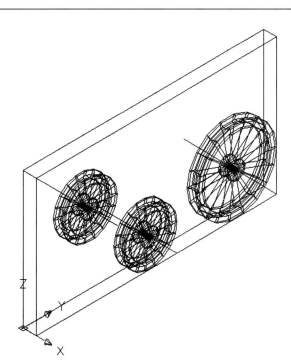

Surftab1 = 18
Surftab2 = 18

Figure 15-63

1. Select Right UCS from the UCS II toolbar.
2. Select Right from the View toolbar and make it the current view.

See Figure 15-64. The origin is located at the lower left corner of the support plate and will not move. Remember that the working plane of this view is the back face of the support plate, even though you are looking at the front face.

3. Type Elev; press Enter.

New current elevation <0.0000>:

4. Type −1; press Enter.

This value moves the working plane 1 inch from the back face of the support plate.

New current thickness <0.0000>:

5. Type 4; press Enter.

The value 4 is the length of the shafts.

6. Select center point for circle.

Specify center point for circle or [3P/2P/Ttr(tan tan radius)]:

7. Type 3,7,0; press Enter.

The 3,7 (X, Y) component values were obtained from the design sketch, Figure 15-53. The Z component is 0 because the working plane has been set to align with the end of the shaft.

Radius/<Diameter>:

8. Type .25; press Enter.
9. Press the right mouse button and select the Repeat Circle option.

Specify center point for circle or [3P/2P/Ttr (tan tan radius)]:

10. Type 7.5,3,0; press Enter

Radius/<Diameter>:

11. Type .25; press Enter.
12. Press the right mouse button and select the Repeat Circle option.

Command: _Circle 3P/2P/Ttr/<Centerpoint>:

13. Type 11,4,0; press Enter.

Radius/<Diameter>:

14. Type .25; press Enter.

To draw the belt

The belt is .50 wide and can be created by constructing the required shape using the Circle, Osnap Tangent, Line, and Trim commands. The working plane will be

Top view of
Pulley assembly
showing shafts
in place

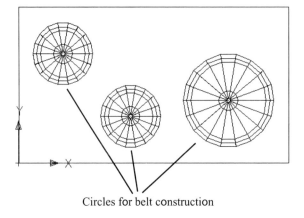

Circles for belt construction

Figure 15-64

All layers turned off, except for the belt layer.
Drawing is still using the Right UCS orientation.

Figure 15-65

Finished drawing

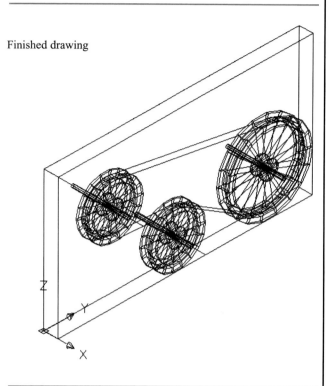

Figure 15-66

moved to a plane .625 from the face of the support plate, and the current elevation thickness set to .50. The .625 value was derived by adding the distance from the front face of the support plate to the edge of the pulleys (.50), and the .125 distance from the edge of the pulleys to the edge of the belt.

The drawing should still be in the Right view orientation. See Figure 15-65. Turn off all layers except for the belt layer.

1. Type Elev.

    New current elevation <−1.0000>:

2. Type 1.625; press Enter.

The additional 1 inch is the thickness of the plate. The origin that you are working from is still located at the original 0,0,0 point of the WCS

    New current thickness <4.0000>:

3. Type .5; press Enter.
4. Select the Layer Control tool, then the Belt layer.

    Turn off any layers that you find visually confusing.

5. Select the Tools pull-down menu, then Drafting Settings.
6. Set the Grid value for 1.00 and the Snap value for .50.
7. Select the Radius option from the Circle tool on the Draw toolbar and draw three circles as shown in Figure 15-65.

The center point coordinate values are 3,7,0; 7.5,3,0; and 11,4,0. The same points were used as the center points for the shafts. Again, the Z component is 0 because the working plane has been moved using the Elev command.

The radius values of 1.625 and 2.625 were derived from the design sketch in Figure 15-53 and define the locations of the interfaces of the pulley surfaces with the belt.

8. Draw the belt path by drawing lines between the circles using the Osnap and Tangent commands.
9. Use the Trim command to remove the excess portions of the circles.

To create the final assembly drawing

1. Select the Layer tool and turn on all layers except the construction layer.
2. Select the World UCS from the UCS II toolbar.
3. Select the SE Isometric tool from the View toolbar and make it the current view.

The final drawing should appear and look similar to Figure 15-66.

4. Select the File pull-down menu, then Save As.
5. Save the drawing as PULLEYS.

15-19 EXERCISE PROBLEMS

Draw surface models of the objects in Exercise Problems EX15-1 to EX15-3.

EX15-1 INCHES

EX15-2 INCHES

EX15-3 INCHES

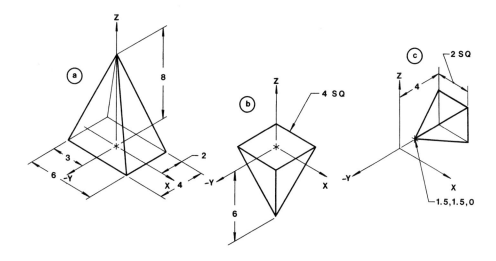

EX15-4 INCHES

Draw the three boxes positioned as shown. The length, width, and height for each box are as follows:

A. X = 6, Y = 5, Z = 2
B. X = 4, Y = 4, Z = 4
C. X = 5, Y = 2, Z = 1

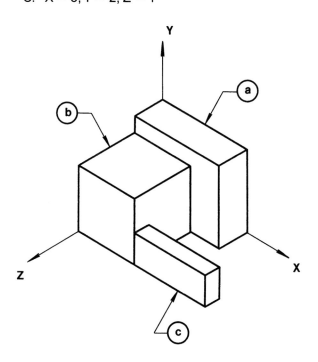

EX15-5 INCHES

Draw the three boxes as shown centered about the Z axis. The length, width, and height for each box are as follows:

A. X = 8, Y = 8, Z = 1
B. X = 6, Y = 6, Z = 2
C. X = 2, Y = 2, Z = 6

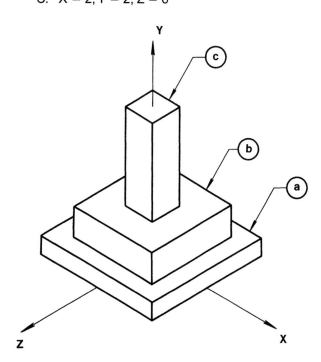

EX15-6 INCHES

Draw the following three cylinders centered about the Y axis positioned as shown. The sizes of the cylinders are as follows. Use either the Revolved Surface or the Ruled Surface command.

A. Diameter = 2, height = 4
B. Diameter = 4, height = 1
C. Diameter = 6, height = 2

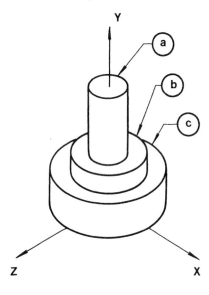

EX15-7 INCHES

Draw the three boxes positioned as shown. The length, width, and height for each box are 2 × 2 × 5.

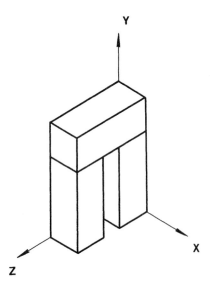

Draw surface models of the objects shown in Exercise Problems EX15-8 to EX15-27.

EX15-8 FEET

EX15-9 MILLIMETERS

EX15-10 MILLIMETERS

EX15-11 MILLIMETERS

EX15-12 MILLIMETERS

EX15-13 INCHES

EX15-14 MILLIMETERS

EX15-15 MILLIMETERS

NOTE: LOWER SURFACE OF BASE IS +5
GREATER THAN THE TOP SURFACE ALL
AROUND.

EX15-16 MILLIMETERS

EX15-17 MILLIMETERS

EX15-19 INCHES (SCALE 4:1)

EX15-18 MILLIMETERS

EX15-20 INCHES

EX15-21 MILLIMETERS

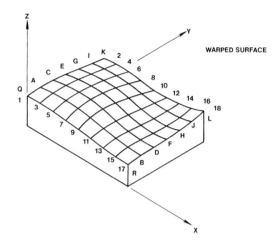

WARPED SURFACE

	LINE Q R		
N	X	Z	Y
1	0	20.0	0
3	10	20.4	0
5	20	20.0	0
7	30	19.6	0
9	40	17.8	0
11	50	16.8	0
13	60	16.0	0
15	70	15.0	0
17	80	14.8	0

	LINE A B		
N	X	Z	Y
1	0	20.5	10
3	10	21.5	10
5	20	22.0	10
7	30	21.5	10
9	40	20.5	10
11	50	18.0	10
13	60	16.5	10
15	70	15.8	10
17	80	15.2	10

	LINE CD		
N	X	Z	Y
1	0	20.0	20
3	10	21.2	20
5	20	22.2	20
7	30	22.7	20
9	40	21.3	20
11	50	17.8	20
13	60	16.0	20
15	70	15.5	20
17	80	15.8	20

	LINE E F		
N	X	Z	Y
1	0	19.3	30
3	10	20.8	30
5	20	22.0	30
7	30	22.5	30
9	40	20.5	30
11	50	17.5	30
13	60	15.8	30
15	70	15.0	30
17	80	16.0	30

	LINE G H		
N	X	Z	Y
1	0	17.5	40
3	10	19.0	40
5	20	20.3	40
7	30	20.0	40
9	40	18.8	40
11	50	16.3	40
13	60	15.2	40
15	70	15.4	40
17	80	16.8	40

	LINE I J		
N	X	Z	Y
1	0	16.5	50
3	10	18.0	50
5	20	18.8	50
7	30	17.8	50
9	40	16.6	50
11	50	15.5	50
13	60	15.3	50
15	70	16.0	50
17	80	18.0	50

	LINE K L		
N	X	Z	Y
1	0	15.0	60
3	10	16.5	60
5	20	17.0	60
7	30	14.5	60
9	40	13.8	60
11	50	14.3	60
13	60	15.6	60
15	70	17.5	60
17	80	20.0	60

EX15-22 MILLIMETERS

EX15-24 MILLIMETERS

EX15-23 MILLIMETERS

EX15-25 MILLIMETERS

EX15-26 INCHES

EX15-27 INCHES

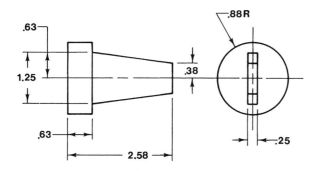

EX15-28 MILLIMETERS

Study the sample problem presented in Section 15-18, then create a similar surface model for the pulley assembly described here.

PULLEY PROFILE

Ø40 – SMALL PULLEY
Ø60 – LARGE PULLEY

If the pulley in the upper left of the plate is turning at 1750 rpm, what is the speed of the other pulley?

EX15-29 MILLIMETERS

Study the sample problem presented in Section 15-18, then create a similar surface model for the pulley assembly described here.

DETAIL A
SCALE:4=1

If the pulley in the upper left of the plate is truning at 1750 rpm, what is the speed of the other pulleys?

EX15-30 MILLIMETERS

Study the sample problem presented in Section 15-18, then create a similar surface model for the pulley assembly described here.

If the pulley in the upper left of the plate is turning at 3550 rpm, what is the speed of the other pulleys?

DETAIL A
SCALE:4=1

CHAPTER 16

Solid Modeling

Figure 16-1

16-1 INTRODUCTION

This chapter introduces solid modeling. The solid modeling commands can be accessed using the Solids toolbar, the Solids Editing toolbar or by using the Solids option on the Draw pull-down menu or the Solids Editing option on the Modify pull-down menu. See Figure 16-1.

Solid modeling allows you to create objects as solid entities. Solid models differ from the surface models created in the last chapter in that solid models have density and are not merely joined surfaces.

Solid models are created by joining together, or *unioning*, basic primitive shapes: boxes, cylinders, wedges, and so on, or by defining a shape as a polyline and extruding it into a solid shape. Solid primitives may also be subtracted from one another. For example, to create a hole in a solid box, draw a solid cylinder, then subtract the cylinder from the box. The result will be an open volume in the shape of a hole.

The first part of the chapter deals with the individual tools of the Solids toolbar. The second part gives examples of how to create solid objects by joining primitive shapes and changing UCSs. The chapter ends with a discussion of the Solids Editing toolbar.

16-2 BOX

The Box tool on the Solids toolbar has two options: Center and Corner. Corner is the default option. The Center tool is used to draw a box by first locating its center point. The Corner tool is used to draw a box by first locating one of its corner points.

Set the drawing for SE Isometric 3D View.

**To draw a box using the Corner option
(See Figure 16-2.)**

1. Select the Box tool from the Solids toolbar.

   *Command: _box
   Specify corner of box or [CEnter] <0,0,0>:*

2. Press Enter.

   This means that the corner of the box will be located on the 0,0,0 point of the XY plane.

   Specify corner or [Cube/Length]:

3. Type 10,10,0; press Enter, or use dynamic input to locate the corner.

   Specify height:

4. Type 6; press Enter.

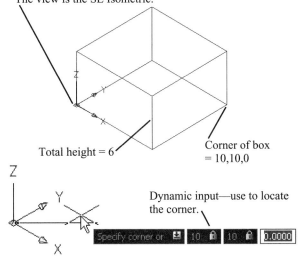

First corner of the solid box is located on the WCS origin. The view is the SE Isometric.

Total height = 6

Corner of box = 10,10,0

Dynamic input—use to locate the corner.

Specify corner or 10 10 0.0000

Figure 16-2

**To draw a box using the Center option
(See Figure 16-3.)**

1. Select the Box tool from the Solids toolbar.

   *Command: _box
   Specify corner of box or [CEnter] <0,0,0>:*

2. Type ce; press Enter.

   Specify center of box <0,0,0>:

3. Type 5,5,0; press Enter.

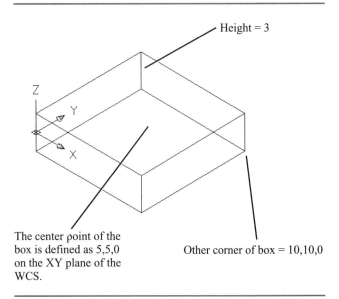

Height = 3

The center point of the box is defined as 5,5,0 on the XY plane of the WCS.

Other corner of box = 10,10,0

Figure 16-3

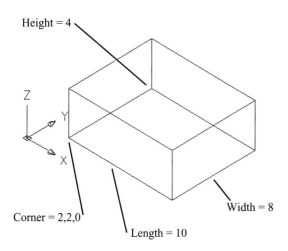

Height = 4
Z
Y
X
Corner = 2,2,0
Length = 10
Width = 8

Figure 16-4

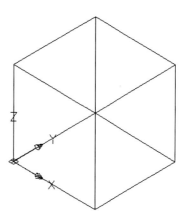

Z
Y
X

The cube option makes the length, width, and height of the box of equal length.

Figure 16-5

Specify corner or [Cube/Length]:

4. Type 10,10,0; press Enter.

    Specify height:

5. Type 3; press Enter.

    The box is centered about the 5,5,0 point. The size of the box along the XY plane is defined by the distance from the center point (5,5,0) to the right corner of the box (10,10,0). The height input of 3 represents the total height of the box centered about the XY plane.

    The box shown in Figure 16-2 has its bottom surface aligned with the XY plane, whereas the XY plane passes through the middle of the box shown in Figure 16-3.

To draw a box from given dimensions

    See Figure 16-4. Draw a box with a length of 10, a width of 8, and a height of 4, with its corner at the 2,2,0 point.

1. Select the Box tool from the Surfaces toolbar.

    Command: _box
    Specify corner of box or [CEnter] <0,0,0>:

2. Type 2,2,0; press Enter.

    Specify corner or [Cube/Length]:

3. Type L; press Enter.

    Specify length:

4. Type 10; press Enter.

    Specify width:

5. Type 8; press Enter.

    Specify height:

6. Type 4; press Enter.

To draw a cube (See Figure 16-5.)

1. Select the Corner tool from the Solids toolbar.

    Command: _box
    Specify corner of box or [CEnter] <0,0,0>:

2. Press Enter.

    Specify corner or [Cube/Length]:

3. Type c; press Enter.

    Specify length:

4. Type 7.5; press Enter.

    AutoCAD automatically makes all three edges of the box equal lengths of 7.5.

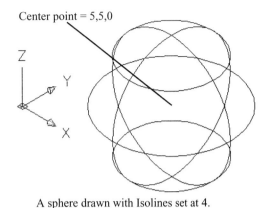

Center point = 5,5,0

A sphere drawn with Isolines set at 4.

Figure 16-6

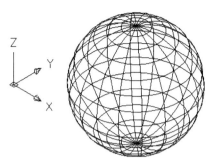

A sphere drawn with Isolines set at 18.

Figure 16-7

16-3 SPHERE

The visual accuracy of solids depends on the settings of the Isolines command. The sphere shown in Figure 16-6 was drawn with an Isolines setting of 4. For this section the Isolines setting will be changed to 18.

To change the Isolines settings

1. Type Isolines; press Enter.

   There is no tool for the Isolines command.

   Enter new value for ISOLINES <4>:

2. Type 18; press Enter.

   Command:

The new value is now in place and will be used for all solids drawn until it is changed or a new drawing is started.

To draw a sphere (See Figure 16-7.)

1. Select Sphere from the Solids toolbar.

   Specify center of sphere <0,0,0>:

2. Type 5,5,0; press Enter.

   Diameter/<Radius> of sphere:

3. Type 4; press Enter.

16-4 CYLINDER

There are two options associated with the Cylinder command: circular and elliptical. This means cylinders may be drawn with either elliptical or circular base planes. The base elliptical shape is drawn using the same procedure as was outlined for the Ellipse command in Chapter 2.

To draw a cylinder with a circular base

See Figure 16-8. Note that Isolines is still set for 18.

1. Select the Cylinder tool from the Solids toolbar.

   Command: _cylinder
   Current wire frame density: ISOLINES=18
   Specify center point for base of cylinder or [Elliptical]<0,0,0>:

2. Type 5,5,0; press Enter.

   Specify radius for base of cylinder or [Diameter]:

3. Type 4; press Enter.

   Specify height of cylinder or [Center of other end]:

4. Type 6; press Enter.

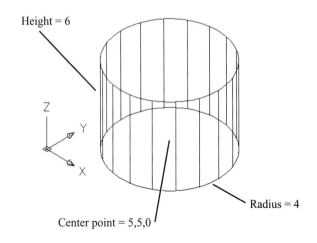

Height = 6

Center point = 5,5,0

Radius = 4

Figure 16-8

Figure 16-9

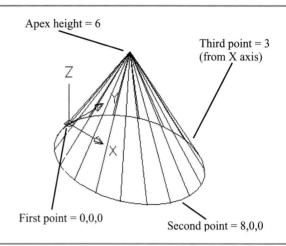

Figure 16-10

To draw a cylinder with an elliptical base

See Figure 16-9. The following sequence uses coordinate value input. The same points could have been selected by moving the crosshairs and pressing the left mouse button.

1. Select the Cylinder tool from the Surfaces toolbar.

   Command: _cylinder
   Current wire frame density: ISOLINES=18
   Specify center point for base of cylinder or [Elliptical]<0,0,0>:

2. Type e; press Enter.

   Specify second axis endpoint of ellipse for base of cylinder:

3. Type 0,0,0; press Enter.

   This input locates one end of the base axis on the 0,0,0 point of the XY plane.

   Specify axis endpoint of ellipse for base of cylinder:

4. Type 10,0,0.

   This input locates the axis line along the X axis.

   Specify length of other axis for base of cylinder:

   Note that the line dragging from the crosshairs has one end centered on the axis just defined.

5. Type 5,3.5,0; press Enter.

   Specify height of cylinder or [Center of base]:

6. Type 4; press Enter.

   An elliptical base can also be defined by first defining a center point for the ellipse, then defining the length of the radii of the major and minor axes.

16-5 CONE

There are two options associated with the Cone tool: circular and elliptical. This means that cones can be drawn with either an elliptical or circular base plane. The base elliptical shape is drawn using the same procedure as was outlined for the Ellipse command in Chapter 2. The Cone command cannot be used to draw truncated cones, as could the Cone tool associated with the Surfaces toolbar. Solid truncated cones are created by subtracting the top portion of the cone.

**To draw a cone with an elliptical base
(See Figure 16-10.)**

1. Select the Cone tool from the Solids toolbar.

   Command: _cone
   Current wire frame density: ISOLINES=18
   Specify center point for base of cone or [Elliptical]<0,0,0>:

2. Type e; press Enter.

   Specify axis endpoint of ellipse for base of cone or [Center]:

3. Type 0,0,0; press Enter.

   This input will locate one end of the ellipse axis at the 0,0,0 point of the XY plane.

   Specify second axis endpoint of ellipse for base of cylinder:

4. Type 8,0,0.

   Specify length of other axis for base of cone:

   Note that the line dragging from the crosshair has one end centered on the axis just defined.

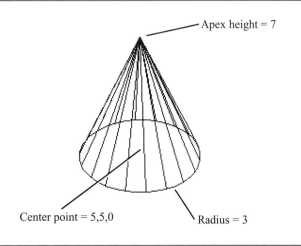

Apex height = 7

Center point = 5,5,0

Radius = 3

Figure 16-11

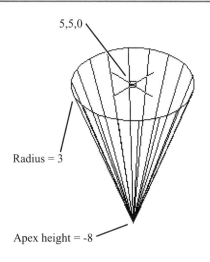

5,5,0

Radius = 3

Apex height = -8

Figure 16-12

5. Type 3; press Enter.

   Specify height of cone or [Apex]:

6. Type 6; press Enter.

A response of A to the Apex/<Height>: prompt allows you to select the height of the cone using the crosshairs.

To draw a cone with a circular base
(See Figure 16-11.)

1. Select the Cone tool from the Solids toolbar.

   Command: _cone
   Current wire frame density: ISOLINES=18
   Specify center point for base of cone or [Elliptical] <0,0,0>:

2. Type 5,5,0; press Enter.

   Specify radius for base of cone or [Diameter]:

3. Type 3; press Enter.

   Specify height of cone or [Apex]:

4. Type 7; press Enter.

A response of A to the Apex/<Height>: prompt allows you to select the height of the cone using the crosshairs. Figure 16-12 shows a cone drawn using a negative height input.

16-6 WEDGE

There are two options associated with the Wedge command: center and corner.

To draw a wedge by defining its corner point
(See Figure 16-13.)

1. Select the Wedge tool from the Solids toolbar.

   Command: _wedge
   Specify first corner of wedge or [CEnter] <0,0,0>:

2. Press Enter.

This input will locate the corner of the wedge on the 0,0,0 point of the XY plane.

   Specify corner or [Cube/Length]:

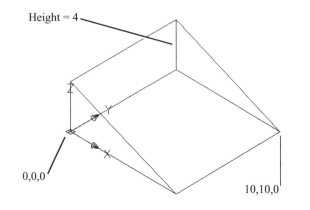

Height = 4

0,0,0

10,10,0

Figure 16-13

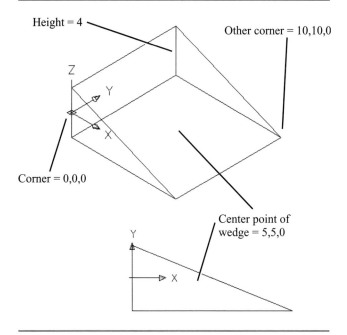

Height = 4
Other corner = 10,10,0
Z
Y
X
Corner = 0,0,0
Center point of
wedge = 5,5,0
Y
X

Figure 16-14

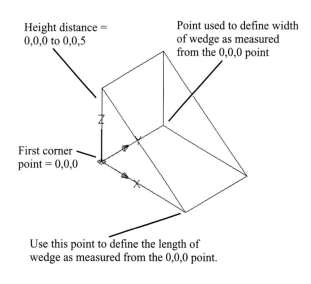

Height distance =
0,0,0 to 0,0,5
Point used to define width
of wedge as measured
from the 0,0,0 point
Z
First corner
point = 0,0,0
X
Use this point to define the length of
wedge as measured from the 0,0,0 point.

Figure 16-15

The default response to this command defines the diagonal corner of the wedge's base.

3. Type 10,10,0; press Enter

Specify height:

4. Type 4; press Enter.

**To draw a wedge by defining its center point
(See Figure 16-14.)**

1. Select the Wedge tool from the Solids toolbar.

    Command: _wedge
    Specify first corner of wedge or [CEnter]
    <0,0,0>

2. Type ce; press Enter.

    Specify center of wedge <0,0,0>:

3. Type 5,5,0; press Enter.

    Specify opposite corner or [Cube/Length] <0,0,0>:

4. Type 10,10,0; press Enter.

    Specify height:

5. Type 4; press Enter.

The wedge shown in Figure 16-14 is centered about the XY plane; that is, part of the wedge is above the plane, and part is below. This is not easy to see even with the grid shown. The far right corner of the wedge is actually located below the grid at the 10,10 point. Figure 16-14 also shows a side view of

the same wedge with a line drawn on the XY plane added. Note how the line bisects the height line of the wedge.

**To draw a wedge using selected points
(See Figure 16-15.)**

1. Select the Wedge tool from the Solids toolbar.

    Command: _wedge
    Specify first corner of wedge or [CEnter]
    <0,0,0>

2. Press Enter.

This input will locate the corner of the wedge on the 0,0,0 point of the XY plane.

    Specify corner or [Cube/Length]:

3. Type L; press Enter.

    Specify Length:

4. Select the 0,0,0 point

    Specify second point:

5. Select a point on the X axis.

The length input values are measured only along the X axis. If you had selected a point within the XY plane, the resulting length distance would have been the X component of the selected point relative to the first point selected. The width distances are measured only in the Y direction, and the height distances in the Z direction.

0,0,0

Figure 16-16

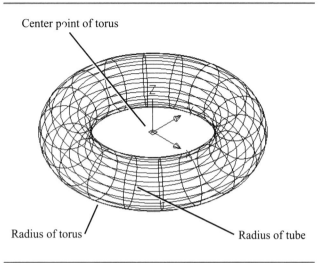

Center point of torus

Radius of torus

Radius of tube

Figure 16-17

Specify width:

6. Select the 0,0 point.

Width: Second point:

7. Select a point on the Y axis.

Specify height:

8. Select the 0,0,5 point; press Enter.

The technique of drawing a wedge by selecting points is best used when another object already exists and the Osnap command can be used to align the selection points with the existing object.

To align a wedge with an existing wedge

This example illustrates how you can use different inputs to position a wedge. Figure 16-15 shows a wedge. The problem is to draw another wedge with its back surface aligned with the back surface of the existing wedge.

1. Select the Wedge tool from the Solids toolbar.

Command: _wedge
Specify first corner of wedge or [CEnter] <0,0,0>:

2. Press Enter.

Specify corner or [Cube/Length]:

3. Type L; press Enter.

Specify length:

4. Select the 0,0,0 point.

Specify second point:

5. Select a point on the X axis.

Specify width:

6. Select the 0,0 point.

Width: Second point:

7. Use Osnap, Endpoint and select the Y-axis corner point of the existing wedge.

Specify height:

8. Select the 0,0,0 point.

Specify second point:

9. Use Osnap, Endpoint and select the Z-axis corner point of the existing wedge.

See Figure 16-16. The model could also have been constructed by using the Copy command to create a second wedge, the Rotate command to rotate the new wedge 180°, and the Move command to align the wedge with the existing wedge. Use Osnap, Endpoint to ensure exact alignment.

16-7 TORUS

A torus is a donutlike shape. See Figure 16-17.

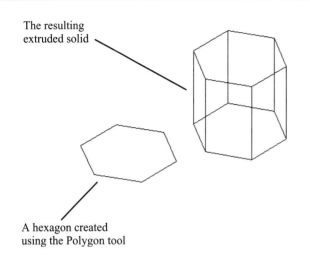

The resulting extruded solid

A hexagon created using the Polygon tool

Figure 16-18

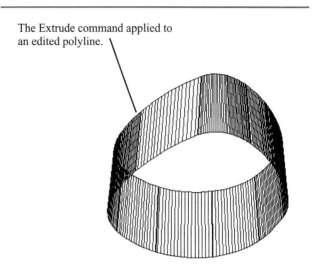

The Extrude command applied to an edited polyline.

Figure 16-19

To draw a torus

1. Select the Torus command.

   Command: _torus
   Current wire frame density: Isolines = 18
   Specify center of torus <0,0,0,>:

2. Press Enter.

   This input will locate the center of the torus at the 0,0,0 point on the XY plane.

   Specify radius of torus or [Diameter]:

3. Type 5; press Enter.

   Specify radius of tube or [Diameter]:

4. Type 1.5; press Enter.

   The torus shown in Figure 16-17 was created with Isolines set at 18.

16-8 EXTRUDE

The Extrude command is used to extend existing 2-D shapes into 3-D shapes. The Extrude tool can be applied only to a polyline.

To extrude a 2D Polyline

Figure 16-18 shows a hexagon drawn using the Polygon command. All shapes drawn using the Polygon command are automatically drawn as a polyline, so the hexagon can be extruded. How to draw a polygon is discussed in Chapter 2.

1. Select the Extrude tool from the Solids toolbar.

   Command: _extrude
   Current wire frame density: ISOLINES = 18
   Select objects:

2. Select the hexagon.

   Select objects:

3. Press Enter.

   Specify height of extrusion or [Path]:

4. Type 6; press Enter.

   Specify angle of taper for extrusion <0>:

5. Press Enter.

   Figure 16-19 shows an irregular enclosed curve created using Polyline, Polyline edit. The Extrude command was applied specifying a height of 5 and a taper angle of 5.

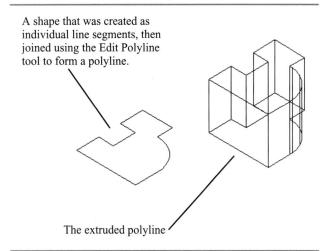

A shape that was created as individual line segments, then joined using the Edit Polyline tool to form a polyline.

The extruded polyline

Figure 16-20

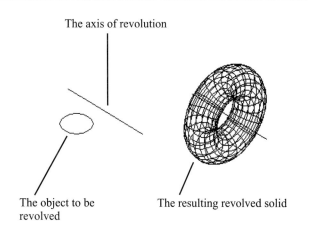

The axis of revolution

The object to be revolved

The resulting revolved solid

Figure 16-21

To create a polyline from line segments

Figure 16-20 shows a 2-D shape that was created using the Line and Circle tools from the Draw toolbar. The object must be converted to a polyline before it can be extruded.

1. Select the Edit Polyline tool from the Modify II toolbar.

   Command: _pedit
   Select polyline:

2. Select any one of the lines in the 2-D shape.

   Object selected is not a polyline
   Do you want to turn it into one? <Y>:

3. Press Enter.

   Enter an option [Close/Join/Width/Edit vertex/Fit/
   Spline/Decurve/Ltype gen/Undo]:

4. Type j (for Join); press Enter.

   The polyline will be defined by joining together all the line segments to form a polyline. A curve is considered to be a line segment.

   Select objects:

5. Window the entire object.

   Enter an option [Close/Join/Width/Edit vertex/Fit/
   Spline/Decurve/Ltype gen/Undo]:

6. Press Enter.

   9 Segments added to polyline
   Close/Join/Width/Edit vertex/Fit/Spline/Decurve/
   Ltype gen/Undo/eXit <X>:

7. Press Enter; then select the Extrude command and create an extrusion 3 units high with a 0° taper angle.

16-9 REVOLVE

The Revolve tool on the Solids toolbar is used to create a solid 3-D object by rotating a 2-D shape around an axis of revolution. Figure 16-21 shows a torus created by rotating a circle around a straight line. The density of the resulting object is controlled by the Isolines command. In this example Isolines is set at 18.

To create a revolved solid object

This procedure assumes that the curve path (2-D shape) and the line that will be used as the axis of revolution already exist on the drawing.

1. Select the Revolve tool from the Solids toolbar.

   Command: _revolve
   Current wire frame density: ISOLINES = 18
   Select objects:

2. Select the circle.

   Select objects:

3. Press Enter.

   Specify start point for axis of revolution or
   define axis by [Object/X (axis)/Y (axis):

4. Select one end of the line to be used as the axis of revolution.

   Use Osnap, Endpoint to ensure accuracy.

   Specify endpoint of axis:

5. Select the other end of the axis line.

   Specify angle of revolution <360>:

6. Press Enter.

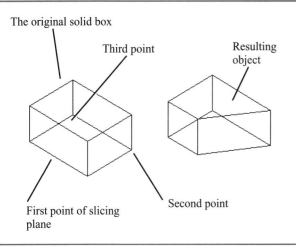

The original solid box

Third point

Resulting object

First point of slicing plane

Second point

Figure 16-22

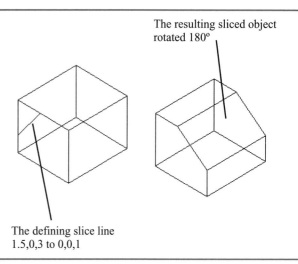

The resulting sliced object rotated 180°

The defining slice line 1.5,0,3 to 0,0,1

Figure 16-23

16-10 SLICE

The Slice tool is used to remove part of an existing solid object. The plane of the slice can be defined using several different methods.

To slice an object — 3 points (See Figure 16-22.)

1. Select the Slice tool from the Solids toolbar.

   Command: _slice
   Select objects:

2. Select the box.

   Select objects:

3. Press Enter.

   Specify first point on slicing plane by [Object/ Zaxis/View/XY/YZ/ZX/3points]<3points>:

4. Press Enter.

   This input means that the cutting plane for the slice will be defined using three points. This is a process similar to that used to define a UCS in Chapter 14.

   Specify first point on plane:

5. Select a point.

   In this example a first point was selected along the X axis of the box.

   Specify second point on plane:

6. Select the far right corner of the box.

   The Osnap, Endpoint tool can be used to ensure accuracy.

   Specify third point on plane:

7. Select the third point on the plane.

In this example a coordinate value (X,Y,Z) was used to define the third point. Remember, the crosshairs move only in the XY plane, so either Osnap commands or an X,Y,Z coordinate value must be used to define the point. It cannot be defined by moving the crosshairs and selecting a point.

   Specify a point on desired side of plane or [keep Both sides]:

8. Select a point on the part of the object you want to remain.

In this example the far left corner was selected. Figure 16-22 shows the resulting 3-D shape.

To Slice an object — Z axis

The Z axis option allows you to specify a slicing plane by defining a line with its origin on the Z axis and its other end in an XY plane. The resulting slice will be generated normal to the defining line. See Figure 16-23.

1. Select the Slice tool from the Solids toolbar.

   Command: _slice
   Select objects:

2. Select the box.

   Select objects:

3. Press Enter.

   Specify first point on slicing plane by [Object/ Zaxis/View/XY/YZ/ZX/3points]<3points>:

4. Type Z; press Enter.

   Specify a point on the section plane:

5. Type 1.5,0,3; press Enter.

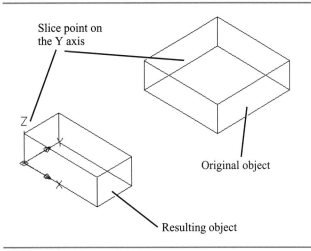

Slice point on the Y axis

Original object

Resulting object

Figure 16-24

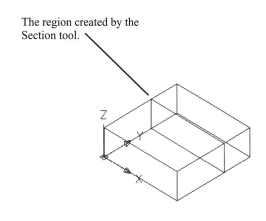

The region created by the Section tool.

Figure 16-25

This point could also have been selected using the crosshairs.

Point on Z-axis (normal) of the plane:

6. Select a point on the Z axis.

In this example the point 0,0,1 was selected. Again, the point could have been selected using the crosshairs.

Specify a point on desired side of plane or [keep Both sides]:

7. Select a point on the object on the side of the plane you want to keep.

In this example, a point on the Y axis was selected. Figure 16-23 shows the resulting sliced object.

To slice an object — ZX

The Slice command lists three plane options: XY, YZ, and ZX. Each of these options allows you to take slices parallel to these principal planes. See Figure 16-24.

1. Select the Slice tool from the Solids toolbar.

Command: _slice
Select objects:

2. Select the box.

Select objects:

3. Press Enter.

Specify first point on slicing plane by [Object/ Zaxis/View/XY/YZ/ZX/3points]<3points>:

4. Type zx; press Enter.

Specify a point on the zx plane <0,0,0>:

This prompt is asking for the location of the ZX slicing plane. The plane will be drawn parallel to the ZX plane based at the 0,0,0 origin, so select a point along the Y axis.

5. Select a point on the Y axis.

Specify a point on desired side of the plane or [keep Both sides]:

6. Select a point on the object on the side of the plane you want to keep.

16-11 SECTION

The Section command is used to define a region within an existing solid. Regions are defined in the same manner as the slicing planes discussed in the previous section.

1. Select the Section tool from the Solids toolbar.

Command: _section
Select objects:

2. Select the box.

Select objects:

3. Press Enter.

Specify first point on slicing plane by [Object/ Zaxis/View/XY/YZ/ZX/3points]<3points>:

Original shown with Hide command applied

Figure 16-26

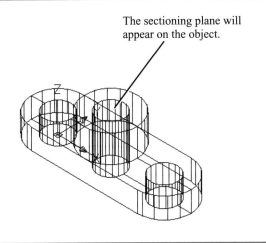

The sectioning plane will appear on the object.

Figure 16-28

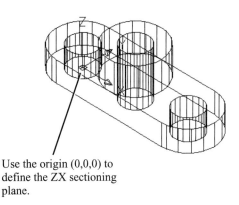

Use the origin (0,0,0) to define the ZX sectioning plane.

Figure 16-27

4. Type zx; press Enter.

Specify a point on the ZX plane <0,0,0>:

This prompt is asking for a location parallel to the ZX plane based at the 0,0,0 origin. In this example the cutting plane will be through the 0,0,0 point, so press Enter to accept the default value.

Figure 16-25 shows the resulting region. The region is an independent object or plane. This can be verified by erasing the box. After the box is erased, the region will remain.

To create a sectional view from a solid object

Figure 16-26 shows a solid object. Use the Section command to create a sectional view along the longitudinal centerline of the object.

1. Select the Section tool from the Solids toolbar.

Command:_section
Select objects:

2. Select the object.

Select objects:

3. Press Enter.

Specify first point on slicing plane by [Object/ Zaxis/View/XY/YZ/ZX/3points]<3points>:

4. Type zx; press Enter.

Point on the ZX plane <0.00>:

5. Select the origin.

See Figure 16-27. The example shown was drawn centered about the X axis, so the origin (0,0,0) can be used to define the location of the ZX sectioning plane. See Chapter 6 for sectional view terminology. The section cutting plane will appear on the object. See Figure 16-28.

6. Select the Move command and move the cutting plane away from the solid object.

Move the sectioning plane away from the object and use the Front and Move UCS origin tools from the UCS II toolbar to create a new UCS.

Figure 16-29

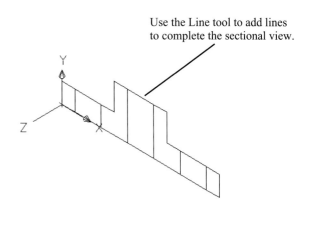

Use the Line tool to add lines to complete the sectional view.

Figure 16-30

See Figure 16-29. To apply Hatch lines to the sectional view just created, you must create a UCS aligned to the sectional view.

7. Select Front UCS from the UCS II toolbar.
8. Select the Move UCS origin tool from the UCS II toolbar and move the Front UCS origin to the lower left corner of the sectional view.
9. Use the Line tool to add the lines needed to complete the sectional view including centerlines.

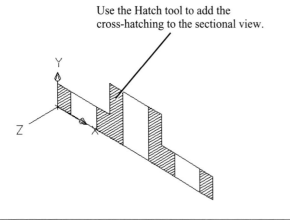

Use the Hatch tool to add the cross-hatching to the sectional view.

Figure 16-31

Use Osnap, Endpoint to ensure accuracy of the point selections. See Figure 16-30.

To add hatching to the sectional view

1. Select the Hatch tool from the Draw toolbar and hatch the appropriate areas on the sectional view.

See Figure 16-31. See Chapter 6 for instructions on the Hatch command.

2. Create a layer called SECTION and use the Properties (Modify pull-down menu) command to move the sectional view to the SECTION layer.
3. Turn off the 0 layer, turn on the SECTION layer and make it the current layer.

Only the sectional view should be seen on the screen.

4. Select the Front tool from the View toolbar and make it the current view.

If the sectional view appears too large for the screen, use the Zoom command to reduce the view size. Figure 16-32 shows the resulting sectional view.

The resulting sectional view taken from a solid model

Figure 16-32

16-12 INTERFERE

The Interfere command is used to define a volume common to two or more existing solid objects. Figure 16-33 shows a solid cylinder and a box that intersect each other. They were both drawn on the XY plane. The follow-

ing procedure will define the volume common to both of them.

1. Select the Interfere tool from the Solids toolbar.

   Command: _interfere
   Select first set of solids:
   Select objects:

2. Select the box.

   Select objects:

3. Press Enter.

   Select second set of solids:
   Select objects:

4. Select the cylinder.

   Select objects:

5. Press Enter.

   Create interference solids ? [Yes/No]/<No>:

6. Type y; press Enter.

   The common volume is now defined but difficult to see.

7. Select the Erase tool from the Modify toolbar and erase the box and cylinder.

   Figure 16-33 shows the resulting common volume.

The Interfere tool used to define the common volume between the cylinder and the box.

The common volume. The Erase tool was used to remove the cylinder and the box.

A cylinder and box both drawn with their bases on the XY plane.

Figure 16-33

Figure 16-34

16-13 UNION AND SUBTRACT

Solid objects may be combined to form more complex objects. Objects can be added together using the Union command and subtracted from each other using the Subtract command. A volume common to two or more objects may be defined using the Intersect command. The tools for these three commands are located on the Solids Editing toolbar or under the Solids Editing command located on the Modify pull-down menu. See Figure 16-34.

To Union two objects

Figure 16-35 shows two solid boxes drawn with adjoining surfaces.

1. Select the Union tool from the Solids Editing toolbar.

    Command: _union
    Select objects:

2. Select the two boxes.

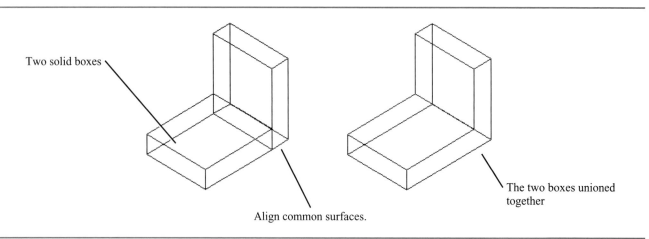

Two solid boxes

Align common surfaces.

The two boxes unioned together

Figure 16-35

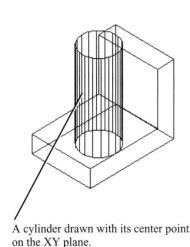
A cylinder drawn with its center point on the XY plane.

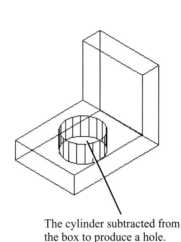
The cylinder subtracted from the box to produce a hole.

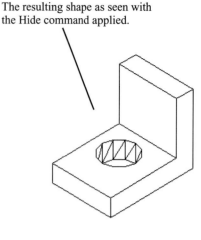
The resulting shape as seen with the Hide command applied.

Figure 16-36

Note the changes in the boxes after they have been unioned. The solid object is no longer two boxes but an L-shaped object.

To subtract an object

Figure 16-36 shows the L-shaped bracket formed. This exercise will add a hole to the front surface. Holes are created in solid objects by subtracting solid cylinders from the existing objects.

1. Select the Cylinder tool from the Solids toolbar.

   Command: _cylinder
   Current wire frame density: ISOLINES=18
   Specify center point for base of cylinder or [Elliptical]<0,0,0>:

2. Select a point on the XY plane approximately in the middle of the front surface.

   Remember, the crosshairs move only in the XY plane, so you can select a point only on the bottom surface of the box.

   Specify radius for base of cylinder or [Diameter]:

3. Select a radius for the cylinder.

   Specify height of cylinder or [Center of other end]:

4. Type 5; press Enter.

   The height of the cylinder was deliberately drawn higher than the top surface of the bracket to illustrate that the two heights need not be equal for the Subtract command. The

only requirement is that the cylinder be equal to or greater than the height of the box surface. See Figure 16-36.

5. Select the Subtract tool from the Solids Editing toolbar.

   Command: _subtract
   Select solids and regions to subtract from...
   Select objects:

   This prompt is asking you to define the main object, that is, the object you want to remain after the subtraction.

6. Select the L-shaped bracket.

   Select objects:

7. Press Enter.

   Select solids and regions to subtract...
   Select objects:

   This prompt is asking you to define the object you want removed by the subtraction.

8. Select the cylinder.

   Select objects:

9. Press Enter.

16-14 SOLID MODELING AND UCSs

In this section we will again work with the L-shaped bracket and add a hole to the upper surface. The procedure is to create a new UCS with its origin at the left intersection

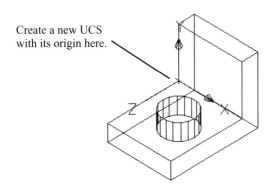

Create a new UCS with its origin here.

Figure 16-37

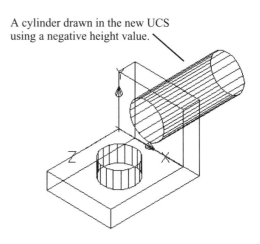

A cylinder drawn in the new UCS using a negative height value.

Figure 16-38

of the two perpendicular surfaces, then create and subtract a cylinder. See Figure 16-37.

1. Select the Origin UCS tool from the UCS toolbar.

   Command: _ucs
   Enter an option [New/Move/orthoGraphic/Prev/ Restore/Save/Del/Apply/?/World]<World>:

2. Type n; press Enter.

   Specify origin of new UCS or [Zaxis/3point/ OBject/Face/View/X/Y/Z]<0,0,0>:

3. Use Osnap, Endpoint and select the new origin.
4. Select the X Axis Rotate UCS tool from the UCS toolbar.

   Specify rotation angle about the X axis <90>:

5. Press Enter.
6. Select the Cylinder tool from the Solids toolbar.

   Command: _cylinder
   Current wire frame density: ISOLINES=18
   Specify center point for base of cylinder or [Elliptical]<0,0,0>:

7. Select a center point in the approximate center of the surface.

   Specify radius for base of cylinder or [Diameter]:

8. Select a radius for the cylinder.

   Specify height of cylinder or [Center of other end]:

9. Type −5; press Enter.

   See Figure 16-38. The negative value is required to project the cylinder into the back surface. The direction on the Z axis is determined using the right-hand rule.

Figure 16-39 shows the right-hand rule. The positive direction of a Z axis relative to a given XY plane is determined by aligning your thumb with the X axis so that the end of your thumb is pointing in the positive X direction. Align your first finger with the Y axis so that it is pointing in the positive Y direction. Extend your second finger so that it is perpendicular to the plane formed by your thumb and first finger. This is the positive Z direction.

10. Select the Subtract tool from the Solids Editing toolbar.

    Command: _subtract
    Select solids and regions to subtract from...

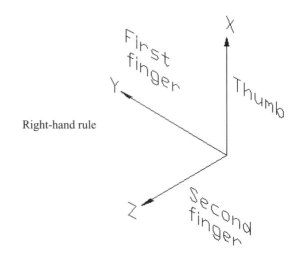

Right-hand rule

Figure 16-39

The finished solid model.

The solid model with the Hide command applied

Figure 16-40

Select objects:

11. Select the L-shaped bracket.

Select objects:

12. Press Enter.

Select solids and regions to subtract...
Select objects:

13. Select the cylinder.

Select objects:

14. Press Enter.

Figure 16-40 shows the resulting solid object.

16-15 COMBINING SOLID OBJECTS

Figure 16-41 shows a dimensioned object. The following section explains how to create the object as a solid model. There are many different ways to create a solid model. The sequence presented here was selected to demonstrate several different input options.

To set up the drawing

Set up the drawing as follows:

Units = decimal (millimeters)
Drawing = Limits 297,210
Grid = 10
Snap = 10

View = SE Isometric
Toolbars = Draw, Modify, Solids, Solids Editing,
   View, UCS, and UCS II

The object is relatively small, so use the Zoom tool to create a size that you find visually comfortable.

To draw the first box

The size specifications for this box are based on the given dimensions.

1. Select the Box tool from the Solids toolbar.

Command: _box
Specify corner of box or [CEnter]:

Figure 16-41

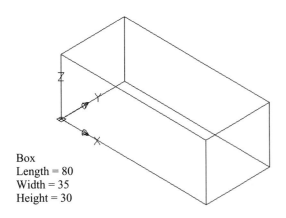

Box
Length = 80
Width = 35
Height = 30

Figure 16-42

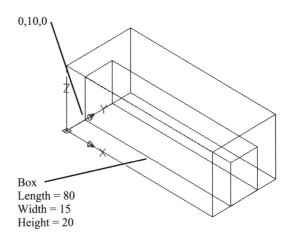

0,10,0

Box
Length = 80
Width = 15
Height = 20

Figure 16-43

2. Select the 0,0,0 point on the WCS by pressing Enter.

Specify corner or [Cube/Length]:

3. Type L; press Enter.

Specify length:

4. Type 80; press Enter, or use dynamic input.

Specify width:

5. Type 35; press Enter.

Specify height:

6. Type 30; press Enter.

See Figure 16-42.

To create the internal open volume

The volume will be created by subtracting a second box from the first box.

1. Select the Box tool from the Solids toolbar.

Command: _box
Specify corner of box or [CEnter]:

2. Select the 0,10,0 point on the WCS.

The point 0,10,0 was selected based on the given 10-millimeter dimension. The point can be selected using the crosshair because it is on the grid located on the XY plane.

Specify corner or [Cube/Length]:

3. Type L; press Enter.

Specify length:

4. Type 80; press Enter.

Specify width:

5. Type 15; press Enter.

Specify height:

6. Type 20; press Enter.

Figure 16-43 shows the second box within the first box.

7. Select the Subtract tool from the Solids Editing toolbar.

Command: _subtract
Select solids and regions to subtract from...
Select objects:

8. Select the first box.

Select objects:

9. Press Enter.

Select solids and regions to subtract...
Select objects:

10. Press Enter.

See Figure 16-44.

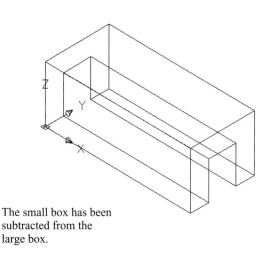

The small box has been subtracted from the large box.

Figure 16-44

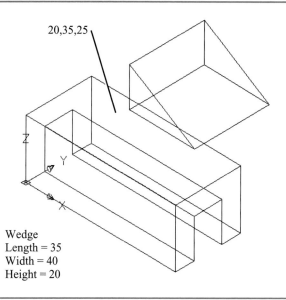

20,35,25

Wedge
Length = 35
Width = 40
Height = 20

Figure 16-45

To create the wedge-shaped cutout

The wedge-shaped cutout will be created by first drawing a wedge based on the given dimensions, then moving the wedge into the correct location. A small box will be unioned to the wedge, and both will be subtracted from the first box.

1. Select the Wedge tool from the Solids toolbar.

   Command: _wedge
   Specify first corner of wedge or [CEnter] <0,0,0>:

2. Type 20,35,25; press Enter.

This corner point locates the corner of the wedge on the back surface of the first box, 5 millimeters below the top surface as specified by the given dimensions.

   Specify corner or [Cube/Length]:

3. Type L; press Enter.

   Specify length:

4. Type 35; press Enter.

The Wedge command always interprets a length dimension as being along the current X axis. In this example, the wedge will be rotated 90° into place, so the 35-millimeter length must be equal to the width of the object.

   Specify width:

5. Type 40; press Enter.

   Specify height:

6. Type 20; press Enter.

   See Figure 16-45.

To rotate the wedge in the XY plane

1. Select the Rotate tool from the Modify toolbar.

   Command: _rotate
   Select objects:

2. Select the wedge.

   Select objects:

3. Press Enter.

   Specify base point:

4. Use Osnap, Endpoint and select the corner point of the wedge.

You may have to turn the Snap command off temporarily to select the point.

   Specify rotation angle or [Reference]s:

5. Type −90; press Enter.

See Figure 16-46. The counterclockwise direction is the positive direction.

To rotate the wedge along the X axis

The Rotate command will rotate only in the current XY plane, so a new UCS is required.

1. Select the Origin UCS tool from the UCS toolbar.

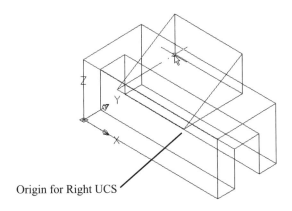

Origin for Right UCS

Figure 16-46

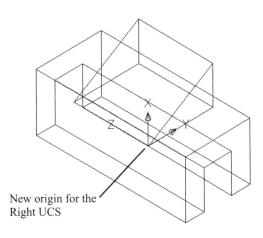

New origin for the
Right UCS

Figure 16-47

Command: _ucs
Enter an option [New/Move/orthoGraphic/Prev/
Restore/Save/Del/Apply/?/World] <World>: _o
Specify new origin point <0,0,0>:

2. Use Osnap, Endpoint and select the new origin.

   See Figure 16-47.

3. Select the Y Axis Rotate UCS.

   Specify rotation angle about Y axis <90>:

4. Type −90°; press Enter.
5. Select the Rotate tool from the Modify toolbar.

   Command: _rotate
   Select objects:

6. Select the wedge.

   Select objects:

7. Press Enter.

   Base point:

8. Use Osnap, Endpoint and select the new origin,
   or type 0,0,0; press Enter.

   Specify rotation angle or [Reference]:

9. Type 180; press Enter.

   See Figure 16-48.

To relocate the wedge

1. Select the Move tool from the Modify toolbar.

   Command: _move
   Select objects:

2. Select the wedge.

   Select objects:

3. Press Enter.

   Specify base point or displacement:

4. Type 0,0,0; press Enter.

   Specify second point of displacement or <use
   first point as displacement>:

5. Type 0,35,0; press Enter.

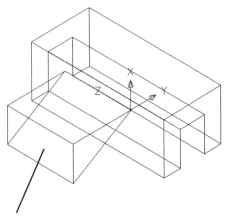

The wedge rotated 180° about the Right UCS

Figure 16-48

SOLID MODELING 651

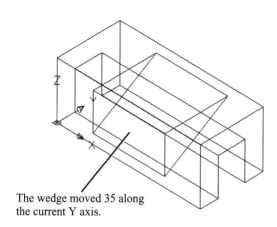

The wedge moved 35 along
the current Y axis.

Figure 16-49

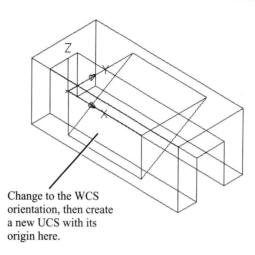

Change to the WCS
orientation, then create
a new UCS with its
origin here.

Figure 16-50

The displacement inputs serve to move the wedge 35 millimeters along the current Y axis. Remember, you are in a new UCS.

6. Select the World tool from the UCS toolbar.

   See Figure 16-49.

To add a small box to the wedge

The wedge is located 5 millimeters from the top surface of the first box. A small box will be added to reach the top surface of the first box.

1. Select the Origin tool from the UCS toolbar.

   Command: _ucs
   Enter an option [New/Move/orthoGraphic/Prev/Restore/Save/Del/Apply/?/World] <World>: _o
   Specify new origin point <0,0,0>:

2. Use Osnap, Endpoint and select the new origin.

   See Figure 16-50.

3. Select the Box tool from the Solids toolbar.

   Command: _box
   Specify corner of box or [CEnter] <0,0,0>:

4. Press Enter.

   The corner of the box could have been defined directly relative to the WCS as point 20,0,25.

   Specify corner or [Cube/Length]:

5. Use Osnap, Endpoint and select the diagonal corner from the origin.

Specify height:

6. Type 5; press Enter.

   See Figure 16-51.

7. Select the World tool from the UCS toolbar and return to the world coordinate system.

To subtract the wedge and small box

1. Select the Subtract tool from the Modify II toolbar.

   Command: _subtract
   Select solids and regions to subtract from...
   Select objects:

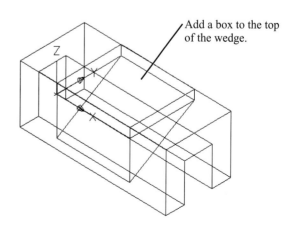

Add a box to the top
of the wedge.

Figure 16-51

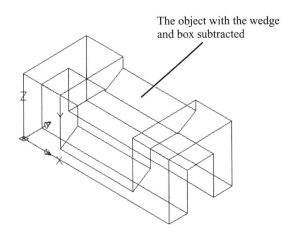

The object with the wedge
and box subtracted

Figure 16-52

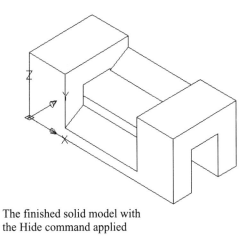

The finished solid model with
the Hide command applied

Figure 16-53

2. Select the first box.

   Select objects:

3. Press Enter.

   Select solids and regions to subtract...
   Select objects:

4. Select the small box.

   Select objects:

5. Select the wedge.

   Select objects:

6. Press Enter.

   See Figure 16-52.

7. Type Hide; press Enter.

   See Figure 16-53.

8. Type Regen; press Enter.

The Regen command will return the screen to a wire frame type of object display.

9. Save the drawing, if desired.

16-16 INTERSECTING SOLIDS

Figure 16-54 shows an incomplete 3-D drawing of a cone and a cylinder. The problem is to complete the drawing in 3-D and show the front, top, and right-side orthographic views of the intersecting objects. If this problem were to be done by hand on a drawing board, it would require extensive projection between views, as well as a

high degree of precision in the line work. Done as a solid model, the problem is much simpler and serves to show the strength of solid modeling as a design tool.

To set up the drawing

Set up the drawing screen as follows.

Grid = 0.50
Snap = 0.50
Units = Decimal
View = SE Isometric
Toolbars = Solids, Solids Editing, View, UCS,
   UCS II, Modify, and Modify II

Figure 16-54

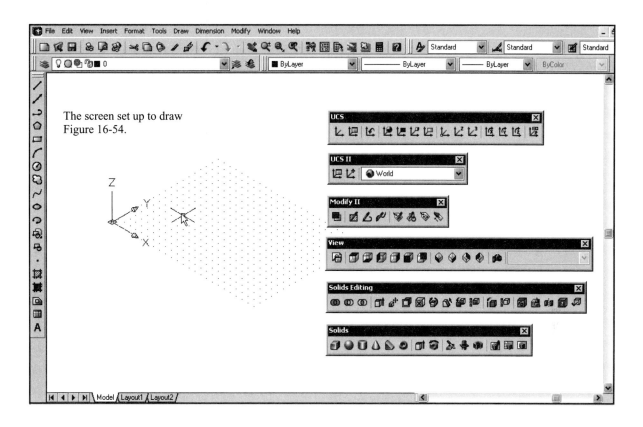

Figure 16-55

Isolines = 18

See Figure 16-55. The objects are small, so use the Zoom Window command to create a comfortable visual size.

To draw the cone

1. Type Isolines and set the value for 18.
2. Select the Cone tool from the Solids toolbar.

   Command: _cone
   Current wire frame density: Isolines = 18
   Specify center point for base of cone or [Elliptical]
   <0,0,0>:

3. Press Enter.

   The center point of the cone will be located on the origin of the WCS.

   Specify radius for base of cone or [Diameter]:

4. Type d; press Enter.

Specify diameter for base of cone:

5. Type 1.50.

   Specify height of cone or [Apex]:

6. Type 2.50; press Enter.

   See Figure 16-56.

The cone drawn about the WCS origin

Figure 16-56

To draw the cylinder

1. Select the Origin UCS tool from the UCS toolbar.

   Command: _ucs
   Enter an option [New/Move/orthoGraphic/Prev/
   Restore/Save/Del/Apply/?/World] <World>: _o
   Specify new origin point <0,0,0>:

2. Type 1.25,0,0; press Enter.

   This input locates the origin in the same plane as the end of the cylinder.

3. Select the X Axis Rotate UCS tool from the UCS toolbar and press Enter, accepting the 90° default value, then select the Y Axis Rotate UCS tool and accept the 90° default value.

   See Figure 16-57.

4. Select the Cylinder tool from the Solids toolbar.

   Command: _cylinder
   Current wire frame density: ISOLINES=18.
   Specify center point for base of cylinder or [Elliptical] <0,0,0>:

5. Type 0,.88,0.

   Specify radius for base of cylinder or [Diameter]:

6. Type d; press Enter.

   Specify diameter for base of cylinder:

7. Type .63; press Enter.

   Specify height of cylinder or [Center of other end]:

8. Type −2.50; press Enter.

   The negative value is used based on the right-hand rule applied to the Right UCS. See Figure 16-58.

To complete the 3-D drawing

1. Select the Union tool from the Solids Editing toolbar.

   Command: _union
   Select objects:

2. Select the cone.

   Select objects:

3. Select the cylinder.

   Select objects:

4. Press Enter.

   Command:

5. Select the World tool from the UCS toolbar.

   See Figure 16-59.

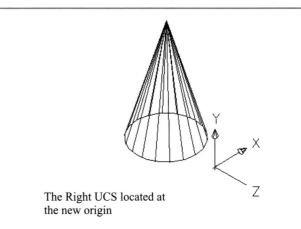

The Right UCS located at the new origin

Figure 16-57

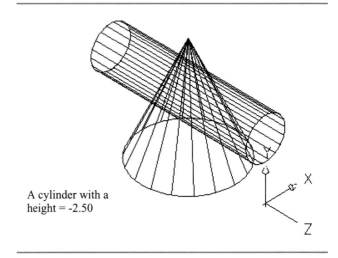

A cylinder with a height = -2.50

Figure 16-58

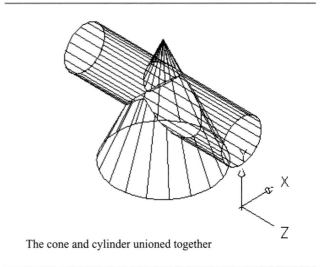

The cone and cylinder unioned together

Figure 16-59

Figure 16-60

To create the viewports for the orthographic views

1. Select the View pull-down menu.
2. Select Viewports, then 4 Viewports.

See Figures 16-60 and 16-61. The toolbars have been deleted from Figure 16-61 for clarity. Only the View toolbar is shown.

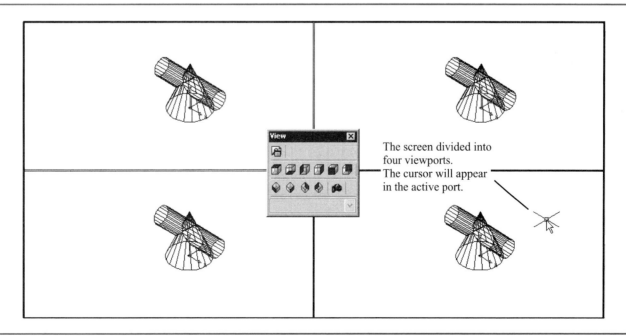

Figure 16-61

To create a top orthographic view

1. Move the cursor into the top left port and press the left mouse button.

   The crosshairs will appear in the port.

2. Select the Top View tool from the View toolbar.

   The View dialog box will appear.

3. Make the Top view the current view.

   An oversized top view of the objects will appear.

4. Type Zoom; press Enter.

   [All/Center/Dynamic/Extents/Left/Previous/Vmax/ Window] <Real time>:

5. Type 3; press Enter.

   See Figure 16-62.

To create the front orthographic view

1. Move the cursor into the lower left port and press the left mouse button.

   The crosshairs will appear in the port.

2. Select the Front View tool from the View toolbar and make it the current view.

3. Type zoom, press Enter, and enter a scale factor of 3.

   See Figure 16-63.

To create the right-side orthographic view

1. Move the cursor to the lower right port and press the left mouse button.
2. Select the Right View tool from the View toolbar and make it the current view.
3. Type zoom, press Enter, and enter a scale factor of 3.

   See Figure 16-64. The model shown in the upper right port has the Hide command applied and has also been zoomed to a scale factor of 3.

16-17 SOLID MODELS OF CASTINGS

Figure 16-65 shows a casting. Note that the object includes rounded edges. These rounded edges can be created on a solid model using the Fillet command found on the Modify toolbar. The Fillet command was explained in Chapter 2.

Figure 16-62

Figure 16-63

Figure 16-64

Figure 16-65

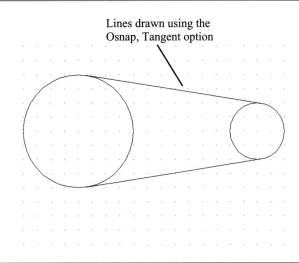

Lines drawn using the
Osnap, Tangent option

Figure 16-66

This example will be presented without specific dimensions and will use a generalized approach to creating the model. Decimal inches are used for all dimensions.

To draw the basic shape

The basic shape will first be drawn in 2-D, then extruded into the 3-D solid model.

1. Set up the drawing screen as needed.
2. Draw the basic shape using the Circle tool and then the Line tool along with the Osnap, Tangent option.

See Figure 16-66. It is important to know the center point locations for the two circles in terms of their X,Y components. In this example the center point location for the large circle is 4.5,5, and the location for the small circle is 11,5.

To create a polyline from the basic shape

Because only polylines can be extruded, some of the lines in the basic shape must be formed into a polyline. The large circle can be extruded, so it need not be included as part of the polyline; however, the polyline must be a closed area, and so it will need part of the circle. The needed circular segment can be created by drawing a second large circle directly over the existing circle and then using the Trim command to remove the excess portion. Remember that two lines can occupy the same space in AutoCAD drawings. If there is difficulty working with the two large circles, trim the circles, then add another larger circle, if needed.

1. Use the Trim tool to remove the excess portion of both the large and small circles.

Figure 16-67 shows the resulting shape that will be joined to form a polyline.

2. Select the Edit Polyline tool from the Modify II toolbar.

    Command: _pedit
    Select polyline:

3. Select the remaining portion of the small circle.

    Object selected is not a polyline
    Do you want to turn it into one? <Y>

4. Press Enter.

    Enter an option [Close/Join/Width/Edit vertex/Fit/
    Spline/Decurve/Ltype gen/Undo/eXit/ <X>:

5. Type j; press Enter.

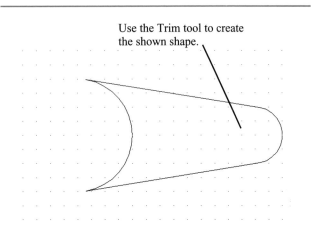

Use the Trim tool to create
the shown shape.

Figure 16-67

Change to a SE Isometric view.

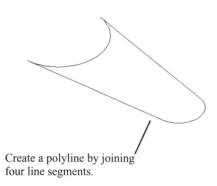

Create a polyline by joining
four line segments.

Figure 16-68

Select objects:

6. Select the line segments for the polyline; press Enter.

   Close/Join/Width/Edit vertex/Fit/Spline/Decurve/ Ltype gen/Undo/eXit/ <X>:

7. Press Enter.

There will be no visible changes to the lines, but they have been combined to form a single polyline.

To extrude the shape

1. Select the SE Isometric tool from the View tool-bar and make it the current view.
2. Use the Zoom tool, if needed, to present the fig-ure at a comfortable visual size.

   See Figure 16-68.

3. Type Isolines and change the value to 18.
4. Select the Extrude tool from the Solids toolbar.

   Command: _extrude
   Current wire frame density: ISOLINES=18
   Select objects:

5. Select the polyline, and assign a height and 0° taper.

   In this example a height of 1 was assigned. See Figure 16-69.

   Command:

6. Select the cylinder tool from the Solids toolbar and create a cylinder whose diameter equals the original large circle diameter and whose height is 3.

   See Figure 16-70.

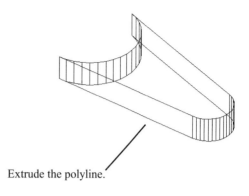

Extrude the polyline.

Figure 16-69

To add the holes

Create the holes by subtracting cylinders from the object.

1. Select the Cylinder tool from the Solids toolbar.

   Command: _cylinder
   Current wire frame density: ISOLINES=18
   Specify center point for base of cylinder or [Elliptical] <0,0,0>:

2. Type 4.5,5,0; press Enter.

   This value came from the original circle's center point location.

3. Enter the appropriate diameter and height values.

The cylinder was created using the Cylinder tool on the Solids toolbar. Center point = 4.5,5.

Figure 16-70

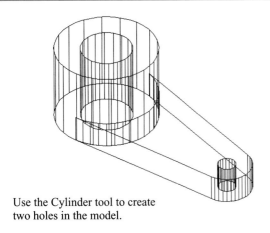

Use the Cylinder tool to create
two holes in the model.

Figure 16-71

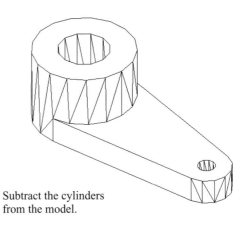

Subtract the cylinders
from the model.

Figure 16-72

Command:

4. Repeat the cylinder command.

   Specify center point for base of cylinder or [Elliptical] <0,0,0>:

5. Type 11,5,0.
6. Enter the appropriate diameter and height values.

   See Figure 16-71.

7. Select the Union tool from the Solids Editing toolbar and join the large cylinder portion of the object to the polyline portion.
8. Select the Subtract tool from the Solids Editing toolbar and subtract the cylinders from the basic shape.

   See Figure 16-72.

To create the rounded edges

1. Select the Fillet tool from the Modify toolbar.

   Command: _fillet
   Current settings: Mode = TRIM, Radius=0.5000.
   Select first object or [Polyline/Radius/Trim]:

2. Type r and enter the appropriate radius value, if necessary.

   In this example a radius of 0.125 was used.

3. Repeat the Fillet command and select the outside edge of the top surface of the large cylindrical portion of the object.

   Enter fillet radius <0.1250>:

4. Press Enter.

   Select an edge or [Chain/Radius]:

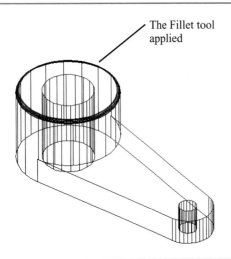

The Fillet tool
applied

Figure 16-73

The Fillet tool
applied

Figure 16-74

Draw a cylinder to represent the body of the thread and arrayed circles to represent the threads.

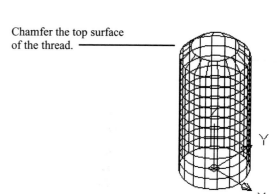

Chamfer the top surface of the thread.

Figure 16-75

5. Press Enter.

See Figure 16-73.

6. Use the Fillet tool to create a fillet along the top edges of the object as shown in Figure 16-74.

Note that the arc edge line between the large cylindrical portion of the object and the extended flat area cannot be filleted.

16-18 THREAD REPRESENTATIONS IN SOLID MODELS

This section explains how to draw thread representations for solid models. The procedure presented represents only a thread. It is not an actual detailed solid drawing of a thread. As with the thread representations presented in Chapter 11 for 2-D drawings, 3-D representations are acceptable for most applications.

1. Select the Cylinder tool from the Solids toolbar and draw a cylinder.

In the example shown, a cylinder of diameter 3 and a height of 6 was drawn centered about the 0,0,0 point of the WCS. See Figure 16-75.

2. Draw a circle with a diameter equal to the diameter of the cylinder using center point 5,0,0.
3. Select the 3D Array command from the Modify pull-down menu, located under the 3D Operation heading.

   Select object:

4. Select the circle.

Rectangular or Polar array:

5. Type r; press Enter.

Enter the number of rows (___)<1>:

6. Press Enter.

Enter the number of columns: (|||)<1>:

7. Press Enter.

Enter the number of levels:

8. Type 11; press Enter.

The number 11 is used because the cylinder is 6 units high, and in this example circles representing threads will be spaced .5 apart. The top edge of the thread will be chamfered.

Specify the distance between levels: (...):

9. Type .5; press Enter.
10. Select the Move tool from the Modify toolbar and move the arrayed circles' center points to the 0,0,0 origin.
11. Select the Chamfer tool from the Modify toolbar and draw a .5 × .5 chamfer around the top edge of the cylinder.

16-19 LIST

The List command is used to display database information for a drawn solid object. Figure 16-76 shows a list for the thread model created for Figure 16-75. There is no icon for the List command. Type list in response to a command prompt and select the object.

The List command output

Figure 16-76

The Massprop command output

Figure 16-77

Figure 16-78

16-20 MASSPROP

The Massprop command is used to display information about the structural characteristics of an object. Figure 16-77 shows the Massprop information for the object shown in Figure 16-75. To access the Massprop command, type Massprop in response to a command prompt and select the object.

16-21 FACE AND EDGE EDITING

AutoCAD 2006 has the capability to edit the faces and edges of existing solids. The solid editing command can be accessed using the Solids Editing toolbar or by using the Solids Editing option on the Modify pull-down menu. See Figure 16-78. The following examples are based on a solid box of dimensions 4×2×3.

To extrude a face (See Figure 16-79.)

1. Select the Extrude faces tool from the Solids Editing toolbar.

   Select faces or [Undo/Remove]:

2. Select the right face.

   Select faces or [Undo/Remove]:

3. Press the right mouse button and enter the face.

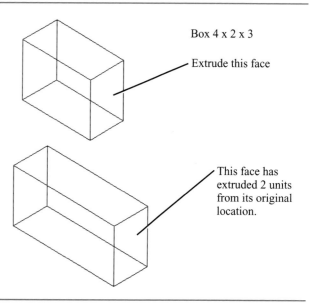

Box 4 x 2 x 3

Extrude this face

This face has extruded 2 units from its original location.

Figure 16-79

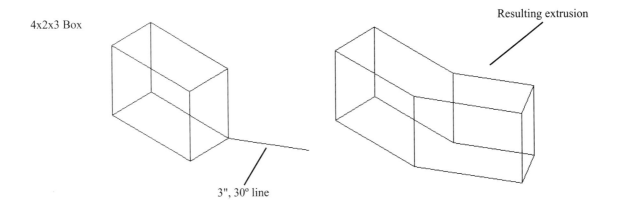

4x2x3 Box

Resulting extrusion

3", 30° line

Figure 16-80

Specify height of extrusion or [Path]:

4. Type 2; press Enter.

    Specify angle of taper for extrusion <0>:

5. Press Enter.

To extrude a face along a path

See Figure 16-80. A line has been drawn from the right corner of the box 3″, 30°. This line will serve as the extrusion path.

1. Select the Extrude faces tool from the Solids Editing toolbar.

    Select faces or [Undo/Remove]:

2. Select the right face.

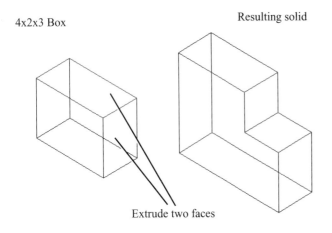

4x2x3 Box

Resulting solid

Extrude two faces

Figure 16-81

Select faces or [Undo/Remove]:

3. Press the right mouse button and enter the face.

    Specify height of extrusion or [Path]:

4. Type p; press Enter.

    Select extrusion path:

5. Select the line.

To extrude two faces at the same time (See Figure 16-81.)

1. Select the Extrude faces tool from the Solids Editing toolbar.

    Select faces or [Undo/Remove]:

2. Select the right face.

    Select faces or [Undo/Remove]:

3. Press the right mouse button and enter the face.

    Specify height of extrusion or [Path]:

4. Type 2; press Enter.

To move a face (See Figure 16-82.)

1. Select the Move faces tool from the Solids Editing toolbar.

    Select faces or [Undo/Remove]:

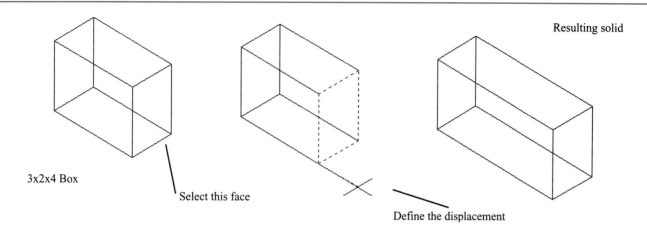

3x2x4 Box

Select this face

Define the displacement

Resulting solid

Figure 16-82

2. Select the right face and enter it.

   Specify a base point or displacement:

3. Select the corner of the box as shown.

   Specify a second point of displacement.

4. Select a second point along the X axis.

To offset faces (See Figure 16-83.)

1. Select the Offset Faces tool from the Solids Editing toolbar.

   Select faces or [Undo/Remove]:

2. Select the right and front faces and enter them.

   Specify the offset distance:

3. Type 1.5; press Enter.

To rotate a face (See Figure 16-84.)

1. Select the Rotate Faces tool from the Solids Editing toolbar.

   Select faces or [Undo/Remove]:

2. Select the front face and enter it.

   Specify an axis point or [Axis by object/View/ Xaxis/Yaxis/Zaxis]<2 points>:

3. Type x; press Enter.

   Specify the origin of the rotation <0,0,0>:

4. Press Enter.

   Specify the rotation angle or [Reference]:

5. Type 15; press enter.

   An input of −15 would have rotated the face in the opposite direction.

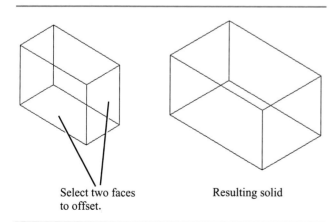

Select two faces
to offset.

Resulting solid

Figure 16-83

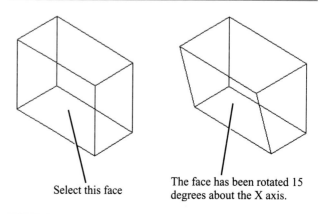

Select this face

The face has been rotated 15
degrees about the X axis.

Figure 16-84

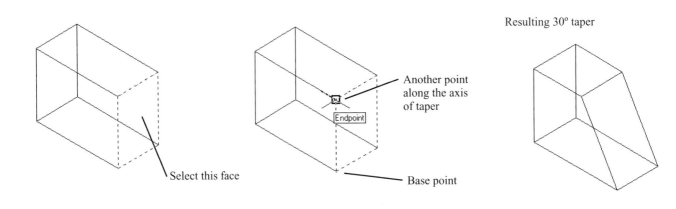

Resulting 30° taper

Another point along the axis of taper

Endpoint

Select this face

Base point

Figure 16-85

To taper a face

See Figure 16-85.

1. Select the Taper faces tool from the Solids Editing toolbar.

   Select faces or [Undo/Remove]:

2. Select the right front face.

   Select faces or [Undo/Remove]:

3. Press the right mouse button and enter the face.

   Specify the base point:

4. Select the lower right corner of the box.

   Specify another point along the axis of tapering:

5. Use Osnap, Endpoint and specify the top corner as shown in Figure 16-85.

   Specify the taper angle:

6. Type 30; press Enter.

   [Extrude/Move/Rotate/Offset/Taper/Delete/Copy/ coLor/Undo/eXit]<eXit>:

7. Type x, press Enter.

To copy a face

See Figure 16-86.

1. Select the Copy faces tool from the Solids Editing toolbar.

   Select faces or [Undo/Remove]:

2. Select the right front face.

   Select faces or [Undo/Remove]:

3. Press the right mouse button and enter the face.

   Specify a base point or displacement:

4. Select the lower right corner of the box.

   Specify a second point of displacement:

5. Select the location for the copied face.

   [Extrude/Move/Rotate/Offset/Taper/Delete/Copy/ coLor/Undo/eXit]<eXit>:

6. Type x, press Enter

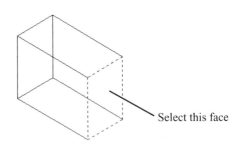

Select this face

Location for copied face.

Figure 16-86

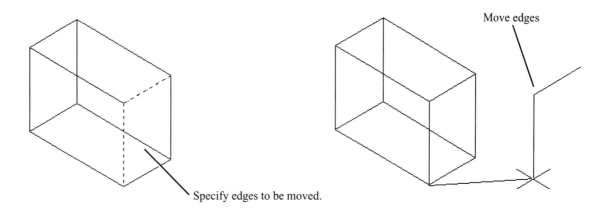

Move edges

Specify edges to be moved.

Figure 16-87

To copy edges (See Figure 16-87.)

1. Select the Copy edges tool from the Solids Editing toolbar.

   Select edges or [Undo/Remove]:

2. Select two edges.

   Select edges or [Undo/Remove]:

3. Press the right mouse button and enter the edges.

   Specify a base point or displacement:

4. Select the lower endpoint of the vertical line.

   Specify a second point of displacement:

5. Select a second point.

   Enter an edge editing option [Copy/coLor/Undo/ eXit] <eXit>:

6. Type x; press Enter.

To imprint an object (See Figure 16-88.)

1. Draw a solid box (4×2×3), then a Ø1.00 circle with its center point on the upper right corner of the box as shown.

2. Select the Imprint tool from the Solids Editing toolbar.

   Select a 3D solid

3. Select the box.

   Select an object to imprint:

4. Select the circle.

   Select the source object <N>:

5. Type y; press Enter twice.

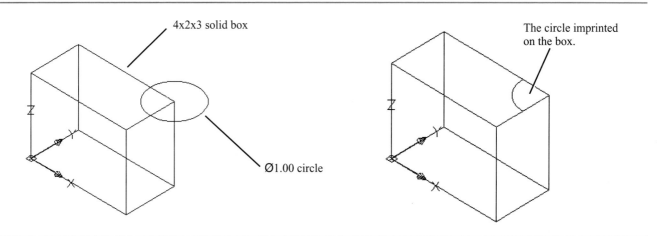

4x2x3 solid box

Ø1.00 circle

The circle imprinted on the box.

Figure 16-88

This is page 726

Shafts in the assembled position

Shaft 1

Shaft 2

Shaft 1: Ø=20±.01

Shaft 2: Ø=16±.01

Figure 16-89

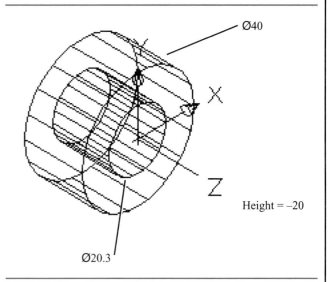

Ø40

Height = −20

Ø20.3

Figure 16-90

16-22 DESIGN PROBLEM

Design a coupling that will hold together the two shafts shown in Figure 16-89. The coupling is to be cylindrical and have an outside diameter of 40. It should also include two threaded holes for M4 set screws to hold the shafts in place. The final design was created as follows.

The two shafts are positioned on the screen so that the intersection of their centerlines is at the 0,0,0 point on the WCS. This was done to make it easier to determine any required coordinate points.

Assume that analysis has determined that the inside diameters of the coupling should be Ø20.3±.05 and Ø16.3±.05.

1. Select the Right UCS preset from the UCS II toolbar.

This step will create a new UCS perpendicular to the longitudinal axis of the two shafts. The origin for the UCS is located on the 0,0,0 point of the WCS.

2. Select the Cylinder tool from the Solids toolbar and draw two cylinders with their center points located at the 0,0,0 point.

The diameter of the smaller cylinder is Ø20.3, and the diameter of the larger cylinder is Ø40, and both have a height of −20. See Figure 16-90. The two shafts were moved to a new layer, Shafts, and the layer turned off.

3. Subtract the smaller cylinder from the larger cylinder.

4. Draw a second set of solid cylinders.

The diameter of the smaller cylinder is Ø16.3, and the diameter of the larger cylinder is Ø40, and both have a height of 20. See Figure 16-91.

5. Subtract the smaller cylinder from the larger cylinder.

6. Union the two resulting hollow cylinders to form the overall shape of the coupling.

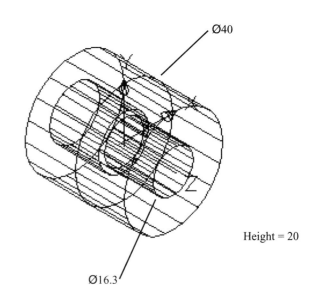

Ø40

Height = 20

Ø16.3

Figure 16-91

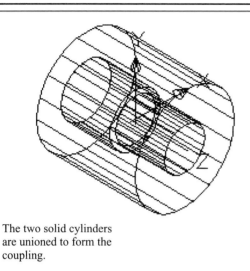

The two solid cylinders
are unioned to form the
coupling.

Figure 16-92

See Figure 16-92.

7. Create a new layer called Coupling and move the unioned cylinder to the new layer.

To draw the holes for the set screws

1. Return to the WCS using the World UCS tool from the UCS toolbar.
2. Draw a solid cylinder centered about center point −10,0,22 of Ø4 with a height of −50.

   See Figure 16-93.

3. Subtract the Ø4 cylinder from the coupling.

   See Figure 16-94.

4. Draw a second Ø4 solid cylinder centered about 10,0,22 with a height of −50.

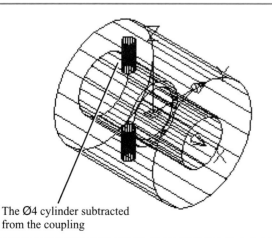

The Ø4 cylinder subtracted
from the coupling

Figure 16-94

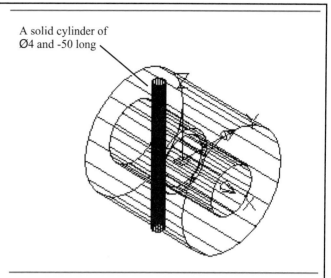

A solid cylinder of
Ø4 and -50 long

Figure 16-93

5. Subtract the Ø4 cylinder from the coupling.

   See Figure 16-95.

To create a sectional view of the coupling

1. Select the Front UCS preset from the UCS II toolbar.
2. Select the Origin tool from the UCS toolbar and move the origin to −20,−20,0.

   The given coordinate values are based on the fact that the new Front UCS has its initial location at the WCS 0,0,0 point.

3. Select the Section tool from the Solids toolbar.

   Select object:

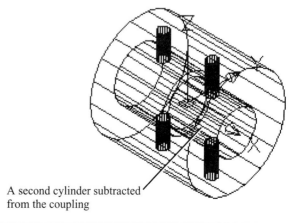

A second cylinder subtracted
from the coupling

Figure 16-95

A section plane created
in the XY plane

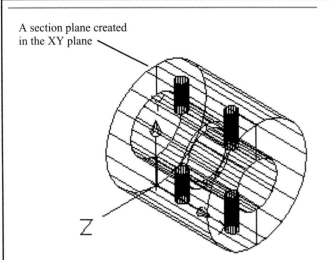

Z

Figure 16-96

Hatching applied to the
section plane

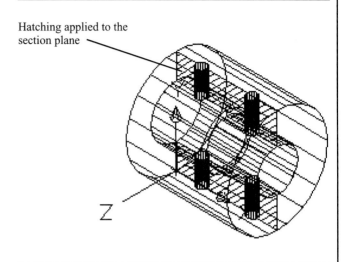

Z

Figure 16-97

4. Select the coupling; press Enter.

Specify first point on Section plane by [Object/ Zaxis/View/XY/YZ/ZX/3points] <3 points>:

5. Type XY; press Enter.

Specify a point on XY plane <0,0,0>:

6. Press Enter.

See Figure 16-96. The default 0,0,0 point can be accepted because the origin for the Front UCS was moved from its original location.

To hatch the sectional plane

1. Select the Hatch tool from the Draw toolbar.

The Hatch and Gradient dialog box will appear. See Chapter 6 for an explanation of the Hatch command. Use the ANSI 31 pattern.

2. Set the Scale factor equal to 5, then select Add: Select objects.

Select internal points:

3. Select the section plane; press Enter.

The Hatch and Gradient dialog box will reappear.

4. Select OK.

The section plane will be hatched. See Figure 16-97.

To add centerlines to the holes

See Figure 16-98. The values used here are based on the current origin location ($-20,-20,0$ relative to the WCS).

1. Select the Line tool from the Draw toolbar.

Specify first point:

2. Type 10,50,0; press Enter.

Specify next point

3. Type 10,$-$10,0; press Enter.
4. Press the right button and enter the line.
5. Select the Format pull-down menu, then Linetype.

The Linetype Manager dialog box will appear.

6. Select the Load button and load the Center linetype; select OK.

The Centerline option appears on the Linetype Manager listing.

7. Select OK and return to the drawing screen.
8. Select the vertical line.

It changes to a broken blue line.

9. Select the Modify pull-down menu, then Properties.

The Properties dialog box appears. See Figure 16-99.

10. Select Linetype and change the type to CENTER.
11. Select the X in the upper right corner of the dialog box to exit the dialog box.

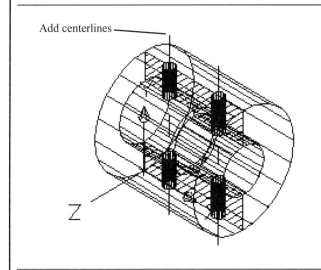

Add centerlines

Z

Figure 16-98

The selected line will remain blue until the next command is entered.

12.   Select the Copy tool from the Modify toolbar.

The line is already selected, so the base point prompt will appear.

Specify base point or displacement, or [Multiple]:

13.   Type 10,50,0; press Enter.

Specify second point of displacement or <use first point as dsplacement>:

14.   Type 30,50,0; press Enter.

Change the layer here.

Figure 16-99

To create two viewports (See Figure 16-100.)

1.   Select the View pull-down menu, then Viewports, then 2 Viewports.

Enter a configuration option [Horizontal /Vertical]:

2.   Press Enter.
3.   Place the crosshairs in the left port and press the left mouse button.

Figure 16-100

Figure 16-101

Figure 16-102

Figure 16-103

This will make the left port the active port.

4. Select the Front View tool from the View toolbar and make the front view the current view. See Figure 16-101.
5. Type zoom; press Enter.

   Specify corner of window, enter a scale factor 9nX or nXP), or [All/Center/Dynamic/Extents/Previous/Scale/Window] <real time>:

6. Type 4; press Enter.
7. Make the right port the active port and zoom it using a scale factor of 4. Use the Pan tool to center the object.

   See Figure 16-102.

To dimension the coupling

1. Make the port containing the section view the current port.
2. Select the Dimension Style tool from the Dimension toolbar and define the appropriate settings.
3. Dimension the sectional view.

   See Figure 16-103.

To render the 3-D view

1. Make the port with the 3-D view of the coupling the current port.
2. Type render; press Enter.

   The Render dialog box will appear. See Figure 16-104.

Figure 16-104

Figure 16-105

3. Select the Query for Selections box in the Rendering Procedure area of the dialog box.
4. Select the Render box.

   Select objects:

5. Select the coupling; press Enter.

   Figure 16-105 shows the results.

16-23 EXERCISE PROBLEMS

Draw the objects in Exercise Problems EX16-1 to EX16-45 as follows.

A. Draw each as a solid model.
B. Create front, top, and right-side orthographic views from the solid models.
C. Dimension the orthographic views.

EX16-1 INCHES

EX16-2 INCHES

EX16-3 MILLIMETERS

EX16-4 MILLIMETERS

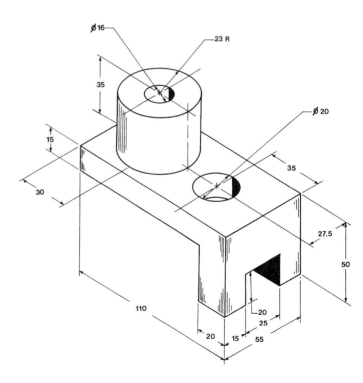

EX16-5 INCHES

.25
1.75
2.25
.88
1.50
.25
.25
.38
.63
.38

EX16-7 MILLIMETERS

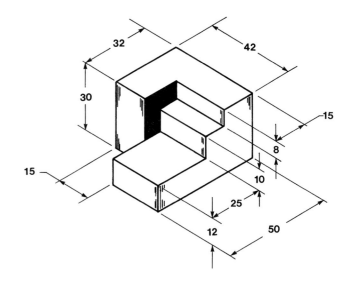

32
42
30
15
8
15
10
25
12
50

EX16-6 MILLIMETERS

Slot is 15 DEEP

25
8
17
10
15
18
50
10
15
40

EX16-8 MILLIMETERS

100
10
75
10
30
10
35
65
30
35
60
25
20
R15

EX16-9 INCHES

EX16-10 MILLIMETERS

EX16-11 MILLIMETERS

EX16-12 INCHES

EX16-13 MILLIMETERS

EX16-14 INCHES

EX16-17 INCHES

EX16-15 MILLIMETERS

EX16-18 MILLIMETERS

Note: Slot is 12 deep
from centerline

EX16-16 MILLIMETERS

EX16-19 MILLIMETERS

EX16-20 MILLIMETERS

EX16-23 MILLIMETERS

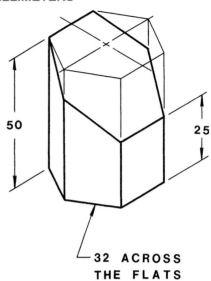

32 ACROSS
THE FLATS

EX16-21 INCHES

EX16-24 MILLIMETERS

EX16-22 MILLIMETERS

EX16-25 MILLIMETERS

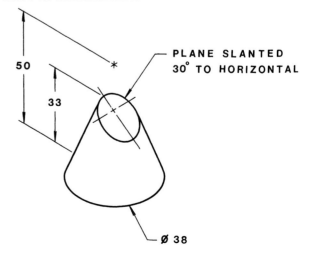

PLANE SLANTED
30° TO HORIZONTAL

EX16-26 MILLIMETERS (SCALE 2:1)

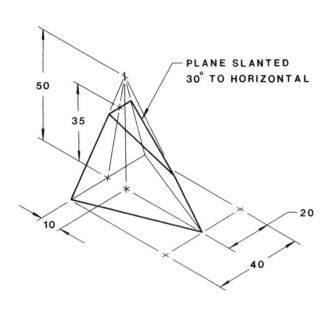

PLANE SLANTED
30° TO HORIZONTAL

50

35

10

20

40

EX16-28 INCHES

Ø .375 x .500 DEEP
4 HOLES

1.75

2.25

.75

.50

1.00

.88

.63

1.63

1.13

1.25

30°

.50

.88

60°

.75

Ø .750 x .25 DEEP
2 HOLES – BOTH
BOTTOM DRILLED

2.00

.25

1.75

EX16-27 MILLIMETERS

CENTERLINE

11

20

20

10

46

11

80

35

7 ALL
AROUND

HEXAGON
95 ACROSS
THE FLATS

14

EX16-29 MILLIMETERS

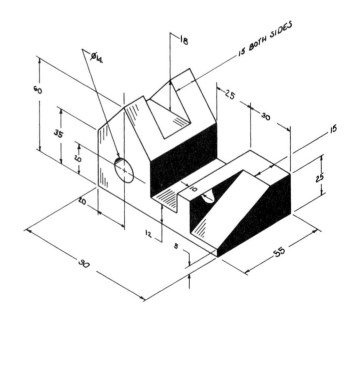

18

15 BOTH SIDES

Ø14

25

60

30

35

15

20

25

20

10

12

5

55

90

EX16-30 INCHES (SCALE 2:1)

EX16-33 MILLIMETERS

ALL FILLETS AND ROUNDS=R5
MATL 5 THK

EX16-31 MILLIMETERS

ALL FILLETS AND ROUNDS = R3
MATL 5 THK

EX16-34 MILLIMETERS

ALL FILLETS AND
ROUNDS=R5

EX16-32 MILLIMETERS (SCALE 2:1)

ALL FILLETS AND ROUNDS= R3

EX16-35 INCHES (SCALE 2:1)

EX16-36 INCHES (SCALE 4:1)

EX16-37 INCHES

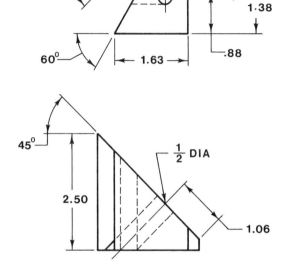

EX16-38 INCHES

TOP

All fillets and rounds = $\frac{1}{8}$ R

EX16-39 MILLIMETERS

EX16-41 MILLIMETERS

EX16-40 MILLIMETERS

EX16-42 MILLIMETERS

EX16-43 MILLIMETERS

EX16-45 MILLIMETERS

EX16-44 INCHES

Draw a solid model of the object, then create the three indicated sectional views from the model.

HOLE	X	Y	DIA
A	1.63	2.00	.44
B	1.13	1.00	.56
C	2.50	2.00 / 1.00	.63
D	3.88	2.00 / 1.00	.50

Redraw the assemblies in Exercise Problems EX16-46 to EX16-48 as solid models with the individual parts located in approximately the positions shown.

EX16-46 MILLIMETERS

First Assembly

EX16-47 MILLIMETERS

Pivot Assembly

M8 x 1.25 Screw
50 Long
15 THD Length

10 x 14 x 3 Washer
2 REQD

Support Block

10 x 13 x 2 Washer
2 REQD

Ø10 – 2 Holes

R7 – 2 Places

Ø10
6 Holes

All parts made from SAE 1020 ST

M 8 x 1.25 Nut

Linkage

EX16-48 MILLIMETERS

REAR VIEW OF
PART 1

Prepare solid models and 3-D orthographic views of the intersecting objects in Exercise Problems EX16-49 to EX16-54.

EX16-49 INCHES

EX16-52 MILLIMETERS

EX16-50 MILLIMETERS

EX16-53 MILLIMETERS

EX16-51 MILLIMETERS

EX16-54 INCHES

EX16-55

Redraw the given objects as solid models and add the bolts with the appropriate nuts at the L and H holes. Add the appropriate drawing callouts. Specify standard bolt lengths.

A. Use inch values.
B. Use millimeter values.
C. Prepare orthographic assembly views from the solid model.
D. Prepare a parts list.
E. Prepare detail drawings of each part.

DIMENSION	INCHES	mm
A	.25	6
B	2.00	50
C	1.00	25
D	.50	13
E	1.75	45
F	2.00	50
G	4.00	100
H	Ø.438	Ø11
J	.50	12.5
K	1.00	25
L	Ø.781	Ø19
M	.63	16
N	.88	22
P	2.00	50
Q	.25	6

EX16-56

Redraw the given objects as solid models and add the hex head machine screws at M and N. Use standard-length screws, and allow at least two unused threads at the bottom of each threaded hole. Add a bolt and the appropriate nut at hole P.

A. Use inch values.
B. Use millimeter values.
C. Draw the front assembly view using a sectional view.
D. Prepare orthographic assembly views from the solid model.
E. Prepare a parts list.
F. Prepare detail drawings of each part.

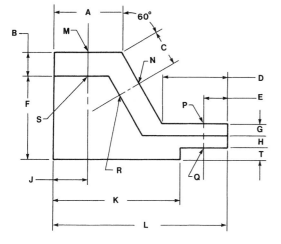

DIMENSION	INCHES	mm
A	1.50	38
B	.50	13
C	.75	19
D	1.38	35
E	.50	13
F	1.75	44
G	.25	6
H	.25	6
J	.75	19
K	2.75	70
L	3.75	96
M	Ø.31	Ø8
N	Ø.25	Ø6
P	Ø.41	Ø12
Q	Ø.41	Ø12
R	.164–32 UNF X .50 DEEP	M4 X 14 DEEP
S	.250–20 UNC X 1.63 DEEP	M6 X 14 DEEP
T	.25	6

EX16-57

Redraw the given objects as solid models and add the appropriate hex head bolts and nuts. Use only standard-length bolts, and include callouts for the bolts and nuts on the drawing.

A. Use inch values.
B. Use millimeter values.
C. Draw the front assembly view using a sectional view.
D. Prepare orthographic assembly views from the solid model.
E. Prepare a parts list.
F. Prepare detail drawings of each part.

DIMENSION	INCHES	mm
A	1.25	32
B	.63	16
C	.50	13
D	3.25	82
E	2.00	50
F	.63	16
G	.38	10
H	1.25	32
J	4.13	106
K	.63	16
L	.50	13
M	.75	10
N	3.38	86

EX16-58

The following objects are to be assembled as shown. Select sizes for the parts that make the assembly possible. (Choose dimensions for the top and bottom blocks and determine the screw and stud lengths.) The hex head screws (5) have a major diameter of either .375 or M10. The studs (3) are to have the same thread size as the screws and are to be screwed into the top part (2). The holes in the lower part (1) that accept the studs are to be clearance holes.

A. Use inch values.
B. Use millimeter values.
C. Draw the front assembly view using a sectional view.
D. Prepare orthographic assembly views from the solid model.
E. Prepare a parts list.
F. Prepare detail drawings of each part.

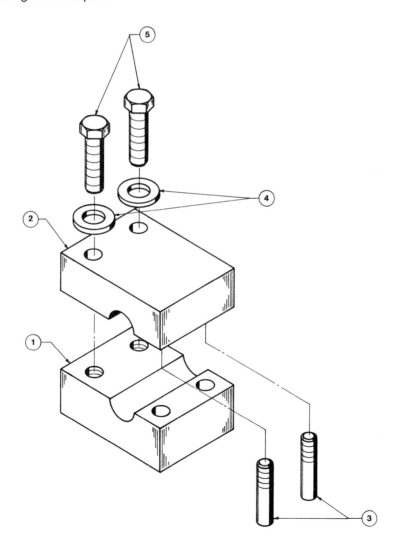

EX16-59

Select values for the dimensions indicated in A through J. Use either inches or millimeters. Use either .375 or M10 as the major diameter of the screws. Assemble the parts using three identical screws.

The holes in part 1 are clearance holes and are threaded in part 2. Allow at least two unused threads in the holes beyond the ends of their assembled screws.

A. Use inch values.
B. Use millimeter values.
C. Draw the front assembly view using a sectional view.
D. Prepare orthographic assembly views from the solid model.
E. Prepare a parts list.

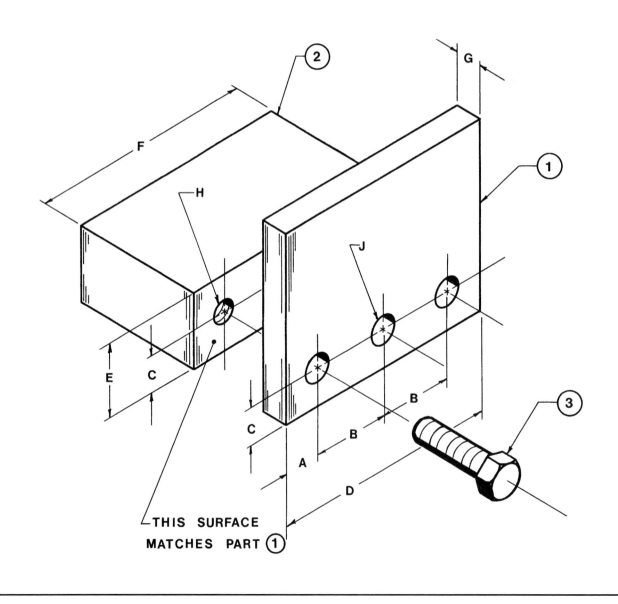

EX16-60

Design an access controller based on the information given. The controller works by moving an internal cylinder up and down within the base to align with output holes A and B. Liquids will enter the internal cylinder from the top, then exit the base through holes A and B. Include as many holes in the internal cylinder as necessary to create the following liquid exit combinations:

1. A open, B closed
2. A open, B open
3. A closed, B open

The internal cylinder is held in place by an alignment key and a stop button. The stop button is to be spring-loaded so that it will always be held in place. The internal cylinder will be moved by pulling out the stop button, repositioning the cylinder, then reinserting the stop button.

Prepare the following drawings.

A. Draw the objects as solid models.
B. Draw an assembly drawing.
C. Draw detail drawings of each nonstandard part. Include positional tolerances for all holes.
D. Prepare a parts list.

INTERNAL CYLINDER

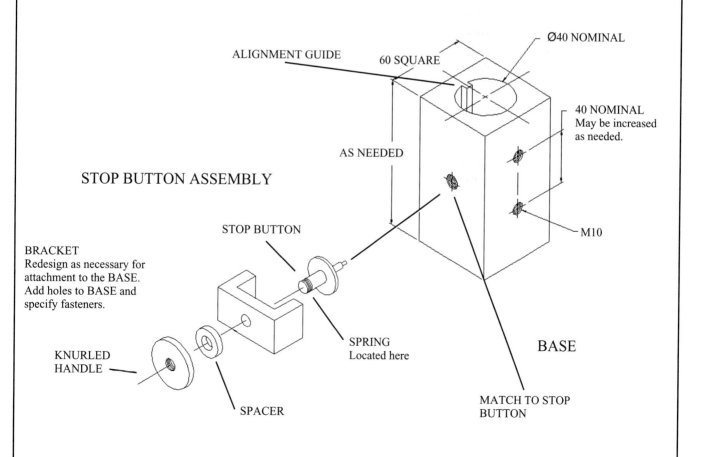

STOP BUTTON ASSEMBLY

EX16-61

Design a hand-operated grinding wheel specifically for sharpening a chisel. The chisel is to be located on an adjustable rest while it is being sharpened. The mechanism should be able to be clamped to a table during operation using two thumbscrews.

A standard grinding wheel is Ø6.00 inch, is ½ inch thick, and has an internal mounting hole with a 50.00±0.3 millimeter bore.

Prepare the following drawings.

A. Draw the objects as solid models.
B. Draw an assembly drawing.
C. Draw detail drawings of each nonstandard part.
D. Prepare a parts list.

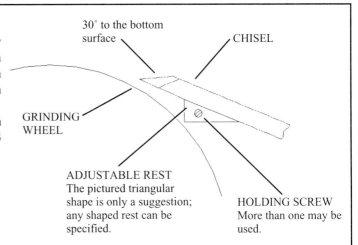

30° to the bottom surface

CHISEL

GRINDING WHEEL

ADJUSTABLE REST
The pictured triangular shape is only a suggestion; any shaped rest can be specified.

HOLDING SCREW
More than one may be used.

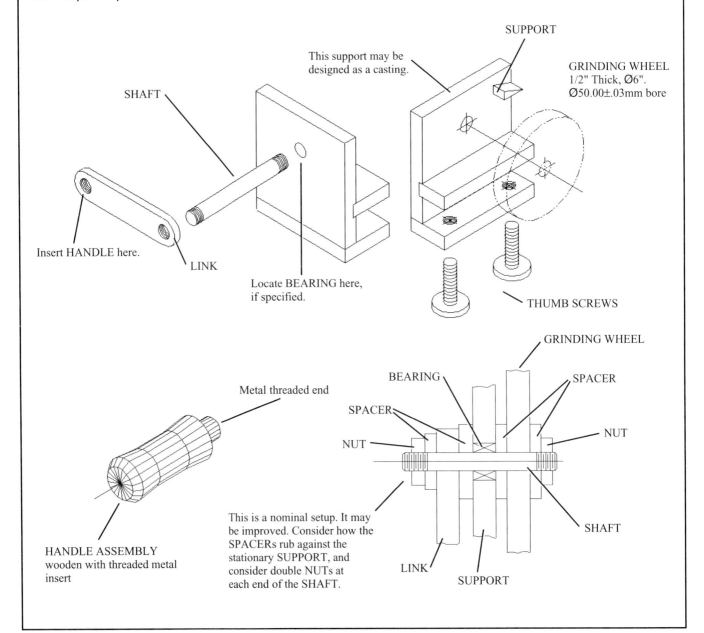

SHAFT

Insert HANDLE here.

LINK

This support may be designed as a casting.

Locate BEARING here, if specified.

SUPPORT

GRINDING WHEEL
1/2" Thick, Ø6".
Ø50.00±.03mm bore

THUMB SCREWS

Metal threaded end

HANDLE ASSEMBLY
wooden with threaded metal insert

This is a nominal setup. It may be improved. Consider how the SPACERs rub against the stationary SUPPORT, and consider double NUTs at each end of the SHAFT.

GRINDING WHEEL

BEARING

SPACER

SPACER

NUT

NUT

SHAFT

LINK

SUPPORT

EX16-62

A. Draw an assembly drawing of the given object.
B. Prepare a parts list.
C. Select appropriate fasteners to hold the object together.
D. Define the appropriate tolerances.

BRACKET ASSEMBLY

C-BRACKET, SAE1020 STEEL, 2 REQD
Part Number: AM311-1

QUAD SPACER, SAE 1020 STEEL
2 REQD, Part Number: AM311-2

EX16-63

A. Draw an assembly drawing of the given object.
B. Prepare a parts list.
C. Select appropriate fasteners to hold the object together.
D. Define the appropriate tolerances.
E. Create a second assembly and bolt it to the back of the given assembly to form a new assembly.

CLIP ASSEMBLY

SUPPORT PLATE
SAE 1040 STEEL, 2 REQD
Part Number: AM312-3

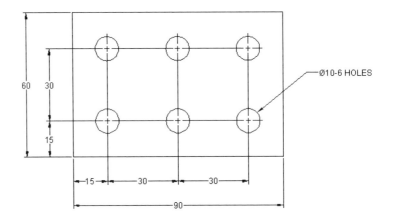

Ø10-6 HOLES

60   30   15

15   30   30   90

L-CLIP
SAE 1040 STEEL, 2 REQD
Part Number: AM312-4

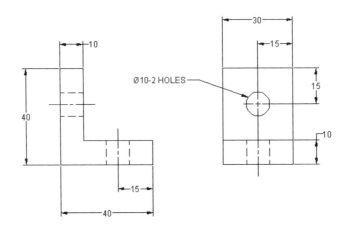

10   40   15   40

30   15   15   10

Ø10-2 HOLES

EX16-64

A. Draw an assembly drawing of the given object.
B. Prepare a parts list.
C. Select appropriate fasteners to hold the object together.
D. Define the appropriate tolerances.

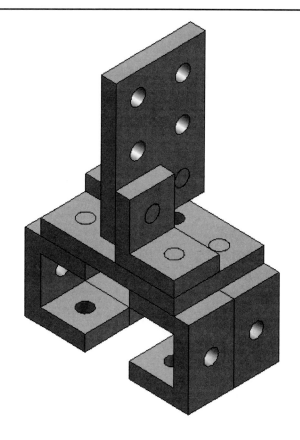

C-BRACKET
SAE 1020 STEEL, 4 REQD
Part Number: AM311-1

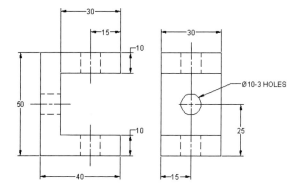

L-CLIP
SAE 1040 STEEL, 2 REQD
Part Number: AM312-4

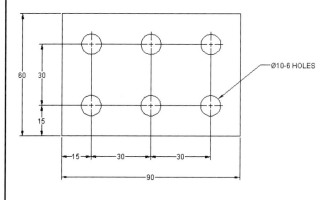

SUPPORT PLATE
SAE 1040 STEEL, 2 REQD
Part Number: AM312-3

EX16-65

A. Draw an assembly drawing of the given object.
B. Prepare a parts list.
C. Select appropriate fasteners to hold the object together.
D. Define the appropriate tolerances.
E. Use phantom lines and define the motion of the CENTER LINK and the ROCKER LINK, if the DRIVE LINK rotates 360°.

ROCKER ASSEMBLY

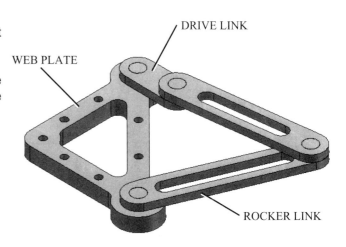

DRIVE LINK, SAE 1040 STEEL
Part Number: AM311-22A
5mm THK

ALL FILLETS AND ROUNDS = R3

ROCKER LINK, SAE 1040 STEEL
Part Number: AM311-22C
5mm THK

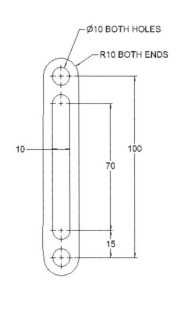

WEB PLATE, SAE 1040 STEEL
Part Number: AM311-22B
10mm THK

CENTER LINK, SAE 1040 STEEL
Part Number: AM311-22D
5mm THK

EX16-66

A. Draw an assembly drawing of the MINIVISE.
B. Prepare a parts list.
C. Select the appropriate fasteners to hold the vise together.

D. Redesign the interface between the Drive Screw and the Holder Plate.

MINIVISE

MINIVISE -ISO

1. BASE
SAE 1040 STEEL

2. DRIVE SCREW
SAE 1040 STEEL

3. END PLATE
SAE 1040 STEEL

4. SLIDER
SAE 1040 STEEL

5. HOLDER PLATE
   SAE 1040 STEEL

R2 - 4 CORNERS
R1 - BOTH SIDES
R3.00

7. HANDLE
   SAE 1040 STEEL

M6x1 - 6g
BOTH ENDS

1×1 CHAMFER
BOTH ENDS

Ø6.00

9. DRIVE PLATE
   SAE 1040 STEEL

Ø6.00 THRU
∨ Ø10.40 X 90.0°
3 HOLES

6. FACE PLATE
   SAE 1040 STEEL

Ø6.00 THRU
∨ Ø10.40 X 90.0°
2 HOLES

8. END CAP
   SAE 1040 STEEL

M6x1 - 6H▽6

1×1 CHAMFER

Ø12.00

10. M5×10 RECESSED COUNTERSUNIT HEAD-STEEL
11. M5×22 RECESSED COUNTERSUNIT HEAD-STEEL

EX16-67

Create the following for the slider assembly shown below.

1. Select the appropriate fasteners.
2. Create an assembly drawing.
3. Create a parts list.
4. Specify the tolerance for the Guide Shaft/Bearings interface.

Hole Plate

Guide Shaft - 1

Lock Plate - 2

RACK ASSEMBLY - 1

RACK ASSEMBLY

Ø19

M2.5x0.45 - 6H ▼ 6
6 HOLES

SIDE PLATE

Ø7-4 HOLES

1.25 MODULE, 20° PRESSURE ANGLE

17.17

282.8

4 50 75 75 50 4

10   M5x0.8 - 6H ▼ 8   VIEW C-C
        6 HOLES   SCALE 1 : 1

5

BASED ON: PRECISION RACK R1M-2
BERG MANUFACTURING CO.

RACK

Ø16
Ø10 THRU
M3.5x0.6 - 6H ▼ 4   10 10

PITCH Ø = 20.00
1.25 MODULE

PRECISION SPUR GEAR
BERG MANUFACTURING CO.
PART NUMBER: PBS86-16

GEAR 16

Ø19

Ø10

5

0.5X0.5 CHAMFER

BALL BEARING
BERG MANUFACTURING CO.
PART NUMBER: B11M-11

BEARING

EX16-67 CONTINUED

BASE SLIDER

LOCK PLATE - 2

GUIDE SHAFT - 1

KNURLED THUMB NUT
BERG MANUFACTURING CO.
STOCK NUMBER: PD1M-15

THUMB NUT

HOLE PLATE

C H A P T E R 17

Descriptive Geometry

17-1 INTRODUCTION

Descriptive geometry is the study of points, lines, and planes in space to determine their locations and true shapes. Classic descriptive geometry solutions involve using projection between both standard and auxiliary orthographic views. This chapter introduces these solutions and shows how they can be done using AutoCAD. The chapter also introduces some different approaches to the problems using AutoCAD's 3-D capabilities.

17-2 ORTHOGRAPHIC PROJECTION

Figure 17-1 shows a point P located in space represented by the box. The front, top, and right-side orthographic views of the point are used to define the location of the point by relating the point's location to the sides of the box or to the orthographic planes. The point's locations in the orthographic views are related to each other using a projection rectangle. The front and side views are related

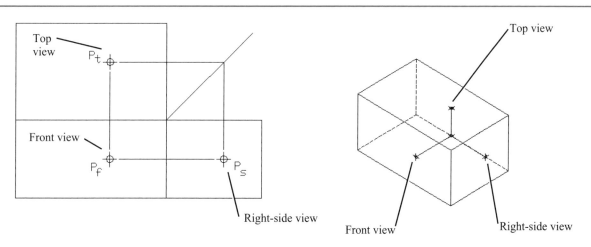

Figure 17-1

Where is the location of line A-P
in the top view?

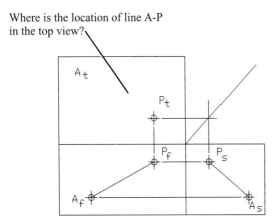

Line A-P is projected
with its endpoints.

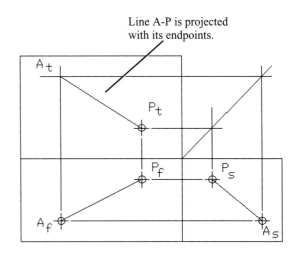

Figure 17-2

by a horizontal line, the top and front views by a vertical line, and the top and side views by a combination of a horizontal line and a vertical line.

Each orthographic view is two-dimensional and includes two pieces of locating information. For example, if the bottom surface of the box representing space were on an X,Y axis, the top view would locate the point using its X,Y coordinates, the front view the X,Z coordinates, and the side the Y,Z coordinates. This means that any two views will generate the X,Y,Z coordinate values for the point. This also means that if any two orthographic views are defined, the third orthographic view, or an auxiliary view, can be derived from the defined views.

To create a third view from two existing views

Figure 17-2 shows the front and side views of a line A-P. The location of the line in the top view can be determined by projecting the endpoints of the line. If the line were curved, it could not be projected by using just its endpoints. Other points would have to be defined and then projected.

To project a curved line

Figure 17-3 shows the front and top views of a curved line. The side view was derived as follows.

1. Draw vertical lines between the front and top views so that they intersect both the front and top views of the curved line.

In this example two vertical lines were drawn.

2. Label the intersections between the vertical lines and the front and top views of the curved line.

These intersections are defined points on the curved line common to both views of the line.

3. Project the points into the side view.
4. Use the Polyline tool from the Draw toolbar to join the endpoints and the projected points with a polyline.
5. Use the Polyline Edit tool from the Modify II toolbar, then the Fit option to change the straight polyline into a curved line through all the defined points.

The resulting elliptically shaped line is the side view of the original curved line.

To project a plane

Flat planes may be projected with their corner points. Projecting a plane's corner points projects the plane's edge lines, and in turn the entire plane. Figure 17-4 shows the projection of a plane 1-2-3-4 from given top and front views into the side view.

Only flat planes can be projected in this manner. Warped or compound surfaces must be projected by defining points on the plane's surface and then projecting the individual points, similar to the method demonstrated for curved lines.

What is the shape of line A-B in the side view?

Define some additional points in the front view and project them into the top view.

Project the defined points into the side view.

Use the Edit Polyline, fit option to create the elliptical-shaped side view.

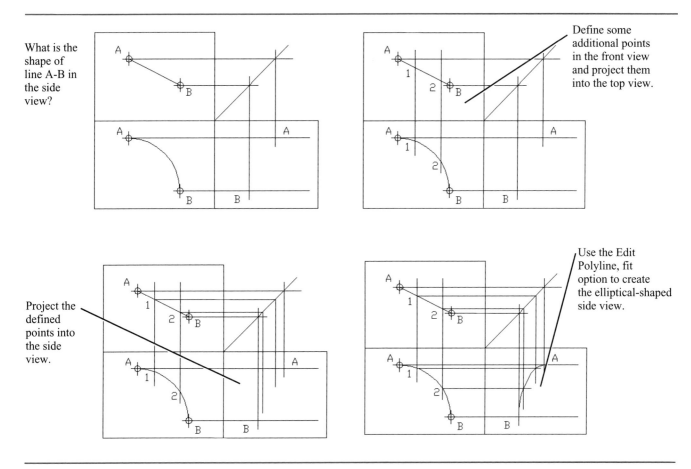

Figure 17-3

Project a plane by projecting its corner points.

Side view?

Figure 17-4

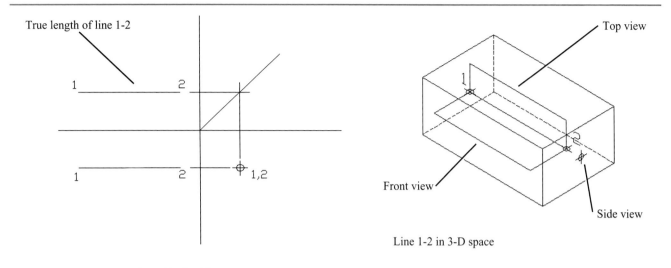

Figure 17-5

17-3 THE TRUE LENGTH OF A LINE

An orthographic view of a line shows the true length of the line only if the line is exactly parallel to the orthographic view's plane. Figure 17-5 shows three orthographic views of a line. Note that the side view is a point, or the end view of a line. If one of the views of a line is an end view, it means that a view 90° to the end view is a true-length view. In the example shown, both the front and top views are true-length views.

To determine the true length of a line

Figure 17-6 shows three views of line 1-2. None of the views is parallel to the front, top, or side orthographic plane, so none of the views is a true-length view. A true-length view can be created by defining an auxiliary orthographic plane parallel to one of the views of the line and then projecting the line into that view. The procedure is as follows.

1. Use the Offset tool from the Modify toolbar and create a line parallel to the side view at any distance from the side view.

This line is a reference plane line for an auxiliary view parallel to the side view of line 1-2.

2. Type Snap; press Enter.

Specify snap spacing or [ON/OFF/Aspect/Rotate/Style] <0.2500>:

3. Type r; press Enter.

Specify base point <0.0000,0.0000>:

4. Use the Osnap, Endpoint option and select point 2 in the side view.

Base point<0.0000,0.0000>: _endp of Rotation angle<0.00>:

5. Use the Osnap, Endpoint option and select point 1 in the side view.

The crosshairs will align with the side view of line 1-2.

6. Draw lines perpendicular to the two endpoints of the auxiliary plane reference line.

7. Use the Snap, Rotation option and return the crosshairs to their normal horizontal and vertical orientation.

Set the base point value to 0.0000,0.0000 and the angle of rotation to 0.

8. Use the Osnap, Endpoint and Perpendicular options to draw lines from the endpoints of the front view of the line perpendicular to the reference plane line between the front and side views.

9. Click the Distance tool from the Standard toolbar.

10. Use the Distance tool to determine the lengths of the perpendicular lines drawn in step 8. Use Osnap to ensure accuracy.

11. Use the Offset tool from the Modify toolbar to draw lines parallel to the auxiliary reference plane line at distances equal to the distances determined in step 10.

In the example shown, the distances are represented by distances A and B.

12. Draw an auxiliary view of line 1-2 between the offset line and the lines drawn perpendicular to the auxiliary plane reference line as shown.

13. Erase any excess lines.

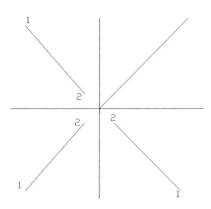

Orthographic views of line 1-2.
What is the true length of the line?

Projection lines into the auxilia
view perpendicular to the refer
plane line.

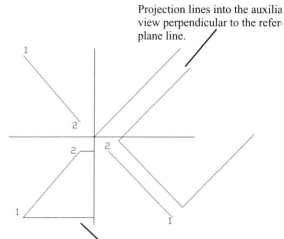

Draw lines from the line's endpoints perpendicular to the
vertical axis line. Use the Distance tool to determine the
distances from the points to the vertical reference line.

This is the true length of line 1-2.

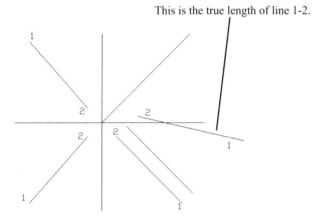

Use Snap, Rotate and align the crosshair
with the side view of line 1-2.

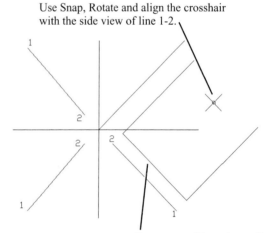

Draw an auxiliary view reference
plane line parallel to the side view
of line 1-2.

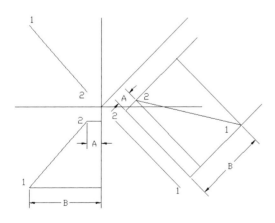

Use Offset to transfer the distances determined in the
last step into the auxiliary view.

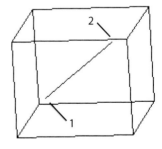

Line 1-2 in 3-D space

Figure 17-6

Figure 17-7

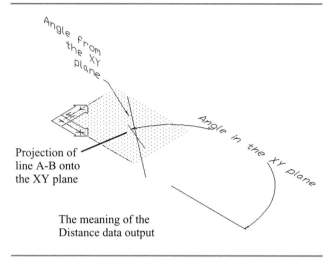

Projection of
line A-B onto
the XY plane

The meaning of the
Distance data output

Figure 17-9

To determine the properties of a line using AutoCAD

Figure 17-7 shows a line A-B in 3-D space. The location of the line's endpoints and the line's true length can be determined using the ID (identification) and Distance commands.

1. Type ID in response to a command prompt.

   Point:

2. Use Osnap, Endpoint and select endpoint A.

   Point:_endp of X = 6.0000   Y = 5.0000 Z = 4.0000

   These coordinate values are the location of point A relative to the WCS origin.

3. Press Enter and repeat the ID command.

   Point:

4. Use OSNAP, ENDPOINT and select endpoint B.

   Point: _endp of X = 12.0000   Y = 2.0000 Z = −3.0000

5. Select the Distance tool.

Specify first point:

6. Use Osnap, Endpoint and select point A.

   Specify second point:

7. Use Osnap, Endpoint and select point B.

   Figure 17-8 shows the resulting value readout that will appear in the command area of the screen. The distance value, 9.6954, is the true length of the line. The values listed as delta values are the changes in the individual component values. For example, the X value for point A is 6 and the X value for B is 12. The change in the values equals 6. Likewise, the Y value for point A is 5 and the Y value for B is 2. The delta value is −3 measured from point A to point B. Figure 17-9 shows the meaning of the two given angle values.

To determine the true length of a line using the rotation method

Figure 17-10 shows the front and top views of a line A-B. The true length of the line can be determined by rotating the line so that one of the views of the line is parallel to one of the orthographic planes. The other view will then be a true length.

Data generated by the Distance tool

```
 Specify second point: _endp of
Distance = 9.6954,   Angle in XY Plane = 333,   Angle from XY Plane = 314
Delta X = 6.0000,   Delta Y = −3.0000,   Delta Z = −7.0000

Command:
```

Figure 17-8

1. Select the Rotate tool from the Modify toolbar.

   Select objects:

2. Select the front view of line A-B.

   Select objects:

3. Press Enter.

   Specify base point:

4. Use Osnap, Endpoint and select point A.

   Specify rotation angle or [Reference]:

5. Rotate line A-B so that it is parallel to the reference plane line between the two views.

   This rotation can be done visually. The line will be smooth only when it is perfectly horizontal or vertical, or

parallel to one of the orthographic view reference plane lines. If the rotation is to be done in another type of orthographic plane, use Offset to create a line parallel to the required orthographic view through one of the point's endpoints, then align the rotated line to the offset line.

6. Turn Ortho on and draw a horizontal line from point B in the top view.
7. Draw a vertical line from point B in the front view as shown in Figure 17-10.

   The intersection of the lines is the new location for point B.

8. Draw a line in the top view from point A to the new point B.

   This line is the true length of line A-B.

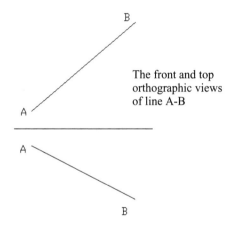

The front and top orthographic views of line A-B

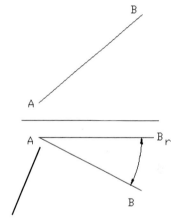

Rotate line A-B about point A so that it is parallel to the horizontal reference line.

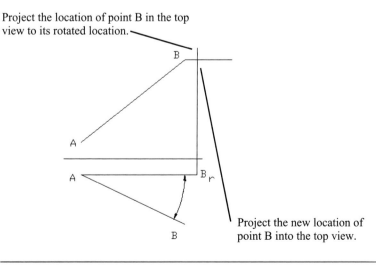

Project the location of point B in the top view to its rotated location.

Project the new location of point B into the top view.

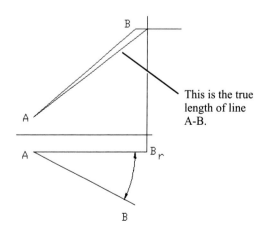

This is the true length of line A-B.

Figure 17-10

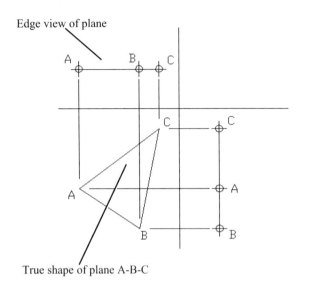

Edge view of plane

True shape of plane A-B-C

Figure 17-11

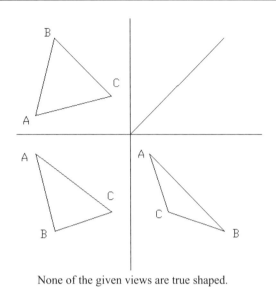

None of the given views are true shaped.

Figure 17-12

17-4 THE TRUE SHAPE OF A PLANE

Figure 17-11 shows three views of a plane A-B-C. The top and side views appear as single lines, or as edge views of the plane. This means that the front view is a view perpendicular to the plane: a view of the plane's true shape.

Figure 17-12 shows three views of a plane A-B-C. None of the views appears as a straight line, so none of the views is the true shape of the plane. All the views are distorted.

The true shape of the plane can be determined by creating an auxiliary orthographic view parallel to the plane. This is done by first creating an auxiliary view that defines an edge view of the plane (a straight line), and then taking a second auxiliary view perpendicular to the first.

To create a secondary auxiliary view of a plane

In this example, only the front and top views will be used. To define an edge view of the plane, we need a reference line that defines the true angle between the plane and the orthographic reference axis. None of the edge lines is parallel to the orthographic axis; there is no appropriate reference line. A plane contains an infinite number of lines, so a line can be drawn parallel to the orthographic axis in one of the views, then projected into the other view to yield a correct reference line. See Figure 17-13, Parts 1 to 3.

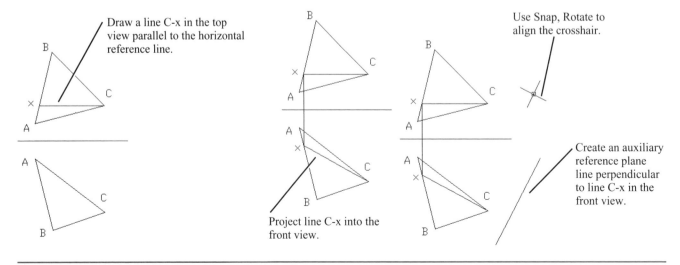

Draw a line C-x in the top view parallel to the horizontal reference line.

Project line C-x into the front view.

Use Snap, Rotate to align the crosshair.

Create an auxiliary reference plane line perpendicular to line C-x in the front view.

Figure 17-13, Part 1

To create an edge view of a plane

1. Draw a horizontal line C-x in the top view.

   Any horizontal line within the plane can be used. It is simply convenient to select one end of the line on a known corner point.

2. Project the line into the front view.
3. Type snap; press Enter.

   Specify snap spacing or [ON/OFF/Aspect/ Rotate/Style/Type] <0.5000>:

4. Type r; press Enter.

   Specify base point <0.0000,0.0000>:

5. Use Osnap, Endpoint and select point x.

   Specify base point <0.0000,0.0000>: _endp of Specify rotation angle <0>:

6. Select point C.

   The crosshairs will rotate and align with line C-x.

7. Turn Ortho on and draw a line to the right of and perpendicular to line C-x.

   This is a reference plane line for the first auxiliary view.

8. Draw projection lines parallel to line C-x from points A, B, and C in the front view into the auxiliary view.
9. Turn Ortho off and draw a line from the corner point in the top view to the reference line between the front and top views.
10. Use the Distance tool to determine the lengths of the projected lines drawn in step 9.
11. Record the lengths and then use Offset to create lines parallel to the auxiliary view reference line in the auxiliary view plane.
12. Use the appropriate intersections to draw the edge view of plane A-B-C.

   The distances measured in step 9 determine where the corner points are located in the auxiliary view along the projected lines created in step 8.

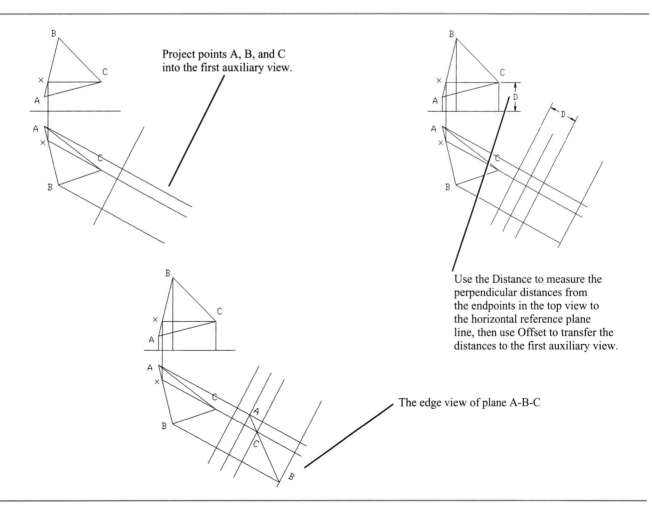

Project points A, B, and C into the first auxiliary view.

Use the Distance to measure the perpendicular distances from the endpoints in the top view to the horizontal reference plane line, then use Offset to transfer the distances to the first auxiliary view.

The edge view of plane A-B-C

Figure 17-13, Part 2

13. Erase the offset lines and trim the projection lines using the edge view as a cutting edge line.

To create a secondary auxiliary view perpendicular to the edge view of the plane

1. Use the Snap, Rotate command to reposition the crosshairs so that they are aligned with the edge view line.
2. Draw a line parallel to and above the edge view line.

This line is the reference plane line for the secondary auxiliary view.

3. Turn Ortho on and draw projection lines from the corner point of the plane in the first auxiliary view into the second auxiliary view.
4. Use the Distance command to determine the distance from the corner point in the front view to the first auxiliary view reference line.
5. Use the Offset command to transfer these distances to the secondary auxiliary view.
6. Draw lines between the appropriate intersections to create the secondary auxiliary view of plane A-B-C.
7. Erase any excess lines.

The secondary auxiliary view is the true shape of plane A-B-C.

Create a secondary auxiliary view reference plane line parallel to the edge view of the plane and project the endpoints into the auxiliary view.

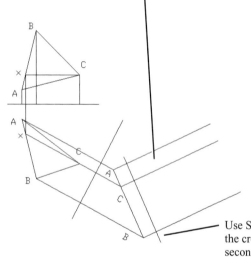

Use Snap, Rotate to align the crosshairs with the secondary reference plane line.

Use Offset to transfer the point locations from the front view to the auxiliary view.

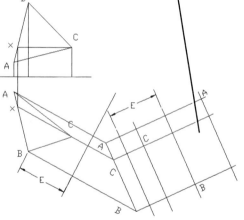

The true shape of plane A-B-C

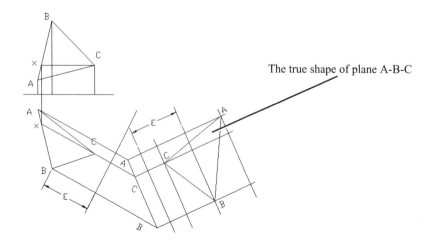

Figure 17-13, Part 3

To determine the true shape of a plane using AutoCAD

Figure 17-14 shows plane A-B-C in 3-D space. The true shape of the plane can be determined by creating a UCS aligned with the plane and then taking a plan view of the UCS.

1. Select the 3-point tool from the UCS toolbar.

    Specify new origin point <0,0,0>:

2. Use Osnap, Endpoint and select point A.

    Specify point on the positive portion of the X-axis <>:

3. Use Osnap, Endpoint and select point B.

    Specify point on the positive-Y portion of the UCS XY plane <>:

4. Use Osnap, Endpoint and select point C.

    The coordinate system will change, creating a UCS aligned with the plane. In the example shown, the UCS icon was located on the UCS's origin.

5. Select the View pull-down menu, 3D Views, then Plan View, then Current UCS.

    The view shown is the true shape of plane A-B-C.

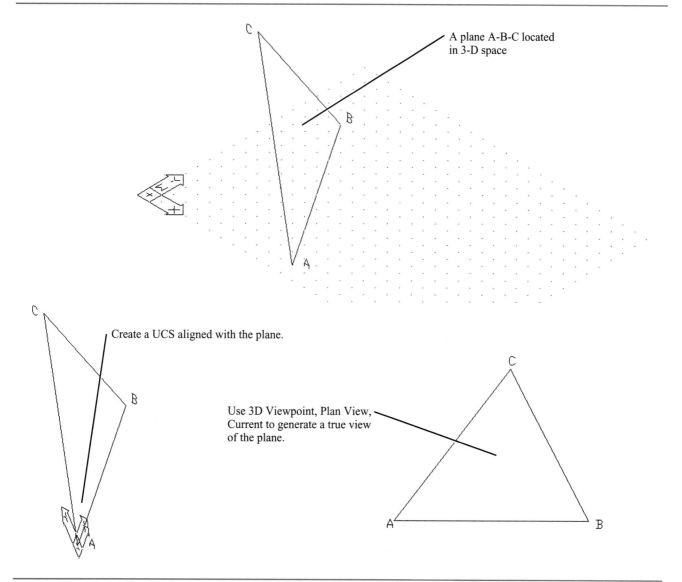

A plane A-B-C located in 3-D space

Create a UCS aligned with the plane.

Use 3D Viewpoint, Plan View, Current to generate a true view of the plane.

Figure 17-14

17-5 LOCATING A LINE IN A PLANE

Figure 17-15 shows the front and top views of plane A-B-C and a line 1-2 in the top view. Line 1-2 may be located in the front view as follows.

1. Define the intersection points of the line with the edge lines of the plane as x and y.
2. Project points x and y into the front view.

This is done by drawing vertical lines from the intersection points in the top view into the front view through the appropriate edge lines. In this example point x is on edge line A-C, and point y is on A-B.

3. Draw a line between points x and y in the front view.
4. Draw vertical lines (Ortho) from the endpoints of the line into the front view.
5. Use the Extend command to extend line x-y to the projection lines from endpoints 1 and 2.

Line 1-2 is now defined in the front view.

The given views
of plane A-B-C
and line 1-2

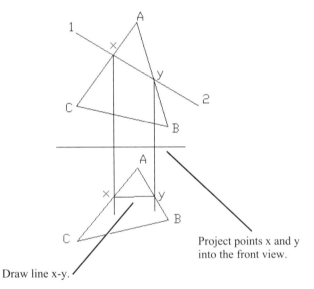

Draw line x-y.

Project points x and y
into the front view.

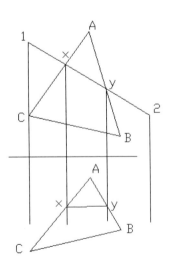

Use Osnap, Endpoint and Ortho to project
line 1-2's endpoint into the front view.

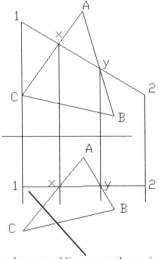

Use Extend to extend line x-y to the projection lines
for points 1 and 2.
This is the front view of line 1-2.

Figure 17-15

To locate a line not in a plane

The line need not actually intersect the plane. Figure 17-16 shows line 1-2 in the top view, which does not intersect plane A-B-C. The line can be located in the front view as follows.

1. Project the endpoints into the front view.

At this point the exact location of the endpoints is unknown, so draw the line into the front view, past the front view of the plane.

2. Use the Extend command and extend line 1-2 into the plane so that it crosses at least two edge lines.

3. Label intersection points x and y, and project them into the front view.
4. Draw a line between points x and y in the front view.
5. Use the Extend command and extend line x-y in the front view to the projection line for endpoint 2.
6. Use the endpoint projection lines to trim line 1-2 to its correct length in both the front and top views.
7. Erase any excess lines.

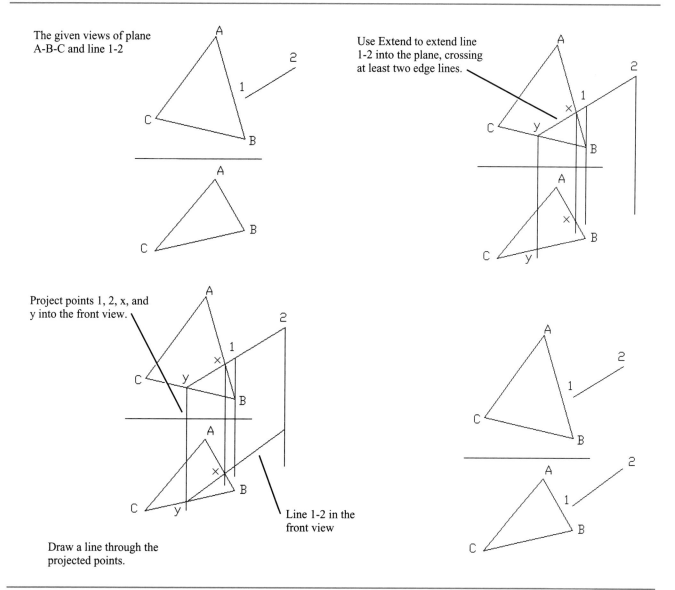

The given views of plane A-B-C and line 1-2

Use Extend to extend line 1-2 into the plane, crossing at least two edge lines.

Project points 1, 2, x, and y into the front view.

Line 1-2 in the front view

Draw a line through the projected points.

Figure 17-16

17-6 LOCATING A POINT
IN A PLANE

Figure 17-17 shows front and top views of plane A-B-C. Point P is shown in the top view. The location of the point can be determined by drawing a line from one of the plane's corner points through point P and intersecting one of the plane's edge lines. This line can then be projected into the front view. It is known that the point's location in the front view is directly below the top view location, so the intersection of a vertical line from the point location in the top view with the projected line in the front view defines the point's location in the front view.

1. Draw a line from corner point A to point P.
2. Use the Extend command and extend line A-P to the edge of the plane.

3. Label the intersection point with edge line x.
4. Project line A-x into the front view.

   Use Osnap to ensure accuracy.

5. Project point P into the front view by drawing a vertical line from point P in the top view so that it intersects line A-x in the front view.

The intersection point is the location of point P in the front view.

The preceding method can also be used to determine the location of a point relative to a known plane. In Figure 17-18, a point is located to the right of plane A-B-C. The point can be located relative to the plane by drawing a line from the point to a corner point of the plane that intersects an edge line. The line can then be projected into the other views, and the point can be projected using the line. See Figure 17-18.

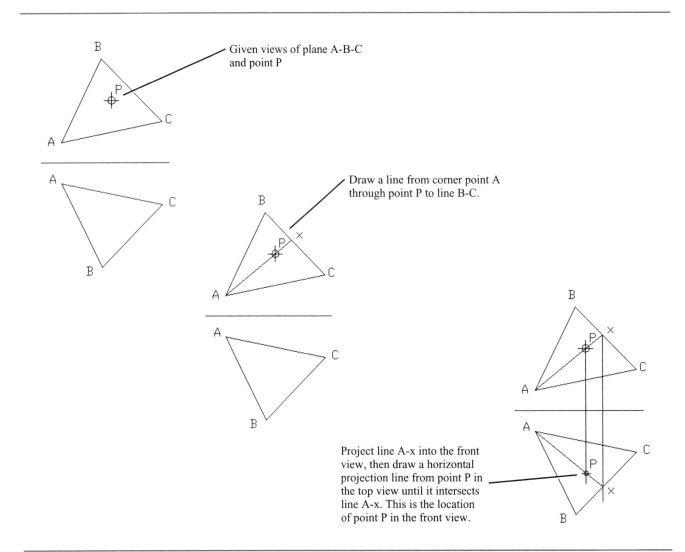

Given views of plane A-B-C and point P

Draw a line from corner point A through point P to line B-C.

Project line A-x into the front view, then draw a horizontal projection line from point P in the top view until it intersects line A-x. This is the location of point P in the front view.

Figure 17-17

Given views of plane A-B-C and a point

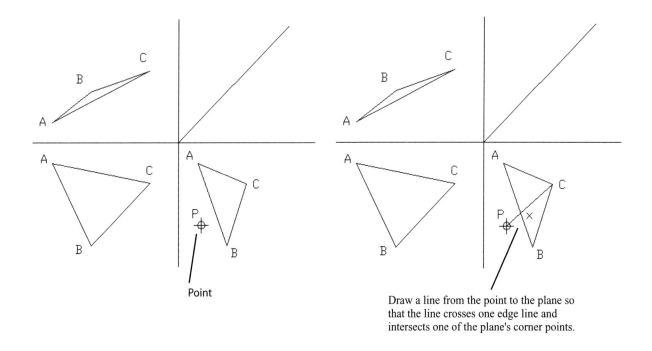

Point

Draw a line from the point to the plane so
that the line crosses one edge line and
intersects one of the plane's corner points.

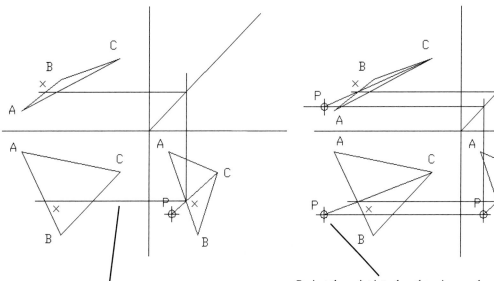

Project line C-x into the other views.

Project the point into the other views and
extend line C-x to create intersections
that define the location of the point in
each of the views.

Figure 17-18

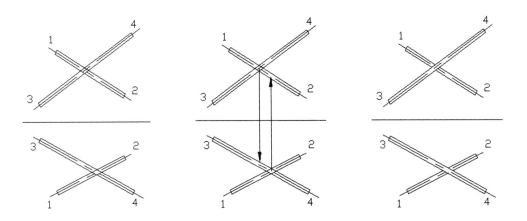

Figure 17-19

17-7 VISIBILITY OF A LINE

When working in 2-D orthographic views it is sometimes difficult to determine the relative position of two lines with respect to each other. In the example presented here, solid bars were used rather than lines so it would be easier to see the visual distinction between the lines' relative locations.

Figure 17-19 shows two intersecting bars. Which bar is closer in the top view, and which is closer in the front view?

For the top view

If the intersection point of lines 1-2 and 3-4 in the top view is projected into the front view by drawing a vertical line downward, the projection line intersects line 3-4 before it intersects line 1-2. Remember that objects near the top of the front view are higher than those near the bottom of the view. If line 3-4 is intersected first, it must be higher than line 1-2 at the intersection point in the top view.

For the front view

If the intersection of lines 1-2 and 3-4 in the front view is projected into the top view by drawing a vertical line upward, the projection line intersects line 1-2 first, indicating that line 1-2 is in front of line 3-4. Points near the bottom of the top view are closer than those located in the top portion of the view.

Figure 17-19 shows the resulting intersections with their visibility displayed.

Figure 17-20 shows two lines in 3-D space. They were both drawn as solid cylinders so that their relative positions could be more easily seen.

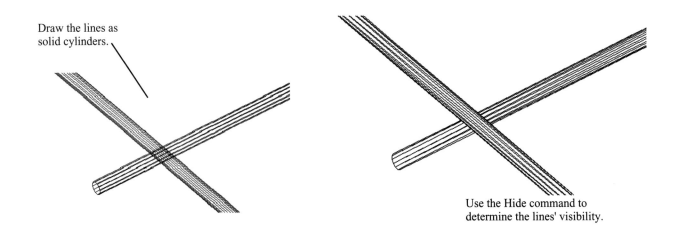

Draw the lines as solid cylinders.

Use the Hide command to determine the lines' visibility.

Figure 17-20

To determine the lines' visibility using AutoCAD

1. Zoom the intersecting area.
2. Type hide; press Enter.

It can be clearly seen that line 1-2 is above line 3-4 from this viewpoint. Different viewpoints would yield different results. This may be verified by returning to the original Zoom scale, then using the Zoom command again and creating a window that includes both lines in their entirety. Use the 3D Dynamic View command to rotate the lines about the screen so you can see their relative positions and different viewpoints. If you are unsure about the lines' visibility at any orientation, use the Hide command to see the current visibility. See Figure 17-20. The Regen command will always return the lines to their original wire frame visibility.

17-8 PIERCING POINTS

Figure 17-21, Parts 1 and 2, shows front and top views of plane A-B-C and line 1-2. What is the position of the line relative to the plane? There are three possible

results: the line pierces the plane, the line is parallel to the plane, or the line is within the same plane as the designated plane. There are two methods that can be used to determine whether the line pierces the plane: the cutting plane method or the auxiliary view method.

Cutting plane method

1. Complete line 1-2 across the top view.
2. Label the intersection points with the plane's edge lines as x and y.

Think of this line as representing the top edge of a plane that includes the line 1-2.

3. Project points x and y into the front view and draw line x-y.
4. Complete line 1-2 in the front view.

The intersection of lines 1-2 and x-y in the front view defines the piercing point between the line and the plane.

5. Project the piercing point into the top view.

The visibility of the line relative to the plane can be determined by using the method explained in Section 17-7

Given front and top views of plane A-B-C and line 1-2

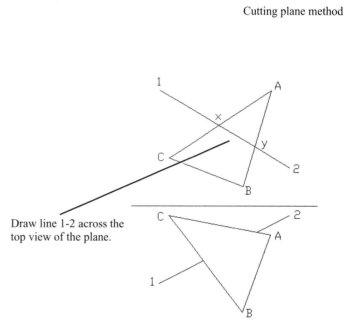

Cutting plane method

Draw line 1-2 across the top view of the plane.

Figure 17-21, Part 1

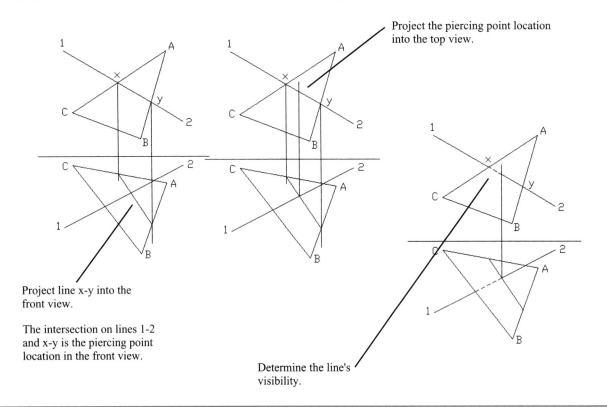

Project the piercing point location into the top view.

Project line x-y into the front view.

The intersection on lines 1-2 and x-y is the piercing point location in the front view.

Determine the line's visibility.

Figure 17-21, Part 2

for the visibility of lines. Note the intersection of lines A-C and 1-2 in the top view, intersection x. Follow the projection line from the intersection down to the front view. Line A-C is intersected before line 1-2, indicating that line A-C is higher than line 1-2. Likewise, the projection of the intersection between lines C-B and 1-2 in the front view strikes line C-B first, indicating that line C-B is closer to the viewer in the front view.

Auxiliary view method

Figure 17-22 shows the same front and top views of plane A-B-C and line 1-2 that were used to explain the cutting plane method in Figure 17-21. In this example, the piercing point location will be determined using an auxiliary view that shows the edge view of the plane. See Section 17-4 for a more detailed explanation of auxiliary views.

1. Determine the projection angle for the plane's edge view by drawing a horizontal line in one of the views and then projecting it into the other view.

In this example, horizontal line C-x was drawn in the top view, then projected into the front view.

2. Use the Snap, Rotation axis and align the crosshairs with the front view of line C-x.

3. Extend line C-x into an area for the auxiliary view.
4. Draw a line perpendicular to the extension of line C-x.

The perpendicular line is the reference plane line for the auxiliary view.

5. Project the endpoints of the plane into the auxiliary plane.
6. Draw a line between the projected endpoints.

The result should be a straight line, or the edge view of plane A-B-C.

7. Project line 1-2 into the auxiliary view.
8. Complete the views of line 1-2 in both the top and front views.
9. Project the piercing point location back to the front and top views.

The auxiliary view generates the piercing point location on line 1-2, and because the location of line 1-2 is known in both the front and top views, the point locations in those views can be found using projection.

The visibility of the line relative to the plane can be determined as explained for the cutting plane method.

Given views of plane A-B-C and
line 1-2

Define line C-x parallel to
the horizontal reference line.

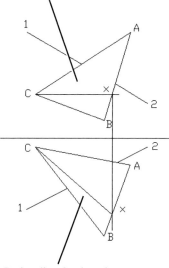

Project line C-x into the
front view.

Create an auxiliary view perpendicular
to the front view of line C-x.

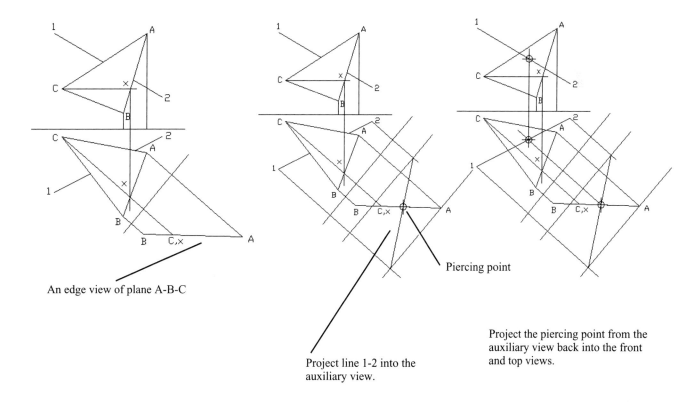

An edge view of plane A-B-C

Project line 1-2 into the
auxiliary view.

Piercing point

Project the piercing point from the
auxiliary view back into the front
and top views.

Figure 17-22

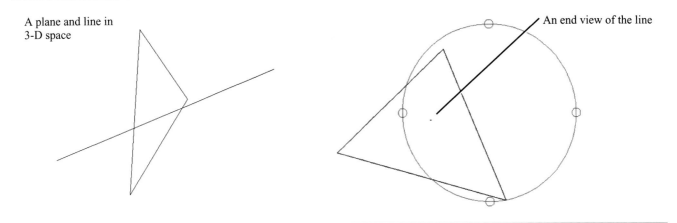

A plane and line in 3-D space

An end view of the line

Figure 17-23

To determine if a plane and a line intersect using AutoCAD

Figure 17-23 shows a plane and a line in 3-D. We can quickly determine if the line pierces the plane, but not the piercing point's exact location, by using the 3D Orbit command. In this example, the plane and line are not solids; they are surface models.

1. Select the View pull-down menu, then 3D Orbit.

A large green circle will appear on the drawing screen with its four quadrant points indicated by small circles.

2. Hold the left mouse button down and move the mouse around.
3. Move the objects around until an end view of the line is found.

The endpoint of line 1-2 appears as a point. If the point appears within plane A-B-C, then the line pierces the plane.

To determine the piercing point of a line and a plane using AutoCAD's solid modeling

In this example the corner points of the plane and the endpoints of the line are used to create solid models, then the Intersection command is used to determine the location of the piercing point relative to the WCS. See Figure 17-24.

1. Use the Draw command and draw the edge lines of the plane using the given coordinate values.
2. Select the 3-Point UCS tool on the UCS toolbar and create a UCS aligned with the plane.
3. Select the Edit Polyline tool from the Modify II toolbar and change the drawn lines into a polyline.

The Edit Polyline command cannot be applied to planes that are not parallel to the current UCS.

4. Select the Extrude tool from the Solids toolbar and create a solid plane .00001 thick (height of extrusion).
5. Save the UCS and return to the WCS.
6. Select the Solid Cylinder command.
7. Draw a cylinder between the two known endpoints of the line of radius .00001.

Because the thickness and radius values are so small, the plane and line will appear as they did as surface models.

8. Zoom the approximate area of the piercing point.
9. Use the Intersection command to determine the piercing point.

The piercing point for two solid models is their common volume. It will appear as a small dot on the screen after the Intersection command has been applied. Be sure

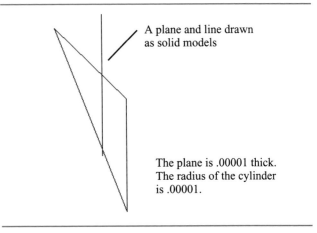

A plane and line drawn as solid models

The plane is .00001 thick. The radius of the cylinder is .00001.

Figure 17-24

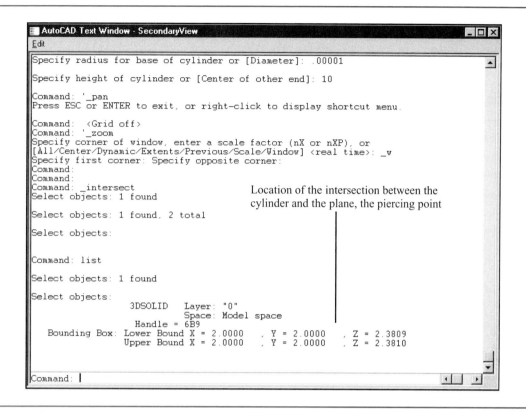

Location of the intersection between the cylinder and the plane, the piercing point

Figure 17-25

to turn off Grid if it is on, so that the intersection volume can be seen.

10. Type List; press Enter.
11. Select the common volume (the dot that represents the common volume).

Figure 17-25 shows the resulting AutoCAD Text Window and the X,Y,Z coordinate values relative to the WCS. Two values are listed for the Y coordinate. Use the upper value to verify the location of the piercing point. If you were working with the plane's UCS, the resulting values would be relative to that UCS.

If you need to work with the piercing point, first use the Point command to define the point as an entity. Then you can use it as a selected object.

17-9 DISTANCE BETWEEN A LINE AND A POINT

Figure 17-26, Parts 1 and 2, shows the front and top views of a line 1-2 and point P. The shortest distance between the point and the line is determined by taking a secondary auxiliary view of the line, which will be a point view of the line. The shortest possible distance can then be measured directly between the end view and the point.

1. Use the Offset command to create a line parallel to the top view of line 1-2.

This line is the first auxiliary view reference plane line.

2. Project line 1-2 and point P into the first auxiliary view.

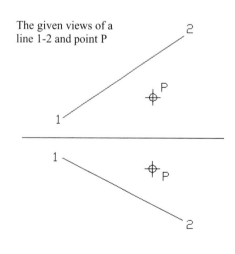

The given views of a line 1-2 and point P

Figure 17-26, Part 1

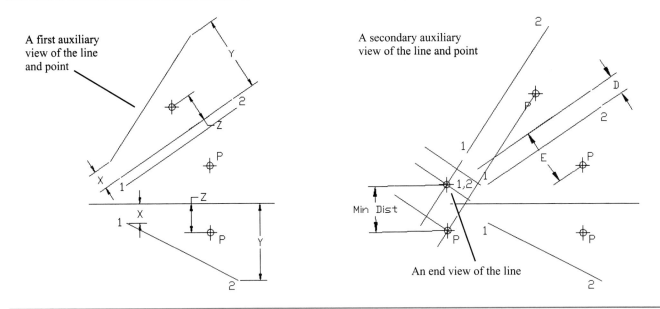

A first auxiliary view of the line and point

A secondary auxiliary view of the line and point

Min Dist

An end view of the line

Figure 17-26, Part 2

3. Use the Snap, Rotate option and align the crosshairs with the first auxiliary view of line 1-2.
4. Create a secondary auxiliary view that shows the end view of the line.

The distance between the edge view of the line and the point in the secondary auxiliary view is the minimum distance between the point and the line. See Section 17-4 for a more detailed explanation of auxiliary views.

To determine the minimum distance between a line and a point using 3D AutoCAD

Figure 17-27 shows line 1-2 and point P. The minimum distance between the point and the line is determined as follows.

1. Select the 3-Point tool from the UCS toolbar.

   Specify new origin point <0,0,0>:

2. Use Osnap, Endpoint and select point 1.

   Specify point on the positive portion of the X-axis:

3. Use Osnap, Endpoint and select point 2.

   Specify point on the positive-Y portion of the UCS XY plane:

4. Use Osnap, Nearest and select point P.
5. Select the View pull-down menu, then 3D views, Plan View, Current UCS.
6. Select the Distance tool.

   Specify first point:

A line and point in 3-D space

The crosshairs in the new UCS orientation

Minimum Distance

A UCS created using the line and point

A plan view of the new UCS

Figure 17-27

Given views of two lines

Create a first auxiliary view parallel to line 1-2.

Create a sceondary auxiliary view and thus an end view of line 1-2.

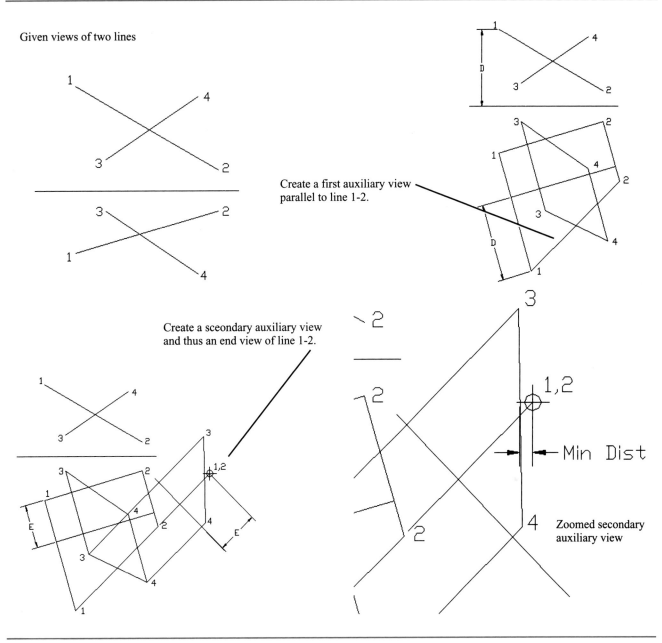

Zoomed secondary auxiliary view

Figure 17-28

7. Use Osnap, Nearest and select point P.

   Second extension line origin:

8. Use Osnap, Perpendicular and select line 1-2.

17-10 DISTANCE BETWEEN TWO LINES

Figure 17-28 shows the front and top views of lines 1-2 and 3-4.

The minimum distance between the lines can be determined by using a secondary auxiliary view to create an end view of one of the lines. The minimum distance can then be measured by drawing a line from the point end view of the line perpendicular to the other line.

The secondary auxiliary view method

1. Use the Snap, Rotate command to align the crosshairs with the front view of line 1-2.
2. Draw a reference plane line for the first auxiliary view parallel to the front view of line 1-2, then project both lines' endpoints into the auxiliary view from the front view.
3. Use the Osnap, Rotate command and align the crosshairs with the first auxiliary view of line 1-2.

4. Create the edge plane line for the secondary auxiliary view by drawing a line perpendicular to the first auxiliary view of line 1-2.
5. Project both lines' endpoints into the secondary auxiliary view.

   Line 1-2 should appear as a point or end view of the line.

6. Draw a line from the end view perpendicular to the view of line 3-4.
7. Use the Linear, Dimension command to measure the length of the perpendicular line or use the Distance command.

The distance found in step 7 is the minimum distance between the two lines.

Using AutoCAD's 3-D capabilities

Figure 17-29 shows two lines in 3-D space. The minimum distance between them may be determined by rotating the lines until one appears as an end view, then measuring the perpendicular distance between the end view and the other line. The Osnap commands cannot be applied in this situation. The resulting distance is an approximation. It is, however, a very close approximation.

1. Select the View pull-down menu, then 3D Orbit.
2. Hold down the left mouse button and rotate the lines until one appears as a point.
3. Zoom the area around the end view and draw a line from the end view perpendicular to the line.

Draw the line by eye; that is, select the endpoints on the screen. Do not use Osnap.

4. Use the Distance command to determine the length of the line.

This distance is the approximate minimum distance between the two lines.

17-11 ANGLE BETWEEN A PLANE AND A LINE

Figure 17-30 shows front and top views of plane A-B-C and a line 1-2. The true angle between them can be

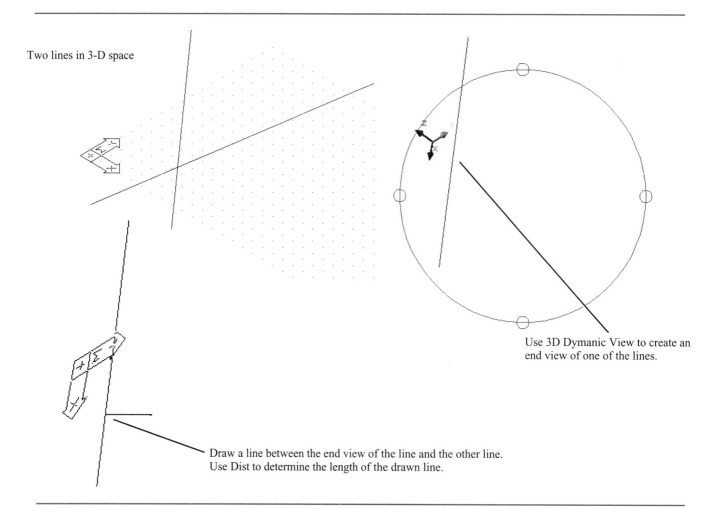

Two lines in 3-D space

Use 3D Dymanic View to create an end view of one of the lines.

Draw a line between the end view of the line and the other line. Use Dist to determine the length of the drawn line.

Figure 17-29

determined by taking several auxiliary views so that the plane appears as an edge view and the line appears as a true length. See Section 17-6 for additional explanation of how to create the end view of a plane.

The auxiliary view method

1. Create a first auxiliary view that shows plane A-B-C as an end view (a straight line).

This view shows the edge view of the plane but not the true length of the line, so the angle between them is not a true angle.

2. Draw a secondary auxiliary view of the line and plane that shows the true shape of the plane.
3. Draw a third auxiliary view so that its edge plane line is parallel to the secondary auxiliary view of line 1-2.

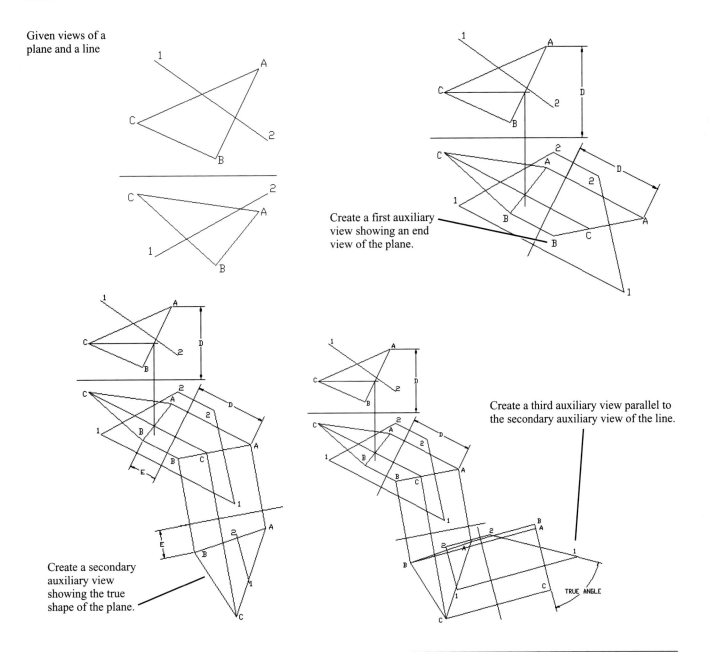

Given views of a plane and a line

Create a first auxiliary view showing an end view of the plane.

Create a secondary auxiliary view showing the true shape of the plane.

Create a third auxiliary view parallel to the secondary auxiliary view of the line.

Figure 17-30

A plane and a line in 3-D space

Create a UCS aligned with the plane.

Use Distance to determine the angle between the line and current UCS, the plane.

```
Command: '_dist Specify first point: _endp of  Specify second point: _endp of
Distance = 7.5498,  Angle in XY Plane = 98,  Angle from XY Plane = 68
Delta X = -0.4036,  Delta Y = 2.8393,   Delta Z = 6.9840
Command:
```

Figure 17-31

Using 3D AutoCAD

Figure 17-31 shows plane A-B-C and line 1-2 in 3-D space. The angle between them can be determined by first defining a UCS aligned with the plane, then using the Dist command.

1. Select the 3-Point tool from the UCS toolbar and define a UCS aligned with plane A-B-C.

   Use Osnap, Endpoint to ensure accuracy.

2. Select the Distance tool.
3. Use Osnap, Endpoint and select points 1 and 2.

The value listed in the command box at the bottom of the screen for "Angle from XY plane" is the angle between the line and the plane. In this example, the angle from the XY plane is defined as 9.65°. See Figure 17-31. If the endpoints had been selected in the opposite sequence, the resulting angular value would have been 350.35°, or the complementary angle of the 9.65° initially determined.

17-12 ANGLE BETWEEN TWO PLANES

Figure 17-32 shows front and top views of two intersecting planes, A-B-C and B-C-D. The true angle between the planes can be determined by using a secondary auxiliary view positioned to show an edge view of each plane. This can be done only by aligning the secondary view so that it shows an end view of the line common to the two planes.

The auxiliary view method

1. Create a first auxiliary view aligned with line B-C, the line common to both planes.
2. Create a secondary auxiliary view perpendicular to the projection line aligned with line B-C in the first auxiliary view.

The resulting auxiliary view shows end views of both planes.

3. Use the Angular Dimension command to determine the angle between the two planes.

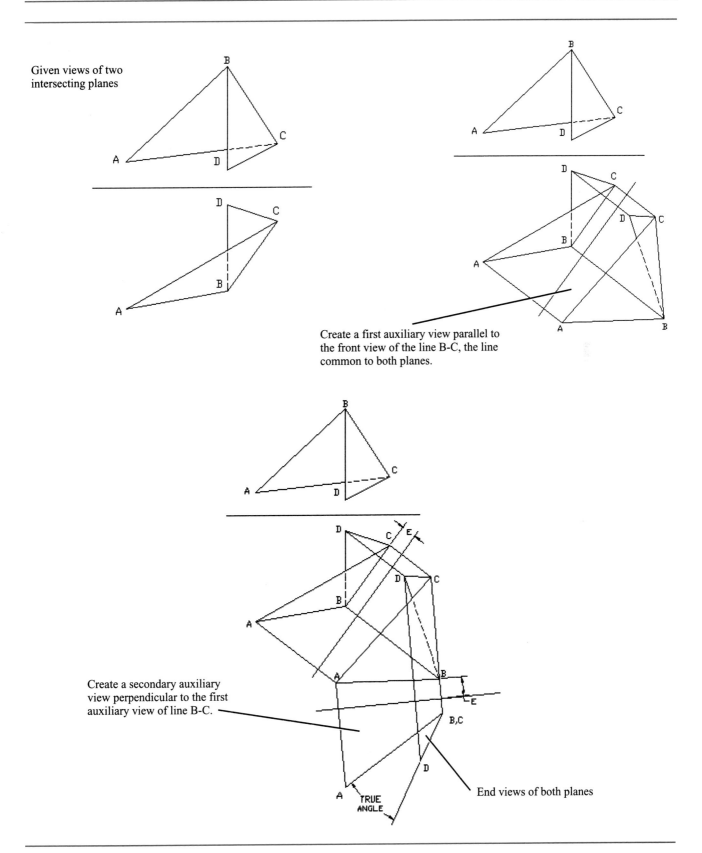

Given views of two intersecting planes

Create a first auxiliary view parallel to the front view of the line B-C, the line common to both planes.

Create a secondary auxiliary view perpendicular to the first auxiliary view of line B-C.

End views of both planes

TRUE ANGLE

Figure 17-32

Using AutoCAD's solid modeling

Figure 17-33 shows two planes in 3-D space: A-B-C and D-E-F. The planes were drawn using the Line command. The endpoints were defined by X,Y,Z coordinate values. This example will explain how to determine the angle between the planes using solid modeling.

The two planes will be changed to solid models .00001 thick, then unioned to determine their intersection line, if any. A UCS will then be created and aligned with the common intersection line. A preset viewpoint of this UCS set to 0° will yield an edge view of both planes, which in turn can be used to determine the angle between the planes. The Origin icon will appear in most of the illustrations to help clarify the different UCSs used.

1. Use the UCS toolbar and create a UCS aligned with plane A-B-C, with point A as the origin.
2. Select Edit Polyline from the Modify II toolbar.

   Command: _pedit
   Select polyline:

3. Select line A-B.

   Object selected is not a polyline.
   Do you want to turn it into one? <Y>

4. Press Enter.

   Enter an option [Close/Join/Width/Edit vertext/Fit/
   Spline/Decurve/Ltype gen/ Undo]:

5. Type j; press Enter.

   Select objects:

6. Select the three lines in plane A-B-C.

   Enter an option [Open/Join/Width/Edit vertex/Fit/
   Spline/Decurve/Ltype gen/Undo]:

7. Press Enter to return to a Command prompt.
8. Select the Extrude command.

   Select objects:

9. Select plane A-B-C.

   Specify height of extrusion or [Path]:

10. Type .00001; press Enter.

    Specify angle of taper for extrusion <0>:

11. Press Enter.

There is no visible change in the plane, but it is now a very thin, solid model.

12. Select the 3-Point UCS tool from the UCS toolbar and create a UCS aligned with plane D-E-F, with point D as the origin.
13. Change plane D-E-F into a solid model as explained previously for plane A-B-C.
14. Use the UCS toolbar, and make the WCS the current UCS.
15. Use the Union command to join the two planes (solid models) together.

A line will appear on the planes. This is their common intersection line.

16. Type hide to see how the two planes intersect.
17. Type regen; then press Enter to return to a wire frame view of the planes.

In this example, the intersection line is labeled 1-2.

18. Select the UCS toolbar and create a third UCS aligned with intersection line 1-2.
19. Select point 1 as the origin, point 2 as a point on the positive portion of the X axis, and point D as a point on the positive portion of the X axis.
20. Select the View pull-down menu, then 3D Views, Viewpoint Presets.

The Viewpoint Presets dialog box will appear.

21. Select the Relative to UCS button at the top of the dialog box, then set both the Angle from X Axis and the XY Plane equal to 0°.

The planes will appear as two intersecting lines.

22. Change the drawing to paper space by clicking the word Model at the bottom of the drawing screen.
23. Use the Angular Dimension tool to determine the angle between the two planes.

17-13 INTERSECTION

AutoCAD's solid-modeling capabilities are particularly well suited to solving intersection problems. Examples of 2-D solutions to intersection problems are presented in Chapter 5, and solid-model solutions are presented in Chapter 16.

Two planes in 3-D space

Create a UCS aligned with one of the planes.
Change the plane to a solid .00001 thick.

Create a second UCS aligned with the
other plane.
Change the plane to a solid .00001 thick.

Line of intersection

Union the two solid planes.

The Hide command may be used to verify
the intersection.
Use Regen to return to the original drawing.

Create a third UCS aligned with the
intersection line.

Select the
Relative to
UCS option

Change the drawing to
Paper space.

ANGLE BETWEEN
PLANES

Set the angle from the X Axis and
the XY Plane equal to 0°.

Use Angular Dimension to determine the angle
between the planes.

Figure 17-33

17-14 EXERCISE PROBLEMS

For Exercise Problems EX17-1 to EX17-12:

A. Locate the line or plane in the missing view.
B. Determine the true length of the line.
C. Determine the true shape of the plane.

The grid spacing for the dot background is either .5 inch or 10 millimeters.

EX17-1

EX17-2

EX17-3

EX17-4

EX17-5

EX17-6

EX17-7

EX17-10 INCHES, SCALE 4:1

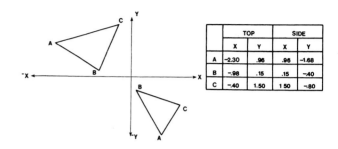

	TOP		SIDE	
	X	Y	X	Y
A	-2.30	.96	.96	-1.68
B	-.98	.15	.15	-.40
C	-.40	1.50	1.50	-.80

EX17-8

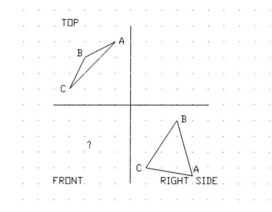

EX17-11 MILLIMETERS, SCALE 3:1

	TOP		SIDE	
	X	Y	X	Y
	-49	35	35	-26
	-11	27	27	-11
	-35	6	6	-37

EX17-9

EX17-12 INCHES, SCALE 4:1

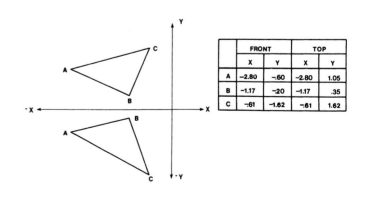

	FRONT		TOP	
	X	Y	X	Y
A	-2.80	-.60	-2.80	1.05
B	-1.17	-.20	-1.17	.35
C	-.61	-1.62	-.61	1.62

Find the true shape of the triangular planes in Exercise Problems EX17-13 to EX17-16. The three corner points of the planes are defined as A, B, and C with the following coordinate values.

EX17-13 INCHES

A = 2,6,−5
B = 3,2,−4
C = 6,5,1

EX17-14 INCHES

A = 0,7,3
B = 8,0,−1
C = 5,5,−6

EX17-15 MILLIMETERS

A = 50,50,125
B = 175,50,−100
C = 150,125,25

EX17-16 MILLIMETERS

A = 20,200,80
B = 200,0,−30
C = 120,120,−160

Determine the length of each of the lines in Exercise Problems EX17-17 to EX17-20 and the minimum distance between the two lines. The lines are defined as A-B and C-D.

EX17-17 INCHES

A = 1,1,1
B = 8,8,−3

C = 3,4,5
D = 9,6,−7

EX17-18 INCHES

A = 2,6,−4
B = 7,1,6

C = 0,1,3
D = 8,6,−2

EX17-19 MILLIMETERS

A = 30,20,20
B = 200,200,−70

C = 60,100,130
D = 200,150,−170

EX17-20 MILLIMETERS

A = 50,150,−100
B = 180,20,150

C = 0,20,70
D = 200,150,−60

Determine the minimum distance between the points and planes in Exercise Problems EX17-21 to EX17-24.

EX17-21 INCHES

Plane:

A = 1,6,4
B = 3,3,−4.5
C = 6,5,0

Point:

P = 4,3,6

EX17-22 INCHES

Plane:

A = 0,7,3
B = 7,1,−1
C = 5,5,−6

Point:

P = 2,3,5

EX17-23 MILLIMETERS

Plane:

A = 55,150,120
B = 75,50,−100
C = 140,130,20

Point:

P = 100,60,130

EX17-24 MILLIMETERS

Plane:

A = 20,180,85
B = 200,0,−35
C = 120,130,−150

Point:

P = 50,75,130

Determine the true shape of each plane in Exercise Problems EX17-25 to EX17-30 and the perpendicular distance from the point to the plane.

EX17-25 INCHES

EX17-27 MILLIMETERS

EX17-26 MILLIMETERS

EX17-28 MILLIMETERS

EX17-29 INCHES

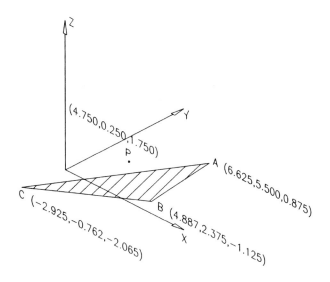

Determine the intersection line and angle of intersection between the planes in Exercise Problems EX17-31 to EX17-34.

EX17-31 INCHES

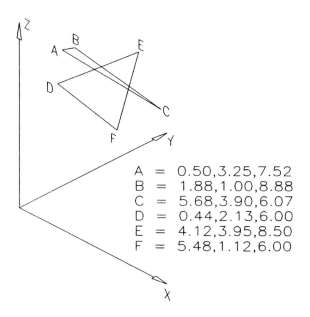

```
A  =  0.50,3.25,7.52
B  =  1.88,1.00,8.88
C  =  5.68,3.90,6.07
D  =  0.44,2.13,6.00
E  =  4.12,3.95,8.50
F  =  5.48,1.12,6.00
```

EX17-30 MILLIMETERS

EX17-32 MILLIMETERS

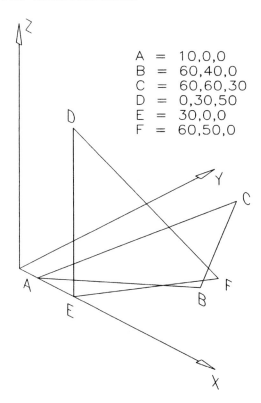

```
A  =  10,0,0
B  =  60,40,0
C  =  60,60,30
D  =  0,30,50
E  =  30,0,0
F  =  60,50,0
```

EX17-33 MILLIMETERS

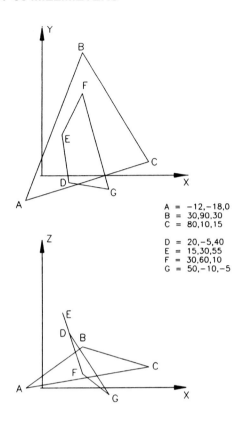

A = -12,-18,0
B = 30,90,30
C = 80,10,15

D = 20,-5,40
E = 15,30,55
F = 30,60,10
G = 50,-10,-5

Determine the minimum distance between the given lines in Exercise Problems EX17-35 and EX17-36.

EX17-35 MILLIMETERS

EX17-34 MILLIMETERS

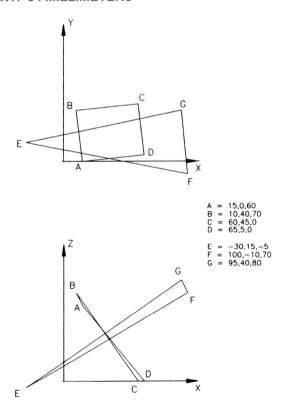

A = 15,0,60
B = 10,40,70
C = 60,45,0
D = 65,5,0

E = -30,15,-5
F = 100,-10,70
G = 95,40,80

EX17-36 MILLIMETERS

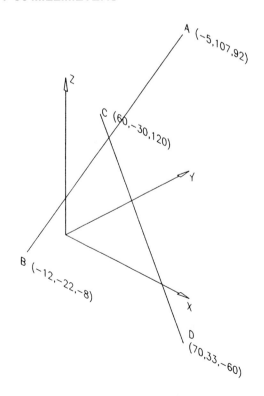

Determine the minimum distance between the given line and the point in Exercise Problems EX17-37 to EX17-40.

EX17-37 MILLIMETERS

EX17-39 INCHES

EX17-38 INCHES

EX17-40 MILLIMETERS

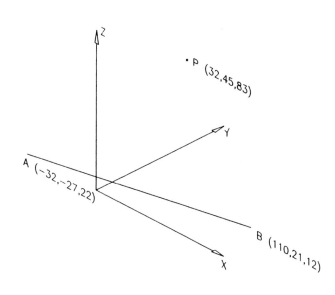

In Exercise Problems EX17-41 to EX17-45, determine the point on the plane where the line intersects. Label the point and specify its X,Y,Z coordinates relative to the WCS.

EX17-41 MILLIMETERS

EX17-43 MILLIMETERS

EX17-42 MILLIMETERS

EX17-44 INCHES

EX17-45 INCHES

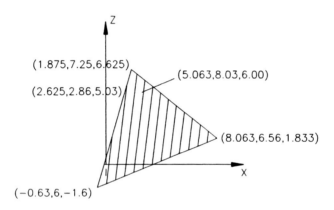

EX17-46

A pole 19.7 feet high is supported by three guy wires. Wire 1 is attached to the pole 1.00 foot from the top, wire 2 is attached 2.00 feet from the top, and wire 3 is attached 2 feet 6 inches from the top. The location of the pole and the location of the ground positions of the three guy wires are as shown. What is the true length of each of the guy wires?

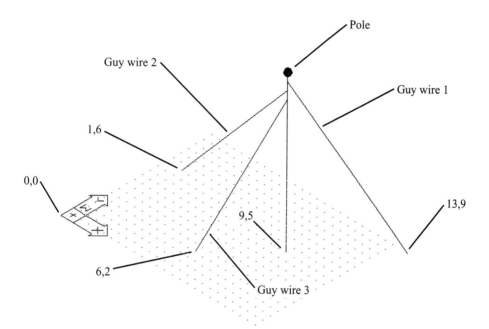

EX17-47

A work platform is to be added to the cowling of a helicopter. It is to fold down, giving access to the transmission area and supplying a place for the mechanic to sit while working. The platform is to be 24 by 24 inches.

Two support wires will be required to support the mechanic's weight and tools. The wires are to attach to the platform 1 inch from each of the outside edges and attach to the cowling 6 inches to the left and right of the top edge of the platform opening as shown.

What is the true length of the support wires?

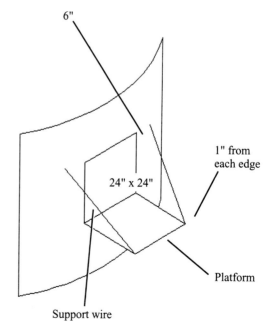

EX17-48

A satellite for scientific experiments involving the solar wind is to be made in an approximately spherical shape. The diameter of the sphere is 20 cm, but the top and bottom portions have to be truncated so that they are 19 cm apart. See below.

The satellite is to be made from 6 rows of 8 flat panels with straight edges. The satellite is symmetrical about its central horizontal axis. The symmetry allows the satellite to be made from just three different-sized panels.

What is the true shape of each of the three different panels?

Solar Wind Satellite

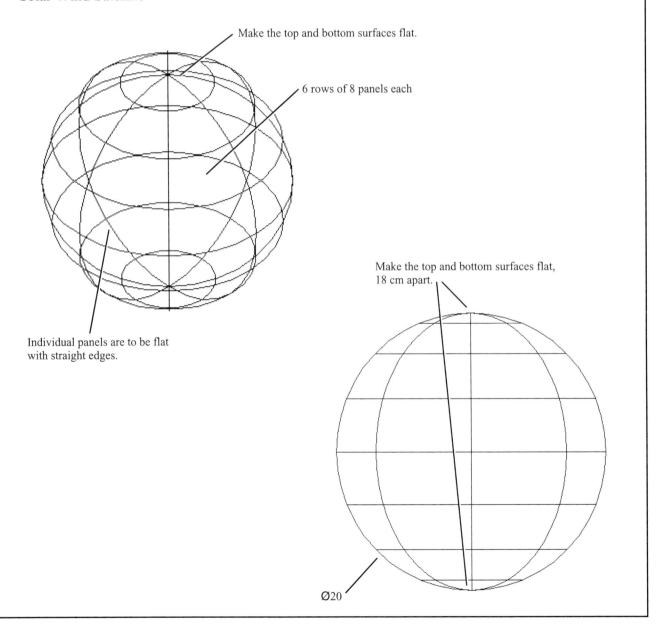

Make the top and bottom surfaces flat.

6 rows of 8 panels each

Individual panels are to be flat with straight edges.

Make the top and bottom surfaces flat, 18 cm apart.

Ø20

Appendix

Wire and Sheet Metal Gauges

Gauge			Thickness	Gauge	Thickness
000	000		0.5800	18	0.0403
00	000		0.5165	19	0.0359
0	000		0.4600	20	0.0320
	000		0.4096	21	0.0285
	00		0.3648	22	0.0253
	0		0.3249	23	0.0226
	1		0.2893	24	0.0201
	2		0.2576	25	0.0179
	3		0.2294	26	0.0159
	4		0.2043	27	0.0142
	5		0.1819	28	0.0126
	6		0.1620	29	0.0113
	7		0.1443	30	0.0100
	8		0.1285	31	0.0089
	9		0.1144	32	0.0080
	10		0.1019	33	0.0071
	11		0.0907	34	0.0063
	12		0.0808	35	0.0056
	13		0.0720	36	0.0050
	14		0.0641	37	0.0045
	15		0.0571	38	0.0040
	16		0.0508	39	0.0035
	17		0.0453	40	0.0031

Figure A-1

American Standard Clearance Locational Fits

Nominal Size Range Inches Over — To	Limits of Clearance	Class LC1 Standard Limits		Limits of Clearance	Class LC2 Standard Limits		Limits of Clearance	Class LC3 Standard Limits		Limits of Clearance	Class LC4 Standard Limits	
		Hole H6	Shaft h5		Hole H7	Shaft h6		Hole H8	Shaft h7		Hole H10	Shaft h9
0 — 0.12	0 0.45	+0.25 0	0 -0.2	0 0.65	+0.4 0	0 -0.25	0 1	+0.6 0	0 -0.4	0 2.6	+1.6 0	0 -1.0
0.12 — 0.24	0 0.5	+0.3 0	0 -0.2	0 0.8	+0.5 0	0 -0.3	0 1.2	+0.7 0	0 -0.5	0 3.0	+1.8 0	0 -1.2
0.24 — 0.40	0 0.65	+0.4 0	0 -0.25	0 1.0	+0.6 0	0 -0.4	0 1.5	+0.9 0	0 -0.6	0 3.6	+2.2 0	0 -1.4
0.40 — 0.71	0 0.7	+0.4 0	0 -0.3	0 1.1	+0.7 0	0 -0.4	0 1.7	+1.0 0	0 -0.7	0 4.4	+2.8 0	0 -1.6
0.71 — 1.19	0 0.9	+0.5 0	0 -0.4	0 1.3	+0.8 0	0 -0.5	0 2	+1.2 0	0 -0.8	0 5.5	+3.5 0	0 -2.0
1.19 — 1.97	0 1.0	+0.6 0	0 -0.4	0 1.6	+1.0 0	0 -0.6	0 2.6	+1.6 0	0 -1.0	0 6.5	+4.0 0	0 -2.5

Figure A-2A

Nominal Size Range Inches Over — To	Limits of Clearance	Class LC5 Standard Limits		Limits of Clearance	Class LC6 Standard Limits		Limits of Clearance	Class LC7 Standard Limits		Limits of Clearance	Class LC8 Standard Limits	
		Hole H7	Shaft g6		Hole H9	Shaft f8		Hole H10	Shaft e9		Hole H10	Shaft d9
0 — 0.12	0.1 0.75	+0..4 0	-0.1 -0.35	0.3 1.9	+1.0 0	-0.3 -0.9	0.6 3.2	+1.6 0	-0.6 -1.6	1.0 3.6	+1.6 0	-1.0 -2.0
0.12 — 0.24	0.15 0.95	+0.5 0	-0.15 -0.45	0.4 2.3	+1.2 0	-0.4 -1.1	0.8 3.8	+1.8 0	-0.8 -2.0	1.2 4.2	+1.8 0	-1.2 -2.4
0.24 — 0.40	0.2 1.2	+0.6 0	-0.2 -0.6	0.5 2.8	+1.4 0	-0.5 -1.4	1.0 4.6	+2.2 0	-1.0 -2.4	1.6 5.2	+2.2 0	-1.6 -3.0
0.40 — 0.71	0.25 1.35	+0.7 0	-0.25 -0.65	0.6 3.2	+1.6 0	-0.6 -1.6	1.2 5.6	+2.8 0	-1.2 -2.8	2.0 6.4	+2.8 0	-2.0 -3.6
0.71 — 1.19	0.3 1.6	+0.8 0	-0.3 -0.8	0.8 4.0	+2.0 0	-0.8 -2.0	1.6 7.1	+3.5 0	-1.6 -3.6	2.5 8.0	+3.5 0	-2.5 -4.5
1.19 — 1.97	0.4 2.0	+1.0 0	-0.4 -1.0	1.0 5.1	+2.5 0	-1.0 -2.6	2.0 8.5	+4.0 0	-2.0 -4.5	3.0 9.5	+4.0 0	-3.0 -5.5

Figure A-2B

American Standard Running and Sliding Fits
(Hole Basis)

Nominal Size Range Inches Over – To	Class RC1 Limits of Clearance	Class RC1 Standard Limits Hole H5	Shaft g4	Class RC2 Limits of Clearance	Class RC2 Hole H6	Shaft g5	Class RC3 Limits of Clearance	Class RC3 Hole H7	Shaft f6	Class RC4 Limits of Clearance	Class RC4 Hole H8	Shaft f7
0 – 0.12	0.1 0.45	+0.2 0	−0.1 −0.25	0.1 0.55	+0.25 0	−0.1 −0.3	0.3 0.95	+0.4 0	−0.3 −0.55	0.3 1.3	+0.6 0	−0.3 −0.7
0.12 – 0.24	0.15 0.5	+0.2 0	−0.15 −0.3	0.15 0.65	+0.3 0	−0.15 −0.35	0.4 1.12	+0.5 0	−0.4 −0.7	0.4 1.5	+0.7 0	−0.4 −0.0
0.24 – 0.40	0.2 0.6	+0.25 0	−0.2 −0.35	0.2 0.85	+0.4 0	−0.2 −0.45	0.5 1.5	+0.6 0	−0.5 −0.9	0.5 2.0	+0.9 0	−0.5 −1.1
0.40 – 0.71	0.25 0.75	+0.3 0	−0.25 −0.45	0.25 0.95	+0.4 0	−0.25 −0.55	0.6 1.7	+0.7 0	−0.6 −1.0	0.6 2.3	+1.0 0	−0.6 −1.3
0.71 – 1.19	0.3 0.95	+0.4 0	−0.3 −0.55	0.3 1.2	+0.5 0	−0.3 −0.7	0.8 2.1	+0.8 0	−0.8 −1.3	0.8 2.8	+1.2 0	−0.8 −1.6
1.19 – 1.97	0.4 1.1	+0.4 0	−0.4 −0.7	0.4 1.4	+0.6 0	−0.4 −0.8	1.0 2.6	+1.0 0	−1.0 −1.6	1.0 3.6	+1.6 0	−1.0 −2.0

Figure A-3A

Nominal Size Range Inches Over – To	Class RC5 Limits of Clearance	Class RC5 Hole H8	Shaft e7	Class RC6 Limits of Clearance	Class RC6 Hole H9	Shaft e8	Class RC7 Limits of Clearance	Class RC7 Hole H9	Shaft d8	Class RC8 Limits of Clearance	Class RC8 Hole H10	Shaft c9
0 – 0.12	0.6 1.6	+0.6 0	−0.6 −1.0	0.6 2.2	+1.0 0	−0.6 −1.2	1.0 2.6	+1.0 0	−1.0 −1.6	2.5 5.1	+1.6 0	−2.5 −3.5
0.12 – 0.24	0.8 2.0	+0.7 0	−0.8 −1.3	0.8 2.7	+1.2 0	−0.8 −1.5	1.2 3.1	+1.2 0	−1.2 −1.9	2.8 5.8	+1.8 0	−2.8 −4.0
0.24 – 0.40	1.0 2.5	+0.9 0	−1.0 −1.6	1.0 3.3	+1.4 0	−1.0 −1.9	1.6 3.9	+1.4 0	−1.6 −2.5	3.0 6.6	+2.2 0	−3.0 −4.4
0.40 – 0.71	1.2 2.9	+1.0 0	−1.2 −1.9	1.2 3.8	+1.6 0	−1.2 −2.2	2.0 4.6	+1.6 0	−2.0 −3.0	3.5 7.9	+2.8 0	−3.5 −5.1
0.71 – 1.19	1.6 3.6	+1.2 0	−1.6 −2.4	1.6 4.8	+2.0 0	−1.6 −2.8	2.5 5.7	+2.0 0	−2.5 −3.7	4.5 10.0	+3.5 0	−4.5 −6.5
1.19 – 1.97	2.0 4.6	+1.6 0	−2.0 −3.0	2.0 6.1	+2.5 0	−2.0 −3.6	3.0 7.1	+2.5 0	−3.0 −4.6	5.0 11.5	+4.0 0	−5.0 −7.5

Figure A-3B

American Standard Transition Locational Fits

Nominal Size Range Inches (Over – To)	Class LT1 Fit	Hole H7	Shaft js6	Class LT2 Fit	Hole H8	Shaft js7	Class LT3 Fit	Hole H7	Shaft k6
0 – 0.12	-0.10 / +0.50	+0.4 / 0	+0.10 / -0.10	-0.2 / +0.8	+0.6 / 0	+0.2 / -0.2			
0.12 – 0.24	-0.15 / -0.65	+0.5 / 0	+0.15 / -0.15	-0.25 / +0.95	+0.7 / 0	+0.25 / -0.25			
0.24 – 0.40	-0.2 / +0.5	+0.6 / 0	+0.2 / -0.2	-0.3 / +1.2	+0.9 / 0	+0.3 / -0.3	-0.5 / +0.5	+0.6 / 0	+0.5 / +0.1
0.40 – 0.71	-0.2 / +0.9	+0.7 / 0	+0.2 / -0.2	-0.35 / +1.35	+1.0 / 0	+0.35 / -0.35	-0.5 / +0.6	+0.7 / 0	+0.5 / +0.1
0.71 – 1.19	-0.25 / +1.05	+0.8 / 0	+0.25 / -0.25	-0.4 / +1.6	+1.2 / 0	+0.4 / -0.4	-0.6 / +0.7	+0.8 / 0	+0.6 / +0.1
1.19 – 1.97	-0.3 / +1.3	+1.0 / 0	+0.3 / -0.3	-0.5 / +2.1	+1.6 / 0	+0.5 / -0.5	+0.7 / +0.1	+1.0 / 0	+0.7 / +0.1

Figure A-4A

Nominal Size Range Inches (Over – To)	Class LT4 Fit	Hole H8	Shaft k7	Class LT5 Fit	Hole H7	Shaft n6	Class LT6 Fit	Hole H7	Shaft n7
0 – 0.12				-0.5 / +0.15	+0.4 / 0	+0.5 / +0.25	-0.65 / +0.15	+0.4 / 0	+0.65 / +0.25
0.12 – 0.24				-0.6 / +0.2	+0.5 / 0	+0.6 / +0.3	-0.8 / +0.2	+0.5 / 0	+0.8 / +0.3
0.24 – 0.40	-0.7 / +0.8	+0.9 / 0	+0.7 / +0.1	-0.8 / +0.2	+0.6 / 0	+0.8 / +0.4	-1.0 / +0.2	+0.6 / 0	+1.0 / +0.4
0.40 – 0.71	-0.8 / +0.9	+1.0 / 0	+0.8 / +0.1	-0.9 / +0.2	+0.7 / 0	+0.9 / +0.5	-1.2 / +0.2	+0.7 / 0	+1.2 / +0.5
0.71 – 1.19	-0.9 / +1.1	+1.2 / 0	+0.9 / +0.1	-1.1 / +0.2	+0.8 / 0	+1.1 / +0.6	-1.4 / +0.2	+0.8 / 0	+1.4 / +0.6
1.19 – 1.97	-1.1 / +1.5	+1.6 / 0	+1.1 / +0.1	-1.3 / +0.3	+1.0 / 0	+1.3 / +0.7	-1.7 / +0.3	+1.0 / 0	+1.7 / +0.7

Figure A-4B

American Standard Interference Locational Fits

Nominal Size Range Inches (Over – To)	Limits of Interference	Class LN1 Standard Limits Hole H6	Shaft n5	Limits of Interference	Class LN2 Standard Limits Hole H7	Shaft p6	Limits of Interference	Class LN3 Standard Limits Hole H7	Shaft r6
0 – 0.12	0 / 0.45	+0.25 / 0	+0.45 / +0.25	0 / 0.65	+0.4 / 0	+0.63 / +0.4	0.1 / 0.75	+0.4 / 0	+0.75 / +0.5
0.12 – 0.24	0 / 0.5	+0.3 / 0	+0.5 / +0.3	0 / 0.8	+0.5 / 0	+0.8 / +0.5	0.1 / 0.9	+0.5 / 0	+0.9 / +0.6
0.24 – 0.40	0 / 0.65	+0.4 / 0	+0.65 / +0.4	0 / 1.0	+0.6 / 0	+1.0 / +0.6	0.2 / 1.2	+0.6 / 0	+1.2 / +0.8
0.40 – 0.71	0 / 0.8	+0.4 / 0	+0.8 / +0.4	0 / 1.1	+0.7 / 0	+1.1 / +0.7	0.3 / 1.4	+0.7 / 0	+1.4 / +1.0
0.71 – 1.19	0 / 1.0	+0.5 / 0	+1.0 / +0.5	0 / 1.3	+0.8 / 0	+1.3 / +0.8	0.4 / 1.7	+0.8 / 0	+1.7 / +1.2
1.19 – 1.97	0 / 1.1	+0.6 / 0	+1.1 / +0.6	0 / 1.6	+1.0 / 0	+1.6 / +1.0	0.4 / 2.0	+1.0 / 0	+2.0 / +1.4

Figure A-5

American Standard Force and Shrink Fits

Nominal Size Range Inches (Over – To)	Limits of Interference	Class FN 1 Standard Limits Hole	Shaft	Limits of Interference	Class FN 2 Standard Limits Hole	Shaft	Limits of Interference	Class FN 3 Standard Limits Hole	Shaft	Limits of Interference	Class FN 4 Standard Limits Hole	Shaft
0 – 0.12	0.05 / 0.5	+0.25 / 0	+0.5 / +0.3	0.2 / 0.85	+0.4 / 0	+0.85 / +0.6				0.3 / 0.95	+0.4 / 0	+0.95 / +0.7
0.12 – 0.24	0.1 / 0.6	+0.3 / 0	+0.6 / +0.4	0.2 / 1.0	+0.5 / 0	+1.0 / +0.7				0.4 / 1.2	+0.5 / 0	+1.2 / +0.9
0.24 – 0.40	0.1 / 0.75	+0.4 / 0	+0.75 / +0.5	0.4 / 1.4	+0.6 / 0	+1.4 / +1.0				0.6 / 1.6	+0.6 / 0	+1.6 / +1.2
0.40 – 0.56	0.1 / 0.8	+0.4 / 0	+0.8 / +0.5	0.5 / 1.6	+0.7 / 0	+1.6 / +1.2				0.7 / 1.8	+0.7 / 0	+1.8 / +1.4
0.56 – 0.71	0.2 / 0.9	+0.4 / 0	+0.9 / +0.6	0.5 / 1.6	+0.7 / 0	+1.6 / +1.2				0.7 / 1.8	+0.7 / 0	+1.8 / +1.4
0.71 – 0.95	0.2 / 1.1	+0.5 / 0	+1.1 / +0.7	0.6 / 1.9	+0.8 / 0	+1.9 / +1.4				0.8 / 2.1	+0.8 / 0	+2.1 / +1.6
0.95 – 1.19	0.3 / 1.2	+0.5 / 0	+1.2 / +0.8	0.6 / 1.9	+0.8 / 0	+1.9 / +1.4	0.8 / 2.1	+0.8 / 0	+2.1 / +1.6	1.0 / 2.3	+0.8 / 0	+2.1 / +1.8
1.19 – 1.58	0.3 / 1.3	+0.6 / 0	+1.3 / +0.9	0.8 / 2.4	+1.0 / 0	+2.4 / +1.8	1.0 / 2.6	+1.0 / 0	+2.6 / +2.0	1.5 / 3.1	+1.0 / 0	+3.1 / +2.5
1.58 – 1.97	0.4 / 1.4	+0.6 / 0	+1.4 / +1.0	0.8 / 2.4	+1.0 / 0	+2.4 / +1.8	1.2 / 2.8	+1.0 / 0	+2.8 / +2.2	1.8 / 3.4	+1.0 / 0	+3.4 / +2.8

Figure A-6

Preferred Clearance Fits — Cylindrical Fits
(Hole Basis; ANSI B4.2)

Basic Size		Loose Running			Free Running			Close Running			Sliding			Locational Clear.		
		Hole H11	Shaft c11	Fit	Hole H9	Shaft d9	Fit	Hole H8	Shaft f7	Fit	Hole H7	Shaft g6	Fit	Hole H7	Shaft h6	Fit
4	Max	4.075	3.930	0.220	4.030	3.970	0.090	4.018	3.990	0.040	4.012	3.996	0.024	4.012	4.000	0.020
	Min	4.000	3.855	0.070	4.000	3.940	0.030	4.000	3.978	0.010	4.000	3.988	0.004	4.000	3.992	0.000
5	Max	5.075	4.930	0.220	5.030	4.970	0.090	5.018	4.990	0.040	5.012	4.996	0.024	5.012	5.000	0.020
	Min	5.000	4.855	0.070	5.000	4.940	0.030	5.000	4.978	0.010	5.000	4.988	0.004	5.000	4.992	0.000
6	Max	6.075	5.930	0.220	6.030	5.970	0.090	6.018	5.990	0.040	6.012	5.996	0.024	6.012	6.000	0.020
	Min	6.000	5.885	0.070	6.000	5.940	0.030	6.000	5.978	0.010	6.000	5.988	0.004	6.000	5.992	0.000
8	Max	8.090	7.920	0.260	8.036	7.960	0.112	8.022	7.987	0.050	8.015	7.995	0.029	8.015	8.000	0.024
	Min	8.000	7.830	0.080	8.000	7.924	0.040	8.000	7.972	0.013	8.000	7.986	0.005	8.000	7.991	0.000
10	Max	10.090	9.920	0.260	10.036	9.960	0.112	10.022	9.987	0.050	10.015	9.995	0.029	10.015	10.000	0.024
	Min	10.000	9.830	0.080	10.000	9.924	0.040	10.000	9.972	0.013	10.000	9.986	0.005	10.000	9.991	0.000
12	Max	12.112	11.905	0.315	12.043	11.950	0.136	12.027	11.984	0.061	12.018	11.994	0.035	12.018	12.000	0.029
	Min	12.000	11.795	0.095	12.000	11.907	0.050	12.000	11.966	0.016	12.000	11.983	0.006	12.000	11.989	0.000
16	Max	16.110	15.905	0.315	16.043	15.950	0.136	16.027	15.984	0.061	16.018	15.994	0.035	16.018	16.000	0.029
	Min	16.000	15.795	0.095	16.000	15.907	0.050	16.000	15.966	0.016	16.000	15.983	0.006	16.000	15.989	0.000
20	Max	20.130	19.890	0.370	20.052	19.935	0.169	20.033	19.980	0.074	20.021	19.993	0.041	20.021	20.000	0.034
	Min	20.000	19.760	0.110	20.000	19.883	0.065	20.000	19.959	0.020	20.000	19.980	0.007	20.000	19.987	0.000
25	Max	25.130	24.890	0.370	25.052	24.935	0.169	25.033	24.980	0.074	25.021	24.993	0.041	25.021	25.000	0.034
	Min	25.000	24.760	0.110	25.000	24.883	0.065	25.000	24.959	0.020	25.000	24.980	0.007	25.000	24.987	0.000
30	Max	30.130	29.890	0.370	30.052	29.935	0.169	30.033	29.980	0.074	30.021	29.993	0.041	30.021	30.000	0.034
	Min	30.000	29.760	0.110	30.000	29.883	0.065	30.000	29.959	0.020	30.000	29.980	0.007	30.000	29.987	0.000

Figure A-7

Preferred Transition and Interference Fits — Cylindrical Fits
(Hole Basis; ANSI B4.2)

Basic Size		Locational Trans.			Locational Trans.			Locational Inter.			Medium Drive			Force		
		Hole H7	Shaft k6	Fit	Hole H7	Shaft n6	Fit	Hole H7	Shaft p6	Fit	Hole H7	Shaft s6	Fit	Hole H7	Shaft u6	Fit
4	Max	4.012	4.009	0.011	4.012	4.016	0.004	4.012	4.020	0.000	4.012	4.027	−0.007	4.012	4.031	−0.011
	Min	4.000	4.001	−0.009	4.000	4.008	−0.016	4.000	4.012	−0.020	4.000	4.019	−0.027	4.000	4.023	−0.031
5	Max	5.012	5.009	0.011	5.012	5.016	0.004	5.012	5.020	0.000	5.012	5.027	−0.007	5.012	5.031	−0.011
	Min	5.000	5.001	−0.009	5.000	5.008	−0.016	5.000	5.012	−0.020	5.000	5.019	−0.027	5.000	5.023	−0.031
6	Max	6.012	6.009	0.011	6.012	6.016	0.004	6.012	6.020	0.000	6.012	6.027	−0.007	6.012	6.031	−0.011
	Min	6.000	6.001	−0.009	6.000	6.008	−0.016	6.000	6.012	−0.020	6.000	6.019	−0.027	6.000	6.023	−0.031
8	Max	8.015	8.010	0.014	8.015	8.019	0.005	8.015	8.024	0.000	8.015	8.032	−0.008	8.015	8.037	−0.013
	Min	8.000	8.001	−0.010	8.000	8.010	−0.019	8.000	8.015	−0.024	8.000	8.023	−0.032	8.000	8.028	−0.037
10	Max	10.015	10.010	0.014	10.015	10.019	0.005	10.015	10.024	0.000	10.015	10.032	−0.008	10.015	10.037	−0.013
	Min	10.000	10.001	−0.010	10.000	10.010	−0.019	10.000	10.015	−0.024	10.000	10.023	−0.032	10.000	10.028	−0.037
12	Max	12.018	12.012	0.017	12.018	12.023	0.006	12.018	12.029	0.000	12.018	12.039	−0.010	12.018	12.044	−0.015
	Min	12.000	12.001	−0.012	12.000	12.012	−0.023	12.000	12.018	−0.029	12.000	12.028	−0.039	12.000	12.033	−0.044
16	Max	16.018	16.012	0.017	16.018	16.023	0.006	16.018	16.029	0.000	16.018	16.039	−0.010	16.018	16.044	−0.015
	Min	16.000	16.001	−0.012	16.000	16.012	−0.023	16.000	16.018	−0.029	16.000	16.028	−0.039	16.000	16.033	−0.044
20	Max	20.021	20.015	0.019	20.021	20.028	0.006	20.021	20.035	−0.001	20.021	20.048	−0.014	20.021	20.054	−0.020
	Min	20.000	20.002	−0.015	20.000	20.015	−0.028	20.000	20.022	−0.035	20.000	20.035	−0.048	20.000	20.041	−0.054
25	Max	25.021	25.015	0.019	25.021	25.028	0.006	25.021	25.035	−0.001	25.021	25.048	−0.014	25.021	25.061	−0.027
	Min	25.000	25.002	−0.015	25.000	25.015	−0.028	25.000	25.022	−0.035	25.000	25.035	−0.048	25.000	25.048	−0.061
30	Max	30.021	30.015	0.019	30.021	30.028	0.006	30.021	30.035	−0.001	30.021	30.048	−0.014	30.021	30.061	−0.027
	Min	30.000	30.002	−0.015	30.000	30.015	−0.028	30.000	30.022	−0.035	30.000	30.035	−0.048	30.000	30.048	−0.061

Figure A-8

Preferred Clearance Fits — Cylindrical Fits
(Shaft Basis; ANSI B4.2)

Basic Size		Loose Running			Free Running			Close Running			Sliding			Locational Clear.		
		Hole C11	Shaft h11	Fit	Hole D9	Shaft h9	Fit	Hole F8	Shaft h7	Fit	Hole G7	Shaft h6	Fit	Hole H7	Shaft h6	Fit
4	Max	4.145	4.000	0.220	4.060	4.000	0.090	4.028	4.000	0.040	4.016	4.000	0.024	4.012	4.000	0.020
	Min	4.070	3.925	0.070	4.030	3.970	0.030	4.010	3.988	0.010	4.004	3.992	0.004	4.000	3.992	0.000
5	Max	5.145	5.000	0.220	5.060	5.000	0.090	5.028	5.000	0.040	5.016	5.000	0.024	5.012	5.000	0.020
	Min	5.070	4.925	0.070	5.030	4.970	0.030	5.010	4.988	0.010	5.004	4.992	0.004	5.000	4.992	0.000
6	Max	6.145	6.000	0.220	6.060	6.000	0.090	6.028	6.000	0.040	6.016	6.000	0.024	6.012	6.000	0.020
	Min	6.070	5.925	0.070	6.030	5.970	0.030	6.010	5.988	0.010	6.004	5.992	0.004	6.000	5.992	0.000
8	Max	8.170	8.000	0.260	8.076	8.000	0.112	8.035	8.000	0.050	8.020	8.000	0.029	8.015	8.000	0.024
	Min	8.080	7.910	0.080	8.040	7.964	0.040	8.013	7.985	0.013	8.005	7.991	0.005	8.000	7.991	0.000
10	Max	10.170	10.000	0.260	10.076	10.000	0.112	10.035	10.000	0.050	10.020	10.000	0.029	10.015	10.000	0.024
	Min	10.080	9.910	0.080	10.040	9.964	0.040	10.013	9.985	0.013	10.005	9.991	0.005	10.000	9.991	0.000
12	Max	12.205	12.000	0.315	12.093	12.000	0.136	12.043	12.000	0.061	12.024	12.000	0.035	12.018	12.000	0.029
	Min	12.095	11.890	0.095	12.050	11.957	0.050	12.016	11.982	0.016	12.006	11.989	0.006	12.000	11.989	0.000
16	Max	16.205	16.000	0.315	16.093	16.000	0.136	16.043	16.000	0.061	16.024	16.000	0.035	16.018	16.000	0.029
	Min	16.095	15.890	0.095	16.050	15.957	0.050	16.016	15.982	0.016	06.006	15.989	0.006	16.000	15.989	0.000
20	Max	20.240	20.000	0.370	20.117	20.000	0.169	20.053	20.000	0.074	20.028	20.000	0.041	20.021	20.000	0.034
	Min	20.110	19.870	0.110	20.065	19.948	0.065	20.020	19.979	0.020	20.007	19.987	0.007	20.000	19.987	0.000
25	Max	25.240	25.000	0.370	25.117	25.000	0.169	25.053	25.000	0.074	25.028	25.000	0.041	25.021	25.000	0.034
	Min	25.110	24.870	0.110	25.065	24.948	0.065	25.020	24.979	0.020	25.007	24.987	0.007	25.000	24.987	0.000
30	Max	30.240	30.000	0.370	30.117	30.000	0.169	30.053	30.000	0.074	30.028	30.000	0.041	30.021	30.000	0.034
	Min	30.110	29.870	0.110	30.065	29.948	0.065	30.020	29.979	0.020	30.007	29.987	0.007	30.000	29.987	0.000

Figure A-9

Preferred Transition and Interference Fits — Cylindrical Fits

(Shaft Basis; ANSI B4.2)

Basic Size		Locational Trans.			Locational Trans.			Locational Inter.			Medium Drive			Force		
		Hole K7	Shaft h6	Fit	Hole N7	Shaft h6	Fit	Hole F7	Shaft h6	Fit	Hole S7	Shaft h6	Fit	Hole U7	Shaft h6	Fit
4	Max	4.003	4.000	0.011	3.996	4.000	0.004	3.992	4.000	0.000	3.985	4.000	-0.007	3.981	4.000	-0.011
	Min	3.991	3.992	-0.009	3.984	3.992	-0.016	3.980	3.992	-0.020	3.973	3.992	-0.027	3.969	3.992	-0.031
5	Max	5.003	5.000	0.011	4.996	5.000	0.004	4.992	5.000	0.000	4.985	5.000	-0.007	4.981	5.000	-0.011
	Min	4.991	4.992	-0.009	4.984	4.992	-0.016	4.980	4.992	-0.020	4.973	4.992	-0.027	4.969	4.992	-0.031
6	Max	6.003	6.000	0.011	5.996	6.000	0.004	5.992	6.000	0.000	5.985	6.000	-0.007	5.981	6.000	-0.011
	Min	5.991	5.991	-0.009	5.984	5.992	-0.016	5.980	5.992	-0.020	5.973	5.992	-0.027	5.969	5.992	-0.031
8	Max	8.005	8.000	0.014	7.996	8.000	0.005	7.991	8.000	0.000	7.983	8.000	-0.008	7.978	8.000	-0.013
	Min	7.990	7.991	-0.010	7.981	7.991	-0.019	7.976	7.991	-0.024	7.968	7.991	-0.032	7.963	7.991	-0.037
10	Max	10.005	10.000	0.014	9.996	10.000	0.005	9.991	10.000	0.000	9.983	10.000	-0.008	9.978	10.000	-0.013
	Min	9.990	9.991	-0.010	9.981	9.991	-0.019	9.976	9.991	-0.024	9.968	9.991	-0.032	9.963	9.991	-0.037
12	Max	12.006	12.000	0.017	11.995	12.000	0.006	11.989	12.000	0.000	11.979	12.000	-0.010	11.974	12.000	-0.015
	Min	11.988	11.989	-0.012	11.977	11.989	-0.023	11.971	11.989	-0.029	11.961	11.989	-0.039	11.956	11.989	-0.044
16	Max	16.006	16.000	0.017	15.995	16.000	0.006	15.989	16.000	0.000	15.979	16.000	-0.010	15.974	16.000	-0.015
	Min	15.988	15.989	-0.012	15.977	15.989	-0.023	15.971	15.989	-0.029	15.961	15.989	-0.039	15.956	15.989	-0.044
20	Max	20.006	20.000	0.019	19.993	20.000	0.006	19.986	20.000	-0.001	19.973	20.000	-0.014	19.967	20.000	-0.020
	Min	19.985	19.987	-0.015	19.972	19.987	-0.028	19.965	19.987	-0.035	19.952	19.987	-0.048	19.946	19.987	-0.054
25	Max	25.006	25.000	0.019	24.993	25.000	0.006	24.986	25.000	-0.001	24.973	25.000	-0.014	24.960	25.000	-0.027
	Min	24.985	24.987	-0.015	24.972	24.987	-0.028	24.965	24.987	-0.035	24.952	24.987	-0.048	24.939	24.987	-0.061
30	Max	30.006	30.000	0.019	29.993	30.000	0.006	29.986	30.000	-0.001	29.973	30.000	-0.014	29.960	30.000	-0.027
	Min	29.985	29.987	-0.015	29.972	29.987	-0.028	29.965	29.987	-0.035	29.952	29.987	-0.048	29.939	29.987	-0.061

Figure A-10

American National Standard Type A Plain Washers
(ANSI B18.22.1-1965, R1975)

Nominal Washer Size		Series	Inside Diameter			Outside Diameter			Thickness		
			Basic	Tolerance		Basic	Tolerance		Basic	Max.	Min.
				Plus	Minus		Plus	Minus			
#6	.138		.156	.008	.005	.375	.015	.005	.049	.065	.036
#8	.164		.188	.008	.005	.438	.015	.005	.049	.065	.036
#10	.190		.219	.008	.005	.500	.015	.005	.049	.065	.036
1/4	.250	N	.281	.015	.005	.625	.015	.005	.065	.080	.051
1/4	.250	W	.312	.015	.005	.734	.015	.007	.065	.080	.051
5/16	.312	N	.344	.015	.005	.688	.015	.007	.065	.080	.051
5/16	.312	W	.375	.015	.005	.875	.030	.007	.083	.104	.064
3/8	.375	N	.406	.015	.005	.812	.015	.007	.065	.080	.051
3/8	.375	W	.438	.015	.005	1.000	.030	.007	.083	.104	.064
7/16	.438	N	.469	.015	.005	.922	.015	.007	.065	.080	.051
7/16	.438	W	.500	.015	.005	1.250	.030	.007	.083	.104	.064
1/2	.500	N	.531	.015	.005	1.062	.030	.007	.095	.121	.074
1/2	.500	W	.562	.015	.005	1.375	.030	.007	.109	.132	.086
9/16	.562	N	.594	.015	.005	1.156	.030	.007	.095	.121	.074
9/16	.562	W	.625	.015	.005	1.469	.030	.007	.109	.132	.086
5/8	.625	N	.656	.030	.007	1.312	.030	.007	.095	.121	.074
5/8	.625	W	.688	.030	.007	1.750	.030	.007	.134	.160	.108
3/4	.750	N	.812	.030	.007	1.469	.030	.007	.134	.160	.108
3/4	.750	W	.812	.030	.007	2.000	.030	.007	.148	.177	.122
7/8	.875	N	.938	.030	.007	1.750	.030	.007	.134	.160	.108
7/8	.875	W	.938	.030	.007	2.250	.030	.007	.165	.192	.136
1	1.000	N	1.062	.030	.007	2.000	.030	.007	.134	.160	.108
1	1.000	W	1.062	.030	.007	2.500	.030	.007	.165	.192	.136
1 1/8	1.125	N	1.250	.030	.007	2.250	.030	.007	.134	.160	.108
1 1/8	1.125	W	1.250	.030	.007	2.750	.030	.007	.165	.192	.136
1 1/4	1.250	N	1.375	.030	.007	2.500	.030	.007	.165	.192	.136
1 1/4	1.250	W	1.375	.030	.007	3.000	.030	.007	.165	.192	.136
1 3/8	1.375	N	1.500	.030	.007	2.750	.030	.007	.165	.192	.136
1 3/8	1.375	W	1.500	.045	.010	3.250	.045	.010	.180	.213	.153
1 1/2	1.500	N	1.625	.030	.007	3.000	.030	.007	.165	.192	.136
1 1/2	1.500	W	1.625	.045	.010	3.500	.045	.010	.180	.213	.153
1 5/8	1.625		1.750	.045	.010	3.750	.045	.010	.180	.213	.153
1 3/4	1.750		1.875	.045	.010	4.000	.045	.010	.180	.213	.153
1 7/8	1.875		2.000	.045	.010	4.250	.045	.010	.180	.213	.153
2	2.000		2.125	.045	.010	4.500	.045	.010	.180	.213	.153
2 1/4	2.250		2.375	.045	.010	4.750	.045	.010	.220	.248	.193
2 1/2	2.500		2.625	.045	.010	5.000	.045	.010	.238	.280	.210
2 3/4	2.750		2.875	.065	.010	5.250	.065	.010	.259	.310	.228
3	3.000		3.125	.065	.010	5.500	.065	.010	.284	.327	.249

Figure A-11

American National Standard Helical Spring Lock Washers (ANSI B18.21.1-1972)

Nominal Washer Size	Inside Diameter, A Max	Min	Regular O.D., B Max	Section Width	Section Thickness	Heavy O.D., B Max	Section Width	Section Thickness	Extra Duty O.D., B Max	Section Width	Section Thickness
#2 .086	.094	.088	.172	.035	.020	.182	.040	.025	.208	.053	.027
#3 .099	.107	.101	.195	.040	.025	.209	.047	.031	.239	.062	.034
#4 .112	.120	.114	.209	.040	.025	.223	.047	.031	.253	.062	.034
#5 .125	.133	.127	.236	.047	.031	.253	.055	.040	.300	.079	.045
#6 .138	.148	.141	.250	.047	.031	.266	.055	.040	.314	.079	.045
#8 .164	.174	.167	.293	.055	.040	.307	.062	.047	.375	.096	.057
#10 .190	.200	.193	.334	.062	.047	.350	.070	.056	.434	.112	.068
#12 .216	.227	.220	.377	.070	.056	.391	.077	.063	.497	.130	.080
1/4 .250	.262	.254	.489	.109	.062	.491	.110	.077	.535	.132	.084
5/16 .312	.326	.317	.586	.125	.078	.596	.130	.097	.622	.143	.108
3/8 .375	.390	.380	.683	.141	.094	.691	.145	.115	.741	.170	.123
7/16 .438	.455	.443	.779	.156	.109	.787	.160	.133	.839	.186	.143
1/2 .500	.518	.506	.873	.171	.125	.883	.176	.151	.939	.204	.162
9/16 .562	.582	.570	.971	.188	.141	.981	.193	.170	1.041	.223	.182
5/8 .625	.650	.635	1.079	.203	.156	1.093	.210	.189	1.157	.242	.202
11/16 .688	.713	.698	1.176	.219	.172	1.192	.227	.207	1.258	.260	.221
3/4 .750	.775	.760	1.271	.234	.188	1.291	.244	.226	1.361	.279	.241
13/16 .812	.843	.824	1.367	.250	.203	1.391	.262	.246	1.463	.298	.261
7/8 .875	.905	.887	1.464	.266	.219	1.494	.281	.266	1.576	.322	.285
15/16 .938	.970	.950	1.560	.281	.234	1.594	.298	.284	1.688	.345	.308
1 1.000	1.042	1.017	1.661	.297	.250	1.705	.319	.306	1.799	.366	.330
1 1/16 1.062	1.107	1.080	1.756	.312	.266	1.808	.338	.326	1.910	.389	.352
1 1/8 1.125	1.172	1.144	1.853	.328	.281	1.909	.356	.345	2.019	.411	.375
1 3/16 1.188	1.237	1.208	1.950	.344	.297	2.008	.373	.364	2.124	.341	.396
1 1/4 1.250	1.302	1.271	2.045	.359	.312	2.113	.393	.384	2.231	.452	.417
1 5/16 1.312	1.366	1.334	2.141	.375	.328	2.211	.410	.403	2.335	.472	.438
1 3/8 1.375	1.432	1.398	2.239	.391	.344	2.311	.427	.422	2.439	.491	.458
1 7/16 1.438	1.497	1.462	2.334	.406	.359	2.406	.442	.440	2.540	.509	.478
1 1/2 1.500	1.561	1.525	2.430	.422	.375	2.502	.458	.458	2.638	.526	.496

Figure A-12

American National Standard Internal-External Tooth Lock Washers (ANSI B18.21.1-1972)

Size	A Inside Diameter Max.	Min.	B Outside Diameter Max.	Min.	C Thickness Max.	Min.	Size	A Inside Diameter Max.	Min.	B Outside Diameter Max.	Min.	C Thickness Max.	Min.
#4	.123	.115	.475	.460	.021	.021	5/16	.332	.320	.900	.865	.040	.032
	.123	.115	.510	.495	.021	.017		.332	.320	.985	.965	.045	.037
			.610	.580				.332	.320	1.070	1.045	.050	.042
										1.155	1.130		
#6	.150	.141	.510	.495	.028	.023	3/8	.398	.384	.985	.965	.045	.037
			.610	.580				.398	.384	1.070	1.045	.050	.042
			.690	.670						1.155	1.130		
										1.260	1.220		
#8	.176	.168	.610	.580	.034	.028	7/16	.464	.448	1.070	1.045	.050	.042
			.690	.670						1.155	1.130		
			.760	.740				.464	.448	1.260	1.220	.055	.047
										1.315	1.290		
#10	.204	.195	.610	.580	.034	.028	1/2	.530	.512	1.260	1.220	.055	.047
	.204	.195	.690	.670	.040	.032				1.315	1.290		
			.760	.740				.530	.512	1.410	1.380	.060	.052
			.900	.880				.530	.512	1.620	1.590	.067	.059
#12	.231	.221	.690	.670	.040	.032	9/16	.596	.576	1.315	1.290	.055	.047
	.231	.221	.760	.725				.596	.576	1.430	1.380	.060	.052
			.900	.880				.596	.576	1.620	1.590	.067	.059
			.985	.965	.045	.037				1.830	1.797		
1/4	.267	.256	.760	.725	.040	.032	5/8	.663	.640	1.410	1.380	.060	.052
	.267	.256	.900	.880				.663	.640	1.620	1.590	.067	.059
			.985	.965	.045	.037				1.830	1.797		
			1.070	1.045						1.975	1.935		

Figure A-13

British Standard Bright Metal Washers – Metric Series (BS 4320:1968)

Nominal Size of Bolt or Screw	Inside Diameter			Outside Diameter			Thickness					
							Form A (Normal Range)			Form B (Light Range)		
	Nom.	Max.	Min.	Nom.	Max.	Min.	Nom.	Max.	Min.	Nom.	Max.	Min.
M 1.0	1.1	1.25	1.1	2.5	2.5	2.3	.3	.4	.2			
M 1.2	1.3	1.45	1.3	3.0	3.0	2.8	.3	.4	.2			
M 1.4	1.5	1.65	1.5	3.0	3.0	2.8	.3	.4	.2			
M 1.6	1.7	1.85	1.7	4.0	4.0	3.7	.3	.4	.2			
M 2.0	2.2	2.35	2.2	5.0	5.0	4.7	.3	.4	.2			
M 2.2	2.4	2.55	2.4	5.0	5.0	4.7	.5	.6	.4			
M 2.5	2.7	2.85	2.7	6.5	6.5	6.2	.5	.6	.4			
M 3	3.2	3.4	3.2	7	7	6.7	.5	.6	.4			
M 3.5	3.7	3.9	3.7	7	7	6.7	.5	.6	.4			
M 4	4.3	4.5	4.3	9	9	8.7	.8	.9	.7			
M 4.5	4.8	5.0	4.8	9	9	8.7	.8	.9	.7			
M 5	5.3	5.5	5.3	10	10	9.7	1.0	1.1	.9			
M 6	6.4	6.7	6.4	12.5	12.5	12.1	1.6	1.8	1.4	.8	.9	.7
M 7	7.4	7.7	7.4	14	14	13.6	1.6	1.8	1.4	.8	.9	.7
M 8	8.4	8.7	8.4	17	17	16.6	1.6	1.8	1.4	1.0	1.1	.9
M 10	10.5	10.9	10.5	21	21	20.5	2.0	2.2	1.8	1.25	1.45	1.05
M 12	13.0	13.4	13.0	24	24	23.5	2.5	2.7	2.3	1.6	1.80	1.40
M 14	15.0	15.4	15.0	28	28	27.5	2.5	2.7	2.3	1.6	1.8	1.4
M 16	17.0	17.4	17.0	30	30	29.5	3.0	3.3	2.7	2.0	2.2	1.8
M 18	19.0	19.5	19.0	34	34	33.2	3.0	3.3	2.7	2.0	2.2	1.8
M 20	21	21.5	21	37	37	36.2	3.0	3.3	2.7	2.0	2.2	1.8
M 22	23	23.5	23	39	39	38.2	3.0	3.3	2.7	2.0	2.2	1.8
M 24	25	25.5	25	44	44	43.2	4.0	4.3	3.7	2.5	2.7	2.3
M 27	28	28.5	28	50	50	49.2	4.0	4.3	3.7	2.5	2.7	2.3
M 30	31	31.6	31	56	56	55.0	4.0	4.3	3.7	2.5	2.7	2.3
M 33	34	34.6	34	60	60	59.0	5.0	5.6	4.4	3.0	3.3	2.7
M 36	37	37..6	37	66	66	65.0	5.0	5.6	4.4	3.0	3.3	2.7
M 39	40	40.6	40	72	72	71.0	6.0	6.6	5.4	3.0	3.3	2.7

Note: The table is headed "NORMAL DIAMETER SIZES"

Figure A-14

American National Standard and Unified Standard Square Bolts (ANSI B18.2.1-1972)

SQUARE BOLTS

Nominal Size or Basic Product Diameter	Body Diam., E	Width Across Flats, F			Width Across Corners, G		Height, H			Radius of Fillet, R
	Max.	Basic	Max.	Min.	Max.	Min.	Basic	Max.	Min.	Max.
1/4 .2500	.260	3/8	.375	.362	.530	.498	11/64	.188	.156	.03
5/16 .3125	.324	1/2	.500	.484	.707	.665	13/64	.220	.186	.03
3/8 .3750	.388	9/16	.562	.544	.795	.747	1/4	.268	.232	.03
7/16 .4375	.452	5/8	.625	.603	.884	.828	19/64	.316	.278	.03
1/2 .5000	.515	3/4	.750	.725	1.061	.995	21/64	.348	.308	.03
5/8 .6250	.642	15/16	.938	.906	1.326	1.244	37/64	.444	.400	.06
3/4 .7500	.768	1 1/8	1.125	1.088	1.591	1.494	1/2	.524	.476	.06
7/8 .8750	.895	1 5/16	1.312	1.269	1.856	1.742	19/32	.620	.568	.06
1 1.0000	1.022	1 1/2	1.500	1.450	2.121	1.991	21/32	.684	.628	.09
1 1/8 1.1250	1.149	1 11/16	1.688	1.631	2.386	2.239	3/4	.780	.720	.09
1 1/4 1.2500	1.277	1 7/8	1.875	1.812	2.652	2.489	27/32	.876	.812	.09
1 3/8 1.3750	1.404	2 1/16	2.062	1.994	2.917	2.738	29/32	.940	.872	.09
1 1/2 1.5000	1.531	2 1/4	2.250	2.175	3.182	2.986	1	1.036	.964	.09

Figure A-15

American National Standard and Unified Standard Hex Head Screws
(ANSI B18.2.1-1972)

Nominal Size or Basic Diam.		Body Diam., E	Width Across Flats, F			Width Across Corners, G		Height, H			Radius of Fillet, R	
		Max.	Basic	Max.	Min.	Max.	Min.	Basic	Max.	Min.	Max.	Min.
HEX BOLTS												
1/4	.2500	.260	7/16	.438	.425	.505	.484	11/64	.188	.150	.03	.01
5/16	.3125	.324	1/2	.500	.484	.577	.552	7/32	.235	.195	.03	.01
3/8	.3750	.388	9/16	.562	.544	.650	.620	1/4	.268	.226	.03	.01
7/16	.4375	.452	5/8	.625	.603	.722	.687	19/64	.316	.272	.03	.01
1/2	.5000	.515	3/4	.750	.725	.866	.826	11/32	.364	.302	.03	.01
5/8	.6250	.642	15/16	.938	.906	1.083	1.033	27/64	.444	.378	.06	.02
3/4	.7500	.768	1 1/8	1.125	1.088	1.299	1.240	1/2	.524	.455	.06	.02
7/8	.8750	.895	1 5/16	1.312	1.269	1.516	1.447	37/64	.604	.531	.06	.02
1	1.0000	1.022	1 1/2	1.500	1.450	1.732	1.653	43/64	.700	.591	.09	.03
1 1/8	1.1250	1.149	1 11/16	1.688	1.631	1.949	1.859	3/4	.780	.658	.09	.03
1 1/4	1.2500	1.277	1 7/8	1.875	1.812	2.165	2.066	27/32	.876	.749	.09	.03
1 3/8	1.3750	1.404	2 1/16	2.062	1.994	2.382	2.273	29/32	.940	.810	.09	.03
1 1/2	1.5000	1.531	2 1/4	2.250	2.175	2.598	2.480	1	1.036	.902	.09	.03
1 3/4	1.7500	1.785	2 5/8	2.625	2.538	3.031	2.893	1 5/32	1.196	1.054	.12	.04
2	2.0000	2.039	3	3.000	2.900	3.464	3.306	1 11/32	1.388	1.175	.12	.04
2 1/4	2.2500	2.305	3 3/8	3.375	3.262	3.897	3.719	1 1/2	1.548	1.327	.19	.06
2 1/2	2.5000	2.559	3 3/4	3.750	3.625	4.330	4.133	1 21/32	1.708	1.479	.19	.06
2 3/4	2.7500	2.827	4 1/8	4.125	3.988	4.763	4.546	1 13/16	1.869	1.632	.19	.06
3	3.0000	3.081	4 1/2	4.500	4.350	5.196	4.959	2	2.060	1.815	.19	.06
3 1/4	3.2500	3.335	4 7/8	4.875	4.712	5.629	5.372	2 3/16	2.251	1.936	.19	.06
3 1/2	3.5000	3.589	5 1/4	5.250	5.075	6.062	5.786	2 5/16	2.380	2.057	.19	.06
3 3/4	3.7500	3.858	5 5/8	5.625	5.437	6.495	6.198	2 1/2	2.572	2.241	.19	.06
4	4.0000	4.111	6	6.000	5.800	6.982	6.612	2 11/16	2.764	2.424	.19	.06

Figure A-16

Coarse-Thread Series, UNC, UNRC, and NC — Basic Dimensions

Sizes	Basic Major Diam., D	Thds. per Inch, n	Basic Pitch Diam., E	Minor Diameter		Lead Angle at Basic P.D.		Area of Minor Diam. at D-2h	Tensile Stress Area
				Ext. Thds., Ks	Int. Thds., Kn				
	Inches		Inches	Inches	Inches	Deg.	Min.	Sq. In.	Sq. In.
1 (.073)	.0730	64	.0629	.0538	.0561	4	31	.00218	.00263
2 (.086)	.0860	56	.0744	.0641	.0667	4	22	.00310	.00370
3 (.099)	.0990	48	.0855	.0734	.0764	4	26	.00406	.00487
4 (.112)	.1120	40	.0958	.0813	.0849	4	45	.00496	.00604
5 (.125)	.1250	40	.1088	.0943	.0979	4	11	.00672	.00796
6 (.138)	.1380	32	.1177	.0997	.1042	4	50	.00745	.00909
8 (.164)	1.640	32	.1437	.1257	.1302	3	58	.01196	.0140
10 (.190)	.1900	24	.1629	.1389	.1449	4	39	.01450	.0175
12 (.216)	.2160	24	.1889	.1649	.1709	4	1	.0206	.0242
1/4	.2500	20	.2175	.1887	.1959	4	11	.0269	.0318
5/16	.3125	18	.2764	.2443	.2524	3	40	.0454	.0524
3/8	.3750	16	.3344	.2983	.3073	3	24	.0678	.0775
7/16	.4375	14	.3911	.3499	.3602	3	20	.0933	.1063
1/2	.5000	13	.4500	.4056	.4167	3	7	.1257	.1419
9/16	.5625	12	.5084	.4603	4723	2	59	.162	.182
5/8	.6250	11	.5660	.5135	.5266	2	56	.202	.226
3/4	.7500	10	.6850	.6273	.6417	2	40	.302	.334
7/8	.8750	9	.8028	.7387	.7547	2	31	.419	.462
1	1.0000	8	.9188	.8466	.8647	2	29	.551	.606
1 1/8	1.1250	7	1.032	.9497	.9704	2	31	.693	.763
1 1/4	1.2500	7	1.572	1.0747	1.0954	2	15	.890	.969
1 3/8	1.3750	6	1.2667	1.1705	1.1946	2	24	1.054	1.155
1 1/2	1.5000	6	1.3917	1.2955	1.3196	2	11	1.294	1.405

Figure A-17

Fine-Thread Series, UNC, UNRC, and NC — Basic Dimensions

Sizes	Basic Major Diam., D	Thds. per Inch, n	Basic Pitch Diam., E	Minor Diameter		Lead Angle at Basic P.D.		Area of Minor Diam. at D-2h	Tensile Stress Area
				Ext. Thds., Ks	Int. Thds., Kn				
	Inches		Inches	Inches	Inches	Deg.	Min.	Sq. In.	Sq. In.
1 (.073)	.0730	72	.0640	.0560	.0580	3	57	.00237	.00278
2 (.086)	.860	64	.0759	.0668	.0691	3	45	.00339	.00394
3 (.099)	.990	56	.0874	.0771	.0797	3	43	.00451	.00523
4 (.112)	.1120	48	.0985	.0864	.0894	3	51	.00566	.00661
5 (.125)	.1250	44	.1102	.0971	.1004	3	45	.00716	.00830
6 (.138)	.1380	40	.1218	.1073	.1109	3	44	.00874	.01015
8 (.164)	.1640	36	.1460	.1299	.1339	3	28	.01285	.01474
10 (.190)	.1900	32	.1697	.1517	.1562	3	21	.0175	.0200
12 (.216)	.2160	28	.1928	.1722	.1773	3	22	.0226	.0258
1/4	.2500	28	.2268	.2062	.2113	2	52	.0326	.0364
5/16	.3125	24	.2854	.2614	.2674	2	40	.0524	.0580
3/8	.3750	24	.3479	.3239	.3299	2	11	.0809	.0878
7/16	.4375	20	.4050	.3762	.3834	2	15	.1090	.1187
1/2	.5000	20	.4675	.4387	.4459	1	57	.1486	.1599
9/16	.5625	18	.5264	.4943	.5024	1	55	.189	.203
5/8	.6250	18	.5889	.5568	.5649	1	43	.240	.256
3/4	.7500	16	.7094	.6733	.6823	1	36	.351	.373
7/8	.8750	14	.8286	.7874	.7977	1	34	.480	.509
1	1.0000	12	.9459	.8978	.9098	1	36	.625	.663
1 1/8	1.1250	12	1.0709	1.0228	1.0348	1	25	.812	.856
1 1/4	1.2500	12	1.1959	1.1478	1.1598	1	16	1.024	1.073
1 3/8	1.3750	12	1.3209	1.2728	1.2848	1	9	1.260	1.315
1 1/2	1.5000	12	1.4459	1.3978	1.4098	1	3	1.521	1.581

Figure A-18

American National Standard General-Purpose Acme Screw Thread Form—
Basic Dimensions (ANSI B1.5-1977)

Thds. per Inch	Pitch	Height of Thread (Basic)	Total Height of Thread	Thread Thickness (Basic)	Width of Flat	
					Crest of Internal Thread (Basic)	Root of Internal Thread
16	.06250	.03125	.0362	.03125	.0232	.0206
14	.07143	.03571	.0407	.03571	.0265	.0239
12	.08333	.04167	.0467	.04167	.0309	.0283
10	.10000	.05000	.0600	.05000	.0371	.0319
8	.12500	.06250	.0725	.06250	.0463	.0411
6	.16667	.08333	.0933	.08333	.0618	.0566
5	.20000	.10000	.1100	.10000	.0741	.0689
4	.25000	.12500	.1350	.12500	.0927	.0875
3	.33333	.16667	.1767	.16667	.1236	.1184
2 1/2	.40000	.20000	.2100	.20000	.1483	.1431
2	.50000	.25000	.2600	.25000	.1853	.1802
1 1/2	.66667	.33333	.3433	.33333	.2471	.2419
1 1/3	.75000	.37500	.3850	.37500	.2780	.2728
1	1.0000	.50000	.5100	.50000	.3707	.3655

Figure A-19

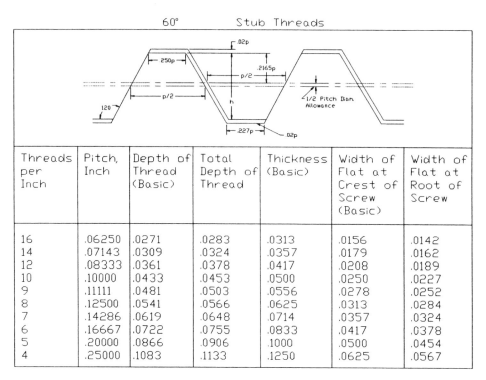

Threads per Inch	Pitch, Inch	Depth of Thread (Basic)	Total Depth of Thread	Thickness (Basic)	Width of Flat at Crest of Screw (Basic)	Width of Flat at Root of Screw
16	.06250	.0271	.0283	.0313	.0156	.0142
14	.07143	.0309	.0324	.0357	.0179	.0162
12	.08333	.0361	.0378	.0417	.0208	.0189
10	.10000	.0433	.0453	.0500	.0250	.0227
9	.11111	.0481	.0503	.0556	.0278	.0252
8	.12500	.0541	.0566	.0625	.0313	.0284
7	.14286	.0619	.0648	.0714	.0357	.0324
6	.16667	.0722	.0755	.0833	.0417	.0378
5	.20000	.0866	.0906	.1000	.0500	.0454
4	.25000	.1083	.1133	.1250	.0625	.0567

Figure A-20

American National Standard Slotted 100° Flat Countersunk
Head Machine Screws (ANSI B18.6.3-1972, R1977)

Nominal Size or Basic Screw Diam.		Head Diam., A		Head Height, H	Slot Width, J		Slot Depth, T	
		Max., Edge Sharp	Min., Edge Rounded or Flat	Ref.	Max.	Min.	Max.	Min.
0000	.0210	.043	.037	.009	.008	.005	.008	.004
000	.0340	.064	.058	.014	.012	.008	.011	.007
00	.0470	.093	.085	.020	.017	.010	.013	.008
0	.0600	.119	.096	.026	.023	.016	.013	.008
1	.0730	.146	.120	.031	.026	.019	.016	.010
2	.0860	.172	.143	.037	.031	.023	.019	.012
3	.0990	.199	.167	.043	.035	.027	.022	.014
4	.1120	.225	.191	.049	.039	.031	.024	.017
6	.1380	.279	.238	.060	.048	.039	.030	.022
8	.1640	.332	.285	.072	.054	.045	.036	.027
10	.1900	.385	.333	.083	.060	.050	.042	.031
1/4	.2500	.507	.442	.110	.075	.064	.055	.042
5/16	.3125	.635	.556	.138	.084	.072	.069	.053
3/8	.3750	.762	.670	.165	.094	.081	.083	.065

Figure A-21

American National Standard Slotted Truss Head Machine Screws
(ANSI B18.6.3-1972, R1977)

Nominal Size or Basic Screw Diam.		Head Diam., A		Head Height, H		Head Radius, R	Slot Width, J		Slot Depth, T	
		Max.	Min.	Max.	Min.	Max.	Max.	Min.	Max.	Min.
0000	.0210	.049	.043	.014	.010	.032	.009	.005	.009	.005
000	.0340	.077	.071	.022	.018	.051	.013	.009	.013	.009
00	.0470	.106	.098	.030	.024	.070	.017	.010	.018	.012
0	.0600	.131	.119	.037	.029	.087	.023	.016	.022	.014
1	.0730	.164	.149	.045	.037	.107	.026	.019	.027	.018
2	.0860	.194	.180	.053	.044	.129	.031	.023	.031	.022
3	.0990	.226	.211	.061	.051	.151	.035	.027	.036	.026
4	.1120	.257	.241	.069	.059	.169	.039	.031	.040	.030
5	.1250	.289	.272	.078	.066	.191	.043	.035	.045	.034
6	.1380	.321	.303	.086	.074	.211	.048	.039	.050	.037
8	.1640	.384	.364	.102	.088	.254	.054	.045	.058	.045
10	.1900	.448	.425	.118	.103	.283	.060	.050	.068	.053
12	.2160	.511	.487	.134	.118	.336	.067	.056	.077	.061
1/4	.2500	.573	.546	.150	.133	.375	.075	.064	.087	.070
5/16	.3125	.698	.666	.183	.162	.457	.084	.072	.106	.085
3/8	.3750	.823	.787	.215	.191	.538	.094	.081	.124	.100
7/16	.4375	.948	.907	.248	.221	.619	.094	.081	.142	.116
1/2	.5000	1.073	1.028	.280	.250	.701	.106	.091	.161	.131
9/16	.5625	1.198	1.149	.312	.279	.783	.118	.102	.179	.146
5/8	.6250	1.323	1.269	.345	.309	.863	.133	.116	.196	.162
3/4	.7500	1.573	1.511	.410	.368	1.024	.149	.131	.234	.182

Figure A-22

American National Standard Plain and Slotted Hexagon Head
Machine Screws (ANSI B18.6.3-1972, R1977)

Nominal Size or Basic Screw Diam.	Regular Head Width Across Flats A Max.	Min.	Across Corn. W Min.	Large Head Width Across Flats A Max.	Min.	Across Corn. W Min.	Head Height H Max.	Min.	Slot Width J Max.	Min.	Slot Depth T Max.	Min.
1	.125	.120	.134				.044	.036				
2	.125	.120	.134				.050	.040				
3	.188	.181	.202				.055	.044				
4	.188	.181	.202	.219	.213	.238	.060	.049	.039	.031	.036	.025
5	.188	.181	.202	.250	.244	.272	.070	.058	.043	.035	.042	.030
6	.250	.244	.272				.093	.080	.048	.039	.046	.033
8	.250	.244	.272	.312	.305	.340	.110	.096	.054	.045	.066	.052
10	.312	.305	.340				.120	.105	.060	.050	.072	.057
12	.312	.305	.340				.155	.139	.067	.056	.093	.077
1/4	.375	.367	.409	.375	.367	.409	.190	.172	.075	.064	.101	.083
5/16	.500	.489	.545	.438	.428	.477	.230	.208	.084	.072	.122	.100
3/8	.562	.551	.614				.295	.270	.094	.081	.156	.131

SHAPE OF INDENTATION

INDENTED HEAD

TRIMMED HEAD OR FULLY UPSET HEAD

Figure A-23

Slotted Round Head Machine Screws
(ANSI B18.6.3–1972, R1977 Appendix)

Nominal Size or Basic Screw Diam.		Head Diameter, A		Head Height, H		Slot Width, J		Slot Depth, T	
		Max.	Min.	Max.	Min.	Max.	Min.	Max.	Min.
0000	.0210	.041	.035	.022	.016	.008	.004	.017	.013
000	.0340	.062	.056	.031	.025	.012	.008	.018	.012
00	.0470	.089	.080	.045	.036	.017	.010	.026	.018
0	.0600	.113	.099	.053	.043	.023	.016	.039	.029
1	.0730	.138	.122	.061	.051	.026	.019	.044	.033
2	.0860	.162	.146	.069	.059	.031	.023	.048	.037
3	.0990	.187	.169	.078	.067	.035	.027	.053	.040
4	.1120	.211	.193	.086	.075	.039	.031	.058	.044
5	.1250	.236	.217	.095	.083	.043	.035	.063	.047
6	.1380	.260	.240	.103	.091	.048	.039	.068	.051
8	.1640	.309	.287	.120	.107	.054	.045	.077	.058
10	.1900	.359	.334	.137	.123	.060	.050	.087	.065
12	.2160	.408	.382	.153	.139	.067	.056	.096	.073
1/4	.2500	.472	.443	.175	.160	.075	.064	.109	.082
5/16	.3125	.590	.557	.216	.198	.084	.072	.132	.099
3/8	.3750	.708	.670	.256	.237	.094	.081	.155	.117
7/16	.4375	.750	.707	.328	.307	.094	.081	.196	.148
1/2	.5000	.813	.766	.355	.332	.106	.091	.211	.159
9/16	.5625	.938	.887	.410	.385	.118	.102	.242	.183
5/8	.6250	1.000	.944	.438	.411	.133	.116	.258	.195
3/4	.7500	1.250	1.185	.547	.516	.149	.131	.320	.242

Figure A-24

AMERICAN NATIONAL STANDARD SQUARE HEAD SETSCREWS
(ANSI B18.6.2)

Nominal Size of Basic Screw Diameter		Width Across Flats		Width Across Corners		Head Height		Neck Relief Diameter		Max Neck Relief Fillet Radius	Min Neck Relief Width	Min Head Radius
		Max.	Min.	Max.	Min.	Max.	Min.	Max.	Min.			
10	0.1900	0.188	0.180	0.265	0.247	0.148	0.134	0.145	0.140	0.027	0.083	0.48
1/4	0.2500	0.250	0.241	0.354	0.331	0.196	0.178	0.185	0.170	0.032	0.100	0.62
5/16	0.3125	0.312	0.302	0.442	0.415	0.245	0.224	0.240	0.225	0.036	0.111	0.78
3/8	0.3750	0.375	0.362	0.530	0.497	0.293	0.270	0.294	0.279	0.041	0.125	0.94
7/16	0.4375	0.438	0.423	0.619	0.581	0.341	0.315	0.345	0.330	0.046	0.143	1.09
1/2	0.5000	0.500	0.484	0.707	0.665	0.389	0.361	0.400	0.385	0.050	0.154	1.25
9/16	0.5625	0.562	0.545	0.795	0.748	0.437	0.407	0.454	0.439	0.054	0.167	1.41
5/8	0.6250	0.625	0.606	0.884	0.833	0.485	0.452	0.507	0.492	0.059	0.182	1.56
3/4	0.7500	0.750	0.729	1.060	1.001	0.582	0.544	0.620	0.605	0.065	0.200	1.88
7/8	0.8750	0.875	0.852	1.237	1.170	0.678	0.635	0.731	0.716	0.072	0.222	2.19
1	1.0000	1.000	0.974	1.414	1.337	0.774	0.726	0.838	0.823	0.081	0.250	2.50
1 1/8	1.1250	1.125	1.096	1.591	1.505	0.870	0.817	0.939	0.914	0.092	0.283	2.81
1 1/4	1.2500	1.250	1.219	1.768	1.674	0.966	0.908	1.064	1.039	0.092	0.283	3.12
1 3/8	1.3750	1.375	1.342	1.945	1.843	1.063	1.000	1.159	1.134	0.109	0.333	3.44
1 1/2	1.5000	1.500	1.464	2.121	2.010	1.159	1.091	1.284	1.259	0.109	0.333	3.75

Figure A-25

AMERICAN NATIONAL STANDARD SQUARE HEAD SETSCREWS

(ANSI B18.6.2)

Nominal Size or Basic Screw Diameter		Cup and Flat Point Diameters		Dog and Half-Dog Point Diameters		Point Length				Oval Point Radius +0.031 -0.000	Cone Point Angle 90° ± 2° for these Nominal Lengths or Longer, 118° ± 2° for Shorter Screws
						Dog		Half-Dog			
		Max.	Min.	Max.	Min.	Max.	Min.	Max.	Min.		
10	0.1900	0.102	0.088	0.127	0.120	0.095	0.085	0.050	0.040	0.142	1/4
1/4	0.2500	0.132	0.118	0.156	0.149	0.130	0.120	0.068	0.058	0.188	5/16
5/16	0.3125	0.172	0.156	0.203	0.195	0.161	0.151	0.083	0.073	0.234	3/8
3/8	0.3750	0.212	0.194	0.250	0.241	0.193	0.183	0.099	0.089	0.281	7/16
7/16	0.4375	0.252	0.232	0.297	0.287	0.224	0.214	0.114	0.104	0.328	1/2
1/2	0.5000	0.291	0.270	0.344	0.334	0.255	0.245	0.130	0.120	0.375	9/16
9/16	0.5625	0.332	0.309	0.391	0.379	0.287	0.275	0.146	0.134	0.422	5/8
5/8	0.6250	0.371	0.347	0.469	0.456	0.321	0.305	0.164	0.148	0.469	3/4
3/4	0.7500	0.450	0.425	0.562	0.549	0.383	0.367	0.196	0.180	0.562	7/8
7/8	0.8750	0.530	0.502	0.656	0.642	0.446	0.430	0.227	0.221	0.656	1
1	1.0000	0.609	0.579	0.750	0.734	0.510	0.490	0.260	0.240	0.750	1 1/8
1 1/8	1.1250	0.689	0.655	0.844	0.826	0.572	0.552	0.291	0.271	0.844	1 1/4
1 1/4	1.2500	0.767	0.733	0.938	0.920	0.635	0.615	0.323	0.303	0.938	1 1/2
1 3/8	1.3750	0.848	0.808	1.031	1.011	0.698	0.678	0.354	0.334	1.031	1 5/8
1 1/2	1.5000	0.926	0.886	1.125	1.105	0.760	0.740	0.385	0.365	1.125	1 3/4

Figure A-26

American National Standard Slotted Headless
Setscrews (ANSI B18.6.2)

| Nominal Size or Basic Screw Diameter | | Crown Radius | Slot Width | | Slot Depth | | Cup and Flat Point Diameters | | Dog Pont Diameters | | Point Length | | | | Oval Point Radius | Cone Point Angle 90°±2° For These Nominal Lengths or Longer 118°±2° For Shorter |
| | | | | | | | | | | | Dog | | Half-Dog | | | |
Basic Diameter		Basic	MAX	MIN	MAX	MIN	MAX	MIN	MAX	MIN	MAX	MIN	MAX	MIN	Basic	
0	0.0600	0.060	0.014	0.0010	0.020	0.016	0.033	0.027	0.040	0.037	0.032	0.028	0.017	0.013	0.045	5/64
1	0.0730	0.073	0.016	0.012	0.020	0.016	0.040	0.033	0.049	0.045	0.040	0.036	0.021	0.017	0.055	3/32
2	0.0860	0.086	0.018	0.014	0.025	0.019	0.047	0.039	0.057	0.053	0.046	0.042	0.024	0.020	0.064	7/64
3	0.0990	0.099	0.020	0.016	0.028	0.022	0.054	0.045	0.066	0.062	0.052	0.048	0.027	0.023	0.074	1/8
4	0.1120	0.112	0.024	0.018	0.031	0.025	0.061	0.051	0.075	0.070	0.058	0.054	0.030	0.026	0.084	5/32
5	0.1250	0.125	0.026	0.020	0.036	0.026	0.067	0.057	0.083	0.078	0.063	0.057	0.033	0.027	0.094	3/16
6	0.1380	0.138	0.028	0.022	0.040	0.030	0.074	0.064	0.092	0.087	0.073	0.067	0.038	0.032	0.104	3/16
8	0.1640	0.164	0.032	0.026	0.046	0.036	0.087	0.076	0.109	0.103	0.083	0.077	0.043	0.037	0.123	1/4
10	0.1900	0.190	0.035	0.029	0.053	0.043	0.102	0.088	0.127	0.120	0.095	0.085	0.050	0.040	0.142	1/4
12	0.2160	0.216	0.042	0.035	0.061	0.051	0.115	0.101	0.144	0.137	0.115	0.105	0.060	0.050	0.162	5/16
1/4	0.2500	0.250	0.049	0.041	0.068	0.058	0.132	0.118	0.156	0.149	0.130	0.120	0.068	0.058	0.188	5/16
5/16	0.3125	0.312	0.055	0.047	0.083	0.073	0.172	0.156	0.203	0.195	0.161	0.151	0.083	0.073	0.234	3/8
3/8	0.3750	0.375	0.068	0.060	0.099	0.089	0.212	0.194	0.250	0.241	0.193	0.183	0.099	0.089	0.281	7/16
7/16	0.4375	0.438	0.076	0.068	0.114	0.104	0.252	0.232	0.297	0.287	0.224	0.214	0.114	0.104	0.328	1/2
1/2	0.5000	0.500	0.086	0.078	0.130	0.120	0.291	0.270	0.344	0.334	0.255	0.245	0.130	0.120	0.375	9/16
9/16	0.5625	0.562	0.096	0.088	0.146	0.136	0.332	0.309	0.391	0.379	0.287	0.275	0.146	0.134	0.422	5/8
5/8	0.6250	0.625	0.107	0.097	0.161	0.151	0.371	0.347	0.469	0.456	0.321	0.305	0.164	0.148	0.469	3/4
3/4	0.7500	0.750	0.134	0.124	0.193	0.183	0.450	0.425	0.562	0.549	0.383	0.367	0.196	0.180	0.562	7/8

Figure A-27

Lengths for Threaded Fasteners

DIAMETER	LENGTHS																
	.250	.313	.375	.438	.500	.563	.625	.750	.875	1.000	1.250	1.500	1.750	2.000	2.500	3.000	3.500	4.000
5(.125)	●	●	●	●	●	●	●	●	●	●		●						
6(.138)	●	●	●	●	●	●	●	●	●	●	●	●		●				
8(.164)	●	●	●	●	●	●	●	●	●	●	●	●		●				
10(.190)	●	●	●	●	●	●	●	●	●	●	●	●	●	●				
12(.216)	●	●	●	●	●	●	●	●	●	●		●		●				
.250	●	●	●	●	●	●	●	●	●	●	●	●	●	●	●			
.313	●	●	●	●	●	●	●	●	●	●	●	●	●	●	●			
.375	●	●	●	●	●	●	●	●	●	●	●	●		●	●	●		
.438	●	●	●	●	●	●	●	●	●	●	●	●		●	●	●		
.500	●	●	●	●	●	●	●	●	●	●	●	●		●	●	●	●	●
.563			●	●	●	●	●	●	●	●		●		●	●	●	●	●
.625			●	●	●	●	●	●	●	●		●		●		●		●
.750					●	●	●	●	●	●		●		●		●	●	●
.875						●	●	●	●			●		●		●	●	●
1.000												●		●	●	●		●

Figure A-28

Lengths for Metric Threaded Fasteners

DIAMETER	LENGTHS														
	4	5	8	10	12	16	20	24	30	36	40	45	50	60	70
1.6	●	●	●												
2	●	●	●												
2.5	●	●	●	●	●										
3		●	●	●	●										
4			●	●	●	●	●								
5			●	●	●	●	●	●							
6				●	●	●	●	●							
8					●	●	●	●	●	●	●				
10						●	●	●	●	●	●	●	●	●	
12					●	●	●	●	●	●	●	●	●	●	●
16						●	●	●	●	●	●	●	●	●	●
20							●	●	●	●	●	●	●	●	●
24								●	●	●	●	●	●	●	●
30									●	●	●	●	●	●	●

Figure A-29

American National Standard Square and Hexagon Machine Screw Nuts
(ANSI B18.6.3-1972, R1977)

Nom. Size	Basic Diam.	Basic F	Max. F	Min. F	Max. G	Min. G	Max. G1	Min. G1	Max. H	Min. H
0	.0600	5/32	.156	.150	.221	.206	.180	.171	.050	.043
1	.0730	5/32	.156	.150	.221	.206	.180	.171	.050	.043
2	.0860	3/16	.188	.180	.265	.247	.217	.205	.066	.057
3	.0990	3/16	.188	.180	.265	.247	.217	.205	.066	.057
4	.1120	1/4	.250	.241	.354	.331	.289	.275	.098	.087
5	.1250	5/16	.312	.302	.442	.415	.361	.344	.114	.102
6	.1380	5/16	.312	.302	.442	.415	.361	.344	.114	.102
8	.1640	11/32	.344	.332	.486	.456	.397	.378	.130	.117
10	.1900	3/8	.375	.362	.530	.497	.433	.413	.130	.117
12	.2160	7/16	.438	.423	.619	.581	.505	.482	.161	.148
1/4	.2500	7/16	.438	.423	.619	.581	.505	.482	.193	.178
5/16	.3125	9/16	.562	.545	.795	.748	.650	.621	.225	.208
3/8	.3750	5/8	.625	.607	.884	.833	.722	.692	.257	.239

Figure A-30

Standard Twist Drill Sizes (Inches)

SIZE	DIAMETER	SIZE	DIAMETER	SIZE	DIAMETER	SIZE	DIAMETER
40	.098	19	.166	C	.242	U	.368
39	.0995	18	.1695	D	.246	3/8	.375
38	.1015	11/64	.1719	1/4(E)	.250	V	.377
37	.104	17	.173	F	.257	W	.386
36	.1065	16	.177	G	.261	25/64	.3906
7/16	.1094	15	.180	17/64	.2656	X	.397
35	.110	14	.182	H	.266	Y	.404
34	.111	13	.185	I	.272	13/32	.4062
33	.113	3/16	.1875	J	.277	Z	.413
32	.116	12	.189	K	.281	27/64	.4219
31	.120	11	.191	9/32	.2812	7/16	.4375
1/8	.125	10	.1935	L	.290	29/64	.4531
30	.1285	9	.196	M	.295	15/32	.4688
29	.136	8	.199	19/64	.2969	31/64	.4844
28	.1405	7	.201	N	.302	1/2	.5000
9/64	.1406	13/64	.2031	5/16	.3125	9/16	.5625
27	.144	6	.204	O	.316	5/8	.625
26	.147	5	.2055	P	.323	11/16	.6875
25	.1495	4	.209	21/64	.3281	3/4	.750
24	.152	3	.213	Q	.332	13/16	.8125
23	.154	7/32	.2188	R	.339	7/8	.875
5/32	.1562	2	.221	11/32	.3438	15/16	.9375
22	.157	1	.228	S	.348		
21	.159	A	.234	T	.358		
20	.161	B	.238	23/64	.3594		

NOTES FOR TWIST DRILL SIZES - INCHES
1. This is only a partial list of standard drill sizes.
2. Whenever possible, specify holes sizes that correspond to standard drill sizes.
3. Drill sizes are available in 1/64 increments between .5000 and 1.2500.
4. Drill sizes are available in 1/32 increments between 1.2500 and 1.500.

Figure A-31

Standard Twist Drill Sizes (Millimeters)

0.40	2.05	5.10	8.60	15.25	30.00
0.42	2.10	5.20	8.70	15.50	30.50
0.45	2.15	5.30	8.80	15.75	31.00
0.48	2.20	5.40	8.90	16.00	31.50
0.50	2.25	5.50	9.00	16.25	32.00
0.55	2.30	5.60	9.10	16.50	32.50
0.60	2.35	5.70	9.20	16.75	33.00
0.65	2.40	5.80	9.30	17.00	33.50
0.70	2.45	5.90	9.40	17.25	34.00
0.75	2.50	6.00	9.50	17.50	34.50
0.80	2.60	6.10	9.60	17.75	35.00
0.85	2.70	6.20	9.70	18.00	35.50
0.90	2.80	6.30	9.80	18.50	36.00
0.95	2.90	6.40	9.90	19.00	36.50
1.00	3.00	6.50	10.00	19.50	37.00
1.05	3.10	6.60	10.20	20.00	37.50
1.10	3.20	6.70	10.50	20.50	38.00
1.15	3.30	6.80	10.80	21.00	40.00
1.20	3.40	6.90	11.00	21.50	42.00
1.25	3.50	7.00	11.20	22.00	44.00
1.30	3.60	7.10	11.50	22.50	46.00
1.35	3.70	7.20	11.80	23.00	48.00
1.40	3.80	7.30	12.00	23.50	50.00
1.45	3.90	7.40	12.20	24.00	
1.50	4.00	7.50	12.50	24.50	
1.55	4.10	7.60	12.80	25.00	
1.60	4.20	7.70	13.00	25.50	
1.65	4.30	7.80	13.20	26.00	
1.70	4.40	7.90	13.50	26.50	
1.75	4.50	8.00	13.80	27.00	
1.80	4.60	8.10	14.00	27.50	
1.85	4.70	8.20	14.25	28.00	
1.90	4.80	8.30	14.50	28.50	
1.95	4.90	8.40	14.75	29.00	
2.00	5.00	8.50	15.00	29.50	

Figure A-32

Index